TO THE END
OF THE
EARTH

TO THE END
OF THE
EARTH

THE US ARMY AND
THE DOWNFALL OF JAPAN, 1945

JOHN C. McMANUS

CALIBER

DUTTON CALIBER

An imprint of Penguin Random House LLC
penguinrandomhouse.com

Copyright © 2023 by John C. McManus
Maps by Rick Britton

LIBRARY OF CONGRESS CATALOGING-IN-PUBLICATION DATA
has been applied for.

ISBN 9780593186886 (hardcover)
ISBN 9780593186909 (ebook)

Printed in the United States of America
1st Printing

To Nancy, with all my love . . .

To the Pacific theater veterans, so many of whom experienced
far more anonymity than glory . . .

To Reverend Nelson Woody, beloved father-in-law, who only saw
the completion of this book in spirit . . .

Contents

1

Crusade

Like a faithful steed, USS *Boise* plunged through the deep blue waters of the South China Sea, the ship's prow knifing gracefully through the relentless waves, bound for Luzon. Below deck, inside a snug, well-appointed private cabin, General Douglas MacArthur sat at a desk, pen in hand, preparing to write a letter to his wife on January 8, 1945, the eve of the largest invasion to date in the war against Japan. At once a magisterial and vexing figure, MacArthur oozed a sense of captivating uniqueness. He was the only US Army field commander who had once served at the very top of the Army as chief of staff. Only he among all the Army ground generals in the Pacific had been decorated with the Medal of Honor, a distinction he shared with his late father, Lieutenant General Arthur MacArthur, who had four decades earlier led American military forces in the Philippines. During World War II, Douglas MacArthur had experienced, by far, more frontline combat than any other American general of four-star rank, only adding to a record of valor that he had already carved out as a younger officer in the First World War. In 1929, he had endured a difficult, stormy divorce from his first wife, Louise Cromwell, putting the lie to Army conventional wisdom that a failed marriage for an officer would inevitably lead to a failed career. Eight years later, he married Jean Faircloth, daughter of a Nashville banker and his true soul mate, who bore him a son named Arthur the next year.

Astonishingly, MacArthur subsequently chose—in direct defiance of a War Department order to evacuate military families—to keep them with him in 1941–42, when he led the ill-fated Allied defense of the Philippines. He thus became the only high-level American commander to expose his family to combat in World War II. With unrepentant

1

independence, he continued to live with his family throughout much of the war, seemingly indifferent to the fact that his many thousands of subordinates enjoyed no such option. In yet another characteristic action that revealed much about his broke-the-mold distinctiveness, he had willfully crossed the red line that sensibly separates the civil and the military in the American system by running an unsuccessful clandestine campaign to win the presidency in 1944. Complex to the point of near convolution, an intimate aide once said of the general, "None of us knew MacArthur. We all saw fragments of the man."

Over three long years of war, he had carved out a record as a thoughtful military strategist, an innovator with a strong grasp of the potency of airpower and sea power, and an inspirational figure whose keen understanding of image approached the savant level. But far too often, he had also revealed himself to be a petty, paranoid, insecure, vainglorious, egomaniacal schemer who seemingly viewed Washington policy makers as adversaries on par with the Japanese. An ardent opponent of the Allies' Europe First policy, he believed with an almost evangelical fervor that America's geopolitical future lay in Asia and the Pacific. His greatest objective—perhaps as much as or more than defeating Japan—was to liberate the Philippines. His invasion of Leyte a couple months earlier had served only as a warm-up act for what he envisioned as an archipelago-wide liberation, most notably of Luzon, his former home, with himself playing an almost predestined, messianic role. Lieutenant Colonel Weldon "Dusty" Rhoades, his personal pilot and a close intimate, once opined of his chief that "he had some feeling that he was a man of destiny. He seemed to believe that he was especially protected so that he could fulfill a mission." MacArthur loved the people of the Philippines with almost familial intensity. In his mind, the impending invasion of Luzon equated to something of a twentieth-century crusade. Only a few weeks shy of his sixty-fifth birthday, MacArthur remained physically robust, though he now combed strands of black hair over his balding pate in an apparent effort to conceal the encroachment of senior citizenship. He seldom allowed photographs of himself bareheaded, preferring instead to wear a specially designed braided cap most everywhere he went. Upscale sunglasses and a corncob pipe completed a look that seemingly only he could pull off.

Hunched over the desk inside his cabin aboard *Boise*, MacArthur scrawled his letter to Jean on personal stationery. "The *Boise* is the most comfortable cruiser on which I have traveled. The suite I occupy is much larger, has artificial ventilation and better cooking than the others." Battle-hardened *Boise*'s modernity reflected the stupendous and growing power of the US Navy by 1945. By the same token, MacArthur and his Southwest Pacific Area (SWPA) command could be said to symbolize the corresponding maturation of the US Army during the war with Japan. He had once led a poorly equipped, sparsely fed colonial-style army in the Philippines but now presided over the largest ground force ever assembled for amphibious island warfare, and these legions were only one component of a larger army that had now grown to full maturity. Indeed, nearly 1.4 million soldiers were now serving throughout the Pacific and Asia. By war's end, the number would swell to 1.8 million, the third-largest ground force ever sent overseas by the United States to fight a war. Superbly equipped, highly mechanized, well fed and well led, the Army of the Pacific/Asia theater reflected the bounty of the nation that produced it, and it was shouldering the onerous responsibility of expeditionary-style warfare in far-flung, inhospitable locales. Army soldiers were doing the lion's share of the fighting and dying in the Pacific, particularly in the Philippines, the true nexus of the American war against Japan. And yet, contemporary and subsequent popular memory tended to focus on the more publicity savvy and extraordinarily valorous Marines, who had carved out a distinguished combat record but were far fewer in number than the soldiers. Even now, in 1945's infancy, the Army labored in an almost unbelievable diversity of missions—combat and noncombat—that included ostensibly everything from the logistics of loading and shipping to guerrilla warfare, from diplomacy to cutting-edge medical care, and from civil affairs to engineering of such sophistication as to lay foundations of knowledge to benefit future generations. Spread over nearly one-third of the globe's surface of island, sea, and continent, it was an army of such size and diversity of purpose as to make one unified command nearly impossible—MacArthur controlled only about 60 percent of Army combat formations.

Over three years, the Army had steadily fought its way northward from the South Pacific to the Central Pacific and now beyond. The

Army's evolution into an extraordinarily potent, modern military force paralleled the maturation of the US Navy into the most powerful maritime force in global history, a behemoth of sea power upon which rested the foundation of the American war against Japan. The Army Air Forces, particularly the B-29 formations that were beginning to bomb Japan itself, only added to this prodigious combination of American military strength that, in tandem with America's theater allies, now amounted to a dagger at the Japanese throat. Allied victory now seemed certain, and yet the tasks ahead, especially for the US Army, were daunting in the extreme. The impending liberation of the Philippines, the opening of a viable landward supply route to China, and the seizure of key islands on the doorstep of Japan all loomed as costly enterprises on the immediate drawing board. And somewhere beyond, like an Everest on the horizon, a horrendously bloody invasion of Japan beckoned as a serious possibility, perhaps even a necessity. So the essential question now was how much it would cost the Allies, and most notably the Army, in lives, treasure, and time to subdue Japan, a country still tightly controlled by a defiant cabal of civil and military elites who were loyally supported by millions of soldiers, sailors, and even ordinary citizens, most of whom seemed more than willing to fight on indefinitely, unto the death.

The first answers to this disquieting question would now come at Luzon, the target of an enormous American task force of which USS *Boise* was only one relatively small component. For nearly forty miles in any direction around *Boise*, the huge invasion armada of some 700 ships carried or escorted 203,000 soldiers from all over General MacArthur's enormous SWPA empire; about one-third of these men were noncombat service troops. The soldiers hailed from a geographically diverse network of bases, ranging from Leyte to the picked-over South Pacific burgs of Nouméa, Sansapor, Aitape, Finschhafen-Toem, Hollandia, Oro Bay, Noemfoor, Cape Gloucester, and Bougainville, places whose vast distances from one another would have encompassed a substantial chunk of the United States itself.

Once boarded, most of the soldiers never returned to these places, their very absence a powerful reminder that the war had moved forever northward to enter its final bloody phase. Perhaps sensing this, base commanders on Bougainville staged a memorable send-off for Major General Oscar Griswold, the XIV Corps commander who had masterminded the American victory on that island and had since spent over half a year there preparing his men to go back into combat. Under a bright tropical sun, as LSTs and other troopships loaded with soldiers from the 37th Infantry Division and XIV Corps stood just offshore, color guards gathered at a dock to honor the popular general. "Marine band played honorary concert at old CP," Griswold tersely related to his diary. "Guard of honor at beach."

Army and Navy honor guards stood at attention alongside Griswold. At the pier he shook hands with several dozen officers who lined up respectfully to send him off. Perhaps most significantly, the well-wishers included Lieutenant General Stanley Savige, whose II Corps of the Australian Imperial Force now took over the unglamorous task of garrisoning the backwater island and containing the remnants of the Japanese forces, a mute microcosm of Australia's diminished role in the war. Only a few days before, the introspective Griswold had attended a memorial service at the military cemetery where many Marines and XIV Corps soldiers who had died fighting for Bougainville were buried. For Griswold, the visit was a sober reminder of the grave responsibilities of corps command. Once aboard USS *Mount Olympus,* the command ship for Griswold's good friend Vice Admiral Theodore Wilkinson, the general gravely intoned in his diary, "The time is growing short—may God give us his blessing and his help in the dark days up ahead, that we may draw this thing to a close and that peace once again may grace this war-torn world."

MacArthur had once habitually kvetched about a supposed paucity of manpower and resources allotted by Washington decision makers to his theater. The complaints now seemed an embarrassment, almost akin to a man in a mansion crying poor. MacArthur's sizable army was larger than the US Army forces that had fought campaigns in North Africa, Sicily, Italy, and Southern France. Its size exceeded even the entire Allied ground complement at Sicily. Indeed, the SWPA armies now ranked behind only the large American ground forces fighting in western Europe. MacArthur's headquarters now directly controlled, or soon would control, impressively formidable combat forces. The order of battle included two armies, four corps, and fifteen divisions, plus regimental combat teams, independent tank formations, guerrilla units, and other attachments that only added to the girth. He earmarked Lieutenant General Walter Krueger's Sixth Army to carry out Mike I, the SWPA code name for the invasion of Luzon. The obvious place to invade was over the expansive beaches of Lingayen Gulf, where the Japanese had landed in late 1941. MacArthur and his staff initially hoped to surprise General Tomoyuki Yamashita, the Japanese commander, by landing elsewhere, but eventually they bowed to the reality that only Lingayen could accommodate the huge numbers of troops, tanks, and other vehicles that the Americans intended to fling ashore. Moreover, Lingayen offered a nice gateway to the roads that snaked through Luzon's central plains to the crowning prize of Manila some 120 miles to the southeast.

Krueger planned to land four divisions, plus an engineer special brigade and two boat and shore regiments. The 43rd Infantry Division was slated to land on the extreme left flank, from the invader's point of view, near San Fabian. The 6th Infantry Division would land immediately to the right. The two divisions would serve under the control of Major General Innis Palmer Swift's I Corps. Swift had commanded the 1st Cavalry Division at Los Negros, successfully enough that Krueger had since promoted him to corps command. Both divisions had fought in the South Pacific, the 43rd at New Georgia and the 6th at New Guinea, most notably Lone Tree Hill. To the right of I Corps, the 37th Infantry Division, hardened veterans of Bougainville, would land near Dagupan while the 40th Infantry Division, a California, Nevada, and Utah National Guard unit new to combat, was picked by the Sixth Army planners to hit the beaches on the extreme right flank near the town of Lingayen. These two divisions were controlled by Griswold's XIV Corps. In terms of American amphibious combat units, the landing forces exceeded those that had carried out the Normandy invasion at Utah and Omaha beaches. Follow-on forces under the control of the respective corps headquarters included the 32nd and 33rd Infantry Divisions, the 1st Cavalry Division, the 25th Infantry Division, the 158th Regimental Combat Team, the 112th Cavalry Regimental Combat Team, the 6th Ranger Infantry Battalion, and the 13th Armored Group, the latter of which possessed nearly as many tanks as the typical European theater

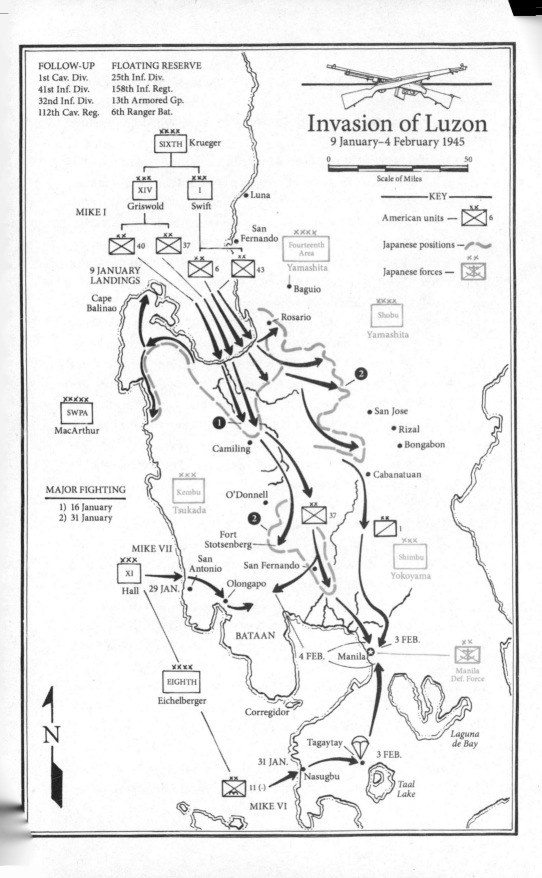

Invasion of Luzon
9 January–4 February 1945

FOLLOW-UP
1st Cav. Div.
41st Inf. Div.
32nd Inf. Div.
112th Cav. Reg.

FLOATING RESERVE
25th Inf. Div.
158th Inf. Regt.
13th Armored Gp.
6th Ranger Bat.

SIXTH Krueger

XIV Griswold

I Swift

MIKE I

40

37

9 JANUARY LANDINGS

6

43

Luna

San Fernando

Fourteenth Area
Yamashita

Baguio

0   50
Scale of Miles

KEY
American units — ☒ 6
Japanese positions — 〜
Japanese forces — ☒

Cape Balinao

Rosario

Shobu
Yamashita

2

SWPA
MacArthur

1

Camiling

San Jose
Rizal
Bongabon

Cabanatuan

MAJOR FIGHTING
1) 16 January
2) 31 January

Kembu
Tsukada

O'Donnell

2

37

1

Shimbu
Yokoyama

MIKE VII

XI Hall

29 JAN.

San Antonio

Fort Stotsenberg

Olongapo

San Fernando

BATAAN

3 FEB.

4 FEB. Manila

Manila Def. Force

EIGHTH
Eichelberger

Corregidor

N

Tagaytay

3 FEB.

Laguna de Bay

31 JAN.

Nasugbu

Taal Lake

11 (-)

MIKE VI

armored division. Six more infantry divisions, plus the 11th Airborne Division and the 503rd Parachute Infantry Regiment, would eventually become available for MacArthur's operations on Luzon and elsewhere in the archipelago.[1]

In the meantime, the invasion armada under Vice Admiral Thomas Kinkaid, who had worked closely with MacArthur for more than a year, sailed through the narrow waters of the Surigao Strait and then inexorably north, past the western coastlines of Negros, Panay, and Mindoro, along with many smaller islands, and then off Luzon itself. In response, the Japanese scraped together their few remaining planes in the Philippines to launch a series of frantic kamikaze attacks. Lieutenant General Kyoji Tominaga, the air commander, routinely gave an eloquent farewell speech to these idealistic, extraordinarily courageous young pilots. "I know what you feel now as you put the sorrows and joys of life behind you because the Emperor's fortunes are failing. Do not worry about what happens when you die and what you leave behind you—for you will become gods. Soon I hope to have the privilege of joining you in glorious death." The appalling reality about the kamikaze fliers, and one that has never since abated in relation to suicide bombers, was that it took only one or two to cause serious damage. The law of averages dictated that, even against well-orchestrated combat air patrols and a wall of effective antiaircraft fire, some of the suicide planes were assured of surviving long enough to crash into a ship. A twin-engine bomber smashed into the flight deck of the escort carrier USS *Ommaney Bay*. The plane's bombs penetrated belowdecks and exploded, touching off a fire that the crew could not control. "Pandemonium broke out," Aviation Ordnanceman José "Andy" Chacón, an air crewman, recalled. "A barber jumped right into the turning propeller screw with a bag of money he kept in the barber shop. All we saw of him was a blotch of red sea water."

The ship sank after several hours of agony. Watching its death throes from USS *Mount Olympus,* a shaken Griswold took to his diary and noted, with a mixture of revulsion and grudging admiration, "You've got to hand it to the Jap—he has guts!" On January 6 alone, kamikazes scored hits on sixteen ships, including the battleship USS *New Mexico,* where Lieutenant General Herbert Lumsden, Prime Minister Winston

Churchill's SWPA liaison officer and a good friend of MacArthur's, was blown from a ladder and killed instantly. Saddened, MacArthur wrote to the prime minister, "His general service and usefulness to the Allied cause was beyond praise. My own personal sorrow is inexpressible." The kamikazes sank three minesweepers, including the USS *Long,* whose skipper, Lieutenant Stanley Caplan, later told a Navy debriefer that when the enemy plane hit the ship, "immediately there was a terrific flash of flame which went up to the bridge . . . and did burn some of the men who were on the starboard wing of the bridge. This flash went across the well deck down through the galley house passageways." The flames were so intense that they actually incinerated the clothes and shoes off one unfortunate sailor and burned most of his body.

The suicide planes inflicted damage on over two dozen Allied ships, most notably the battleship USS *California* and five cruisers, killing 503 sailors. "The suicider is quite deliberate in his approach, remaining outside of range of . . . automatic weapons until he has looked the situation over and obtained the desired position from which to strike," Vice Admiral Theodore Wilkinson, a task force commander, commented succinctly in a post-battle study. In the wake of the flurry of attacks, MacArthur vowed to his staff, "If the Lord will let me land this one, I'll never ask so much of him again."

By unleashing the kamikazes, the Japanese regained some tactical initiative, albeit at a gratuitous cost in human beings and planes. Even so, they failed to impede the movement of Kinkaid's fleet or the timetable of MacArthur's invasion. The Americans were fortunate in two respects. First, the kamikaze pilots focused mainly on the escort ships rather than the transport ships. No soldiers lost their lives to the suicide planes. One of the many reasons why the war had turned so decisively against Japan was the wasteful loss of so many Imperial Army soldiers whose transport ships were sunk by Allied planes or submarines. The kamikazes might well have given the Americans a taste of this horrible, demoralizing experience, but missed their opportunity. Second, the Japanese had lost so many planes in the Philippines since the onset of the Leyte invasion that the kamikaze attacks on Kinkaid's fleet represented a last gasp of sorts. For obvious reasons, the suicide pilots, and their planes, were a steadily diminishing asset. Within a few days in

January, the Japanese in the Philippines no longer possessed any usable aircraft. This, in turn, forced Imperial General Headquarters to choose between reinforcing the Philippines or the home islands and Okinawa, where Admiral Chester Nimitz's forces would soon invade. Tokyo decided to deploy its remaining kamikazes to defend Okinawa rather than the Philippines. In terms of aerial support, Yamashita's Fourteenth Area Army was on its own, once the last Philippines-based kamikazes had expended themselves by January 12. General Tominaga, who had professed a desire to die a "glorious" death alongside his kamikaze pilots, instead ignominiously fled to Formosa with his staff. An outraged Yamashita tried unsuccessfully to have him court-martialed.

In addition to suicide planes, the Japanese also sent midget submarines against the American armada. One of these subs fired a pair of torpedoes at *Boise*. Captain Willard Downes, the skipper, skillfully maneuvered the ship out of harm's way and the torpedoes missed. "As I watched, I couldn't help thinking of my cabin at the waterline with those watertight doors locking me in," Lieutenant Colonel Roger Egeberg, MacArthur's physician, later wrote of the tense moments he and the general spent watching the torpedoes run their course. Once the fleet was in place near the invasion beaches, the Japanese employed, with less success, explosive-laden suicide boats and even suicide divers. MacArthur took all this in stride with his usual calm resolution. During quiet moments of the voyage, he stood at the ship's railing, corncob pipe theatrically jutting from his mouth, and studied the familiar Luzon coastline, just discernible in the distance. "There they were, gleaming in the sun far off on the horizon," he later wrote eloquently, "Manila, Corregidor, Marivales [sic], Bataan. I could not leave the rail. I was alone with my memories. At the sight of those never-to-be-forgotten scenes of my family's past, I felt an indescribable sense of loss, of sorrow, of loneliness, and of solemn consecration."[2]

With Japanese airpower and sea power largely swept from the archipelago, and having inflicted heavy losses on Yamashita's Leyte ground forces, MacArthur expected to encounter a substantially weakened army on Luzon. From the earliest days of the war, his intelligence chief, Brigadier General Charles Willoughby, had too often demonstrated—at least for a man with so many resources at his disposal—poor judgment of

enemy intentions, faulty predictions, and a seeming talent for miscalcu-
lating enemy strength. In this sense, Luzon was Willoughby's magnum
opus of inaccuracy. By the eve of the invasion, he presided over a gargantuan intelligence fiefdom that included skilled linguists of the Allied
Translator and Interpreter Section (ATIS); the Central Bureau, an organization that daily intercepted huge numbers of Japanese signals
communications; and the Allied Intelligence Bureau, a sophisticated
human intelligence network whose information came from the burgeoning coterie of Filipino guerrilla organizations, special operators
such as Alamo Scouts and coast watchers, in addition to prisoner interrogations. Willoughby's most potent asset was probably Ultra, the remarkably successful Allied effort to break Japanese codes. A little over
a week before the invasion, he assessed Japanese strength on Luzon at
about 152,000 soldiers, an eye-popping underestimate, by over 100,000,
of the true number of 287,000. Colonel Horton White, Krueger's intelligence officer, seriously disagreed with Willoughby about the size of Yamashita's Luzon forces. White placed Japanese strength at 234,000, still
an underestimate but closer to reality. It is remarkable that these two
highly experienced intelligence officers could arrive at such dramatically different conclusions after studying more or less the same data.
Whereas Willoughby confined his calculations to a simple estimate from
the enemy's known order of battle, White correctly deduced the presence of large numbers of unaffiliated combat soldiers and service troops
who either augmented or supported the combat formations.

The tension over their disagreement had played out when Brigadier
General Clyde Eddleman, Krueger's operations officer, briefed MacArthur on the final invasion plan. When Eddleman shared White's estimates of Japanese strength, MacArthur repeatedly interrupted him,
"Bunk! Bunk!" Eddleman chuckled and said, "General, apparently you
don't like our intelligence briefing." MacArthur retorted, "I don't. It's
too strong. There aren't that many Japanese there." The SWPA commander had embraced Willoughby's predictions, probably because they
conveniently fed MacArthur's larger narrative to the Joint Chiefs that he
could liberate the Philippines quickly and at minimal cost. He seemed
not to realize, or admit, that fierce enemy resistance at Leyte had already
unraveled that narrative. Given this immutable truth, neither Luzon nor

any other objective in the Philippines was likely to prove much different from Leyte. Eddleman replied to MacArthur, "Sir, most of this information came from your headquarters." At that, Willoughby, uptight and severe as always, leapt from his chair and declared, "Didn't come from me!"

Eddleman sidestepped the disagreement and instead briefed MacArthur on the invasion plans, which the commander quickly approved. Later, at MacArthur's behest, the two men met privately. In Eddleman's recollection, the general told him "that he knew of only two outstanding intelligence officers in all of military history and added, 'Mine is not one of them.' The two he had in mind were Hannibal's and Grant's intelligence officers. Yet he went on to explain some of Willoughby's intelligence-gathering problems and showed great sympathy for his G-2." MacArthur's oddly transparent conversation with Eddleman might have indicated that he knew Willoughby's estimates were questionable, or perhaps the discussion indicated total support for his intelligence officer. Regardless, the discrepancy between Willoughby and White laid the groundwork for significant strategic differences between MacArthur and Krueger. MacArthur envisioned Luzon as a lightning campaign, the primary objectives of which were to secure the runways of Clark Field, a major American-built air base complex; take Manila; liberate the population centers; and in so doing, break the back of Japanese resistance, a redemptive crusade with himself as the central figure. In typical deliberative fashion, Krueger saw Luzon as a campaign of multiple phases for the ultimate purpose of eliminating the Japanese presence on the island. This outlook reflected the circumspect nature of an autodidactic, self-made man who had emigrated from Germany to the United States as a child, joined the Army as a seventeen-year-old private during the Spanish-American War, earned a field commission, and over a forty-year career, ascended to three-star rank (remarkably, without even a high school diploma to his credit). Krueger planned to get ashore, carve out a beachhead in central Luzon, and then develop the situation according to what kind of resistance he encountered. The intelligence discrepancies between SWPA and Sixth Army either reflected or exacerbated those profound conceptual differences, a divergence of outlook that festered unattended, seemingly waiting for the moment when it would mature into a full-blown conflict between these two otherwise compatible partners.[3]

Neither American general fully understood Japanese intentions. Like every other intelligent Japanese commander at this stage of the war, Yamashita favored a protracted inland defense. Fourteenth Area Army had little mobility. In total, it had 4,600 vehicles, half of which were damaged or diminished in some way. Fuel stocks were minimal; some units were even attempting to utilize distilled pine-root oil in lieu of gasoline. Yamashita knew he could not stop the Americans at the beaches, nor could he hold Luzon's central plains. "I realized that . . . decisive battle was impossible," he commented after the war. "Therefore I decided on a delaying action to divert as much American forces in Luzon so as to keep them from attacking Japan as much as possible. I realized the American air forces and Navy were exceedingly superior to ours and also the firepower of the ground forces were superior and very mobile. Therefore I knew that I could not conduct . . . warfare on flat land. I employed a delaying action in the mountains." Lieutenant General Akira Muto, his chief of staff, later asserted, "To the question of what could be expected from a clash on an open plain and without air support between the Japanese Army and its adversary, the most steadfast believer in the power of spiritual factors had perforce to answer that the outlook was dark for Japan." Yamashita understood that the best way he could enhance Japan's strategic position would be to bleed the Americans and fight on as long as he possibly could. In this way, defense could become like offense if it affected the American will to spend copious amounts of lives and resources to consummate a total-victory conquest of Japan.

So, Yamashita elected to hunker his forces into Luzon's many mountains and hills and fight to the death, thus emphasizing the intrinsic strength of Japanese soldiers for defense. To this end, he divided his command into three major components. The Shobu Group, under his direct command, would defend the northern half of Luzon, roughly from Lingayen Gulf to the north coast. With 152,000 soldiers it was the largest of the three groups, and headquartered at Baguio, the pleasant mountain city where Yamashita himself had recently located his head-quarters. The Kembu Group, numbering about 30,000 men under Major General Rikichi Tsukada, defended Clark Field, Bataan, and the Zam-bales Mountains along the western coast opposite Manila. Another 80,000 troops, lumped into the Shimbu Group under Lieutenant Gen-eral Shizuo Yokoyama, defended the rest of the island, massing espe-cially in the mountainous areas east of Manila and the hilly parts of the Bicol Peninsula.

Though Yamashita exercised direct control over the Shobu Group, his ascendance over the other two groups was less sure. In part this re-sulted from geographic and communication issues. Yamashita's phys-ical remoteness and the chaotic state of Japanese logistics and tenuous lines of communication all but guaranteed to mitigate his influence. But some of the troops were actually from the Imperial Navy and the Army Air Force. They consisted of sailors marooned from sunken ships, naval special base force units, aviation ground crewmen whom Tominaga had abandoned, and the like. The ever-continuous divisions and rivalries among Japan's military services made it difficult for Yamashita to place these units comfortably within his chain of command. During the weeks leading up to the invasion, Lieutenant General Muto expended great effort to bring these men under his boss's command. "In order to bring about these changes in chain of command a great deal of time and negotiation was required." Even once they were integrated into Four-teenth Area Army, as they generally were by early January 1945, their commanders were not always certain to acknowledge Yamashita's au-thority and obey his orders. Many of the non-Army personnel were lo-cated in Manila, as part of the Shimbu Group's order of battle, but only loosely under its authority.

Interestingly, Yamashita did not intend to defend the capital. "I de-cided to put the Manila area outside the battle area," he later explained. "First, the population is approximately one million . . . it is impossible to feed them. The second reason is that the buildings are very inflam-mable. The third reason is that because it is a flat land it requires tremendous . . . strength to defend it." Muto contended that Manila's "underground water was so close to the surface that the construction of tunnels was impossible." He also estimated—on what basis he never said—that the defense of the city would absorb an astronomical, untenable garrison of eight divisions. "It was considered not only impossible but disadvantageous." Ominously, after Yamashita issued orders through Yokoyama's headquarters to evacuate Manila, most of the garrison failed to carry them out, owing to American bombing raids, a lack of transportation, and sheer defiance because many Japanese officers did not agree with the notion of abandoning the city. In this respect, they understood the defensive value of an urban cluster better than did the Fourteenth Area Army commander. If indeed Yamashita actually believed that Manila's buildings were too inflammable and the area too demanding of combat manpower to defend effectively, then he was amazingly deficient in his understanding of urban combat, where a rubble-littered landscape of ruined buildings and the funneling of firepower greatly enhance the effectiveness of small numbers of defenders.

It is hard to believe that the need to feed Manila's population actually factored much into Japanese strategic and military decision-making. As the Americans had sensed from the first day they set foot on Leyte, the Japanese cared little about the health and welfare of Filipinos, especially with guerrillas plaguing them on nearly every sizable island. Humanitarian considerations aside, though, Manila represented a valuable opportunity for Yamashita to fulfill his defensive vision. In every building and on every block, he could bleed the Americans terribly, at minimal cost to his own forces in manpower and firepower. Similar to what the Soviets did to the Germans at Stalingrad, he could force them to forfeit their mechanized mobility as well as their airpower to take the place in a meat-grinder battle. Manila was a powerful political symbol to both the American and Philippine peoples. Its liberation, in many minds, would equate to the liberation of the country itself; to deny its liberation, the opposite. The capital's harbor facilities, infrastructure, and communication nodes also comprised a major strategic objective for the Americans, in fact the most crucial one of the entire campaign. Indeed, the Americans badly needed Manila to feed the logistical requirements of MacArthur's sizable armies (not unlike the value of French harbors to sustain Eisenhower's forces in Europe). They could not bypass or besiege Manila. They simply had to have the place as quickly as possible. It made little military sense, then, for Yamashita to abandon such a prize to his adversary without a fight. While it was true that he could very well destroy the harbor facilities before evacuating the city, thus denying this valuable objective to his enemies at least for the short term, it actually made even more strategic sense to turn the entire area into a battleground, since this could compromise Manila as a logistical base even more. By compelling the Americans to fight for Manila, he could have forced them to confront a terrible moral choice, a kind of hostage-rescuer dilemma, and one that actually applied to the country as a whole: Should they risk destroying the city in order to liberate it? Surprisingly, the Japanese commander did not seem to grasp this fundamental truth. Or perhaps, from a kinder historical viewpoint, humanitarian impulses won out over his best military judgment. The true answer must remain unknown.[4]

In any event, as Kinkaid's fleet settled into Lingayen Gulf for the invasion, the fate of Manila remained for the moment ensconced in the nebulous, partially glimpsed future. Ever hopeful of eclipsing Eisenhower, MacArthur dubbed the January 9 invasion date "S Day" rather than the more famous and ubiquitous D-Day term. Aboard *Mount Olympus,* Griswold almost dreaded the arrival of S-Day. "As I looked at the ships bearing XIV Corps, my heart was sad," he jotted mournfully in his diary. "I know that some of my boys who are on these ships will, by this time tomorrow, have laid down their lives. I pray . . . for strength and wisdom and Divine Guidance that I may lead them right. War is a terrible thing." Many of the soldiers had been at sea for weeks by now. They had settled into a shipboard routine that they looked forward to renouncing soon. "The cram-packed men on the LST's and LSM's struggled for 'lebensraum,'" quipped the 37th Division historian in a descriptive report about life for the troops aboard the transports. "Amazing bivouacs sprang up as shelter halves and ponchos were hung, draped, stretched from every possible ships [sic] fitting to which a rope could be secured. Packing boxes, deck loaded cargo were pressed into service to provide additional weather-proofing." Few looked forward to combat; even fewer relished living this transient life.

The sun peeked in and out of drifting clouds, framing a formidable panoply of horizon-to-horizon naval hardware that had, by now, simply become a typical setting for invasion day. "The approach, the formation of ships as they maneuvered into position for their tactical jobs, no backfield has ever functioned with such precision and perfect timing," Lieutenant Howard McKenzie, an antiaircraft platoon leader, wrote in a letter to his wife. "There were so many vessels in the water that you were reminded of a whirlpool." The mild weather made for calm waters. Landing craft laden with troops plowed relentlessly to their beaches, all the while under a massive umbrella of supporting firepower from the battleships, cruisers, and other bombardment ships. "No one can exaggerate in words such fire-power," Lieutenant McKenzie marveled. "It was so great . . . so horrible, that one just couldn't think. All you could do was just look."

With little Japanese presence in the landing areas, the firepower might have done more harm to Filipino friends than damage to the enemy. Rear Admiral Jesse Oldendorf—by now an experienced guru of naval bombardment—wrote ruefully in his post-action report, "Japanese tactics of withdrawal from beach areas probably made much of the bombardment unnecessary." Aboard many dozens of landing craft, the assault troops watched the shells explode or, even more commonly, hunkered down and waited to debark into the unknown. "The men smoked nervously, made a few weak smiles at their buddies, and squirmed as if their cartridge belts were buckled too tightly across their stomachs," the 129th Infantry Regiment, 37th Division's after-action report vividly chronicled. One observer professed surprise at how many of them were praying. "They were fingering their rosary beads, or had a New Testament or Old Testament."

In a matter of a few hours, from 0930 onward, some 68,000 troops landed against little resistance and established a beachhead about fifteen miles long. Some of the soldiers quickly advanced as far as 6,000 yards inland. "S Day landings were made with an almost unbelievable lack of enemy opposition," Krueger's Sixth Army after-action report commented, with the faintest air of mystified ignorance. From a commanding perch atop Mount Santo Tomas near Baguio, General Yamashita watched the landings impassively. The location of the invasion did not surprise him, though its timing did. He had not expected the Americans to arrive for several more weeks. Initially, he and Lieutenant General Muto had mistaken the invasion force for a friendly resupply convoy. "We had been awaiting the arrival of rice and petroleum," Muto later wrote, "but the Americans came in their stead." Yamashita dispatched a messenger to Tokyo with the news and included a private missive to his wife, Hisako. "The American Army has landed and is already at my knee but everyone is in good spirits. We are brave enough to deal them a heavy blow but our main difficulty is ammunition. I may be silent for some time as I am very busy." As Yamashita watched enviously, the usual gaudy array of American vehicles, supplies, and specialized equipment soon followed in the wake of the assault troops. Typical of so many others, Transport Division Six, in landing the 43rd Division's 103rd Infantry Regiment near San Fabian, disgorged 447 trucks, jeeps, trailers, tractors, and guns, as well as 2,283 short tons of ammunition, fuel, rations, medical supplies, and other cargo.

General MacArthur had spent the morning and early afternoon watching the landings from his vantage point aboard *Boise*. At 1400, he gathered his entourage and headed for the beach in the 6th Division sector. Whereas his wet landing at Leyte the previous fall had been spontaneous, this landing was as orchestrated as a symphony performance. At MacArthur's behest, Major General Richard Marshall, the deputy chief of staff, had prepared a detailed roster assigning staff members to specific landing craft, with each person placed precisely according to plan in proximity to MacArthur. "Group D" consisted of the general; Lieutenant General Richard Sutherland, his chief of staff; General Marshall; Colonel Lloyd "Larry" Lehrbas, a public relations aide; Lieutenant Colonel Egeberg, the physician; and Staff Sergeant Francisco Salveron, MacArthur's Philippine-born enlisted aide. Although Seabees had already built a pier to accommodate dry landings, MacArthur deliberately eschewed it in favor of wading ashore for beachside photographers, a conscious decision to reprise the photographic gold of the Leyte landing. As he sloshed ashore, he affected a grim, determined facial expression, yet another deliberate recapitulation of Leyte for this master of political-military theater.

With the beachhead secured, MacArthur immediately pressed inland. He visited the 6th Division headquarters and met with Major General Edwin Patrick, the volatile, courageous commander whose staff privately referred to him as "The Green Hornet" because of the gaudy green jumpsuit he wore in combat. MacArthur jeeped south and established an advance headquarters in a school building at Dagupan before heading back to *Boise*. Almost everywhere he went, Filipinos cheered and mobbed him. "The people of Luzon seem quicker to recognize MacArthur . . . or else they are more demonstrative," CBS News correspondent Bill Dunn told his radio audience. One local man told Dunn that the general should someday be buried in Manila under a huge monument alongside his deceased friend President Manuel Quezon. Dunn concluded that MacArthur "makes a strong appeal to the Filipino sense of the dramatic." In a postwar memoir, the general wrote of the adoring crowds. "Everywhere I went jubilant Filipinos lined the roads and rent the air with cheers and applause. They would crowd around me, try to kiss my hand, press native wreaths around my neck, touch my clothes, hail me with tears and sobs." He added, perhaps with just a touch of disingenuous modesty, "It embarrassed me no end." Excited and relieved at the success of the invasion, he returned to *Boise* and gobbled down a quart of ice cream "like a kid at a circus," in the estimation of one aide. "He is very happy tonight."[5]

For several days, even as Krueger's divisions kept advancing against weak resistance, and increasing numbers of reinforcements and matériel largesse arrived over the beaches, MacArthur commuted back and forth between *Boise* and the beachhead. Krueger did the same from his floating command post aboard USS *Wasatch*. Griswold had already left USS *Mount Olympus* and had set up XIV Corps headquarters in the town of Binmaley. "Our troops now 15 miles inland," he jotted in his diary. "Killing a few Nips. Opposition light in XIV Corps sector. I Corps having a tough time with enemy shelling." On January 12, MacArthur and Krueger met aboard *Boise*. Krueger brought Eddleman along and Sutherland sat in as well. Krueger and MacArthur agreed to launch a follow-up invasion in late January with Major General Charles Hall's XI Corps to cut off and secure the Bataan Peninsula. When the discussion turned to Manila, though, the mood soon grew tense. "It's the only time I ever saw the two of them when they had cross words," Eddleman said. MacArthur made it clear that he wanted Krueger to push speedily for the capital. He also badly wanted Clark Field. MacArthur understood that improvised airfields in the Lingayen Gulf area could not sustain the kind of air support he would need for his armies in the weeks ahead. Moreover, he needed Clark's mature runways to base heavy bombers to support Nimitz's forthcoming invasions of Iwo Jima and Okinawa, both of which had been postponed because of the protracted battle for Leyte, an embarrassment for the SWPA commander. MacArthur wanted no such delays this time. He wanted Clark and Manila, the two strategic crown jewels of Luzon, and he wanted them quickly, while he seemingly had the Japanese off guard.

The safety and security of POWs and civilian internees who remained in Japanese captivity in Manila and its environs also loomed large in MacArthur's mind. His impatience had nothing to do with some sort of self-centered desire to take Manila in time for his birthday on January 26, a birth date he shared with Krueger, who was a year younger. In a postwar memoir and in comments to an Army historian, Krueger made a passing mention about having an abstract desire to take Manila in time for MacArthur's birthday, in part because he sensed that MacArthur wanted this. Latter-year historians somehow took this to mean that MacArthur was motivated mainly by preoccupation with his birthday, a ludicrous claim that had no basis in any evidence. MacArthur never made any such statements to Krueger nor anyone else. The SWPA commander had sound strategic and humanitarian reasons for wanting a speedy advance, though he did not of course fully appreciate the inherent risks. In the Sixth Army commander's recollection, MacArthur "seemed extremely anxious to have that advance made rapidly. He maintained that the advance would encounter little opposition and that the Japanese would not attempt to defend Manila." Krueger believed they would, but he left this unsaid. As MacArthur saw it, Sixth Army had so far encountered little resistance and had suffered minimal losses. "Where are your casualties?" he chided Krueger. "Why are you holding I Corps back?"

The SWPA commander's outlook must have been influenced, at least partially, by Willoughby's lowball estimates of Japanese strength on Luzon. The enemy's seemingly apathetic response to the Lingayen landings—though I Corps was beginning to encounter heavier resistance on the northern flank—probably only reinforced notions of

Japanese weakness in MacArthur's mind. In his opinion, the capital lay open for the taking, so he must lose no time in grabbing it. Fortified by more accurate intelligence data, and more deliberate by nature, Krueger disagreed. He emphasized that I Corps was holding a tenuous flank that protected the entire Lingayen beachhead against the possibility that the Japanese might threaten it with formidable counterattacks, rather than contenting themselves, as they currently were, with hurling periodic and largely ineffective artillery fire at the Americans. "What other base do I have?" he asked rhetorically. He later wrote of the conversation, "I pointed out that the enemy had such strong forces in the northeast that the troops I had assigned to insure [*sic*] the security of our base on Lingayen Gulf and protect the Army's left were indispensably necessary, but that this left me only XIV Corps of two divisions for the advance on Manila, 120 miles away." He did not believe he could supply XIV Corps under these conditions and he had no stomach for sallying them far away from Sixth Army's beachhead bases into the face of unknown enemy opposition and across numerous rivers and streams, most of which were bereft of bridges due to American air strikes or Japanese demolition. In a postwar speech to Command and General Staff College students, Krueger summarized the gist of his argument: "Although naturally anxious to seize the Central Plains–Manila area quickly, I did not consider a precipitate advance for that purpose feasible with the forces initially available to me."

Krueger emphasized to MacArthur that he could not hope to move on Manila until he received reinforcements to protect the beachhead and help secure the XIV Corps's logistical lifeline for the advance. "General MacArthur did not seem to be impressed by my arguments," Krueger later wrote. "He did not appear to take very seriously the danger that the enemy might well take advantage of any over-extension of our forces to attack them in the flank as we moved south." The two men clearly had significant philosophical differences, a divergence of outlook that was bound to impact future events. Nonetheless, MacArthur refrained from overruling Krueger, who, in the wake of the meeting, bolstered the I Corps front with the newly arrived 25th Infantry Division and continued a steady, but slow, advance with XIV Corps to the southeast, an average of about four miles per day. In deed, if not necessarily word, Krueger continued to consolidate, protect his flanks, and marshal his resources before pushing in earnest for Manila.

If any larger historical meaning can be divined from the courteous disagreement between the top two American commanders, it was that Krueger better grasped the tactical realities of the unfolding Luzon campaign while MacArthur had a keener understanding of the strategic picture. In that sense, both were right and both were wrong. Given the nascent nature of the Lingayen beachhead, and the tenuous logistical lifeline inherent in any substantial advance, Krueger's logistical concerns held much merit. From a logistician's point of view, Luzon's sheer size presented challenges more akin to littoral operations and yet without offering the advantage of many high-capacity harbors. Liberty ships were forced to anchor half a mile from the coast and discharge cargo aboard DUKWs or landing craft rather than directly onto docks. Unloading of supplies was hindered by heavy surf, bad weather, and uneven beaches. For a time, the waves became so unruly in the XIV Corps sector at Lingayen that Krueger was forced to reroute all unloading to San Fabian, where I Corps had landed, creating an inefficient bottleneck in the inland movement of supplies. In the estimation of the Army's transportation historian, the effort was continually plagued by "muddy roads, shortage of trucks, lifting equipment, and spare parts, and lack of drydock facilities." Far too much cargo remained aboard ships for too long, a persistent problem throughout the entire Pacific War. Transport Division 5, a reinforcement and resupply convoy composed of eight attack transport and attack cargo ships, did well to disgorge about half of its matériel within a twenty-four-hour period, a typical if unsatisfying circumstance.

In spite of the challenges, 11,000 short tons of supplies and equipment moved across the beaches each day. Shore parties and newly hired Filipino laborers manhandled crates and boxes into hastily organized supply dumps or loaded them directly onto trucks. Often operating without guides, drivers did the best they could to get the supplies to forward units, sometimes dodging enemy shellfire, more frequently dealing with traffic jams, bridge outages, or just simple confusion. Already a shortage of trucks plagued Sixth Army. The intensity of resupply operations and the ever-expanding distance between the beaches and the front de-graded vehicles quickly, only adding to the problem. "There were times when the base was so hard pressed for trucks that G-4 [supply] and G-3 [operations] of Sixth Army had to pull badly needed vehicles from divi-sions already short of transportation," lamented Colonel Herbert Vogel, commander of the beachhead logistical base.

Inland supply depots were established. The typical depot spanned seventy-five acres and processed 1,500 tons of supplies daily. Even with these forward supply nodes in place, it was nearly impossible for quar-termasters to provide Krueger with everything he needed. "Serious dif-ficulties were caused by shortage of spare parts, tires, recoil mechanisms, gun tubes, 60 mm mortars and 30 caliber machine gun mounts," he later wrote. As always seemed to be the case in this war, the Americans managed, in spite of an oft state of chaos and confusion, to keep front-line units supplied adequately if not lavishly, though every forward step of leading units only added to the boilerplate-like pressure of daily lo-gistics.

Many of Krueger's engineers were absorbed with the vital task of constructing usable airfields in the beachhead area. The support of the Navy's escort carriers was temporary, confined to a seven-day period beyond S Day so that Nimitz could use the ships for his pending inva-sions. Land-based planes from Mindoro and Leyte contributed some support, but not enough to meet Sixth Army's needs. Both MacArthur and Krueger had known since the planning stages of Mike I that they must develop their own beachhead airfields for close air support, at least until they could capture Clark. MacArthur had bluntly asked Brigadier General Leif "Jack" Sverdrup, the theater engineer, if he could get fields ready in time to take over when the escort carriers left. "General Mac-Arthur looked stern as he asked the question," Lieutenant Colonel Ege-berg, a witness to the conversation, later wrote. "Jack waited two or three seconds (he had this sense of drama). Then, using his forefinger for emphasis and exuding confidence, he took a step forward and said, 'You'll have it, sir.'"

Sverdrup was especially confident that a preexisting airstrip near the town of Lingayen could become a productive airfield for fighters and medium bombers. In some ways, though, the Americans were their own worst enemy. On S Day, Sverdrup had to personally intercede, with his service pistol drawn, to keep newly landed tanks from tearing up the airstrip. When engineers and newly hired local laborers went to work on it, they spent much of their time filling craters and clearing fragments left by the preinvasion bombardment. The work crews used beach sand to fill the craters, then smoothed the surface with a coating of palm fronds before laying 5,000 feet of steel matting for the runways. "After the steel mat was in place the entire surface, except where woven bamboo mats had been used, was shot with tar in an effort to control dust and erosion," the Sixth Army engineer reported months later. A hastily constructed control tower, alert shack, and some five dozen revetments completed the facilities necessary for operations. True to Sverdrup's promise, numerous fighter squadrons and several cargo-ferrying C-47s arrived at the little base by the afternoon of January 16 and formally relieved the escort carriers of duty. After an abortive attempt to construct a medium-bomber field at an unsuitable site near Dagupan, the engineers completed a base with a 7,000-foot runway and enough parking for 350 aircraft at Mangaldan on January 22. "This strip had a surface of compacted earth, treated with oil as a dust palliative," wrote the Army Air Forces official historian. The base accommodated fighters and medium bombers. Perhaps most impressively, the engineers constructed fuel pipelines that spanned from barges offshore to the respective bases. The two fields provided Krueger with just enough air cover until he could secure Clark Field, a short-term solution whose shelf life diminished with every passing day.[6]

Armed with better intelligence than MacArthur about the size of Yamashita's forces, Krueger was right to at least consider the possibility that Japanese units, most notably the Imperial Army's 2nd Tank Division, might emerge from eastern Luzon's mountainous spine to hit XIV Corps with flanking attacks. He correctly anticipated that in addition to dislodging the Japanese from Clark Field, he might very well have to fight for Manila in a manpower- and firepower-intensive, bloody struggle. In a larger sense, though, Krueger had surprisingly little grasp of the strategic purpose behind the invasion of Luzon, nor of its impact on the wider war in the Pacific. Like a brilliant civil engineer who fully appreciates every nut and bolt of a construction project but not necessarily its larger societal effect, Krueger seemed to look past what was most important. The twin objectives of Clark and Manila and, to a lesser extent, the liberation of the population and Allied prisoners represented Luzon's true strategic value. The engagement and destruction of the Japanese armies meant less, and MacArthur knew it. Yamashita and his isolated soldiers were not going anywhere. They were at the mercy of an enemy that controlled the air and sea. Their greatest strength lay in the defense of formidable terrain; their potency diminished in any other scenario save perhaps the hypothetical possibility that they could unleash mass suicide attacks by turning themselves into explosives-laden human bombs. If they decided to emerge from the hills and fight amid the valleys, rivers, and roads of central Luzon, they would immediately risk destruction from US air strikes and mobile firepower. No one understood this better than Yamashita, hence his intention to do little more than launch local counterattacks. Unfortunately, the Americans did not quite realize this just yet. MacArthur correctly anticipated Yamashita's unwillingness to fight for the capital, but little else about enemy intentions and capabilities, including the Japanese commander's inability to make subordinates in Manila bend to his will. MacArthur's acceptance of Willoughby's deeply flawed estimates warped the SWPA commander's mindset in relation to the many difficulties of what securing Luzon would cost in lives, resources, and time, and brought out one of his worst qualities, namely the tendency to dismiss unpleasant facts that did not suit his larger agenda (a series of erroneous, starry-eyed communiqués pronouncing a premature end to the Leyte campaign the previous fall served as only the most recent example).

Even so, MacArthur keenly understood, arguably better than anyone else, the big-picture riches that would flow from fulfilling, as soon as possible, the strategic purpose of invading Luzon. The logistical advantages of controlling Clark Field and Manila were of course beyond dispute. The establishment of powerful air bases would mean that SWPA had done its part to justify the resources it absorbed; to date in his dealings with Admiral Nimitz, he had largely been an importer of air and sea support, but now he could become an exporter, a bold statement of SWPA's importance in the Pacific War. More than this, MacArthur realized the tremendous effect on morale: for ill among the Japanese; for well in the Allied world, where liberations seemed to encompass larger national war aims. The attainment of a rapid strategic victory on Luzon would wordlessly communicate an obvious reality that Japan itself might well become the next invasion target. In this context, then, he felt, quite rationally, that a fast dash for Manila was worth the considerable risk. More than a few of the soldiers on the ground shared his viewpoint. "There is no doubt in my mind that we could have reached Manila a week to ten days sooner than we did, if Sixth Army had permitted us to move as fast as possible rather than worrying about its left flank," Lieutenant Colonel Loren Windom, executive officer of the 37th Division's 145th Infantry Regiment, later contended. "It was heartbreaking to have to stop the advance around four p.m. and see [a] barrio just a few miles ahead being burned by the Japs."

Perhaps because MacArthur felt that rewards were well worth the risks, he soon began breathing down the neck of the Sixth Army commander, though he was still careful to refrain from interfering directly with Krueger's battle plans. MacArthur peppered Krueger with messages urging more aggressive action. He made frequent visits to Sixth Army headquarters. To Egeberg, a disappointed MacArthur remarked perceptively, "I think he feels that every side valley on our east is full of Japanese ready to storm out. Well, there are plenty of Japanese back there, but they're defending . . . and they are not going to come charging down into the plain with all that we have here." In the wake of one typically unproductive, frustrating visit, MacArthur told Egeberg, "Walter's pretty stubborn. Maybe I'll have to try something else." MacArthur soon relocated his headquarters from Dagupan to a sugar plantation site at Hacienda Luisita, about halfway between the landing beaches and Manila, and a full forty-seven miles ahead of Sixth Army headquarters at Calasiao. The move made the not-so-subtle point that if the theater commander felt secure enough to move his headquarters so far forward, then perhaps the Army commander might consider moving more rapidly without consideration for his flanks.

Krueger refused to give in to this blatant attempt to shame him into what he considered to be undue recklessness. "Our advance toward the south was slower than desirable," he later admitted. "But its pace depended upon the reconstruction of the many destroyed bridges, some very large ones, rehabilitation of the roads and the Manila-Dagupan railroad. Shortage of vital bridge material, lack of locomotives and limited rolling stock complicated matters." Many of the bridges of central Luzon had indeed been destroyed or degraded by American planes in order to restrict Japanese mobility; some had been wrecked by the Japanese themselves as they retreated. The bridging troubles were significant enough that Krueger asked the headquarters of General George Kenney, MacArthur's air commander, not to bomb any bridge unless by specific request from ground units. A worried Griswold, whose XIV Corps was leading the way for Sixth Army, admitted to his diary, "The bridging problem is considerable." Engineers worked to build pontoon, treadway, and Bailey bridges over the many rivers and streams. Even more frequently, their efforts were absorbed in repairing damaged, but intact, structures. In the path of Griswold's XIV Corps, engineers encountered 217 destroyed timber bridges, of which they repaired 138 and completely rebuilt another 79. Over wider rivers and streams, Griswold's engineers constructed 26 Bailey bridges, 10 steel treadway bridges, and 14 pontoon bridges. They also rebuilt roads that had degraded during the Japanese occupation. "There was practically no road maintenance, and it was necessary to refill numerous and deep chuck-holes, and in some instances, to remove all the topping," explained the XIV Corps after-action report.[7]

The bridging problem presented an obstacle to Sixth Army's progress, but it was not the primary reason for Krueger's deliberate pace. Just as MacArthur had sensed, Krueger would not set aside concerns about the security of his flanks. As with Carigara on Leyte the previous fall, he was preoccupied with what the enemy might do rather than what he himself could achieve. In the South Pacific and on Leyte he had occasionally become too tethered to his headquarters, mainly due to the diffusion and remoteness of his battlefields rather than any paucity of courage. This ran counter to Krueger's personality of hands-on leadership. "The commander must see as much as possible of his troops, especially at the front, go through the various hospitals and talk to the wounded, and personally inform himself of the state of supply, housekeeping, discipline, medical care, mail deliveries and so on," he once said.

By contrast to his previous campaigns, suitable roads and the more fluid military situation on Luzon allowed him to visit frontline units frequently, and he seemingly grew more discomfited with the tenuousness of his army's logistics and security the more it advanced. He spent most of his days in a jeep convoy, constantly visiting frontline units, often under the watchful protection of military policemen or Alamo Scout bodyguards. "To cover his schedule we had to travel fast with sirens going most of the way, pebbles and dust flying in all directions and chickens scurrying for cover," Lieutenant Colonel David Gray, a staff officer in Krueger's operations section, later wrote. The general apparently observed everything, with a keen eye for detail. He especially made sure to speak to enlisted men. He asked about their food, their socks, the condition of their feet, their weapons, their morale, and anything else that related to the job of soldiering; no matter was too trivial to escape his attention. "As we talked, it was obvious to me that he was taking everything in, sizing everything up," one regimental commander later fondly recalled of a typical Krueger visit; "vehicles, wire, weapon positions, the condition of the men and the equipment. He could tell by looking at the troops how often they shaved or got cleaned up, and he could tell how weapons were emplaced and equipment cared for by looking at the positions."

Unassuming, bereft of any charm or charisma, but exuding the sort of authentic savvy that accrued from soldiering over four decades, Krueger had a down-to-earth, gruff demeanor that fostered honest conversations, so much as this was ever possible between a general and an average citizen soldier. "He was out in the field himself, seeing what the troops were doing and what their commanders at all echelons were doing to take care of their troops," wrote Lieutenant Colonel Jack Tolson, an Airborne liaison officer with Sixth Army headquarters who, like many who worked on Krueger's staff, admired him greatly. Krueger's subordinate commanders almost universally respected him. Few of them, though, felt even a modicum of affection for him. "I give him credit for being completely sincere in every single thing he did," Major General Roscoe Woodruff, commander of the 24th Infantry Division, once told a latter-year historian. "He was not a pleasant man to get along with. I had great admiration for his staff, who must have had to put up with a lot." Some, like Griswold, came to dislike him. "[He] was nasty and critical about things in general," the exasperated XIV Corps commander complained to his diary of Krueger at one point during the Luzon campaign. "Nothing seemed to please him. Damndest man to serve with I ever saw!" Though Krueger was lacking in any niceties, his rise from private to general bespoke an impressive achievement that reflected his extraordinary competence and dedication. "There are many occasions when I don't know what to do, but from long experience I know what not to do," he once told his indispensable chief of staff, Brigadier General George Decker. Krueger's son Walter Junior, a West Point graduate and engineer officer serving in the European theater, wrote revealingly of his father, "He never hurried. He was deliberate. He had the strongest character of any man I ever knew. His integrity, loyalty, and iron will were fundamental."

Arguably, General Krueger understood the rank-and-file soldier better than did any of his senior officer peers. When he found out one morning that officers at a division headquarters had eaten fresh food for breakfast but the frontline troops had not, he immediately made it clear to the commander that the best food should go to the combat soldiers, not staff officers. Nor was this just talk. During another typical visit with a frontline infantry battalion, he made a point of inspecting the field kitchens to ask the mess sergeant what the troops were eating. Upon learning that the unit had eaten only powdered eggs since leaving the States, he told one of his aides to find fresh eggs and get them forward. "They arrived two days later," Lieutenant Colonel Ellis Blake, the battalion commander, marveled. "I was impressed by his genuine concern for us." After listening to a pre-attack briefing at a division command post, Krueger emotionally shook the hand of the young battalion commander whose unit was scheduled to lead and said, "God bless you, son, and God bless your soldiers." One day he stopped on a pontoon bridge to speak with an engineer who was using a sledgehammer to pound beams back into place after they had been loosened by jeep and truck drivers who drove too fast across the bridge. Krueger expressed regret that the man had to expend this effort because of the speeders. He authorized the man to use the sledgehammer on the offending vehicles to slow them down. The soldier's face lit up with a smile. He saluted and enthusiastically said, "Yes, sir!" Krueger doubted that the soldier actually beat on any vehicles, but he figured the story would spread far and wide, and impart the necessary message to take better care of the bridges.

He took pride in never raising his voice to an enlisted man, though he was anything but shy about correcting them. As his jeep passed a careless sentry who had leaned his rifle against a tree, well beyond his reach, Krueger immediately ordered the driver to stop. The jeep skidded to a halt "in a shower of flying gravel," according to one aide. Krueger jabbed a finger at the young soldier and barked, "The next time I catch you without your rifle it will cost you one hundred dollars." He proceeded to explain to the soldier, in a fatherly tone, that without his rifle he could not protect himself or his comrades. He emphasized, quite correctly, that his rifle equated to his life. At night, after a long day of touring the Sixth Army front, Krueger returned to the midsize house that served as his command post and discussed what he had seen that day with Decker and other staffers, many of whom he instructed to correct deficiencies or problems he had noticed. He ate with his staff each evening at 1800 sharp. He had no interest in frills or personal conversations. He consumed only small amounts of heavily salted food and incessantly smoked Camel cigarettes or cigars or a pipe. For relaxation he took in the occasional movie, or far more commonly, he read detective novels. His reading habits leaned toward the voracious. Already a pile of nearly seventy-five paperbacks had accumulated in the front room of his command post.

Krueger had served multiple tours in the Philippines. He especially knew Luzon. It was here that he had come of age as a soldier. During one visit to a division command post, he actually stumbled over "an obstruction in the tall brush," as he later described it, only to realize that the obstruction was a monument he himself had placed there in 1908. On one occasion he even pointed out to Lieutenant Colonel Tolson the exact spot where he had been commissioned from the ranks in 1901. As a young lieutenant, Krueger had conducted a topographic survey of the island. "I was amazed!" Tolson later wrote to a historian. "I wondered if there was any general who knew the geography of the Philippine Islands like Gen Krueger." When the MP in Krueger's lead jeep misguided his group on one trip to the front, the general took the lead and flawlessly guided them to their objective. "Either he had studied his map assiduously or he had one helluva memory of the area he had known forty odd years before," Lieutenant Colonel Gray marveled.

Indeed, few knew the terrain like Krueger. But regretfully, this institutional memory did not translate into the sort of aggressive advance that the situation warranted. By the last week of January, Krueger's leading units had closed to within striking distance of Clark Field but not Manila. Sixth Army's ponderous southerly advance had by now become such an irritant that Krueger's name became proverbial mud at Hacienda Luisita. "GHQ [General Headquarters] bubbled and boiled with exasperation with Krueger," longtime SWPA stenographer Paul Rogers, newly promoted to second lieutenant, wrote. "All of them joined the hue and cry, echoing and inflaming MacArthur's own impatience." To the surprise of no one who knew him, Sutherland's voice was the loudest. The chief of staff was blessed with a sharp, incisive mind, and his indefatigable work ethic put younger men to shame, but his waspish egotism, caustic condescension, and penchant for self-serving connivance made him perhaps the most uniformly hated person at MacArthur's headquarters. Once, after dining with him, a three-star colleague privately vented to his diary, "I have never at any time in my life listened to anyone with such colossal conceit" and bluntly assessed him as "an inconsiderate, pompous ass." With characteristic brusque insensitivity, Sutherland derided the sixty-four-year-old Krueger as an old man using outmoded tactics. The chief of staff forcefully urged MacArthur to sack Krueger and send him home. A year and a half later, Sutherland cuttingly told an Army historian, "If I had worked for Krueger instead of General MacArthur, I would still be in New Guinea." Open rumors swirled that Sutherland wanted to take over Sixth Army himself. "If I were commanding the Sixth Army," he told a reporter, "we'd be in Manila by now."

If Sutherland really did intend to maneuver himself into command of Sixth Army, then he undoubtedly was soon disappointed to realize that his sideline carping came to nothing. MacArthur conceded intense frustration with Krueger, and Lieutenant General Robert Eichelberger, the Eighth Army commander, later claimed the SWPA commander bluntly told him that he "had many times considered relieving Krueger on the way to Manila." Regardless of what MacArthur might have said in unguarded moments, he refused to fire Krueger. The SWPA commander had handpicked him for command of Sixth Army and worked closely with him for two years. He had just put him in for promotion to four-star general. Like it or not, Krueger was MacArthur's protégé. As such, MacArthur understood that any relief of Krueger would reflect just as poorly on him as it would on Krueger. Nor did he wish to inflict the humiliation of relief upon an honest and reasonably effective commander whom he held in high personal regard.

MacArthur's loyalty to Krueger did not preclude him, though, from continuing to complain to other intimates about his slowness. In one such conversation with the aggressive, cocksure Kenney, who had brilliantly presided over the assemblage of a powerful aviation arm in SWPA, earning MacArthur's highest trust and esteem, the airman bluntly asserted, "You will never be able to get any speed until you put Eichelberger in command." Kenney's candid remark cut to the quick of the matter. MacArthur really had only himself to blame for this situation. He should have understood Krueger well enough to realize that he was ill-suited for this mission. Similar to British Field Marshal Bernard Montgomery, Krueger was a set-piece thinker, a master professional who planned much better than he improvised. Krueger often said, "It is sometimes difficult to be patient, but patience is necessary in war." As the statement indicates, he valued an actuarial-style diminution of risk rather than audacity. He too easily preoccupied himself with enemy intentions and capabilities, to the detriment of his own progress. He was endlessly sensible, to the point where this admirable quality could actually become a liability when a situation called for the supremacy of speedy action over safe steadiness.

Krueger possessed a sharp, analytical mind, and he had a passion for learning from military history. It is surprising, then, that he did not seem to understand that, almost from the beginning of the war, the Imperial Army had demonstrated little facility for ground attacks against American and Australian troops. Almost all the early Japanese ground victories in the South Pacific had stemmed from invading sparsely defended or undefended areas, Rabaul being a prime example of the former and the Gilbert Islands the latter. Even their invasion of the Philippines in 1941–42 owed its success primarily to control of the air and sea, and the resulting logistical collapse of their Fil-American opponents, rather than to any tactical proficiency in ground attacks. Their subsequent record when on the attack in ground combat read like a litany of epic military disasters—Guadalcanal, the Kokoda Trail, Bougainville, the Driniumor, Guam, Saipan. Though the Imperial Army could cause consternation and losses to the Americans through wasteful, self-defeating suicide assaults, the unvarnished truth was that it lacked the combined arms capability, firepower, and staff coordination to pose a serious threat to alter the strategic balance of any campaign against the Americans through offensive ground operations. Nowhere was this more true than on Luzon in 1945, where Yamashita's armies faced crippling logistical shortcomings and a near total absence of mobility. In this context, one cannot escape the conclusion that Krueger gave them too much credit. He worried far too much about the possibility of Japanese flanking attacks from Luzon's eastern hills onto the road net that led to Manila, an unlikely scenario, so much so that one wonders if his worries served as little more than a justification for the methodical deliberation he so constitutionally favored.

To the point, MacArthur should have anticipated during the planning for Mike I that Krueger was the exact wrong commander for a quick bolt into Manila. MacArthur correctly foresaw that the Japanese would not defend the central plains and that his armies could make it to the capital quickly. And yet he did not seem to foresee that the hard-charging Eichelberger would have been a far better fit for this assignment. Glib, cordial, energetic, and physically robust, the fifty-eight-year-old Eighth Army commander had carved out a record as one of the finest American ground generals of the war. At Buna in 1942, he had won the first American land victory of World War II by leading from the front, with tremendous courage and skill. At Hollandia in April 1944, he had deftly implemented MacArthur's bold amphibious stroke to outflank the Japanese on the northern New Guinea coast, rapidly accelerating the SWPA advance to the Philippines. Perhaps just as importantly, he had then successfully overseen a massive construction program to convert Hollandia from a swamp-pocked wilderness into a thriving air and sea base without which the Allied return to the Philippines would have been next to impossible. In June, when an American attempt to seize a key airfield at Biak had bogged down into a nightmarish stalemate, MacArthur sent Eichelberger there as his own personal "fixer" of sorts. True to form, Eichelberger had led from the front, often with a tommy gun in hand. Within a week, he had turned the situation around, provided for the security of the airfield, and achieved the strategic purpose of the invasion. By 1945, Eichelberger had become a master of combined arms warfare, keenly attuned to the synergistic melding of logistics, maneuver, and morale. Like his West Point classmate and close friend George Patton, he believed in boldness and rapid offensive operations. Undoubtedly, he would have been well cast to lead a Manila dash. Thus, if MacArthur wanted a sprinter rather than a distance runner, then he should have chosen his commanders accordingly, but he seems not to have thought in these terms. Perhaps he simply felt—quite incorrectly, as events turned out—that once ashore he could prod Krueger into making a rapid advance, a chancy plan since it meant transforming the Sixth Army commander from his comfort zone as a careful, sensible tactical clinician into an aggressive strategist eager to embrace substantial risk for great reward. The best commanders fully understand the strengths and weaknesses of their personnel and utilize them accordingly. Though Eichelberger lacked Krueger's laudable self-effacement and his attention to the minute details of operational planning, he would have embraced a Lingayen-to-Manila (and Clark) sprint with tremendous gusto and probably more success. "Eichelberger . . . would have gone on and hit them when they were retreating," Brigadier General Bonner Fellers, MacArthur's military secretary, commented after the war. "There was a great difference."[8]

Instead, MacArthur consigned himself to weeks of frustration by miscasting his two key commanders. Eventually, he told Krueger firmly that he must make it to Manila by February 5. The arrival of the 1st Cavalry Division on January 27 added some welcome heft to XIV Corps, and more momentum to Krueger's previously unspectacular advance. Griswold now had three divisions in his cupboard—the 37th, the 40th, and of course the 1st Cavalry. His leading units bounded down Route 3, the main highway that led to Clark and Manila. Clark was a sprawling complex that straddled both sides of the highway for nearly fifteen miles. Most of the fifteen runways were located west of the road. A dizzying array of revetments, hangars, and outbuildings honeycombed the area. Adjacent to the western edges of Clark was venerable Fort Stotsenburg, prewar home of the Philippine Scouts, gallant local professional soldiers who dedicated their lives to the US Army, and the 26th Cavalry Regiment, the Army's last horse-mounted combat unit whose brokenhearted troopers had resorted to consuming their beloved horses in an attempt to stave off starvation during the 1942 Bataan fighting. Soldiers from the 129th Infantry Regiment, 37th Division, fought a bitter battle to reclaim Stotsenburg. When the fighting had only just begun, MacArthur's head-quarters, in characteristic fashion, prematurely announced the capture of the fort. "This erroneous news release had considerable detrimental effect on the morale of the regiment at that time," Major Morris Naudts, executive officer of a leading assault battalion, bitterly complained in a postwar analysis. A vexed Griswold fumed to his diary, "Japs hold Stot-senburg in strength, though Gen. MacArthur has already announced its capture. Why does he do this?" Contrary to MacArthur's cheery pro-nunciations, the 129th needed five hard days of fighting to take Stotsen-burg.

To the west of Clark, a series of rugged hills and ridgelines brooded over the entire area. Understandably, the Japanese focused on defending this high ground rather than the lowlands of the airfield complex and the fort, though individual riflemen and machine gunners concealed in abandoned planes and hangar buildings posed a constant threat. In-comprehensibly, the Japanese had contented themselves mainly with sowing mines and booby traps around Clark rather than destroying it altogether. Though, in fairness, American bombing raids had already done much of the job for them by badly cratering many of the runways and destroying numerous buildings. "Japanese defenses within the area were characterized by improvisation," Major Naudts explained. "Mines, barricades, and the use of weapons of all types."

Major General Tsukada, the Kembu Group commander, the qualita-tively weakest and numerically smallest of Fourteenth Area Army's three major components, dispersed about 8,500 defenders in layered defensive lines among the ridges and caves. Griswold hoped to grab

Clark with just one regiment from the 40th Division. The Americans had little trouble taking the runways and their environs; the ridges were another matter. From caves and trench lines atop the hills, the Japanese showered the low ground with mortar shells and automatic weapons fire, necessitating an onerous battle to root them out of each ridge lest the fire prevent the Americans from using the air base. "Murderous infantry and artillery fire from cave positions in the cliffs made any advance almost certain death," the Sixth Army's after-action report grimly intoned.

Aided by high-powered naval telescopes, Tsukada's men wheeled 75-millimeter artillery pieces and antiaircraft guns out of the mouths of their caves, took a few shots, and then ducked back inside. The Americans replied with massive saturations of artillery fire, much of it directed by observers in liaison planes circling overhead. "It took a lot of ammunition and precision adjustments to drop high explosive shells into those caves, but there was many a direct hit which buried many a Jap alive," Tech Sergeant Philip Hauser, a communications NCO in the 40th Division's 222nd Field Artillery Battalion, wrote to his wife. His unit was equipped with 155-millimeter guns, fearsome and effective weapons that pummeled the Japanese mercilessly while infantrymen painstakingly ascended the ridges to kill them at close range. Tank destroyers, tanks, and self-propelled guns provided the infantry soldiers with direct-fire support. "As infantry advanced, small arms fire and hand grenades were used to clean out the positions, and flame thrower teams destroyed possible survivors in the larger caves," the 40th Division's after-action report explained. "So close were the opposing forces that on some instances hand grenades were traded by tossing them over the pointed crests of hills."

Japanese resistance was stubborn and formidable enough that Griswold had to commit elements of four infantry regiments from both the 37th and 40th Divisions to the fight. By the end of January, the Americans had pushed Tsukada's holdouts back far enough to consolidate their occupation of Clark and start cleaning it up and preparing it to become a major hub for Kenney's planes. "Wrecked and burned-out airplanes were all over the place," he later wrote of what he found when he first visited the place. "Rusty piles of burned gasoline drums dotted the edges of the field, and hangars, shops, and operations buildings were tangled piles of steel and concrete." Sergeant Hauser, the artilleryman, marveled at the "mass of twisted, melted girders . . . planes in them were melted to the ground." The unglamorous, bitter fighting in the hills continued for another three weeks while engineers and construction crews worked constantly to reclaim the vast airfield complex. The 37th Division's 117th Engineer Combat Battalion alone neutralized 1,300 buried aerial bombs, disarming them manually one by one. "They turned down the arming collar on the fuze spindle, unscrewed the nose fuze, and inserted the bomb plug in the nose-well," one engineer wrote. "Using an A-frame [crane] or a truck winch, they pulled the bomb out of the ground," and then disposed of it or, if need be, blew it in place. Around Clark and its surroundings, the Americans captured or destroyed an incredible quantity of weaponry and supplies: 538 vehicles, 463 machine guns, 335 antiaircraft guns, 3,483 cases of ammunition, and 8,050 sacks of rice. By mid-February, Clark began to welcome transport planes and soon thereafter fighters and medium bombers.[9]

With this modern airfield complex now in tow, Griswold amassed in early February the newly arrived 1st Cavalry Division and elements of the 37th Division for a two-pronged drive into Manila. The XIV Corps commander more than sensed MacArthur's impatience to reach the capital. "He is insane on this subject!" Griswold vented to his diary. The supreme commander seemingly had an Emerald City type of yearning for Manila, as if he could hardly stand another minute away from it now that his armies were so tantalizingly close. Almost from the first minute he had set foot on Luzon, he had behaved with near reckless bravery, exposing himself to dangers that might have been too much for a regimental commander, much less a theater commander.

Most of the time he traveled with little security. On a typical day, he climbed into the passenger's seat of a jeep, with a driver and Egeberg alongside, and roamed all over the battle area. On one occasion, his jeep actually wandered in between the two sides during the fighting for Clark. The driver hastily reversed course and returned safely to American lines. Another time, MacArthur found himself enmeshed in ferocious fighting between the 2nd Tank Division and the 25th Division around San Manuel. "Our lines reeled, and I became so concerned over a possible penetration that I personally hastened to the scene of action of the 161st Infantry," MacArthur later wrote. The lines held, though the fighting remained intense. "It is impossible to describe the absolute height of noise produced," Lieutenant Floyd Radike, a young platoon leader in the 161st, later wrote. "We could see enemy soldiers and tanks about a half block away, and everybody in our CP [command post] began firing while the artillery escalated to an unbearable fury. Tanks were hit and went up in deafening explosions." The surviving Japanese tanks and infantrymen eventually retreated, harassed all the way by American planes. Radike claimed that his unit counted 775 enemy bodies in the area.

Another day as MacArthur's jeep ambled along Route 3, a tank commander noticed the five stars on the bumper and used his tank to block the general's vehicle. "My God, sir, you can't go beyond this point," the commander, a major, told him. "They're shelling the road down there and hitting this part too." Explosions were visible just down the road, but MacArthur would not relent. "Thank you, Major, but I think I'll just go down and have a look." Like Krueger, he knew the terrain intimately and he sometimes encountered emblems of the past, as on the day when he found the exact spot where his father, Lieutenant General Arthur MacArthur, had fought in a battle during the Philippine-American War about half a century earlier. "On that spot, Doc . . . my father's aide-de-camp was killed standing at his side," he told Egeberg. As January came to an end and Manila beckoned more tangibly, the frontline journeys intensified. "He certainly was in some ways a restless man," Egeberg later reflected. "There was fighting all around us. He was anxious to get a feel of it all first-hand. Sometimes he would stop at division headquarters and ask the division general to join him. Sometimes he would go directly to the front. The fighting was so often near a road that we would drive forward till we heard, saw, or smelled it; then he would get out and walk until we found somebody who could tell us what the General wanted to know. The General always stood up to talk and seemed unmindful of rifle fire. As we came closer to Manila, the number of visits to the front increased. What the General considered the front was usually where rifle and machine-gun fire was going on."

MacArthur's almost fantastical displays of courage reprised previous

moments in his life, such as in the trenches during World War I, Corregidor during the early days of this war, and Leyte when he had com-
ported himself with similar degrees of calm valor. By nature, he had a
tendency to embrace, maybe even disdain, danger. But his almost fool-
hardy bravery during these weeks of the Luzon campaign was probably
rooted in more than just his intrinsic courage. By visiting the front so
often, he might have wanted to shame Krueger into moving more
quickly, or at least convey the notion that he was watching Sixth Army's
operations closely. Certainly, the welfare of the prisoners could not have
been far from his mind. Perhaps the most important factor, though, was
the personal nature of the campaign to such a self-centered personality.
Luzon represented a beloved home away from home, but also the focal
point of his earlier humiliation, when he had unceremoniously abandoned his troops in the field, albeit at the express orders of the president.
But to a man with MacArthur's personal sense of honor, this probably
seemed little more than a nettling detail, especially now that he knew so
much about the terrible realities of captivity for his erstwhile soldiers.
For MacArthur, the liberation of Luzon and, really more specifically
and symbolically, Manila offered the allure of redemption, something
for which he yearned as if craving water in a desert. "Doc, I want to get
in there early," MacArthur revealingly told Egeberg of his intense desire
to reach Manila. "Three years ago I was driven out of there."[10]

News of a dramatic event might have whetted MacArthur's appetite
even more for his Manila redemption. On January 27, guerrillas reported to Krueger's headquarters the exact location of more than five
hundred prisoners of war at the Cabanatuan POW camp. This golden
information hinted at the growing prominence and significant contributions of Filipino insurgent groups as the campaign to liberate the
archipelago unfolded. The men at Cabanatuan were among the few
American POWs remaining in the Philippines after hell ship evacuations of the previous months. The Japanese had held these prisoners
back primarily because of their poor physical condition. "Those
remaining had been declared by the Japanese to be totally incapacitated," one of the prisoners, Lieutenant Colonel Stephen Sitter, a

neuropsychiatrist, later commented. Actually, most were not so much incapacitated in the strictest meaning of the word as they were in frail health. They were still in the camp as Krueger's forces approached to within twenty-four miles. Krueger and his intelligence officer, Colonel Horton White, knew that when the Japanese thought the Americans were about to invade Palawan in mid-December, they had reacted by packing 150 US prisoners into a trench and setting them afire. Those who attempted to flee were mercilessly machine-gunned. Only 11 men escaped to relate the story of this grisly massacre. On Luzon, Krueger and other American commanders, especially MacArthur, worried that the Japanese would carry out similar, though exponentially larger, executions rather than allow the Americans to liberate their people. Lieutenant General Muto later dismissed such concerns as "sheer nonsense" and claimed that Yamashita had ordered his subordinates to hand over the prisoners through third-party neutral country intermediaries.

Yamashita probably had no intention of harming the prisoners but, from his remote headquarters in the mountains of northern Luzon, he had little control over subordinate commanders at the various camps, whose intentions might have been far different. By the end of January, the Japanese had technically "freed" the Cabanatuan prisoners, but this was a mere semantic charade. The supposed free men were told that if they left their enclosure, they would be shot as combatants. The camp guards left. But other groups of Japanese soldiers continually migrated to and from the area and, more or less, performed the same duties. Sitter described them as "a transient garrison which changed every two or three days." The most the prisoners could do was to plunder a Japanese warehouse for food and butcher some local animals to sustain themselves. The fact remained that they, and most other Allied prisoners on Luzon, military and civilian, remained incarcerated, under guard. Sixth Army had no intention of leaving them to the tender mercies of captors who had compiled a uniquely disgraceful record of barbarity, cruelty, and neglect. In fact, the guerrilla leader, twenty-eight-year-old Iowa-born Major Robert Lapham—who had fought on Bataan three years earlier, evaded captivity, and since built an effective insurgent network in this part of Luzon—told Colonel White that he feared for the safety of the prisoners. The same was true for Lapham's two key Filipino confederates, Captains Juan Pajota and Eduardo Joson, both of whom had once fought in the Philippine Army's 91st Division.

With Krueger's eager blessing, Colonel White conceived of a rescue mission involving Lieutenant Colonel Henry Mucci's 6th Ranger Infantry Battalion, two teams of Alamo Scouts, Pajota and Joson's guerrillas, and even fighter planes from the Army Air Forces. The West Point–trained Mucci selected 121 Rangers belonging to his C Company and his headquarters, plus a platoon from F Company, to act as the strike force to infiltrate to the camp and, at a prearranged signal, ambush the guards, eliminate all opposition, and then retrieve the prisoners for evacuation. Mucci placed his C Company commander, Captain Bob Prince, in operational command.

By extreme stealth, the Alamo Scouts and several handpicked guerrillas preceded the Rangers and staked out the camp, in essence functioning in a similar role as long-range reconnaissance patrol teams and Special Forces soldiers of the Vietnam era. The Scouts and guerrillas later linked up with the Rangers to provide Mucci and Prince with real-time intelligence on routes of advance, the camp layout, and Japanese strength and dispositions, as well as the condition of the prisoners. "The reconnaissance mission was carried out with vigor and enthusiasm as evidenced by the completeness and exactness of detail which were indicative of intelligence reports," Captain George Monsarrat, the headquarters company commander, later wrote admiringly of the Scouts and guerrillas. The main concern was not so much the camp garrison of a couple hundred soldiers as the presence of sizable enemy units in the area that possessed the strength to destroy the Fil-American rescue forces, not to mention the prisoners, in a toe-to-toe fight. Indeed, Lapham estimated the presence of as many as 5,000 Japanese within a five-mile radius of the camp. Enemy units were constantly traversing the nearby road, either in retreat or advancing to meet Krueger's oncoming forces, and this added an unwelcome element of unpredictability to the enterprise. In fact, the reconnaissance teams detected the presence of so many Japanese soldiers in the area on the planned day of the raid that they persuaded Mucci to postpone the mission for a day, until these forces had moved on.

To further prevent nearby Japanese units from interfering with the rescue, the planners assigned Pajota and Joson to set up blocking positions on either side of Cabanatuan. Captain Joson and 80 armed guerrillas manned a roadblock several hundred yards to the south while Captain Pajota and 90 armed men did the same a few hundred yards to the north. In this fashion, the two guerrilla forces acted as brackets to hold open a corridor. Another 150 of Pajota's troops manned twenty-five carabao-powered carts about a mile and a half away to carry the emaciated prisoners back to friendly lines. The guerrillas also secured the villages on the infiltration route, warning the population not to breathe a word of the raiders' presence, and even going so far as to muzzle all dogs and shelter all other animals. Before the Rangers set out for the compound, the flinty, hard-edged Lieutenant Colonel Mucci told them, "This will be a tough but rewarding task. The guerrillas tell us there will be about two hundred fifty Japs in the camp. We'll jump them at night. Get inside quick and knife 'em up! I don't want any of our boys from Bataan and Corregidor killed. Bring out every prisoner. Bring 'em out even if every Ranger has to carry a man or two on his back!" Mucci then asked his men, all of whom were volunteers, to sacrifice their lives, if need be, to save the prisoners. "I did that because I believe in it," he later wrote. "Everybody on the mission took that oath." True to the Ranger credo, they also vowed that, dead or alive, no one would be left behind. They also all understood that the key to success hinged on maintaining strict operational security. "One thing was certain, speed and surprise were of the essence," Captain Monsarrat succinctly wrote.

Late in the afternoon on January 30, guerrillas and scouts guided them expertly to the camp site, where the Rangers quietly went to ground and crawled, with tremendous stealth and more than a little tension, into position over the open ground that led to the compound. The attackers traveled light. They carried only weapons and ammunition. They wore soft caps instead of steel helmets. Several hundred yards away, Pajota's and Joson's units quietly set up their roadblocks. Overhead, a lone P-61 Black Widow fighter from the 547th Night Fighter Squadron, piloted by Lieutenant Kenneth Schrieber, suddenly appeared. Earlier that day, Mucci had radioed a request for air support to Sixth Army headquarters. In response, Krueger's people had arranged for this plane, nicknamed "Hard to Get," to provide a distraction to the Japanese guards. For twenty minutes, Schrieber circled some five hundred feet above, diving and parrying, wheeling about, engaging in aerobatics that transfixed the Japanese, whose initial fear of an aerial attack gave way to dumbfounded fascination with Schrieber's airmanship. Meanwhile, the Rangers crawled ever closer, undetected. "The pilot's moves were so skillful and deceptive that the diversion was complete," Captain Prince later said. "I don't know where we would have been without it."

Inside the camp, some of the prisoners watched the plane, just as absorbed as the Japanese. Many weeks before, the prisoners had jury-rigged a clandestine radio from which they learned of MacArthur's invasion and the approach of his armies. For days they had heard the rumble of artillery and had seen many American fighters. They sensed that true liberation was at hand, though they knew nothing of the raid. "Tension among us was at the breaking point," Sergeant Bill Seckinger, one of the prisoners, later testified. "Any minute, we feared, the Japs might open fire and kill all of us." After the onset of darkness, the Rangers crept even closer. At precisely 1944 hours, they opened fire and began their lightning attack. "The whole world seemed to explode outside," one of the prisoners later said. "I fell to the floor and tried to dig a hole with my fingers." The compound stretched about eight hundred yards in length and six hundred yards in width. Fortified with effective intelligence, the Rangers knew much about the camp layout, especially the location of the Japanese-inhabited buildings and the prisoner barracks. "There was a barbed wire fence about ten feet high running around the outside, and two more lines of barbed wire fences running the length of the camp on the inside," Mucci wrote. "There were two main guardhouses at the front and rear gates and two pillboxes at the northeast and northwest corners."

Armed with bazookas, grenades, submachine guns, and rifles, the well-trained Rangers breached the gates, destroyed the pillboxes, and annihilated the stunned, disorganized Japanese garrison in less than thirty minutes of close-quarters fighting. "Surprise had been complete," Captain Monsarrat affirmed. "The rapidity of the action had so overcome the enemy that only feeble resistance had been encountered." The Americans claimed that they killed at least two hundred enemy soldiers. The men the Rangers had come so far to save were just as surprised as the Japanese. Racked with disease, diminished by years of malnutrition and privation, most were slow to realize what was happening. "We were convinced that the Japs had begun to wipe out all of us," one of them later shuddered. Isolated from the outside world for so long, few recognized the newer weapons and uniforms of their liberators. "Into our midst swarmed many armed American soldiers who told us we were free Americans and to start for the main gate," Major Emil Reed, the camp's executive officer, testified later in a postliberation report.

The Rangers spent many anxious moments calming the prisoners, herding them to the front gate, and carrying those who could not walk. "Getting those prisoners out was quite a job," Mucci wrote. "Some were dazed. Some couldn't believe it was true." Most were clothed in rags. Some had no shoes. Many could only limp. One refused to be carried even though he could hardly hobble on his rickety legs. "I made the death march from Bataan, and I can certainly make this one," he declared proudly. It took half an hour just to get the newly liberated men to the carts, something that would not even have been possible if not for hospitable terrain and the assistance of the guerrillas. "It was past the harvest period so the rice paddies instead of being wet were dry, hard-caked mud, which was fortunate because . . . when we brought out the POWs . . . it would have been very difficult if it had been wet and muddy," Captain Prince later remarked. Of the intrepid guerrillas, Captain Monsarrat raved, "Their bravery and loyalty are worthy of the highest praises." As Prince and his men gently but insistently prodded the 512 former prisoners along, Pajota's guerrillas, exactly as planned, fought off a Japanese column that attempted to break through to the camp. "We couldn't have done it without the guerrillas," Prince insisted. "They protected our flank and then on the way back they formed our rear guard in case anybody should come after us."

The odyssey to ultimate freedom proved anything but easy. The ragged column, stretching at times to a mile and a half in length, moved all night long, on foot and in carts, protected by Rangers and guerrillas. Two of the former prisoners died from heart attacks. In many instances, friendly villagers along the way provided the fugitives with food and water. At midday on January 31, a convoy of American ambulances and trucks met them in the village of Sibul at the leading edge of Sixth

Army's advance. The vehicles took the evacuees to the 92nd Evacuation Hospital, where their long journey to recuperation commenced. After years of near starvation, they gorged themselves on great quantities of hearty American food, something the medics should not have allowed since their shrunken stomachs and malnourished digestive systems could not handle the rich fare. "They were clad in gray hospital pajamas," CBS News correspondent Bill Dunn reported in a broadcast to his audience back home. "In their hands as they shuffled past the mess attendants were porcelain plates, granite pie pans, aluminum mess kits—anything that would hold the great helpings of canned meat, fruit and vegetables that were being dished out. Their expressions were as varied as the moods of man. Some were dazed, some alert, some soberly silent, others jubilantly talkative." As one of the prisoners gobbled down six eggs, a slice of ham, seven biscuits smeared with jam, and a whole can of sliced grapefruit, accompanied by five cups of coffee, he told another correspondent, "This will probably make me sick as hell, but I don't give a damn!"

In saving these unfortunate men, the Rangers, the Alamo Scouts, and their Filipino partners had pulled off an incredible coup de main. The Rangers lost two men killed and two wounded; the guerrillas lost twenty-six killed; two of the Alamo Scouts were wounded. The former prisoners greatly appreciated what these men had done. "My night of liberation was one which will be with me forever," Sergeant Harry Pinto, a Marine rescued at Cabanatuan, said reverently. "The memory of those who broke us out of hell is part of my life. To them I owe my life." A grateful Major Reed called the liberation "wonderful and spectacular." The Army soon shared the thrilling news with the families of the liberated men. "Official confirmation has now been received that your husband, Lieutenant Colonel Albert Fields, returned to Military control thirty-one January," the adjutant general telegraphed the colonel's wife, Bess, in a communication typical of many hundreds. A jubilant Bess immediately wrote to a support group of POW families to which she belonged and announced "my wonderful news—that Albert was among those men rescued from Cabanatuan." Bess shared with the support group the contents of a letter from Albert himself, who expressed regret that "others of my army friends whose loved ones are held by the

Japanese could not have the supreme joy we are experiencing, but sincerely hope it won't be much longer." The family members of the great majority of American prisoners who remained in dismal captivity elsewhere in the Japanese Empire must have had much the same thought, and perhaps some pangs of jealousy.

In the afterglow of the successful mission, an elated General MacArthur visited the survivors during their convalescence at the 92nd. As war correspondents looked on, the general reconnected with these men who had served under him three years earlier. "I'm a little late, but we finally made it," he said, with emotion dripping from his voice. Many congregated around him, shook hands, and thanked him for returning. "You are a little better off than the last time we met," he said in oblique reference to the dark days of 1942.[11]

The general hoped the same would soon be true for the other prisoners on Luzon, who were still under Japanese control. As February dawned, Griswold had positioned two of his divisions to drive into Manila—in the west the 37th Division was advancing on Route 3, to the east the 1st Cavalry Division moved along Route 5. Bypassing Krueger and even Griswold, MacArthur ordered Major General Verne Mudge, the 1st Cavalry Division commander, "Go to Manila. Go around the Nips, bounce off the Nips, but go to Manila. Free the internees at Santo Tomas. Take Malacañang Palace and the Legislative Building." The orders called for a swift advance over ninety miles to Manila from the division's assembly area at Guimba. Mudge created two mechanized maneuver convoys, nicknamed "Flying Columns," under the redoubtable Brigadier General William Chase, an exceptional combat commander well suited for the job. "He was . . . full of pep, very charming," Lieutenant Colonel Glines Perez, executive officer of one of the units chosen for the mission, later said of Chase. "He was very aggressive." In fact, Chase was so hardened by his many months in intense combat that he frequently fired up his soldiers by yelling, "Kill, kill, kill, that is all you need to remember! That's all you need to do!"

Chase's columns embodied the Army's growing sophistication in combined arms mechanization and rapid exploitation mobile warfare. Each column consisted of a cavalry squadron riding in trucks, a tank company, a mobile 105-millimeter howitzer battery, plus engineers, medics, and reconnaissance units. Generous numbers of jeeps and armored cars added to the mobility. In all, Chase had about 2,000 soldiers. They were determined, as a point of pride, to become the first Americans into Manila. They would be protected by planes from a pair of newly arrived Marine air groups whose forward controllers rode with the ground units. To travel as quickly as possible, Chase stripped his columns down to "bare essentials and travelled light with arms, ammunition, water, and four days rations," he later wrote. "What we had a great deal of . . . was high spirit and morale and a grand desire to get into Manila first."

Strikingly similar to thunder runs of the twenty-first century, the convoys drove almost nonstop. Ever so relentlessly, they careened southward, annihilating or bypassing disorganized jags of enemy resistance. "We went right on," Private Fred Faiz, a machine gunner, recalled; "we didn't hunt them down or nothing. We just blew up their . . . machine gun nests or something beside the road." Chase masterfully employed bounding overwatch tactics: Well-organized series of vehicles alternated taking the lead, covered one another as they advanced, and then repeated the process for miles on end. According to the 5th Cavalry Regiment after-action report, vehicle drivers pushed "their trucks to the limit . . . [maintaining] a speed of from 40 to 50 miles per hour down the two lane paved road, with the men ready to spit fire at anything that would attempt to stop their race." In one almost surreal incident at a crossroads, the 5th approached a quartet of Japanese trucks loaded with troops and equipment. "They were waved back by our leading elements and then received the surprise of their life as each passing truck load of American soldiers placed burst after burst into the trucks and Japs. All trucks were set on fire and several Japs killed and the rest scattered."

Chase could not hope to keep his columns on the move constantly. Roadblocks and occasional heavy resistance forced several halts, as did the need for the troopers to catch a few hours of rest and maintain their vehicles. As they progressed down the central neck of Luzon, they were, in the recollection of Lieutenant William Swan, a staff officer, "frequently held up for reconnaissance, blown bridges, and river fordings where troopers dismounted from trucks [and] waded, sometimes waist deep, holding weapons overhead while vehicles were pushed or pulled through engineer improved fords." Earthmoving bulldozers created those fords in a matter of moments, aided substantially by favorable conditions. Whereas the Americans had dealt with the worst of the Leyte rainy season during the fall, Luzon was in the midst of its dry season, greatly abetting movement through many hard-packed ravines, gullies, trails, and even rivers with low water levels.

In many spots, jubilant Filipinos lined the roads or descended on the American vehicles. "We would pass through barrio after barrio, where every man, woman and child would be out waving, shouting victory, handing us flowers, eggs, asking for cigarets [sic], and there could be no doubt of where their warm and deep convictions lay," wrote Carl Mydans, a Life magazine correspondent and photographer who embedded with one of the columns. Mydans had chronicled the first Philippines campaign. He had himself been interned at Santo Tomas for about a year before he was repatriated and eventually made it back to the United States. He had subsequently covered the war in Europe as well. Probably because of that personal history in the Philippines, he found himself even more moved by the liberation scenes here than those he had witnessed the previous summer in France. His colleague Bill Dunn, also along for the ride, marveled at the ecstatic reception as "thousands of people thronged the streets, screaming, singing, and dancing about our armored column until it was difficult to move. Women threw flowers at us and literally fought to touch our hands. I had two eggs pressed into my hands. Another correspondent was handed an offering of sweet corn. People demanded autographs of everyone and women and girls struggled to kiss the passing soldiers." The troopers excitedly returned the kisses, bedecked themselves in flowers, and, in the recollection of Lieutenant Swan, laughed joyously "with a great glee of youth that had seldom appeared in Leyte."

After two and a half days of this breakneck advance, they fulfilled their goal of entering Manila first. Chase's leading vehicles crossed the Manila city limits around 1900 hours on Saturday, February 3, and continued rumbling warily through the northern edges of town, bound straight for Santo Tomas University, where some 3,700 Allied civilians had been incarcerated since 1942. Founded over three hundred years earlier by the archbishop of Manila and named for St. Thomas Aquinas, the university was one of the foremost Catholic institutions of higher education in the world. Twelve-foot-high walls of stone and concrete, interspersed with iron fencing and large iron gates, surrounded the sixty-acre campus. The inmates were shoehorned into the venerable university's dormitories and other buildings that dotted the compound; some people had built modified shanties for themselves on the grounds.

Not all the prisoners were civilians. The Japanese had captured sixty-eight female US Army nurses at Corregidor in 1942 and, out of deference to their gender, had confined them here rather than in POW camps with their male military colleagues. By now, this remarkable group of women had managed to survive the fighting on Bataan and Corregidor, plus three years of extraordinarily difficult captivity in which most functioned as health-care givers to their fellow prisoners. They treated the impoverished, malnourished prison population as best they could, despite equipment and supply shortages. They were now caring for about thirty patients per day who had a wide range of injuries and illnesses that included heart attacks and communicable diseases. The nurses sterilized surgical instruments by baking them in ovens or boiling them over Bunsen burners. For almost a year, food rations had steadily declined at Santo Tomas. On the eve of liberation, the average prisoner was somehow subsisting on eight hundred calories a day, with no protein or fat. From January onward, a day had seldom passed without the death of an inmate; the most vulnerable seemed to be men over the age of sixty. Somber Filipino laborers carted their wasted bodies to a local cemetery. When the camp's physician, Dr. Theodore Stevenson, refused to remove the words "malnutrition" and "starvation" as a cause of death for the inmates, the Japanese promptly put him in solitary confinement.

Most of the nurses had by now lost between twenty and thirty pounds or even more. "I saw my friends faces with the skin drawn tightly against the bones, eyes unnaturally bright and deeply circled," Lieutenant Frances Nash later wrote of their gradual starvation. "I would find myself standing absolutely still, staring into space. I had trouble remembering the days and the dates. There was nothing beautiful in our lives except the sunsets and the moonlight." They worked four-hour shifts in the infirmary, the longest their diminished state allowed them to function. "It was about all one could do to get out of bed for four hours duty and then go back to bed," recalled Lieutenant Alice Zwicker, a nurse who had lost over thirty pounds. Like nearly every other nurse, Lieutenant Madeline Ullom's health had declined dangerously. "I had bacillary dysentery and I had beriberi and scurvy and I had quite a bit of trouble with my teeth and I had lost forty pounds." Still, she and the others held on, determined, almost defiant, to survive. "Several of us said we wouldn't die to please the Japs," joked Lieutenant Rose Rieper.[12]

Like the Cabanatuan prisoners, the Santo Tomas internees sensed that their liberation was imminent. For several days, they had heard the sounds of explosions and the engine rumbles of vehicles in the distance. "We had grown accustomed to nighttime gunfire, but the shooting that evening seemed louder and nearer," wrote Rupert Wilkinson, an eight-year-old child interned with his mother and sister. Wilkinson and the others had seen numerous American planes overhead, including late on the afternoon of February 3, when, at General Chase's request, Marine SBD dive-bombers overflew the area. The prisoners waved and cheered. One of the SBD gunners had tossed a pair of aviator goggles into the compound with a note attached: "Roll out the barrel. Santa Claus is coming." The Marine fliers reported to Chase through their liaison officer that "there were lots of people there waving at them, but that there were many big fires breaking out all over the city," the general wrote. "This worried me as we feared that the Japanese would blow up the whole internment camp." Many of the internees feared much the same thing, a silent testimony to the awful reputation the Japanese had earned for themselves after three years of execrable behavior rather than to any tangible plans on their part. Similar to Cabanatuan, Santo Tomas crackled with tension over this fear. As evening shadows settled over Santo Tomas, the internees heard several guards singing together as if in farewell and immediately figured this must be a bad omen. At almost the same time, the power went out, shrouding the campus in inky darkness, only adding to the tension. Earlier that day, when several inmates witnessed guards storing barrels under the staircase of the main campus building, they had assumed malevolent intentions. Lieutenant Rieper snuck a look and claimed that the barrels were soaked with kerosene. "So all they had to do was ignite it," she later claimed.

Now in the darkness, she and many others became convinced that the commandant, Lieutenant Colonel Toshio Hayashi, intended to blow Santo Tomas up. In truth, Hayashi and his motley garrison of sixty or seventy soldiers, many of whom were Formosans who had been coerced into Imperial Army service, wanted little more than to bolt the camp. Hayashi had hoped to take his troops and leave Santo Tomas many weeks earlier, but his superiors ordered him to remain in place. He knew now that the Americans were very close and, orders or not, he intended to withdraw before they arrived. Indeed, he had already begun preparations to gather his men and leave when one of Chase's lead spearheads closed in on Santo Tomas around 2330. Guided by thirty-eight-year-old Captain Manuel Colayco, a Filipino guerrilla leader, Lieutenant Colonel Haskett Conner, half a dozen Sherman tanks, and about two hundred soldiers approached the main gate. The troopers dismounted their vehicles and moved forward in quiet, dispersed columns. "Fires were burning over much of the city and the red-lighted sky and stealth of the scene and pitch of the emotion had me shaking so that my camera bag pounded against me," Mydans, the *Life* photographer, wrote eloquently. The lead tank, nicknamed "Battlin' Basic," smashed into the gate. "The gate groaned, cracked and crashed under the treads," Dean Schedler, an Associated Press correspondent on the scene, wrote. The tank rumbled through the opening, scraping against the wall, shaking pieces of concrete loose to cascade onto the helmets of the dismounted troopers who warily entered the compound. Aside from a short firefight, the sentries offered little resistance.

For most of the internees, the first indication of their long-anticipated liberation was the ubiquitous, prevailing odor of gasoline, a unique smell after so many years in the Japanese-occupied, fuel-deprived Philippines. Then they heard the unmistakable cadence of American voices. "Hello, folks!" the soldiers called out. An almost electrical excitement spread among the prisoners. "They're here! The boys are here!" people cried joyously. Guided through the darkness by the excited voices, many people, including some of the nurses, poured out of their buildings and shanties and descended on the soldiers. "Thank God you are here," many cried. "It's been so long!" In Lieutenant Ruby Motley's recollection, "Everyone tumbled out to greet the men, laughing, crying and shouting." The hungry internees hugged the soldiers, enthusiastically pounded them on the back, even summoned unknown reserves of strength to lift them up. A wave of happy people surrounded Carl Mydans, the *Life* correspondent, and swept him away. "Crowds pressed in on me so closely that I could not move and then suddenly the crowd picked me up, 40-pound camera kit and all, and passed me from hand to hand overhead," he wrote in wonderment.

The jubilant former internees sang "God Bless America" and "The Star-Spangled Banner" with an almost spiritual emotion. "I've never heard it sung better," commented Private George Fisher, a loader on a tank nicknamed "Georgia Peach." Kids "swarmed over the tanks," Private John Hencke, a gunner on "Battlin' Basic," later said. The singers shouted at the top of their lungs, almost for the sheer excitement of it, an emotional release three years in the making. "It was just the most wonderful feeling," Lieutenant Bertha Dworsky gushed. "It was just indescribable. The feeling of joy and relief to see an American after all that time." To Dunn, the CBS newsman, the euphoria represented "the culmination of thirty-seven months of never dying hope!" Some survivors, such as Lieutenant Marcia Gates, were almost overcome with emotion: "Everyone was weeping with joy and we were almost unable to believe that it had finally happened." Lieutenant Minnie Breese felt the same sense of dreamy unreality over the presence of the liberating soldiers, to the point where, she said, "I had to go and touch one of them. I cried like a baby, everybody cried, even the men in the camp and some of the soldiers too."

To the gaunt nurses, the well-fed, well-armed cavalry troopers seemed like giants; no one recognized their uniforms and equipment. "I never would have recognized [them]," Lieutenant Phyllis Arnold marveled. "They were in camouflage. They looked like tigers." To Lieutenant Helen Cassiani, the GIs seemed like men "from another planet. They were so young, healthy-looking, pink cheeks, filled-out . . . all of them. I felt as high as a kite." One person even blurted out, "How come you fellows are so big?" The cavalrymen handed out chocolate bars and K rations. When one of them gave a K ration meal to Lieutenant Rieper and saw her tremendous enthusiasm, he joked, "Ma'am, if you'll eat that you *must* be hungry." A later official report to MacArthur on the state of the internees bluntly assessed, "Their physical condition is poor," and estimated that most of the women weighed between 70 and 80 pounds, and the men between 110 and 120. Most could not handle the rich American food. By consuming it, they actually imperiled their health. "Many developed gastro-intestinal upsets, so that at first many of the internees lost weight and became weaker than before," an Army physician who treated them related to an interviewer a few months later.

Amid the pandemonium, there were heartwarming reunions. Carl Mydans saw Betty Wilborne, a woman he had known during his time as a Santo Tomas internee. Overcome with emotion, Wilborne "threw her arms around my neck and cried." Lieutenant Swan, the staff officer, searched intently for Margie Bukeley, his onetime girlfriend at the University of Arizona. "I found Margie. What a happy reunion! She was, as were all the prisoners, gaunt and pale. They looked like skeletons, but Margie hadn't lost her buoyancy." Frank Hewlett of the United Press had been one of the last reporters to escape from Corregidor in 1942. He had not seen his wife, Virginia, since New Year's Eve 1941 when she had insisted on staying behind to work as a nurse at a Manila hospital. Beyond knowing that she had been interned at Santo Tomas, he had received little news of her since. He found her in the camp infirmary, severely undernourished and recuperating from a nervous breakdown. "Doctors said she would have fully recovered now if she had had sufficient good food," he told his readers. "Her weight had dropped to 80 pounds, but I found her in excellent spirits." He saw his friend Bill Dunn, the CBS reporter, and exclaimed, "I found her!" The two newsmen bear-hugged each other. An emotional Dunn later told his radio audience of Virginia and the other survivors, many of whom he also knew personally. "Their condition is truly pitiful and if our arrival had delayed another thirty days the results might have been completely tragic. Three years have taken a terrific toll of human endurance and these people were near the end of their string."

The soldiers enjoyed the adulation. "It was one of the proudest things in our lives," one of them later remarked. For countless troopers like Sergeant Warren Matha, the sight of the grateful internees generated an instant clarity, after months of grim combat, as to why they were fighting the war. "We had been killing all across the Pacific and now we were

going to save all those people," he later commented. "What a feeling."
Even so, they could not relax as long as Japanese soldiers remained at
large on the Santo Tomas campus. Troopers in search of enemy soldiers
tried to push their way through the crowds. Officers urged the internees
to return to their beds, lest they get hurt in a firefight. Ironically, when
the tanks entered the compound, Lieutenant Colonel Hayashi had been
meeting in his office on the ground floor of the campus Education
Building with two Japanese-speaking Westerners, Frank Cary and Ernest Stanley, to plan for his exit. Hayashi had no intention of surrendering, nor did he want to fight. He had hoped the American soldiers could
wait outside until he and his men left, but this was an impossibility now
that Lieutenant Colonel Conner's men had entered Santo Tomas and
liberated the prisoners. Instead, Hayashi and 65 of his men hunkered
down, refused to surrender, and held 221 internees, including many
children, as hostages. Tense negotiations, with Cary serving as an interpreter and intermediary, bore no fruit. Hayashi promised not to harm
the hostages. But he would not surrender and he demanded safe passage
out of Santo Tomas. The Americans foolishly opened fire on the building multiple times. The firefights lasted only a few minutes but accomplished nothing. They also led to pointless casualties among soldiers on
both sides. An elderly internee collapsed and died of a heart attack. True
to form, the nurses immediately went on duty and set up a new hospital
in a dormitory, where they helped Conner's medics treat the wounded
American soldiers. As Lieutenant Sally Blaine made her rounds, she
stopped at one bed and told a sergeant, "You have no idea how good you
look to me." The sergeant touched her cheek and replied, "You don't look
so bad yourself, kid!"

Brigadier General Chase arrived during the night and continued the
negotiations throughout the next day, as both sides recognized a truce.
The general disliked the idea of letting Hayashi's people go but felt he
had little other choice. His mission was to liberate the internees un-
harmed, not to destroy the camp garrison. As the situation stood right
now, he and his men had provided only the equivalent of a shared life
raft to the internees. Only time and more security from reinforcements
could furnish them with the necessary medical care, food, and repatriation necessary for true liberation. All of this might be imperiled by

fighting it out with Hayashai. Chase also realized that his forces comprised a mere salient in enemy territory, with a tenuous supply line, and he did not want Hayashi to know just how vulnerable he was to a counterattack. "We were short of food and ammunition and would have been hard pressed to hold the compound," he later wrote. "They really had me in a bind." Finally, through their intermediaries, Chase and Hayashi arrived at a compromise. The Japanese could leave, under American protection, but they had to relinquish their automatic weapons and keep only rifles and sidearms. At first light on February 5, the odd procession left Santo Tomas under escort by cavalry troopers, many of whom fidgeted menacingly with their trigger assemblies. "There was nervousness all around," Mydans wrote. For an uncomfortable moment, Sergeant Matha even made eye contact with Hayashi. "I stared him right in the eye and he stared right back. I wanted to kill him right there. But orders were orders." Flanked by the armed troopers, a helmeted Hayashi led his men into the street. "Some Santo Tomas residents jeered, but GIs shushed them," the boy Rupert Wilkinson later wrote. "Our old jailers maintained order for a few blocks, but once their American escorts turned back toward the campus, the former guards broke ranks and scattered, as a mortified Hayashi angrily tried to rein them in."[13]

The 37th Division's progress into northern Manila had been slower than that of Chase's flying columns, primarily due to blown bridges and an inherently weaker mechanized capability rather than as a result of Japanese opposition. An incredible discovery on the morning of February 4 also did little to hasten the speed of the advance. Leading the division, the 2nd Battalion, 148th Infantry Regiment, found itself halted for a few hours by a destroyed bridge over the Tullahan River. As engineers built a new bridge, some of the infantrymen searched the area. A squad investigated a nearby deserted complex of warehouses and office buildings, where they found vats and faucets that poured a cool brownish liquid onto the floor. They scooped up the liquid, tasted it, and poured it onto their sweaty heads. To their amazed delight, they soon realized that they had stumbled upon a brewery, generally known as the San Miguel Brewery. The Japanese had taken over the facility and renamed it the Balintawak Beer Brewery. The GIs cared little for the name of the place. They knew only that gallons and gallons of cold beer flowed freely, just waiting for them to imbibe. Truly, it was an infantryman's dream come true, a once-in-a-lifetime mini miracle.

Word of the cold beer excitedly spread around the battalion and then the regiment. Cynical dogfaces who were used to fending off disappointment and absurd rumors could not believe their ears. A veteran sergeant trudging along a street about a quarter mile away scoffed, "You don't run across cold beer when you want it most. We'll probably find beer one of these days when we're in a flurry of snow at Baguio." But he was wrong, deliciously, improbably, fantastically wrong. As word spread, deliriously happy soldiers converged on the brewery buildings. "The dirty, thirsty GIs were indulging in the soldier's dream," Lieutenant Stanley Frankel, commander of the 2nd Battalion's Headquarters Company, later wrote. "They swam in beer. Bathed in beer. Lapped it off the floors, filled up their helmets, canteens, mess gears, ration cans, jugs, and even soaked their handkerchiefs with it. The beer was ice cold. No rationing. No standing in line. Some guys just sat on the floor and drank. Others put their mouths against some of the small holes in the vats like a calf on a teat and hung on beyond all reason or understanding. Thank God the brew was mild. The men were comfortably lit, not dead drunk. They were more intoxicated with delight than with alcohol." Unit officers either imbibed themselves or looked the other way. Happily pickled, most of the troops gradually migrated back to a shady assembly area where they resumed waiting for the engineers to finish the bridge. Many filled up any possible receptacle with beer and continued sipping as they lounged.

In the meantime, Griswold and Major General Robert Beightler, the 37th Division commander, arrived in the area to see what had held up the division's progress. They heard many of the GIs singing and laughing. Initially, Griswold complimented Beightler on their spirit, until he almost collided with a soldier who was carrying a helmet full of beer in one hand and his rifle in the other. "He immediately straightened up, dropped his precious weapon on the ground, shifted the beer gingerly from the right to the left hand, came up with a snappy salute and followed it up with a deep bow," Frankel wrote jovially. The nonplussed generals failed to see the humor in the situation. They immediately attempted to find the relevant commanding officers but could track down only an overawed second lieutenant who explained the unit's amazing discovery after its long, hot march from the landing beaches over one hundred miles and several weeks to Manila. Then he adventurously asked the brass what they would have done in the same situation. "We can't sanction this sort of thing but as long as we know nothing about it, Old Man Krueger can't burn us," an unsmiling Griswold replied. "Just be sure those men are in condition to fight when the bridge goes across." He and Beightler turned away and left.

With the bridge ready by midafternoon, the pleasantly buzzed soldiers of the 2nd Battalion crossed the Tullahan River and resumed the advance deeper into northern Manila, through the blue-collar Tondo district. Within a few hours they approached Bilibid, the old Spanish-built prison where, only a few months earlier, thousands of American prisoners had languished before boarding ships for their hellish journeys to the Japanese home islands and other places in the empire. Similar to Cabanatuan, Bilibid now functioned as something of a dumping ground for prisoners whom the Japanese considered to be in failing health. By early evening on February 4, spoke-shaped Bilibid still held about 810 Allied POWs and 465 civilian internees within its unhappy walls. The previous night they had heard the sounds of Conner's columns fighting their way to Santo Tomas, about a mile to the northeast. They had even heard American voices and dared to imagine imminent liberation. "Last night everyone KNEW it was over," a disappointed but still hopeful Sergeant Ike Thomas jotted in his POW diary. "This morning there was much talk of last night's activity being just a commando raid."

He and the other prisoners were racked by disease and malnutrition. Clothed in rags, they slept on concrete floors, lucky to have a blanket or a poncho to cover themselves. As at Santo Tomas, food supplies had dwindled to starvation levels. The daily ration consisted of 100 grams of cornmeal, 50 grams of rice, and 50 grams of soy. "All of it could be held in the palm of one hand," according to one SWPA report on conditions. The Japanese commandant at Bilibid, a Major Ebiko, might have known of the standoff unfolding at Santo Tomas. Regardless, he had no intention of staying put to take on any potential liberation force. Earlier in the day on February 4, he and his garrison had left with the declaration that the prisoners were now free but advised, for their own safety, to stay in place. Before leaving, the guards posted a sign in Japanese alerting any of their comrades who might wander into Bilibid, "Lawfully released prisoners of war and internees are quartered here. Please do not molest them unless they make positive resistance." Major Warren Wilson, an eye doctor and the ranking military prisoner, armed his healthiest soldiers with clubs and baseball bats and posted them on guard duty, "to keep all inside and [keep] unauthorized persons out."

For hours they remained in limbo, technically free but not really liberated. In the early evening, an advance squad from the 148th led by Sergeant Rayford Anderson made the first contact with them. Anderson and his soldiers cautiously cleared a building adjoined to Bilibid's stone walls. Through a hole in the wall, they conversed with several prisoners who remained suspicious and wary. Only by throwing them several packs of Philip Morris cigarettes did they convince them that rescue was really at hand. "By Jesus, it's the Yanks!" someone on the inside exclaimed after retrieving one of the packs. "We're all around you," Anderson told them. "You got nothing to worry about." After a few minutes of excited conversation, Sergeant Anderson's squad left to report their find to their superiors.

Within a couple of hours, most of the battalion converged on Bilibid and quickly secured it. "We've come to free you," a soldier told one bedraggled prisoner who promptly replied, "Where the hell have you been? We've been waiting three years for you." Liberators and liberated mixed together in fellowship that night. "Everything was calm, except our emotions," one of the former POWs later told an Army interviewer. Still, a mood of barely restrained elation seemed to prevail, in contrast to the carnivalesque scenes of joy that had unfolded at Santo Tomas. "Strangely they seemed happier to see us than we were to see them," Sergeant Thomas wrote in his first postliberation diary entry of the 148th Infantry Regiment soldiers. "They liberally passed out their cigarettes and K rations to us ex-prisoners, thereby doing without themselves. They even gave away to us their whiskey, beer and cigars which Filipinos had given them." Still, he made sure to add, "It is obvious that we were overjoyed to see Americans." To Sergeant Charles Sadler, a medic who had been captured on Bataan, the liberators "were a very tough-looking bunch of fellows. They could have had anything they wanted, we were so glad to see them." They also seemed tired, understandably so after a long day of marching, fighting, liberating, and beer drinking.[14]

The 37th Division and the 1st Cavalry Division soon linked up, an important development because this secured a supply line for Chase's flying column troopers who had become cut off during their foray into Japanese territory. Griswold established new boundaries between the two divisions, with the cavalry swinging east to isolate the city and prevent the Japanese from sending reinforcements into Manila, a vital component of any urban combat. The troopers also captured water pipelines—the Balara Water Filters, the San Juan Reservoir, the Novaliches Watershed, and La Mesa Dam—all of which were vital to maintaining Manila's water supply. He charged the 37th Division with the main mission of capturing the heart of the city. By now, Griswold had begun to sense the Japanese determination to defend Manila. He correctly feared that his men were in for a hard fight. Yamashita's directive to abandon the city amounted to a meaningless order from a distant proconsul, mostly because of the persistently toxic schism between the Imperial Army and the Imperial Navy. The ranking naval officer on Luzon, Vice Admiral Denshichi Okochi, reported to Combined Fleet, not Yamashita. In early January, as most of the Imperial Army's soldiers were leaving Manila, Okochi had personally relocated from the city to Yamashita's headquarters in Baguio, a seeming indication of willingness to accede to the general's concept. But he also organized the Manila Naval Defense Force, appointed his principal subordinate in the capital, Rear Admiral Sanji Iwabuchi, to command it, and ordered him to defend the Imperial Navy's extensive complex of bases in the city, as well as Nichols Field on its southern edges. Once Iwabuchi could no longer defend the naval installations, he was to destroy them, the land-based equivalent of scuttling a ship lest it fall into enemy hands.

In effect, these orders had led by early February to Iwabuchi hunkering his garrison down, cut off from the outside world with no hope of escape or resupply, and resolving to defend Manila to the last. He had 17,000 troops at his disposal, about two-thirds of whom were Imperial Navy sailors. These men came from a mishmash of units such as the 31st

Naval Special Base Force, and occupational specialties that included aviation ground crewmen, shipless sailors, construction troops, civilian
employees, and the like. A stay-behind Army contingent under Colonel
Katsuzo Noguchi defended northern Manila above the Pasig, the major
river that flowed east to west through the heart of the city into the bay.
From there, the soldiers resisted as best they could the encroachments
of Griswold's two divisions. Iwabuchi placed the bulk of his naval personnel south of the Pasig. The Central Force defended the heart of the
city; the Southern Force defended Nichols Field, nearby Fort McKinley,
and southern Manila, where Iwabuchi incorrectly expected the main
American attack. Many of his men had no training for ground combat,
much less urban combat. He lacked the organic artillery, combat engineers, and heavy mortars that the presence of an infantry division or
larger ground formation would have provided. But he and his people
still had access to plenty of formidable heavy weapons, many of them
scrounged from marooned or sunken ships, grounded airplanes, and
ordnance depots. By one estimate, Iwabuchi's forces possessed a
staggering array of deadly weaponry: 600 machine guns of various calibers, 990 20-millimeter guns salvaged from aircraft, 110 25-millimeter
cannons, 15 37-millimeter guns, 15 40-millimeter antiaircraft guns, 5
47-millimeter antitank guns, 10 75-millimeter pieces, 25 dismounted
naval guns ranging in caliber from 3 to 6 inches, 60 120-millimeter dual-
purpose naval guns, 5 120-millimeter mortars, plus a few rocket launch-
ers. Buried artillery shells, torpedoes, depth charges, and mines made
for excellent booby traps.

Most of the men were armed with rifles and grenades. Those who did
not have firearms affixed spears to poles or concocted Molotov cocktails.
They also had access to barbed wire and small stocks of high-octane
fuel. The fact that they had little training for the task at hand hardly
mattered. "It is possible to defend a city for a time without prior doctrine, training, or equipment for urban warfare," a leading scholar of the
Manila battle later wrote insightfully. The sturdy urban landscape, by
its very nature, provided Iwabuchi with ideal ready-made fortifications
for defensive warfare. The willingness of his people to fight to the death
only made his forces that much more potent. In order to wreak tremendous havoc, they needed little else besides some weapons and a stubborn

determination to sell their lives dear. "When shall I see those American . . . beasts?" one typically fanatical fighter mused in his diary. "If I expend all my ammunition, I shall attack and kill them by Japanese spirit alone. If my bayonet breaks, I'll assault them and kill them anyhow. If my rifle breaks, I will bite them in the throat."

For a few days in early February, the problematic bridge situation kept General MacArthur out of Manila, only adding to his overall impatience to liberate the city. "The going was bad," Brigadier General Bonner Fellers, the SWPA commander's military secretary, wrote succinctly to his wife, Dorothy, of MacArthur's abortive attempts to embed himself with the leading troops. When MacArthur finally made it across the Tullahan River, he immediately visited Bilibid and Santo Tomas with SWPA staffers and reporters at his side. The general's elation and relief at the successful liberation of so many prisoners and internees, tempered as it might have been by guilt at leaving them behind three years before, knew no bounds. "I cannot recall . . . a more moving spectacle," he later wrote. Major Wilson, the doctor, greeted and guided him at Bilibid. "Thin he was, and tired he looked, but the warmth of his smile and welcome touched both the General and me deeply," Lieutenant Colonel Egeberg reflected.

A somber, almost reverential mood prevailed. In spite of the former prisoners' degraded physical condition, they stood at attention as the general circulated among them. "They remained silent, as though at inspection," MacArthur recalled in his memoirs. "I looked down the lines of men bearded and soiled, with hair that often reached below their shoulders, with ripped and soiled shirts and trousers, with toes sticking out of such shoes that remained, with suffering and torture written on their gaunt faces." MacArthur moved along the lines, shaking hands, conversing quietly and somberly. "You're back," some said. Others said fervently, "God bless you." MacArthur repeatedly replied, "I'm a little late but we finally came." He lingered to speak with Lieutenant Colonel Joseph Chabot, a West Pointer who had served as a corps-level staff officer during the first Philippine campaign and survived the Bataan Death March. His weight had deteriorated to 88 pounds. He greeted MacArthur warmly and the general replied, "How do you feel about getting back in the fight?" Chabot replied gamely, "I know a lot about the islands and the Japanese. I think I could help after a week." MacArthur said, "Well, I admire your spirit, but you are going home for six months. Then you can come back." Some could not hold back tears. Even MacArthur murmured repeatedly to Egeberg, as if trying to maintain his own composure, "My boys, my men. It's been so long." Brigadier General Chase had tagged along with the general's entourage. As he watched MacArthur reverently greet these men whom he had thought so much about but had not seen in three years, he was struck by the obvious raw emotions on display in a man who usually oozed composure. "I have never seen him so moved," Chase later commented. The intimacy of the moment was inevitably frittered by the presence of a media horde. "There was a battery of news cameramen who took pictures of us everywhere as the Gen. and I led the parade," Major Wilson later told his diary.

The tenor of MacArthur's visit to Santo Tomas could not have been more different from the austere military correctness at Bilibid. Crowds of ebullient former internees converged on MacArthur, almost suffocating him with their excitement and affection. "There was uproarious cheering as people struggled forward to get closer to him and if possible to grasp his hand," wrote Abraham Hartendorp, an American civilian who had survived three years in Santo Tomas. "Some old friends succeeded in doing so and MacArthur spoke to them by name." Lieutenant Gaetano Faillace, the general's personal photographer, remembered that in response to the ecstatic clutches of old friends and acquaintances, he "would sort of embrace them emotionally and talk to them." Lieutenant Colonel Sidney Huff, a longtime MacArthur aide, remembered that "hoarse cries came from their mouths. Tears flowed down their cheeks. I thought I had never seen such an unhappy sight, until I realized that this was not a demonstration of sorrow; it was an outburst of pure, unalloyed joy!" One man threw his arms around the general, leaned his head against his chest and sobbed. Some of the nurses, including Lieutenant Edith Shacklette, still resented MacArthur for abandoning his command three years before. In spite of her bitterness, though, even she got caught up in the spirit of the moment. When he approached her, she leaned close to him and kissed his cheek.

MacArthur left after about an hour, pensive and almost completely drained mentally. "This has been a bit too emotional for me," he told Egeberg and Chase. "I want to get out and I want to go forward until I am stopped by fire and I don't mean sniper fire." The adventurous Chase dutifully took him on a whirlwind tour around the embattled parts of northern Manila. Civilians who saw him shouted, "Viva MacArthur!" He smiled and waved grandly. The party ended up at the newly liberated San Miguel Brewery, where 37th Division soldiers had so recently immersed themselves in suds. MacArthur's group included Colonel Andres Soriano, an old friend who had fought on Bataan in 1942 and was now attached to SWPA as a representative of the Philippine government. Soriano had also once been president of the brewery. He joyfully greeted many of his old employees. Meanwhile, the irrepressible Chase could not help but wonder if any beer might still be available. "My tongue was hanging out a foot," he colorfully wrote in his memoir, "so I asked Soriano just who we had to know to get some cold beer." Soriano quickly arranged for everyone to receive beer, including nearby mortar crews from the 5th Cavalry Regiment. Chase drank a pitcher. MacArthur drank a bottle.

MacArthur had already ordered his staff—absurdly, as events turned out—to plan for a grand Manila victory liberation parade that would dwarf the one staged by the Allies the previous August in Paris. A SWPA communiqué claimed that "our forces are rapidly clearing the enemy from Manila. Their complete destruction is imminent." Amazingly, considering how often he was visiting the front and risking his own life, he seemed not to understand much about the intensity of the fighting, and certainly next to nothing of Japanese intentions. He remained mentally imprisoned by Charles Willoughby's inaccurate estimates and his own unrealistic hopes. MacArthur met with Griswold and repeated his familiar mantra for more speed, even fantastically asserting that a single platoon could probably clear the rest of the city, a statement that prompts one to wonder if MacArthur had consumed much more than just a single bottle of beer. In the emotional aftermath of visiting the camp survivors and in his understandable zeal to liberate the rest of Manila, he was stunningly slow to grasp the resolve and strength of Iwabuchi's forces. "He seemed to think the enemy had little force here," a concerned Griswold confided to his diary. "Was quite impatient that more rapid progress was not being made. He was much affected by the pitiful sights and utter thankfulness of our starved people at Santo Tomas and Bilibid. Gen. MacArthur has visions of saving this beautiful city intact. He does not realize, as I do, that the skies burn red every night as they systematically sack the city. Nor does he know that enemy rifle, machine gun, mortar fire and artillery are steadily increasing in intensity. My private opinion is that the Japs will hold that part of Manila south of Pasig River until all are killed."[15]

Griswold could not have been more correct. As the battle migrated south of the river, into the heart of Iwabuchi's defenses, the fighting had already become increasingly intense and destructive. According to Sixth Army's after-action report, "every building and every wall became a strong point. The streets were mined and barricaded with obstacles. These in turn were covered by fire from antitank guns and automatic weapons located in buildings and pillboxes at key street intersections. Artillery was emplaced in the upper stories of buildings where it could deliver fire against our forces advancing down the main thoroughfares." A ubiquity of buried mines, embedded steel rails six to eight feet in height, makeshift barricades constructed from urban detritus, and even, in a few spots, wired lines of abandoned trucks made the streets even more perilous. In many cases these formidable defenses were buttressed by "steel drums filled with sand, soil or cement, and additionally, wired for demolition and covered by fire," in the dreary recollection of one American officer. "In front of these, artillery shells, bombs of all sizes, naval depth charges and floating mines were fused with regular mine detectors and were countersunk in the streets." Some of these massive booby traps were even wired for command detonation by observers peering from a neighboring building. "From the piles of fallen debris, from sand-bagged entrances and barricaded windows, the approaching American troops were met on every hand by devastating machine-gun and small-arms fire," a XIV Corps post-battle analysis grimly lamented. All too often, when the Japanese were forced to retreat or couldn't defend a block, they simply blew it up or put it to the torch. Already, flames were raging out of control in many parts of Manila. "The wind was favorable to [their] efforts and soon the fires had spread to such huge proportions that our forward positions were untenable,"

Major Herald Smith, the intelligence officer of the 148th Infantry Regiment, later wrote.

Japanese commanders were determined to lay waste to Manila. "The Jap is a fiend," Brigadier General Fellers fumed in a letter to his wife and daughter. "He is burning and murdering indiscriminately." Demolition teams blew up 39 of Manila's 101 bridges. Rear Admiral Iwabuchi ordered his men to destroy factories, warehouses, and any other useful installations. This included not just the vital harbor facilities but most anything else his troops felt like wrecking. He cautioned his men to carry out their destructive work "secretly for the time being so that such actions will not disturb the peace and tranquility of the civil population." Actually, the defenders had begun to target the "civil population" on the pretext that they might all assist the Americans by becoming guerrilla fighters. Commanders disseminated chilling secret orders to kill all Filipinos they could in Manila. "All people on the battlefield with the exception of Japanese military personnel, Japanese civilians . . . will be put to death," one of them declared, with bloodthirsty, clinical finality. Another instructed, with grotesque precision, "When Filipinos are to be killed, they must be gathered into one place, and disposed of with the consideration that ammunition and manpower must not be used to excess. Because the disposal of dead bodies is a troublesome task, they should be gathered into houses which are scheduled to be burned or demolished. They should also be thrown into the river." The order revealed that the Japanese propensity to set buildings aflame stemmed from much more than military considerations.

Iwabuchi's men carried out their orgy of destruction against people and property with such mercilessness, enthusiasm, callousness, and inventive brutality as to compare even with the infamous Rape of Nanking. In one respect, Manila perhaps proved even more troubling. The perpetrators at Nanking came as conquerors who expected to live on and exploit their new subjects as overlords of a newly established empire. By contrast, the defenders of Manila all knew they faced imminent death and defeat on the battlefield, and yet they still chose to commit monstrous crimes. In one bloodcurdling, prophetic conversation with a local girl, a Japanese sailor pointed north across the Pasig River and said, "Although you cannot see them, the Americans are just over there and will soon be [here]. By that time, nothing will matter, because we will both be dead." One perpetrator kept a ghoulish tally of his victims in a small notebook: "150 guerrillas were disposed of last night. I stabbed 10. Burned 1,000 guerrillas tonight." Another who apparently had more of a self-reflective conscience noted that he had "already killed over 100. The innocence I possessed at the time of leaving the homeland has long since disappeared. Now I am a hardened sinner and my sword is always stained with blood. Although it is for my country's sake, it is sheer brutality. May God forgive me. May my mother forgive me." Many Japanese servicemen had grown to hate and fear the Filipinos—especially the guerrillas—and resent them as cowardly, ungrateful race traitors for their loyalty to the Americans. "They are the enemies of Asia," one young Japanese officer raged of the Filipinos in his diary. "Though they look like Orientals, they are really Occidentals, no better than Americans." He derided them as "orientals who will not act like orientals, wretches who have neither initiative nor national soul, they are a miserable sort of people. They are therefore our enemies, and their presence in Asia must be eliminated to the last man."

Such hostile feelings undoubtedly played a role in the bloodlust displayed by Iwabuchi's troops at Manila. One American postwar investigator characterized their actions as typified by "wanton cruelty, bestiality and bloodthirstiness that stagger the imagination." Women were gang-raped, beaten to a pulp, disfigured, bayoneted, or left for live cremation inside burning buildings. "Her screams were unbearable," an anguished survivor later wrote of one woman who was burned alive in her house. Babies were impaled on the ends of bayonets. Groups of people, ranging from a few family members to hundreds at a time, were herded inside buildings, shot, stabbed, tortured, and ordered to stay while the buildings were set afire. Japanese troops slashed and beat untold thousands to death. The luckiest victims were shot. Usually, the Japanese sought other ways to kill rather than expend ammunition they preferred to use against the Americans. In some cases, the Japanese lined people up, tied their hands behind their backs, shot or stabbed them to death, and roughly pushed their bodies into ditches. "The children were from two to ten years old," the investigator of one massacre site later wrote. "Some of the women had been pregnant." Most victims were clubbed or burned or bayoneted. "Because of the burned or seared condition of the bodies it was difficult to determine if they had been subjected to bayonet, bullet, or shell fragment wounds," another researcher reported somberly of maggot-ridden corpses he found inside a building. "At the officer's command the soldiers began bayoneting all of us, men, women, and children without provocation," one survivor remembered of a typical anonymous killing. "When the Japanese had finished, they threw our bodies into a heap. The dead were thrown over the living. Not many died outright, a few died within one or two hours, the rest slowly bled to death. The soldiers retired and we heard them later drinking outside. Frequently they returned to laugh and mock at our suffering."[16]

As the fighting and the atrocities tragically raged around the burning city, MacArthur played a new card, one he had already decided to employ in spite of his expectations of minimal enemy resistance in the capital. As far back as November, MacArthur had spoken to Eichelberger about the possibility of landing troops somewhere in southern Luzon. "The objective was to disrupt the Japanese lines of communication, create a diversion . . . and, if possible, even occupy Manila itself," Eichelberger explained in an official report. By late January, the concept had evolved into a plan, called Mike Six, to land one regiment on January 31 from the 11th Airborne Division on Luzon's west coast at Nasugbu (pronounced "Nah-soog-boo") about forty-five miles south of Manila as a reconnaissance in force. If these troops from the 188th Glider Infantry Regiment did not meet strong enemy resistance, and if Eichelberger saw an opportunity for an inland advance, he was authorized to land the 187th Glider Infantry Regiment over the beaches and then drop the 511th Parachute Infantry Regiment at Tagaytay Ridge, a prominent finger of high ground about twenty-five miles inland that could serve as a nice pivot point onto Route 17, the main two-lane road that led to Manila. "In other words, it was up to me to decide whether to hit or run," Eichelberger later wrote, "and also whether to advance on Manila." In one conversation, MacArthur told Eichelberger, "Go in and cut the enemy to pieces. Break up his rear areas."

In the weeks before the invasion, several officers from the 11th Airborne landed clandestinely by submarine and rubber rafts in the Nasugbu area, where they worked with guerrillas to gather valuable intelligence on the landing beaches and what appeared to be a minimal Japanese military presence. An unopposed landing on January 29 by Major General Charles Hall's XI Corps in the San Antonio area of the Bataan Peninsula augured well for Mike Six. On the day before the invasion, Eichelberger, tanned from a swimming regimen he had recently maintained until boarding ship and, as always, eager for action, wrote to his wife and soul mate, Emma, "The weather is fine and we now have the pleasure of seeing many good old American planes flying overhead. We are offshore about five miles with beautiful mountains in the distance. The water is as blue as indigo. The sun is shining through a light overcast." The 11th Airborne commander, Major General Joseph Swing, excitedly described the plan to his father-in-law, retired General Peyton March, as "an end run with a forward pass as a climax. These youngsters of mine are raring to go again and I don't believe we'll get our noses bloodied too badly."

At 0815 on January 31, the 188th hit the beach at Nasugbu against minimal resistance. "There were no enemy obstructions on the beach and with the calm sea no beach swells to interfere with the landing boats," one soldier wrote of the first-wave landings. Like many other American officers in SWPA, Lieutenant Colonel Ernest LaFlamme, the 1st Battalion commander, knew Luzon well from prewar tours of duty. In fact, he had spent many weekends with his wife on Nasugbu beach. Led by his battalion, the 188th quickly seized the town, where excited locals plied them with papayas, eggs, bananas, and even chickens. "Victory! God bless you!" the Filipinos bellowed joyously. Smiling soldiers were sorely tempted to stick around and party, but they knew they could not afford to linger. "We couldn't stop," the division historian later explained. "The Japs were on the run and we had to take advantage of their being off balance."

Barely impeded by any enemy resistance, they lunged inland more than eight miles, captured a small airfield, a sugar refinery, and the key steel-trussed Palico River bridge where Japanese guards were caught by such surprise and so decimated by the fire of the advancing American formations that they failed to detonate demolition charges. Guerrillas materialized to assist the Americans as guides, intelligence gatherers, and light infantry support. Aboard USS *Spencer*, Eichelberger digested promising reports of the successful landing. "Everything is going forward very nicely so far," he wrote in a quick letter to Emma. At midday he decided to reinforce rather than withdraw. Given his innate aggressiveness, it is difficult to imagine that he ever took the reconnaissance-in-force concept very seriously. MacArthur undoubtedly understood this, too—after all, one does not unleash a sleek racehorse from a starting gate with anything other than the expectation that he will run. Years later, Eichelberger admitted his intentions: "I made up my mind that if conditions ashore were okay, I would land the rear elements not over three hours behind the others."

MacArthur could have decided to place the Nasugbu invasion under Krueger's control, but instead he chose Eichelberger to carry it out, a choice that stemmed from a deep appreciation of the latter's suitability for the job at hand. In one conversation, MacArthur had actually told Eichelberger, "This is your only chance to take part in the capture of Manila, Bob. You can be the Patton of the Pacific!" MacArthur understood the similarities between Patton and Eichelberger and how he might use this to his advantage. Eichelberger had kept in touch with his friend Patton during the war. Their similarities were striking. Both had a near brilliant grasp of modern combined arms operations. Both had a keen sense of personal honor. Both thirsted for the public acclaim of military glory, though Patton valued this significantly more than did the comparatively unassuming Eichelberger, who had a deeper affinity for the war's terrible effect on the average soldier.

MacArthur knew that invoking Patton's name would dangle the delicious carrot of military immortality in front of the history-conscious Eichelberger. More than this, MacArthur understood the deep antipathy that the Eighth Army commander now felt for Krueger, whom he viewed as little more than an unimaginative plodder, an attitude startlingly similar to Patton's private view of Omar Bradley as a stolid commander of commonplace ability. "Bradley is a man of great mediocrity," Patton once confided tellingly to his diary. Over the course of nearly a year and a half of working closely with Krueger, including a stint as a corps commander in Sixth Army, Eichelberger had come to think of him as rude and mean-spirited, qualities that were unimaginable to a person of Eichelberger's sensitive affability. In letters to Emma, Eichelberger had taken to deriding Krueger as "Old Molasses in January." Contemptuous of what he viewed as Krueger's excessive caution, he told her in one missive, "If he is a great general or has any of the elements of greatness, then I am no judge of my fellow man. Beyond a certain meanness, which scares those under him, and a willingness to work, he has little to offer." MacArthur well understood the full-blown rivalry that had now developed between his two army commanders. He especially knew of Eichelberger's particular eagerness to eclipse Krueger, and he shrewdly resolved to exploit this as a means to liberate Manila as soon as possible.

In the early afternoon of January 31, Eichelberger went ashore, hopped into a jeep, and visited Swing's newly established command post, where he ordered him to send in the 187th Glider Infantry Regiment, plus accompanying antiaircraft and antitank units, all of which were ashore and on the move by late afternoon. The Japanese were now confronted with another flying column of sorts, albeit one composed this time of foot soldiers with a few trucks, but nonetheless poised to threaten Manila from the south. "My orders to General Swing called for advance all day and throughout the night," Eichelberger wrote. "Enemy troops were confused and retreating, and a halt at dark would have permitted them to reorganize."

Eichelberger's refreshing mandate to fight at night as a means of keeping the bewildered Japanese on their heels found a willing executor in the innovative, enterprising Swing. If opposites can be said to attract, then surely the same must be true far more frequently for those of similar or even identical outlook. Eichelberger and Swing were strikingly alike and as well matched as peanut butter and jelly. Both had an enduring passion for leading from the front. "Where can one find out more than from actual conditions when bullets are flying?" Eichelberger liked to ask rhetorically. Once in action, neither had patience for much of anything besides hastening tactical and strategic victory. Lieutenant Colonel Douglass Quandt, Swing's operations officer, once described his boss as "so energetic and so purposeful that he could tend to break under pressure were it not for the safety valve provided by his sense of humor and his ability to relax completely. In combat, General Swing's quick, incisive mind enabled him to reach decisions rapidly, and he never hesitated to make them. He thinks big, and has amazing perspective."

Blue eyed, prematurely snow haired at age fifty, ramrod straight in his posture, lean, and physically fit, Swing had once served as Airborne adviser to his West Point classmate Eisenhower during the Sicily operation. As a general, Swing could have attained a waiver rather than go through jump school; instead, he insisted on completing the requisite five jumps to earn his wings, just like every other trooper. Equally prone to outbursts of furious but focused temper and good-natured jags of laughter, Swing fervently believed that a highly motivated, well-trained combat soldier was the ultimate weapon of war. Few senior officers connected so personally with their soldiers as did Swing. "A dynamic personality," Major General Innis Swift, the current I Corps commander for whom Swing had once worked as a colonel, wrote of him in an official efficiency report. "Has all the qualities essential in a combat leader. Has a sympathetic and thorough understanding of the enlisted man. Considerate of and intensely interested in his subordinates—officers and enlisted, but is very exacting and is never satisfied with a mediocre performance."

Swing's hale and hearty exterior masked a stupendous intellect that proved a powerful asset for him as a commander. He expected leaders to be thinkers every bit as much as doers. "You've got to be thinking to get young men to do what you want [them] to do, and keep their spirits up," he once told an interviewer. During lulls in battle, he would sequester himself in his tent and devour half a dozen paperback books at a time, "one after the other, utterly oblivious to what was going on around him," in Quandt's recollection, and then return to his command post, seemingly mentally refreshed. Eichelberger deeply admired Swing and enjoyed his company. "Joe Swing is grand to deal with," he told Emma in one letter. Aboard ship, the Eighth Army commander had listened intently for nearly two hours as Swing discussed the Sicily campaign and explained the nuances of Airborne operations. "He saw a great deal of the interplay of personalities," Eichelberger further related to

Emma about the conversation. The insightful Swing fully understood the depth of tension between Eichelberger and Krueger, and he figured this would work to his own advantage. The 11th Airborne commander wrote to his father-in-law that "there is no love lost between [Eichelberger] and Krueger. He's going to give me all the support he can."

True to Eichelberger's orders, Swing's division maintained a steady advance all through the first night after the invasion and into the next day as well, mainly against artillery fire and sporadic resistance. "The Japanese defenders fought short but fierce defensive actions throughout the day, but abandoned successive positions and supply dumps," stated the division after-action report. The 11th Airborne was only about half the size of a regular infantry division that could mobilize about 16,000 soldiers, and only two-thirds of the 11th Airborne had landed. With only about 6,000 troops ashore, the Americans sought to create the impression of a much larger force, an objective that suited Swing's command style perfectly. "General Swing . . . realized that the best way to overcome the shortcomings of the division was by audacious tactics," Captain Harrison Merritt, a company commander in the 187th, commented. Jeeps and trucks roared in both directions along the narrow roads. Artillery pieces spewed generous quantities of shells. Planes strafed any Japanese movement. Dispersed infantry formations attacked relentlessly. So confident and crisp were the American movements that the Japanese commander in southern Luzon, Colonel Masatoshi Fujishige, believed that he was facing two full infantry divisions. Fujishige's misapprehension was crucial to the success of an operation that Eichelberger later described as a "monumental bluff we were running against the Japanese."

The two key bluffers, Swing and Eichelberger, ate lunch at the division command post on the afternoon of February 1. The Eighth Army commander was pleased with the state of the "bluff" and especially the troopers who were carrying it out. He had personally visited the frontline positions and witnessed them in action. He knew that the 11th Airborne had advanced nineteen miles, mostly on foot, in just under thirty hours. "The 11th Airborne was living up to its reputation," he later wrote approvingly. "The troops stood up unflinchingly under artillery fire and performed flawlessly. All combat equipment had been unloaded, a port and an airstrip had been established." Highly impressed with Swing's men, Eichelberger described them to a war correspondent as "the fightingest goddamn troops" he had ever seen. To Emma, he raved, "I am very keen on this 11th Airborne. They are small in number but they are willing to fight." Their proficiency only added to Eichelberger's intentions to exploit the successful Nasugbu landing. He had received no guidance from MacArthur on what to do next. He knew this meant not only that the decision was his but also that the supreme commander supported his penchant for bold action. On the afternoon of February 1, Eichelberger authorized, without a shred of hesitation, the 511th Parachute Infantry Regiment's jump on Tagaytay Ridge and thus, in effect, an all-out push for Manila. At the same time, he arranged for elements of the 24th Division's 19th Infantry Regiment to land at Nasugbu and protect the ever-growing, tenuous supply line that led from the beach to the front.[17]

Early on the morning of February 3, the first of two waves of paratroopers boarded C-47 transports from the 317th Troop Carrier Group on Mindoro and took off for the forty-five-minute flight to Tagaytay Ridge. They were escorted by P-38 fighters from the Fifth Air Force. To draw Japanese attention away from the drop zone, more C-47s dropped dummy paratroopers at Mount Malepunyo, about twenty miles to the southwest. Pathfinders from the division's reconnaissance platoon, along with guerrillas, had infiltrated through Japanese-controlled territory to set up smoke pots on the drop zones. According to one post-battle analysis, the drop fields were located "in rolling country composed of parallel ravines running north from Tagaytay Ridge line to lower successive ridgelines. These ravines were about 100 yards from crest to crest and 35–50 feet deep from crest to trough. Most of the ground had been freshly cultivated and the bottoms of ravines were laced with narrow drainage ditches from 3 to 8 feet deep, overgrown with vines and fringed with trees." Flying in V formation, the leading echelon of 18 C-47s dropped the first wave of 345 troopers right on target at 0820. But a mistaken parapack-bundle drop from a succeeding plane caused the rest of the serial to jump too early, about five miles to the east of their intended zones. This, in turn, sowed confusion when the second wave of C-47s overflew the area at 1210. Many jumpmasters saw the chutes on the ground from the earlier misdrops, assumed this must mean they were over the drop zone, and jumped. In all, 1,750 men dropped during the day. Only 425 landed in the right place. The rest landed between four and six miles astray. But fortune smiled on the 511th. The troopers encountered no opposition and, in spite of the misdrops, they suffered only 3 percent jump casualties, most of whom were just slightly injured.

Once on the ground, commanders needed a couple of hours to organize their units, in part because of the well-meaning intervention of Filipinos. "Considerable interference was encountered when hundreds of Filipino civilians swarmed in the area and along the roads, carrying the soldiers' weapons, packs, parachutes, etc.," Captain John Coulter, a company commander, later wrote. "Maintenance of control was difficult." Civilians helped the troopers out of their harnesses, gave them coconuts, and shook hands excitedly. Private First Class Walter Cass affectionately compared them to "a crowd of collegians after a gridiron victory over an arch rival. I was grinning nearly all the way up the road I walked to the assembly area." The paratroopers linked up at 1300 with soldiers from the 188th Glider Infantry Regiment who had fought their way east over the course of the morning. Eichelberger and Swing participated in this advance, as did the 188th's inspirational commander, Colonel Robert "Shorty" Soule, who was wounded in the fighting, refused evacuation, and, under heavy enemy fire, directed a successful attack. Soule's valor earned him a Distinguished Service Cross and a promotion to brigadier general. Respectful troopers who observed Soule and the generals in the thick of combat began proudly referring to their frontline units as "a spearhead tipped with brass."

Swing's division by late afternoon controlled the most commanding high ground in southwestern Luzon. Tagaytay Ridge loomed 2,400 feet over descending lowlands and a concrete road that led to Manila. Swing and Eichelberger both set up their headquarters in the looted remnants of what had once been an annex to the resplendent Manila Hotel. From this vantage point they enjoyed visibility for many miles across the Hagonoy Isthmus, the narrow neck of land that bridged the salt waters of Manila Bay on the left and the fresh waters of Laguna de Bay on the right. The Hagonoy beckoned like a causeway into southern Manila. Eichelberger later wrote that he could "see the city of Manila gleaming whitely in the sunshine. I could see Corregidor, and the hook of the Cavite peninsula, which curves into Manila Bay. In another direction I could see Balayan and Bantangas Bays on the sea, and, inland, Lake Taal in the crater of an extinct volcano and the shimmer of Laguna de Bay." Like many other American commanders, Eichelberger had spent much time in this area as a young officer. As he gazed at the breathtaking sight of Manila in the distance, he could not help but feel a twinge of nostalgia. "It was strangely like a homecoming."

That night, Swing sent his reconnaissance platoon north up Route 17 as far as Imus at the southern outskirts of Manila. They returned before dawn and reported no opposition. Even before sunrise on February 4, Swing sent troopers from the 511th north on Route 17, some on foot and some packed into newly arrived trucks rushed forward from the Nasugbu beachhead. The weather was idyllic, a stark contrast with what these same men had so recently experienced on Leyte. "We, the mudrats of Leyte, could hardly believe it," the division historian marveled. "We left a cloud of dust instead of the ripples we had left in the not so *terra firma* of Leyte. It seemed incredible that now the only use for our ponchos was as pillows." As the sun steadily rose over the eastern sky, the trucks rumbled north unimpeded. In their trail, long lines of troopers quick marched. In the many small towns and barrios along the route, happy Filipinos cheered them on and happily flung mangoes at them. A few even plied the GIs with fried chicken and cucumbers. In one spot, a brass band blared John Philip Sousa marches. "Guerrillas, equipped with an assortment of arms, both Japanese and American, and displaying a large American flag, were drawn up at Present Arms along the roadway," Captain Edwin Jeffress, the intelligence officer for the 511th's 2nd Battalion, happily wrote. Only at Imus, where they fought a sharp battle with about seventy Japanese who had holed up in stone buildings, did they encounter any substantial opposition.[18]

The joyride lasted until that evening, when they reached the Parañaque River at Manila's southern boundary, where Rear Admiral Iwabuchi had located the first of an incredibly formidable network of defenses. The 11th Airborne troopers still fostered vain hopes of being the first into Manila. From Eichelberger on down, no one on this side of the American advance knew that the 1st Cavalry Division had already made it to Santo Tomas the night before. Eichelberger had received only a brief message from Krueger to the effect that the cavalry troopers had made it to the northern suburbs. Otherwise, communication between Sixth Army and Eighth Army remained minimal to nonexistent, though Eichelberger did send multiple unanswered messages to both Krueger and MacArthur requesting clarification. "I have not been able to find out where our supporting troops are," he complained in a letter to Emma. "I do not seem to be able to get an answer. I am sitting here with my little force without any knowledge where [Sixth Army] is and what help I can expect from them when I hit the outskirts of Manila."

The desire to know the location and progress of friendly units, and coordinate with them, made perfect sense, especially in view of the fact that the two armies were, after all, attacking directly toward each other, a situation fraught with friendly fire peril. Without question, Sixth Army did a poor job of communicating with Eichelberger. But the truth was that both he and Krueger shared the blame. Well before the Nasugbu landings, they should have taken concrete steps to establish clear lines of communication, perhaps by exchanging trusted liaison officers or by establishing mutually agreed-upon times to share updates between their respective headquarters. Instead, neither made any substantial effort to work closely with the other, a clear by-product of their mutual antipathy, and one that could possibly have led to disastrous friendly fire incidents; as it was, their poor coordination eroded the cohesiveness of the American push for Manila.

In the space of just a few days, the 11th Airborne had dashed almost seventy circuitous road miles from Nasugbu to the Parañaque River, sweeping aside all opposition. Troopers joked that their supply line ran "sixty-nine miles long and five hundred yards wide." Eichelberger protected that supply line with guerrillas and a battalion from the 19th Infantry. Now, having reached the proverbial southern gates of Manila, his lead troops ran into heavy resistance from Iwabuchi's Southern Force. The admiral had expected the main American push from this direction, so in this narrow urban corridor he had placed his most formidable fortifications in what soon became known as the Genko Line. This nest of 1,200 pillboxes and fortified buildings extended from Nichols Field near the sea all the way eastward to Fort William McKinley and beyond to Laguna de Bay. The depth of the line layered some six thousand yards to the Manila Polo Club, where teams of US Army officers had once competed in spirited tournaments, and locals were often imperiously excluded from membership.

A terrifying array of powerful weapons proliferated among the Genko Line positions, ranging from 20- and 40-millimeter guns, 90-millimeter antiaircraft guns, 150-millimeter mortars, 5- and 6-inch naval guns, and heavy artillery pieces. "Roads were heavily mined with 500 pound aerial bombs armed with low pressure detonators," the 11th Airborne's after-action report testified. "Mutually supporting concrete pillboxes defended each block." In some instances, tunnels or zigzag trenches connected the pillboxes. The Japanese had augmented some of these mini forts with camouflaging sod and dirt. A few were three stories deep and made of reinforced concrete. Other than 75- and 105-millimeter artillery pieces and close air support, the Americans had few heavy weapons for fire support. In spite of these limitations, the troopers forced the river and tore into the defenders, steadily rooting them out block by block. "It was hand grenades *versus* 150mm mortars," the division historian affirmed with just a whiff of hyperbolic exaggeration, "carbines and M-1's with bayonets *versus* 20mm all-purpose guns; pack 75s *versus* 6-inch naval guns; sawed-off 105's *versus* steel-and-concrete pillboxes." Fighting boiled from building to building. The Americans made liberal use of white phosphorous grenades, flamethrowers, 81-millimeter mortars, and direct-fire support from artillery pieces. Self-propelled tank destroyers blasted pillbox apertures point-blank "with their high velocity 76mm [shells]," General Swing wrote to his father-in-law. "Then when the garrison would try to escape through communication trenches, [we] put time fire on them with 105's." Booby traps and buried bombs lay in malevolent wait, seemingly on every sidewalk and street. The Japanese even booby-trapped their own dead comrades. In one terrible incident, an aerial torpedo that was wired to the armpit of a corpse exploded in the face of a searching American soldier, instantly killing him and two nearby comrades.

Swing attempted to overwhelm the Genko Line by repeatedly attacking with one regiment while another maneuvered right to outflank the enemy. "It was like an end run in football with the ball-carrier lateraling the pigskin to another back who in turn would sweep around," one observer noted. The well-conceived tactics produced steady, block-by-block gains, but the strength of the Genko Line, the tenacity of the defenders, and the urban terrain negated any possibility of the lightning victory for which Swing and Eichelberger yearned. Traumatic, time-consuming room-to-room combat offered the only way forward. "The air was constantly filled with artillery and mortar salvos, the banging of rifle fire, the chatter of machine-guns, the whine of ricochets," PFC Cass wrote to his mother. Japanese troops became attuned to the unique pinging sound when an empty clip ejected from the breech of an M1 Garand rifle. They took to waiting for the ping and then charging. In response the GIs baited them. "We would put a full clip in the rifle, hold an empty clip in our mouths or free hand, fire one or two rounds, then bang the empty clip on a metallic part of the rifle," Sergeant James Augustin of the 187th Glider Infantry commented. "This made a sound similar to an empty clip being ejected. Of course, the result was disastrous to the Japanese."

The fighting laid waste to block after block of warehouses, homes, and shops. Refugees streamed south, "pushing, pulling and driving every conceivable form of conveyance, bearing on their backs their personal belongings and the aged and infirm," wrote Captain Jeffress, the intelligence officer. Sadly, they left behind their wrecked houses that now looked, in the somber reminiscence of one American, "as though a giant can-opener had sliced through them." Everywhere the Japanese fought fanatically, unto the death, especially at Nichols Field, where, in the estimation of the 11th Airborne's historian, they resisted "as if the Emperor's Palace itself were sitting in the center of the runway." The field bristled with so many dismounted naval guns that one wiseacre company commander quipped in a note to Swing, "Tell Halsey to stop looking for the Jap fleet. It's dug in on Nichols Field."

It took nearly a week to subdue resistance in the area. Senior leaders were constantly involved in the heavy fighting all over the division front. Swing survived numerous near misses. Two of his key subordinates were less fortunate. He lost his chief of staff, Colonel Irving Schimmelpfennig, and the 511th's well-regarded commander, Colonel Orin Haugen. Eichelberger visited the forward units constantly and found himself pinned down several times by heavy fire. His headquarters commandant, Colonel Rinaldo Coe, was killed by shell fragments. Amid the rubble, infantrymen attempted to recover and evacuate the bodies of their dead buddies. Private Deane Marks somberly remembered that when his company's first sergeant was killed, his body quickly swelled to twice its size. "The skin had turned black from the afternoon sun." Marks and three others attempted to manhandle the corpse onto a litter. "The swelling of his body had caused his uniform to act as a rigid envelope. His helmet strap had cut through his chin and cheeks. As we moved the body, the skin broke and gas and fluids came out. Someone threw up and that made the other of us do the same. Body fluids ran down the litter onto Porteous and myself. The reality of war cannot be imagined by anyone who has not been there."

Late on the afternoon of February 11, paratroopers from the 511th made contact with the 5th Cavalry Regiment, joining the two American pincers and snapping a noose shut around Manila, trapping all of Iwabuchi's people inside. Ironically, Yamashita, Vice Admiral Okochi, and even Lieutenant General Yokoyama, the Shimbu Group commander, had by now ordered the admiral to evacuate Manila. The continuous American front made this an impossibility—whether the admiral would have complied if he had had the opportunity to evacuate remains an imponderable.

The day before, MacArthur had placed the 11th Airborne under Sixth Army control. Krueger immediately assigned it to Griswold's XIV Corps to assist the 1st Cavalry Division and 37th Infantry Division in Manila. The move ended Eichelberger's involvement in the battle, an oddly anticlimactic moment for a man so used to achieving dramatic results. Even so, he had presided over a successful amphibious landing and a remarkable dash through southwestern Luzon, killing or marginalizing many thousands of enemy troops, and he had made it to Manila, though he had not gotten there first, nor could he claim to have liberated it whole. "I think it is high time for me to be getting out," he wrote to Emma before returning to his headquarters on Leyte. "I do not want you to believe that I am going to risk myself any more like I did during the last week. This was a special raid that required special action. Personally I think we pulled one of the most daring feats of the war."

Brigadier General Clovis Byers, his trusted chief of staff, wrote excitedly to his wife, Marie, that "the speed with which we have done our part has overjoyed our many friends and delighted the Chief [MacArthur] because it indicates a freedom of action which is anything but typical of Walter's organization."

As Byers's statement indicated, Eichelberger knew from his communications with SWPA staffers that his performance had impressed MacArthur. In one letter, Willoughby gushed warmly, "I . . . watched your brilliant advance via Tagaytay with great interest. I always believed (and attempted to influence C/S [Sutherland] and G-3 [Major General Stephen Chamberlin, the operations officer] at the time) that your operational axis was a decisive one." Willoughby felt that Eichelberger's forces should have received reinforcements and priority to take Manila. Another senior officer attached to SWPA wrote to Eichelberger and claimed that "when you were pushing on Manila so rapidly, I visited 6th Army Headquarters and found them greatly agitated over the fact that you would be in Manila before they were, and I believe . . . that we could have saved more of Manila if they had given you the means to come in by way of Nasugbu." The petty side of Eichelberger took solace in these assurances. Privately he commented, "Krueger was woefully slow in his advance," and added that he had handled his army with "all the dash of a circus elephant."[19]

Heedless of the egos of army commanders, the Manila battle raged on, like an enduring disease. MacArthur quietly shelved his parade plans. He forbade air strikes for fear of abetting the destruction of the city he so loved. "The use of air on a part of a city occupied by a friendly and allied population is unthinkable," he declared. A disappointed Griswold confided to his diary that "I hated to ask for it since I know it would cause the death of civilians held captive by the Japs. We know, too, that the Japs are burning large numbers to death, shooting them, and bayoneting them. Horrid as it seems, probably death from bombing would be more merciful." Only reluctantly did MacArthur even agree to permit the use of heavy artillery. These difficult choices strongly indicated the depth of the unfolding tragedy. The horrified Americans had finally come to realize that they must destroy Manila in order to take it back, the precise scenario that Admiral Ernest King, the chief of naval operations, had envisioned many months earlier when he had argued for bypassing the Philippines. No one was more dismayed than Griswold. From New Georgia to Bougainville to Manila, he always seemed to get the dirtiest jobs. No American corps commander in the Pacific, except those who served in the Philippines in 1941–42, dealt consistently with more adversity. "This is rough," he wrote plaintively in his diary of the fierce urban combat. "I'm getting a lot of unavoidable casualties."

To date, the Americans in the Pacific had not faced the task of taking a major city. Manila's urban sprawl covered an area of 110 square miles. The population had swollen during the war from 625,000 people to nearly 1.1 million. The heart of the city, where the fighting now centered, spanned about 5.5 miles along the bay, and inland to a depth of some 4 miles. Manila's modern structures, particularly the thick stone and pillars of government buildings, reflected a strong American influence, mirroring architectural styles prevalent in Washington, DC, as well as the early-twentieth-century vision of Daniel Burnham, perhaps the greatest of all American architects. Many of the buildings were specially reinforced with extra concrete to withstand earthquakes, making them ideal fortifications. "These buildings, together with the solid city walls . . . formed mutually supporting fortresses of great strength and extent which resisted artillery fire except from the heaviest guns and howitzers available, and were defended in the typical Japanese manner, floor-by-floor and room-by-room," Colonel Ingomar Oseth, a Sixth Army observer, wrote gravely. The once bustling arteries of the city, such as Taft Avenue and Dewey Boulevard, offered such wide vistas as to make concealed advances nearly impossible. "Wide streets . . . precluded anything except direct assault over open ground," one Sixth Army study commented.

The XIV Corps had now wedged the Japanese defenders into a semi-circular perimeter, with their backs to the bay. Atavistic, intimate, no-quarters fighting blazed among the honeycomb of alleys, streets, and structures. Exhausted infantrymen hopscotched methodically from building to building, fighting death duels with an enemy for whom surrender was unthinkable. "When a squad was used to search an isolated building half the squad remained outside covering the grounds and entrances while the other half entered and search the building," a XIV Corps post-battle analysis explained of the assault unit's typical methods. "On larger buildings where platoons were used, the support squad covered the advance of the assault squads which moved in by rushes." Assault squads carried flamethrowers, bazookas, satchel charges, grenades, and submachine guns. A typical unit comprised a two-man flamethrower team, a man with a Browning Automatic Rifle (BAR) and his assistant, a demolition specialist, a pair of Thompson submachine gunners, a two-man bazooka team, plus three riflemen and a squad leader. They saturated all doors, windows, and apertures with fire before assaulting. "Day in and day out, we fought street by street, block by block, building by building, floor by floor, room by room," Sergeant Warren Matha of the 5th Cavalry Regiment shuddered. "Kick in the door. Stick in the flame thrower nozzle. Roast the Japs alive. I can still hear them screaming. I can still smell the burning flesh. The flame thrower has to be the most horrible weapon imagined by man." Wherever possible, they blasted new openings into buildings instead of venturing through the doors and any large windows, where they were likely to run into preplanned kill zones. Often they leapt from the roof of one structure to another and fought their way down, room to room, floor to floor, blowing up the Japanese defenders with grenades or explosives, raking them with rifle and submachine-gun bullets, roasting them with flamethrowers, sometimes even pouring gasoline onto them and setting them afire. Even then, according to one intelligence officer, the survivors fought on, necessitating the American infantrymen to "actually enter . . . dugouts, caverns and pillboxes and annihilate [them] before . . . resistance ceased." In the estimation of Colonel Oseth, the observer, the "horrible wounds on many of these" last holdouts demonstrated the effectiveness of the American weapons.

The rapidly decomposing, swollen bodies of dead Japanese and Filipinos lay seemingly everywhere, in the streets, in gutters, inside buildings, in parks. The Americans sprinkled them with lime to stifle their stench. Wary of ambushers who played dead, the GIs pumped a bullet into the forehead of every Japanese corpse and then stacked it against a wall. "It was a grotesque, gruesome picture to see these row-by-row bodies along the wall," one combat soldier later commented with more than a tinge of revulsion. "These were the day-by-day necessities to survive one day more."

The shocking reality of Japanese atrocities against the population blanketed the area like some sort of malevolent stench. Staff Sergeant Warren Fitch, a squad leader in the 37th Division, heard nearby screams one evening. When he and his men investigated, they made a grisly discovery. "Behind a corrugated sheet metal fence . . . there were perhaps twenty-five Filipino civilians, men, women, children, half-stripped, hands tied behind them, all bayoneted, all dead." After seeing similar scenes, another 37th Division infantry soldier, PFC Edwin Hanson, wondered sadly how many Filipinos "must have either been burned, shot down, or just left homeless—all in a last few days of vengeful orgy by some 'so called' people named Japs." At one concealed observation post, PFC Thomas Howard, a gunner in the 745th Tank Battalion, watched helplessly as distant Japanese sailors whipped nuns and then set upon several other women. "We had to endure the sight of a group of Japanese soldiers drag Filipino women out into the open and then rape them. There was no way to describe the emotion of hate of the Japanese and the anguish of not being able to help the women." Howard's group could not open fire for fear of revealing their position, but they were probably too far away to save the victims.

All over the heart of Manila, the desperate, intimate battles inevitably spread from one iconic building to another, among them the New Police Station, City Hall, the University of the Philippines campus, the National Assembly of the Philippines Commonwealth Legislative Building, the government mint, the Philippine General Hospital, the General Post Office, and the Manila Hotel, where General MacArthur had once lived with Jean and their son, Arthur, in an air-conditioned penthouse that featured a breathtaking view of the city. Without massive fire support, the Americans would have had difficulty taking any of these objectives or making any headway at all. Attackers had little chance of survival without the protection offered by blankets of firepower. This of course guaranteed widespread destruction, a timeless but tragic reality of urban combat and one that could have been strategically self-defeating under different circumstances. Sherman tanks, M7 self-propelled guns, and 4.2-inch mortars all provided direct-fire support to the infantrymen. By far, artillery proved the most effective. Had MacArthur not authorized its use, Griswold's casualties undoubtedly would have been prohibitive. Soon the Americans were unleashing torrents of shellfire to take every objective. They pumped 680 155-millimeter rounds into the police station and still lost 25 dead, 80 wounded, and three tanks to take this objective. They saturated the university campus with 3,400 artillery shells, and incurred 500 casualties over ten days of fighting. They battered City Hall with 145 155-millimeter shells, most of which were fired from the point-blank range of 250 yards, to collapse the eastern wall through which infantrymen unleashed a final assault.

By necessity, they let loose an especially prodigious cocktail of firepower upon venerable Intramuros, a walled mini city abutting the Pasig River, constructed by the Spanish nearly four hundred years earlier, where colonizing Spanish families and soldiers had once lived. Built in the medieval fashion as a fortified city, the sturdy walls of Intramuros were twenty to forty feet thick. At the northwestern corner of Intramuros, behind even more walls, was Fort Santiago—a fortress within a fortress—the Lubyanka of the Philippines, a haunted, unhappy place in whose dungeons Spanish Inquisition torturers had once set upon nonbelievers, and more recently, the Japanese had imprisoned and tortured many hundreds of Allied prisoners and Filipino civilians. Griswold had serious misgivings about the prospect of destroying Intramuros. "I am going to have to breach walls in several places," he told Brigadier General Decker, Krueger's chief of staff, in a worried phone conversation. "It is an all-historic thing. I think it is a military necessity. I am just wondering if General Krueger or yourself have any advice."

"General Krueger's advice is to take Manila," Decker replied. "I think, insofar as he is concerned, you can use such means as are necessary."

"In other words, as I understand you, the responsibility is mine."

"That is the way General Krueger feels about it, and I think he will back you up in anything you do which you feel is necessary or justified by military necessity."[20]

Though grateful for the validation from Krueger's headquarters, Griswold still hoped to avoid fighting in Intramuros. He sent a surrender ultimatum to Iwabuchi, but got no response, so he went forward with his plans. To prepare for the assault by two infantry battalions, the

Americans positioned no fewer than nine field artillery battalions, plus tanks, tank destroyers, mortars, and innumerable machine guns. Artillery observers holed up on the top floors of fire-damaged modern office buildings and made themselves at home "to establish very business-like offices . . . including several swivel chairs, desks for their feet, and lounging chairs for their guests," one artillery officer later wrote. Comfortably ensconced in these perches, they could see practically every inch of the walled city. From 0730 to 0830 on February 23, the artillerymen unleashed a terrifying torrent of firepower onto Intramuros. The average tube fired two rounds per minute, each at a carefully planned target. "Such was the organization of fire that each gun had its own part of the area in the wall to be destroyed," explained a XIV Corps post-battle analysis. In the duration of an hour, they and the armor pumped 7,896 rounds of varying caliber into the old city, an avalanche of ordnance totaling nearly 370,000 pounds, with 3 tons and 131 shells per minute that crumbled walls and dazed or killed untold numbers of Japanese. Most of the shells contained M78 fuses geared specifically toward piercing concrete. "The noise and concussion was so great even on the sending end that one wondered how any of the recipients could possibly survive," one artilleryman marveled. An awestruck Griswold termed the barrage "the fiercest artillery fire ever seen in the southwest Pacific area." Major Nelson Randall, an artillery officer, later commented with a touch of pithy pride, "We shot the works, literally as well as figuratively."

The barrage worked. In many places, the walls caved in or crumbled. A battalion from the 129th Infantry Regiment rowed unmolested across the Pasig in small engineer boats while another from the 145th Infantry Regiment assaulted Intramuros on foot. Under the cover of a smoke screen laid down by the artillery batteries and mortar crews, they made their way across the rubble of the crumbled walls into the mini city, where they fought street to street and subdued Japanese resistance within one day, at the cost of 25 dead and 265 wounded. The Americans killed about 1,000 Japanese in this fighting and took 25 prisoners, almost all of whom were actually Formosan. In a few instances, they encountered Japanese soldiers who had disguised themselves in American uniforms and wielded American weapons. The unfooled GIs shot them down mercilessly.

Predictably, the heaviest opposition came inside the grounds of Fort Santiago, where infantrymen had to secure every square foot of rubble and dungeon ruthlessly "and numerous tunnels and recesses which harbored enemy, and which one by one were turned into death-traps by hand grenades, flamethrowers, and gasoline poured down into the holes and ignited," the XIV Corps after-action report somberly stated. Some 400 Japanese died defending Santiago. The 37th Division managed to save and evacuate about 2,000 local women and children, only to discover that the Japanese had separated the men from this group and killed or left to starve some 2,000 of them, mostly in dungeons. The Americans found their corpses charred, starved, shot, and stabbed, often in heaps so densely packed together—sometimes hundreds inside a cell the size of a modest bedroom—that the GIs could not hope to count them accurately. "Bodies were piled on each other, in some places four deep," one soldier witness grimly recounted. "All of their feet pointed to the only doorway into the room. I noted that their hands were tied behind their backs." An evil, suffocating odor pervaded all of Fort Santiago. "The stench from the bodies was virtually unbearable and the stage of decomposition precluded detailed investigation," Colonel John Frederick, commander of the 129th, avowed.

Even with Intramuros under control, the Americans needed another ten days to subdue the last resistance, primarily in a complex of government buildings where they simply bludgeoned the enemy into submission with point-blank artillery fire and unrelenting infantry assaults. "We are destroying our communications equipment and charging the enemy," the signals operator of one doomed group of defenders radioed Field Marshal Count Hisaichi Terauchi's theater headquarters in Saigon. Cornered inside the Agriculture Building, Rear Admiral Iwabuchi committed ritual hara-kiri rather than face justice for the enormous crimes he and his people had perpetrated.

The wrecked husk of Manila brooded on. Private First Class Hanson sadly beheld "blocks and blocks of open ground with nothing standing— no movement, no nothing—just ashes." Private First Class Joseph Jones, a young signalman, wrote soberly to his parents, "I can truly say that I saw a city practically destroyed. Flames were shooting up into the air hundreds of feet and over the city a great pall of smoke hung like a curtain. At night the fire lit up the sky so brightly that you could read a paper by the light of the glare. You could go for blocks and blocks throughout the city and not a single building would be left standing. You just can't imagine the utter destruction of the city. Every building showed the effects of artillery fire, rifle fire, and the Japs' demolition work." Brigadier General Clovis Byers, Eichelberger's chief of staff, estimated that the flames rose as high as one thousand feet into the air and the smoke twenty times that. "The burning of Rome and the Chicago and San Francisco fires had nothing on this," he asserted in a letter to a friend. Like many other Americans, he seethed with rage, and a casually dismissive racism, against the Japanese, whom he viewed as beyond redemption. "I only wish that more Americans could have seen the devastation. There would then be no more of this drivel about forgiving the dear, little, brown brothers. The quicker that race of savages is eliminated from the face of the earth the better off the world will be."

Those soldiers who had experienced better times in prewar Manila were filled with a sense of profound gloom. Lieutenant Rogers, MacArthur's stenographer, felt so depressed at what had become of a city he once loved that he sat down and scribbled an epitaph: "Manila is a graveyard. Wrapped in a shroud of biting dust. Her gaunt grey shell-scarred fire-blackened walls and torn twisted girders reach mutely to the sky. The pungent stench of charred bodies permeates the air!" In the wake of the fighting, an equally somber MacArthur visited the remains of his beloved Manila, including the Manila Hotel, where he found on the fifth floor his onetime home destroyed. Most of the books from his remarkable personal library were missing or reduced to inert ashes, as were his other personal possessions. Walls had collapsed. A baby grand piano was shattered. A dead Japanese colonel lay at the front door. Decades earlier, in more harmonious days, Emperor Meiji, grandfather of Hirohito, had given a beautiful vase to MacArthur's father as a gift. When MacArthur and Jean had evacuated the apartment on Christmas Eve in 1941, she had made a point of prominently placing the vase on a table where the Japanese could not miss it, in a vain hope that they might respect the sanctity of the home. Now, as MacArthur picked through the ruins, he discovered the shattered remnants of the vase scattered near the colonel's corpse, a symbolic reminder of the war's waste and tragedy. "I was tasting to the last acid dregs the bitterness of a devastated and beloved home," MacArthur later sadly reflected.

Indeed, with the exception of Lieutenant General Jonathan Wainwright and other high-ranking POWs, no other senior American commander in World War II experienced the war at such a personal level and paid such a steep price for victory. The destruction of Manila deeply depressed MacArthur and eroded his usual composure. His moods swung from impatient to morose to outright angry. He became so enraged when he learned that a war correspondent wrote a story entitled "Manila Is Dying" that he ordered Colonel LeGrande "Pick" Diller, his public relations chief, to censor that headline and any other that alluded to the death or destruction of the city. The supreme commander exuded a distinct sadness. In Rogers's estimation, "MacArthur was shattered by the holocaust. [He] had destroyed the city he loved." In one month's fighting, XIV Corps had fired 45,000 artillery and mortar shells. Destitute survivors picked through the ruins, searching for the bodies of loved ones or attempting to salvage the remnants of their homes. Much of the city was without power and water. Public transportation did not exist anymore. Sewage systems were heavily damaged. Garbage collection had ceased. Harbor facilities were almost totally destroyed. Cultural and scientific damage was profound. The National Library of the Philippines and the National Museum, the Scientific Library, and the Philippine General Hospital lost hundreds of thousands of books, paintings, sculptures, and medical volumes, as well as untold millions of patient histories and records. The Manila Observatory lost nearly four centuries' worth of irreplaceable records about typhoons and earthquakes.

The Americans counted 16,655 Japanese bodies in Manila. Countless others probably lay under the ruins; a few enemy soldiers probably escaped. Some 100,000 Filipinos lost their lives due either to Japanese atrocities or to US firepower, the exact breakdown between the two, and the long-term emotional trauma of this holocaust on survivors, forever impossible to determine. The Army lost 1,010 soldiers killed in action and 5,565 wounded. Almost half of the killed and wounded came from the 37th Division. Among the American casualties was Major General Mudge, the 1st Cavalry Division commander who was badly wounded in the abdomen by a Japanese grenade and evacuated. Brigadier General Hugh Hoffman succeeded him (MacArthur had already promoted Chase to major general and given him command of the 38th Division on Bataan, though eventually Chase returned to command the 1st Cavalry Division). The XIV Corps kept no records on how many men were debilitated by combat fatigue, nor could anyone know how many of the survivors were forever haunted by the experience of fighting in this Armageddon-esque battle. A chastened Griswold, though relieved to have won yet another hard-fought victory, somberly scrawled in his diary, "It has been a great strain and responsibility." The price was steep, and the prize seriously diminished, but at least the Americans now controlled the key objective of the entire Philippines campaign.[21]

Like an upbeat subplot in the midst of a Greek tragedy, one final prisoner rescue mission offered a glimmering counterpoint to the Manila cataclysm. As of mid-February, over two thousand Allied civilian internees remained incarcerated at Los Baños, a dreary sixty-acre barbed wire compound located on the grounds of the University of the Philippines agricultural college, about 1,200 yards inland from the southern shore of Laguna de Bay, some twenty-five miles behind Japanese lines. The Imperial Army's 8th Division controlled much of the area. American civilians and a handful of US Navy nurses comprised about two-thirds of the Los Baños population; the rest were primarily from Western Allied countries, with a strong presence of priests, nuns, and Protestant clergy. They knew the Americans were getting closer by the day. In the gloaming distance, especially at night, they could see flashes and hear the rumble of fighting. "Everyone is very heartened by the sounds," internee George Mora told his diary; "it's a big thing to be able to hear the battle and know that it is coming our way."

As with the other camps, MacArthur and his commanders worried deeply about the possibility of a massacre, especially in light of the ongoing Rape of Manila. The internees worried about much the same thing, and yearned eagerly each day for liberation. As early as February 4, MacArthur's headquarters called for a rescue mission, after which the planning details worked down the chain of command from Sixth Army to XIV Corps to the elite 11th Airborne Division, the logical candidate to pull off such a coup de main. By the third week of February, General Swing's staff had prepared a sophisticated, inventive plan. The two key authors were Lieutenant Colonel Henry "Butch" Muller, a twenty-seven-year-old intelligence officer and UCLA graduate, and Lieutenant Colonel Quandt, the operations officer who had arguably become Swing's most indispensable aide following the death of Colonel Schimmelpfennig, the division chief of staff. Muller and Quandt were greatly assisted by access to outstanding intelligence sources. The Fifth Air Force provided them with excellent detailed aerial photographs. Even more important, they drew upon a rich vein of human intelligence. Guerrillas shared good information on the camp layout, the surrounding area, and the location and strength of nearby 8th Division units. At least 6,000 enemy soldiers were currently in the province. Only 80 low-morale dead enders guarded the camp, but just 3,000 yards to the west, a well-equipped infantry company was bivouacked in a gravel quarry.

Escapees gave the planners the most vital information. In particular, Pete Miles, an American mining engineer, stole away from the camp and, with the assistance of guerrillas, made it to the 11th Airborne Division's headquarters at Parañaque in southern Manila. Blessed with an encyclopedic memory as well as an engineer's gift for spatial cognition, Miles had carefully studied the layout of Los Baños and the habits of the guards. Once at Parañaque, he spelled out an incredible array of granular detail about the camp. He knew the precise location of every pillbox, every machine gun, the orientation of the guns, their fields of fire, the position of every guard post, and the exact locations of the huts that served as prisoner barracks. Most impressively, he informed Muller and the other planners that the garrison rose each day at 0700, unarmed and only partially clad, for morning exercise. During that time, only soldiers in the guard posts were armed. All other weapons were locked inside a small connecting room between the two main guard barracks buildings.

Miles made a point of stressing the poor physical condition of the internees. Some were nearing starvation or death from disease. Food in the camp had just about run out. "We were eating anything we could put our hands on, including . . . indigestible weeds," Ensign Dorothy

Still, one of the nurses, later recalled. Miles outlined this dire food situation and even provided a solid estimate as to how many internees were likely to require evacuation by stretcher. Lieutenant George Skau and Sergeant Terry Santos from the division's reconnaissance platoon infiltrated by local banca boats into the area, alongside guerrillas and an escapee, and, once on the ground, by practiced stealth. Strikingly similar to the Alamo Scouts, they lay hidden for hours and observed Los Baños, confirming all of Miles's claims. In the estimation of one key Airborne commander, Miles "gave us that vital information that no aerial photo or guerrilla could supply." Skau also determined that a dry rice paddy a few hundred yards outside the camp could serve as a sufficient drop zone for paratroopers.

With such a rich composite of relevant intelligence information at hand, Swing's people prepared a detailed plan that reflected the division's unique airborne and amphibious capabilities. From the beginning they understood that they could not even consider trying to fight their way overland in a linear fashion to liberate the camp. Even if they succeeded in punching through enemy lines, the Japanese would almost certainly have plenty of time to evacuate or harm the prisoners. Similar to Cabanatuan, the only feasible option was to launch a deep-penetration raid, utilizing a variety of assets, with surprise as the crucial element for success. Skau's reconnaissance platoon of thirty-two soldiers would act as the advance element. These were handpicked, highly motivated men; some had trained with the Alamo Scouts. "We were a small group, mostly college men, crazy as h—," Private Martin Squires later wrote. "Most of us were outdoorsmen to begin with and grew up with a familiarity to hunting, hiking and camping." Skau's troopers and fifty guerrillas would infiltrate by bancas across the lake and into position the night before the raid. While the guerrillas acted as guides and secured the drop zone, the reconnaissance men were supposed to mark the amphibious landing area and the drop zone, then get into their proper places, with some guerrillas alongside, to kill specific sentries at a prearranged signal. "In addition, one squad was to open fire on the Japs massed at calisthenics while the other was to cover arms racks, all on the signal arranged for the 'sentry-shooters,'" Lieutenant Colonel Louis Walsh, an early student of the raid, wrote a few months later.

The aforementioned signal would be an Airborne drop at the stroke of 0700 into the adjacent rice paddy by B Company, 1st Battalion, 511th Parachute Infantry Regiment, plus an attached mortar section and machine-gun platoon. These troopers would assist the reconnaissance men in subduing any remaining Japanese resistance, secure the internees, and move them out of the camp. Perhaps the most ingenious aspect of the plan involved the evacuation. Swing's staff called upon the services of 54 LVTs from the 672nd Amphibian Tractor Battalion. The amtracs would carry the balance of Major Henry Burgess's 1st Battalion—about 400 troopers—and use the Laguna de Bay as a means of flanking around the Japanese lines. Under cover of darkness, the noisy LVTs were to depart from American lines at Mamatid, plunge eastward into the lake, and then somehow find their way over a seven-mile route in the inky blackness to an exact prearranged landing spot. Once ashore, Burgess and his men were supposed to secure a mini beachhead from which the newly freed internees and their liberators would be evacuated by the LVTs back across the lake to 11th Airborne lines. The last piece of the plan involved a diversionary attack down Highway 1 on the main front by the 1st Battalion, 188th Glider Infantry Regiment, to draw Japanese attention and troops north, away from the camp.

Swing and his staff chose February 23 for the day of the raid and submitted their plan to Griswold, who readily approved. Less than two days before the operation, Burgess's battalion was hastily withdrawn from the fighting around Fort McKinley and briefed. The evening before the raid, troopers of B Company were trucked to newly captured Nichols Field, where shell craters still pockmarked the runways, and the men were thoroughly schooled on their new mission. They feasted on spaghetti and meatballs and listened to a last-minute talk from their commander, Lieutenant John Ringler. "We're going to do the most important thing we've ever done, and maybe we'll ever do," he told them earnestly. With full bellies and much anticipation, they drifted off to sleep under the wings of nine C-47s from the 65th Troop Carrier Squadron that would soon ferry them into action.

That evening, as other 1st Battalion troopers prepared to board their amtracs and Skau's operators laboriously moved into position, Swing received a disturbing report, one that necessitated the sort of soul-searching decision that accompanies senior-level command. At about midnight, an Army Air Forces P-61 Black Widow night reconnaissance plane observed a long column of truck headlights moving near Los Baños, raising the disquieting possibility that the Japanese had found out about the raid and were reinforcing the camp. Abject disaster might result if the mission proceeded. As Lieutenant Colonel Muller pointed out, though, the presence of trucks conveyed nothing of enemy intentions or knowledge. "All we know from this report is that a long column of vehicles was observed entering Los Banos," he told Swing. "We don't know how many or from which direction they came or went. We don't know if it was reinforcements heading for the prison camp. We don't know if they were just passing through town. We're not even sure how many trucks there were."

The high-strung Swing had sometimes been very demanding, almost to the point of harshness, with his young intelligence officer. "Mueller [sic] was scared to death of Swing, and had had his tail eaten out on a number of occasions by General Joe," Major Burgess, the 1st Battalion commander, later claimed. In this case, Swing listened calmly to Muller's analysis and pondered for a moment. He could order Burgess's unit to disembark, call off the diversionary force attack, and cancel the Airborne drop. But Skau and the guerrillas were out of contact, fully committed to carrying out the mission. At 0700, regardless of what anyone else did, they would attack the Los Baños guards. If Swing canceled the mission, Skau and his people were doomed. On the other hand, if Swing went ahead with the operation, everyone might just be walking into an enemy ambush. Turning all this over in his mind for a few seconds, he arrived at a decision. "Let's go ahead." The only adjustment he made was to alert another battalion from the 511th Parachute Infantry to beef up the diversionary attack, and perhaps assist in a crisis evacuation.

Remarkably, after a long, tense night, all the strike elements found themselves in nearly perfect position by 0700. Major Burgess's amphibious force arrived at the precise landing spot and began to disembark. The reconnaissance troopers lay in wait to ambush the guards—some had closed to within only a few feet of their prey. Lieutenant Ringler's company had successfully boarded their C-47s for the twenty-minute flight to Los Baños, and arrived over the drop zone to see it marked perfectly with smoke grenades. In a synchronized shock wave, they struck. The recon troopers and their guerrilla partners killed the sentries and mowed down the rows of exercising, half-naked guards. "[They] didn't really know what the heck was happening," Sergeant Ronald Morgan, one of the recon troopers, recalled. "They were just sort of milling around."

At nearly the same moment, Lieutenant Ringler and the B Company paratroopers jumped from their aircraft. He had wisely decided to have his men jump from five hundred feet in order to minimize their exposure to enemy fire as they descended and enhance the chances of a rapid assembly once on the ground. The plan worked well. The company landed with no casualties, quickly assembled, and assisted the recon men in destroying the Japanese garrison. Most of the guards were killed within fifteen minutes; a few managed to flee. Almost eerily similar to Cabanatuan, the Americans took no casualties and their fire hit only enemies, probably because internees and guards were so rigidly segregated from one another in the compound. The emaciated internees were just as stunned as the Japanese, and many needed several minutes before they realized that the soldiers in the compound were Americans who had come to save them. An awestruck Ensign Still, the nurse, remembered them as "young, healthy men wearing camouflage uniforms, something we were not familiar with . . . they had a new kind of helmet." When one elderly woman saw the soldiers, she blurted disappointment that she had not been rescued by Marines, a humorous but telling reflection on the ubiquity of the notion in many American minds that the Corps had fought most of the war against Japan. Elsewhere, a nun threw her arms around a harried paratrooper and hugged him so hard that the busy soldier pulled away and said, "Hold your horses a second, sister, and I'll be right back." Moments later, the paratrooper, who turned out to be a devout Catholic, returned and made a proper introduction to the nun, who had by then settled down considerably.

Once more the challenge of rapidly rounding up the liberated masses and herding them to salvation proved formidable. "We had an awful time getting the prisoners out of the barracks," Sergeant Morgan said. Some were in such a state of shock or so reluctant to leave behind possessions or meager remnants of food that the soldiers resorted to setting the huts on fire with white phosphorous grenades. At the same time, the troopers tried to organize them to figure out who could walk and who would need to ride to safety. "The internees were very jubilant and excited," Lieutenant Ringler later wrote. "With over two thousand individuals this became a turbulent mass of human beings. Trying to control them and keeping them in one place was almost an impossible task." Under Major Burgess's supervision, LVTs crashed through the barbed wire fence, and the troopers began to load people aboard the vehicles. "I was appalled at the condition of the internees," he shuddered. "None of us were prepared for what we found. The prisoners were in a condition of hysteria and euphoria, most of the larger men weighed no more than 110 pounds and the women resembled sticks. A few children had survived and they were very weak."

Soldiers made sure to place the camp's 130 hospital patients aboard first. They also carried out the withered corpses of patients who had recently died. This tragedy coexisted with humorous irony. One group of priests and nuns clambered into an LVT nicknamed "The Impatient Virgin." Soldiers who saw it amble past could not keep from bursting out laughing. Perhaps even more ironically, the 11th Airborne troopers had, with sarcastic pride, embraced the nickname "Angels" for themselves two years earlier during their training at Camp Mackall when Quandt had caustically asked one commander if his angels had all returned safely from liberty.

The evacuation took the entire day, during which the Japanese offered mainly just harassing fire. By 1700 the 11th Airborne Division troopers had succeeded in rescuing 2,147 men, women, and children and ferrying them aboard the LVTs across Laguna de Bay and to the safety of American lines, where they received the welcome surcease of food, medical care, and love. Every one of the paratroopers made it out alive. By any measure, the operation was a massive success. The "Angels" had pulled off a complex, daring rescue, right under the noses of the Japanese, and quite possibly saved the lives of the internees. It was an incredible accomplishment and one that pointed to the professional excellence of the 11th Airborne Division. An ebullient Swing wrote jauntily to his father-in-law, General March, "All in all, it was a nice party."

The "party" did exact some cost, though. The 188th Glider Infantry Regiment lost three men killed and two wounded in the diversionary attack, the only serious casualties during the operation for Swing's division. Paul Leary, father of a rescued priest, wrote gratefully to the mother of PFC John Doiron, one of the men who had been killed, "I know that nothing which I may now say can restore your loved one to you. Only a father or a mother can understand what the loss of a child means." Doiron's company commander, Lieutenant William Mayberry, also wrote to let his mother know that the dead soldier's "excellent character and devotion to duty had won him the admiration and respect of all the officers and men. He had proven himself a capable soldier and a gentleman." Among the rescued was Walter Scott Price, the successful entrepreneur in whose home MacArthur had made his headquarters on Leyte. Unfortunately, Price was in very poor condition. On March 18, just a few weeks after liberation, he died of pneumonia at the 5th Field Hospital and was buried in the University of Santo Tomas cemetery.

With the Americans gone from the Los Baños area, the Japanese unleashed in late February an all-too-typical series of abominable reprisal atrocities against civilians from surrounding villages. By one historical estimate, they tortured and killed 1,500 people, thus further staining their already odious human rights record and creating an uncomfortable legacy of bitterness between the Filipinos and the Americans, whom locals blamed for leaving them to the tender mercy of the enemy. In fact, during the raid, Swing had contemplated leaving the rescue force in place to link up with the troopers from the 188th, something Burgess considered to be tantamount to suicide because they remained so deep in enemy-controlled country. The major actually feigned radio trouble rather than discuss the matter with Swing. Clearly, he wanted no part of such a mission, for which he and his tiring soldiers would have been less than well prepared. Neither he nor any other paratrooper on the scene could have foreseen the Japanese reprisals. By any fair measure, the historical blame for these terrible crimes should affix solely upon the perpetrators, and certainly not the liberators of Los Baños, who, even had they stayed in place, would hardly have been in position to provide true protection for local civilians.[22]

2

Grind and Dash

I n order to utilize the port of Manila fully—once engineers could rebuild it—MacArthur needed Corregidor, the fortress island located at the entrance to Manila Bay, where he and his family had endured numerous shellings and bombings during the desperate early months of 1942 and from which he had secretly sallied forth to make his escape to Australia. The Japanese had captured Corregidor following a sharp, bloody fight on May 5–6, 1942, to force the surrender of General Wainwright and his last holdouts. To MacArthur and many thousands of other Americans, the place was hallowed ground that must be reclaimed, but they also needed it for solid military reasons. If the Japanese remained in control of the island, they could harass passing ships with shellfire and probably menace them with suicide boats. A Japanese-held Corregidor would serve as an uncomfortable stone in the American shoe, sapping the vitality and usefulness of Manila to the Allied cause. In early February, MacArthur ordered Krueger to take it as soon as possible.

Willoughby once again demonstrated his seemingly inexhaustible talent for inaccuracy. He calculated the Japanese garrison at 850, a fivefold underestimate. Colonel White, the Sixth Army intelligence officer who had come close to pinpointing Japanese strength on Luzon, this time shared in Willoughby's mistaken notions. Krueger later dolefully termed their collective calculations as "an underestimate of major proportions." In fact, Corregidor was defended by about 5,000 Japanese, most of whom were naval personnel under the command of Captain Akira Itagaki, who answered to Rear Admiral Iwabuchi. Alamo Scouts might have detected their presence. Sixth Army intended to recon Corregidor by shuttling a team onto the island via PT boat. But two

97

missions were aborted due to the skipper's concerns about mines and Japanese surface opposition. Perhaps this was for the best. Sixth Army's after-action report claimed that "the Japanese had set a trap for the landing parties, and had it succeeded, the Scout teams would have been annihilated."

Most of the Japanese were hunkered down inside the island's many tunnels and caves. Corregidor had absorbed a tremendous pounding during the 1942 battle. The skeleton of a three-story concrete-and-steel barracks building, stretching 1,500 feet in length and once proudly inhabited by a US Army garrison, lay in shattered ruins now, as did some of the old American battery positions. Bomb and shell craters pockmarked the whole island. Shattered trees and boulders lay in random shambles. Jagged tree stumps menaced the troubled landscape.

Starting on January 23, General Kenney's aviators began working the place over even more. For three weeks, B-24s, A-20s, and a mixture of fighter planes dumped bombs and bullets onto the tortured remnants of the little tadpole-shaped island that measured two square miles and little more than four miles in length. "Everything must have been shaken up over there," an impressed Seaman James Fahey aboard the cruiser USS *Montpelier* noted in his diary after witnessing a typical raid. "It seemed as if a powder factory had exploded. Corregidor was blacked out for some time. It was covered with smoke and dust. Bombs were exploding everywhere like big balls of fire. It was quite a sight to see." The aircraft flew 2,028 sorties, during which they dropped an eye-popping 3,128 tons of bombs and fired untold thousands of .50-caliber machine-gun bullets onto hapless Corregidor. Krueger later called the bombardment "the heaviest bombing to which any comparable area had been exposed in the whole Southwest Pacific Area fighting." The Japanese could do little besides take shelter and weather the ordnance storm. "We could not move except at night," Sadashichi Yamagishi, a member of an Imperial Navy construction battalion on Corregidor, later reflected soberly. "It was as if a child were fighting a man."

While the planes unleashed their hell from the sky, XI Corps ground troops fought a bitter battle to clear the adjacent Bataan Peninsula of Japanese resistance. The 38th Infantry Division needed almost the entire first half of February to secure the Zig Zag Pass in northern Bataan, where Route 7 snaked crazily along a seemingly endless series of hills and knolls, each of which offered nearly perfect defensible ground for the stubborn Japanese defenders who had constructed mutually supporting pillboxes, bunkers, and tunnels. "Few pieces of ground combine to the same degree both roughness and dense jungle," wrote Robert Ross Smith, the Army's official historian. The Americans could not seal off and control Bataan until they took Zig Zag. The protracted, bloody nature of the fighting prompted a frustrated Major General Charles Hall, the XI Corps commanding officer, to relieve Major General Henry Jones, the 38th's commander, in favor of newly promoted Major General Chase, who came over from the 1st Cavalry Division and quickened the pace of the advance, though he needed nearly a week to take the pass and clear the way for soldiers from the 6th Infantry Division to begin moving south along Bataan's coastal roads.

The heavy fighting at Zig Zag Pass forced Krueger to postpone the invasion of Corregidor from February 12 to 16. On February 15, Chase's 151st Infantry Regiment successfully landed at Mariveles on the southern tip of Bataan, just opposite Corregidor, eliminating any Japanese threat from that flank and providing Krueger with a nice sally point. The Sixth Army commander had planned a joint airborne-amphibious operation to take the island. He chose the 503rd Parachute Infantry Regiment to make a combat jump onto Corregidor. The unit had spent nearly two years in theater and had yet to take on a mission that truly challenged its high caliber. The troopers had logged combat jumps in September 1943 at Nadzab on New Guinea and at Noemfoor in July 1944. They had met almost no resistance at Nadzab. Although they did some sharp fighting at Noemfoor, they suffered almost as many casualties from the jump as in battle. Subsequently, the regiment's unopposed amphibious landing on Mindoro in mid-December had yielded little ground combat, something of a disappointment for an all-volunteer unit populated by adventurous, aggressive young men. Like a powerful college football program without membership in a conference, the 503rd inexplicably remained independent of any affiliation with the 11th Airborne Division—home to the only other parachute infantry regiment in theater—an odd anomaly of the sort that seems to happen all too often in the Army. The troopers, though, reveled in that independence. "They looked on themselves proudly as being <u>the</u> veteran parachute outfit of the SWPA," Lieutenant Colonel Jack Tolson, the executive officer, later wrote. "They had no desire to be assigned to the . . . 11th A/B Division."

For a brief time, General Swing had considered, and discarded, the possibility of attaching the 503rd to his division for the Tagaytay Ridge jump. Soon thereafter came an alert for a jump on Nichols Field that never materialized. At last, a couple of days later, Sixth Army headquarters alerted the 503rd for the Corregidor mission. The regimental commander, Colonel George Jones, a West Pointer on the cusp of his thirty-fourth birthday, embodied the unit's youthful élan. Grandson of a Confederate soldier, the Memphis native and natural fighter had once boxed at the academy. Among his troopers he had picked up the jocular nickname "The Warden" for restricting miscreant men to quarters aboard ship during the unit's long journey to the South Pacific, as well as for the notorious reputation his men earned for stealing from other units. Soldiers throughout SWPA took to calling the 503rd, not always affectionately, "Panama Jones and His Three Thousand Thieves."

Jones had assumed command of the 503rd in October 1943 when the original CO, Colonel Kenneth Kinsler, killed himself. At the time, Krueger apparently suspected that Jones was too young for such an important assignment. In a meeting between the two, the general emphasized that he had actually been in the Army longer than Jones had been alive. With characteristic brusqueness, Krueger told the young West Pointer, "Jones, I don't know anything about you. You have assumed command . . . because you are the senior lieutenant colonel. I am not going to recommend your promotion. Of course, if you do well at some future date, I will recommend your promotion. If not, I'll be forced to relieve you." Krueger need not have worried. Jones performed well and had since earned his promotion to full colonel.

To plan for the operation, the young colonel boarded a B-25 on a bombing mission and studied the terrain intently through the plexiglass nose of the aircraft. He realized that the island's diminutive size and the proliferation of debris and craters would make jumping perilous. He proposed to jump onto tiny Kindley Field at the southeastern tip of Corregidor, the lowest point of the island, and the only spot he deemed remotely suitable for a drop zone. Krueger overruled him on the grounds that the troopers would be highly vulnerable to fire from the higher ground known as Topside—the location of the ruined barracks—and Malinta Hill, the intricate network of concrete-reinforced tunnels built before the war by US Army engineers and where MacArthur, his family, and his staff had taken refuge three years earlier. "It seemed better to me to make the drop on Topside itself, where the Japanese were not likely to expect it to be made," Krueger later wrote. Jones worried that he might incur prohibitive jump casualties amid Topside's concrete ruins, craters, and tree stumps. But Krueger's contention made good sense. The wrecked barracks at Topside were surrounded by a parade ground and a nine-hole golf course that provided as much open space as Corregidor had to offer. Not only was Topside physically larger than the Kindley Field area but its central location offered Jones's troopers the opportunity to split the enemy garrison in two and control the high ground.

Captain Itagaki, the Japanese commander, dismissed the notion of an airborne landing as impossible, so he neglected to have his men fortify the area with mines, sharpened stakes, barbed wire, and fixed gun positions that could have turned Topside into a death zone. "Our Corregidor jump would, I believe, have been impossible if the Japs had prepared against a jump landing in the selected area," Colonel Jones later opined. Instead, Itagaki emphasized coastal defense in the deployment of his troops and defenses solely in anticipation of an amphibious landing. The final American plan called for the 3rd Battalion to jump at 0830 on February 16 and the 2nd Battalion around midday. At the same time, soldiers from Lieutenant Colonel Edward Postlethwait's 3rd Battalion, 34th Infantry Regiment, 24th Division, would board LCMs at Mariveles and then land at 1030 on Corregidor's south coast, just underneath Malinta Hill. Colonel Jones would then decide whether to land his remaining battalion by air or sea the following day.[1]

On Mindoro the night before the operation, the troopers clustered at an outdoor theater to watch captured Japanese footage of Corregidor's fall in 1942. "The film showed the Japs mistreating American PWs and stomping the American flag into the ground," Captain Magnus Smith, a staff officer, wrote angrily. The images were upsetting enough to prompt one private to express amazement that no one did more than simply sit and watch. "It was hard to imagine this bunch jumping the next day as everything was perfectly normal," he wrote home soon thereafter. The movie exemplified the personal feel to the operation; for many it felt like avenging a crime against a family member, or at least completing unfinished business. "The memory of General Wainwright surrendering a handful of half starved but gallant soldiers . . . lingered in the minds of members of the regiment," Captain Donald Crawford, an assistant personnel officer, remembered poignantly. A few men had actually served on Corregidor before the war. West Point classmates of both Colonel Jones and Lieutenant Colonel Tolson had fought there in 1942. "Morale was extremely high," Lieutenant Edward McCash, a young platoon leader, asserted. "Aside from the sentimental aspects of the retaking of 'The Rock', the urge for revenge surged in every man." To Lieutenant Donald Lundy, a C-47 pilot who observed the troopers closely, "they seemed very eager to go. No complaining or anything like that."

Two years of pent-up yearning for major action had morphed into a general mood of enthusiasm. "Now we are getting somewhere," Major Harris Mitchell, the executive officer of the 3rd Battalion, excitedly thought to himself. Lieutenant William Calhoun, a twenty-two-year-old platoon leader, later ruminated, "We were so keen to get into action that I doubt if many of us paused to reflect upon what could be awaiting us. We were paratroopers, dammit, and Corregidor was the best shot at being Paratroopers that our training and years overseas could ever have afforded us, and wild horses would not have stopped us from it." The eagerness did not forestall mischief in a unit with a well-deserved reputation for bending the rules. Corporal Walter Gonko and a buddy bought a fifth of Black & White Blended Scotch Whisky for thirty dollars from someone they knew in the 317th Troop Carrier Group, the unit assigned to fly them to Corregidor. As the three men steadily hollowed out the bottle's contents, Gonko's Airborne buddy grew maudlin and asked him to look after his fiancée back in Connecticut if anything happened to him. "I assured him I would and maybe do more than that—ask her to marry me," Gonko rejoined with typical Airborne irreverence.

The next morning the troopers rose at 0500 and chose from a breakfast menu of either powdered eggs or soggy pancakes with gobs of sticky syrup, washed down by liberal quantities of strong coffee. As they ate, a layer of island dust settled over food and men alike. With full bellies, they boarded trucks that shuttled them to their assigned C-47s, where they began kitting up with heavy loads of gear, such as extra ammunition, equipment bags, main and reserve chutes, personal weapons, radios, grenades, knives, a pair of canteens, a quartet of K ration meals, and the like, so typical for an Airborne drop. To reduce their vulnerability after landing, they strapped to their chests under their reserve chutes or along their right sides every kind of weapon except .50-caliber machine guns, 81-millimeter mortars, flamethrowers, and, quite obviously, artillery pieces. "They worked in complete silence," wrote Lieutenant Dick Williams, an Airborne-qualified leader of a photographic unit assigned to jump with the troopers. "This was important business, the job of putting yourself in a harness of cotton and silk that would hold your life in its grip."

By now, they had absorbed several days of detailed briefings, but some leaders gave last-minute speeches. Lieutenant Colonel John Erickson, whose 3rd Battalion was slated to drop first, told his men, with barely controlled fury, "Get those Japs, knife 'em, shoot 'em, then drop 'em over the cliffs and listen to 'em scream." Another commander concluded his talk by assuring his troopers, "Yes, you shall go down in history." One of his men, Sergeant Frank O'Neill, a smart-aleck young infantryman, later wrote to his mother, "That didn't seem new to me as I had gone down in it for years—I still can't recall a year I ever made as high as a 75." Groaning under their heavy burdens, they waddled to their planes and struggled aboard. In some cases, jumpmasters told their charges to don most of their equipment once on the plane, a process that made boarding easier but kitting up more difficult in a confined environment.

At 0715 the first of the 317th Troop Carrier Group's 51 C-47s took off. The flight to Corregidor absorbed an hour, during which they slept, rechecked their gear, or just sat and fretted. Engine noise made meaningful conversation nearly impossible. One trooper looked around at his buddies and noticed "the strange yellow-toned pallor in their faces which spelled strain." A nearby man was so bathed in sweat that thick droplets from his chin repeatedly splashed against his rifle stock. Clear skies and idyllic warm weather blessed them with a perfect day for jumping. Successive waves of B-24 and B-25 bombers, followed by A-20 Havocs, worked Corregidor over one last time. Cruisers and destroyers soon joined the fray. "Our ship shakes from the terrific explosions," Seaman Fahey aboard the light cruiser *Montpelier* jotted in his diary. "Corregidor is covered with smoke. I cannot see the high cliffs . . . on account of it. The troops who were on Corregidor when it fell to the Japanese in 1942 would have enjoyed the script."

The tiny size of the parade ground and golf course drop zones necessitated changes to the usual practice of disgorging entire planeloads of troopers from aircraft flying in a V formation. Instead, the C-47s flew in a pair of opposite columns like long conveyer belts, and dropped abbreviated sticks of seven or eight paratroopers at a time. "The planes in the left column would fly over Field 'A', drop eight jumpers, circle to the left, join the tail of the column and in a 'round robin' fashion continue this until all men and equipment were dropped," Captain Crawford explained of the unique practice. The other column did the same over the "B" field. Each plane circled three times before disgorging all its troopers. To one staff officer observing from the vantage point of an aircraft flying overhead, the C-47s "seemed to fly so slowly that I thought they would never get there." Even directly over the proper drop zone, jumpmasters counted three or four seconds before leaving their planes in order to account for stiff 22-knot-per-hour winds that otherwise might have blown men over the cliffs and into the sea. The unique jump tactics were time-consuming and required enormous concentration and skill on the part of everyone involved, most notably the pilots. "The target was so small, the wind so strong," Lieutenant Lundy later commented. The whole practice would not have been possible if not for the paucity of enemy antiaircraft guns and the complete American domination of the air.

Lieutenant Colonel Erickson's first troopers jumped at 0833, and it took over an hour for his entire battalion to land. A multicolored kaleidoscope of white and camouflage chutes now honeycombed the island. Before jumping himself, Colonel Jones spent much of that time circling overhead in a C-47 piloted by Lieutenant Colonel John Lackey, commander of the 317th. Jones directed the drops and made downward adjustments to the drop altitude to maximize the chances of accuracy and to minimize the time the troopers spent in vulnerable descent at the mercy of the wind and perhaps the enemy. "We started off by jumping . . . [at] 550 feet, but we successfully lowered this altitude to 500 feet, and then to 400 feet," he later wrote. Dropping at midday, Major Lawson Caskey's 2nd Battalion needed about the same amount of time to touch down on Corregidor. Most of the equipment and supporting weapons made it to the ground intact.

Individual batteries of the 462nd Parachute Field Artillery Battalion dropped with the infantrymen. The artillery troopers utilized eleven of their battalion's fifteen 75-millimeter pieces. One tube was lost. The other three were damaged in the drop but were cannibalized for parts. The artillery troopers recovered about 75 percent of the shells for these weapons. Twenty-two of twenty-four .50-caliber machine guns made it into action, providing a powerful source of fire support. As Colonel Jones had anticipated, the perilous drop zones took a toll on his troopers, though not quite as much as he feared. Of the 2,050 paratroopers who jumped in the two waves, he lost 280, a nearly 14 percent casualty rate. Some 210 were injured on landing, including Lieutenant Colonel Tolson, who broke a bone in his foot; about 50 were wounded in the air or on the ground by enemy fire; 3 died as a result of malfunctioning parachutes and 2 others from the trauma of crashing into buildings; 15 were killed by the Japanese before they could get out of their chutes.

The official casualty numbers underestimated the full extent of the damage the 503rd suffered from making such a low-altitude jump onto perilous, cratered fields, strewn as they were with so many dangerous impediments. One chastened trooper termed the drop zone as "the worst jump field ever used for an airborne operation." Many paratroopers suffered painful bruises and scrapes or injuries that would have been more serious under less adverse circumstances. "We did not consider a man a casualty unless he was immobile as a result of a broken bone or was suffering shock as the result of wounds or injuries," Lieutenant Colonel Erickson later told an interviewer. "Otherwise he was treated, bandaged, and continued to fight." Captain Hudson Hill, a company commander, landed hard enough against the top of a ruined concrete building to collapse his chute and fall unaided to the ground. "The only serious result of the fall was to have seven teeth knocked out or broken off," he later wrote without any hint of sarcasm. "The loss of the teeth was a fair exchange for possible death." Dismissive of the missing teeth, he carried out his duties without reporting himself as a casualty. The same was true for PFC Tony Sierra, whose rifle smashed him in the face and knocked out three teeth when he landed in a shell crater on the golf course. Concussed, bleeding, and confused, it took him several minutes to come to his senses. "My chute was snagged on a piece of concrete. I was scared and I thought I had been shot." After receiving first aid from another trooper, he got on his feet and headed for his objective. Colonel Jones himself was nearly impaled by a tree stump that "took off the flesh of my thighs on each leg, which was painful but did not require attention from the medics." He managed to extract a five-inch-long splinter from his inner thigh. He later joked that if the splinter had "hit only a few inches farther up, I would be talking . . . now a pitch or two higher." Unlike some Airborne officers, Jones viewed jumping into combat as a necessary evil rather than a rite of passage. "I felt that entering combat by parachute should never be done unless it gave you a tactical advantage," he once wrote revealingly. Once on Corregidor soil, he saw no profit in any more jumps, so he took steps to make sure his remaining battalion came to the island by sea the next morning.[2]

Similar to Los Baños and Tagaytay Ridge, the Airborne drop at Corregidor did confer upon the Americans a major advantage of surprise. As troopers landed, organized, and began fanning out over the island, the Japanese were caught almost completely off guard, none more so than Captain Itagaki, whose operational myopia now cost him dearly. At 0830, just as the first troopers prepared to jump, he had hastened to an observation post at Breakwater Point to watch soldiers from Lieutenant Colonel Postlethwait's 3rd Battalion, 34th Infantry, board their landing craft a few miles across the bay at Mariveles. Their impending amphibious assault seemed to confirm his expectations that the Americans intended to invade Corregidor by sea and not air. Itagaki, an aide, and a security detail watched the landing craft, transfixed, seemingly unaware of the Airborne landings happening all around them. A platoon-size group of paratroopers soon landed nearby, assembled, and attacked Itagaki's group, killing him and eight members of his security

detail. Captain Itagaki's early death, along with the near complete decimation of all Japanese communications systems on the island, robbed
the garrison of any cohesion. Physically separated groups of defenders
simply hunkered down inside their caves, tunnels, craters, and foxholes
to fight self-sacrificial defensive actions, spiced with limited counterattacks, mostly at night.

When Postlethwait's people, plus supporting tanks and self-propelled
artillery, landed at 1028 on Corregidor's south coast, mines comprised their main opposition. Within a few moments, as infantrymen
charged ashore and worked their way inland, mines destroyed a tank, a
self-propelled gun, and an antitank gun. "My outfit lost over fifty percent of its vehicles within twenty yards of the water line," Postlethwait
later said. The mines and some accompanying 20-millimeter-gun and
machine-gun fire could not prevent the 3rd Battalion from quickly securing Malinta Hill and linking up with the paratroopers, where they
came under the control of Colonel Jones, the senior officer on the island.
With the Americans in control of Corregidor's heart and enjoying almost complete aboveground freedom of maneuver, they focused on methodically killing group after group of stubborn Japanese. The defenders'
fragmentation into disparate groups with no cohesion proved a fortunate break for the Americans, as the Japanese outnumbered them almost
by a factor of two to one. In other circumstances, this could have been
fatal to an attacking force.

The unpleasant reality of enemy numbers became apparent to Colonel Jones and his commanders within a day or two of the invasion,
largely thanks to the efforts of Sergeant Harry Akune, a Japanese
American translator. Loaned to the 503rd by the Sixth Army's intelligence section, Akune had never even made a parachute jump, and yet he
managed to land safely. Captain Francis Donovan, the regimental intelligence officer, so mistrusted Akune that he discouraged him from gain-
ing access to a weapon, much less making use of his language and cultural
skills. "How am I supposed to give him information and have him believe me?" Sergeant Akune wondered gravely. In spite of Donovan's ma-
lignant stupidity, Akune quickly set to work translating captured
Japanese documents and interrogating the few enemy soldiers who
ended up in captivity. In the process, Akune learned of Captain Itagaki's

death, the surprisingly large size of the Corregidor garrison, their paucity of communications, and the presence of nearly one hundred
explosives-laden suicide boats that might threaten Allied vessels, most
notably a pair of destroyers that stood offshore to provide supporting
fire. Indeed, this single man found out more about the Japanese on Corregidor in the space of a couple of days than Willoughby and his retinue
had learned over the course of months, a classic real-world lesson in the
limitless value of bona fide human intelligence.

Fortunately, Akune caught the ears of more intelligent, open-minded
officers than Donovan. Sergeant Akune reported his valuable information to Lieutenant Colonel Tolson, whom he already knew from serving
with him at Sixth Army, and to Colonel Jones. "Through his unique and
valuable skills . . . Akune was able to obtain information . . . that, without
any doubt, materially assisted me and my staff in planning most effective measures to destroy the enemy," Jones later gratefully wrote. "I
can make the unqualified statement that he was essential in obtaining
enemy information which shortened the operation and saved an untold
number of American casualties." Captain William McRoberts, a staff
officer who dealt frequently with Akune, later testified that "within two
hours after the capture of prisoners, he obtained valuable information
about Jap dispositions and weapons." Acting on the tip about suicide
boats, destroyers located and blasted most of the Japanese soldiers in
their caves and other hiding places.

Thanks to Akune, Jones knew his forces were outnumbered but that
the Japanese were leaderless and incapable of an organized counterattack. He assigned each of the four infantry battalions under his
control—collectively known as the Rock Force—to clear out a specific
section of Corregidor. Each morning, commanders briefed their men
and then led patrols to take the day's objectives. "Moving silently they
would plod under the hot sun, sweating and stinking and not knowing
what they would run into," Lieutenant Williams, the Signal Corps photographer, later wrote of the monotonous action. "Every day was different. Sometimes being ambushed, crawling on their bellies for hours,
running out of ammunition, dropping in exhaustion, and at the end of
the day struggling back to the command post bearing their wounded
and malaria ridden comrades. Each day their beards grew longer, their

faces dirty, the very clothes becoming a stinking combination of sweat, dirt and death."

Day by day for nearly two weeks, they fought from crater to crater, cave to cave, tunnel to tunnel, sometimes back clearing when small groups of Japanese re-infiltrated positions they had previously lost. "The Japs placed their automatic weapons in well selected positions on forward slopes, protected by riflemen," one officer told a post-battle analyst. "Several hundred yards to the front they would place a ring of snipers. The snipers would hold their fire until the automatic weapons opened on our troops, then they would go to work in the confusion." Even more frequently, they fought to the death from fortified caves or tunnels where they were literally ripped to shreds by the frightening potency of American firepower. "You couldn't find a whole limb or a body, just a piece," Sergeant Ben Guthrie later commented of surveying the gruesome remnants in many captured caves.

Artillerymen fired point-blank at any suspected target. "When the infantrymen would back off, our gunners bore-sighted their tubes on targets and fired several rounds," Lieutenant Joe Gray, a young section leader in the 462nd Parachute Field Artillery Battalion, later wrote. "In all cases that I can recall our fire was 100 percent effective." In one typical forty-eight-hour period, gunners disgorged 889 shells and claimed to have killed 392 Japanese. Guided by a shore fire control party that had jumped with the paratroopers, destroyers closed to within one thousand yards of the coast to saturate Japanese positions. In the course of the battle, they unleashed 10,688 5-inch projectiles at various targets. Close air support from fighters added another powerful fist to the onslaught, relentlessly pounding the Japanese. In a single small unit action to support one rifle company, 31 P-47 Thunderbolts dropped 4,000 gallons of napalm and 38 500-pound bombs, and fired 31,000 rounds of .50-caliber ammunition.

Enough of the Japanese managed to survive the hurricane of firepower to make any cave the potential site of a desperate struggle to the death. "Each one in itself presented a difficult and dangerous operation," bemoaned an XI Corps post-battle report. Nor could they be outflanked. "The element of maneuver was virtually nonexistent," Captain Hudson Hill commented. "The very nature of the terrain left no choice but direct assault on enemy positions." Combined arms teams of riflemen, machine gunners, explosives-wielding engineers, bazookamen, and flamethrower teams, occasionally supported by tanks, blasted them at close range. "The infantry would pin down the enemy in position by delivery of heavy fire while the demolitionists moved in with explosives and flamethrowers to reduce the position," Captain Crawford wrote. "If the position was such as to require a great deal of time and demolition work to eliminate, the infantry, after initial assistance, would push on and the demolitionists would remain to complete the job." On average, the explosives teams expended between 20 and 30 TNT blocks per cave.

When flamethrower operators started getting hurt by the backblast that sometimes occurred in hosing down shallow caves, they took to spraying unignited fuel and then setting it ablaze with white phosphorous grenades. To destroy the many underground fortified positions, the teams tied five-gallon cans of fuel together with white phosphorous grenades and a fuse. "The infantry would cover the position while the demolition team crawled forward to a ventilator shaft or other similar opening, ignited the time fuse and dropped the explosive into the shaft," Crawford explained. The noise of the explosion seldom drowned out the agonized screams of the dying. "All in all it was a hell of a messy, stinking job," Private Ralph Frey, a young infantryman, wrote to his sister-in-law with searing honesty about clearing caves and tunnels. "We came out all covered with sweat, dirt and blood. I never want to go thru anything like that again." Once cleared, some of the caves yielded a bizarre diversity of booty, including sewing machines, car tires, cloth, and a Studebaker automobile, alongside sixty tons of rice and canned fish and innumerable bottles of sake.[3]

At night, under the half-light of fires flickering thirty miles away in embattled Manila, as the Americans settled into their usual wary perimeters, groups of Japanese launched fruitless banzai assaults. "The Japanese had a way of yelling," PFC Sierra shuddered. "We don't know if they were drunk or drugged up. It was almost like an Indian dance." To Sergeant O'Neill, they seemed more like "a rat or a vampire getting blood wherever he can and dying for the Emperor. Our knowledge of being outnumbered 2 to 1 made sleep a little less frequent." The Americans mowed them down in droves. By the time the battle neared its merciful end, the little island had seemingly become choked with Japanese bodies and body parts. "We couldn't walk in the clear," one paratrooper claimed, "too many Japs laying [sic] on the ground . . . just a carpet of them." The frenetic pace of combat and the rocky soil made it nearly impossible to bury them. Another trooper later wrote sadly of a landscape practically coated with human flesh. "Hundreds of bodies laid [sic] about, unburied and by the fourth or fifth day, maggots were eating the bodies." Sergeant O'Neill wrote of one typical corpse "with back side bared, pointing to the sky, and in addition to the normal cavity that from the lower part of the great intestine, he had another cavity on the left cheek about the depth and proportion of a large cantaloupe, and chuck full of flies—about a thousand of them."

A plague of flies, nearly biblical in proportion, descended on Corregidor. By the millions they swarmed, feasting on the dead, harassing the wounded, tormenting everyone by their sheer relentless numbers. "When we attempted to eat our rations, we had to place our chow on the ground so we could wave away the flies that tried to crawl into our mouths," a nauseated Lieutenant Gray wrote. In PFC Victor Erdahl's recollection, "You could not open your mouth without eating a fly." The simple act of eating became something of a gymnastic exercise. Tight-lipped soldiers ate with one hand while, according to one infantryman, "the other waved the fifty or one hundred flies away." More than a few men inadvertently ingested dozens of flies each day. Corporal Gonko, the machine gunner, grew so repulsed by this that he nearly lost any appetite. "I never ate unless I was really hungry as it was almost impossible to put anything in your mouth without a dozen flies landing on it." The troops could not even sip coffee from canteen cups without first waving away a cloud of the flies. An inevitable wave of dysentery swept through the ranks. By one estimate, almost half the men were afflicted. "It was well nigh impossible to care for the wounded and to prepare food without contamination," a Sixth Army study of the fly problem affirmed. At the behest of the Sixth Army's surgeon, C-47s soon inundated the island with DDT powder. Over a four-day period, the planes dumped 1,400 pounds of the insecticide on Corregidor, destroying the adult fly population.

The nearly suffocating stench of death and decay persisted, especially in the tropical heat. "Everything began to smell bad, the food, the very breath you sucked between dried and burning lips and the men that you slept beside and fought with," Lieutenant Williams wrote. In SWPA circles it was said that for many weeks Corregidor's stench was so overwhelming that even people aboard ships sailing past the island got sick. Reflecting on the filth of the battlefield in which he found himself enmeshed, Private Arthur Smith of the 34th Infantry wrote to his family that "war is boredom and discomfort and fear and pain, destruction and death and waste."

A paucity of potable water on the island made a mockery of good hygiene. Soldiers barely had enough to drink, much less to use scarce water for anything else. The paratroopers had jumped with two canteens apiece and quickly drank them dry within a day or so, after which many became nearly crazed with thirst. "The weather was hot and dry and the sun beat down on us to make matters worse," wrote Captain Henry Gibson, a battery commander in the 462nd. The men resorted to sucking on pebbles or looting canteens off enemy corpses. "Tongues would swell and parched lips would crack in thirst," Sergeant Guthrie lamented. To maintain the bare minimum of subsistence, C-47s dropped water—and other supplies—to the troops until more necessities could be brought in from Mariveles to Corregidor's beaches. On a typical supply run, the planes dropped 1,250 gallons of water in durable five-gallon cans from a height of 400 feet. "More than 80% of it was recovered intact and undamaged," Major Caskey, the 2nd Battalion commander, later avowed. The arrival by ship of water trailers enhanced the water supply enough to allow for a ration of four quarts per man per day. The infusion made it far easier for a pair of Red Cross canteens, one of which had actually jumped in with the paratroopers, to serve coffee.

By February 26, after ten days of intense fighting, the Americans had snuffed out all but a few scattered remnants of the Japanese garrison. The Rock Force killed 4,464 Japanese and captured only 20. Perhaps as many as 200 enemy soldiers were killed or drowned as they desperately attempted to swim from Corregidor to Bataan. Another 500 might have been trapped inside caves. "Many were buried alive when our demolitionists sealed the caves, as enemy screams rang in their ears, and the Japs committed harikari [sic] with hand grenades," the 503rd's after-action report soberly recounted. The Rock Force lost 210 killed, 5 missing, 450 wounded, and another 340 injured. The 503rd suffered over three-quarters of the American casualties, including a mind-boggling 52 killed and 144 wounded in a single instant on February 26 when an underground arsenal detonated at Monkey Point near the eastern tip of the island. The blast resulted either from a deliberate Japanese suicide effort or an American tank shell. Bodies were blown to bits, torn in half or hurled dozens of feet into the air. A reverberating wave of concussion spread across the bay. Debris was ejected as far as one thousand yards out to sea; rocks actually hit a destroyer. A thirty-five-ton Sherman tank flipped end over end and landed upside down more than fifty feet away. Rescuers needed to borrow an acetylene torch from a destroyer to retrieve the one badly wounded, traumatized surviving crewman. The blast decimated Major John Davis's 1st Battalion. "I have never seen such a sight in my life," he mourned; "utter carnage, bodies laying [sic] everywhere, *everywhere*."

Harried, appalled medics saved as many lives as possible and cleaned up the gruesome aftermath. "As soon as I got all the casualties off, I sat down on a rock and burst out crying," one medic recalled. "I couldn't stop myself and didn't even want to. I had seen more than a man could stand and still stay normal." Medics tallied the dead by simply counting the number of arms they found and dividing by two. Dazed, shocked survivors limped away, never to forget. "The sight of these men was revolting," Lieutenant Williams, the photographer, shuddered. "All of them were covered with grime and blood and mud, most of them that could move at all were in semi-coma." Among the Rock Force dead was Tech 5 Clarence Miller, a medic in the 1st Battalion of the 503rd who left behind a wife and a three-year-old daughter whom he had never met. "I would have done anything in my power for him when he was alive, and I know he would have done the same for me," Miller's best friend wrote to his shattered widow. "So nothing you could ask would be too great a favor. I know you are taking it very hard and I only wish there was some way I could make it easier, but there isn't. I won't even try to tell you how I am taking it, because I think you know."

On March 2, shortly after the last of the fighting on Corregidor died down, Generals MacArthur and Krueger and a copious entourage of staffers and brass visited the island. In a conscious reenactment of Mac-Arthur's troubled exit from the island almost exactly three years earlier, he and his people arrived aboard a quartet of PT boats. An exhausted Colonel Jones proudly led the supreme commander and the other senior officers on a tour of MacArthur's many old haunts. The party walked past disposal teams working to cremate Japanese bodies. "I watched as the soldiers poured gasoline on the bodies and then threw in a match," Lieutenant Rogers, the stenographer, later wrote. "The bodies burned like logs. The stench of burning flesh added to the stench of decaying flesh still lying in the brush and debris."

In a ceremony on the parade ground near the Topside barracks, as an honor guard stood at attention, Colonel Jones saluted MacArthur and said, "Sir, I present you the Fortress Corregidor." Delighted and moved, MacArthur responded with a short speech. "Colonel Jones, the capture of Corregidor is one of the most brilliant operations in military history. Outnumbered two to one, your command by its unfaltering courage, its invincible determination, and its professional skill overcame all obstacles and annihilated the enemy. I see the old flagpole still stands. Have your troops hoist the colors to its peak, and let no enemy ever haul them down." At the same flagpole where General Wainwright's men had once sadly lowered the colors, Jones's men now proudly raised them, closing the book not just on the struggle for Corregidor but, in a larger sense, Manila as well.[4]

Even with this strategic victory, the campaign for Luzon ground on, seemingly in perpetuity, as SWPA troops experienced their first northern hemispheric spring and summer since the war's onset. By springtime, the SWPA order of battle on Luzon alone (not including the forces still "mopping up" on Leyte) had swollen to twelve divisions, plus three independent regimental combat teams and numerous tank and engineer combat battalions, supported by tens of thousands of service troops. With the notable exception of northern Europe, MacArthur's legions represented the largest overseas deployment of US Army power anywhere on the globe. Ironically, for a man who fancied himself a skilled practitioner of maneuver warfare, adept at producing big results from meager resources, and one who had breezily promised War Department planners that he would secure Luzon in a matter of six weeks with "inconsequential" losses, he instead presided over nothing less than a brutal, blunt-force, protracted campaign of attrition.

Like a brawny but overtaxed strong man, Sixth Army was enmeshed in a bloody, manpower-intensive struggle to gain ground on two primary Luzon fronts—in the north against the Shobu Group and to the east of Manila, where the Shimbu Group, until late May, held dams that controlled much of the city's water supply. Both parts of Luzon bristled with the sorts of jungle-covered ridges, mountains, caves, hairpin passes, and raging rivers that made for excellent defensive terrain from which Yamashita's men simply hunkered down and sold their lives as expensively as they could. Of the scenery, Lieutenant Bob Guhl, an artilleryman in the 32nd Infantry Division, wrote to his family, "This would be great country to be sightseeing in with a nice hi-way. But it's sure tough to fight in." Sergeant James Augustin, a combat medic in the 11th Airborne Division, later described the rugged terrain as "extremely difficult on which to maneuver. There were heavily wooded ridges, tree covered knobs of hills, sharp bamboo and deep gorges. The Japanese had dug their usual cave defense system, well hidden by bamboo and brush. Even when located, the caves were hard to hit with artillery or mortar fire. Each cave had to be reduced by foot soldiers with hand grenades, rifles and flame throwers." All too often, to clear a cave, American troops had to approach almost within spitting distance of the enemy. "Fighting the Japs in caves means that you have to take what they dish out until you can get in and blow it or neutralize it prior to closing in," Lieutenant Colonel Robert Vance, a battalion commander in the 32nd Division, wrote in a post-battle analysis. His men took to building three-pound TNT grenades and hurling them into holes or the mouths of caves. "One block . . . would knock the Japs temporarily goofy from the concussion. This method was extremely successful in allowing the demolition teams to approach the position close enough to place a heavy charge." Commanders increasingly placed a premium on killing as many Japanese as possible, with the bare minimum of friendly losses, creating a preoccupation with body counts and kill ratios well before the Vietnam War made those terms infamous. "The only thing that makes

me happy is dead Japs!" declared Major Arndt Mueller, a battalion commander in the 6th Infantry Division, in a fervent speech he gave to Private Russell McLogan and a group of newly arrived replacements before
they went into action. "It's your job to keep me happy. If you don't, you
men are going to have a very miserable time here." A ruthless phrase,
"The only good Jap is a dead Jap," proliferated on the lips of many GIs.
The executive officer of one company that experienced the bloody fighting at Zig Zag Pass on Bataan later commented, "It was an easy job to
convince the men . . . that it was either kill or be killed." After entering
combat for the first time, one company history reported, with almost
morbid enthusiasm, "Francis (Heil Hitler) Fricke had the honor of killing the first Jap. Of course, we don't have to mention the fact that the Jap
was so sick and crippled he was ready to die in a few minutes anyway."
Unit after-action reports studiously documented enemy losses, and often related kill claims that so strained credulity as to lean toward ghoul-
ishness. In one representative example, the 7th Cavalry Regiment's
post-Luzon report claimed that the unit killed 3,141 Japanese at the cost
of 184 regimental fatalities, a 17-to-1 kill ratio that almost certainly could
not have reflected reality. The 1st Infantry Regiment, 6th Infantry Division, reported the killing of 6,338 Japanese against 269 of its own dead,
another unlikely 17-to-1 kill ratio. Major General Hall, the XI Corps
commander, told Krueger's chief of staff that, in one firefight, a single
regiment under his command had killed 873 enemy soldiers with minimal friendly losses. "It was from napalm and everything else. They were
riper than hell; the stench was terrible. The ones killed were armed and
wouldn't give up. Just mowed them down."

In essence, Luzon had turned into a giant, ungainly clearing operation analogous—in terms of its perpetual sameness—to the Brittany
and Colmar battles in France and the ongoing Allied conquest of Germany. "Each week brought new inhumanities, new fears, new horror,"
Lieutenant Milton Pearce, a young rifle platoon leader in the 38th Division, later remarked. "Nothing mattered much any longer except to
hunt and kill and somehow to keep ourselves alive. We dragged ourselves up one mountain after another, cleaned out the enemy from numerous jungle covered draws. We went weeks without taking off our

clothes or bathing or getting away from our own stink. We were half starved . . . torn with dysentery, malaria and dingue [*sic*] fever. Physically and mentally we were spent." A pervasive, unspoken throb of abject fright infused most everyone. "Every action and reaction, every thought and impulse is blanketed in a sweaty hiatus of fear," PFC Robert Myerson, a young medic from the 55th Field Artillery Battalion, told his father in a heartfelt letter. "It permeates the atmosphere and wraps itself around one like a clammy shroud. It accents individualities, meanness, pettiness, magnanimity, sacrifice—everything acquires a sharper pulse; the fear is almost tangible."

The after-action report of the 103rd Infantry Regiment, 43rd Division, asserted bluntly about the endless fighting in rugged eastern Luzon, "No hill . . . in a military maneuver is just a hill. It is a complete, self-contained chain with innumerable twists, turns, gorges, cut-outs, and a minimum of seventeen distinct peaks—each one of which, when one is on it, is dominated by all the others. The 'commanding ridge' is the next one after the one you just took. The men of the regiment, who have been chasing the 'commanding ridge' across six thousand miles of Pacific war zone, now believe themselves placed eternally at the foot of a steadily rising series of ridges, the ultimate one of which is probably located in Tibet." Riflemen like Private Ralph Frey now lived deep in Luzon's hills "where we patroled [*sic*], fought, sweated and stunk without much water and eating C rations. The only time we got to wash was when we found a stream or river and then sometimes we only had time to fill our canteens." Trailers brought as much water forward as possible, but their range remained limited. "In the final analysis we had to depend on the five-gallon can and the carrier to bring water to the men," attested one regimental post-battle report. The carrying parties could seldom fully quench the insatiable thirst of the frontline troops. "The terrific heat, together with the dust of the hills, made what seemed to be a sufficient supply actually inadequate," the chagrined surgeon of the 130th Infantry Regiment reported. A weekly ration of warm beer in some fortunate units raised spirits far more than it actually slaked any thirst. "Everyone is dripping with perspiration," PFC Henry Burger of the 20th Infantry Regiment, 6th Division, wrote to his father. "You certainly wish it would cool off. Later in the afternoon . . . it starts to rain, and it feels pretty good. But the rain keeps on and the wind blows, and you start to shiver from the cold."[5]

The fighting amounted to little more than a labor-intensive slog, with productive gains measured in yards rather than miles. "One ridge was cleared only after a bulldozer, a medium tank, and a flamethrowing tank joined the assaulting infantry platoon," recounted a Sixth Army study of a small unit action in the caves and hills around the Wawa Dam east of Manila. "The bulldozer scraped a road on the knife-edged ridge for the tanks to follow and apply direct fire and flame against the Japanese emplacements. Infantrymen, following behind the flamethrower, saw 30 enemy soldiers die in as many seconds when the heat reached them." The offensive plod contained little ambiguity. The Americans simply pummeled Yamashita's stubborn defenders with the standard array of massive firepower, an absolute must to achieve any objectives and avoid existential casualty rates. "When engaging our forces, their method is to completely destroy our positions by . . . intense artillery shellings and bombings prior to the infantry advance," one Japanese lieutenant noted in his diary. During four months on the line, the 130th Infantry Regiment documented the expenditure of 43,793 mortar shells, 6,396 105-millimeter rounds from self-propelled guns, 29,945 hand grenades, and an eyebrow-raising 1,392,336 machine-gun bullets. The ratio of firepower expended versus casualties inflicted tended toward an appalling level of inefficiency. The 130th's staff calculated that the firing of "637 tons of ammunition resulted in 4,000 enemy casualties or an average of 300 pounds per Jap." Army small-unit commanders hardly blinked an eye at routine outlays of such firepower, understandably much preferring to lose ordnance than men. "The U.S. soldier had courage as well as sense," Lieutenant Floyd Radike, now a company commander in the 25th Division, wrote proudly. "If he couldn't make any progress, he stopped and got out of there. Armchair theorists who think that the American soldier is too prone to hunker down and let airplanes, tanks and guns do the dirty work, seem to regard only the red badge of courage as worthy of praise. But it is not part of our ethos, tradition or training to have men killed or wounded when time and materiel can avert such needless losses."

With visibility generally limited to only a few yards and the sight of live enemy soldiers rare, experience taught the Americans to shoot at sectors rather than targets in order to "sweep the roots of trees and bushes with distributed small arms fire, whenever fired upon," in the estimation of one commander. A nearly universal respect, bordering on awe, was perasive among the Japanese for the overwhelming nature of the American firepower. "We have underestimated the importance of material power and are suffering the consequences," one of them scribbled in his diary, probably speaking for tens of thousands of others. To even the odds, the Japanese continued their usual practice of infiltrating or attacking at night, capitalizing on the American tendency to fight the war on banker's hours. "You're always glad to see the sun go down, because that means the end of the day's 'work,'" Lieutenant Noel Seeburg, a platoon leader in the 37th Division, wrote revealingly to his family of this self-deceptive mindset. Seeburg and thousands of others even urinated or defecated in their own foxholes at night rather than risk leaving them and getting shot by their own side. "Sanitary facilities were nonexistent," Private McLogan wrote.

Japanese attackers roamed under the cover of darkness, confident in finding the Americans passively ensconced in foxholes; many of the infiltrators wrote final letters to family or concluding diary entries before setting out on their suicidal expeditions. "I say this strongly for the last time," one of them asserted to his diary. "Even though my body has wasted away in the Philippines, my spirit carries on undaunted, and I go out bravely. I have nothing to regret." A characteristic Japanese tactical memo urged soldiers to take full advantage of the American propensity to hunker down at night. "Determine the halting location of the enemy, reconnoiter with patrols, effect an infiltration and destroy him. The objective of infiltrating attacks will be tanks, heavy guns, commanders, supply dumps, etc." A few units like the newly arrived 33rd Infantry Division under the thoughtful Major General Percy Clarkson, a Texas A&M graduate and combat veteran of World War I, learned to buck this custom. "This division has conducted night operations freely on Luzon and all our commanders favor them," he wrote in a battle analysis for Army Ground Forces. "Not only do they achieve surprise and reduce losses but they are far less fatiguing. Movements can frequently be made more rapidly by night than by day." Ironically, as Clarkson's testimony indicated, the necessity of maintaining wary, oft-terrified perimeters generally wore on the troops more than did night attacks or patrols.

Fatigue hung like a dark cloak over Sixth Army as combat units spent weeks and then months in action. "After an outfit has been fighting steadily and hard for fifteen or more days, then men begin to get haphazard and sluggish in everything they do," one infantry commander lamented. "Holes are not dug as deep as they should be, sanitation drops off markedly, and the usual cautions such as taking cover, not bunching up, etc., are ignored." Weariness led to mistakes, and mistakes led to death. An exhausted Lieutenant Howard Cooksey, a young platoon leader in the 158th Infantry Regiment, let his men take cover in folds of ground one evening rather than dig proper foxholes. "We were hit during the night and those folds in the ground weren't good enough. We lost some people . . . and it was my responsibility." The nearly universal exhaustion eroded morale and initiative, prompting Krueger to tell an Army Ground Forces observer that "the most important need and greatest lack in our forces is resourcefulness on the part of individuals and leaders of small groups—squads and platoons."

The unrelenting, enervating heat, the nighttime mountain chill, and the natural filth and privation of the jungle environment hardly helped. "The weather over here is so terrible hot we can march 1/4 mile real slow & our clothes will be soaked with perspiration," Private Raymond Lansford wrote to his parents. Cat-size rats proliferated everywhere. The 158th Infantry actually discovered nests of them living underneath their foxholes. The explosions of enemy shells tore holes in the ground, exposing the rats and sending them into an attacking frenzy against the horrified soldiers, who could get rid of them only by grabbing their tails and hurling them away. Insects of every type and description tormented the troops. "[They] are thick as raindrops here and much more demoralizing," Staff Sergeant Jay Gruenfeld of the 43rd Division wrote to a former teacher. "Ants from 1/32" to 1-1/2" long and they all bite." The prevalence of rivers, streams, and so much jungle foliage guaranteed the major presence of leeches. "Wherever there was water, you'd have these leeches that would dig into you with their heads and they'd suck your blood," Sergeant Keith Barress of the 25th Division recalled many years later. To remove these hated pests, Barress and legions of other soldiers poured turpentine on them or burned them off with cigarettes. "They're not so tough as they are slimy. It's like a slug. I'd mash them with my feet. I'd do anything. I just hated leeches. I hate them to this day." A company commander in the 1st Cavalry Division remembered that leeches "were all over everyone's body, including some that had crawled under eye lids, completely closing the eyes of many men."[6]

As the fighting dragged on, casualties inevitably ate away at Sixth Army ranks. Many of the combat units had gone into Luzon under strength. Most fought their battles at somewhere between half and two-thirds strength. Not until April did Sixth Army begin to receive replacements in any quantity. Even then the newbies could not truly flesh out the ranks of the hard-fighting infantry outfits, where 90 percent of American casualties occurred. Krueger's command reported 37,854 battle casualties, including 8,140 killed in action and 157 missing, over the course of the Luzon fighting. The fatalities included Lieutenant William Clark of the 38th Division, who was felled by Japanese machine-gun fire as he led his platoon at Zig Zag Pass on Bataan. "War inevitably takes the best of our nation's youth and it is a source of grief to me that so many American families are saddened by the loss of their loved ones," General Krueger wrote in a personal letter to Clark's grieving father. "He must indeed have been a 'good soldier' as all who knew him respected and admired him greatly." Nor were the senior ranks immune to the grim reaper's scythe. Major General Edwin Patrick—once Krueger's chief of staff, onetime victor at Lone Tree Hill in New Guinea, and now commander of the 6th Division—was mortally wounded by Japanese machine-gun fire during a visit to the front. "This was a great shock to the whole division," Captain Charles Hanks, an artilleryman, later wrote. Colonel Bruce Palmer, Patrick's chief of staff, commented that the troops "knew he was a fighting soldier and they were pretty upset about it." In a consolation letter to Patrick's widow, Krueger assured her that "his passing leaves a gap in our ranks that cannot be filled. I wish that I could extend my heartfelt sympathy to you in person, but since this is not possible, at least I can tell you how much I am thinking of you."

A legion of some 10,000 medical personnel provided cutting-edge care for the many thousands of combat wounded and, with most of the battles raging in remote areas, dealt with the familiar problem of evacuation. A long chain of treatment centers stretched along the Sixth Army front, from the combat medics to portable surgical hospitals, forward aid stations, and collecting and clearing companies near the front to field hospitals and general hospitals well behind the lines. "Evacuation from the front to the aid station was rendered difficult because of the rugged terrain," Major Louis Sass, the surgeon for the 127th Infantry Regiment, 32nd Division, wrote in a post-battle report. "The ridges were steep and devoid of vegetation, making litter parties excellent targets for the enemy-occupied surrounding hills." In many units, medics adjusted by moving closer to the action. Fortified with plasma and other medical supplies, surgeons, litter teams, and technicians stationed themselves a few hundred yards behind advancing troops, ready to help at a moment's notice. Sixth Army went into Luzon with 25,000 pints of whole blood, a number that remained steady throughout the spring and summer as soldiers donated blood. To save vital time that might mean the difference between life and death, surgical teams at forward aid stations set up special teams equipped with whole blood, ready to administer to patients within a matter of seconds. "It was organized with definite duties assigned to each man, assuring a continuous rapid flow of blood to the patient," Major John Olwin, a physician, reported to the Sixth Army surgeon. In one instance, a litter team brought in a grievously wounded, unconscious infantry sergeant with no pulse and only shallow breathing. Machine-gun bullets had shattered his right leg, the remnants of which, according to hospital records, "lay in a pool of fluid feces and clotted blood." In less than thirty seconds, the whole blood team began giving him a lifesaving transfusion. "In five minutes his pulse and color had returned, his breathing was considerably improved and one hour after admission, he was talking to us intelligently." He received a total of 17 pints of blood, enough to save his life, though the surgeons had to amputate the leg.

Buoyed by the Leyte experience, the efficiency of medical evacuations by air and ground improved. A combination of L-5 liaison planes, C-47s, ambulances, jeeps, litter teams, and even a few helicopters steadily moved casualties to safety. The average journey for a wounded soldier from the front line to a fixed medical facility was three and one-third miles. Some 17,000 patients were evacuated from Luzon's mountains and hills by air. Air and ground vehicles made 160,000 lifesaving trips over the course of the campaign. Once treated, many of the patients were sent either to Leyte, other Pacific bases, or home to the United States for more treatment. Sixty-eight percent left Luzon by air, the rest by sea. During the three-month period of heaviest fighting, an average of 269 patients left the island by air in any given twenty-four-hour period. The official Sixth Army battle casualty statistics encompassed only soldiers who were hit by some sort of enemy fire. As one physician in the 33rd Division wrote, this basically meant "bullet wounds, shrapnel wounds, usually from 'knee' mortars and artillery shells, grenade fragment wounds, and white phosphorous burns from grenade, mortar and artillery shells."

The Sixth Army measuring system did not include casualties from disease, accidents, and combat fatigue, a disingenuous approach that ignored huge numbers of battle-related casualties as well as the direct causal link between combat and all these maladies. In a six-month period, Krueger's army lost 93,400 men to supposed "nonbattle" casualties, a whopping total that, in combination with the men lost directly to enemy fire, actually exceeded American losses incurred during the Normandy campaign. On Luzon, diseases savaged the ranks. In the course of the fighting, nearly 87,000 men—enough manpower for two full corps-size formations—needed hospitalization for some kind of battle-related sickness. Skin infections and yellow jaundice were common. Earlier in the war, during the New Guinea campaign, malaria in SWPA had become so rampant as to incapacitate four of MacArthur's soldiers for every one he lost to the Japanese. Ruthless efforts to eradicate the mosquito population and strong standing orders to take the malaria-suppressing drug atabrine led thereafter to a steep decline in hospitalizations, as did the progression of the fighting to more hospitable islands. The lull led to complacency by the time the Americans invaded the Philippines.

Exhaustion also played a part. Combat units in action for weeks at a time had little inclination to observe strict atabrine discipline. Indeed, with death and maiming staring many soldiers in the face each day, the prospect of contracting a survivable disease to get off the line grew increasingly tempting. "It is not unlikely that a good many troops deliberately evaded the taking of atabrine in the hope that an attack of malaria would take them to the comparative luxury of a hospital," the Sixth Army surgeon acknowledged. The data more than backed up this assertion. One-third of malaria evacuees admitted to Army medics that they intentionally stopped taking atabrine as a means of escaping combat, if only temporarily—one suspects the actual percentage was probably higher, because many soldiers were understandably reluctant to make such a confession to any authority figure. Some 2,000 men were hospitalized for dengue fever. "You get very, very weak and it's a matter of not having any appetite," Private V. G. Rowley, a member of the 112th Cavalry Regiment, later told an interviewer. "When you are in combat with that sort of experience, it's very scary." Another 10,000 soldiers went down with infectious hepatitis. During a three-month period, operating mainly in support of the 25th Infantry Division, the 36th Evacuation Hospital recorded 5,787 admissions, of which only 1,671 had actually been hit by enemy fire; 458 were admitted for malaria and 393 for infectious hepatitis. During the three months of fighting in northern Luzon, the 127th Infantry Regiment, 32nd Division, lost 153 men to hepatitis, 169 to gastroenteritis (dysentery), and 233 to fevers of unknown origin, most of which were probably caused by malaria, dengue, or some other tropical disease. During February alone, the 3rd Field Hospital in support of the 38th Infantry Division on Bataan recorded a stunning 1,452 admissions due to disease, compared with 839 battle casualties.

Another battle-related malady, combat fatigue, sapped the vitality of the fighting formations, and yet commanders inexplicably did not tabulate these losses among their battle casualties. The Army's medical historian estimated that "psychological causes accounted for about 20 percent of the total casualties among combat divisions of the Sixth Army." A steady stream of crying, shaking, haunted, debilitated men was evacuated from the front. Lieutenant Floyd Gilbert of the 33rd Division saw one of them helped to the rear by a pair of medics who physically held him up. "His head and neck were wobbling on his right shoulder, his eyes rolling out of their sockets, his battle fatigues streaked with blood—a disheveled zombie. A perfect example of battle fatigue." After one heavy stretch of action, PFC Leon Clement, a 37th Division rifleman, reported in a letter to his mother the sad sight of incapacitated buddies. "We had about 10 fellows go out of their heads from battle shock. It's a terrible sight seeing them hysterical, yet, you get used to seeing that stuff over here." A deeply troubled soldier in PFC Robert LaChausee's company unconsciously assumed a chaplain's role and incessantly went from foxhole to foxhole blessing everyone until medics gently led him to the rear. On another occasion, a soldier from his unit drifted away from a carrying party "and shot himself in the hand. He was right handed and had been an artist." Between January and July, an astonishing 23,631 patients were admitted to SWPA hospitals with psychiatric or neurological problems. One typical station hospital treated 80 combat fatigue cases per month. Neuropsychiatrists were so scarce that physicians with other specialties treated these men as best they could with sedation, rest, fresh food, and occasional therapeutic discussions. "It was striking that these men showed marked resentment reactions [to] . . . prolonged continuous intensive combat," one consultant reported to the theater surgeon. The average hospital stay spanned from seven to ten days. Between half and three-quarters of the patients were then sent back to their units. The rest were evacuated for more specialized treatment elsewhere in the Pacific or back home.[7]

Sixth Army's many tribulations paled in comparison with the steady deterioration of General Yamashita's Fourteenth Area Army. By late spring and summer, his remaining soldiers were experiencing a living nightmare. Harassed constantly by air strikes, artillery, and relentless American attacks all over Luzon, every day represented a defiant struggle to resist and perhaps survive long enough to do it again the next day. "Cold, hunger, exhaustion, lack of sleep, incessant enemy shell fire, and when the weather became fair, the bombing by enemy planes," wrote one officer, "all this is a rough sketch of life on the front lines." Roads, hillsides, and valleys were increasingly littered with the shattered husks of vehicles, equipment, and men. "Every hundred yards or so Jap trucks and civilian automobiles are strewn along the sides of the road," PFC Burger of the 6th Division told his father. "Some are already stripped of their tires and other valuable parts. Most of them had been bombed and strafed to pieces, the rest were probably abandoned for lack of gas. Not dozens, but hundreds of them all along the road for miles; and the Jap dead are the same way. Nothing left but the stink, a few ribs and a pelvic bone held together with rags that were once uniforms. You'd kick some of their ridiculous little tin helmets out of the way, and sometimes the head would still be in it."

Dysentery, beriberi, malaria, and a host of other diseases had by now debilitated innumerable Japanese soldiers, many of whom did not have access to proper medical care, nor the option of leaving the front lines. By Yamashita's estimate, disease was now killing more of his soldiers than US firepower. Scattered deep into the mountains and hills of northern and eastern Luzon, all too many of his units had no reliable line of supply. A wave of desperate hunger prevailed. Eerily reminiscent of Fil-American formations during the 1942 Philippines campaign, entire Japanese battalions spent most of their time looking for food rather than focusing on fighting. "My suffering surpasses even that of death," one man bemoaned to his diary. "I have just one ball of rice to eat. I'm hungry! I want to eat rice, fish, and vegetables. I want to eat everything. My bowels are growling. The friends, who promised to die together, have died, but I am still wandering around the fighting zone." He eventually resorted to eating grass. Others caught and consumed the very same rats that the Americans saw as a disgusting nuisance. "For those who had to use body and soul in furious combat the food shortage was a critical matter," Lieutenant General Muto, the Fourteenth Area Army chief of staff, later wrote. "Front line fighting strength decreased before our eyes." Officers and NCOs sometimes had to break up death struggles between soldiers over morsels. One lieutenant halted a knife fight between two men over "a little frog about the size of your thumb." In mid-April, Sergeant Teruo Furunishi documented in his diary a scrounged meal: "Satisfied my appetite by eating a dinner of dog meat. Potatoes are my daily food. Rice is available only once a week." Two months later he found himself nearly dead from starvation and trapped behind American lines. "I can easily watch the movement of my honorable enemy, but I must not reveal myself," he wrote in a final entry. "We are planning to make a suicide charge against the enemy tents."

Officers enforced strict rationing as best they could. "The precious-
ness, the importance of each grain of rice," wrote Lieutenant Obara Fukuzo in his diary, "until now this vital concern had been something I
had been lectured on and in turn had lectured my men countless times.
Now here in this mountain fastness I am for the first time made em-
phatically to see that these words have meaning in terms of our own
survival." Sergeant Hara Yutaka and his men plundered grains of red
rice from the body of a dead soldier whom they did not know. "His face
was already decomposed, and from his mouth and nose maggots tumbled to the ground." Paying no attention to the maggots, they cooked the
red rice in their mess tins and wolfed it down. Perhaps inevitably, given
the wanton cruelty of Japanese military forces in the Philippines, Yamashita's forlorn troops generally had no qualms about plundering food
and other valuables from the local population. On Bataan, men from the
Imperial Army's 39th Infantry Regiment raided local rice fields with
impunity. "It was terrible for the Filipino farmers, but there was no other
way for the men . . . to survive," one of them later wrote. In the course
of the looting, some units also murdered as many Filipinos as they
could. "For security reasons all inhabitants of the town were killed and
all their possessions were confiscated," one Imperial Army soldier wrote
with chilling insouciance in a diary entry. "Until yesterday we lived in
the hills or in fishing barrios and we had only salt to go with our rice.
But today we are in Paradise. There is nothing we cannot obtain. Although there were tremendous number of watches, rings, suits, shoes
and dresses, we couldn't take them back with us, and so we had to burn
them with great regret. Everyone has 3,000 or more pesos in cash. We
had all we wanted of good things to eat." A few days later he added, "because 90% of the Filipino people . . . are anti-Japanese, Army HQ issued
orders . . . to punish them. In various sectors we have killed several
thousands (including young and old, men and women). Their houses
have been burned and valuables have been confiscated." Far too few had
the humane attitude of a Lieutenant Hasegawa, who mournfully told his
diary, "Burning the town of peace loving people, I feel sorry for them. I
am sure they are resenting the Japanese Army. To the civilians we have
been of more trouble to them than the guerrillas. For this reason, the
drifting of the civilians to the enemy side is unavoidable."

Wounded men could expect to receive little medicine nor much treatment beyond the basics. "Some had arms or legs cut off, some had their innards sticking out of their bodies, some had their lower jaws shattered by gunfire," Private Nishihara Takamaro recalled. "Countless wounded men writhed, getting no treatment. When a person dies, his internal organs start to decompose first. As they breathe, flies gather, attracted by the rotten stench exhaled. Maggots hatch on the nose and mouth of soldiers still alive. When the maggots begin to crawl in the eyes, the men die. Spending every day among dead bodies makes one doubt whether one can know where the dividing line is between life and death." Terrified of abandonment, many of the wounded begged their comrades to kill them. In one typically surreal incident, a dying soldier pointed to his buttocks and told a buddy, "If I die, go ahead and eat this part." The buddy demurred but later admitted, "I couldn't take my eyes off the flesh on his rear." Retreating commanders occasionally ordered their soldiers to kill abandoned wounded men lest the Americans capture them and find out vital information. One soldier found himself in the position of leading his best friend to believe that he had come back to rescue him. Instead, in the darkness of night, he stabbed him to death. "No matter how many years had passed since the War's end, he was unable to rid himself of the heavy burden on his heart," another soldier sadly commented years later.

The battlefields seemed coated with the rotting or newly skeletonized remains of the Japanese dead. "At nighttime it seemed as if their spirits were crying out," a messenger attached to Fourteenth Area Army headquarters remarked eerily. "Every river had swollen corpses floating on the surface." The dead were so numerous as to defeat any efforts by headquarters to document their fate or dispose of their remains. In northern Luzon, General Yamashita held his forces together as best he could and continued the struggle against this incredible array of adversity. Diminished by hunger himself, he and Lieutenant General Muto, his chief of staff, spent hours counting insects they found hiding beneath rocks. Yamashita refused to bathe, not just out of solidarity with his filthy troops but also, in Muto's estimation, "because if he had placed his huge body in the tub, the water would have overflowed leaving not enough for others." One of Yamashita's soldiers summarized the

Japanese plight in an anguished diary entry: "The enemy has taken every advantage of the latest weapons, while we depend on the old Japanese spirit. I wonder who will win the war in the end? We are out of food, airplanes, and guns. It is a battle in which the enemy can do whatever they please."[8]

The Americans could not quite do whatever they pleased, but they could do a lot. MacArthur's forces could not possibly have sustained operations, especially in such remote areas, without an impressive foundation of logistical brawn. From the Lingayen beaches to a host of smaller harbor enclaves, the Americans landed enormous amounts of cargo that progressed to the fighting fronts via truck, jeep, railroad, aircraft, and carrying parties. The quartermasters juggled an almost overwhelming array of responsibilities that included, according to Lieutenant Colonel Charles Ritchie, a base quartermaster, "maintenance of proper stock levels within bases . . . proper methods of receipt, storage and issue of Quartermaster supplies; proper inventory and stock control methods . . . Graves Registration service; Baggage Agencies; bakeries; laundries; cold storage plants; ice plants; ice cream plants; operation of overland refrigerated vans; sales stores and sales commissaries; operation of salvage and reclamation activities; operation of Petroleum drum cleaning and drum filling plants." Typical of many, the little port of Batangas matured from a small railroad terminal into a fully developed harbor equipped with a modern concrete pier and five Liberty ship piers that could accommodate fifty-three cargo vessels at a time. Subic Bay was soon home to a modern wharf and a 600-foot-long fuel jetty.

At the height of the Leyte campaign, SWPA had received nearly 750,000 measurement tons of matériel per month. By June 1945, the number had swollen to 1,000,000 tons per month, a mandatory amount to support the needs of a military force whose size had grown to 858,698 soldiers, plus tens of thousands of Filipino guerrillas. To store and process the largesse, engineers built 2.6 million square feet of covered warehouse storage, leased another 1 million square feet, and constructed over 30.6 million square feet of outdoor storage. Some 180,000 gallons of fuel flowed each day through the two Lingayen pipelines, enough not only to feed the dizzying array of vehicles and aircraft but also for the average airfield to store 10,000 barrels in reserve. Mobile bakeries produced a steady supply of bread and other food that augmented prepackaged rations. "They knew what it was to set up in areas that were ankle-deep in mud," one quartermaster wrote. "It was generally possible to pick out a warehouse or a market center, and, in one instance, a cockfight arena, for the bakery installations. Wells or established water systems were already going, which made quick set-ups possible."

To move the prodigious tonnage of supplies, the Army employed every possible transportation node, including railroads. Engineers and railway operating battalions repaired track and rolling stock for immediate usage. During a five-month period, they moved 163,550 passengers and 471,126 tons of cargo to railroad depots all over Luzon. Throughout much of the campaign, nine quartermaster truck companies, five of which were African American, accounted for the bulk of the Army's supply movement via the roads. A fleet of 454 two-and-a-half-ton trucks—a Pacific theater equivalent to the more famous Red Ball Express in Europe—operated in twelve-hour shifts, hauling 320,023 tons over a distance of nearly nine million passenger miles. The traffic put inevitable stress on the road net. Engineers, in addition to their normal duties building bases, clearing mines, and fixing bridges, spent untold man hours maintaining the roads. In support of I Corps alone, the engineers repaired or maintained 576 miles of road. Records of the 65th Engineer Combat Battalion, representative of many others, revealed that the unit spent almost 44 percent of its time on road maintenance and construction, a far greater percentage than any other activity. In support of the 25th Division's drive in northern Luzon, the 339th Engineer Combat Battalion maintained a treacherous stretch of road through the Cagayan Valley. "We worked that road 24 hrs. a day for nearly two months and we worked under constant armed guard provided by ourselves, of course," the unit history chronicled. "When bridges were swept away, we built them over again. When the usual torrential rains caused heavy landslides blocking the road, our bulldozers knifed and plowed through the great debris of rock and mud, and when actions of the road itself would wash out, we built huge cribs into the deep banks."

The Americans especially capitalized on one of their greatest advantages, airpower. Airdrops sustained more than a few combat units as they operated in remote, almost inaccessible areas. From January to June, planes dropped an astounding five million pounds of supplies, 87 percent of which were successfully recovered by friendly troops. In the end, though, as was true at Leyte, forward-deployed units ultimately depended upon enervated carrying parties of Filipino civilian employees, guerrillas, and American soldiers to deliver most of their supplies. "Every bite of food the men eat, the clothes they wear, and the ammunition they expend, has to be carried on the backs of carriers up hills which the average person couldn't climb empty-handed," Lieutenant Colonel Lawrence Swope, one of Krueger's quartermasters, sagely commented. By his estimate, one carrier could support only three soldiers.

The impressive wealth of matériel pouring into the theater hardly guaranteed against shortages, especially during intense fighting. At one point, the Army was expending 12,400 rounds of 105-millimeter ammunition per day, an amount that could not be sustained by available shipping and infrastructure. "Operations were always on a shoestring," wrote Colonel Herbert Vogel, a logistical base commander. "It was impossible to bring up great stocks." Occasionally, Krueger had to enforce strict rationing of artillery and mortar shells. At one point, he even restricted artillerymen to just under 10 percent of their daily needs. His preoccupation with conserving ammunition manifested itself during visits to frontline units. When he heard artillerymen firing repeatedly one day in support of an infantry regiment, he pointedly asked the regimental commander what they were shooting at and followed up the question with a monologue about the logistical situation. "He gave me a lesson in resource conservation," Lieutenant Colonel Arthur Collins, the commander, later wrote. "He told me how many artillery tubes there were in the Sixth Army; how many rounds would be fired if all the artillery pieces fired at once, five times, or ten times a day; how much tonnage each rate of fire added up to; and how many ships would have to ply the Pacific to get that amount of ammunition to all the different places where Sixth Army troops were fighting."[9]

At the heart of the growing American presence in the Philippines lay Manila, deeply scarred from the terrible combat. "The dreadful cost of liberation had been paid," Lieutenant Rogers, MacArthur's longtime stenographer, wrote despondently. "Much of the city was destroyed or heavily damaged. The public transportation system had gone. Water and sewage systems required extensive repair. There was no electric power." Homes were destroyed or badly damaged. Abraham Hartendorp, the former Santo Tomas internee, sadly described the city as "for the greater part a shack-town, a sprawling, giant slum." Colonel Maurice Pincoffs, a preventive medicine specialist charged by the Army's ranking surgeon in the Pacific with stemming the spread of disease and starvation in Manila, described the place, in a letter to a friend, as "dust, ruins, garbage, smells, swarming humanity—and flies, flies, *flies*. There is one obvious advantage: whatever I accomplish can only be an improvement."

Nowhere was this more true than in the harbor area, where the Japanese had systematically demolished one of the world's premier ports. The waters were cluttered with 500 sunken barges and ships, some of which were actually layered or tied on top of one another. Sunken freighters and mines blocked any entry to the harbor. Piers and wharves were blown to pieces. Japanese demolition teams tore the adjacent waterfront area to shreds, pocked with bomb craters and heaped with mounds of jagged rubble. "Oil tanks and water reservoirs were destroyed," the Army's transportation historian vividly wrote, "the main pipe of the municipal water system was cut in several places, and city power facilities were methodically dismantled." Lieutenant Colonel Ritchie, the quartermaster who found himself trying to run a major logistical base among the ruins, later wrote plaintively, "I was faced with many problems. No covered storage was available. No lights were available. No dunnage was available. No materials handling equipment was available. It was necessary to handle all supplies by hand, in open storage, on improvised dunnage, and by light of flares made of burlap wicks in empty beer cans."

The Japanese engineers had done an incredibly thorough job, inflicting more destruction upon Manila's harbor than did the Germans on any European port. MacArthur's naval salvage expert, Commodore William Sullivan, had overseen the successful reclamation of many ports, including Naples and Cherbourg, the latter of which the Germans had completely ruined in June 1944. Sullivan took one look at the Manila mess and declared his mission to rehabilitate the harbor as "the greatest salvage task in history." Starting in early March, his teams of engineers, divers, port companies, and construction crews set to work with a vengeance. Mines were cleared or blown in place, as were sunken ships. Waters were surveyed, dredged, and buoyed. Mountains of rubble were cleared; piers, wharves, warehouses, storage tanks, streets, and cranes were repaired or razed and rebuilt. Hired Filipino laborers, many of whom were still malnourished and, with no access to working public transportation, forced to walk miles to work, contributed immeasurably to the steady rehabilitation. In one radio address, William Dunn, the CBS correspondent, succinctly described this flurry of activity: "The determined growl of bulldozers, forever pushing the ruins aside to make room for more and more military areas, is always in evidence."

Reflecting the Army's growing genius for improvisation, cargo vessels and troopships found ways to sidestep the obstacles and begin unloading badly needed food and clothing—much of it for the impoverished local population—onto improvised piers with the help of 535 pieces of lighterage equipment. A thirty-ton crane soon began operating, as did a fleet of barges, tugs, and landing craft shuttling matériel from ships to shore. Among the valuable cargo was a shipment of cutting-edge water purification units that provided the city with two million gallons of water per day until, bit by bit, engineers repaired pipes and mains to restore water service. Generators produced varying amounts of electricity per day while the power grid was slowly but steadily restored. According to one official Army report, the various service commands charged with cleaning up Manila utilized detailed overlay maps "showing current conditions of highways, power lines and power installations, storage and warehouse areas, and water distribution for Manila and its environs."

By summertime, the resuscitated harbor counted 35 mobile cranes, 11 tractor cranes, 17 turnabout cranes, and 484 forklifts among its growing complement of equipment, all of which improved efficiency and capacity. On a typical evening, one observer counted 756 separate ship lights in the bay. The amount of cargo unloaded and processed in the harbor shot up from 143,186 tons in March to nearly 400,000 tons in

July, more than twice the amount that entered the island each month via the Lingayen landing beaches. In that short span, Manila, now dubbed Base X by the quartermasters, had already become the largest Allied logistical base in theater. Untold thousands of tons of the newly arrived matériel went to feed, clothe, and care for the local population, on the assumption that each person required at least 2,000 calories per day and one yard of cloth per person over a three-month period. Colonel Pincoff's command organized the city into eight districts and dispensed, through specially trained Philippine Civil Affairs Units, food, medical care, and other necessities. An admiring Dr. Karl Compton, an MIT physicist attached to MacArthur's headquarters as a scientific adviser, expressed surprise at "the cheerfulness of the people, and their general cleanliness despite the large portion living in little shanties built out of the corrugated iron roofing left in the ruins of the hundreds of acres of burned houses."

The remarkable efforts of Colonel Pincoff's team, and the general American attention to the welfare of civilians, undoubtedly prevented widespread disease in an otherwise problematic environment. All too commonly, the locals pilfered from the American cornucopia or bought items from corrupt soldiers, who made handsome profits selling supplies on the growing local black market, which Krueger later described as assuming "serious proportions as the campaign progressed. Military property, principally food and clothing, but also medicines, was illicitly acquired by Filipinos by gift, barter or theft." Military police attempted to guard cargoes and storage facilities, but they had neither the manpower nor the resources to solve the problem. "The Operations Section of the Provost Marshal's Office encountered a high incidence of pilfering and . . . uncovered large black market operations," declared one official Army report. Attempts to embed a military police officer with the port command "to check each ship arriving in the harbor for pilferable goods, and to make arrangements for the protection of such goods" failed miserably. Sixth Army's provost marshal reclaimed 291,000 dollars' worth of property in May and June, a pittance compared to the losses. A criminal undercurrent coursed from the docks outward. "The fearsome Japs are gone," asserted an editorial in the *Manila Post,* "but the hoodlums and hold-up gangs infest the streets, waylaying peaceful, law-abiding citizens." Petty thievery became an ordinary part of everyday life. "The 'little brown people' were clever at appropriating what they wanted," one American officer wrote with a characteristic mixture of annoyance and patronizing racism. "Even on the street, one might suddenly be jostled and then find a pen or cigarettes missing from a shirt pocket. Even under lock and key possessions were not safe. Very few thieves were caught."[10]

Though not by any means fully recuperated, Manila became home to SWPA's vast headquarters complex and a lodestone for copious numbers of pleasure-seeking soldiers. Thousands of SWPA staffers set up operations at Far Eastern University, or inside relatively undamaged office buildings, warehouses, or homes in northern Manila, where the fighting had been lightest. In some cases, they even pitched their own tents. The rot of mass death still hung over much of the city. "There was an overpowering stench of death and decay," Lieutenant Rogers later wrote. "It pervaded the air, and there was no escape." Weeks of cleanup efforts by US engineers and their Filipino partners, plus the infusion of the new life inherent in the arrival of so many young soldiers and the return of thousands of locals to reclaim their homes, slowly squelched death's odor. "Manila is a modern city which would fit in the States," one SWPA ordnance officer wrote optimistically to a friend of the city's rebirth. "Wide blvds along which race traffic. The supply depots are scattered and the trucks are numerous. Women everywhere, many of them rather beautiful. Some [buildings] are being used despite the gaps and holes in their sides or roofs." At first they experienced water and power shortages, similar to the local population. For a short time, parts of Willoughby's intelligence section had access to only twenty minutes of water per day and no usable toilet facilities in their offices. "Trucks were run on a schedule to the living quarters where there were latrines," Lieutenant Colonel N. B. Sauve wrote. "At the worst of the shortage, naturally, everybody got the 'trots,'" leading to the unforgettable image of "hard benches, rough roads, thoughtful, preoccupied expressions." Sponge baths gradually gave way to full-blown showers and daily access to electrical power for most of the Americans. Mess halls served fresh food, even occasional steaks. "The meals here have been exceptionally good and we have enjoyed fresh eggs several times," one sergeant wrote home. "Vegetable salad sure added interest to our meals and big smiles to the faces of most of us. I never appreciated fresh fruit, vegetables & meat before. Life is beginning to take on new interest."

For some, service in Manila became an attractive billet with access to luxuries unimaginable to the sweating dogfaces on the increasingly remote front lines. "If we keep living in this luxury I'll not be wanting to go home," Corporal Robert Landers wrote in wonderment to friends. "We have everything a soldier in the States has at a regular camp. We have swimming pools, volleyball courts, boxing, movies, symphonies, stage show theater tickets, boat rides . . . ice cream, cokes, every day. We have electric lights, music and radio programs relayed over loudspeakers." Some of Manila's best musicians and singers played three concerts per week under the title "Interlude of Fine Music." Two other local groups, Cesar Velasco and His Society Band, and Pete Aristorenas and His Symphony, played a total of forty-seven concerts. Former Los Baños and Bilibid internees with theater backgrounds teamed with local professionals to stage a production of Irving Berlin's *This Is the Army*.[11]

Unavoidably, most everyone in Sixth Army wanted in on this kind of action and more. With or without authorization, soldiers descended on the city in droves, mostly looking for the welcome release offered by women and booze after weeks or months in the jungle and, quite often, years away from home. As a testament to the long American presence in the archipelago, most Manileños were either fluent or at least minimally conversant in English, a communication flow that greatly aided business transactions. Before long a small army of adolescent boys began accosting soldiers with an endless drone of propositions, almost all of which centered around prostitution. "Want pom pom? Want fun? I take you my big sister, she clean." The brazen sales pitches by family members bespoke the poverty and hardship prevalent among all too many of the Filipinos—few of whom would have resorted to prostitution under more stable circumstances—and the imperial holdover of economic inequity in their relationship with the Americans.

Similar to other places around the world, the relative wealth and power of the GIs made almost anything accessible for those who were willing to pay. "The streets teem with people, little shops have sprouted everywhere on the rubble . . . and the people are busy buying and selling," Sergeant Joseph Steinbacher, a hard-fighting veteran of the 169th Infantry Regiment, 43rd Division, noted in his journal after earning a liberty visit to the city. "Children are present everywhere, the little girls in their mother hubbard style dresses, the little boys with a shirt on top and nothing below. Young pimps, many not over ten years old, are everywhere hawking their sisters's [sic] charms. Every American soldier is a Joe to the little rascals eagerly hunting for customers. Cathouses . . . in some places are every other building on the street. Most are mom and pop operations, the mother coaches the daughter while the old man sits out front collecting from the eager American soldiers."

Animated negotiations in overweening English buzzed on seemingly every street corner. Sellers tried to collect more from tall men on the theory that the larger the man, the larger the penis and, by logic, the more taxing the encounter promised to be for the woman. Regardless of size, most GIs eventually settled on a price of about six pesos, the equivalent of no more than three dollars. The women ranged in age and experience. "Some are real young, not over fifteen years old, and these places are real busy," Sergeant Steinbacher told his journal. "Others of the hookers look quite jaded, probably from being overworked by the oversexed Japanese. The Americans appear just as oversexed and all the houses do a good business. The older married soldiers are the most sexually active and some just about live in a cathouse. So much for love, faith, and fidelity to the ones back home." Fidelity was nowhere to be found in Tech 4 Melvin Benham's unit when the men pooled their money for sex. "The fellas were getting hard up for some love, so an old Philippine woman about 50 satisfied the wants of 20+ GIs," he wrote bluntly, years later. "The officers were last in line—ahem!"

Not surprisingly, the partying had some consequences. According to one official SWPA analysis, 11 Americans died and 3 were blinded from consuming poisoned alcoholic drinks. Venereal disease rates skyrocketed to levels not seen since almost two years earlier when large numbers of American soldiers had convened in Australia. Some 10 percent of Sixth Army soldiers contracted some form of sexually transmitted disease in 1945. The closer to Manila, the higher the infection rates. By April, Base X reported 268 cases per 1,000 men. A few small units even recorded truly mind-blowing rates of 2,000 to 4,000 cases per 1,000 soldiers. MacArthur's headquarters had vainly attempted to forestall this problem by establishing eight prophylactic stations around the city, one of which even used penicillin. "This treatment was to consist of urination, washing with soap and water, urethral injection of four cc penicillin solution and application of four gms. [grams] penicillin ointment," declared one medical report. More commonly, the station attendants handed out tubes of medicinal jelly to soldiers with orders to smear it on their genitals. The stations administered 23,013 preventive treatments in a one-month period, but could not stem the tidal wave of cases. "The very high venereal disease rate in the Philippines could be partially explained by sexual promiscuity, partially by the fact that troops in New Guinea had not been 'pounded' with v.d. prevention thus the importance of precautionary measures were not fresh in their minds, and partially by the fact that the troops have gained the impression that penicillin 'answers all problems,'" wrote Colonel Floyd Wergeland in a 1945 medical survey of the theater.

The other issue was the paucity of medical treatment for prostitutes and other local women who had liaisons with the troops. As a result, far too many GIs came down with telltale symptoms of a "red swollen penis with pus running out the end," in the recollection of one soldier. A quarterly report of the 36th Evacuation Hospital actually found that 12 percent of their cases did not even respond to penicillin. So great was the problem that SWPA had to dedicate the entire services of one major medical unit, the 93rd Field Hospital, to the exclusive treatment of venereal disease patients. At any given time, thousands of men were hospitalized or forced to curtail their duties in some fashion.

The expansion of education programs and prophylactic stations still did not completely squelch the problem in Manila. By one estimate, three-quarters of Manila prostitutes were infected with one or more strains of venereal disease. Two visiting doctors from the Surgeon General's Office—Earl Moore, a civilian, and Lieutenant Colonel Thomas Sternberg—as well as Colonel Pincoff and Lieutenant Colonel Roger Egeberg, MacArthur's personal physician, eventually grew so concerned that they urged him to make the city off-limits to any troops who were not on duty. MacArthur would not hear of it. "Doc, do you know what you're asking me to do?" he replied to Egeberg, who made the request

on behalf of the other doctors. "You're asking me to tell the soldiers—
grown men—who have fought their way through the jungles of New
Guinea and the mud of Leyte . . . to stay out of the first city they have
seen where they can have any fun, where they can go and perhaps have
a drink or two, maybe dance a bit, buy some trinkets, see civilian life?
Besides that, you're asking me to cut off one of the main sources of
money for the people of Manila, selling things, having restaurants, giving our men relaxation when they're off duty. No, Doc, that's an insult
to the soldiers and hard on the disrupted economy of this war-torn city.
I shall not declare Manila out of bounds to our soldiers." Chastened but
sympathetic to the reasoning behind MacArthur's decision, Egeberg
and the other doctors focused on containing the problem. "The venereal
disease rate continued to climb, but not much more," he wrote. "With
the normal efforts on the parts of . . . doctors . . . and the line officers
conscious of the rate, it was gradually brought down to a more acceptable level."[12]

An infusion of female soldiers, most belonging to the Women's
Army Corps (WAC), hinted at the beginnings of an embryonic gender
diversity and maturity in MacArthur's armies. It also spoke volumes
about the increasingly secure American presence in the Philippines, because almost no one in 1940s America favored the notion of having
women face any sort of danger from enemy action. Female nurses had,
of course, served under MacArthur's command since the beginning of
the war, most notably those who were captured on Corregidor and survived internment in Santo Tomas, earning nearly universal esteem and
a hero's welcome when they were sent home in February 1945. "The admiration and deep respect . . . could not be adequately expressed in
words," Lieutenant Margaret Carlson, an Army nurse, wrote to a friend
of conversations she had with former Santo Tomas internees whom
these caregivers had helped during their long months together in captivity, "but their eyes told more than their lips ever could when they
spoke of the high morale of these girls."

A cadre of nurses had comprised a tiny female minority in New
Guinea. Most were guarded day and night, ostensibly to protect them
from Japanese patrols but, more likely, to shield them from the amorous
encroachments of lonely GIs, some of whom were so starved for

feminine companionship that they took to writing racy proposition letters to women whom they had never even met. "Now don't think that
I'm jiving you because I say that I love you," Private Al Carleton wrote
in one typical letter to Ms. Jessie White. "I dreamt last night that me and
you were together and you were in my arms making love to each other.
Oh! How I hated to wake up and find it was a dream. As you know
dreams sometimes come true. I am hoping this one will. Maybe we can
get something out of life."

From New Guinea to the Philippines, as the SWPA medical complement grew, the number of female nurses under MacArthur's command
rose even as the Army began to face a significant shortage due to the
rising number of casualties from the various fighting fronts around the
globe. As of mid-1944, the Army had a shortfall of 10,000 nurses from
its targeted mobilization of 50,000, prompting the government to briefly,
and absurdly, contemplate drafting nurses from civilian life at the very
same time its segregation policies made it difficult for African American
nurses to volunteer. To date, the Army had accepted only 330 African
American nurses for service, mainly with segregated units. In March
1945, a consortium of women's groups, unions, and nurses' advocacy
organizations urged the Roosevelt administration to end this hypocrisy.
"As sweethearts, wives and relatives of our brave fighting men, we know
that an important group of qualified trained nurses have been seriously
neglected, and that their abilities are denied our wounded, because a
policy of discouragement, discrimination and segregation is yet practiced by the Army and Navy." In a similar statement, the National Nursing Council for War Service and the National Association of Colored
Graduate Nurses lobbied, "Acceptance of more Negro nurses by the
Army and Navy is urged as an immediate step toward meeting current
shortages." The two organizations estimated that at least 2,000 nurses
were available, properly trained, and willing to serve. Their efforts came
to nothing. As of summer 1945, the number of Black nurses in the Army
had risen to only 479.

Though largely shielded from danger, and seldom viewed as equals
by their male colleagues, the SWPA nurses dealt with heat, privation,
and the trauma of working long hours to care for the sick and wounded.
"These boys don't complain and wouldn't dream of asking for relief

from pain," an admiring Lieutenant Carlson wrote of her patients. "There is little they can write in their letters to their folks, but they don't forget. My roommates and I spend hours looking at family snapshots with them and fastening up their 'pin-up girls' which are usually children that they've never seen." The nurses' status as officers and medical professionals afforded them some level of authority over enlisted male orderlies and, more often than not, deferential respect from the wounded or sick soldiers whose lives they helped to save. "They were there because of their devotion to American men," one soldier later declared; "of course we were prepared to fight for them."

The same was true of the WAC soldiers, the first of whom had arrived in Australia the previous May, dressed in Class A winter uniforms and helmets with full field packs. "Gee, they're real American girls," an awestruck GI had remarked at the time. Activated in the summer of 1943 for the purpose of recruiting women to perform administrative and other support duties to free up men for combat, the Women's Army Corps reflected the Army it served, with an officer and an NCO corps, and an enlisted force. Their training included military courtesy, close-order drill, physical fitness, and orientation for military occupational specialties. In a telling sign of the times, WAC officers and NCOs had no authority over men, nor did the female soldiers receive any weapons or combat training (the same was largely true for nurses). The corps sent its soldiers all over the globe, including even New Guinea by the middle of 1944, where the inappropriate Class As had given way to cotton trousers and shirts far better suited to the tropics, and Leyte in the fall of 1944, where the women wallowed in the same mud and typhoon rains as everyone else.

The first of an eventual 5,500 WACs arrived in Manila on March 7. Most were housed in the dormitories of De La Salle University, near the waterfront, just a short walk from the remnants of the Intramuros. The vast majority, nearly 70 percent, performed office work as typists, stenographers, message center clerks, postal laborers, and, in the case of officers, censoring mail. Most of the rest worked as mechanics, switchboard operators, code clerks, and finance and food service specialists. A small complement of 150 WACs, including some Japanese Americans, served with the Allied Translator and Interpreter Section as linguists and interrogators. The WAC censors quickly earned a reputation for attention to detail. "I don't know what there is about women that makes them so sharp-eyed in reading letters, but the ones I have here possess an uncanny knack for picking up hidden security breaches, such as tricky codes a soldier may devise to tell his wife where he is," one supervisor marveled. "They are turning out more and better work than the male officers they released to the combat area." The work took its toll, though, mainly because the edgy content of all too many letters proved disturbing and shocking to WAC officers, many of whom came from relatively sheltered backgrounds. "Much of what the men wrote was so obscene that the women became demoralized from having to read it all day," Captain Jeanne Letallier, a WAC inspector general, later commented. "The WAC censors became nervous, temperamental, and complaining; first they thought they would lose their eyesight, then their minds. By the end of the war . . . many of them had become definitely neurotic if not actually psychotic." When she investigated the problem, she found that 20 percent of the censors were listed on sick call each day, 50 percent experienced eyestrain, and 8 percent were evacuated due to tropical disease or psychoneurotic issues.

Most of the women toiled six days a week, twelve hours a day, with a three-hour siesta at midday to escape the heat as per Filipino custom. They lived under strict curfews, with military-style restrictions on their movements and activities. They endured snarky sexist barbs from male soldiers, the general tone of which painted them, at best, as useless adventurers or, at worst, opportunistic comfort women. Krueger viewed them as a distraction and banned all females from eating in his Sixth Army mess halls. Some men even went so far as to lodge written complaints with MacArthur's headquarters. "As far as replacing men, that is purely a myth," one claimed; "it takes more GIs to work for them, and more to guard them, than they come anywhere near replacing." Another asserted that "for every WAC that is sent overseas it required approximately eight soldiers to take care of her." At the time the WACs arrived in theater, an overwhelming 90 percent of comments from enlisted soldiers about them were negative. But this changed dramatically as male soldiers actually met WACs and realized that they were making important contributions to the SWPA mission. Within a month, only

28 percent of incoming comments were unfavorable, and most of these came from men in units that had no interaction with WAC outfits. By July an encouraging 72 percent of GI comments were favorable. Nor was there any truth to the notion that the women absorbed more male manpower than they freed up for other duties. A careful theater-wide study revealed that they required only a minimal cadre of guards, and proved themselves self-sufficient in terms of housing, food, labor, and equipment. Their venereal disease rates were nonexistent—certainly that was more than could be said for most male units. Only 111 of 5,500 WACs were sent home due to pregnancy, a 2 percent rate; half of these returnees were married.

The low disease and pregnancy rates belied the reality of a vibrant dating scene for WAC soldiers in a theater where men outnumbered women by a factor of something like 100 to 1. For SWPA enlisted men who were prohibited from dating officers—thus eliminating nurses from the equation, though illicit liaisons undoubtedly did occur—enlisted WACs provided the only available option to go out with an American woman. "We dated constantly," PFC Mildred Ferguson later wrote, "as many nights as we could spare. Every GI outfit varied with its neighbor in thinking up attractions to lure the WACs to parties. Food was the most successful." As an officer, Lieutenant Martha Wayman enjoyed a range of social advantages. She lived in a rehabilitated house with other WAC lieutenants and operated in a privileged social circle that encompassed some of SWPA's Manila-based officer corps. During her months in the city, she dated a war correspondent and two Army officers, including one who had fought for three years as a guerrilla and another who was stationed near the harbor in Manila. "Earl and I ate, went out to a club a few miles out, near Quezon City," she wrote to her sister of a typical date. "They had a pingpong table and a nickelodeon, so we played and danced. Then we came back to the house. Earl left fairly early that evening, for a change."

Besides offering food or drinks, male units organized bands, games, and other entertainment to induce WACs to attend their parties or accept dating proposals. Like carnival ringleaders, men coated WAC unit bulletin boards with colorful posters and invitations. "Some listed the menu, promising ice cream or some other rare delicacy, for the WACs soon became blase about masculine company and refused to stir without the guarantee of food," wrote Mattie Treadwell, the Army's official historian of the Women's Army Corps. "No WAC was so old or unattractive as to be neglected." The competition for the attention of the women occasionally grew intense and underhanded. In one instance, the soldiers of one unit posed as another to hijack a truckload of women and drive them to their own dance.[13]

Similar to the Army Nurse Corps, most all the WACs were white, an unspoken indication of the repressed anonymity that defined the status of African American soldiers in theater. Excluded from frontline combat duty by the ludicrously racist, and ahistorical, notion that Blacks inherently lacked the ability to fight, they formed a segregated subculture of quartermasters, cooks, engineers, truck drivers, and stevedores. Their efforts undergirded the growing potency of the SWPA logistical empire. "We were hauling . . . gasoline, in some cases ammo, things of that sort," Private George Ridout, a truck driver in the 3524th Trucking Company, recalled of his unit's indefatigable efforts to circulate vast quantities of matériel to the fighting fronts. Ridout and other Black GIs occupied an oddly ambivalent status—much better off than the oft-displaced, poverty-stricken Filipinos and the hard-pressed Japanese, but hardly equal to white soldiers. Segregation guaranteed mistreatment by inherently favoring an overwhelming white majority over a comparatively powerless Black minority. At times, white base commanders attempted to keep African American soldiers from fraternizing with any locals, sparking tremendous resentment and anger. "Bitter over the new orders," one soldier complained to *The Pittsburgh Courier,* the famous African American newspaper. "The orders do not pertain to white soldiers who continue their association with the Filipinos, thus bringing about unpleasant attitudes on the part of the natives toward the Negroes. This is the bitterest act of discrimination we have seen in our twenty-one months overseas." A white chaplain, Captain Joseph Pruden, opined in an official letter of complaint that the order caused "very serious damage which can be repaired only by a modification of the restriction."

Unsurprisingly, most of the tension flared over competition for the attention of women and access to entertainment. Many USO clubs, YMCA buildings, bars, restaurants, and even Red Cross clubs were segregated. When African American soldiers attempted to dance with Filipinas at one integrated event in Manila, a white captain bellowed, "You niggers are not going to dance with the Filipino girls!" An angry and humiliated Black GI later told a correspondent, "This is one of the causes of constant friction between white and Negro men in the armed forces. We are all fighting together for the preservation of all that we know and love, but behind the scenes, the Negro is still the goat so far as white America is concerned." White soldiers circulated pernicious, grossly racist rumors among local women that Black men had tails and were imbued with the intellectual capacity of apes. "We are not allowed to even leave the area," one Black GI related in an exposé letter he sent to his minister back home. "The white soldiers are permitted to do anything. We have to do all the dirty work, and our food is different from that served to white troops. And worst of all, the white officers and soldiers are teaching the people in the Philippines that the Negro soldier has a tail like a dog that comes out at night and goes back in during the day." Violent clashes broke out between Black and white servicemen. In one ugly incident, a white guard at a quartermaster depot shot and killed a Black soldier whom he suspected of stealing clothing. The tension over the shooting metastasized into a fistfight between African American soldiers and white military policemen that might have escalated into something worse if not for the joint efforts of white and Black MPs to break up the fights and return troops to their quarters.

The veritable leper status of the primarily African American 93rd Infantry Division proved another sore point. Unfairly consigned to backwater patrolling, garrison duties, and stevedore duty for its supposed failures in combat at Bougainville, elements of the division now performed the same tertiary role in the Philippines. Relegated to an obscure spot deep on the SWPA bench, these soldiers who had trained to fight struggled to maintain their morale. "This is just another rear area now," one wrote despondently to his wife. "Yep, 93rd stuff—drag ass along behind." A well-meaning but nonetheless segregation-minded Eighth Army operations section analysis of the 93rd Division recommended "that there be no mixing of white and Negro enlisted personnel in any type unit; that Negro units be provided with capable and efficient leadership; that the same consideration and treatment be given Negro troops as that given to white troops; that the tendency to favor and pamper Negros [sic] be discontinued."

Walter White, former executive secretary of the NAACP and a close friend of Eleanor Roosevelt, toured the theater in his new capacity as a war correspondent, quickly learned of the 93rd's plight and conducted a personal investigation. He dubbed the 93rd's treatment as "one of the most shameful episodes of the Pacific War—a widespread and apparently deliberate attempt on the part of certain persons to brand Negro combat troops as failures and cowards." He sent President Roosevelt a detailed, exculpatory memo in which he decried this slander campaign and urged frontline duty for the division. White also met with General MacArthur to voice his concerns. MacArthur expressed complete disgust at any disparagement of the 93rd's fighting acumen. "Race has nothing whatsoever to do with a man's ability to fight," he told White. "Any man who says another man's fighting ability can be measured by color is wrong." He assured White that the 93rd Division would see combat like any other unit.

The general's laudable words reflected his intellectual belief in racial equality and the inherent sense of fair play that reflected one of the best aspects of his personal character. His actions, though, bespoke little commitment to bringing his ideals to practical fruition. Focused on fighting the Japanese and rehabilitating the Philippines, he had little interest in spending time and effort to push for more racial equality in his command, even if that meant sidelining combat troops who might otherwise have assisted his mission. Prodded by Roosevelt, General George Marshall radioed a chagrined MacArthur to request clarification of the issues raised by White. "[He] mentions local hearsay reports that you personally do not favor use of Negro troops in combat in the Pacific. Because it may be anticipated that [this] department will be required to make specific reply, your early comments . . . would be appreciated." MacArthur responded with a detailed analysis in which he argued that the 93rd Division simply ranked below other available divisions in combat readiness, but that he intended to make the best possible use of the outfit. In a concluding sentence, he revealed his true feelings about White and his efforts. "The violent opinions and unfounded statements of Mister White would seem to mark him as a troublemaker and a menace to the war effort." MacArthur never took any meaningful action to send the 93rd Division into battle. Given the constant paucity of manpower in frontline units, MacArthur's inaction spoke volumes about the Army's inherent institutional prejudice against Black soldiers, as did the fact that neither Krueger nor Eichelberger nor any of the corps commanders seem ever to have even considered asking for the services of the 93rd Division. Unfortunately, the sentiments of one Army Air Forces general on the issue of race proved to be all too true: "The real solution to the problem lies in the overall education on the subject and will undoubtedly take generations to accomplish."[14]

While the ongoing fighting raged in remote jungles and mountains, MacArthur settled back into the place that, more than anywhere else on the planet, he thought of as home. "In this city," he later wrote affectionately of Manila, "my mother had died, my wife had been courted, my son had been born." MacArthur moved into a beautiful two-story mansion known as Casa Blanca in the city's upscale Santa Mesa district. Adorned with a circular driveway, a swimming pool, gardens, four exquisitely crafted pillars, a gymnasium, a theater, a bowling alley, a billiard room, and about ten other rooms, the house belonged to Emil Bachrach, a Russian-born American businessman who had moved to the Philippines in the early twentieth century and made a fortune in the automotive business. Bachrach had died in 1937. His wife, Mary, who had once been a prominent Manila hotelier, fled the house when the Japanese took over the city. "The main floor has walls and ceilings of exquisitely paneled and beautifully polished mahogany," Brigadier General Byers related in a letter to his wife, Marie, after one visit. "I know that sounds dark but the many full length windows give so much light that the heavy tapestry hangings and the golden walls combine to give an atmosphere of comfortable luxury and coolness. It is the most restful place that I have seen since leaving home." Ironically, General Yamashita had lived at Casa Blanca before relocating to northern Luzon. His exodus to the privation of jungle life and MacArthur's appropriation of the house spoke volumes about the direction of the war.

Bits and pieces of MacArthur's property began to resurface. Soldiers found his black Cadillac sedan at Santo Tomas University. They salvaged a few intact books from the burned-out remains of his onetime apartment at the Manila Hotel. At the former residence of a Japanese official, a Filipino gardener recovered a box of MacArthur's silver. At a waterfront storehouse, troops found a box labeled "Medical Supplies—for Shipment to Tokyo" that actually contained tea sets, serving bowls, and other silver that belonged to MacArthur and his wife, Jean. Once in place at Casa Blanca, MacArthur gravitated away from his earlier mobile, adventure-seeking ways and returned to a structured, adventive lifestyle. For the rest of the war, he left Manila only three times, once to visit the Sixth Army front and twice to board ship and observe amphibious invasions. With the Japanese firmly confined to Luzon's hinterlands, he summoned Jean and seven-year-old Arthur to join him. They made the journey by sea, with Brigadier General Fellers, the military secretary, as an escort, and arrived on March 6 to a joyous welcome from MacArthur, who had not seen them since October 14, six days before the Leyte invasion the previous fall.

In an attempt to head off any criticism over their presence in Manila, a SWPA spokesman claimed that Jean had come solely "to aid and assist in such way as she can in the care of internees and rehabilitation of the city and its inhabitants." Though, undoubtedly, Jean had much to offer in this respect, the real reason for her presence had much more to do with MacArthur's megalomaniacal self-centeredness than any humanitarian impulse. No other American overseas commander, in this or any previous or future war, and certainly no one else in SWPA, enjoyed the company of his family while on duty. Only MacArthur. This jarring contrast seems never to have occurred to him, or if it did, he likely did not care. He once told Lieutenant Colonel Egeberg, his physician, who had not seen his own wife in years, "Doc, you have a long life ahead of you, time to enjoy and appreciate each other. I can't count too many years." Sutherland, in his own self-interested way, heartily disapproved. He could not understand how MacArthur could prohibit the presence of Sutherland's Australian girlfriend, Captain Elaine Bessemer-Clark, while he himself got to enjoy Jean's company (the distinction of wife versus extramarital foreign mistress seemed lost on the chief of staff). At one point, he even vented to Eichelberger about it, calling

MacArthur's decision the "greatest mistake of his life." Sutherland was incorrect. Army and War Department authorities simply chose to look the other way. One Pentagon official said, "MacArthur is not a young man. Maybe he needs his wife." Egeberg wholeheartedly agreed. "Reunited with his family, he was relaxed and happy in a different manner from that of his campaign days."

By contrast, Arthur was initially frightened to return to Manila, where three years earlier he had experienced the evacuation of his home and the siege of Corregidor, an especially traumatic event for such a young child. The first night at Casa Blanca, he heard the booming of heavy artillery in the distance. Jean found him trembling and wide-eyed. "Are those our guns, Mom?" he asked. When she assured them that they were, he went to sleep and thereafter settled into a happy daily schedule of play mixed with tutoring sessions from a personal teacher whom his parents hired. Jean spent her days visiting with former internees, touring military and civilian hospitals, and working hard to alleviate the poverty and suffering of as many Filipinos as possible. She was appalled at the devastation she witnessed, and she held the Japanese responsible. "You can't possibly conceive of the destruction wrought by the enemy here," she wrote to a friend. "His brutality is something that, to me, isn't even paralleled in the darkest ages. He destroyed, killed, massacred and looted. Entire families that I knew were murdered. Others have completely disappeared from the face of the globe. Even as much as I had been told before I arrived, I couldn't grasp it until I got here."

Meanwhile, MacArthur settled into a daily routine. From March 5 to May 12, he located his headquarters inside the Wilson Building in northern Manila. After that he moved it into Manila's spacious City Hall. Both sites, and the Malacañang Palace, home to President Sergio Osmeña's newly reestablished government, were located within easy driving distance of Casa Blanca. Each day he woke at 0700, ate breakfast, and got to the office at 0930. He returned home for lunch in the early afternoon, took a nap in the tradition of a Filipino siesta, and then returned to the office for more work until 1930. He and Jean generally kept a low profile, hosting only a few occasional dinner parties for prominent visitors such as Lord Louis Mountbatten. In the evenings, MacArthur played with Arthur, ate a quiet dinner, and wound down by taking in a movie with Jean and other intimates. "There were usually ten or twelve in the room, which had several rows of seats," Dr. Egeberg later wrote, "General and Mrs. MacArthur customarily sitting alone in the front row." In choosing films, MacArthur had only one rule—no war movies. Though he was more at ease than before the arrival of Jean and Arthur, the general's acerbic side did not recede altogether. When he learned from Fellers of President Roosevelt's death on April 12, he ungraciously said, "Well the old man has gone. A man who never told the truth if a lie would suffice."[15]

From his newly established domestic haven in Manila, MacArthur continued to manage SWPA's ongoing operations. All along he had intended to liberate as much of the archipelago as possible. He worried about the possibility that bypassed Japanese garrisons on southern islands would perpetrate atrocities against Filipinos, and he wanted new air bases from which to menace any remaining enemy shipping in the Dutch East Indies (Indonesia) or elsewhere in the South China Sea, and to support scheduled Australian landings to seize the oil fields of Borneo. Part of him also felt that true liberation for the Philippines must mean immediate freedom for all the major islands, regardless of whether this might be necessary for the ultimate defeat of Japan. For this purpose, as Sixth Army continued slugging away on Luzon, MacArthur had kept Eichelberger and Eighth Army in his back pocket for an eventual campaign to liberate the southern Philippines. The concept was fraught with multiple strategic problems. On Luzon and Mindoro, MacArthur already had all the air bases he really needed to keep advancing north to Japan. The Imperial Navy hardly posed any more threat in the waters around the Dutch East Indies. The successful landings on Leyte, Mindoro, Samar, and Luzon, as well as the defeat of the Imperial Navy and the suppression of Japanese airpower, had already severed Japan's lines of communications with most any remaining Japanese-controlled areas in the south and western Pacific. In that context, any invasion of an island south of Leyte amounted to moving backward—quite similar to Eisenhower and Bradley's decision in France to clear Brittany after

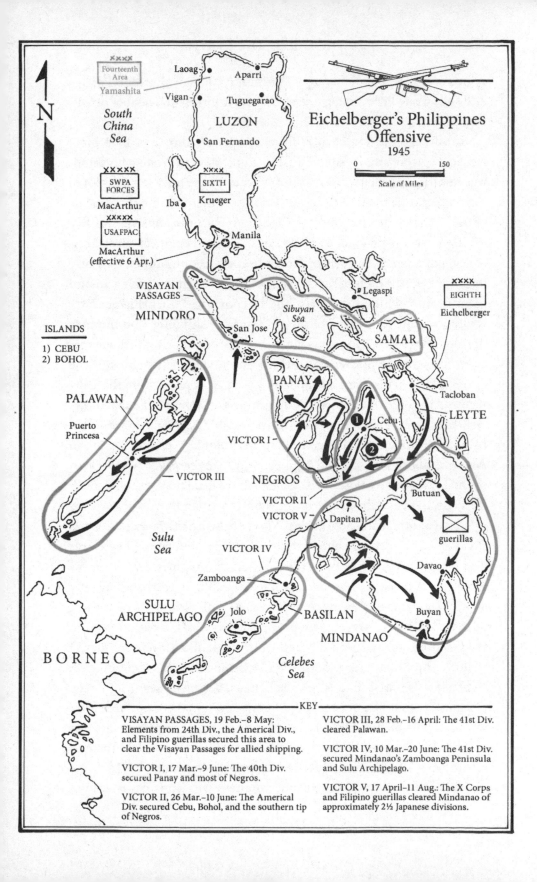

Eichelberger's Philippines Offensive
1945

N

South China Sea

XXXX Fourteenth Area — Yamashita

LUZON

Laoag • Aparri • Vigan • Tuguegarao • San Fernando

XXXXX SWPA FORCES — MacArthur

XXXX SIXTH — Krueger

Iba • Krueger

XXXXX USAFPAC — MacArthur (effective 6 Apr.)

Manila

VISAYAN PASSAGES

MINDORO

San Jose

Sibuyan Sea

Legaspi

XXXX EIGHTH — Eichelberger

SAMAR

ISLANDS
1) CEBU
2) BOHOL

PALAWAN

Puerto Princesa

PANAY

VICTOR I

① Cebu **②**

Tacloban

LEYTE

VICTOR III

NEGROS

VICTOR II

VICTOR V

Dapitan

Butuan

guerillas

Sulu Sea

VICTOR IV

Zamboanga

SULU ARCHIPELAGO

Jolo

BASILAN

Davao

Buyan

MINDANAO

BORNEO

Celebes Sea

0   150
Scale of Miles

— KEY —

VISAYAN PASSAGES, 19 Feb.–8 May: Elements from 24th Div., the Americal Div., and Filipino guerillas secured this area to clear the Visayan Passages for allied shipping.

VICTOR I, 17 Mar.–9 June: The 40th Div. secured Panay and most of Negros.

VICTOR II, 26 Mar.–10 June: The Americal Div. secured Cebu, Bohol, and the southern tip of Negros.

VICTOR III, 28 Feb.–16 April: The 41st Div. cleared Palawan.

VICTOR IV, 10 Mar.–20 June: The 41st Div. secured Mindanao's Zamboanga Peninsula and Sulu Archipelago.

VICTOR V, 17 April–11 Aug.: The X Corps and Filipino guerillas cleared Mindanao of approximately 2½ Japanese divisions.

Allied armies had broken out of Normandy and advanced on Paris—and thus made little strategic sense for the fundamental goal of defeating Japan.

To liberate the southern Philippines, MacArthur had to deprive Krueger of troops and resources, a decision certain to prolong his grinding campaign to shatter Yamashita's forces in the hills and jungles of Luzon. Regardless, MacArthur wanted the southern Philippines, and he chose Eichelberger for the job. Eighth Army now consisted of five divisions, two regimental combat teams, and two engineer special brigades, not a particularly large force to seize what amounted to nearly two-thirds of the archipelago. "At times Eighth Army . . . felt a wistful identification with Oliver Twist and his porridge," Eichelberger later wrote jovially. "In matters of supply, available shipping, and infantry divisions, we learned to make out with what we had." But Eichelberger enjoyed complete mastery of the sea and air, with the ships of the Seventh Fleet at his disposal and land-based air support from the Thirteenth Air Force. He could also count on the support of substantial, well-organized guerrilla forces, most notably 33,000 insurgents on Mindanao under the able command of Colonel Wendell Fertig, an American-born local mining engineer and Army reservist who had coordinated his efforts closely with MacArthur's headquarters to establish the equivalent of a shadow government on the island.

Lieutenant General Sosaku Suzuki's 35th Army, the Japanese formation that had so fiercely contested the American presence on Leyte, was also responsible for defense of the southern Philippines. On paper, his force of 102,000 Japanese sounded impressive. But, in truth, he had only about 30,000 Imperial Army combat soldiers with little artillery; the rest of his people were service troops, naval personnel, aviation ground crewmen or construction laborers, and civilians. Moreover, Suzuki himself and Major General Yoshiharu Tomochika, his chief of staff, were enmeshed in a state of personal chaos, fleeing by sea from Leyte. Not until the middle of March did Suzuki even make it to Cebu, after which he lost his life at sea as he attempted to get to Mindanao. Tomochika did not get to the latter island until late April, fortunate to escape with his life after a meandering, perilous odyssey.

Similar to many other isolated Japanese garrisons, 35th Army's strength lay in the terrain it commanded and the willingness of its troops to fight to the death. Eichelberger understood this well. He had no intention of playing into the hands of such a doomed but dangerous foe with frontal attacks or battles of annihilation. Instead, he stressed audacity and lightning-fast maneuverability. "I was convinced . . . that the way to keep your losses down and to get ahead with the Japanese was to never give them time to get set," he later commented. He told his commanders to get ashore, move fast, and not worry about their flanks. "[My] remarks pertained particularly to the need for rapid advances and the avoidance of any of the sit-still-and-patrol method," he noted in his diary, of a talk he gave to subordinates. "Also stressed the importance of complete cooperation between the services." He focused on seizing ports, controlling lines of communication, securing populated areas, and forcing the Japanese units to retreat into useless, remote jungle areas where guerrilla fighters could effectively harass and destroy their remnants.

Knowing that he faced no real threat to his supply lines, he amended his logistical plans to facilitate rapid operations. "There can be, under certain circumstances, too much supply—odd as that may sound," he once wrote. Instead of insisting upon the standard sixty days of provisions for any landing, he and his excellent supply officer, Colonel Henry "Tubby" Burgess, pared that number down to fifteen days. In case of emergency, they maintained floating stores of ammunition, food, and other vital items at sea, where Eichelberger could rush them forward to wherever he might need them. Eichelberger's innovative, lean logistical structure afforded tremendous, and much-needed, agility to Eighth Army. Over a six-week period, from February 28 to the middle of April, Eighth Army conducted thirty-eight successful invasions at a dizzying variety of islands that included Palawan in the west, Mindanao in the east (as well as Zamboanga on this island's extreme southwest coast), and Panay, Bohol, Negros, and Cebu in between. The invasions ranged from company to division level in size. Each one required a complex web of intelligence gathering, interservice coordination, staff planning, on-site combat leadership, and liaison with guerrilla units. At the height of these "Victor" operations, as the planners officially dubbed them, Eighth Army launched an invasion, on average, every day and a half, demonstrating a unique level of proficiency in amphibious operations unequaled by any other military organization during World War II. Ever conscious of posterity, Eichelberger proudly took to referring to his army as "the Amphibious Eighth," in tribute to his troops' mastery of this most challenging of military operations. "There was never a time . . . when some task force of my command was not fighting a battle," he wrote. "And most of the time, hundreds of miles apart, separate task forces were fighting separate battles simultaneously."

If ever anyone was well suited to the difficult task of commanding such a fast-paced, unorthodox operation, it was the energetic Eichelberger. He maintained a frenetic pace of the sort made possible by the cutting-edge automation of the US Armed Forces and the increasing sophistication of their communications. "We have been using every type of conveyance there is, starting with a cub, an L-5, the tiniest of artillery observation planes, through the C-47, B-25, Navy Catalinas and Mariners on up to our B-17," Brigadier General Byers, the chief of staff, wrote to a friend. "We have troops in so many different localities that no one type of conveyance will permit us to reach them all." Eichelberger nicknamed his B-17 the "Miss Em," in tribute to his beloved wife. This and the other aircraft, as well as ships on several occasions, made it possible for him to observe invasions or frontline action without risk of losing touch with his Leyte headquarters and the bigger picture. Eichelberger jokingly called himself "one of the Orient's busiest air commanders. The airplane was a magic carpet for me. I could rise early, be in the air by seven, take off for a conference with GHQ [MacArthur's General Headquarters] in Manila, and be back at my desk for a staff conference before sundown."

All of this proved crucial for a man so committed to immersing himself in the action. With the exception of occasional desk days on Leyte, and several visits to Manila, he spent nearly every day in motion, almost always somewhere in the field, where fighting raged. "You understand, of course, that when I go in on these operations I do not assume personal command," he wrote to Emma in late March from Cebu, where the Japanese lined the landing beaches with rows of mines, aerial bombs, and obstacles, and the beautiful capital Cebu City was almost entirely destroyed by the fighting between the Americal Division and the Imperial Army's 102nd Division. "I merely land there as an Army commander. Of course what I want done is done, but I try to keep out of the tactical handling of troops."

Eichelberger's commanders appreciated the balance he struck between hands-on leadership and micromanaging. Years later, the Americal's commander, Major General William "Duke" Arnold, told an interviewer, "Eichelberger was a fine commander. Never gave me any restrictions whatsoever. He gave me a mission to do and he left it entirely up to me how I did it." To wit, at the peak of the fighting on Cebu, when Japanese troops in caves had pinned down Arnold's two leading regiments for a week, Arnold secured Eichelberger's permission to release his third regiment, the 164th Infantry, from Army reserve to land on Cebu and, guided expertly by guerrillas, smash into the Japanese right flank. The new pressure forced the Japanese to retreat north into a dead-end life of hunger and marginality in the island's inhospitable jungles. "By the time you and I returned to Leyte, Duke's morale was high beyond imagination," Byers fondly wrote to Eichelberger years later of the turnaround on Cebu. Another factor in the improvement of Arnold's morale and, more important, the battlefield situation was a personal talk he had with Eichelberger in which the Eighth Army commander expressed great confidence in him and his plans. "This determination at the critical point in battle is one of Bob's remarkable qualities of leadership," Byers wrote to his wife, Marie, a few days later. "He bolsters the courage of his subordinates and doesn't permit their doubts and worries to shake his faith."

On Mindanao, the second-largest island in the Philippines, Eichelberger utilized excellent intelligence information provided to him by Colonel Fertig, the guerrilla leader, to land on undefended beaches at Parang and Malabang rather than the more populated areas of Davao City and Sarangani Bay, where the Japanese garrison of some 43,000 troops expected them. To avoid becoming enmeshed in the massive island's confining jungles, he used the Mindanao River as his main supply route. Amphibian engineers aboard landing craft shuttled supplies, artillery pieces, and a regiment from the 24th Infantry Division to make multiple landings and link up with another regiment moving along the degraded remnants of Highway 1, where, in Eichelberger's recollection, he and his men found "the highway just a tunnel through green vegetation. That section of Mindanao was moist, dank, and insufferably hot." The troops knifed across the island in ten days, cutting the Japanese defenders in two.

Eventually the battle involved the entire 24th and 31st Divisions, as well as regimental combat teams from the 40th and 41st Divisions, and a battalion from the Americal Division. They fought a pincers-style battle, constantly displacing and outflanking the befuddled Japanese defenders, who fought hard but were plagued by guerrillas, supply problems, and poor communications, in addition, of course, to the constant battering inflicted upon them by Eichelberger's forces. They did, though, succeed in blowing most of the island's key bridges, mainly costing the Americans time as engineers steadily rebuilt them. In characteristic fashion, the Eighth Army commander frequently visited Mindanao and the fighting. Ordinarily, he circled the area in his plane to view the battlefield from that vantage point and then landed to get a firsthand feel for the fighting on the ground. During the fighting in early May to secure Davao City, the largest on the island, he and Byers were driven back one afternoon by accurate enemy fire. "Early the next morning I crossed the swift tidal Davao River on a shaky footbridge which sometimes was a single plank," Eichelberger later wrote of his experiences in the fight for the city. "Then I walked into Davao City with the infantry. The town had been wrecked. Japanese positions were being gradually liquidated by the 19th Infantry." Though the campaign was nowhere near as intense as the fight for Manila, the Americans did not snuff out the last Japanese resistance in Davao until the middle of May. On another typical occasion, Eichelberger watched firsthand as combat troops fought an anonymous small unit action among Mindanao's caves and jungled ravines. "The Japs are in caves down there and since the vegetation is thick it is going to be hard to get them out," he wrote to Emma. "A battalion of men waded across the river and came up the other bank of the canyon where they were in position on the other side of a young mountain. From the observation post on the side of the canyon I could look all around with my glasses and watched the tanks shooting into the caves."[16]

In the space of three months, Eighth Army troops secured all the key objectives of the Victor operations, including Palawan to Negros, Cebu,

Panay, Bohol, and Mindanao, though small unit fighting still continued on Mindanao and elsewhere. The liberation of the central and southern portions of the archipelago, and nearly 7 million Filipinos, cost Eichelberger's army 2,070 soldiers killed and nearly 7,000 wounded, with few losses to disease and combat fatigue. The campaign accrued little, if any, strategic advantage to the Americans since, in essence, they had simply reclaimed a relative backwater and inflicted more losses on an already beleaguered enemy. For Eichelberger, though, Victor represented a tactical masterpiece of the first order, a signal, capstone accomplishment. "These were great moments," he later reflected, almost wistfully. "At no time in my whole life have I been so happy from a military standpoint. We were doing what seemed to me the impossible. Striking out in all directions; asking no one for help; taking the initiative; it made me very happy."

Throughout SWPA, his stature grew, a welcome tonic for such a sensitive man who yearned almost desperately for military distinction. When he boarded the USS *Montpelier* for the Mindanao invasion, the ship's crewmen eagerly clustered around just to catch a glimpse of him. "When the General arrived, everyone wanted a look at him," Seaman James Fahey recorded in his diary. "His outfit has made quite a name for itself. The Japs will see plenty of him and his troops before the war is over with." Eichelberger's old friend and classmate George Patton raved in one letter, "In my limited experience with amphibious attacks, I found them the most dangerous form of sport yet devised. If I should be so fortunate, I am going to sit at your feet and learn how to do it." Patton was being unduly modest. He had extensive, and quite successful, experience with amphibious operations, so his complimentary comments were probably especially meaningful to Eichelberger. Colonel Fertig, who knew both men well, described their relationship as "extremely close," so much so that Fertig claimed that Patton actually offered to serve as a division commander under Eichelberger.

No one was happier with Eichelberger than General MacArthur. Eager to deflect the attention of the Joint Chiefs away from the attritional realities of his Luzon campaign, and locked in a high-stakes struggle with naval leaders to carve out a major role for SWPA in the anticipated invasion of Japan, MacArthur was thrilled at the speed with which

Eighth Army completed the Victor operations. Throughout the spring and early summer, he showered Eichelberger with praise in long, intimate personal conversations or through his staff when Eichelberger was in the field. "You run an army in combat just like I would like to have it done," MacArthur told him once. He lauded Eighth Army's excellence and spoke of the Victor operations as a classic "model of what a light but aggressive command can accomplish in rapid exploitation." After one meeting with MacArthur, an upbeat Eichelberger wrote to Emma, "I never received so many bouquets in my life. He said that my operations . . . had been handled just the way he would have wanted to have done it had he been an Army commander—speed, dash, brilliance, etc." After another similar discussion, Eichelberger told Emma that "the praise from him and everyone up there [in Manila] is really embarrassing. Of course it was a grand psychological moment for me." When MacArthur met one day with Byers, he could hardly contain his enthusiasm. "There was a distinctly jubilant note in his voice when he greeted me," Byers documented in a memo shortly after the meeting. "He said that Bob's progress in these Eighth Army operations was brilliant and that nothing in the history of this war would surpass what Bob had done with the meager forces available to him in such lightning-like strokes." In a letter to Marie, Byers related the almost ecstatic attitude of MacArthur and his key staffers in relation to Eichelberger's performance. "Bob's successes are becoming increasingly brilliant to the point that those around the Chief [MacArthur] tell me he talks about Bob's work incessantly. Roger Egeberg told me that only this morning the Chief said that Bob's leadership was one of the most brilliant things he had ever seen."

In many private conversations with Eichelberger, MacArthur derided Krueger and Sixth Army, an unprofessional but effective way of motivating the Eighth Army commander and stroking his ego (if MacArthur ever uttered a negative comment about Eichelberger and his command in conversation with Krueger or anyone else, it did not make it into the historical record). The main theme seemed to be MacArthur's frustration with Krueger's methodical, almost stodgy nature, and the Sixth Army's inability to snuff out Japanese resistance on Luzon, even with priority of resources. The SWPA commander told Eichelberger that

Sixth Army could not possibly have pulled off the aggressive Victor operations. "He said they are mentally incapable but if given tremendous forces they are able to advance ponderously and slowly to victory," Eichelberger recorded in his diary. "He said that [Krueger] is the old-fashioned Army general who wants to do everything by the rules. If he is given a certain number of troops to do a job with, he wants twice that number." In yet another conversation, MacArthur ripped Krueger as "all infantryman. He would tolerate the artillery and hate the Navy and Air Corps . . . [can't] get along with them." To Byers, MacArthur said during the height of the campaign, "Tell Bob if he keeps going at his present pace he'll have his whole task finished before Walter gets started."

The chief's attitude spread among his staff as well. Colonel Larry Lehrbas, one of MacArthur's key public relations officers, told Major Robert White, his opposite at Eighth Army, that Eichelberger "is absolutely the fair-haired one. At long last the General [Eichelberger] is truely [sic] held in sweetness and light." In response to most any operational problem, the SWPA staffers took to saying, "Give the Eighth Army a couple of squads and they will do it." Major General Steve Chamberlin, MacArthur's low-key, competent operations officer, made a point of thanking Eichelberger for making his job easier. "He said he is crazy about Eighth Army because we don't ask for a tremendous force whenever we have things to do, and he added that that is the way everybody else at GHQ felt," Eichelberger reported to Emma of the conversation. Another time, Chamberlin informed Eichelberger that a group of visiting Pentagon officers "were popeyed while they were watching" Eighth Army's operations. The visitors also spoke with Byers, who duly informed Marie that "these Washington men mentioned that our situation was the high spot in this theater. And don't think for a minute that they won't announce this fact in Washington!" A confident Eichelberger told Emma, "I believe I do not exaggerate when I tell you that the Eighth Army is riding on the crest of the waves." To his sister he crowed, "I know that my army now stands number one by long odds out in this area every place from the top down."

As a reward for his great success, Eichelberger fully expected publicity, promotions, and decorations for himself and his staff, and a leading role in all future operations. Indeed, MacArthur had promised all this, but the Eighth Army commander should have known better than to put much stock in the assurances of such an enigmatic, self-centered figure. In June, Byers did receive a second star, and the Eighth Army's operations officer, Colonel Frank Bowen, was promoted to brigadier general. But Eichelberger did not receive a fourth star, nor any new decorations. To his deep, resentful chagrin, he remained junior to Krueger. Not surprisingly, MacArthur allowed little publicity for Eighth Army's exploits. In SWPA, there was room for only one central figure— MacArthur himself.

Downplayed by MacArthur, overshadowed by the final operations in Europe, and hindered in history's big picture by an undeniable scent of strategic pointlessness, Eighth Army's southern Philippines campaign slipped into the mists of anonymity. For MacArthur's duplicity, Eichelberger came to nurse an acrimony against him that would only grow in time. MacArthur did, though, make good on his promise to assign Eighth Army a lead role. As the Luzon campaign staggered into its seventh month and Yamashita's survivors stubbornly fought on, mainly in the north, MacArthur turned the battle over to Eichelberger's Eighth Army. By this time, MacArthur had learned that he would command all Army forces in the invasion of Japan. He decided to use Sixth Army for Operation Olympic, the invasion of Kyushu, designed to seize bases for the much larger capstone invasion of Honshu, where Eichelberger's Eighth Army would lead the way in what promised to be the largest amphibious operation in history.

As Luzon fighting continued, heedless of SWPA communiqués referring to mop-up operations, and as planning for the invasion of Japan proceeded apace, and as Filipinos began to confront the nettling postliberation, postindependence political issues, the Americans unquestionably controlled everything of any strategic importance in the Philippines. The return to this beloved place—in the manner of a redemptive, almost messianic cause for MacArthur—had become the costly fulcrum for the entire war in the Pacific. A decade and a half later, Eisenhower as president cast doubt on its very necessity. "The President, from a military point of view, considered [it] unnecessary," declared a memo of Eisenhower's discussion of the Pacific War with Australian

Prime Minister Robert Menzies. From a fairer vantage point, the campaign undeniably administered powerful blows to Japan's war-making capacity. Leyte Gulf, the air battles, the slaughter of the Imperial Army's cream, the severing of Japanese communications, and the marginalization of Japan's conquered resource trove in the South and Southwest Pacific all contributed materially to its defeat. The liberation of POWs and internees and pro-American Filipinos and the crucial contributions of guerrillas all mattered morally and politically. The real question, though, is whether this merited the loss of over 10,000 American lives, the expenditure of massive military resources eclipsed only by those at Eisenhower's disposal, and, perhaps most important, the enormous death and destruction wrought upon the Philippines and its people, especially in its once beautiful capital. Considering these troubling realities, perhaps Formosa could have represented a better option, though it, too, would likely have become an equally costly, time-consuming bloodbath, and for no redemptive purpose of liberation. The consequences from this road not taken, by their very hypothetical nature, must remain forever muted. "Hindsight arguments about the desirability and necessity of tying up strong American forces . . . in the reconquest of Luzon and the Southern Philippines may rage for decades to come, with justice and logic undoubtedly to be found on both sides of the argument," Robert Ross Smith, the Army's official historian, wrote presciently in the early 1960s. Alas, as Smith foresaw, the ambivalence has never yet dissipated, and probably never will. The results of the second Philippines campaign were simply too mixed to warrant any other conclusion.[17]

3

Hope and Grief

Major General Albert Wedemeyer was a difficult man to surprise, but he knew that war often confounded the predictable. Born to German American parents in Nebraska, fluent in the tongue of his ancestors, and one of the US Army's few graduates of the Kriegsakademie, Germany's war college, he did not expect to succeed General Joseph Stilwell in China. The news of this had come to Wedemeyer in the form of an urgent message from General George Marshall on the evening of October 27, 1944, just as Wedemeyer drifted off to sleep in his bunk at Kandy on the island of Ceylon (present-day Sri Lanka). At the time, Wedemeyer served as deputy chief of staff to Admiral Lord Louis Mountbatten, the British commander of Southeast Asia Command, the polyglot theater that included Burma and India. True to his diplomatic, propitiative nature, Wedemeyer had gotten along well with Mountbatten, no easy feat given the divergence of American and British interests in Asia, where the Yanks hoped that the rise of a modern, independent, continent-leading China would hasten the demise of colonial empires, while the British wanted little else but to preserve the old imperial order. The Americans also deeply valued China's participation in the war in order to tie down as many Imperial Army soldiers as possible. The strategic objective of dispersing Japanese resources in Asia remained so important to US interests that, to hedge against the possibility that the Chinese could not continue the war, President Roosevelt at the Yalta Conference had even negotiated an agreement with Joseph Stalin for the Soviet Union to enter the war in Asia three months after the conclusion of the war in Europe.

Tall, stately, impeccably groomed and neatly coiffed, Wedemeyer's pleasing physical appearance accurately suggested a man more at ease

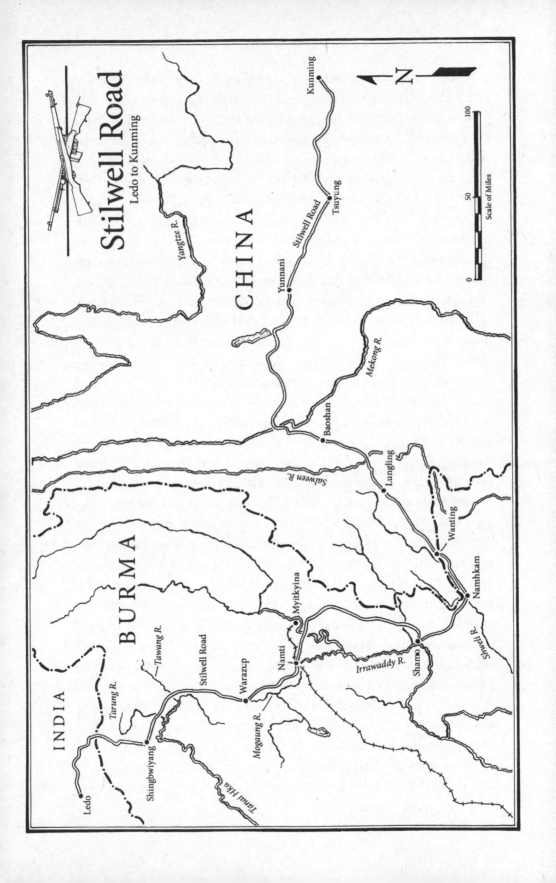

Stilwell Road
Ledo to Kunming

CHINA

Kunming

Tsuyung

Stilwell Road

Yunnani

Yangtze R.

Baoshan

Mekong R.

Lungling

Salween R.

Wanting

Namhkam

BURMA

Myitkyina

Shweli R.

Shamo

Irrawaddy R.

Namti

Tawang R.

Stilwell Road

Warazup

Mogaung R.

INDIA

Tarung R.

Shingbwiyang

Ledo

Tanai Hka

Scale of Miles

0   50   100

N

in a boardroom than a foxhole. A 1919 West Point graduate with two and a half decades of loyal service to his credit, he had no combat experience, little command time, and almost nothing in common with the average soldier. Clever minded, diplomatic, and adept at under-the-radar self-promotion, Wedemeyer counted himself among George Marshall's many protégés. He also found an influential sponsor in Lieutenant General Stanley Embick, whose daughter Elizabeth he had married in 1925. Wedemeyer clearly lacked the inspirational characteristics of a frontline commander. On one occasion, when he described his experiences observing the Sicily invasion, he said, with more than a touch of drawing-room naivete, "I put on for the first time my war regalia." To some senior colleagues, such as Lieutenant General Robert Richardson, he came across as little more than a convivial upstart with greater political than military talents. "He is a very nice young man but he is immature in his ideas," Richardson tartly assessed in a private diary entry after meeting Wedemeyer; "talks a lot and advertises himself."

Much more a manager than a leader, with considerably more Courtney Massengale than Sam Damon in his military DNA, Wedemeyer had an understanding of modern combat that tended more toward the intellectual than the experiential. But he possessed an incisive strategic mind, one that marked him as an insightful military thinker who was blessed with a strong understanding of geopolitics. On the eve of the war, when Wedemeyer was only an overaged major in the War Plans Division at the Pentagon, an organization his father-in-law had recently commanded, Marshall had chosen him to work on a team to produce a comprehensive plan for mobilization and victory when the United States entered the conflict. Wedemeyer's significant contributions to this so-called Victory Plan had catapulted his career in a relentlessly upward direction, with a rapid two-year rise from major to major general, and led historical posterity, with his gentle prodding, to afford him a bit too much credit for the plan's success. For the first two years of the war, Wedemeyer had remained part of the War Plans Division, functioning as a roving planner and consummate military insider, and an intimate participant in high-level conferences from London to Casablanca and Washington, DC, helping to craft Allied grand strategy. He emerged as one of the Army's leading experts on German military capabilities, a skill set that he expected—incorrectly, as things turned out—would lead him to spend the war in Europe. He argued passionately for a cross-Channel invasion of France in 1942 and 1943, butting heads with Churchill, who advocated successfully for Mediterranean operations. Wedemeyer's strategic views were so adamantly opposed to those of Churchill that it was said in high-command circles—and Wedemeyer came to believe—the prime minister himself orchestrated his assignment to Mountbatten's headquarters in October 1943 just to prevent him from having any influence on European grand strategy.[1]

If Wedemeyer was something of a map board and typewriter officer, his appointment to China did make some sense in a theater bereft of US ground combat units and where the American military presence never rose above 60,000 soldiers, over half of whom belonged to the Army Air Forces. The situation called for a strategy-savvy military diplomat, not necessarily a warrior. As Wedemeyer served Mountbatten ably for a year, he had observed China's many problems and Stilwell's demise, albeit from a distance. Wedemeyer respected Stilwell's extensive experience on the ground in China and his obvious expertise about the country and its people. But he could not fathom Stilwell's inability to get along with Chinese leader Chiang Kai-shek when the success of his mission, and American strategic aims, so conspicuously depended upon it.

Once in-country Wedemeyer was stunned to discover that Stilwell, after more than two rocky, stressful years working closely with Chiang's Nationalist government, had left the country without bequeathing him strategic and operational plans of any kind, nor even a good luck note. Honest and upright yet prone to small-minded pettiness, Stilwell loved China and its people, but he had grown to detest, in equal measure, Chiang as little more than a third-rate despot and his government as a corrupt, repressive oligarchy with little inclination to fight the Japanese, at least in a manner he thought appropriate. Stilwell thoroughly lacked the diplomatic skills to keep his opinions to himself for the greater good of productive Sino-American relations. Lieutenant General Robert Richardson, who had known Stilwell since their cadet days at West Point almost forty years earlier, once insightfully described him as "very intolerant and caustic . . . a hater of all sham and pretense." Indeed, Stilwell's unvarnished contempt for Chiang, and its inevitable toxic residue, finally, in October 1944, exhausted Stilwell's welcome in China when the Chinese leader demanded his relief after an especially stormy meeting. Stilwell's recall pointed to the larger failure of American grand strategy in China, and President Franklin Roosevelt had no wish to draw voter attention to this deficiency of his administration during the home stretch of his final bid for reelection that fall. As a result, Stilwell's relief unfolded under a veil of secrecy that mandated a rapid, anonymous exit from China. Wedemeyer seemed not to realize that the hasty, secret nature of his predecessor's recall had negated the usual change-of-command customs. The courtly Wedemeyer viewed Stilwell's omissions as an appalling, inexcusable discourtesy, and he developed a lifelong grudge against him. "There was nothing whatsoever, no message wishing me good luck, or go to hell, or anything else," Wedemeyer later groused. He professed that "my feelings were hurt . . . by General Stilwell's apparent attitude of hostility." In a private letter to Major General J. Edwin Hull, a War Department planner and an old friend, he ripped Stilwell's "lack of coordination and organization among the Americans in the China Theater." To General Embick, his father-in-law, he bluntly asserted that "my predecessor has made a botch of the job. He spent so much time in the jungles in Upper Burma commanding a few battalions and acquiring a great deal of publicity as a great tactician that he neglected sorely the responsibilities inherent in his position as Chief of Staff to the Generalissimo and as Commanding General of American Forces in the China Theater." The letter revealed not only Wedemeyer's burning resentment against his predecessor but also his philosophy that a commander's proper place was not at the front but far to the rear. Wedemeyer later exacted some public revenge in a 1958 memoir, published during the midst of serious Cold War tensions, in which he unfairly and ungraciously portrayed Stilwell as a careless, pro-communist stooge who had blundered in his mission. To one latter-year historian he dismissed Stilwell as "a very good division commander, but he wasn't much beyond that level." To another historian he conceded Stilwell's inspirational qualities of combat leadership but derided him as "incapable of maintaining high morale in peacetime or in situations requiring tact, diplomacy, and a broader knowledge of the humanities as well as of history."

Stilwell, for his part, had little regard for Wedemeyer, whom he once called "the world's most pompous prick." The earthy Stilwell saw Wede-meyer as a stuffed shirt, a military poseur better suited for staff work than theater command, and he probably resented being supplanted by him. Given Stilwell's unappealing tendency toward prejudicial contempt, it is worth pondering whether he might have left behind a more helpful foundation for someone whom he held in higher regard. Unfortunately, the bad blood between these two key figures and their adherents led to a simplistic Cold War notion—cultivated very much by Wedemeyer in many postwar writings and interviews—that Stilwell and his charges had abetted the Chinese communists while Wedemeyer, as an anticom-munist crusader, had seen through their devious machinations and held fast against them.[2]

These elemental ideas belied the complex realities that actually con-fronted Wedemeyer when he arrived in China at the end of October. After eight terrible years of war and the loss of millions of lives, three main power brokers besides the Japanese continued to vie for domi-nance over a country in which one out of every five people had, at some point, become a refugee. In Japanese-occupied China, the Reorganized National Government of the Republic of China under Ching-wei Wang, an ardent follower of the great Chinese nationalist Dr. Sun Yat-sen, saw itself as the best hope to salvage an autonomous China from the ashes of Japanese continental dominance. The Americans and their Chinese allies dismissed this regime as little more than a Japanese puppet (similar to the Allied view of Vichy France). In Yan'an province and nearby portions of northern China, Mao Zedong's communist shadow government continued to grow in power and influence. By the end of 1944, 90 million people lived under communist rule. The communists implemented educational and land reforms that solidified much grass-roots support from locals. "The government was perhaps more honest and beneficient [sic] than any they had before experienced," one US Army study ventured; "at least they were made to feel that way." Party membership had swollen to one million. Mao now controlled an army of 900,000 soldiers, augmented by a similar number of militia and guer-rilla fighters. Communist propaganda perpetuated the notion that Mao's troops were fighting stubbornly and effectively against the

Japanese. In reality, they were doing little besides observing mutual back-scratching truces with the Japanese, though communist military formations, by their very existence, did function as an impediment to Japanese influence and expansion in northern China. Instead of fighting, Mao focused on enhancing the political position of his movement and preserving his military strength to fight Chiang and the Nationalists. Both leaders saw the other as the main adversary, far more dangerous than the Japanese and Wang's so-called puppets; both knew they must one day either destroy or neutralize the other in order to establish real control over China.

Chiang once opined that the Japanese were like a skin disease, the communists like heart disease. Colloquially known as "The Generalissimo" in acknowledgment of his days as the army's commander in chief, he remained the face of legitimate public government in China, a flawed but respectable, patriotic figure who had managed to preserve the notion of an independent, modern China through nearly a decade of war. He nominally controlled southern and western China. But his armies were hollow. His government was still plagued by corruption and sapped by the disloyalty of all too many local officials who pursued their own personal agendas, often to the point of defying Chiang's orders or observing backhanded cease-fire arrangements with the Japanese. The hated foreigners remained in control of Manchuria, the entire coastline, major cities such as Canton and Shanghai, and much of the Chinese heartland. Their ongoing Ichi-Go offensive now menaced the eastern frontiers of Nationalist-controlled China, placing the key transit point town of Kweilin in danger, as well as perhaps even the Generalissimo's capital city of Chungking, 480 miles to the north, and the western Chinese city of Kunming, a vital supply hub and the location of air bases for American Major General Claire Chennault's Fourteenth Air Force. Newly established B-29 bases at Chengtu, located some 240 miles northwest of Chungking, were probably well beyond the reach of the invaders, but these fields would inevitably become compromised logistically if the Japanese succeeded in taking any of the other objectives.

Wedemeyer received a multipoint directive from the Joint Chiefs stipulating that his "primary mission with respect to Chinese Forces is to advise and assist the Generalissimo in the conduct of military operations against the Japanese." He would command all American military forces in the country and serve as Chiang's chief of staff, just as Stilwell had done before him. Unlike Stilwell, though, Wedemeyer's authority did not extend beyond China. Instead, the Chiefs, at Roosevelt's behest, split the theater up, placing all American military forces in India and Burma under Lieutenant General Dan Sultan, an efficient logistician and engineer who had once served as Stilwell's deputy. The split-theater arrangement inevitably enhanced Mountbatten's influence, since he no longer had to contend with an American commander affiliated with Chiang, but it also allowed Wedemeyer to focus his efforts on China—the only country in the region of any real long-term strategic importance to the Americans—at a time when the campaign in Burma neared its final stage. No doubt with an eye on the looming death struggle for power between Chiang and Mao, the Chiefs cautioned Wedemeyer not to let his troops become embroiled in Chinese domestic strife "except insofar as necessary to protect United States lives and property."[3]

Wedemeyer believed that the key to accomplishing his mission hinged on establishing a good relationship with Chiang, an objective that Stilwell had so famously and glaringly failed to achieve. Though Wedemeyer lacked Stilwell's Chinese linguistic skills, he understood many nuances of Chinese culture, especially the notion of saving face. He had served in China with the 15th Infantry Regiment in the early 1930s and of course learned much during his year on Mountbatten's staff. He had already met Chiang on several occasions, so he simply built upon the existing relationship. Constitutionally even tempered, the tactful Wedemeyer spoke nary a sharp word to the Generalissimo. He unfailingly treated Chiang with courtesy and respect, and the Chinese leader responded in kind. The two men got on well. They met nearly every day, often to discuss the long, thoughtful daily memos that Wedemeyer composed for Chiang. Wedemeyer favored a solicitous but not quite deferential persona. Even when he and Chiang disagreed, Wedemeyer always made sure to keep the conversation cordial. A few weeks after taking command, he wrote proudly to General Marshall, "My approach to the Generalissimo has been friendly, direct and firm. I believe that he likes and respects me now. I have been uniformly careful to massage his ego and to place myself in an advisory position so that he will not lose face or feel that I am trying to coerce him in action not in consonance with sound military plans."

Wedemeyer's private view of Chiang differed little from his public face. Unlike Stilwell, he refrained from making any derogatory remarks to his staff about Chiang and seldom, if ever, criticized him in private conversations with fellow Americans. He was stunned at the attitude of Clarence Gauss, the American ambassador and a career Foreign Service officer who had spent decades in China. Cynical and jaded after witnessing so many years of tragedy and byzantine political machinations, Gauss had lost all faith in Chiang and his government. "We should pull up the plug and let the whole Chinese Government go down the drain," he told an astounded Wedemeyer. When Gauss stepped down in November, Wedemeyer found a more hopeful partner in his successor, Patrick Hurley, the eccentric Oklahoma Republican whom Roosevelt had sent to China during the summer as a special envoy. The two men generally got along well, in part because Ambassador Hurley shared Wedemeyer's favorable view of Chiang. "He was the only top flight leader in Asia who was anti-Communist," Hurley once wrote of the Generalissimo, "who was in favor of a government of the people, by the people, and for the people." Wedemeyer evaluated Chiang as "a dedicated leader who was determined to preserve the freedom of the Chinese people. He was subjected to many pressures . . . and could not devote all of his time and energy to the conduct of the war although I am certain he recognized the importance of concentrating on sound strategic decisions." Years later, though, Wedemeyer did acknowledge Chiang's limitations in one interview. "I don't think he was what we call a thoroughly capable general in modern warfare. He knew very little about modern weapons, was not a skillful military man, certainly not a strategist."

Wedemeyer sympathetically recognized that Chiang was surrounded by a poisonous coterie of scheming family members, political advisers, and generals who usurped his power and often served as a negative influence. In viewing Chiang as an unrepentant advocate of freedom, though, the American seemed not to grasp the repressive nature of the Nationalist government, at least in the eyes of many Chinese who resented the regime's confiscatory taxation, its heavy-handed conscription, its wasteful neglect of public health, its inflationary currency, and the tyrannical police state run by the odious but fanatically loyal Lieutenant General Dai Li, Chiang's right-hand man and intelligence chief. Or perhaps Wedemeyer understood all this well, but diplomatically decided that he must overlook the regime's flaws in pursuit of a greater good. Regardless, he implemented changes meant to bring the Chinese and the Americans closer together. When he learned of the existence of regular joint Chinese-American meetings every Thursday— gatherings that Stilwell had initially attended and then eschewed as a waste of time—he resolved to attend regularly along with key members of his staff. Wedemeyer's personal attention soon resulted in the establishment of a joint planning staff that met frequently. At times the Generalissimo himself even went to these meetings. In deference to Chinese sensibilities and to prevent host country commanders from losing face, Wedemeyer also implemented a new system of high-level adjudication to resolve the frequent disagreements that arose between Chinese generals and their American military advisers. A set of instructions he issued directly to the liaison officers ordered them to "create a friendly, cooperative spirit through tactfulness and perseverance."[4]

Without question the new commander's commitment to courteous, open-minded cooperation, and his genial relationship with Chiang, defused some of the tension that had accumulated, like clogged arteries, during the Stilwell years. But Wedemeyer, with his bird's-eye approach to military life, tended erroneously to equate this with success. "[He] is the kind of man who sees only the great picture, strategy on a global scale," one of his public affairs officers analyzed confidentially, "but he seems utterly incapable of adjusting his grandiose ideas to practicable conditions and facts. This situation is probably the result of being a 'book soldier' with little practical experience." As General Wedemeyer soon discovered, a nicer work environment could not paper over ugly ground-level realities. An in-depth assessment he sent to General Marshall nearly mirrored many of Stilwell's reports. "They are not organized, equipped, and trained for modern war," Wedemeyer wrote of the Nationalist government. "Psychologically they are not prepared to cope with the situation because of political intrigue, false pride, and mistrust of leaders' honesty and motives. Frankly, I think that the Chinese officials surrounding the Generalissimo are actually afraid to report accurately conditions for two reasons, their stupidity and inefficiency are revealed, and further the Generalissimo might order them to take positive action and they are incompetent to issue directives, make plans, and fail completely in obtaining execution by field commanders."

Chiang's underfed, overmatched armies reeled under the weight of a new phase of the Ichi-Go offensive launched by the Japanese in response to China-based B-29 raids against southern Japan. The Japanese took Kweilin on November 10. "The Chinese are not fighting," a dejected Wedemeyer confided to his friend Hull in one gloomy missive. "It is indeed disconcerting to take over under [these] . . . depressing circumstances." For several weeks thereafter, it seemed that the enemy might actually capture Kunming and Chungking, a nightmare scenario that would have compromised the American position in China and might well have destroyed the Nationalist government. "It was highly discouraging when even the highly touted divisions which at great effort we have moved by air or motor transport to the Kweilin-Liuchow area also fell back," Wedemeyer later wrote.

He found himself in crisis mode, wondering if the military situation was so dire that the Allies might have to choose between hanging on to Chungking or Kunming. To Army Air Forces Major General Larry Kuter, an old friend, he confided his deep concerns in colorful terms. "I feel that the War Department has made me Captain of a Chinese junk whose hull is full of holes, in stormy weather, and on an uncharted course. If I leave the navigator's room to caulk up the holes, the junk will end up on the reef and if I remain in the navigator's seat, the junk will sink." With admirable resolve, Chiang vowed to stay in Chungking and, if necessary, die there. Wedemeyer made it clear to the Generalissimo that he had no such intentions. Secretly, he and his staff prepared evacuation plans to Chengtu and Kunming, the latter of which he viewed as an irreplaceable supply node whose military value far exceeded the threadbare Nationalist capital.

During the spring and early summer of 1944, at the dawn of Ichi-Go, Chiang had understandably chafed at the notion of having his best troops fighting in northern Burma while the Japanese threatened to overrun his country. Once again in the late fall he pushed for their return to defend Chinese soil. A supplicating Wedemeyer managed to persuade his old boss Mountbatten to agree to airlift two divisions, the 14th and the 22nd, back to China throughout December. American transport planes managed to move 25,105 soldiers and 1,596 horses and mules, plus weapons and equipment, into western China. Fortunately, the crisis passed, more due to Japanese limitations than the intervention of these divisions. Had the Allies understood more about enemy intentions, they might not have even gone to the trouble of airlifting these troops home. As always seemed to be the case in China, the Japanese could take territory, inflict tactical defeats on Nationalist forces, and unleash untold horrors upon the population. But they seldom possessed the manpower and logistical heft to establish real control over large swaths of territory, especially the farther inland they advanced from their coastal bases. Plus, relentless attacks from Chennault's aviators limited their mobility. Japanese objectives during this last phase of Ichi-Go were confined to compromising the security of American strategic air bases, particularly in Kweilin, and establishing land links to their occupation forces in northern Vietnam, goals they largely achieved. They had no intention, nor really the capability, of pushing for Kunming and Chungking, both of which remained firmly under Allied control.[5]

Japanese limitations in China hinted at larger problems. Under serious pressure now from the advance of the MacArthur-Nimitz dual onslaught as well as the beginnings of an American strategic bombing campaign against the home islands and an economic decline that resulted from the loss of access to resource-rich Pacific conquests, strategists at Imperial General Headquarters in Tokyo were forced into retrenchment mode. With the decimation of the Imperial Navy and the Allies nearing Japan's doorstep, Tokyo could hardly afford to invest any more assets in Burma. As recently as the spring of 1944, when the Japanese besieged the Imphal-Kohima area on India's eastern frontier, the campaign in Burma had offered the tantalizing possibility of demolishing the British Empire in Asia and permanently severing China's line of communication with the outside world. By late fall, though, the pixie dust had turned to ashes, with shattered Japanese divisions turned back from India by the British Fourteenth Army, prompting a full retreat into central and southern Burma, and Stilwell's capture of Myitkyina in the northern part of the country. Imperial General Headquarters now wanted nothing more from the Burma Area Army than to delay the Allied advance as long as possible.

Lieutenant General Sultan had inherited Northern Combat Area Command from Stilwell. After sending the Chinese 15th and 22nd Divisions to Wedemeyer to deal with the Ichi-Go crisis, he still had three Chinese divisions, the British 36th Division and the American 5332nd Brigade or Mars Task Force, the only American ground combat troops in Asia. Most of the Chinese formations had been trained and equipped by the Americans at Ramgarh in India. The 36th was a colonial unit of combined British and Indian manpower. Mars Task Force consisted of three major components: the 475th Infantry Regiment; the newly arrived 124th Cavalry Regiment, a dismounted infantry unit in the mold of the 1st Cavalry Division; and the highly trained 1st Chinese Infantry Regiment (Separate), plus supporting artillery and medics. One of the 475th's battalions was composed of survivors from the traumatic 1944 Myitkyina campaign when Allied troops, including a regimental-size American light infantry force known as "Merrill's Marauders," had laboriously dislodged the Japanese from northern Burma. Sultan's strategic objective now was to fulfill the long-held Allied goal of establishing road access from Ledo in India all the way to China. From mid-October to late January, his formations steadily pressed southeast through heavy jungle, hills, and grasslands against stubborn but poorly organized and supplied Japanese defenders. Similar to Merrill's Marauders, the Mars Task Force soldiers made extensive use of mules, moved in long columns screened by reconnaissance units, and drew much of their resupply by air. On average, friendly planes dropped 91.31 tons of supplies to the task force per day. Kachin guerrillas of Colonel William Peers's OSS Detachment 101 continued to act as guides for friendly troops and, operating in small, mobile light infantry formations, savaged Japanese rear areas. As many as 10,000 of them participated in the campaign, paralyzing Japanese communications and mobility.

Meanwhile, the Americans of Mars Task Force, in concert with their Chinese and British allies, battled nature and the Japanese in nearly equal parts, crossing rivers and mountains, fighting numerous sharp engagements. "I couldn't speak," Tech 5 Walter Pippin, a radioman, wrote to his parents of the terror he experienced in one typical firefight. "My vocal chords [*sic*] seemed to have jelled. It was as though my legs had been severed at the knee. Floating about in the mild . . . lethargy, I saw, but did not perceive, heard but did not hear. Screaming shells, screaming men, screaming souls. Even the wounded, choking on their own blood, and becoming ill at the sight of their own shuddering mass of torn flesh and muscle could know no relief except the soul-stealing effect of morphine administered in the hopes that they might forget the pain." Over weeks of movement and fighting, the stresses of protracted privation and action accumulated like debts to the psyche. The camaraderie forged during their difficult training intensified into an almost mystical bond among the troops. "What guts these kids have," Lieutenant Robert Jones, a young platoon leader, marveled of his men in a remarkably searing, honest letter to his mother. "Most of them are young and their ability to do their job, no matter what the cost, is amazing! People in the states don't realize what it is to see men die beside you, to be filthy, and live in a hole for days, your nerves on edge, no food cause your guts get tied in knots. Being an officer you must not show your feelings, must bolster the men when they falter, kid them when they are about to give up. You get to know each man like a son. You read his letters, you get him chow, fight to get him a rating, chew him out for not taking atabine [*sic*] or not using DDT to prevent typhus. You love, you work, and then sometimes you hate it. It takes your all. What do you get in Return? You get a SATISFACTION OF THE SOUL that you can't get anywhere else in the world. You get heartbreak when one of them is killed. New men and officers come in and fill the ranks. The awful grist of war goes on. You wonder why they had to die. You're talking, laughing, swearing, fighting, digging TOGETHER, and then all at once, they lie a still quiet form."

By late January, the Allied formations had crossed the border into China and even, on January 20, linked up at Wanting with Nationalist troops pushing toward them from the east, uniting two major Allied fronts, effectively dooming the Japanese in northern Burma. The Mars Task Force transferred to the rear on February 10. In some five weeks of action, the unit lost 115 killed, 938 wounded, and 1 missing. Another 929 men were evacuated, often by air, due to disease, combat fatigue, or injuries. The British Fourteenth Army and its brilliant commander, General William Slim, did most of the heavy lifting for the Allies in Burma that spring, crossing the Irrawaddy River—Burma's equivalent to the Mississippi—on March 3, seizing the major hub of Mandalay in late March and the checkmate objective of Rangoon on May 2, before the onset of monsoon rains. Slim's victories destroyed the bulk of Japanese combat power in Burma and severely weakened the enemy's ability to resist in the northern part of the country. Small-unit fighting did rage throughout February and part of March along the border of northern Burma and western China, but the remaining Japanese formations were shattered, isolated, or retreating.[6]

The road link could now become a reality. Engineers, about half of whom were African American, had busily extended the road 116 miles beyond Myitkyina to Bhamo in the wake of the advancing frontline troops. The construction crews worked through "jungles so thick daylight never penetrates, rains so heavy earth dissolves into a sea of mud, climate so hot it saps all vitality," one awestruck war correspondent wrote. In highland areas, they removed, on average, 100,000 cubic yards of earth per mile of highway built; in the lowlands the average per mile was 25,000 cubic yards. Truckers were already using the completed highway to haul some 550 tons of supplies forward per day. In China, from Kunming westward to the Burmese border, a detachment of 500 American engineers under Lieutenant Colonel Robert Seedlock worked alongside 12,000 Chinese laborers to prepare the confusingly named Burma Road. Supplied by mule trains and airdrops, they succeeded in converting almost one hundred miles of jungle wilderness and peaks as high as 8,500 feet into a winding but usable one-lane road. A January 9 report on the status of both road projects predicted, "No major delaying factors are foreseen. A direct link with the Burma Road will be completed pronto."

By the end of the month, this had become a reality. Brigadier General Lewis Pick, the seasoned engineer commander who had masterminded most of the road construction from Ledo to Myitkyina and beyond, assembled, amid great fanfare, a Chinese and American convoy of 113 jeeps, trucks, and trailers loaded with artillery ammunition and other supplies for the first trip into China. Lieutenant General Sultan showed up in khakis, shook hands with Pick, and formally ordered the convoy to proceed. The roster of participants included sixty-five war correspondents, ten African American truck drivers, and of course Pick himself in the lead jeep. Unimpressed with the majesty of the moment, jeep driver PFC Oscar Green complained to Sergeant Dave Richardson, "To me this is just another dirty detail. Damned if I don't always catch 'em." Escorted by a pair of military policemen on motorcycles, the column left Ledo on January 12 for the beginning of a long odyssey over the gravel and dirt road that many soldiers had dubbed "Pick's Pike." A banner stretched across the back of one truck proudly blared, "Pick's Pike, Lifeline from India to China." Chinese and American flags adorned the fronts of vehicles. "We passed American engineers, bulldozers and graders, Indian soldiers digging a drainage ditch, and Chinese engineers building a plank bridge," Richardson wrote of the journey.

As the miles unfolded, Pick could not resist studying the road with a professional eye. When he noticed that one unit had built a stretch of road on a ridge shelf rather than adjacent valley and asked a grader operator why, the man replied irreverently, "Don't ask me, General, I just work here." The convoy soldiers consumed K rations or ate more substantial meals with other Allied units along the highway. At night they slept in tents or on portable cots, or on the ground. Twice they were forced to halt until combat units could clear Japanese holdouts from border areas that intersected with the road. At newly captured Bhamo in eastern Burma, they topped off their fuel tanks at a burgeoning supply depot. It took the column sixteen days just to make it to the Chinese border. By this time, another mini convoy of two trucks and a wrecker under Lieutenant Hugh Pock had already made it from Myitkyina to Kunming.

Heedless of this upstaging, Pick's convoy pressed on and made it, on January 28, to Wanting, where T. V. Soong, Chiang's brother-in-law and the foreign minister, welcomed them with a brief speech. Once they were in China, a carnival atmosphere prevailed. At Baoshan, a Chinese Army band played welcoming tunes while children waved banners and shot off fireworks. A raucous party that night at a local Confucian temple featured windy speeches, a belly-stuffing meal, and acrobats who performed feats of agility that seemed to defy gravity. The Americans attempted to manipulate chopsticks and, along with their hosts, guzzled tremendous quantities of rice wine that, according to one soldier, "tastes like wood alcohol and is called jing bao or air raid juice by GIs stationed in China."

At last on February 4, after twenty-four days and 1,079 road miles, they arrived in Kunming, where raucous overflow crowds lined the streets, and Yun Lung, the provincial governor, warmly welcomed them. "The Chinese put on a real demonstration," Pick wrote a friend a couple of weeks later. "There was speech making, flag waving, pop-cracker [firecracker] shooting, and everything in true Chinese style." Deton Brooks, a correspondent for *The Chicago Defender,* marveled at the colorful scene in which excited, adoring crowds greeted "the dust-covered, road-weary soldiers as they wheeled their way into the city." That evening, Lung staged a sumptuous banquet for the newly arrived Americans, with Pick as the guest of honor. Once again, they ate and drank in style. "Entertainment consisted of two short Chinese operas and a concert by Lily Pons, American opera star, whose husband, Andre Kostelanetz, directed a soldier orchestra in accompaniment," the theater historian recorded of the convivial party.[7]

The initial excitement over the reestablishment of the road link between India and China—its very existence, by any measure, a remarkable achievement of resolve and engineering—soon gave way to the realities of utilizing it and maintaining such an elaborate creation. The theater historian calculated that to build the road, engineers had to move 22,235,000 cubic yards of earth, enough soil to build a continuous six-foot-high wall from New York to San Francisco. The job had absorbed 6,618,000 man-days for US Army engineers, another 735,000 for Chinese engineers, and 7,800,000 for hired Indian and Burmese laborers. The line of communication infrastructure of 60,000 telephone poles, 95,000 electrical crossarms, 1,000,000 insulators, and 25,000 miles of wire bordered on staggering. A specially designed 6-inch pipeline also paralleled the road and became operational in April, pumping, over a five-month period, 9,220,452 gallons of aviation and motor fuel into Chinese receiving stations. Much of the fuel went to the Army Air Forces rather than Chiang's poorly automated armies. In Fourteenth Air Force alone, the average heavy bomber consumed 13,200 gallons per month, and the average medium bomber 9,000 gallons. A sobered, nearly overwhelmed Pick wrote to a friend confidentially, "Trying to operate the road one's head is filled with sharp, excruciating pains from morning till night. I sometimes think it would be better to give it back to the aborigines." Even the name was confusing; the terms Ledo Road, Burma Road, and Pick's Pike all proliferated freely. Fortunately, Chiang resolved the name issue by graciously suggesting the moniker Stilwell Road to refer to the entire Ledo-to-Kunming route, a nickname that eventually stuck.

A force of 12,000 engineers worked full-time to repair bridges, clean up rock slides, and resurface innumerable hard-pressed stretches of tortured roadway torn apart by the incessant galloping of heavy vehicles. The Burma sections alone included over 700 bridges, of which the most elaborate crossed the mighty Irrawaddy with six floating spans stretching for 1,600 feet from bank to bank. In hopes of avoiding delays to the convoys that now routinely rolled along the highway, maintenance crews worked to exhaustion. "Day and night their 'dozers' chug, moving restlessly, inching back the jungle so it cannot strangle this supply line," an amazed war correspondent reported to his readers. "Cliffs have been sheared away to prevent landslides; hilltops moved to lower steep grades, new traces cut to straighten dangerous curves. The whole land contour has been transformed."

Like on a new thoroughfare in a growing city, traffic increased steadily. Between February and August, no fewer than 368 convoys with 21,807 vehicles and 6,081 trailers traversed the Stilwell Road, hauling 157,874 tons of cargo. Their movements were closely coordinated and serviced by a growing support infrastructure. Nine way stations provided maintenance, fuel, and bathing facilities for the crewmen. Ordnance and repair teams offered servicing at twenty-two different spots. Refrigeration companies operated ice plants that preserved meat for consumption by the troops. Military policemen patrolled constantly in a vain attempt to eliminate black market theft by locals (and more than a few Americans) along the route. Similar to modern-day state troopers, the MPs tried to enforce a blanket 25-mile-per-hour speed limit. The average trip from Ledo to Kunming took between ten and fifteen days with a 10 percent loss of vehicles.

Each journey was enervating and stressful. "The drive was rather lonely," Corporal Walter Orey recalled. "Most of our vehicles had only one person in them. The convoy would begin rolling at 0600 each day, and except for short breaks we would drive until the sun went down." They ate K and C rations, slept beside their trucks, and often conducted their own maintenance. The combination of the road's crudeness and vehicles designed for utility rather than comfort made for a bone-crunching ride. "The rocky and rough roadbed jolts the truck and the passengers within like a churn," Sergeant Clifford Miller, a medic who often traveled the route, wrote to his sister. Bad weather, rough terrain, and difficult road conditions challenged the nerves of even the most experienced drivers. "Only those who have actually driven . . . have a true picture of the many precarious sections where the road clings to the mountain side and sheer drops of hundreds of feet beckon the unfortu-nate driver forced too near the edge of that ledge called a road," one unit history testified. Sheer drops of ten thousand feet or more were not un-common. "Life could be pretty short if you were to go off a cliff," Private Robert Chisman wrote to his parents. Another nervous driver told a journalist, "I just can't get used to looking down from the road and see-ing all those airplanes flying around down below me."

Any moisture made it difficult to brake, prompting the typical driver, according to the same history, to skid "down steep grades and around sharp curves with a prayer on his lips and a lump in his stomach, creep-ing by treacherous landslides, dodging trucks by hair breadths." An-other soldier commented with wonderment on the many perils inherent in any of these thousand-mile journeys: "Being a convoy driver was dif-ficult and dangerous. In the dry, winter weather, the vehicles would kick up huge clouds of dust that obscured vision and covered the wind-shields. To see the truck ahead—which was essential to avoid collisions—a driver had two choices. He could tailgate the vehicle ahead, risking a collision if that truck slowed or stopped suddenly. Or he could lag far behind where the dust thinned out, greatly stretching the convoy. Sun-light reflecting off the dusty windshield prevented the driver from see-ing anything in the dark shadows ahead. In addition, the gravel road developed corduroy-like bumps with heavy travel. On curves, these had the same effect as ice—greatly reducing friction. At significant speeds this could cause a vehicle to spin and go over the side of the road. In the rainy season the roads got muddy, causing similar problems with spat-tered windshields and slick roads."

Sultan's headquarters documented 439 accidents, 199 of which were classified as major, between February and September. Incredibly, given the circumstances of young men routinely driving such a dangerous route in heavy, overburdened vehicles, only seven of the accidents led to fatalities. Five Americans were killed, 3 Chinese, and 2 Indians. Occasional attempts by overzealous, deskbound officers to prevent accidents and damage to vehicles by deducting the cost of repairs from the pay of drivers fizzled quickly as grossly unfair and irrational, an example of petty harassment in a theater where an Army survey revealed that nearly two-thirds of enlisted men and 41 percent of officers agreed with the statement "There is too much 'Chicken[shit]' to put up with for an overseas theater."

Mile markers and frequent road signs offered a pleasant, benign di-version from the monotony, blaring such safety-conscious pronuncia-tions as "Accidents Go Up When the Sun Goes Down, Take It Easy" and "Don't be a Sad Sac, Be Alert, Obey Traffic Rules, Speed Limit 25 M.P.H," and one from a hat-bedecked Uncle Sam figure urging men, "Be Smart, Be Careful." Long stretches of the route in China contained such sharp curves as to appear, from the vantage point of the air, like a coiled snake or winding river. "If you think some of those movie stars have curves, you should travel on the Burma Road," one driver quipped in a letter to a friend. Love-starved GIs painted safety-conscious signs portraying sexy, curvaceous women and placed them in known danger spots. One sprawled-out brunette, with dress uniform blouse pulled back from her bare chest and a military cap jauntily perched on her head, urged the truckers, "Drive slow. Curves on me may look swell but on Ledo Road they can be hell." Another partially naked roadside beauty with tanta-lizingly wide hips and a small waist smiled suggestively and admon-ished, "No you can't get that any more! Unless you drive carefully around these curves." At another spot, a sign specially geared to attract the attention of African American soldiers portrayed a curvy, impec-cably dressed black woman looking suggestively over her shoulder and advising her presumably transfixed observer, "Listen, cats, I ain't jivin', take it easy while you're drivin'."

Because the route from Myitkyina into China was only one lane, American drivers usually returned to India by air. The vehicles, and of course their cargo, stayed in-country. The weary drivers might have been dismayed to realize that all their noble efforts paled in comparison to the aerial resupply effort of the transport crews who continued to fly from bases in India to Kunming and other airfields in China. Before the opening of the road, they had provided the only option to get matériel to Chiang. As the northern Burma campaign progressed and the Allies gained almost total control of the air, their efforts were bolstered by the construction of new bases and the implementation of safer, more efficient flight routes than earlier in the war. The ground tonnage moved over the road in 1945 averaged 22,553 per month, a respectable total that proved the road offered some value, though perhaps not enough to justify its immense cost. Over nearly the same span of time, the aviators more than doubled those numbers at 46,226 tons a month, almost calling into question, at least from an actuarial point of view, the road's necessity, especially given the time, manpower, and resources necessary to keep it in operation. Prime Minister Churchill had always opposed operations in northern Burma as wasteful, though it is well to remember that he cared little for keeping China in the war, or fostering the rise of the country as a true world power. Still, given the disparity in tonnages moved by ground and air, his concerns about the inherently diminishing returns offered by the road seemed to have merit. Without a doubt, it became less relevant with every passing day in 1945 as Japan's power in China, and elsewhere, receded, and as the Allied airlift capability grew. Churchill later aptly described the effort to construct the road as an "immense laborious task, unlikely to be finished until the need for it had passed." Ironically, the road would have made more sense in 1943, when the Allies could not possibly have brought it to fruition, than in 1945, when they could and did. In that respect, the road invited comparison with Eichelberger's campaign to liberate the southern and central Philippines—brilliant in implementation, but with a dubious strategic return.[8]

The completion of the Stilwell Road inevitably grew the American presence in Asia and brought about more cultural discourse, especially in China. American wartime propaganda tended to portray all Allied countries as similar to the United States, and the China theater proved no different. The *Pocket Guide to China* issued to every US soldier asserted, "Of all the peoples of Asia, the Chinese are most like Americans. Those who know both peoples often remark at the likenesses. One of the reasons is that we both live in countries where there is plenty of space and a great variety of climate and food. We are alike, too, because we both love independence and individual freedom." The lofty rhetoric did not seem to apply to the inherently unequal relationship between the well-heeled Americans and the Chinese in a country rife with runaway inflation and poverty. The same guidebook, with a distinct tone of racial condescension that hearkened to the recent past of Open Door imperialism, advised GIs to make extensive use of Chinese servants. "A good 'boy' not only will see that you are fed and comfortable, your clothes clean and in order, your shoes shined and your rooms neat, but he will get many things done for you which you cannot do for yourself. More than that, he has his own way of getting information you may want."

The overall theme of all official pronouncements to the troops emphasized good discipline, politeness, and respect for local customs. Anything less might imperil what senior commanders assured their men was a vital mission. Another instructive pamphlet, titled *What You Should Know About China*, counseled the GIs with a tenor of grave sincerity, "You must realize that every minute of the day hundreds of eyes are watching and judging the U.S.—and what we claim it stands for—by watching and judging *you*." Few soldiers disagreed with this worthwhile point, and relations were generally correct. But even fewer could consistently live up to the lofty standard of functioning as daily grassroots diplomats among people and places that seemed alien and backward. A troubling survey revealed that 62 percent of soldiers professed little faith in the value of China's contribution to the Allied war effort. Another 53 percent expressed a low opinion of Chinese soldiers. All too many viewed their Chinese allies as corrupt and deceptive, if not outright barbaric. "The life of the individual soldier meant very little," one disapproving American contended.

Negative attitudes especially tended to permeate among medical personnel who witnessed the callous indifference with which the Chinese often treated wounded soldiers. "My opinion, based on observation, is that the Chinese are as sadistic and bestial as the Japanese," Major George Kuite, the executive officer of a medical battalion, fumed to an Army interviewer. "They enjoy their comrades' suffering and seem to derive a great deal of pleasure in seeing a soldier lying on the ground with his hand or arm blown off." More commonly, differing standards of hygiene, especially when Chinese patients were treated in American hospitals, colored the attitudes of Americans. To the revulsion of the Americans, Chinese troops carelessly threw half-eaten food to and fro, and stored garbage, and even live chickens, under their beds, attracting swarms of flies, which did not seem to bother them in the least. They attended evening movies "in various stages of undress," according to one American source. They eschewed bathing, spat anywhere, even indoors, and urinated immediately outside their wards rather than using latrines. "The majority are illiterate and have come from isolated farms and small villages where life has often been hard and for many a persistent struggle for existence," the unit history of the 48th Evacuation Hospital recounted with indulgent disapproval. "This poverty and ignorance has caused them to develop habits and attitudes which are often undesirable, but which one cannot expect them to abandon as soon as they enter an American Army Hospital."

The Americans had plenty of their own issues as well. Some of the worst corruption in theater stemmed from a highly organized GI smuggling ring whose members stole millions of dollars' worth of drugs and other supplies for sale through Chinese collaborators. "Many of these items found their way into occupied China and eventually into the hands of the Japanese," the theater historian claimed. The thievery became so rampant and troubling that General Wedemeyer eventually convened a major investigation by the Criminal Investigation Division and the Counterintelligence Corps to apprehend the perpetrators.

Similar to the Philippines, most of the trouble with locals centered around the insatiable GI quest for women. The Chinese deeply resented the American tendency to make use of their seemingly limitless wealth to coax women into liaisons. Chinese journalists took to calling any woman seen with an American a "jeep girl," with strong implications of prostitution. In some villages, angry crowds descended on mixed couples, hurling angry epithets and sometimes even stones as well. "This left no doubt about what the words might have meant," one Army report deadpanned. Hundreds gathered outside Chungking bars frequented by the Americans, intending to pounce on any woman they saw inside with them. The situation grew so tense that American military policemen were forced to hide the women in jeeps and other vehicles and drive them to safety. "Rocks and mud were thrown at Army vehicles in the area," the same report testified.

Disapproving civilians could not begin to put an end to the expansion of prostitution that eventuated from the arrival of more GIs over the Stilwell Road. In one typical instance, a dance hall in the front of a house provided a facade for a thriving sex business in the rear of the building. "Between the two was a pro [prophylactic] station," Captain Malcolm Bouton, a venereal disease control officer, later commented. "This establishment was winked at by the authorities, but I found out about it. We closed the place." In many villages along the Stilwell Road, amorous liaisons proliferated between American truckers and local women whom the Yanks dubbed "Rice Paddy Girls." An Army physician whose mission was to prevent the spread of venereal disease claimed in one report of the average local girl on the make, "By walking along the roads . . . she could easily be detected by a GI who was 'out for business.' Rice paddies were eventually placed 'Out of Bounds.'" Baoshan soon teemed with convoy crewmen who were eager to find a good time after numerous stressful days of driving. "This being the first adventure into China for thousands of men, celebration was in order," the same doctor wrote. "At times due to the competition or possibly jealousy between American and Chinese troops from Burma . . . there was fighting, gun play, and the town was off limits to Americans." Nonetheless, the Army operated a large prophylactic station in the heart of town that averaged between five and six thousand treatments per month. Wedemeyer's headquarters did not stipulate specific statistics on sexually transmitted diseases, but the medical professionals charged with prevention came to believe that the infection rates were at least twice as high as those in India, where most units reported a rate of thirty to forty cases per one thousand men.[9]

A troubling odor of racism also sparked some tension between the hosts and their visitors when Chiang issued an informal order prohibiting African American soldiers from entering China. Considering the culture shock that ensued from the infusion of whites into western China, the Generalissimo apparently felt that adding black men to the mix would prove to be especially upsetting for his people. Undocumented and enmeshed in a web of double-talk, as so much institutional racism tended to be in that era, the news of this policy spread more in the manner of rumor than order when Chinese authorities seemed to limit the number of African American drivers on the first convoy into their country. Sniffing injustice and controversy, war correspondents soon began asking difficult questions of surprised and unprepared American commanders, who found themselves in the uncomfortable position of being associated with a directive they neither created nor supported. Their wrongheaded, knee-jerk reaction was to deny the existence of any exclusionary policy even as black soldiers were diverted from driving on convoys that entered China. "James Crow lurks somewhere within the 'august' body," a suspicious Frank Bolden, an African American correspondent with *The Pittsburgh Courier*, wrote to a friend. "The pattern is familiar and works in the same manner."

He and his colleague Deton Brooks of *The Chicago Defender*, along with Harold Isaacs, a white correspondent, refused to let the matter drop, in part as a matter of principle, but also because nearly two-thirds of the GIs who had built the road were African American. In that context, their exclusion from China was especially egregious. Isaacs's persistence had already brought him into conflict with one public relations officer, Lieutenant Colonel George Hibbert, who scornfully wrote in one private memo of the reporter, "It is the opinion of this writer that Isaacs' interest in the Negro troop situation is a 'party line' which fits in with some of his personal political views and which crops out in almost all his writing. It is the further belief of the writer that his personal political background and beliefs do not fit him to be helpful to the current policies of US forces in China." During one contentious press conference with Major General Gilbert Cheves, the theater supply officer, and Brigadier General Pick, an uncompromising Isaacs said, "I want information about the colored boys and I want it straight." Cheves replied lamely, "I like colored troops and they like me." Then, incredibly, he launched into a defense of segregation. "The best way to have colored

and white men get along is to give each group its own recreational facilities. If they get to mixing in bars and cafes disciplinary trouble de-
velops." Pick hailed from segregated Virginia and had received his
engineering degree from Virginia Tech. His origins belied a man who
disliked segregation and felt a strong loyalty toward the hardworking
black engineers who had built the road, in the face of privation and difficult conditions. In a private conversation with another reporter, he
fumed, "These correspondents think that because I'm a southerner, I'm
against having Negro drivers [in China]. They're wrong! I want those
drivers. But Generalissimo Chiang Kai-shek has made it clear he does
not want them coming into China." Pick later told Brooks, the reporter
from *The Chicago Defender*, that he thought every engineer, white or
Black, had earned the right to spend time in China. "In this way they
will see what they have accomplished."

Chiang soon came under steady pressure to change his mind, from
Pick and other commanders, including Wedemeyer, who disliked any
negative public relations implications and felt he needed African
American troops to support his future plans in China. Wedemeyer and
others focused on practical rather than moral arguments. "These colored troops would primarily be operating away from the larger cities of
China and slight opportunity for friction should arise," Major General
Robert McClure, Wedemeyer's chief of staff, wrote to the Generalissimo
on behalf of his boss. Chiang relented and agreed to accept Black soldiers into his country, but only as far as Kunming. Even then, only one
African American aviation engineer battalion deployed permanently
into China while three engineer regiments, four engineer battalions, a
pair of dump truck companies, and other Black units remained in
Burma to maintain the road. As late as August, Wedemeyer secretly
wrote to MacArthur hoping to trade a Black port company for a white
one to use once he captured a Chinese harbor, because he anticipated
that Chiang would not budge from his decision to forbid the presence of
Black soldiers east of Kunming. "It is realized that this request for
change comes at a difficult time for you," Wedemeyer admitted to Mac-
Arthur. "It is only made because of the very firm policy established by
Generalissimo and our tight situation with regard to qualified personnel."

The fiasco over Chiang's ill-conceived directive proved ironic for a theater that had relatively little racial discrimination and tension, at least by the mortifying standards of the time. Merrill's Marauders and Mars Task Force combat soldiers forged a tight bond with African American troops who supported them in Burma. One group of white soldiers felt so strongly about racial discrimination back home that they wrote an impassioned letter to *Yank*, the soldier's magazine. "There are many Negro outfits working with us. They are doing more than their part to win this war. We are proud of the colored men here." They concluded their letter with a furious denunciation of Jim Crow laws that allowed German prisoners to eat at whites-only restaurants while Black soldiers were turned away. "If this sort of thing continues, we the white soldiers will begin to wonder: what are *we* fighting for?"

Throughout India and Burma, most—though not quite all—military bases, Red Cross clubs, soldiers' clubs, entertainment venues, rest camps, and sports facilities were integrated. "The so-called color problem is practically non-existent here," a pair of physicians in the 14th Evacuation Hospital proudly asserted in one official report. "The colored and white patients share the same ward and often occupy adjoining beds. One of the favorite topics for discussion is the race situation; under careful leadership, usually the Chaplain. Since many of our patients are negroes, we often select one of them to lead the discussion." The Army's provost marshal in India created an all-Black MP platoon, disseminating authority that had almost always remained solely in the hands of whites and had generated much tension and considerable injustice. "In numerous cases colored soldiers when brought under police supervision felt that they were being unjustly treated because of their color," wrote Brooks, the correspondent. "This same charge would have no validity when Negro MPs are used, headquarters feels." These changes did not prevent one investigator from blaming most of the Army's crimes in Burma on Black soldiers. "The Negro problem . . . is extremely serious. CID [Criminal Investigative Division] reported that many units have individual stills operated by the men, utilizing stolen sugar, canned fruit, etc. and that the smoking of Gangi or Marihuana has caused a great deal of trouble. Crimes of violence in this area are very numerous and in many cases are motivated by the Negro soldiers' desire for normal or abnormal sexual gratification." As evidence, the investigator cited eight incidents of assault, rape, thefts, and shootings over a ten-month period. In actuality, though, such criminal events were unusual. Court-martial rates for 1945 hovered just below 4 per 1,000 men.

With white-dominated imperialism in Asia and elsewhere simmering as a major point of tension and anti-imperialist, anti–white nationalistic sentiments growing, especially in India, locals naturally took notice of any relaxed racial mores among the Americans. When one group of Indians observed Black and white soldiers eating together, one of them sagely remarked, "That's the best war propaganda in favor of the United Nations that has ever been put out there." A wealthy white couple in Calcutta hosted regular Wednesday afternoon tea parties at which officers and enlisted, white and Black, Indians and British, all socialized together convivially. A lively sports scene featured highly competitive, integrated tournaments in golf, tennis, baseball, basketball, swimming, Ping-Pong, boxing, and track. Over a four-day period in mid-April, 90,000 spectators packed into the Royal Calcutta Turf Club to watch a series of boxing matches. One study revealed that, on average in any typical unit, 45 percent of men participated in at least one sport. Sixteen USO troupes toured India, Burma, and China, playing to audiences that ranged, according to one theater report, "from 20-bed patients in hospital wards to thousands of enthusiastic soldiers in GI-built theaters." By June 1945, 90 percent of American soldiers in Asia could tune in to Armed Forces Radio Network. Prominent entertainers such as Paulette Goddard, Ann Sheridan, Pat O'Brien, and Joe E. Brown performed live before integrated audiences, even in remote areas along the road. "Working and living are hard but we never heard a gripe," an admiring O'Brien later commented. "All we ever heard was 'thanks' and questions about what it was like back home and what it would be like when they got back." One official report claimed that "there was a marked absence of those incidents normally associated with interracial conflicts." The Army operated four eccentrically named universities that offered integrated courses: Foxhole University in Ledo, North Assam

Arts and Business Institute in Chabua, Pentagon University in Myitky-ina, and Basha University in Tezgaon. By the summer of 1945, over 13,000 students were enrolled in classes.

Like mold growing in an otherwise tidy room, some racial discrim-ination occasionally persisted. Black GIs on liberty in Calcutta were initially shunted into a threadbare rest camp in one of the city's rough-est neighborhoods. Conditions were so demoralizing that many men simply left and went instead to a nearby Red Cross club until Army authorities arranged for a new and cleaner rest area. The segregation of a Red Cross swimming pool prompted Black GIs to stage a boycott. The Continental Club, one of the leading gathering places for British and American enlisted men in Calcutta, refused to admit Black soldiers. "The British make it perfectly clear that they are barred by express order of the American provost marshal in the Calcutta area," a disgusted Deton Brooks informed readers of *The Chicago Defender*. Fortunately, these incidents of segregation proved to be outliers amid a reasonably fair racial environment.[10]

Newly promoted to lieutenant general, Wedemeyer focused mean-while on reforming the Chinese Army, just as Stilwell had before him. "Sometimes I feel like I am living in a world of fantasy, a never never land, but we are going to continue our efforts . . . despite discouraging experiences along the way," Wedemeyer confided in a private letter to Hull. Ichi-Go's limited success had revealed, once again, the persistent problems of inefficiency, corruption, poor leadership, and low morale that had plagued the Nationalist forces for many years. For all of Wede-meyer's famous tact, he laid out the army's many deficiencies for Chiang in frank terms, especially in relation to the paucity of food for the sol-diers and the tyrannical nature of the draft system in which men were forcibly taken into custody, sometimes bound and tied like prisoners. "Conscription comes to the Chinese peasant like famine or flood, only more regularly—every year twice—and claims its victims," he wrote to Chiang in a detailed memo urging immediate reform. "Famine, flood and drought compare with conscription like chicken-pox with plague." While poor and illiterate people were brutally forced into service, the educated and the wealthy could evade the draft by hiring a substitute or paying an official. "One can readily see that it was the poor, weak, and those with insufficient money who were forced to defend their more fortunate countrymen against the Japanese invader," one of Wedemeyer's staff reports bemoaned.

He asserted that the abysmally poor treatment of drafted soldiers, many of whom starved to death or were casually abandoned when they got wounded, amounted to a death sentence. Scarce supplies of food, weapons, ammunition, and other resources were spread too thin among hundreds of hollow divisions whose officers were incentivized to keep them that way in order to skim money and food owed to phantom soldiers who existed only on paper. "As soldiers are primarily a source of income for officials and a source of political power and influence for generals, which general will allow himself to be robbed of his army?" he asked Chiang rhetorically, before adding provocatively, "Armies are instruments to win wars. Does the Chinese Government not want to win the war?" Wedemeyer told the Generalissimo that the time had come to cut the size of the army in half and redistribute resources more efficiently. To improve the treatment, care, training, and effectiveness of the average soldier, and thus the army as a whole, he urged sweeping reforms and reorganization.

He proposed the creation of a new fighting force, known as Alpha, comprising between thirty-six and thirty-nine divisions of 10,000 soldiers apiece, plus supporting troops. They were to be entirely trained, equipped, armed, and advised by the Americans. The plan bore an almost uncanny resemblance to one that Stilwell had proposed, in vain, to the Generalissimo a year and a half earlier. The only major difference was that Stilwell envisioned a sixty-division force. Thanks to the Ichi-Go scare, and perhaps owing to Wedemeyer's more nimble diplomacy, Chiang agreed this time. The core of Wedemeyer's strategy centered around launching an offensive with the Alpha Force in the latter half of 1945 designed to advance to the coast to reclaim the port cities of Hong Kong and Canton. This would achieve the dual objective of opening up another supply route for China and providing staging bases for the invasion of Japan. He spent most of his 1945 time and energy preparing to fulfill this objective.

Chiang's newfound tractability might well have owed just as much to his looming showdown with the communists as to any other factor.

The Generalissimo continued to walk a perilous tightrope. The difficulties of holding together his own government, dependent as it partially was on alliances with corrupt, exploitive local leaders, while also pursuing reforms that inevitably diminished their power, would have challenged the acumen of even the most skilled political practitioner. Nor could Chiang afford to alienate the Americans on whom he depended for crucial Lend-Lease economic and military aid, not to mention the international prestige he received from their political support. For nearly four years, they had helped him stave off the Japanese; in turn, he had played a crucial role for the Americans by absorbing, at terrible human cost, substantial Japanese manpower and resources.

As the power of the enemy now receded and serious conflict with the communists bubbled, he could not afford any deterioration in relations with the Americans, though they continued to prod him to consummate some sort of power-sharing agreement with Mao. "American diplomacy really has no center, no policy, no morals," he complained to his diary. He understood that both he and Mao had to be seen by the Americans, the Chinese people themselves, and internationally as open to negotiation, regardless of whether their intentions were serious or not. "The Communists are [Chiang's] principle [sic] foe," one American diplomat wrote in an analytical memo, "for in the long run it is they and not the Japanese who challenge his supremacy in China. They are the next in the line of succession. The Generalissimo realizes that if he accedes to the Communist terms for a coalition government, they will sooner or later dispossess him and his Kuomaintang [sic] of power." Nonetheless, in an attempt to broker a settlement and establish a coalition government without undercutting Chiang's ultimate authority, Patrick Hurley, the American ambassador, engaged in feverish trilateral negotiations that, through numerous ups and downs, ultimately achieved nothing. "At the heart of the problem was a stubborn fact that the Americans could not or would not see," Rana Mitter, a leading historian of China in World War II, aptly wrote. "Neither Chinese side was sincere about a coalition government for its own sake. Both Chiang and Mao saw it as a temporary arrangement while their parties prepared to vie for absolute power."

Indeed, the same issues persisted in 1945 as in the year before. Mao had no intention of submitting his troops to Nationalist authority, and Chiang knew that recognizing the political legitimacy of the communists could prove mortal to his own government. Mao and his Chinese Communist Party (CCP) envisioned no real endgame that did not include the triumph of their revolution, inevitably at Chiang's expense. "Chinese revolution is an integral part of world revolution against imperialism, feudalism, and capitalism," Mao bluntly affirmed in a prescient conversation with Wedemeyer. "We are definitely committed to the struggle for political and economic revolution in China so that the people will have a new system of politics, economy, and culture." His charismatic, English-speaking colleague Chou En-lai, the Western-friendly face of the CCP, added to Mao's uncompromising points with a quote from Vladimir Lenin. "The proletariat must continue the struggle against capitalism until it is destroyed." In this context, Chiang well understood, perhaps better than did his allies, that any attempt to share power with such zealots was like trying to divvy up freshly killed meat with a hungry lion—by its nature it tended toward a zero-sum game. Wedemeyer could make all the plans he wanted to hasten the demise of the Japanese in China. But, with each passing day, this mattered less compared to the burgeoning brawl that loomed between the Nationalists and the CCP, a conflict of world historical importance. In truth, neither Wedemeyer nor Hurley nor any other American truly had the power to prevent this civil war, one that ironically grew likelier and nearer as the war's end finally came into view.[11]

4

Doorstep

For two years, the Japanese had stepped ever backward, losing buffer after buffer in the Pacific from Guadalcanal to Saipan and beyond. They were now trapped in their own real-world version of the domino theory that would so preoccupy later generations of American strategists. The ferociousness of their resistance, a potent and yet perishable asset, now endured as their only remaining lifeline. Nowhere was this more apparent than at Iwo Jima, where a committed garrison of 21,000 men bled three US Marine divisions terribly from mid-February to late March for possession of a hunk of volcanic rock measuring only 2.5 miles wide and 5.5 miles long. The Marines killed nearly every defender and captured valuable airfields to assist the ongoing bombing campaign of the Japanese home islands, but at terrible cost. The Corps lost 5,931 dead, 17,262 wounded, and another 2,648 to combat fatigue. The Navy also paid dearly. A total of 881 sailors died and another 1,917 were wounded. At Iwo, American total casualties exceeded Japanese, unusual for this war, though Japanese fatalities outnumbered American by a factor of about three to one. Iwo demonstrated disquieting evidence of Japanese resolve to fight on—even when checkmated tactically—and inflict heavy losses upon their increasingly war-weary enemies. The closer Allied military forces came to the Japanese home islands, the more tenacious the response, no matter how hopeless the enemy's abysmal strategic position might have appeared to American eyes.

With hard-won Iwo Jima in tow, the Ryukyu Islands now loomed as the last major objective for Admiral Nimitz's forces before Japan itself. This chain of 140 volcanic islands stretched in a 775-mile crescent from south of Kyushu to Formosa. Most of the islands were deserted, tiny, sparsely populated, or bereft of any strategic value. The largest and most

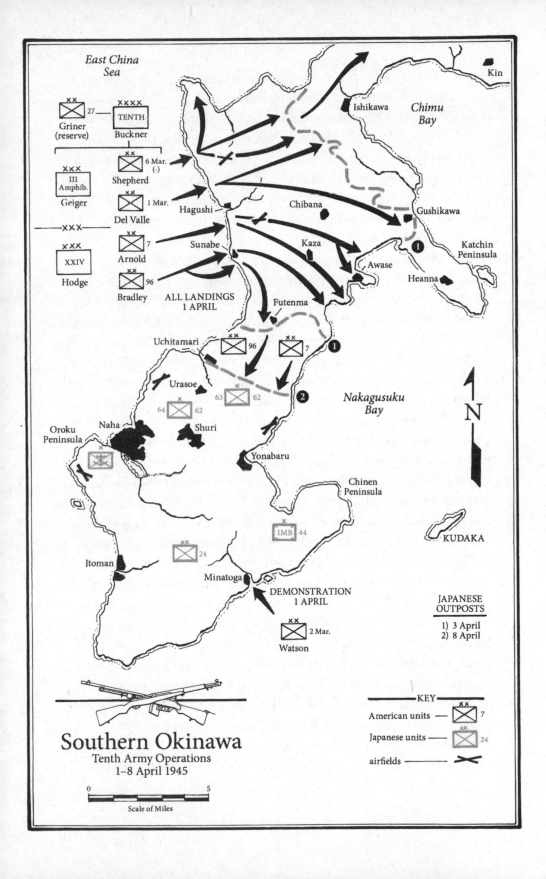

East China
Sea

Kin

Chimu
Bay

Ishikawa

27 Griner (reserve)

TENTH Buckner

6 Mar. (-) Shepherd

III Amphib. Geiger

1 Mar. Del Valle

XXIV Hodge

7 Arnold

96 Bradley

Hagushi

Chibana

Gushikawa

Katchin
Peninsula

Kaza

Sunabe

Awase

Heanna

ALL LANDINGS
1 APRIL

Futenma

Uchitamari

96

7

1

Nakagusuku
Bay

Urasoe

63 62

2

64 62

Naha

Shuri

Oroku
Peninsula

Yonabaru

Chinen
Peninsula

KUDAKA

IMB 44

Itoman

24

Minatoga

DEMONSTRATION
1 APRIL

2 Mar.

Watson

JAPANESE
OUTPOSTS

1) 3 April
2) 8 April

KEY

American units —— 7

Japanese units —— 24

airfields ——

Southern Okinawa
Tenth Army Operations
1–8 April 1945

0   5

Scale of Miles

populous island, Okinawa, lay at the geographic and figurative center of the chain. Claw shaped, 60 miles long and between 2 and 18 miles wide, with 485 square miles of space and a population approaching half a million, Okinawa offered the prospect of excellent air and sea bases in close proximity to Japan. Naha, the capital, was located a mere 360 nautical miles from Kyushu and 850 miles from Tokyo, within medium-bomber range of the home islands. Okinawa amounted to Japan's front step. Anyone hoping to invade the rhetorical Japanese house must first secure and pass over that step.

The Okinawan people owed their heritage to Chinese, Malay, Japanese, and Mongolian origins. Isolated, insular, and peaceful, with a reputation for inveterate aversion to weapons, they had operated for centuries at the intersection of Chinese and Japanese influence. It was said that when a British officer who had spent time on Okinawa later visited Napoleon during his exile on St. Helena and informed him of the people's pacifism, the perplexed former emperor huffed discontentedly, "No army. No soldiers. No war. What sort of barbarians are these?!"

Imperial Japan formally annexed the entire island chain in 1879, turning it into a domestic prefecture and forcing the locals to adopt the Japanese language and customs. The Okinawans were hardly physically imposing. The average man stood five feet two inches tall, the women four feet ten inches. They were slighter of build, darker in complexion, and less well fed than their northern overseers, who contemptuously dubbed them "little brown monkeys." As the racist nickname implied, the Japanese looked down on the Okinawans and their laid-back lifestyle as racially and constitutionally inferior. "Most Japanese saw Okinawans as lazy yokels," one insightful analyst wrote. "[Their] lack of concern for racial purity, national destiny, and the emperor's divinity galled . . . governors from Tokyo." For over fifty years, they worked diligently to Japanize the island, dominating the economy, disseminating the Japanese language and culture in the schools, and administering the island with an iron hand. In general, they treated the inhabitants poorly, sometimes even worse than Koreans, another colonized people for whom the Japanese felt little but disdain. It took four decades for the island to attain legislative representation on par with other prefectures.

On the eve of the war, Okinawans were not even allowed into Naha's nicest hotels and shopping districts.[1]

Like several other Pacific islands, Okinawa had transitioned from a strategic backwater early in the war to a strategic centerpiece as the Americans advanced ever closer to Japan. As early as March 1944, Tokyo strategists had anticipated the distinct possibility that Okinawa might become a battleground. To defend the island, and the Ryukyus as a whole, they created the 32nd Army under Lieutenant General Masao Watanabe, a sensitive officer who had successfully commanded a division in China but who was now so plagued by gastroenteritis that he struggled just to get out of bed each day. Initially, his army was a hollow force that focused mainly on constructing airfields. Had the Americans somehow found a way to invade in the summer of 1944, they would have faced only skeleton formations capable of little else besides fending off a raid. By that fall, though, Imperial General Headquarters had heavily reinforced the 32nd Army with the 9th, 24th, and 62nd Divisions, plus the 44th Independent Mixed Brigade. This revival process exemplified a common pattern in the Pacific War. The Japanese ability to reinforce and fortify most key islands ran about six to nine months ahead of the American invasion timetable. Seldom did the Americans assault a major island before the Japanese could prepare to defend it in some formidable fashion. Still, Watanabe felt he had little chance to defeat the Americans and had no qualms about publicly displaying his pessimism. "An enemy landing means just three things," he told Okinawan leaders. "Death for you, death for me, death for all of us." He described Japanese weapons and equipment as "just so much junk."

Inevitably, word of the general's poor physical condition and his less-than-sanguine attitude filtered back to Tokyo, leading Imperial General Headquarters to replace him in August 1944 with fifty-seven-year-old Lieutenant General Mitsuru Ushijima, one of the most ethical, committed officers in the entire Japanese armed forces. Captain Kunishige Tanaka of the 62nd Division once described Ushijima as "a very gentle and warm hearted person and . . . a man of high character." Lean and physically imposing, hailing from a samurai family, the mustachioed Ushijima favored a consensus command style. He empowered his staffers to make decisions on his behalf, but also took full responsibility himself. Ushijima had successfully commanded the Imperial Army's 11th Division, winning early war battles in China and Burma, before moving on to the superintendency of the army's military academy. An American intelligence analysis described him as a "quiet-spoken officer with a faculty for choosing capable subordinates. He had the quality of inspiring confidence among his troops and was held in great respect by them." Some of his men even compared him to Saigo Takamori, a legendary samurai of the Meiji Restoration era.

Two diametrically opposite, dominant members of his staff held sway over Ushijima, with a sort of latter-day Hamilton-versus-Jefferson vibe. The chief of staff, Lieutenant General Isamu Cho, was an authentic old-school firebrand who, in 1930 as a thirty-five-year-old captain, had joined a radical clique of Imperial Army officers known as the Cherry Blossom Society. To many Japanese, the beautiful but short-lived blossoms of a cherry tree symbolized the youthful, perishable splendor of the warrior. A common Japanese saying held that "as the cherry is the first among flowers, so is the warrior first among men." Cherry Blossom Society officers favored an expansionist Japan controlled by military dictatorship. They rejected capitalism, representative government, and all Western influences. In 1931, Cho was involved in multiple plots to assassinate Japan's civilian prime minister and even once advocated abducting the emperor at knifepoint to force him to appoint a general as head of the government. The plots unraveled. In most any other country, Cho might well have faced treason charges and a firing squad. Instead, his superiors dispatched him to the Kwantung Army in Manchuria, where he found common cause with like-minded adventurers. As a staff officer, he probably ordered the slaughter of Chinese prisoners at Nanking. Later, in 1938, he and another officer orchestrated an attack against a Soviet force in Mongolia, nearly prompting an all-out war between their two countries at a time when Japan was already bogged down in China.

Cho's political radicalism, owlish spectacles, and stocky frame, and his propensity to bully subordinates by subjecting them to verbal harangues and even physical beatings, obscured a fun-loving, humorous side to his personality. He had a passion for fine liquor, rich food, cigarettes, and attractive women, especially geishas. During drunken, exuberant evenings at red-light-district establishments, he sometimes brandished his sword and danced with it. At Okinawa, as elsewhere, he usually favored aggressive offensive tactics to the point where he hoped to repel the Americans at the waterline. In this he differed sharply with his alter ego, the cerebral, low-key, forty-two-year-old Colonel Hiromichi Yahara, the 32nd Army's operations officer, a scholarly realist who advocated an inland defense at Okinawa similar to Yamashita's concept in the Philippines. An American intelligence officer once described Yahara as "quiet and unassuming, yet possessed of a keen mind and a fine discernment . . . from all reports, an eminently capable officer described by some . . . as the 'brains' of the 32nd Army." Captain Tsuneo Shimura, a battalion commander in the 24th Division, described Yahara as someone who "regarded rationality with utmost importance and he was faithful to such a way of thinking."

In spite of the facts that Yahara was junior to Cho and radically different in temperament, and that they often vociferously disagreed on proper strategy, they got along reasonably well. They had known each other for almost two decades. Both had spent time in the United States on an officer exchange program. They served together in Southeast Asia on the eve of the war when Colonel Yahara had worked as a military attaché. In Saigon one night during a mutual stay at the Hotel Majestic— a place later made famous by American war correspondents during the Vietnam War—they had even taken in a movie and then gone on a drunken bender together. "We were thoroughly besotted," Yahara once commented of the evening. "I had always held an image of the general as a fine, spirited fellow. Our revels that night confirmed it."[2]

The 32nd Army's initial dispositions reflected Cho's preference for a blanket defense of the island with the goal of annihilating the Americans before they could establish a beachhead. But in mid-November 1944, Imperial General Headquarters insisted on transferring the well-trained 9th Division away from Okinawa for service in Formosa, greatly angering nearly everyone in the 32nd Army and eliminating any possibility that it could effectively defend more than just part of the island. In late January 1945, headquarters communicated an intention to send the 84th Division to replace the departed 9th. But Lieutenant General Shuichi Miyazaki, head of the strategy branch at Imperial General

Headquarters, scotched the idea. He felt he could not justify sending the 84th to Okinawa when it might soon be needed to defend the home islands. Such were the agonizing Peter-or-Paul choices confronting Japanese leaders by this stage of the war. Better than any other Japanese officer, Colonel Yahara understood that 32nd Army had little chance to repel the Americans on the beaches even with the 9th Division in the fold, much less without it. Given American firepower and predominance in the sea and air, a beach battle made no sense. Yahara possessed a geostrategic grasp well beyond his age and rank. Strategically, he recognized that Japan had few other military options remaining except to bleed the Americans badly enough to stave off total defeat. Tactically, the best way to serve that strategic objective in ground warfare was to dig in, fortify, and make use of the Japanese soldier's formidable proficiency for selling his life dear in defensive combat. The removal of the 9th Division, and Miyazaki's refusal to replace it, only reinforced Yahara's logic. It also helped him sell both Cho and Ushijima on inland defense.

The sparsely populated northern half of the island offered plenty of defensible rugged mountains and hills. But Yahara knew it held little value for the Americans. By contrast, he knew they wanted the airfields, harbors, roads, towns, and population centers of southern Okinawa, where they could more easily develop modern bases and lines of communication along the coastal cities of Naha and Yonabaru. If the Japanese concentrated their troops in the north, the Americans could simply grab the valuable south, cordon off Ushijima's isolated defenders, and profit strategically from control of what mattered most on Okinawa. He knew that the smooth Hagushi beaches stretching for five miles along Okinawa's central western coast offered the only realistic site for the Americans to land multiple divisions. He anticipated that they would then sever Okinawa in two and turn south. The terrain of this part of Okinawa, home to some three-quarters of the population, offered excellent ground for defenders, even more so than the north. The US Army's official historian described the area as "broken by terraces, steep natural escarpments, and ravines. The limestone plateau and ridges are ideal for defense and abound in natural caves and burial tombs, easily developed into underground positions. Generally aligned east and west, the hills

offer natural lines of defense, with frequent steep slopes created by artificial terracing. Rice paddies fill the lowlands near the coasts."

Yahara successfully advocated for the construction of successive defensive lines south of Hagushi. The heart of these defenses was situated
from Naha on the west coast to Yonabaru on the east coast, with the
most powerful positions anchored in the center at Shuri. Similar to on
Iwo Jima, the Japanese planned to fight a subterranean battle from within
expertly camouflaged tunnels, dugouts, and caves. For weeks, Ushijima's soldiers and conscripted Okinawans labored mightily to build a
cobweb-like maze of powerful defensive positions. Three groups worked
eight-hour shifts round the clock. "Confidence in victory will be born
from strong fortifications," the soldiers exhorted one another. Few
shirked the work; most understood the vital importance of their task.
Some even missed unit roll calls to keep working. "They could feel
through their skins that an attack was coming and in digging . . . they
felt as if they were digging holes for their corpses," Captain Shimura, the
battalion commander, later commented. They built sixty miles of tunnels and untold numbers of fortified caves, pillboxes, firing pits, antitank trenches, bunkers, blockhouses, and limestone block tombs.
Planning documents urged the troops to "take advantage of the
American Army's respect for tombs and its avoidance thereof" and featured instructional diagrams that showed how to connect tombs to one
another with tunnels and where to place machine guns near openings.

The troops did almost all their arduous work with picks and shovels,
hacking their way through so many layers of coral that their tools commonly broke or wore down into stumps. Thirty-second Army had only
two bulldozers, very few trucks, and almost no construction materials.
Combat units dispatched special detachments to cut down trees in the
forests of northern Okinawa. Working under the cover of night for fear
of attack by American planes, these men manhandled the logs onto
boats that then carried them southward for incorporation into Yahara's
fortifications. The island's ubiquitous layers of coral made many cave
walls hard as concrete, especially those that were already embedded
by nature into ridgelines. Some caves were large enough to have room
for hundreds of people, and substantial amounts of ammunition and
supplies. More than a few had space enough to accommodate a

headquarters or a hospital. Construction crews camouflaged the caves expertly with live brush and mounds of dirt. A common 32nd Army motto claimed, "Camouflage is better than concrete." An order issued slightly before the invasion stated grandly, "Our object is to conceal all dispositions." Cleverly hidden caves were guarded by obstacles, machine guns, antitank pieces, and other weapons. Wet mats and blankets were put in place to ward off flames or poison gas. Crews cut special air shafts through the coral and, in some cases, L-shaped patterns beyond cave mouths to negate the effects of tank and naval shells.

Ushijima ordered the total mobilization of the local population. About 80,000 Okinawans were evacuated to Kyushu and 60,000 more, especially elderly people and children, were moved to the northern part of the island. About 39,000 men between the ages of eighteen and forty-five were drafted into Japanese military service. Many were used as laborers or service troops; 24,000 were organized into special Home Guard (or Boeitai) militia units. Some were armed only with spears. The Japanese appropriated 1,500 teenage boys from Okinawan schools into special "Blood and Iron for the Emperor" units where they received military indoctrination and hasty combat training, mostly to serve as runners. Six hundred teenage girls were organized into the Himeyuri Student Corps or "Lily Corps" to work as nurses. Substantial numbers of these idealistic teenagers were proud to serve Japan, their parents much less so. When Miyagi Kikuko, a newly minted member of the Lily Corps, bade her parents farewell, her father exclaimed, "I didn't bring you up to the age of sixteen to die!" She was taken aback at his lack of patriotism and left with a chip on her shoulder. "I thought he was a traitor to say such a thing," she commented sadly years later. "I went to the battlefield feeling proud of myself."

A 32nd Army directive to newly conscripted Okinawans emphasized their duty to fight for their homes. "You are within your native land; each and every one of you serves as a representative of that land. Each of you must shoulder his share of the burden; you are a direct part of the army, assuming your part of its load, and charged with a grave responsibility to the Empire." By late March, the 32nd Army had grown into a formidable force numbering between 100,000 and 110,000 men. The order of battle included nearly 70,000 Imperial Army soldiers and 9,000

Imperial Navy sailors, many of whom had been reorganized into anti-aircraft units, plus the Okinawan conscripts. The army's strength in artillery distinguished it from the Japanese formations that had fought in other Pacific battles. Colonel Yahara had successfully lobbied Tokyo to send as much artillery as possible. As a result, Ushijima had 5,300 artillerymen, enough to organize into a brigade-size unit called 5th Artillery Command under Lieutenant General Kojo Wada, a highly respected artillery officer. Wada had 287 guns and howitzers, ranging in caliber from 70 to 150 millimeters, in addition to dozens of antiaircraft guns, nearly 100 81-millimeter mortars, and 24 320-millimeter spigot mortars. Wada had less artillery and fewer mortars than the Americans, but even so, he possessed a devastating array of firepower, made only more dangerous by Yahara's expert efforts to conceal the tubes so well in caves and bunkers.

Although many of the soldiers held no illusions about their slim chances for survival, the considerable firepower and strong fortifications did boost the confidence of more than a few as they worked so hard to bolster Yahara's defensive lines. "The feeling that we will crush the enemy is running high!" one private exulted in his diary. Ushijima's headquarters attempted to stoke the self-sacrificial enthusiasm so common among average Japanese soldiers by circulating throughout 32nd Army a nihilistic, hyperpatriotic set of instructions whose rhetoric was probably influenced by the fiery Cho: "To have faith in ultimate victory each one of us must kill ten of the enemy. They who perform the highly commendable duties of combat soldiers will become heroes. Hells fire! Each one dash forward and accomplish your mission with an aggressive spirit. Entrust your life to heaven. Your fate was determined when you were born, and because you are powerless to do anything about it, dash forward killing ten for one. You will be honored for your boldness and bravery. You must prepare yourself for the sake of the Emperor."[3]

As Ushijima's charges prepared for their version of Armageddon, the unassuming Admiral Nimitz assembled one of the most powerful military expeditionary forces in history. For the objective of taking the Ryukyus, dubbed Operation Iceberg by the planners, the Americans compiled a colossal multiservice invasion force, one that, in retrospect, might well have represented the historical apogee of American military effectiveness, if not necessarily its destructive power. Tried-and-true Admiral Raymond Spruance commanded an impressive armada of 1,300 ships. The fleet included a Royal Navy task force under Vice Admiral Sir Bernard Rawlings, as well as Vice Admiral Marc Mitscher's carrier-rich Task Force 58 and also Task Force 51 under Vice Admiral Richmond Kelly Turner. Spruance had 40 carriers of varying tonnage and 18 battleships at his disposal. Mitscher alone controlled 11 fleet carriers and 6 light carriers with a complement of 1,400 aircraft, plus 7 battleships, 18 cruisers, and 46 smaller vessels. Rawlings added 5 carriers, 2 battleships, and 7 cruisers.

By now the Allies had mastered, to the point of maestro-like skill, the logistical process of maintaining large naval operations for sustained periods. Spruance's staff estimated the minimum need for 6 million barrels of fuel for every month at sea. Stocks of oil, diesel, and aviation gasoline were positioned at bases all over the Pacific. A blue-collar fleet of 40 oil tankers under Commodore Augustine Gray, nicknamed the "Oil King of the Pacific," operated a shuttle refueling service. Day after day, their crews edged to within thirty feet of their recipients, connected hoses to them, and pumped fuel into their bunkers, sometimes persisting even in the choppiest of seas. By all accounts, the acrid odor of the tankers' oil could be smelled on the salt air as far as a mile away (one can only imagine how overwhelming the fumes must have been for the oiler crews).

The tankers replenished the fleet's mail, too, delivering a mind-blowing 24,117,599 pieces of mail over a five-week period. A quartet of specially outfitted escort carriers hauled replacement planes for those that would soon be lost in action. Cargo ships performed the same function for the vast assemblage of provisions, equipment, and specialty items that accompanied humans at sea. In the space of two days, they transferred 64,000 tons of matériel, more than Boston Harbor could manage in a week. A single ship, the USS *Mercury*, delivered 252.5 tons of food, clothing, life jackets, helmets, blankets, signal equipment, toilet paper, cooking utensils, cigarettes, candy, stationery, crockery, gunsights, and myriad other items to a lone carrier group. In the early stages of the war, the attack cargo and attack transport ships so vital to the job of carrying large ground units and their considerable amount of freight were in scarce supply. Now the Okinawa invasion fleet included 168 such vessels, enough to bear, along with 184 LSTs, seven fully equipped infantry divisions and their attachments, the equivalent of an entire field army. A single infantry division accounted for 18,879 tons of supplies and equipment.[4]

These prodigious ground forces were organized into the newly created Tenth Army. Similar to many other American senior leaders in World War II, the commander hailed from a military tradition. Lieutenant General Simon Bolivar Buckner Jr. was the son of a Confederate general with a similar name. Simon Sr. was a classmate and friend of Ulysses Grant at West Point and surrendered Fort Donelson to him in 1862 after a tough fight that earned him plaudits throughout the South. After the war, he served as governor of Kentucky. His first wife died of tuberculosis in 1874. His second wife was more than three decades younger. In 1886, when Buckner was sixty-three years old, his wife gave birth to Simon Jr. The boy followed in his father's footsteps by attending West Point and graduating as an infantry officer in 1908. He soldiered honorably for more than thirty years with no combat and little command experience. He spent the early years of the war heading up the Alaska Defense Command at Fort Richardson in Anchorage. He had played a tangential supervisory role during the invasion of Attu in May 1943 but logged no combat time.

On the surface, Buckner's paucity of battle experience seemed to bode ill for his ability to handle a command of Tenth Army's magnitude. But the eclectic Buckner did possess some characteristics that equipped him well for leadership of an army in Operation Iceberg. For two years he had worked closely with Marine and Navy colleagues, forging intimate, trusting relationships. He detested interservice rivalry. In Alaska and at Tenth Army, he worked assiduously to forge soldiers, Marines, and sailors into a common team. He knew firsthand the poisonous strategic dangers that stemmed from bickering among the services. He had headed up the board that investigated the self-defeating ugliness that boiled among senior Navy, Marine, and Army officers after Marine Lieutenant General Holland Smith had impulsively cashiered Army Major General Ralph Smith at Saipan in 1944. Affable and plainspoken, with an infectious laugh, he had a passion for mixing with troops, no matter the service. "It starts with a little chuckle in his throat and then he really lets go and shakes the walls," a subordinate once commented affectionately of the general's laugh.

For a man in his late fifties, Buckner cut an impressive physical figure. Sturdy and muscled, he had lively blue eyes and a thick head of snow-white hair. His skin was ruddy and bronzed in the manner that oozes a final vitality before the inevitable transition to prunish elderly wrinkles. Married, with two sons and a daughter, he wrote frequent, descriptive letters to his wife, Adele. "I miss your arms and your lips," he told her in one missive. "It will take a long time to get caught up when I get back." A strong believer in physical fitness, he kept himself in fine condition with an exercise regimen that included long hikes and an austere diet. He was not without vices, though. "He takes a drink in congenial company, and though he swears off smoking now and then, he relapses," a correspondent wrote after spending time with him in Alaska.

During Buckner's tenure as commandant of the corps of cadets at West Point, he raised physical training standards, prompting one disapproving parent to complain, "Buckner forgets that cadets are born, not quarried." Once, during a long field march with full packs, he easily outpaced cadets who were less than half his age, to the point where he carried the kit of several who fell out. As a nod to his penchant for alpine hiking, his soldiers nicknamed him the Old Man of the Mountain. An avid outdoorsman, Buckner loved sports, hunting, and fishing. An amateur photographer, he carried a camera with him everywhere, snapping pictures of the Alaska wilderness. "He was a good father," his youngest child, William, who entered West Point as a plebe in 1944, later commented. During one summer visit to Alaska, father and son spent most of their time together outdoors. "We had marvelous duck hunting. We had some wonderful trout fishing." The general was a regular participant in softball games with his men. He learned to ice-skate in his late forties, took up skiing at age fifty-seven, and spent many of his Alaska leisure hours spearfishing or hunting alongside a beloved pair of springer spaniels he sadly left in the care of friends when he transferred to Hawaii in the late summer of 1944. His appointment to high command resulted from personality-driven institutional momentum rather than any kind of linear choice by a superior. Nimitz and Marshall seem to have selected him by mutual consensus for command of Tenth Army after Buckner met with Nimitz and assured him of his commitment to interservice cooperation.

Once in place, Buckner found himself in charge of the Army's largest Pacific theater combat formation outside of MacArthur's purview. By the eve of Operation Iceberg, Tenth Army had grown into a uniquely diverse multiservice organization, unlike any other in the entire American armed forces. Buckner had three Marine divisions and four Army divisions under his direct control, organized into two corps, along with another Army division in theater reserve at his disposal. The III Amphibious Corps was composed of the 1st, 2nd, and 6th Marine Divisions under the trustworthy command of Major General Roy Geiger, a close friend of Buckner's from their interwar days together at the Army's Command and General Staff College at Fort Leavenworth. The Army's 7th, 27th, 77th, and 96th Infantry Divisions comprised the XXIV Corps under hard-bitten, cocksure veteran Major General John Hodge. While all seven of these divisions were afloat by late March 1945, the 81st Infantry Division, veterans of the awful Peleliu and Angaur fighting, remained in reserve on New Caledonia.

Unlike Buckner, nearly every one of his ground combat formations had seen battle. Even the newly created 6th Marine Division contained two regiments that had fought at Guam. Most commanders preferred to lead veteran units. But not all the effects of previous battle experiences were good. Weariness had sapped the fighting proficiency of more than a few experienced combat soldiers, many of whom were now far less enthusiastic about the prospect of seeing action than were well-trained rookies. "The morale and spirit of the Division was in a curious condition at this time," Lieutenant Russell Gugeler, a combat historian embedded with the highly experienced 7th Infantry Division—the unit had already fought three major battles—wrote of the soldiers' mindset aboard ship on the way to Okinawa. "Only the replacements were eager. To the older and experienced men it was a dreary business and their chief concern was the expected length of the battle and the nature of the terrain. There was little evidence of the tense anticipation that is often attributed to men going into combat." Instead, an undercurrent of fear pervaded, like a dark cloud, over those who knew exactly what lay ahead. "Ever since the Leyte landings I had dreaded making our next assault," PFC Ellis Moore, a 96th Division radioman who had seen much action on that island, wrote to his girlfriend. "Whenever I thought of our next landing . . . I knew . . . I would be scared to death. Most of the other guys felt that way too."[5]

Just as Colonel Yahara had anticipated, Buckner chose to land on the Hagushi beaches. The Iceberg plan called for the 6th and 1st Marine Divisions to land on the left while the 7th and 96th Infantry Divisions hit the beach to their right. To distract the Japanese and siphon enemy reinforcements away from Hagushi, the 2nd Marine Division would feint a landing at Minatoga, a smaller beach on Okinawa's southern coast. Nimitz had hoped to invade Okinawa by March 1, but the protracted nature of the Leyte campaign had led to a ripple effect of delays, postponing the invasions of Luzon, Iwo Jima, and Okinawa for about a month apiece. At Okinawa the Americans settled instead on April 1 as L Day, a short-term moniker for Love Day, an ironically chosen word that could not have been more inappropriate for what was in the offing. April 1 was of course universally recognized among Americans as April Fools' Day, but that year it was also Easter Sunday. Needless to say, the participants fervently hoped that divine protection would prevail over court jester absurdity. Lieutenant General Buckner had yet another reason to mark the date—it had been his father's birthday.

The Kerama Retto, a group of diminutive islands ten to twenty miles west of Okinawa, offered attractive long-range artillery platforms and naval anchorages for Vice Admiral Turner's cargo and transport ships. As a prelude to the main landings, Buckner assigned the redoubtable Major General A. D. Bruce's 77th Infantry Division to seize them. Between March 26 and 29, the division took five Kerama Retto islands against ineffective resistance from a surprised skeleton garrison of 400 suicide boat operators and support troops. Bruce's soldiers captured 250 boats that might have wreaked havoc on the fleet. They also came upon a disturbing scene reminiscent of the Marpi Point suicides the year before on Saipan. In a small valley they found the bloody bodies of 250 civilians who had chosen suicide rather than subjecting themselves to American control. "Children had been killed or terribly wounded,"

Lieutenant Paul Leach, a combat historian embedded with the division, later wrote. "Whole families had committed suicide by grenades and strangling, and others had committed Hari Kari with knives. It was a scene of awful sacrifice of lives by innocent people deluded by the military into thinking that suicide would be better than falling into the hands of the Americans who would 'ravish the women and children and torture the rest.'" Contrary to these absurd claims, the GIs fed and cared for many hundreds of others who had wisely resisted the Japanese pressure to kill themselves. Medics saved as many of the wounded as they could. "I won't forget the look on a young mother's face when she realized that her dead babe-in-arms had died unnecessarily," Private Glenn Searles wrote of the sad scene.[6]

As the 77th Division fulfilled its mission, the Americans unleashed an epic bombardment on Okinawa. The softening-up process had actually begun many months earlier on October 10, when American planes had pasted it with 541 tons of bombs, 652 rockets, and 21 torpedoes, killing 1,000 civilians and about half that many Japanese. The raid was arguably Okinawa's first-ever taste of war, certainly of the modern variety. American aviators shot down 23 Japanese planes and destroyed another 88 on the ground or in the water. They also sank dozens of small ships. The bombing unleashed flames that laid waste to Naha, consuming 80 percent of the city. "The enemy is brazenly planning to destroy completely every last ship, cut our supply lines, and attack us," one Japanese soldier morosely commented in his diary. The raid shocked the Okinawans so much that they simply referred to it by its date as "Ten-Ten," a term that became infamous in the local lexicon. Air strikes and photo reconnaissance missions became almost routine throughout February and much of March. "The ferocity of the bombing is terrific," another Japanese private moaned to his diary. "It really makes me furious."

Naval bombardment of the island by Spruance's surface ships began on March 25 and, in a garish, uniquely American display of profligate, misdirected firepower, continued daily for the next week. Destroyers, cruisers, and battleships played the leading parts in the orchestra of destruction. They hurled 13,000 shells of between 6 and 16 inches in caliber and 28,250 5-inch shells of varying types, totaling a suffocating 4,684 tons of ordnance. Task Force 58 planes flew 3,095 supporting sorties. Sheltered by these sheets of steel, underwater demolition teams cleared 2,900 wooden posts that might have restricted the mobility of landing craft. The swimmers reported that reefs off Hagushi would not impede LVTs. Warships poured on 44,825 more shells and 33,000 rockets, plus air strikes on Love Day in what one Tenth Army official report accurately termed "the heaviest concentration of naval gunfire ever delivered in support of the landing of troops." Most of the fire missions focused on the beaches, the inland airfields, and the central areas of Okinawa where the invaders expected to encounter the nexus of resistance. So, instead of degrading Ushijima's actual defensive lines, the bombardment did little besides squander taxpayer money to the winds and unleash wanton destruction upon undefended parts of the island. Its ineffectiveness revealed yet another intelligence failure that rivaled even Charles Willoughby's greatest misses. Relying mainly on aerial photographs and observer information gathered from reconnaissance flights, Tenth Army's intelligence section on the eve of the invasion calculated the size of the enemy garrison at 65,000 troops, an underestimate by one-third.

The paucity of human intelligence available to the American analysts and their general unfamiliarity with the Okinawan political situation made this lowball assessment somewhat understandable. Far more mystifying, though, was their assumption that the Japanese would expend most of their strength to defend the beaches. In reality, the pattern for the previous nine months, including most recently at Iwo Jima and Luzon, had indicated precisely the opposite. Although central Okinawa did offer the Japanese some useful ridgelines on which they could place artillery and bombard the beaches, the area as a whole yielded far less defensible ground, and considerably more vulnerability to Allied naval gunfire, than did southern Okinawa. Nonetheless, the American planners seemed not to grasp this elemental reality, much less the lessons of recent Japanese behavior. A XXIV Corps preinvasion intelligence report asserted, with almost befuddling inaccuracy, "It is unlikely . . . that the enemy forces will be concentrated in the southern portion of the island or that he will abandon all other possible landing sites in effecting a concentration of his forces." An Army historian later ruefully commented on these misapprehensions: "It must be granted, looking at the matter with the evidence available after the event, that the Japanese had successfully cloaked their plan of battle from our eyes. We had been wrong in estimating their plan of battle and the disposition of their forces." The upshot was that, once again, the Americans were embarking upon a major operation with less than a full appreciation of Japanese capabilities and intentions.[7]

Love Day dawned clear and bright, unfolding a breathtaking panoply upon history's last great amphibious invasion. Aboard USS *Eldorado*, Lieutenant General Buckner and his staff attended an Easter service. The assault troops, meanwhile, consumed a steak and eggs breakfast, by now an almost hallowed preinvasion tradition. One veteran Marine cynically referred to it as "the usual feast before the slaughter." Many savored the meal with the knowledge, in the recollection of one infantry officer, "that they would not be eating so well again for some time to come." Like many others, Corporal Aram Philibosian, a signalman scheduled to go in with an infantry unit, spent these last lonely moments contemplating the possibility of death. "I sat on the deck homesick as all hell," he later wrote to his brother-in-law. "I actually bawled tears, but it made me feel much better." Captain Lauren Soth with the 96th Division remembered that in these last moments before receiving orders to go ashore, he and the other soldiers "huddled around the doorways of the sleeping compartments . . . trying not to act nervous. Rifles or carbines over our shoulders, packs or musette bags on our backs, we waited for the call to the boats." The flower of America's shipyards, totaling many hundreds of vessels of all types and description, choked the waters off the Hagushi beaches. "What a sight!" Private Donald Dencker of the 96th Division later marveled. "About a mile from the beaches, a line of battleships and cruisers engaged in the softening-up process. Flame and smoke belched from their guns as they fired repeated salvos. Shell bursts sent up clouds of smoke and dust from the beach area inland to a distance of perhaps a mile." To another infantryman, the concussion of each mighty salvo made the ships look as if "they moved sideways in the water." An awestruck Japanese lookout told his superiors that the sea looked like it was composed of 30 percent water and 70 percent ships. "My God, what kind of enemy do we face?" he worriedly murmured to himself.

Because of the honed expertise that eventuated from experience, know-how, and careful coordination at staff and senior levels, hundreds of troop-laden LVTs and amtanks emerged, seemingly at the same instant, from the innards of the LSTs that had carried them across thousands of miles of ocean. Guided by naval patrol craft, each of which contained a liaison officer from the ground units, the landing craft coalesced into precise formations, spanning across eight miles of coastal waters. Almost as one, they headed for the Hagushi beaches, like an avenging fleet of metal monsters. With appropriate hyperbole, one historian of the battle called this "the finest moment in the history of amphibious operations." Indeed, when the landing craft touched Okinawa's sand at 0830, it marked both the apex of an era and the end of it. Over three hard years of war, the Americans had innovated and refined amphibious warfare to a near science, even as the advent of deadlier aircraft, nuclear weapons, and more sophisticated international communications would eventually make it more problematic. To be sure, amphibious landings did not perish—a mere five years later the 1st Marine Division assaulted the sand spits of Inchon in Korea—but never again would they manifest on anything approaching this scale.

In the space of an hour, 16,000 assault troops from Buckner's four divisions landed against negligible resistance; another 45,000 arrived by nightfall. The 7th Division landings exemplified those of all four divisions. Totally unimpeded by the Japanese, the salty 7th put ashore 17,023 soldiers, 1,145 vehicles, and 9,209 short tons of supplies. Ignorant of Japanese intentions, the Americans were stunned at the lack of resistance. "The rapidity and ease with which the beaches were secured was the antithesis of what had been expected," the 96th Division's after-action report asserted, with an insouciance typical of the prevailing mindset. A giddy 7th Division infantryman marveled gratefully, "I've already lived longer than I thought I would."

His mood might have been less upbeat had he known that a dozen and a half miles to the south, Lieutenant General Ushijima and his staff stood atop the heights of Shuri in the heart of the general's defensive line, peering through binoculars, watching the invaders hurriedly exit their landing craft and warily advance inland. The fervent Lieutenant General Cho observed them like a lion stalking his prey. Others were more relaxed. Some of the officers smoked and casually exchanged familiar jokes. One young lieutenant noticed many of the Americans chewing on something as they hit the beaches. He asked his superiors why the enemy soldiers would eat at a time like this. In response, several of his elders laughed and asked if he had never heard of chewing gum. He actually had not. The sublimity of these empowering moments, when they examined their adversaries like scientists studying organisms under a microscope, was not lost on these officers. In a way, they were mocking the Americans, relishing the knowledge that they had no idea of the trap that awaited them. Even the circumspect, constitutionally pessimistic Colonel Yahara felt emboldened to the point of exultation. He smiled and chuckled to himself. "Advancing with such ease, they must be thinking gleefully that they have passed through a breach in the Japanese defense," he later wrote, with characteristic introspection. "They will be wrong. What a surprise it must all be. It is amusing to watch the American army so desperately intent in its attack on an almost undefended coast, like a blind man who has lost his cane, groping on hands and knees to cross a ditch. So extraordinary is this opening scene of what is to be a historic and decisive battle. It is almost unbelievable."

The Americans, for their part, did find the ease of their initial advance hard to believe. "From the opening bombardment and air attack to the landing of the last tank and gun our assault against Okinawa today was as beautiful a piece of teamwork as I have ever seen," a relieved Buckner wrote to his wife, Adele, on the evening of April 1. "Opposition was light, the Japs evidently having expected us to land elsewhere on the island. We gained more ground today than we had hoped to get within three days." The Tenth Army cut the island in two and easily captured Yontan and Kadena airfields, two of the key objectives of the campaign. Within five days, Marine fighter squadrons were already operating from the two bases. The 1st and 6th Marine Divisions turned left to clear out the northern part of the island. The 7th Division smoothly advanced to the eastern coast. "There was a look of wonder upon the faces of the infantrymen as they traveled along the narrow and dusty highway, or through the small but carefully tended fields," Lieutenant Gugeler, the embedded historian, wrote of the prevailing befuddlement. "They were beginning to wonder, now, where the Japanese Army was hiding and even if the Japanese had an army on Okinawa." Rumors circulated that the Japanese had been fooled by the 2nd Marine Division's feint into moving all their troops to the southern coast. Some incurable optimists even claimed that they had evacuated their entire garrison to Formosa. Indeed, the division's old-timers, who had two years earlier invaded Kiska, where the Japanese had left before the Allies arrived, could not help but ponder if the same scenario was now unfolding here.[8]

In truth, the Japanese response at sea indicated their defiant intentions to resist Operation Iceberg to the utmost. Any remote aspirations they harbored for actually defeating the American invasion centered around aerial attacks, with the kamikazes playing the starring role. In a best-case scenario, they nursed hopes that the suicide planes might so devastate the Allied fleet as to strand Buckner's army, allowing Japanese reinforcements to arrive and annihilate it. This proved no more than an idle fantasy, but the same could not be said for the lethal effectiveness of the kamikazes. Love Day caught the Japanese in the middle of their preparations. Admiral Soemu Toyoda, commander of the Combined Fleet, needed a few days to muster what turned out to be a massive offensive called Ten-Go. Starting on April 6 and continuing periodically through June 22, he launched ten separate major aerial attacks, totaling 1,900 suicide sorties by 1,465 planes, against the Allied fleet. Almost all the attackers originated from airfields on Formosa and Kyushu, the latter of which American B-29s pummeled repeatedly. To the Americans, most of whom could not begin to fathom how any rational human being could willingly volunteer to turn himself into a suicide bomber, the kamikaze pilots seemed like heartless, fanatical, unthinking, sinister automatons. To one horrified Yank, they appeared as "sudden fantastic bolts of destruction that frequently converted both crashing plane and its victim into a flaming torch."

But no matter how terrifying and confounding their choice to become human missiles, they hardly conformed to the stereotype. Many were former university students who had excelled in the sciences,

An overhead glimpse at one part of the vast Luzon invasion fleet as it nears the Lingayen Gulf landing beaches. Vice Admiral Thomas Kinkaid's Seventh Fleet comprised more than 700 ships carrying 203,000 soldiers. Japanese kamikaze raids damaged two dozen ships and killed 503 sailors but could not begin to stop the invasion. US ARMY

On "S-Day," January 9, 1945, in one of the largest invasions in human history, the Americans landed 68,000 troops and carved out a beachhead seventeen miles long and four miles deep. They also unloaded and moved thousands of tons of supplies and equipment inland. In a single regimental sector at San Fabian on S-Day, soldiers disgorged 447 vehicles, as well as 2,883 short tons of supplies. During the days that followed, an average of 11,000 short tons of matériel crossed the landing beaches for points inland. US ARMY

The two masterminds of the successful Lingayen Gulf Invasion. On the right, General Douglas MacArthur, commander of the Southwest Pacific Area theater, a famous, vexing figure of enormous egomania, megalomania, and strategic innovation. On the left, General Walter Krueger, Sixth Army commander, a German-born, self-made autodidact who had once joined the Army as a private and ended up in direct command of more ground troops than any other American in the Pacific. As the Luzon campaign unfolded, the two conflicted sharply over the strategy and pace of operations. NARA

Filipino laborers and Army engineers lay steel mat for the construction of an airfield. MacArthur's vast armies on Luzon were supported mainly by land-based aircraft, many of which sallied forth from hastily constructed fields near the landing beaches. The capture and rehabilitation of Clark Field in late January 1945 ultimately proved to be the key to controlling the skies over Luzon. US ARMY

Army infantrymen cross a makeshift plank bridge somewhere on Luzon. Wrecked bridges comprised perhaps the greatest impediment to the American advance on Manila. XIV Corps engineers encountered 217 destroyed timber bridges. In a matter of weeks, they repaired 138 and rebuilt another 79. At the same time, they constructed 26 Bailey bridges, 10 steel treadway bridges, and 14 pontoon bridges. US ARMY

American combat troops pick through the ruins of Manila. The determination of Rear Admiral Sanji Iwabuchi and about 17,000 Japanese stalwarts to hunker down and fight to the death in the city initiated a ferocious five-week struggle for the Philippines capital, "street by street, block by block, building by building, floor by floor, room by room," as one American infantry soldier later described it. US ARMY

The heart of Manila burns during the height of the battle in February 1945. Bilibid Prison is visible at the bottom of the image above, and the tower of city hall at the right of the image below. According to a stark Sixth Army After Action Report, "Every building and every wall became a strong point." Fought with a savagery on par with Stalingrad, the tragic battle wrecked a once beautiful city and led to a humanitarian catastrophe. About 100,000 Filipinos lost their lives due to horrific Japanese atrocities or U.S. firepower. The U.S. Army lost 1,010 soldiers killed in action and 5,565 wounded. The Japanese garrison of 17,000 fought to extinction. US ARMY

Staff Sergeant Bill Seklecki unleashes a streak of fire from an M2 flamethrower. In the Battle of Manila and elsewhere in the Pacific during the 1945 battles, the flame-thrower proved to be a devastating, effective weapon in close combat. One soldier who fought in Manila described it as "the most horrible weapon imagined by man." US ARMY

Lieutenant General Robert Eichelberger, commander of the Eighth Army. Glib, garrulous, friendly, extremely aggressive, and courageous almost to a fault, Eichelberger was arguably the finest American ground commander in the war against Japan. A master of combined arms warfare with a predilection for rapid offensive operations, in 1945 he led a lightning dash for Manila followed by a brilliantly executed, but strategically pointless, series of amphibious invasions to liberate much of the Philippines archipelago. US ARMY

Paratroopers from the 503rd Parachute Infantry Regiment land on Corregidor during the morning of February 16, 1945. Highly motivated and superbly trained, most had been in theater for nearly two years but had seen only limited action. "They looked on themselves proudly as being *the* veteran parachute outfit of the SWPA," the executive officer once commented. Most were eager to get into combat on Corregidor and exact revenge against the Japanese for taking the island three years earlier. US ARMY

The tiny, perilous drop zones along the Topside portion of Corregidor. Joined by amphibious troops from the 34th Infantry Regiment, 24th Infantry Division, troopers from the 503rd Parachute Infantry Regiment fought for nearly two weeks to destroy a Japanese garrison of 5,000 troops and reclaim U.S. control of the vital island.
US ARMY

(All this page) The unglamorous reality of fighting on Luzon: mud, swamps, jungles, mountains, and stubborn Japanese resistance. From January 1945 until the end of the war, Krueger's Sixth Army, and attached Filipino guerrilla units, fought an enervating, frustrating campaign against the soldiers of General Tomoyuki Yamashita's Fourteenth Area Army but never truly subdued them. Sixth Army reported 37,854 battle casualties, including 8,140 killed and 157 missing. These eye-popping numbers did not even include the Army's 93,400 supposed nonbattle casualties from disease, injuries, and combat fatigue.
US ARMY

The rebuilt docks of Manila Bay. The massive Japanese destruction of the city's harbor facilities, in addition to the violent fighting, necessitated an enormous American reclamation and rebuilding effort in March 1945. By summertime, Manila had become the largest American logistical base in theater, handling 400,000 tons of cargo per month. The massive influx of supplies through Manila sustained MacArthur's armies in the field and helped assuage rampant hunger and disease among the local population. US ARMY

Soldiers from the Americal Division land on the island of Cebu in March 1945 as part of Eichelberger's campaign to seize the central and southern portions of the Philippines. From late February until the middle of April, Eighth Army conducted 38 successful amphibious invasions, liberating 7 million Filipinos at the cost of 2,070 American soldiers killed and another 7,000 wounded. Although brilliantly executed by Eichelberger and well-fought by the troops, the campaign accrued few strategic results for the Americans and has thus been largely forgotten. US ARMY

U.S. soldiers are warmly welcomed by residents as they enter Cebu City. The vast majority of Filipinos favored the Americans and viewed them as liberators from a harsh Japanese occupation, especially when the U.S. government immediately began transitioning the country to independence. The support of the locals, and the efforts of pro-American guerrillas, proved to be a major asset, contributing to the success of Allied operations in the Philippines. US ARMY

Lieutenant General Albert Wedemeyer poses with Chinese civilians in 1945. A consummate Army insider and first-rate strategic thinker, Wedemeyer improved relations with Chinese leader Chiang Kai-shek and oversaw the opening of a supply road into China, but, like his predecessor Joseph Stilwell, he was just as confounded by serious divisions among the Chinese and the rampant corruption of the government. NARA

Pontoon bridge and straightaway sections of the Stilwell Road supply route from India to China. Stretching over 1,000 miles from Ledo to Kunming, and finally completed by Allied engineers in January 1945, the road opened a landward supply line to the embattled Chinese. The Allies poured enormous quantities of labor and other resources into the building of the road: nearly fifteen million man days, 22,235,000 cubic yards of earth, enough to build a six-foot-high wall from San Francisco to New York, plus the construction of rail lines, telephone poles, and fuel pipelines. Between February and August 1945, some 368 vehicle convoys—many driven by African American soldiers—embarked on the perilous journey to China, delivering nearly 158,000 tons of cargo.
US ARMY

Lieutenant General Simon Bolivar Buckner Jr., commander of the Tenth Army in the Battle of Okinawa, tests a 57-millimeter recoilless rifle. Son of a Confederate general of similar name, the affable, plain-spoken general enjoyed mixing with his troops and circulating on the front lines, where he often borrowed a rifle to snipe at the Japanese. Buckner's propensity to lead from the front ultimately cost him his life, when he was killed by Japanese shell fragments on June 18, 1945. NARA

A tank-infantry team works its way forward on Okinawa, the climactic battle of the war. The initial landings faced little opposition, but as the soldiers and Marines of Tenth Army progressed to the populated southern portion of the island, they ran straight into heavily fortified Japanese defenses at Shuri and elsewhere. Lieutenant General Mitsuru Ushijima, the Japanese commander, had a force of more than 100,000 troops at his disposal, and most were determined to make the Americans pay a steep price in blood for every yard of Okinawa real estate. US ARMY

A flame tank, probably from the Army's 713th Tank Battalion, shoots a jet of fiery liquid napalm and gasoline into a Japanese-held cave. Appropriately nicknamed "Zippos" after a popular lighter, these special tanks could shoot steady streams of fire up to a range of eighty to one hundred yards, and they played a major role in destroying Japanese defensive positions in caves and elsewhere. Contrary to popular memory, armor played a major role in the Pacific War. At Okinawa, the Americans utilized enough tanks to equip a standard armored division in the European theater. US ARMY

Major General Andrew D. Bruce, commander of the 77th Infantry Division, whom Admiral Chester Nimitz once referred to as the "finest commander of troops in the Pacific." Highly intelligent, energetic, and solicitous of the welfare of his troops, Bruce joined several of his Army and Marine Corps colleagues in arguing for a second invasion on Okinawa's southeastern coast to outflank Japanese Shuri Line defenses. Buckner thought the operation was too risky and refused to authorize it, a decision that one of Bruce's officers later referred to as "a very great mistake." NARA

Female soldiers of the Army Nurse Corps served all over the Pacific/Asia theater, sometimes even close to front-line fighting. On Okinawa, they wore M1 helmets and carried M1 carbines for their own protection against Japanese infiltrators. As the violence of the battle rose sharply, they worked around the clock for days on end. One nurse recalled "rows of injured, dirty, suffering men in tent after tent. Here was pathos and sorrow for every minute of every day and too much work to be done to think of tears of pity." US ARMY

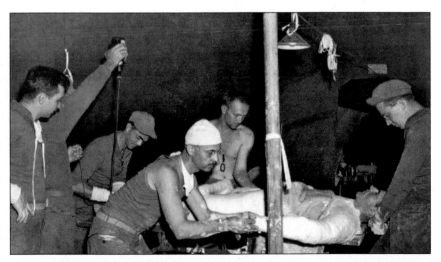

Harried medics treat a badly wounded soldier on Okinawa. In the course of the campaign, 30,848 seriously wounded patients were evacuated, half by boat and half by air. Tenth Army also suffered 26,221 so-called nonbattle casualties, many of whom were debilitated by combat fatigue, accounting for about one in seven hospital admissions. The Americans could replace their losses at something approaching a 50 percent rate. The Japanese had no such luxury. Ushijima received almost no replacements in the course of the fighting, steadily hastening the demise of his 32nd Army. US ARMY

Torrential rains saturated Okinawa during the second half of May 1945, making the landscape nearly impassable with mud, flooded shell craters, and the like. Men and vehicles became enmeshed in a sea of noxious, maggot-filled mud. The horrendous conditions slowed Tenth Army's advance down to a veritable crawl and made life at the front sheer misery for the wet, terrified soldiers and Marines. "Those on the forward slopes of hills slid down, those on the reverse slopes slid back, otherwise no change," one disgusted officer reported to higher headquarters during the worst of the rains. US ARMY

A pair of Japanese soldiers surrenders to their U.S. Army counterparts at the end of the battle for Okinawa. As of late April 1945, there were only 3,260 Japanese prisoners of war in U.S. custody from all previous Pacific theater fighting. During the final stages of the struggle for Okinawa, for the first time, significant numbers of Japanese military personnel began to surrender. In total, the Americans took 7,401 military prisoners, plus 3,339 laborers and 15 civilians. US ARMY

General Douglas MacArthur (left) hugs Lieutenant General Jonathan Wainwright in Japan after the latter's liberation from three years of terrible captivity. Like many other former POWs, Wainwright was deeply scarred, physically and emotionally, by his ordeal, and experienced difficulty adjusting to postwar life. Lionized by the American public and decorated with the Medal of Honor, Wainwright's massive fame became far too burdensome for such a humble man, and he took solace in heavy drinking. A West Point classmate once sadly described him as "alone in his hero's cage." NARA

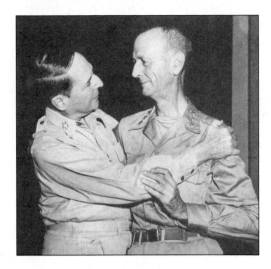

Lieutenant General Toroshiro Kawabe, deputy chief of the Imperial General Staff, arrives at SWPA headquarters in Manila, escorted by Major General Charles Willoughby, MacArthur's occasionally obsequious intelligence officer, to work out the logistics and terms of the Japanese surrender. The initial Japanese surrender communication on August 14, 1945, was equivalent to a handshake business deal with many unresolved issues. During the uncomfortable, anticlimactic weeks that followed, Kawabe and others worked out the specific details with their Allied counterparts. NARA

General Tomoyuki Yamashita (seated center, in front of microphone) surrenders at Baguio on September 3, 1945, to SWPA commanders, a day after the formal Japanese surrender aboard the USS *Missouri*. Yamashita had less than 50,000 troops remaining from an army that had once approached 300,000. Lieutenant General Jonathan Wainwright is visible at the extreme left of this image. Even though he had endured horrible treatment in Japanese captivity, he urged his SWPA colleagues to treat Yamashita and his surrendered soldiers properly, and they were. But later, at the urging of MacArthur, Yamashita was tried and executed for Japanese atrocities in Manila, even though he never ordered them, and had been powerless to put a stop to them. September 3 is still celebrated every year in the Philippines as Yamashita Surrender Day. NARA philosophy, literature, and history, among many other subjects. Their comrades and countrymen revered them as heroes of mythical proportion. Most were in their early twenties, with plenty of life yet to live and no special enthusiasm for death. "When I had first volunteered . . . I did not seriously contemplate my own mortality," Flight Petty Officer Second Class Kanji Suzuki, one of the few who survived the war, later reflected of his mindset as an eighteen-year-old kamikaze. "I was young, sensitive, full of hope, curious even about death; I considered myself to be on a battlefield. However, as the standby period dragged on, I became increasingly anxious and depressed. Only death awaited."

Organized into euphemistically named Special Attack or "Tokko" Squadrons, they whiled away their days in a perpetual holding pattern, like some sort of exalted death row inmates. As they waited, they slept fitfully and rarely laughed. "During the dark hours, delirious utterances and groans could be heard at intervals through the billet, as if we were living in an asylum," Suzuki recalled. When the fateful day came to fly their one-way missions, the Tokko aviators endured a final ceremony, with symbolic toasts and, in Suzuki's recollection, climbed into their planes "with forced smiles on their faces. There was an air of lunatic melancholy in their expressions, in their eyes." Before heading off into their personal death skies, many wrote heart-wrenching letters home or indulged in the Japanese mania for introspective poetry. One erstwhile Tokko poet scrawled, "What is the spirit of Yamato's ancient land?/ It is like wild cherry blossoms/ Radiant in the Rising Sun." As another pilot was about to climb into his plane, he dictated a final letter to his parents, "It is my hope that this last act of striking a blow at the enemy will serve to repay in some small measure the wonderful things you have done for me." Another attempted to console his mother: "I do not want you to grieve over my death. Go ahead and weep. But please realize that my death is for the best and do not feel bitter about it." Cultural expectations made the avoidance of death shameful, perhaps even unthinkable. Their families were left in the terrible position of both hoping for and dreading their demise. "When at last I learned he'd died, people said, 'That's good, congratulations,'" Araki Shegeko, the wife of one dead kamikaze, ruefully commented years later. "I replied, 'Yes, it is. It's for the country,' and then I returned home to cry alone. I let no one see my tears. We were told that with our eyelids we should suppress our tears."

With horrifying repetitiveness, waves of these men hurled themselves at Allied ships. The majority were shot down or missed their targets. "As the flaming plane grew brighter and began to glide toward earth I seemed to remember that God doesn't judge souls by color or creed," Lieutenant Larry McDonnell, a gunnery officer, wrote magnanimously to his family shortly after his gun crews shot down a kamikaze. "Almost mechanically my right arm rose and I was whispering the simple prayer of a Christian baptism and making the Sign of the Cross. Maybe that Jap didn't join his ancestors after all. Maybe he went to purgatory." But a mere few suicide planes could, and did, inflict tremendous damage. By one estimate, they were responsible for sinking 28 ships and damaging 225 others. Destroyers maintained a sophisticated network of radar-aided early-warning pickets, so the kamikazes often singled them out for overwhelming attacks, sinking 11 in the course of the battle. "It's impossible to convey the true picture of a suicide plane attack," Seaman Harry Hymon wrote to his sister after witnessing a kamikaze barely miss his ship and smash into nearby destroyer USS *Luce*, sinking it with the loss of 149 men killed and 94 wounded. "The sky in their vicinity would sometimes be full of flack and bursts and right through it they'd come, as if they were untouchable. Another second and we'd have got it, but good!" Ghastly carnage ensued from most every hit and even some of the near-miss explosions as fire, fragments, and detritus engulfed stricken ships. "All of the men were burned badly, some more than others," one sailor wrote to his parents in the aftermath of a successful attack. "One boy had both legs and one arm broken & a very bad leg wound."

Fifth Fleet's surgeon lamented in an official report prepared during the battle that "bombing by suicide (kamikaze) planes is proving a most effective Japanese weapon. Ship casualties occur quickly and heavily, human bodies and steel ships fall apart. Wounds are frequently destructive, mutilating and fearfully mortal." When the USS *Twiggs* was mortally hit during an evening attack and exploded into a blazing inferno, desperate survivors jumped or were blown overboard into oil-slicked, flaming water that mercilessly consumed them. "It's surely a horrible sight to see men burned alive like that and not be able to do anything about it," Yeoman Second Class W. L. "Bud" Wissel of the neighboring USS *Putnam* wrote somberly to his parents after attempting to rescue survivors. "Many of the men who did make it aboard our ship were badly wounded. One man was dead when he was pulled aboard. Quite a few were so weak they had to be pulled in. I saw one man about 50 ft. from the ship who just couldn't swim any further go down . . . never to come up. Our whole ship was covered with oil."

Perhaps the most egregious strike occurred on the evening of April 28 when a suicide pilot deliberately crashed into USS *Comfort,* a hospital ship operating with its lights on, as mandated by the Geneva Convention. The kamikaze apparently used *Comfort's* large Red Cross emblem as a bull's-eye to smash into the superstructure. The vessel was carrying a full complement of 517 wounded men treated by a joint Army-Navy medical staff. The plane plunged through multiple decks into an operating room, instantly killing 2 sailors, 7 patients, and 20 soldiers, including half a dozen female Army nurses. A gasoline fire ignited an explosion that rocked the ship. "I was blown right off my feet," said Lieutenant Doris Gardner Howard, a twenty-five-year-old nurse. "I was thrown about two yards against a bulkhead and landed with my entire spine against the bulkhead and cracked my head hard. I struggled to get up." The ship survived, but with the loss of 30 dead and 48 wounded. Among the dead was thirty-four-year-old Lieutenant Frances Chesley from Maine, the chief operating room nurse, the first woman from her state to die in World War II. The American Legion in her hometown of Poland, Maine, promptly named a brand-new facility in her honor. Aboard the damaged *Comfort,* the survivors did a remarkable job of restoring order and saving patients. "The calm, precise way in which the Army and Navy went about their duties in the face of such danger and under severe mental strain, gave courage and strength to all and reassurance to the patients," Major Alexander Silverglade, the ranking Army officer, reported with admiration to higher command. "The feeling of security thus established early prevented panic."

By nature, the aerial suicide attacks were episodic, like undulating waves of a heavy storm, at once distant and immediate, especially for the majority of sailors who served belowdecks and would never lay eyes on their attackers. Crewmen spent untold helpless hours tensely watching, listening, and waiting for those dreaded moments. "Through the hours we wait," Seaman Second Class William Oyler jotted reflectively during the battle in a note he later sent to his father. "We sit in small groups and talk of many things. We lie in our bunks and stare into space seeing only the . . . images of our mind. From far away flees the terrified sound; nearer and nearer it comes; the crescendo rises and breaks in a mighty finale. Silence. Quiet. We relax. We wait. We listen. We pray. Some men speak aloud of their fear. Some talk of home and wonder. Some call the enemy 'bastards.' Some say nothing. But we all wait . . . in the eerie glow of the red lights, breathe the stuffy air, listen to the mad thumping of our hearts and feel the fear of others stifle us." Among the capital ships sustaining serious damage and loss of life were fleet carriers USS *Wasp, Bunker Hill,* and *Enterprise,* and the battleships USS *Tennessee* and *Maryland.*

The fleet's desperate struggle against the kamikazes inevitably affected the ground armies as well. The kamikaze victims included SS *Hobbs Victory* and *Logan Victory,* two crucial cargo ships sunk in early April with the loss of 31 dead crewmen and 14,000 tons of ammunition, forcing Buckner's logisticians to scramble for several days to keep ground units supplied with artillery shells. Soldiers who were cooped up aboard troopships and LSTs, almost always belowdecks, were awestruck by the violence of the fighting and agonized by their sense of powerlessness against such impersonal killers. "When the enemy planes appeared, the entire fleet would open up with anti-aircraft weapons, including 20mm and 40mm rapid-fire canon [*sic*] and five-inch guns," Lieutenant Richard Spencer, a staff officer in the 307th Infantry Regiment, 77th Division, freshly reembarked aboard ship after the Kerama Retto operation, later wrote. "The sky would be filled with black puffs of exploding AA fire. Even when these planes were hit, they were a menace if the pilot had any control remaining to him. Waiting out such an attack without being able to see what was going on made the foxholes on land seem preferable."

Indeed, on the evening of April 2, the division tasted the bitterness of the kamikaze war firsthand when a plane slammed into the superstructure of the USS *Henrico,* instantly killing Colonel Vincent Tanzola, the crusty, bald-headed commander of the 305th Infantry Regiment, as well as his executive officer, two staff officers, several headquarters soldiers, the transport division commander, and the ship's captain while they were eating dinner. Tanzola's lack of pretension had captured the hearts of many of his men. "The colonel was more to us than our commanding officer," the regimental historian wrote mournfully; "he was our buddy." Captain Frank Barron, one of his company commanders, later described him as "loved and respected. He was one of us and we looked up to him." The colonel's seasoned regiment had developed a reputation for excessive griping to the point where General Bruce, the division commander, had only a few months earlier reprovingly ordered Tanzola to put a stop to it. "Their growls were not just ordinary soldier growls but vicious remarks," Bruce wrote to Tanzola of the grousing. "Let me impress upon you that this bitching can become very dangerous and it must be stopped." Deeply saddened by the colonel's death, Bruce immediately wrote a condolence letter to his widow and assured her, "His outstanding bit of work was to raise the 305th Infantry from a very low state of morale to that of the highest. We shall miss a comrade but we all are glad that he went without suffering instead of lingering on while under intense pain. Please accept the love of the division for your departed husband."

During the same attack that claimed Tanzola's life, other kamikazes menaced ships carrying other elements of the division. Several of the suicide planes barely missed but crashed into the water close enough to inflict damage and casualties. One that was shot down by an antiaircraft gun crew fell onto the deck of the USS *Goodhue,* severing a cable and igniting a fire that killed 4 soldiers and wounded 34 from the 307th Infantry Regiment. Another sheared off a radio antenna aboard USS *Chilton,* Bruce's command ship, and crashed into the sea, narrowly missing a direct hit; otherwise he himself might have become a casualty. In total, the division lost a sobering 22 men killed, 76 wounded, and 10 missing from the attacks. Lieutenant Colonel Joseph Coolidge, who took over command of the 305th, told a historian with wry seriousness that "he never wanted to get off a ship and to start eating K rations on dry land as much in his life."[9]

He and the other soldiers finally got their chance on April 16, when the division invaded Ie Shima (pronounced "Eeh Shima"), a small oval-shaped island three and a half miles off the northwest coast of Okinawa opposite the Motobu Peninsula, where the 6th Marine Division fought a difficult battle to destroy a reinforced Japanese battalion and captured a pair of 150-millimeter guns that could have savaged American troops on nearby Ie Shima. With these guns negated and Motobu under American control, Buckner felt that an invasion of Ie Shima was now tenable and desirable. The island measured five miles long and two and a half miles wide. A cluster of airfields, appearing like the Roman numeral XI to an aerial observer, gave value to the otherwise nondescript place. In American hands, Ie Shima could become, in the pithy phrase of one soldier analyst, "a massive permanent 'aircraft carrier' at the doorstep of Japan proper." In the near term, Ie Shima–based American planes could provide close air support to the troops on Okinawa. In the long term, they could fly missions against Japan itself. Lieutenant General Ushijima grasped Ie Shima's possibilities well enough to defend it with an infantry battalion from the 44th Independent Mixed Brigade, plus hundreds of hastily retrained ground crewmen from the 50th Airfield Battalion and a specially organized unit of 580 Okinawan laborers who were expected by their Japanese cousins to fight. The local population numbered no more than 5,000 people, but many were unusually militant and determined to fight.

Most of the island consisted of a rolling plateau. But a volcanic peak, known locally as Iegusugu Mountain and to the Americans as the Pinnacle, rose 607 feet high and loomed over the whole island, particularly the houses and buildings of adjacent Ie town, where most of the population lived. Similar to on Okinawa, the Japanese focused on inland defense rather than on any attempt to foil the invaders at the waterline. The defenders used the Pinnacle as their fulcrum, heavily fortifying the mountain and the surrounding area with "hundreds of pillboxes, caves in limestone sometimes three stories high, and emplacements in . . . concrete houses," General Bruce later commented. "They had lots of mortars, artillery and antitank guns. Tunnels connected some of the positions." Beyond this gossamer-like maze, the Japanese contented themselves with sowing mines and booby-trapped aviation bombs to restrict American movement around the undefended majority of the island.

At 0758 on April 16, under an umbrella of suffocating naval gunfire from a fleet of 2 battleships, 4 cruisers, and 7 destroyers, as well as friendly artillery from Motobu, Bruce successfully landed two regiments, followed soon thereafter by another. In the days that followed, the 77th advanced incrementally against resistance that grew more stubborn as the Americans neared Ie town and the Pinnacle. At night, small groups of Japanese soldiers infiltrated the American lines and attempted to pitch grenades and explosives into their foxholes. Some even strapped the explosives to their bodies. "[They] functioned as human bombs, blowing themselves up as they reached the vicinity of the front line troops," Major Mills Brown, the operations officer of the 306th Infantry Regiment, later wrote. Most of the nocturnal attackers were mowed down by the alert GIs. In some cases, American firepower detonated their explosives, but more than a few of the attackers blew themselves up, usually prematurely. "There were parts of bodies flying all over the place," Private Glenn Searles later wrote of the macabre setting. "Fifteen foot lengths of intestines were hanging from bushes, parts of shoulders and arms, you name it." A flying enemy leg actually broke the arm of one 77th Division soldier. A gruesome panoply of random body parts wallpapered the forward areas. One rifleman had brewed a canteen cup of K ration coffee and set it aside during the evening's excitement. The next morning, he found a noxious string of guts draped over the cup and a backbone lying beside it. Artillery made little impression on many of the sturdiest pillboxes and caves. "No words can describe the fury of the fighting nor the difficulties that had to be surmounted," one officer wrote to a friend. By day, infantrymen, tankers, self-propelled gun crewmen, and flamethrower teams hammered away at these fortifications and the town. "All streets were mined," the historian of the 305th Infantry Regiment later wrote; "machine guns firing from coral rock emplacements prevented mine-detector teams from clearing avenues of approach for our tanks. Progress of the attack was slow and costly."

Hardly a structure survived in Ie town. Human remains predominated amid the ruins. For two days, the corpse of a baby lay rotting in the middle of one wrecked street, its presence hardly even distinctive from any other detritus in such a ruthless environment. "Just looking at the body . . . deeply affected the men," the historian of I Company, 305th

Infantry Regiment, sadly chronicled. "They were devastated when they saw it crushed beneath the treads of a tank moving forward to attack." An agitated Bruce found that he could do little to speed up the pace of his advance, not when his men had to methodically destroy every position and, at the same time, assess the varying threat levels posed by the many hundreds of civilians whom they encountered among the ruins. Moreover, they constantly had to back clear against resistance from hidden or bypassed Japanese. "The fighting here has become more bitter every day," Bruce reported to Buckner. "It is a slow, cave-to-cave, pillbox-to-pillbox, house-to-house fight. Base of Pinnacle surrounded despite bitterest fight I have ever witnessed against a veritable fortress."[10]

The arrival on Ie Shima of forty-four-year-old Ernie Pyle, the most iconic American war correspondent of World War II, added a much welcomed bit of glamour to the grim slog. Known for his strong connection with the average combat soldier and his extremely empathetic, compelling portrayals of them, the Scripps-Howard Pulitzer Prize–winning columnist had seen so much frontline action in the European theater that he probably suffered from combat fatigue. With the war against Germany nearing an end, he might well have concluded his frontline reporting and gone home for good. Instead, he chose to go to the Pacific and tell the story of the GIs who were fighting the war. "There is a war on and I'm part of it," he commented simply. He had by now become so famous that he had probably, through no fault of his own, crossed the line from the reporter's role of anonymous observance to becoming part of the story himself.

On Love Day he had gone ashore with the Marines, seen little action, and returned to a ship, where he spent several days laid up sick. When he decided to embed with the 77th Division at Ie Shima, a tinge of excitement surged through the ranks. "He was enthusiastically received during his hours ashore and was frequently asked for his autograph, which he smilingly provided," the division historian recounted. He quickly endeared himself to the troops. In one typical interaction, he watched a group of soldiers clear several pillboxes, took their names, and, in the recollection of Private Walter Sneed, "commented [that] it was the nicest piece of work he had ever seen." Another squad of riflemen complained to him about the poor quality of their drinking water.

"Some bastards in the rear area, or perhaps they were Navy people, had filled used gasoline cans with water and sent them up to the front," one of the infantrymen recalled. "It made some of the guys sick. Ernie said that he would look into it."

On the evening of April 17, he slept in an abandoned dugout that served as the command post for Lieutenant Colonel Joseph Coolidge, the officer who had taken over for the deceased Tanzola as commander of the 305th Infantry Regiment. The following morning, Pyle, after a quick meeting with General Bruce, hopped into a jeep with Coolidge and several others and rode forward behind a trio of trucks and a military police jeep toward Ie town and the front. A burst from a previously bypassed Japanese machine gunner tore into the jeep, flattened two tires, and punched a hole in the radiator. Everyone scrambled for cover in a nearby ditch. After several quiet moments, Pyle stuck his head up and stole a look around. At that exact moment the Japanese gunner opened fire again. A bullet hit Pyle in the left temple, just below the rim of his helmet, and exited from his right temple, killing him instantly, but without even knocking his sunglasses askew. Nearby, a crouched Lieutenant Colonel Coolidge had no idea that Pyle had been killed. He was only cognizant that "one shot kicked dust in my face, but ricocheted over my head." Even when Coolidge looked at Pyle, he could not immediately tell that anything was amiss. "He was lying on his back; his hands, resting on his chest, were holding a knitted arctic cap, which he was known to carry at all times. His face was composed. No blood flowed and only after I looked at him more closely did I see the hole through each temple."

When word of the famous correspondent's death filtered by field phone back to Bruce's headquarters, the general initially did not believe it. At 1115, once he received corroboration, he sent a sad telegram to Buckner. "Regretfully report Ernie Pyle, who so materially aided in building morale of GI troops, was killed instantly by surprise Jap machine gun fire." To the media, he released a grief-stricken statement: "It is hard to say how much Ernie Pyle meant to the men of our services. I have seen units buck up and be thrilled when they knew Ernie Pyle was around and would give them their just recognition for the dirty job they had to do." In a private letter to General Hodge, he expressed regret that the machine gunner had apparently lurked undetected in what many had thought was a secure area. "Apparently we missed this sniper in our rapid advance and he had laid doggo for almost 24-hours before he opened up." Patrols spent hours tracking the gunner down and securing the area for good.

Soldiers scavenged wood from packing crates and built a makeshift coffin for Pyle's body. In a simple service, with the chaplain of the 305th Infantry Regiment officiating, they buried Pyle alongside their fallen comrades in a small cemetery on Ie Shima. At the spot where he was killed, they placed a marker that read, "At This Spot, the 77th Infantry Division Lost a Buddy, Ernie Pyle, 18 April 1945." The news of Pyle's demise spread with lightning rapidity all around Tenth Army and beyond. Private First Class Ellis Moore of the 96th Division expressed the sentiment of most in a letter to his aunt: "Ernie Pyle's death came as quite a blow to all of us. We all sort of felt that we knew him personally. [He] was the only one who seemed to be able to write accurately about this plain day in and day out weariness which is actual combat." Part of what made Pyle so special was that his penchant for portraying the war's true ugliness and the plight of the average soldier appealed to everyone, even high-ranking officers who might naturally have been leery about such baldly realistic portrayals of the war. "Everyone knows that the G.I.s loved that man," General Bruce once wrote, "but I want to say that the 'brass hats' loved him to [sic]." In a condolence letter to Pyle's wife, Jerry, the general related the details of his death and the reverence in which the 77th Division held him: "I am so glad I told him when he lived how much he meant to the men and how his presence inspired them. Too often we wait until too late to let people know what they do." She warmly replied, "I have not the right to thank you or your men for what you have done for my Ernie—love for him, love returned for the love he gave. Bless you each and every one."

The losses on Ie Shima were not, of course, confined to just a famous war correspondent. Around the same time that Pyle was killed, PFC Philip Warman, a member of a wire team from the 77th Division's Signal Company, and just the sort of man about whom Pyle often wrote, lost his life to a deadly mine explosion. Back in Uniontown, Pennsylvania, his grief-stricken parents found time to write to General Bruce and express their support for his leadership, "so you'd know your men . . . loved you." Bruce replied gratefully that this was "the greatest compliment a general can have from his men and his men's parents. I would rather have this than a commendation from the highest General in our Army." Warman's company commander, Captain Vincent Calandrillo, assured Warman's parents that their son was highly respected among his fellow soldiers "for his extensive knowledge of world events and his soft spoken manner of expressing himself. At company orientations Warman would always emerge as the leader of the group."

By the time the 77th Division secured Ie Shima on the afternoon of April 21, 216 other men besides Warman had been killed, 9 were missing, presumed dead, and another 821 had been wounded. Almost 44 percent of their wounds were caused by small arms fire, a strong indication of the close-quarters nature of the fighting. Engineers destroyed 559 caves and pillboxes, disarmed 2,156 mines, and demolished 405 gasoline drums that had been rigged with detonators. The 77th Division killed 4,794 enemy fighters, many of whom were Okinawan. By one divisional estimate, more than 1,500 locals were armed and outfitted in Japanese uniforms. Only 149 enemy surrendered or were forcibly captured. In six days of Ie Shima fighting, the 77th took almost as many casualties as it had incurred the previous summer over three weeks of combat on Guam.[11]

The intensity of the battle for Ie Shima dovetailed with increasingly hardening Japanese resistance in southern Okinawa. While Geiger's two Marine divisions cleared the north, Hodge turned XXIV Corps south with the 96th Division on the left (from a Japanese perspective) and the 7th Division on the right. Starting on April 5, they encountered their first serious opposition as they began to nose into the first outposts of Ushijima's Shuri Line. "The terrain . . . definitely favored the defender," Captain John Blair, a company commander in the 96th Division, later wrote. "It consisted of a series of ridges, one behind the other from the landing beaches to the southern shores, particularly suited to the organization of defensive positions. These ridges and hill masses were liberally sprinkled with wooded areas and native tombs. The latter formed

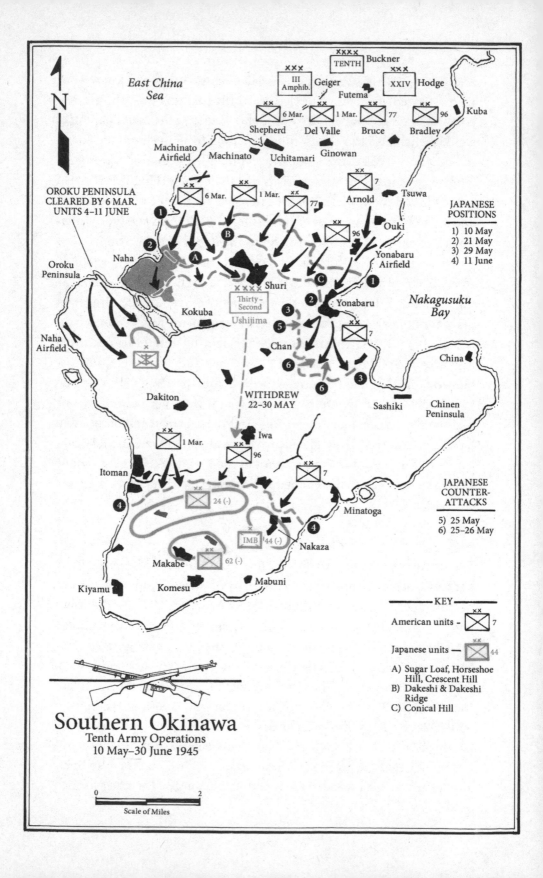

Southern Okinawa
Tenth Army Operations
10 May–30 June 1945

excellent networks of fortified positions, each amounting to a veritable pillbox, as they were constructed with slabs of granite averaging two to three feet in thickness, and capable of accommodating four to twelve armed men and a crew served weapon."

Lead troops of the 7th Division's 184th Infantry Regiment fought a sharp battle to dislodge a company of the 14th Independent Infantry Battalion from a steep hillside on which a fourteenth-century lord had built a stone castle and observation tower, the ruins of which still dominated the area. It was said that in 1853, Commodore Matthew Perry and his uninvited expeditionary party had raised the American flag atop the hill, arguably setting into motion the forces that had led to Okinawa becoming a battleground ninety-two years later. Three times the Americans attacked the hill, and took it only when the surviving 20 of the original 110 defenders, including the commanding officer, fled to the south. "The optimism . . . disappeared and was replaced by the feeling that the 7th Division would now begin paying for gains," the division historian wrote with plaintive accuracy. The 96th Division soon became enmeshed in desperate fighting for the Kakazu Ridge area—the figurative vestibule to Shuri's house—where three battalions from the Imperial Army's 62nd Division cut the attackers to pieces. Enemy artillery and mortars blanketed every route of advance, making it, in the recollection of an Army combat historian who witnessed the fighting, "all but impossible for a human being to stay there and live for long." The experience marked an ominous harbinger for the 96th, a hard-luck, hard-fighting unit that, from this point forward, always seemed to encounter the toughest Japanese resistance on Okinawa. "A complex, interlocking system of coordinated fire-lanes from pillboxes, tunnels and caves on Kakuzu Ridge covered all direct approaches and made them killing grounds," one American officer wrote.

Both sides launched a dizzying series of attacks and counterattacks. Japanese soldiers emerged from caves and flung grenades or live explosives at the Americans. In some cases, they hurled themselves at the GIs and tried to kill them in hand-to-hand fighting. Remnants of some American rifle companies came close to annihilation and, foiled in their attempts to gain objectives, occasionally even had to fight their way back to friendly territory. During the worst of the fighting, bodies of the fallen were left in no-man's-land or in enemy territory. "The color that these men turn as soon as they die is the most horrible part of the scene," PFC Ellis Moore recalled. In most cases that color equated to a brownish black hue. Indifferent GIs treated enemy bodies as so much flotsam. One man leaned over a Japanese corpse and placed a cigarette in its mouth. "Have a cigarette, you yellow son of a bitch," he croaked contemptuously; "sorry I don't have time to light it for you." Hundreds of individual battles to the death solidified a hardness and meanness in soldiers of all ranks. "Never in a thousand years would you expect to get your teeth knocked down to your stomach," Major Art Shaw, an artillery officer who roamed the front line to spot for his gunners, later wrote. "After you've been through some of those firefights and killed a few enemies, the encounters change how you see yourself. You know you can *kill* someone. Sometimes a man gets swallowed by guilt. Other times men recognize that now they know what it means, 'kill or be killed.' Some of the guys just take it in stride. But no one talks about the killing." In a single disastrous day of combat, the 383rd Infantry Regiment suffered 326 casualties and gained nothing. The regiment's L Company was down to 38 upright soldiers. Over three days, from April 7 to 9, the regiment was reduced to 45 percent strength; the 382nd Infantry Regiment was at 61 percent, and the 381st, nominally in reserve, had already lost 18 percent of its men. The XXIV Corps's embedded historian summarized sadly that "the heart of the division had been all but broken on Kakazu Ridge." By the second week of April, the XXIV Corps's front had ground to a near halt, with gains measured in feet.[12]

The stalemate emboldened Lieutenant General Cho and his retinue of aggressive followers on the 32nd Army staff to argue that the time was now right for a counterattack. They were buttressed by similar urgings from Imperial General Headquarters in Tokyo. One hundred feet below the ruins of Shuri Castle, in Ushijima's elaborate subterranean cave headquarters, the staff repeatedly argued the matter. The sturdy walls around them were reinforced with planks and beams that made the cave impervious to American explosives. Electricity, running water, tables, chairs, private rooms, offices, bunks, and a well-stocked kitchen lent a home islands barracks feel to the place. Large stocks of canned goods, beer, and sake added some welcome luxury. Ever attuned to the finer things in life, Cho even had his own personal pastry chef. An office staff of thirty attractive young Japanese and Okinawan women brightened the otherwise dreary underground existence and bolstered morale. A ventilation fan failed to circulate much fresh air. Temperatures generally rose above 90 degrees (outside, they generally ranged from the low 60s to the mid-80s). A dank, sodden humidity suffused the tunnels. The walls sweated so profoundly that dribs of moisture soaked the furniture and documents. The wetness bred mold, fouled cigarettes, and lent a sour taste to rice that had fermented in sacks along the walls.

As early as April 6, Cho had attempted to persuade his chief to attack, but Colonel Yahara had successfully argued, with crystalline rationalism, that the attackers would fall prey to the incredible deadliness of American firepower. He understood, seemingly better than did many of his colleagues, the gravity-like reality that the Japanese soldier in World War II was a far deadlier adversary on the defensive than on the offensive, at least against the Americans in island warfare. Indeed, Major General Archie Arnold, the cool professional who commanded the 7th Division, actually told an embedded historian that he "hoped that the Japanese would counterattack." Regardless, 32nd Army's success in halting the XXIV Corps attacks, in addition to a message from Imperial Navy headquarters in Tokyo claiming that Ten-Go had inflicted crippling damage on the Allied fleet, eventually swung the pendulum in favor of a counterattack. Cho himself climbed the ramparts of Shuri Castle, gazed at the waters off Okinawa's western coast, noted a significant reduction in American ships, and, in a classic self-fulfilling prophecy, attributed this to kamikaze attacks. Actually, he had simply happened to observe the fleet at a time when many ships had unloaded their cargo and were in the process of rotating back to their bases to get more. He persuaded Ushijima, whose laudable consideration for his subordinates had now morphed into a dangerous malleability, to authorize a counterattack.

Cho's mania for self-defeating tactical attacks invites comparison with the similarly courageous but otherwise vacuous, foolishly prideful Confederate General John Bell Hood, who squandered troops and resources in ill-fated attacks against General William Sherman's numerically superior Union Army before Atlanta when the Confederacy would have been far better served strategically to force Sherman into a pro-tracted, defensive battle of attrition to deny him the capture of so great a prize in time to affect the 1864 elections. No doubt ignorant of how this little nugget from American history might have guided them, the staff planned for a pincers-style infiltration assault, involving three in-fantry battalions from the 24th Division and three from the 62nd, with the 44th Independent Mixed Brigade held in reserve as an exploitation force. The end state of the plan was a bit opaque, but it generally cen-tered around the idea of infiltrating the American lines and mixing forces closely enough with the Americans to negate their firepower. With this accomplished, the attackers were to hide out in caves by day and then savage Buckner's rear areas by night.

Cho assigned a leading role to the 62nd Division's 22nd Infantry Regiment under Lieutenant Colonel Masaru Yoshida, whose unit had to move surreptitiously over several difficult miles from the Oroku Penin-sula south of Naha into the front line. The troops moved primarily at night. Under the groaning weight of 110-pound packs, they stumbled over muddy, slippery roads. By day, they hid in sugarcane fields. "The secrecy of our plans must be maintained to the last," Yoshida told his soldiers in a set of final instructions. "March in a sinuous 'eel' line. Al-though you are going to an unfamiliar place, do not make any noise when you arrive, but dig foxholes in hard ground, and camouflage them skillfully." A 32nd Army directive mandated specific infiltration tactics. "The infiltration unit must be divided into the supporting groups (feints, demonstrations, diversions), and the demolition and assault groups. Close liaison must be maintained between them." Colonel Yahara re-mained unreconciled to the attack and knew, with a certainty born of logic, that it would lead to disaster. With no authorization, he personally contacted the two division commanders and persuaded them to reduce the size of the attacking forces by a battalion apiece. So the counterat-tack now consisted of four battalions instead of six. Yahara's insubordi-nate actions would likely have gotten him court-martialed in the US Army. He suffered no such repercussions in the Imperial Army and instead succeeded in saving two irreplaceable infantry battalions from squanderous destruction.

On the evening of April 12, shortly after dusk, a pair of red flares and a dragon flare exploded over the front lines. From signal codes captured several days earlier, American intelligence officers actually knew that the flares were a sign of an imminent attack. The knowledge had little impact on the average soldier for whom this night initially seemed like any other. Soon that changed as the Japanese showered the American lines with hundreds of 105- and 150-millimeter artillery shells. The 96th Division later estimated that its two forward-most regiments absorbed over 1,000 rounds apiece, leading, in the recollection of Captain John Blair, a company commander, to "six to eight hours of miserable existence in foxholes, praying constantly that the next round wouldn't strike home." A single frontline battalion in the 7th Division recorded explosions from 200 105-millimeter shells in less than five minutes. The Japanese added mortar fire to the mix, including 320-millimeter shells from a newly implemented spigot mortar whose terrifying 660-pound rounds descended in a malevolent parabola. The artillery and mortar barrage was less than pleasant, but it did almost no damage to the Americans, most of whom were hunkered deeply into foxholes or bunkers (a cautionary example of artillery's ineffectiveness against dug-in defenders and one the Yanks would have done well to note).

Predictably, Cho's counterattack failed miserably. When the assault troops went forward, they were either decimated by American mortar, artillery, and machine-gun fire, or became involved in intimate close-quarters battles against squad- and platoon-size American units, or they infiltrated and got lost or isolated and were killed in place. The attack on the 7th Division front amounted to little more than sharp probes. The 96th Division absorbed a more powerful blow but, aided by the illumination of Navy star shells, slaughtered the cream of the 62nd Division's 272nd Independent Infantry Battalion's rifle companies. "Deeds of heroism became the rule and not the exception," Captain Blair later noted. The Americans sprayed bullets and shells into the attackers and defiantly taunted them with derisive shouts of "banzai"!

In one remarkable instance, on a forlorn ledge overlooking a draw of Kakazu Ridge, Staff Sergeant Beauford Anderson, a mortar squad leader in the 381st Infantry Regiment, ordered his men to take cover in a tomb while he fought off the assaulting Japanese. Anderson quickly expended all his grenades and carbine ammunition. Out of desperation he grew especially resourceful. He tore 60-millimeter mortar shells out of their casings, removed the safety pins, banged the shells against a wall to release their setback pins, and threw them football style into the roaring Japanese below the ledge. According to one Army report, "their screams were soon reduced to moans. Those who were able to, retreated." In total, he threw 15 live mortar shells at them. He stood guard all night on the lookout for another attack that never came. In the daylight, he and his troops found 25 dead Japanese soldiers who were heavily laden with explosives, machine guns, and knee mortars, probably the better portion of what had been a weapons platoon. In part due to his actions, his battalion did not take a single casualty that evening. Anderson received a well-deserved Medal of Honor. The 96th Division soldiers counted 317 dead enemy, "stacked up like cordwood," according to the testimony of one observer. On the bodies of dead sergeants, the Americans found precise diagrams of their frontline positions, a disquieting testimony to Japanese powers of observance, if not necessarily forbearance. A fortunate Japanese survivor of the battle sadly told his diary, "We, having suffered heavy casualties, withdrew, taking heavy punishment from concussions. Only four of us . . . were left. The Akiyama Tai (1st Company, 272nd) was wiped out while infiltrating. The Shimuzu Tai (2d Company) also suffered heavy losses. The company fell apart during withdrawal."[13]

As the survivors dribbled back to Shuri, a chastened Ushijima hunkered 32nd Army back down into its caves and other fortifications. In the aftermath of the disastrous Japanese counterthrust, General Buckner hoped to overwhelm Ushijima with a renewed offensive. "We are up against the most formidable defenses yet encountered in the Pacific, well backed by artillery and . . . mortars," he opined in a letter to Adele. The methodical Tenth Army commander took several days to reorganize his forces and prepare them for an unambiguous frontal assault offensive that the 96th Division historian dubbed, with a touch of hyperbole, "the greatest land attack in the history of the Pacific War." Buckner fed his reserve unit, the 27th Infantry Division—still smarting from the unfair smearing of its reputation in the Saipan battle—onto the western (or left) side of the XXIV Corps front. The 96th Division moved into the middle, and the 7th remained on the eastern coast.

Beginning on April 19, Buckner hurled the three divisions into the honeycomb of Ushijima's Shuri defenses, initiating yet another desperate, ineffectual bloodbath. Preparation from twenty-seven battalions of artillery, including Marine tubes and naval gunfire, bludgeoned the entire area with 19,000 shells in the space of forty minutes. "It seemed inconceivable that the Japanese troops could have survived our murderous shelling," Private Donald Dencker, the 96th Division mortarman, later wrote. But it barely made any difference. The XXIV Corps artillery commander estimated that, at very best, the barrage killed 190 Japanese, roughly one for every one hundred shells expended. The Japanese simply took shelter in caves and tunnels during the shelling. "He remained below ground, later emerging with large numbers of weapons very close to our front lines," the Tenth Army's after-action report sadly declared of the enemy. "Our infantry as it advanced was subjected to all the rifle, machine-gun, mortar and artillery fire at the enemy's disposal."

The attackers were ripped apart along the nightmarish Golgotha of jagged, fortified ridgelines. One observing officer was deeply shocked at "the huge sacrifice of life in close quarter vicious fighting required to wrest [this ground] from the enemy. The person who sees it for the first time is appalled, as was my feeling upon seeing this 'hell' of [a] battlefield. One is not prepared for what he sees by the news stories. These have failed utterly to give a true account of the . . . bitter fighting." On this first day alone, XXIV Corps suffered 720 casualties for next to nothing, and yet this sort of fighting dragged on for days. "The US infantry had to brave the artillery and enemy infantry weapons because most often they could not be destroyed by our supporting fires," stated the after-action report of the 96th Division's hard-hit 382nd Infantry Regiment. "While the Jap could carry out his defensive mission by remaining under cover, the US infantry in the attack was constantly exposed to Jap fire." Private First Class Melvin Coobs, a young rifleman in the regiment, later testified to the mind-numbing litany of making repeated death-defying attempts to keep moving forward. "Most of the time we were on the attack. Sometimes our advances could be measured in feet or yards and every night was filled with the tension of watching for infiltrators. We went from hill to hill and ridge to ridge, always the exposed attacker trying to root out the concealed defender."

As on many other Pacific battlegrounds, the Japanese took advantage of the American propensity to retire into nervous nighttime perimeters by probing them seemingly every evening. "The enemy not being accustomed to night fighting generally has a fixed idea that night is for resting," a 32nd Army training document declared contemptuously. "They fear our night raids to an extreme degree. As a whole they are noisy at night. This affords us many opportunities to surprise them." On the unusual occasions that the Americans did attack at night, they generally succeeded in capturing their objectives, and at less cost. "Often [this] enabled our troops to obtain positions which could not be reached during the day," stated Tenth Army's after-action report. In spite of this intriguing pattern, it seemed never to occur to Buckner nor any other commander to reorient their operations in favor of nighttime attacks. One embedded combat historian in the thick of the action drifted to the rear long enough to report to his superiors that "the instant one unit got ahead of another, it came under withering fire from its exposed flanks." He envisioned no "short cut to victory, no Patton-like thrusts deep into the enemy rear. From now on it was a matter of maintaining relentless pressure, being content with small gains, and killing Japs until there were no more to man the caves and tombs and machine gun nests." Nor was the vision of a Verdun-like meat grinder battle of attrition unique to historical observers. Buckner had deliberately decided to embrace this concept in the expectation that the Japanese would buckle sooner rather than later. "I am not hurrying the attack . . . but am greatly reducing casualties by a gradual and systematic reduction of their works," he told Adele. "This we are doing successfully and can, I feel confident, break their line in ample time for our purposes." Others felt far less certain of this than did Buckner.[14]

Escorted by a dozen fighter planes, Admiral Nimitz flew from Guam, where he had recently relocated his headquarters, to Okinawa on April 22. He brought with him key members of his staff and General Alexander Archer Vandegrift, commandant of the Marine Corps. That evening Nimitz ate dinner with Admiral Spruance aboard the battleship USS *New Mexico* and personally witnessed Japanese aerial attacks against Fifth Fleet ships. The next day, Nimitz gathered his entourage and Spruance for a tour of the American-controlled parts of the island with

Buckner. They were pleasantly surprised to learn that engineers estimated that Okinawa and Ie Shima together could add 22 mature airfields to the American ledger, plus enough harbors to negate the need for any further operations in the Ryukyus, China, or perhaps even Formosa, where previously American war planners had assumed that they would need to seize more bases for the ultimate invasion of Japan.

Nimitz and his retinue were not as sanguine about the state of the bloody, inconclusive fighting along the Shuri Line. When Nimitz ventured that Tenth Army must speed up its operations in order to remove the supporting fleet from harm as quickly as possible, Buckner bristled and said something to the effect of "the ground campaign is an Army operation and that's my business, not yours." The admiral's normally polite veneer evaporated for a moment. He glared at Buckner and retorted, with a hint of menace, "Yes, but ground though it may be, I'm losing a ship and a half a day. So if this line isn't moving within five days, we'll get someone here to move it so we can all get out from under these stupid air attacks." The tense exchange highlighted the conundrum that challenged Army-Navy relations throughout the entire Pacific War. No matter how well versed Army commanders became in amphibious operations, they still had to deal with the blood-and-guts reality of ground combat. Specifically, they had to find ways to maintain the momentum of offensive operations at a time when modern weaponry afforded well-fortified defenders the opportunity to inflict massive casualties, and often a stalemated defeat, on attackers. To overcome this perilous challenge, Army ground commanders knew they must rely on minutely coordinated combined arms operations and overwhelming firepower, an inherently deliberate process that absorbed time and required a steep experiential learning curve. This was especially true for a generation of senior officers who had, in the wake of World War I, been schooled to oversee continental, littoral operations where they would not have to concern themselves much with the security of supporting naval forces.

By contrast, naval officers were imbued with an axiomatic reluctance to lose ships, the very core resource and raison d'être of their service, and precious assets that were far more expensive for the nation to replace than the expendable trucks, tanks, and artillery pieces commonly consumed in land warfare. The potency of aircraft, especially of the suicide variety, as a mortal enemy to ships added a new element of vulnerability to any fleet within range of enemy planes. An admiral of the near past had needed only concern himself with the threats posed by an enemy surface challenger, submarines, and probably mines as well. The advent of aviation made naval warfare three-dimensional, greatly increasing the perils of any naval activity, much less the vulnerability of any stationary fleet charged with babysitting ground operations.

Moreover, the task of sustaining and maintaining large numbers of ships in a combat zone put a logistical strain on even so sophisticated a military instrument as the 1945 US Navy. In the big geostrategic picture of vast American wealth and shipyard production, Nimitz probably could afford to lose a ship and a half a day, but, with his sailors dying in alarming numbers—since L Day, the Navy had lost 1,297 killed in action, primarily to kamikazes—he could be forgiven for looking at the matter stringently. With Tenth Army suffering an average of about 2,800 battle casualties per week since L Day, Buckner was naturally more focused on the welfare of his soldiers and Marines. Both he and Nimitz were reasonable men, partners, even friends. The tension between them lasted only moments and no longer. They fully understood their mutual interests, and Buckner respected Nimitz's ultimate authority. They remained on excellent personal terms; the admiral gifted a bottle of fine liquor to Buckner, who promptly pledged to pop it open when organized Japanese resistance on Okinawa ended. "I am getting thirsty," an eager Buckner later joked to Adele in an allusion to the liquor.

The fundamental question before Nimitz and Buckner was how best to achieve their collective goal of hastening Ushijima's demise and securing Okinawa. When the group had lunch at Major General Geiger's command post, Vandegrift and the III Amphibious Corps commander proposed the notion of launching a new invasion of southern Okinawa to outflank the Shuri Line. Marine Brigadier General Oliver Smith, Buckner's deputy chief of staff, added his own support. Smith understood the considerable risks but liked the notion of forcing the Japanese "to fight on two fronts, one not of their own choosing." The Marine officers suggested the 2nd Marine Division for the job. After carrying out the L Day feint against the Minatoga beaches on the island's southeastern coast, the unit had returned to Saipan a little more than a week earlier. Rear Admiral Forrest Sherman, Nimitz's chief of staff, contended that by the time the division could be reembarked and loaded aboard ships and transported to Okinawa, the need for the invasion would probably be over. "We promised him it could be underway in six hours," Vandegrift later wrote.

Actually, the Marine generals were not the only ones urging Buckner to authorize a new invasion. Well over a week before this April 23 meeting, even before embarking upon the invasion of Ie Shima, Major General Bruce of the 77th Division lobbied Buckner and his staff for the go-ahead to make new landings somewhere on Okinawa's southern coast. The innovative Bruce saw a golden opportunity to reprise the division's successful invasion of Ormoc only four months earlier, an operation that had arguably compromised the entire Japanese position on Leyte and hastened the American capture of the island. Bruce did not see the 77th's battle on Ie Shima as any real obstacle to its usage elsewhere. If need be, he argued in a letter to Buckner, "the division can be reboated in LSTs and LCMs and the like as a shore-to-shore operation similar to that made on Leyte." Bruce was serious enough about the concept to prepare detailed plans and take his case to Major General Hodge, the XXIV Corps commander, who was initially ambivalent about the idea but ultimately supportive. "I know you will want to kick me in the fanny for keeping on talking about landing on the Southeastern portion of Okinawa," he wrote to Hodge on April 19. "You know without my saying so that I will carry out orders, but I still feel that landing there is to the best interest of everybody concerned."

Buckner and his staff closely studied the concept. Owing to reef and beach conditions, they ruled out any spot on the coast except Minatoga, but even that area presented difficulties, as they well knew from their months of planning for Iceberg. "This particular beach is flanked and covered by an escarpment to the west which was one of the most highly developed defensive positions on Okinawa," Brigadier General Lawrence Schick, the Tenth Army's deputy chief of staff, asserted in a postwar letter to an Army historian. "This position also covers all outlets from the beach area. This beach was also within the range of Jap mortar and artillery emplacements on the Chinen peninsula" immediately to the north. Brigadier General David Blakelock, Buckner's supply officer, had also studied the terrain in depth and formed the view that, even in the absence of heavy opposition, "it would be extremely difficult to land and supply more than one division on the whole of the south coast" because of reefs, cliffs, and lack of inland infrastructure. He advised Buckner that he could guarantee only to supply food and not necessarily ammunition to any division that landed at Minatoga.

Bruce had studied the same data, but formed completely different conclusions. After his experiences supplying the 77th Division over a makeshift beachhead at Ormoc, he had no concerns about logistics. He felt strongly that LVTs could move plenty of troops and supplies ashore over the reefs and then develop the beachhead with little difficulty. To negate Japanese control of the high ground overlooking the Minatoga beaches, he planned to seize a smaller adjacent island as an artillery platform and also use "the hundreds of guns in the immense Naval force available which could, by enfilading fire from both sides of the Chinen peninsula, well support the Division. The close support of troops could also be obtained by . . . 81mm and 4.2 mortars. Furthermore, air support was available." He was confident that his men could make it ashore and, with this fire support, seize the Chinen Peninsula and unhinge any Japanese opposition along the whole southeastern coast. Once in their rear, he would force Ushijima either to react to him or face the prospect of having a sizable enemy force threaten the vulnerable backside of the Shuri Line. In fact, Colonel Yahara had worried about just such a possibility and mentioned it to Ushijima and Cho as part of his vain attempt to thwart the ill-fated April 12 counterattack. "What I warned [about] most was that the U.S. forces would land behind and take the Japanese forces in the rear," he later commented.[15]

Careful and deliberate by nature, the Tenth Army commander seriously pondered these contrasting recommendations for several days in mid-April. The decision was a difficult one. The landings entailed real risks, especially in relation to Japanese resistance, probably more so than Bruce admitted, especially considering the fact that the capture of Ie Shima had already cost his division 1,047 casualties. Buckner saw Bruce as brilliant but unstrung, so he dealt with him warily. "Buckner laughs at Bruce for having crazy ideas," General Joseph Stilwell, who visited Tenth Army during the battle, confided with disapproval to his diary. "'Two out of 15 are O.K. The rest are impossible.' It might be a good thing to listen to him." Beyond the idea of outflanking the Japanese, the purpose of the operation centered around the hope of minimizing friendly casualties, at a time when Buckner could not have known that the horrible Shuri fighting would rage on for weeks. The potential defeat of Bruce's regiments would only add to the casualty figures and hand the enemy a propaganda victory. "General Buckner very much wanted to make the landings on the southern shore," Brigadier General Elwyn "E.D." Post, his loyal chief of staff, later claimed. "It was only after he weighed all factors that he dismissed the plan as being too hazardous."

Even so, Buckner's decision to forgo the operation actually owed more to the limitations of a risk-averse, inexperienced commander than to any fatal flaw in the concept. At heart, Buckner was not particularly aggressive or innovative; by comparison, even Krueger seemed positively adventurous. Buckner was also imbued with the understandable caution of a newcomer. He had little direct experience with amphibious warfare, certainly much less than Bruce and the Marine commanders, so he could not quite grasp the game-changing possibilities offered by outflanking invasions. Bruce knew he could make the Minatoga invasion work because he had already done something strikingly similar at Ormoc on Leyte the previous year. The Marine generals had done the same at other points in the Pacific. Buckner had no such muscle memory of success to embolden him now. His staff was similarly inexperienced. Their mindset simply reflected, as aides are wont to do, that of their chief. Together they saw too many risks and too few opportunities. Logistics should not have been their primary concern. What really mattered was dispersing Japanese strength from the Shuri area, not the long-term viability of the invasion area as a base. Even in the unlikely event that the Japanese succeeded in penning the 77th into its beachhead—presumably by expending combat power that could have impacted the Shuri fighting—the overwhelming strength of Allied naval power would have kept Bruce's people adequately supplied.

When Buckner scotched the operation, he revealingly expressed the concern that it would become "another Anzio, only worse," an allusion to the ill-fated attempt by the Allies in January 1944 to outflank German fortifications in Italy by landing troops behind their lines, only twenty-two miles from Rome. But the comparison between a multidivision invasion against an enemy that controlled a continent, had access to major reinforcements, and whose supply lines were intact as opposed to a smaller landing against an isolated foe on an island was patently ridiculous. The Japanese on Okinawa could not have hoped to wield the power that the Germans had at Anzio. The fact that Buckner would even compare the two revealed a gap in his understanding of amphibious warfare. Seemingly, in his mind, all outflanking invasions were alike, regardless of circumstances, a clearly untrue premise. Nonetheless, flawed premises or not, Buckner had made his choice and he stood by it. On April 21, Brigadier General Post dutifully informed a disappointed Bruce of Buckner's decision. "He feels the presence of your Division here [on the Shuri Line] will turn the tide definitely in our favor. In view of the developments, he simply cannot permit you to land as you prefer over the southeastern beaches."

By the time of the April 23 meeting with Nimitz, Spruance, Vandegrift, and company, Buckner had mentally moved on from the concept. Vandegrift's proposal to use the 2nd Marine Division in an equivalent manner to Bruce's 77th put the lie to the incorrect notion that disagreements over the secondary invasion somehow revealed inherent philosophical differences on the issue between the Army and the Marine Corps. In truth, Bruce, Hodge, and the Marines were all simpatico on the notion, as were many other Army officers. "No one will ever convince me that the tactics employed at Okinawa were not contrary to everything our service schools have taught for the last thirty years," Brigadier General Edwin Randle, the 77th's assistant division commander and a long-serving soldier who had earned the Distinguished Service Cross for combat bravery in North Africa, wrote to Bruce after the war. "And after several landings I participated in during the war, and particularly the one at Ormoc, no will ever convince me that a landing anywhere on Okanawa [sic] could not have been supported logistically. With all the veteran amphibiously trained troops, and with all of the array of Naval vessels of all classes in the greatest abundance, there is no question but that a very great mistake in decision was made."

Colonel John Guerard, the XXIV Corps operations officer, told the embedded corps historian during the battle that the invasion plan "would throw the Japanese into a tailspin." Hodge concurred, and even made a personal appeal, in vain, to Buckner. Thus, the Tenth Army commander's choice to forgo an invasion and instead invest his resources in a frontal assault reflected his own personal proclivities, not some sort of doctrinal difference between the Army and the Marines. When Buckner explained his reasoning to Nimitz at their meeting, the admiral accepted the general's plans at face value and declined to overrule him.[16]

Tenth Army now inelegantly bulled ahead, struggling for mastery over southern Okinawa's endless ridges and crags, in fighting that was faintly reminiscent of the Western Front in World War I. At various times the battle involved both Marine divisions and all four Army divisions, with no real difference in the way the two services fought. "They seem to be following the same techniques," wrote one combat historian who observed frontline actions of both Marines and soldiers, "advancing slowly, ferreting out the Japanese positions, using combined weapons against the positions, moving up more men and supporting weapons, and repeating [this] on the next hill." With no sign of another invasion, Ushijima fed in reserves from the southern coast. "Not a single inch of the present line should be yielded to the enemy," a directive for the newcomers exhorted. "The front line is your grave. Anyone retreating will be killed (in the front line or in the rear). We were born to fight for this very day. This is the most important of all the important battles. It is an opportunity to serve the Emperor loyally to the end." Nor was this just mere headquarters cheerleading that had no bearing on the men at the front. The average enemy soldier fought with a ferociousness that prompted one rifle company commander in the 96th to assess, with a sense of vexed, horrified admiration common to almost all Americans on Okinawa, that "the courage of the individual Japanese soldier is unquestioned. Their complete disregard for their own lives was the height of fanatical stupidity. In fire discipline and camouflage, they were undoubtedly better trained than our own men." General Buckner told reporters during a press conference that the only way to defeat the enemy defenses and gain ground was by employing a "corkscrew and blow-torch" approach of total annihilation. He knew of what he spoke. He visited the front lines incessantly, almost every day, a consistent, courageous presence who, in the estimation of one admiring soldier, "was familiar with every nook and cranny of Okinawa." A crack shot, Buckner enjoyed sniping at the Japanese with rifles he borrowed from frontline troops. "He lay there on the ground shooting for ten or fifteen minutes," Private Herman Buffington, a 96th Division rifleman who once lent his weapon to the general, later recalled. "I could see that the 'old fellow' was shooting really well."

The complex Japanese defenses reflected a studied erudition on their part. They had noticed that the Americans tended to relax after ascending to the crest of a hill on the assumption that making it to the highest ground automatically meant control of the entire hill. In response, the Japanese dug deeply into the reverse slopes of hills, where they heavily camouflaged themselves. This put them in perfect position to devastate the Americans when they appeared on the crests or, even better, when they descended the reverse slopes. Dugouts, holes, tunnels, reinforced concrete pillboxes, caves, and the like bristled with Nambu machine guns, knee mortars, 47-millimeter antitank guns, and artillery pieces of varying calibers. "Each hill was prepared for defense by a complete network of caves and tunnels," wrote Captain Joseph Vering, a rifle company commander in the 96th Division. "These were, in most cases, large enough to provide living and storage space for the occupying troops. Mole-like digging turned the hills into fortresses providing cover, concealment and completely safe routes through which troops could move to mass their fires on any attack from any direction. Hundreds of firing positions for all types of weapons were provided by openings leading into the tunnels on several levels in all directions." The proliferation of so many mutually supporting caves and tunnels, with few blind spots, only added to the deadliness of these cobweb-like networks, as did the fact that many were underground and provided impervious shelter to enemy soldiers. "Use of reverse slopes in the siting of caves and all other fortifications was most pronounced," the Tenth Army's after-action report intoned, almost with a tinge of affected outrage. "This added to the difficulty of neutralizing cave mouths by fire and of obtaining fire support for infantry attacking the cave. As most of the caves on those reverse slopes face to the flanks and rear, attacks on fortified positions from these directions were difficult. Staying on the summit [of a hill] was often suicidal."

The Japanese understood, perhaps better than did the Americans, that since the war's migration north of the equator, jungle had now given way to caves as the war's key characteristic, defensible terrain. Lieutenant Colonel Robert Williams, an Army Ground Forces observer attached to Tenth Army, reported soberly to his superiors in Washington on the proliferation of fortified hillside caves: "[They] were at varying levels, some at the base, some half-way up, and some at the summits. Some tunnels were 100 or 200 feet in length. Weapons, including AT guns, were fired from camouflaged positions in the entrances. Entrances were protected by wires and mines. In addition, the Japs had built pillboxes so that the hills on all sides were dotted with gun positions, well dug-in and camouflaged, often connected and mutually supporting. There was very little dead space in the Japs' defensive fire plan."[17]

The only antidote for this powerful bottleneck of defenses was the almost symphonically coordinated application of combined arms firepower over the course of protracted daily, even hourly attacks. The Americans wielded their ordnance like a cudgel to bludgeon the Japanese into lifeless pulp under the weight of unrelenting blows. Spruance's fleet furnished an unprecedented level of support for a ground operation. Each attacking infantry regiment was partnered with a fire support ship, generally ranging in size from a destroyer to a battleship. Every division and the two corps also enjoyed support from their own designated ships. Each day, Buckner's forces were supported on average by 3 battleships, 3 heavy cruisers, 1 light cruiser, and 5 destroyers, plus smaller vessels. Highly trained Army-Navy Joint Assault Signal Companies masterfully coordinated the immense naval firepower. In the course of the fighting, the ships fired an incredible 448,997 shells, ranging in caliber from 5 inches to 16 inches. To riflemen like PFC Martin Allday of the 96th Division, the big shells zooming overhead "sounded like a freight train. It is loud just going through the air, and it knocked a big hole in the hill it was hitting." Venerable Shuri Castle, whose origins dated back at least five hundred years, was reduced to ruins, as was

Yonabaru and whatever remained of Naha. In the evenings, the ships shot another 66,653 star shells that illuminated much of the front and limited the concealment of enemy infiltrators.

Field artillery provided even more firepower. With the possible exception of the Red Army, no other military organization on earth could begin to challenge the supremacy of American artillery. On Okinawa, every infantry division's order of battle contained four battalions of organic artillery, and this total did not even include the self-propelled and antitank guns of Army infantry regiments. Corps artillery added yet more tubes to the equation. The 7th Infantry Division alone consumed 286,757 shells in the course of the campaign, roughly four and a half times the number of projectiles it brought to the island, necessitating a complete resupply of ordnance every two weeks just to maintain normal operations—one can only imagine the immensely strained logistical efforts that underpinned these generous expenditures. Buckner's gunners fired a truly staggering total of 1.75 million shells in the course of the fighting, comprising 130 million pounds of ordnance. By contrast, even though the Japanese mobilized their maximum artillery effort of any island battle, their output amounted to roughly 100,000 shells, or just 6 percent of the American expenditure. Heavy mortar crews poured even more steel onto the enemy. In a little over a week of combat, a single 81-millimeter mortar platoon from the 77th Division lobbed 19,000 shells in support of attacking riflemen. "In every sense of the word, the 81mm mortars were the battalion commander's own artillery," Lieutenant Lawrence Fawcett, a mortar platoon leader, avowed.

The Japanese were so well entrenched that, incredibly, the massive firepower did not do much more than restrict their mobility and shatter their communications network. By the estimate of one captured Japanese officer, his unit needed a full six hours just to transmit a fire mission request to an artillery battery farther to the rear. Air strikes by fighters added to the constant pounding, if not necessarily its lethality. Occasionally, a well-placed 1,000-pound bomb with a delayed fuse might seal a cave or cause its roof to collapse. In the estimation of Tenth Army's air liaison officer, "many defended areas . . . were so honeycombed with organized cave defenses, that the entire hillside had to be practically blown away before the objective was captured." Most typically, the aviators could contribute little else besides dropping napalm to burn off the foliage that camouflaged cave entrances, hillsides, and ridgelines.[18]

The mass firepower masked the disquieting reality of intimate small unit actions that raged for weeks from cave to cave, hill to hill, and ridge to ridge. "With unsurpassed courage, the infantry soldiers waded in and slugged it out with the Jap on his own ground," Colonel Macey Dill, commander of the 96th Division's 382nd Infantry Regiment, wrote in the unit's after-action report. A grizzled rifle platoon sergeant commented brusquely, "I have no faith at all in this artillery, naval, and air fire getting them out of their caves. The infantryman has got to dig them out." Another hard-fighting combat soldier added that "the only solution was assault by small infantry units who could work up to the entrances by fire and movement and either clear or seal the caves. The necessity for the assault infantryman to know demolitions became very evident." The patches of high ground they attempted to capture were named either for their height in meters, such as Hills 95 and 178, or, owing to the American predilection for nicknames, they were assigned individual monikers like Conical Hill, Sugar Loaf Hill, Item Hill, Tombstone Ridge, Kochi Ridge, Dakeshi Ridge, Zebra Hill, Chocolate Drop Hill, Dorothy Hill, and many other terrible death grounds. "This . . . is a slow, inch-by-inch fight," General Bruce bemoaned of the struggle in a letter to Admiral Nimitz. In a separate letter, Bruce had conveyed much the same sentiment to his mother, Martha, and she replied, in a moving Mother's Day missive, "Some of the hardest [fighting] of the war is going on now and yet . . . I seem to feel a certain peace in spite of this fact. I've been trying to march in spirit with you . . . these trying days. I am hoping it will not be long now till all this terrible war will be over and the world rid of so much that is evil."

For the assault troops who were enmeshed in this daily meat grinder, the primary motivation to keep going was, in the recollection of one rifleman, "other guys moving forward. You saw your buddy moving forward, and you moved forward too." Self-propelled guns and tanks hosed down any suspected cave or pillbox in the hopes of exposing entrances and covering the advance of riflemen, demolition teams, and flamethrower operators who mercilessly shot, blasted, or roasted enemy soldiers. "It has been hard on the honorable Nip," Captain Pat LaValle, a company commander in the 77th Division, wrote to his cousin. "He is quite a mole and loves to bury himself into caves . . . which is very annoying. Usually we give him the hot foot . . . with the flamethrower and a few sticks of candy—the kind that goes boom!" A 96th Division after-action report described this process as "slow, systematic destruction." Liberal use of smoke grenades obscured the vision of the defenders and revealed previously unseen caves or holes. "Each of these openings was then spotted and additional demolition crews sent forward with satchel charges to destroy the emplacements. It was usually found that a 20-pound satchel charge with a 30 to 45-second fuse would effectively seal most caves and emplacements." Division records claimed 273 caves sealed and another 317 pillboxes or other emplacements destroyed. Riflemen expended enormous quantities of bullets, debunking the ratio-of-fire myth that no more than 15–20 percent of soldiers fired their weapons in combat during World War II. The 7th Division alone fired 1,685,040 M1 Garand 30.06-caliber bullets—an average of about 481 bullets fired per rifleman!

In a few instances, engineers pumped hundreds of gallons of gasoline into caves and ignited it with tracer bullets or white phosphorous grenades, burning the Japanese to death in showers of flaming fuel. "We look on the Japs . . . as rodents to be exterminated such as a rat that buries itself in caves, gets into attics of buildings, etc.," Bruce wrote to the mother of a 77th Division soldier about the prevalent dehumanizing attitude that proliferated among the combat troops. A 7th Division private echoed the sentiment, commenting with chilling brevity on the prevailing zero-sum attitude. "I did not consider the enemy as a person. They were . . . to be killed as if they were animals." Close-quarters fighting, even sometimes hand-to-hand, was anything but uncommon. The desperate fight for survival left little room for mercy. The GIs killed or they died. "This may be a shocking statement . . . but at one time in my life, I was a hardened killer," Herman Buffington, a 96th Division rifleman, wrote soberly years after the war. "I probably killed more human beings on Okinawa in three months than have been murdered in Jackson County [Georgia], where I live, in the past 10 or 15 years. I am not proud of this but I do know it was a necessary part of my job." After one bitter firefight, Private Glenn Searles and several squad mates found a badly wounded Japanese officer who demanded help. "I know the Geneva Convention. You are required to care for all the wounded!" An unmoved GI retorted, "Piss on you, shithead," and shot him to death on the spot.[19]

The rhythm of this deathly close combat soon centered around repeated assaults by highly exposed, numerically small tank-infantry teams. No single American weapon on Okinawa was more indispensable to the destruction of Japanese defenses than the tank, the first time that armor played such a prominent, starring role in a Pacific War battle. Indeed, General Ushijima asserted in a directive circulated throughout 32nd Army during the fighting that "the enemy's power lies in his tanks. It has become obvious that our general battle against the American forces is a battle against their . . . tanks." In fact, Tenth Army's order of battle included enough Sherman medium tanks to populate a standard armored division in Europe, though the organization was markedly different. European theater armored divisions operated as combined arms entities with armored infantry, armored field artillery, armored engineers, and the like comprising a preponderance of the unit's manpower. On Okinawa, the 20th Armored Group operated as a clearinghouse administrative headquarters overseeing four tank battalions and an armored flamethrower tank battalion, each of which operated independently in support of the infantry divisions (the order of battle also included three amphibious tank battalions and six amphibious tractor or LVT battalions that played a leading role in the invasion but less so after L Day).

The armored battalion commanders parceled out their tanks either platoon by platoon or company by company with attacking infantry battalions. "On the platoon level, control and coordination took several forms," a postwar Armor School study by a team of experienced tank officers related. "If the tank turrets were open, voice or hand signals sufficed for target designation and direct contact. With turrets closed, the telephone attached to the back of each tank provided a ready means of communication." Their teamwork depended too much on close proximity to one another. Far too often the infantrymen became separated from the tanks or pinned down alongside them. The two groups did not have direct radio contact with each other. To communicate in these circumstances, they had to relay radio messages up their respective chains of command, a time-consuming, inefficient process and one fraught with the potential for disastrous miscommunication or misunderstanding. Regardless, they formed a potent team, one that comprised the only real way to destroy Ushijima's defenses and gain ground. "The number of these small units, each engaged in taking a certain pillbox, or of closing a certain cave, or of wiping out a machine gun, or of destroying an entrenched squad of Japanese by grenades, or of hurling satchel charges into a position that could not otherwise be reached, was multitudinous across the whole front," Captain Roy Appleman, the XXIV Corps historian, wrote insightfully after personally witnessing weeks of combat. "Each little action was a desperate adventure in itself, and generally had to be executed in close coordination with the assaults of adjacent small units, each helping to neutralize action against the other. In general it was a fight that required many small groups to think out carefully just how a pinpoint on a map was to be taken, and then by paying a price in blood to wrest the place from the enemy over his dead bodies."

The fighting boiled with an almost industrial intensity. The average tank company burned between 800 and 1,500 gallons of fuel for each day on the front line; each battalion fired 700 main gun 75-millimeter shells per day and sprayed the Japanese with 51,377 .30-caliber machine-gun bullets. The 711th Tank Battalion documented the expenditure of 49,000 main gun 75-millimeter shells for its 51 tanks that fought in support of the 7th Division and asserted that these quantities "are proof of a very stiff fight." The typical Sherman tank carried 100 rounds for its 75-millimeter main gun. Most were high-explosive shells with an identifying coat of yellow paint slathered over their noses; a few were blue-nosed white phosphorous rounds that the tankers used to lay down smoke screens. Due to the paucity of Japanese armor, few American tanks carried armor-piercing rounds in any real numbers.

Aboard the Sherman, the five-man crew worked together with the closeness of proximity and synchronicity that stemmed from the deadly seriousness of their dependence upon one another for survival. Instant, efficient communication meant the difference between life and death. "All five crew members wore leather helmets that contained ear phones and throat mikes," Lieutenant Bob Green, a platoon leader in the 763rd Tank Battalion, explained. "The tank commander could talk to crew members on an intercom system, or, by flicking a switch, to other tanks. As the tank platoon leader did most of the talking, he used a larger, hand-held microphone which transmitted more clearly than did the throat mikes. The large radio was in the upper rear part of the turret, and by pushing buttons the tank platoon leader could talk or listen in to various other units connected into his radio 'net.'" The crew stored a dozen shells in ready racks just behind the breech of the main gun and more in sponsons along the inside hull of the vehicle. A pair of .30-caliber machine guns added a devastating dimension of antipersonnel firepower. Their tracer rounds allowed the tank commander in the turret to site in on targets for the main gun, especially when he and his crew were buttoned up inside the tank with their hatches closed, as they often were for fear of getting hit by Japanese sniper and machine-gun fire. With the hatches closed, the visibility of the crewmen was severely limited to an inadequate periscope and narrow vision slits. "You're out in front, vision very limited, constant roar of guns, motors, radio and . . . looking for your own infantry and trying to distinguish who is friendly and who isn't," one tank commander wrote to his mother. "They all look about alike through a periscope."

In reality, the infantrymen became their eyes and ears. Knowing this, the Japanese sought to separate dogfaces from the tanks and isolate each armored vehicle into a stranded, helpless beast. Hidden mines blew the treads and bogie wheels off Shermans, immobilizing them. Artillery or mortar shells killed, wounded, or scattered infantrymen, damaged tank armor and main guns, or spooked crewmen into abandoning their vehicles. Suicide antitank teams of three to nine men sprang from caves or holes to assault stranded tanks. "The Jap has a nasty habit of running up to tanks with satchel charges, bangalore torpedoes or antitank mines and attempting to stay with the tank until both tank and Jap are destroyed," Lieutenant Colonel Robert Williams, the Army Ground Forces observer, reported during the battle. Tank retrieval vehicles—the unsung heroes of the armor world—and ordnance teams usually recovered and repaired the damaged or abandoned Shermans within a day, so the Japanese tried to finish off immobilized tanks as quickly as possible, preferably with the crew still inside.

To this end, the attackers employed a range of weapons, but followed a predictable pattern. As one of the soldiers pitched a smoke grenade to blind the tank crewmen, others hurled grenades to keep them from evacuating the tank. At the same time, two others attempted to place a mine on the undercarriage or explosives on the tank's rear deck or hurl Molotov cocktails into viewing slits. "The tankers could never relax," an Armor School study later shuddered. "Attacks varied from carefully planned ambushes to fanatic charges across open ground toward the tanks." Similar to the awestruck fear with which sailors regarded the kamikazes, most Tenth Army combat soldiers, including Lieutenant Green, the tank platoon commander with the 763rd, felt that the suicide teams comprised "the spookiest anti-tank weapon the Japanese used against us. At the height of an attack, when several exploding satchel-charges were going off at once, legs . . . along with arms, heads (complete with helmets), and various other body parts would fly off in all directions. If the tank were disabled and isolated from other tank support, then other Japanese would take the place of their blown-up comrades and attack that tank. They would quickly swarm all over it with picks, crow bars and sledge hammers in an effort to pry up a hatch and drop a grenade inside. There was something unsettling about satchel-charge teams. We found it hard to fathom the fact that so many young Japanese soldiers could be influenced or brainwashed to literally blow themselves to bits so nonchalantly. Deliberately killing yourself in droves was beyond the pale for the mind of the ordinary American serviceman to accept."

Unlike the kamikazes, the antitank assault teams were more frightening than they were effective. In most instances, supporting tanks or infantrymen slaughtered them with accurate sheets of machine-gun or rifle fire. Of the 221 American tanks destroyed or severely damaged by enemy action during the battle, suicide attackers accounted for only 8. Mines claimed 64 victims. Antitank guns, especially carefully hidden 47-millimeter wheeled 1,600-pound pieces, represented the gravest threat, inflicting over 50 percent of the losses. Japanese crews moved their guns from prepared spot to prepared spot through tunnels. "Positions void of guns one day, were found occupied during the night by the enemy and ready for action the following day," noted one tank battalion after-action report.

The gun had an effective range up to 800 yards and a 2,700-feet-per-second muzzle velocity that allowed its shell to penetrate all but the thickest armor on a Sherman. The projectile might have torn through the tank and exited cleanly, leaving two unsettling holes behind. Or it might have ricocheted inside, tearing off limbs or smashing torsos; in the worst cases, it exploded and set off high-explosive shells in the ready racks or penetrated the rear fuel tank, touching off a catastrophic fire. Japanese crewmen held their fire until tanks approached within a couple hundred yards and then unleashed rapid shots. "When Jap antitank guns hit a tank, they didn't stop but kept on firing," one 77th Division soldier testified of the Japanese propensity to snap off as many shots, whether well aimed or not, as possible before American tanks could respond. In one cautionary incident on Kakazu Ridge, accurate 47-millimeter fire disabled five tanks "in rapid succession . . . before the gun was spotted and destroyed," according to one on-site analyst. Fortunately, the 47-millimeter gun emitted a telltale muzzle flash that acted as a beacon for adrenaline-charged Sherman gunners, "as if someone . . . quickly flashed a spotlight on and off," according to one tank commander. Gunners poured massive quantities of high-explosive shells at any muzzle flash. "The gun cannot be knocked out by near hits," the commander of one infantry regiment commented with wonderment. "The shells have to go right into the cave with it, on a flat trajectory."

If the tank-infantry and demolition teams comprised Buckner's corkscrew, then the newly introduced 713th Tank Battalion with 55 flamethrower tanks functioned as the blowtorch, spewing jets of a sticky, liquid napalm-and-gasoline mixture to effective ranges of 80 to 100 yards. Appropriately nicknamed "Zippos" by the GIs, after a popular cigarette lighter, the flame tanks were parceled out all over the Tenth Army front and soon proved themselves a powerfully effective weapon without which the battle would have proven even more difficult. "I loved the sight of it shooting that fire," Private John Ryan, a BAR man in the 96th Division's 383rd Infantry Regiment, later commented, expressing a nearly universal opinion among the combat soldiers. Each tank carried 300 gallons of weaponized fuel that would deplete after only about a minute's worth of shooting. Covered by standard tanks and accompanying infantry soldiers who prudently situated themselves to the rear of the flamethrower tank, they saturated the seemingly endless hillsides and caves of Okinawa with liquid flames, consigning enemy soldiers who happened to be in the way to a frightful, painful death as gelatinous burning gasoline stuck tenaciously to them and consumed their skin and organs. "The gunner would discharge his raw napalm at the target," one Marine officer later commented, "and when he saw it hit a pillbox or aperture of a cave, he could press a solenoid switch that lit up the napalm he was now shooting. That thin stream of flame now ignited what was already on the target. It was the ultimate weapon, able to squirt flame right into the position."

They burned away foliage, exposing cleverly hidden positions. In some instances, the tanks poured enough flame into caves to consume the oxygen inside and asphyxiate the defenders. Far more commonly, they motivated the Japanese to do anything to escape the fire, even if that meant leaving shelter to get mowed down by American machine guns and rifles and conventional tank shells. "The Japanese were terrified by the flame tank," Captain Dennis Neill, an armor officer, commented grimly. One unit report clinically claimed that "when all weapons failed to dislodge the suicidal enemy from his last stand defensive position, they would quickly and efficiently dispatch the enemy." A Tenth Army analysis determined that the flamethrower tanks comprised an even more lethal psychological than tangible weapon, one that forced the Japanese to choose between death by fire or death by ordnance. "Its real value lies in its ability to drive the Jap out of his prepared positions into the open to be killed by supporting troops. Regardless of the Jap's fanatical intention to hold his ground, experience has shown that he will not remain in his hole when flame is brought to bear upon him, but will make every effort to get out and away from the flame."[20]

Even with this fearsome weapon, advances were measured in yards, not miles. "Many times we would be pinned down by enemy fire and not be able to move backward or forward," Private Marvin Schroeder, a rifleman in the 96th Division, later wrote, "and as soon as we hit the ground, we started digging." Kakazu Ridge did not even fall until April 24, and by early May, the Americans were still enmeshed in fighting among the ring of highly defensible ridges just north of Shuri. Their stolid progress encouraged Cho to advocate for yet another foolish counteroffensive. At a sake-soaked 32nd Army staff meeting on the evening of April 29, the emperor's birthday and a hallowed holiday in Japan, Cho proposed to launch an all-out attack against the XXIV Corps lines. As Cho saw the situation, if 32nd Army remained on the defensive, it would eventually be overwhelmed and destroyed by the Americans. Instead of waiting to die, it was better to attack and attempt to engulf the enemy in mutual annihilation. Unsurprisingly, Colonel Yahara spoke out against this nihilistic and self-destructive drivel. "To take the offensive with inferior forces . . . is reckless and would lead to certain defeat. The army must continue its current operations, calmly recognizing its final destiny—for annihilation is inevitable no matter what is done."

Cho and Yahara both understood correctly that 32nd Army faced total destruction, but only Yahara comprehended that it could administer far more damage upon the American adversary, and accomplish much more for Japan strategically, through defense than offense. Nonetheless, Cho had a powerful, magnetic personality. His views prevailed with the rest of the staff, the division commanders, and, most importantly, Ushijima. Yahara might have been a voice in the wilderness, but his superiors seemed to respect and perhaps even fear him. The normally polite Ushijima took him aside and warned him not to undercut this offensive as he had the previous one. Yahara assured him of his loyal support even though, in his opinion, the offensive would comprise nothing more than a "meaningless suicide attack." Ushijima actually agreed but said that at least it would be honorable. The admission revealed that the 32nd Army commander had given in to the Imperial Army's propensity for costly symbolism over constructive substance. Cho then personally visited Yahara in his quarters and tearfully asked for the colonel's full support. The reserved Yahara was moved to tears himself and reluctantly replied, "I consent." The mood of aggressive symbolism infused some of the assault troops, too. Captain Koichi Ito, whose 1st Battalion, 32nd Infantry, was assigned a leading role, knew that his unit had little chance to succeed but nonetheless told himself that "pride demanded the attack be conducted as conceived."

On May 3, the night before the offensive, Ushijima and Cho gathered with other general officers in the headquarters cave for a private banquet. Cho's chef prepared a feast of pantry food and canned goods, served by the smiling office women dressed in their finest clothes, and washed down with liberal quantities of Scotch and sake. The well-oiled generals congratulated one another on their impending victory. As these delusional senior leaders sat safely tucked inside their cave, merrily drinking and eating, their soldiers went forward, almost in the manner of sacrificial lambs. "The time of the attack has finally come," one nervous infantryman scrawled in his diary. "I have my doubts as to whether this all-out offensive will succeed, but I will fight fiercely with the thought in mind that this war for the Empire will last 100 years." He was right to have doubts. In less than two days of furious but pointless fighting, 32nd Army lost between five and seven thousand of its best remaining soldiers and untold numbers of irreplaceable artillery pieces, to accomplish nothing more than the attainment of a temporary, and quickly abandoned, salient in the American lines. One dying Japanese soldier scribbled in his diary, "I must fight to the bitter end, for a moment ago a comrade died. I'm certain a battlefield is inconceivable to the people at home."

The 62nd Division now had only one quarter of its original strength left; the 24th Division had lost nearly half of its troops. The 5th Artillery Command's stocks of shells were so depleted that General Kojo Wada, the commander, issued a strict ration of fifteen shells per day for each remaining gun. The debacle prompted a chastened Ushijima to summon Colonel Yahara to his office for yet another heart-to-heart. Sitting cross-legged on the floor, the 32nd Army commander fixed an emotional, pensive gaze on his operations officer: "Colonel Yahara, as you predicted, this offensive has been a total failure. Your judgment was correct." He vowed to follow Yahara's defensive blueprint and authorize no more wasteful attacks. "My instructions to you are to do whatever you feel is necessary." Yahara attempted to suppress anger, not only at his commander's fickle diffidence but at himself for not taking a stronger stand against the offensive. "It was now too late to accomplish anything," Yahara later wrote sadly. "I was not only frustrated, I was furious. Still, I appreciated his sincerity and the fact that he could admit the truth. I could feel his remorse about our situation." Even Cho, who overheard the whole conversation from his adjacent office, now admitted that attacks served no further purpose. Like thousands of other Japanese soldiers, he resigned himself to fight to the end and die a warrior's death. "Hey, Yahara, when will it be okay for me to commit hara-kiri?" he now gibed the operations officer, with the characteristic mixture of humorous irreverence and appalling fanaticism that so marked his personality.[21]

Like a dreary factory working round the clock in multiple shifts, Tenth Army simply resumed its drab offensive, battering away at the Japanese each enervating day, with only negligible gains. Buckner still refused to reconsider the notion of an outflanking amphibious invasion, for which respected *New York Herald Tribune* correspondent Homer Bigart heavily criticized him, describing his tactics as "ultra conservative," and initiating a controversy over the matter that endures to this day. "Instead of an end run, we persisted in frontal attacks. It was hey-diddle-diddle straight down the middle," Bigart wrote. Bigart's opinion mattered because of his reputation in military circles as "the most competent, most hard working, best informed by numerous visits to the front correspondent that has been present during the Okinawa battle," Captain Roy Appleman, the XXIV Corps embedded historian, assessed. At a press conference, an unrepentant Buckner vigorously defended his decisions. "If we'd scattered our forces we might have got licked, or it might have unduly prolonged the campaign . . . or we might have been forced to call on additional troops, which we did not want to do. We didn't need to rush forward, because we had secured enough airfields to execute our development mission."

By now, any semblance of civilization and natural beauty in the Shuri area had been thoroughly destroyed by modern firepower. Naha no longer existed as anything recognizable, nor did any other village. Some 200,000 naval and artillery shells and innumerable 1,000-pound bombs had struck the village of Shuri alone. "The stone walls were battered down," said a XXIV Corps post-battle report. "The rubble of the houses lay in heaps." Shuri Castle's walls were twenty feet thick and had stood for five hundred years, but they lay in shambled ruins now. According to the same XXIV Corps report, adjacent groves of previously beautiful trees "were nothing but bare and gaunt silhouettes on the skyline, stripped of all their life, dismal reminders of the devastating havoc of war that had struck the place. Shell fragments were everywhere under foot, some huge jagged pieces of metal from large-caliber shells, and countless pieces of brown rusting fragments. Pieces of broken pottery and china and tile were strewn over the ground. Foxholes and trenches and dugouts were everywhere. Smashed bits of furniture showed through heaps of rubble and broken red tile. Tattered bits of clothing, Japanese military and Okinawan civilian, lay about in confusion. Over it all hung a smell of death, the stench of rotting human flesh."

Heavy monsoon-like rains in the second half of May only added to the wretchedness and turned southern Okinawa into a flooded, muddy wasteland that did much to bog down Buckner's forces along the hills of the Shuri Line. "Those on the forward slopes of hills slid down, those on the reverse slopes slid back, otherwise no change," one exasperated operations officer reported sardonically to higher headquarters. Captain Lauren Soth, the 96th Division's embedded historian, described the relentless deluge as "a succession of horrors and misery. Even with no Japs around, it would have been bad enough—more than many men could stand. You were wet through all the time. You lived in a hole in the muddy side of a hill. You tried to keep the rain out by stretching a poncho over it—but you couldn't. Your boots and clothes were plastered with adhesive clay. At night you shivered . . . envying the Japs on the other side of the hill [who had] dry caves to live in." Private First Class Horace Floyd, an 81-millimeter mortar crewman in the 96th Division's 381st Infantry Regiment, told his family in a letter he somehow managed to keep dry. "Yesterday it rained, rained and rained. Man your lifeboats men. Yes . . . the rainy season has started, and we are into the mud over knee deep in places." Over the course of one especially heavy ten-day stretch in May, twelve inches of rain showered the island.

The profound wetness fouled ammunition, rusted weapons, spoiled food, and, perhaps worst of all, generated seas of mud, the enduring foot pudding of the Pacific War. To Soth, the mud appeared so thick and deep that "it was like half-set concrete." Roads were so inundated that, in the recollection of one observer, they "became increasingly worse and degenerated into quagmires of yellow reddish sticky clay mud." The muck immobilized vehicles much more effectively than did anything the Japanese could devise, robbing the Americans of their vaunted automation. Tanks, DUKWs, trucks, bulldozers, trailers, and artillery pieces either could not move or sank irretrievably into the maw, like some sort of latter-year mastodons into tar pits. Lieutenant Leach of the 77th Division lamented to his journal that roads and trails had become "so badly mired that it would be impossible to bring up anything heavier than a jeep, and even that couldn't get very far." Typical of most artillerymen, Private Edmund Austin now spent most of his time attempting to keep his crew's 8-inch piece from disappearing into the ooze after each fire mission. "We would spend days trying to dig it out, throwing everything we had under it, powder cans and everything we could find."

The stalemate and its inherent devolution of modernity reeked more of the infamous World War I Western Front than of maneuver amphibious warfare, except that 22,000 tons of vital cargo were landing on the beaches each day and somehow had to be moved forward. With the vehicles on the sidelines, the soldiers themselves functioned as human pack mules. "Supplies had to be hand carried 400 to 1,500 yards to the front line," Captain Appleman chronicled. "Life was miserable. Foxholes dug into the banks of slopes caved in under the influence of unceasing rains. Tanks could not move. Self propelled guns . . . were immobilized. Airplanes could not take to the air to provide observation. These factors made it all but impossible to maintain the pressure that the plans called for. The heavens seemed to come to the aid of the Emperor's cohorts on Okinawa." Nearly everyone on both sides was mired in the moldy, wet filth, rendering them unrecognizable to the point where recently promoted Captain Richard Spencer of the 77th Division contended that "it became difficult to distinguish friend from foe." The profound misery precluded all but a myopic preoccupation with survival. News on May 8 of Germany's surrender was generally greeted with supportive indifference. "Nazi Germany might as well have been on the moon," one Marine quipped. The dead bodies of men from both sides decomposed quickly amid the welter of flooded foxholes, mud banks, and shell holes. Master Sergeant James MacGregor Burns, a combat historian who would one day go on to fame as a presidential biographer, described the bodies he saw on one death ground as "broken and blackened. The bulkiness of our men's bodies as compared with the Japs made them look all the more ghastly."

A horrid curtain of putrefaction and stench hung over southern Okinawa, a kind of hellish degradation that seemed to mark a low point for modern humanity. "Big juicy horse flies would light on a corpse pretty damned quick," PFC Martin Allday of the 96th Division shuddered. "I mean, in thirty minutes they were after the corpse. The maggots were terrible looking, to watch them work in a corpse. That was tough stuff." Private First Class Frank Kittek brusquely referred to his surroundings in a letter to his family as "all torn down and stink. Lots of dead Japs or parts of them are . . . laying all over like horse shit. Sure is a mess." Anyone at the front for more than the briefest time had little choice but to wallow in that disgusting, horrifying "mess." Corporal Eugene Sledge, a mortarman in the 1st Marine Division, attempted to dig a foxhole only to unearth the decaying remnants of a Japanese soldier. "I gazed down in horror and disbelief as the metal scraped a clean track through the mud along the dirty whitish bone and cartilage with ribs attached. The shovel skidded into the rotting abdomen with a squishing sound. The odor nearly overwhelmed me as I rocked back on my heels." Shortly thereafter, one of his friends lost his footing and slid on his belly down a ridgeline through a sea of mud. "He was, of course, muddy from the slide. But that was the least of it. White, fat maggots tumbled and rolled off his cartridge belt, pockets, and folds of his dungaree jacket and trousers. He was as tough and as hard as any man I ever knew. But that slide was almost too much for him. I thought he was going to scream or crack up. Having to wallow in war's putrefaction was almost more than the toughest of us could bear." They grabbed sticks and scraped the maggots off him as best they could. To Sledge, these surroundings were "so degrading I believed we had been flung into hell's own cesspool."[22]

Waterlogged Tenth Army paid in blood for most every forward step. By the middle of May, weekly battle casualties were topping 3,000 men, including at least 500 fatalities. At least 400 wounded men were evacuated from the island each day; another 200 were lost every day to what the Army termed nonbattle casualties. Any attack, no matter how successful or otherwise, exacted a human toll. Sugar Loaf Hill alone cost the 6th Marine Division 2,662 men killed, wounded, and missing. South of Kakazu Ridge, the Japanese tenaciously defended an even more prominent stretch of jagged high ground that the Americans alternately referred to as the Urasoe-Mura Escarpment, the Maeda Escarpment, and, most popularly, Hacksaw Ridge. The combat soldiers who fought for this fortified high ground also gave it "names that can't be printed," one junior officer later wrote, "embodying all the hate [they] felt for this treacherous obstacle and the Japs upon it and inside of it." The 96th Division's embedded historians described it as "a sheer precipice rising for 40–50 feet above the foothills and rocky boulders beneath it, and could be scaled with difficulty only at the extreme western side. At the eastern edge, a rocky crag jutted skyward surrounded by several large boulders of lesser height. To the left of this 'Needle Rock' there was a two hundred yard open saddle which rose on its eastern end into tree-covered Hill 150."

A natural combination of sheer cliffs, escarpment, plateau, rocks, and caves, Hacksaw and its environs dominated the entire area for many miles, to the point where anyone atop it could have seen all the way to northern Okinawa. In the estimation of one officer, the mere sight of this malevolent high ground was enough "to chill the blood of any dough-boy." The Japanese took full advantage of what nature had created. "The Japs had dug in caves and tunnels, all interconnecting and mutually supporting," wrote Lieutenant Paul Leach, the 77th Division historian. "They had shafts dug vertically down into the mountain, with tunnels to the forward and reverse slopes." For nearly ten days in late April and early May, first the 96th Division and then the 77th Division struggled desperately to take this key high ground; many of the assault troops ascended cargo nets up the cliff just to fight atop the plateau. To prepare the way for them, artillery and mortar batteries relentlessly pounded identifiable pillboxes and caves, after which, in the recollection of Captain Richard Spencer, operations officer of the 1st Battalion, 306th Infantry Regiment, "we mixed gasoline and oil and poured this down improvised chutes into the caves. After this was ignited, explosive satchel charges followed."

Still, the fighting was a bloodbath. The 77th Division's 307th Infantry Regiment lost 87 killed, 396 wounded, 3 missing, and 110 others, mostly to combat fatigue. The fatality numbers unquestionably would have been higher if not for the remarkable, courageous efforts of PFC Desmond Doss, a Seventh-day Adventist conscientious objector who refused to carry a weapon no matter how great the danger to his own life. Even through the heaviest of the fighting, he stayed atop the plateau by himself, administering first aid to scores of badly wounded soldiers, hauling them to the edge of the cliff, tying ropes around each man individually, and arduously lowering him to the waiting arms of American soldiers standing thirty-five feet below, at the base of the cliff. "I just kept praying, 'Lord, please help me get one more,'" Doss later recalled of his relentless, and almost spiritual, mindset. It was a feat that demonstrated a brilliant combination of competency, know-how, and valor. According to unit records, Doss saved at least fifty soldiers in this fashion, often under heavy fire and somehow evading nearby Japanese, while wearing a uniform so caked with blood that his platoon leader later personally found a new one for him. "He was one of the bravest persons alive," Captain Jack Glover, his company commander, once opined. Revered throughout the entire division for his compassion and courage, Doss received the Medal of Honor.

Dozens of more anonymous hills claimed their daily victims, proliferating stricken networks of tragedy that spiderwebbed through hundreds and then thousands of American homes like that of Sergeant Bob Heuer, who was killed by machine-gun fire as he led his squad in an attack. "My grief was uncontrollable," his close friend PFC Paul Kaup shortly thereafter wrote poignantly to Heuer's parents of his loss. "The fellows in the company want me to make it plain that he died at the head of his men. I know that each one of them thought as much of Bob as I did, and they'll never forget him." Some of the deceased had eerie premonitions of what soon befell them. When a rifleman who disliked beans tried unsuccessfully to trade them with one of his squad mates as they ate breakfast before one attack, their sergeant urged the rifleman to wait until later. "Sergeant, I won't be here to trade it with anyone later," he replied sadly. "This will be the last hill I'll ever have to climb." Within hours, he was mortally wounded in an attack on that hill.

Callous survivors carried on, none more than the combat medics who constantly battled death. "I remember once I would get sick at seeing blood, but I have seen much more & worse than just blood," Tech 4 Nathan Mandel, an Army medic who treated hundreds of stricken men, wrote to his parents. Similarly, Private Searles of the 77th Division nearly grew used to the sight of his many dead comrades, even one whom he personally retrieved and buried. "Evidently, [a] grenade exploded between his back and the side of [his] hole. He was split up the back from his hips to the back of his head as if a meat cleaver had done the job. His spine was divided neatly and his chest cavity was completely empty above the diaphragm. The occipital portion of the skull was gone, but the brain was intact." The ferocity of the fighting made it impossible to evacuate many of the dead, who, in the recollection of Corporal Eugene Sledge, "lay pathetically just as they had been killed, half submerged in muck and water, rusting weapons still in hand. Swarms of big flies hovered about them."[23]

By a considerable margin, mortars, antitank guns, artillery shells, and grenades presented a greater peril to the Americans than machine guns and rifles. In XXIV Corps, gunshots accounted for 27 percent of the casualties and fragmentation wounds nearly 70 percent. In the 7th Division, half of all surgeries involved bone fractures. According to a study conducted by medics in the 106th Infantry Regiment, 27th Division, the most likely place for a soldier to get hit was in the legs, then somewhere on the arms, and after that the hands and the face. The men might have been comforted to know that hits to the scrotum were relatively unusual, comprising only 4.5 percent of the regiment's wounds.

Tenth Army's elaborate medical infrastructure swelled to include six field hospitals, six portable surgical hospitals, and the organic medical units that were part of every sizable combat formation. A useful variety of neurosurgeons, orthopedic surgeons, dental surgeons, and general surgeons populated most of these units. The hospitals also included female nurses of the Army Nurse Corps who arrived on May 3, in the midst of some of the heaviest fighting. Like any other soldier, they wore fatigues and helmets and carried M1 carbines for their own protection. Unlike the male soldiers, they lived behind barbed wire and were escorted by a pair of armed guards whenever they left their hospitals "because of a few isolated and unpleasant episodes," one of them later wrote with euphemistic mystery. In a constant battle to keep their hospitals clean, they spent hours scrubbing and washing tent floors, clothing, equipment, and patients. Day and night, they cared for the vast population of patients streaming back from the fighting fronts. "Casualties . . . never stopped coming," Lieutenant Catharine Breisacher, one of the nurses, wrote in a history of the Army Nurse Corps on Okinawa. "The wards were in large rectangular pits, covered with tentage and banked with sand bags. The patients were on canvas cots with only blankets for covering, no clean white linens . . . just rows of injured, dirty, suffering men in tent after tent. Here was pathos and sorrow for every minute of every day and too much work to be done to think of tears of pity. Everywhere in these hospitals were men suffering from the brutal, crippling wounds which only war can produce." General Buckner regularly visited the wounded and, unlike many commanders who had difficulty seeing such ghastly results of their orders, usually came away invigorated by the experience. "Blood donations save hundreds who would otherwise die of shock and bleeding," he wrote admiringly of his medics to Adele. "On the whole, the wounded are cheerful and optimistic. It is remarkable how badly a man can be shot up and still recover." Indeed, specially refrigerated Naval Air Service Transport planes flew blood from Los Angeles and San Francisco to Guam and then on to Okinawa. A refrigerated and medically equipped LST stored and dispersed even more plasma and whole blood, making it available for immediate transfusions for those who needed it.

The wounded varied from men who were barely nicked to those who had no chance to survive, and everything in between. Typical of many thousands of others, Lieutenant Gage Rodman, a platoon leader in the 7th Division, fell prey to a mortar shell during an attack to take a well-defended ridge. The explosion knocked him over; hot fragments ripped into his leg and tore his abdomen open. "The next thing I knew I was seated on the ground," he later wrote. "Then I caught sight of what seemed like several yards of pink tubing on the front of my trousers." The "pink tubing" was actually his intestines. A company medic and one of his sergeants gave him first aid, a normal process for combat wounded. He received a syrette of morphine, and his sergeant "made a temporary covering for my exposed intestines." Tenth Army employed fleets of jeeps and DUKWs to function as ambulances. The automation saved countless lives. At times during the Okinawa campaign, wounded were removed from the battlefield in only fifteen minutes and made it to collecting stations within thirty minutes. In Rodman's case, a litter team hauled him to a jeep that took him to a portable surgical hospital where doctors immediately operated on him to install a colostomy bag and remove fragments from his exposed abdomen. After a ten-day stay, he was transported aboard the USS *Anne Arundel* to the 148th General Hospital on Saipan, where he endured three months of operations and convalescence.

Rodman was just one of 30,848 patients evacuated in the course of the campaign from Okinawa, about half by water and half by air, to more permanent installations throughout the Pacific. At the height of the battle, the 148th once admitted 505 patients in a single day. On Saipan, Rodman reluctantly wrote about his wounding to his parents in hopes of keeping them from worrying. "I've been hesitating about saying where I was hit because it sounds worse than it is," he ventured diplomatically. "I guess you'll worry more if you didn't know, so I'll tell you. I got a fragment of mortar shell right on my old appendicitis scar. I am doing fine and will be perfectly all right given enough time." But he was actually less than all right. Though he survived, he was afflicted with brain abscesses that probably stemmed from infections of his colostomy bag. He suffered from chronic, violent headaches and partial paralysis, and he sometimes had difficulty speaking.

Although no medical personnel faced more privation and danger than combat aidmen like Desmond Doss who were directly attached to frontline units, battalion surgeons generally functioned in an exposed role as the forward-most physicians. Most worked within a mile of the front, close enough to become involved in combat, but just far enough away to conduct emergency surgery. Casualties streamed into their overwhelmed aid stations in such disturbingly high numbers as to turn the doctors into highly trained crisis managers. Over a twelve-day period in May, Lieutenant James Wong, the surgeon for the 77th Division's 3rd Battalion, 305th Infantry Regiment, personally cared for an almost unbelievable 532 battle casualties, including 84 in a single day.

"The vicious hand to hand battles resulted in an unusually large number of serious mutilations and Lieutenant Wong, with extraordinary medical skill, saved many amputations and lives," read his citation for a well-deserved award of the Legion of Merit. When a tank repairman was horribly wounded by a mine, Wong personally led a stretcher team more than one thousand yards through the minefield to administer first aid to the man, who was, according to the citation, "in a semiconscious condition, in deep shock, and screaming in agony. His right leg and thigh were almost completely severed, his left leg was blown off at the calf, and his arms were badly mangled and had compound fractures. Multiple fragmentation wounds mutilated the entire front of his body and face beyond recognition. Within a two-yard radius of the place where the man lay, there were four exposed mines." Wong somehow managed to save the soldier's life and calmly lead the litter team out of the minefield. The surgeons regularly made split-second life-and-death decisions amid terrible carnage. "It is beyond the talent of this historian to fully describe the atmosphere," a troubled combat historian, Lieutenant Paul Leach of the 77th Division, wrote in his journal after visiting a battalion aid station. "The men all have the same color, a dirty gray. They are all very dirty, their clothes have been on them, day and night, for at least a week. They realize they are . . . badly hurt. Very few of them can smile. Humor is not present. They have been completely and utterly embroiled in a war, of man to man fighting under very disturbing conditions of semidarkness, artillery, filth, wholesale killing, and seeing their friends of years standing being knocked off. It is not a pretty sight."

Some wounded men were beyond saving, and, typically with far more patients than time to care for them, the doctors had to make the traumatic judgment to set the mortally wounded aside to die as peacefully as possible. "You provided what care and comfort you could and watched him die," Captain John Tobey, surgeon for the 3rd Battalion, 307th Infantry Regiment, wrote sadly. Like nearly every other battalion surgeon, he struggled to find some way to maintain a balance between providing empathetic care and maintaining a clinical distance. "The average soldier or marine might be devastated by the loss of a buddy but the Battalion Surgeon had to endure all the losses—the ones he knew personally and the ones he only vaguely recognized. There were too many. But one took refuge in the fact that there were even more who might have died or become permanently disabled, but who would survive & perhaps recover fully because of the work that you did, while sharing the same jeopardies. One had to remain calm—at least outwardly—in order to think clearly & not permit fear to interfere with your work."[24]

As with Krueger's Sixth Army on Luzon, the Tenth Army was plagued with combat fatigue, especially as the fighting wore on, and in terrible conditions, with no apparent end in sight. The Tenth suffered 26,221 so-called nonbattle casualties (15,613 Army and 10,598 Marines), a substantial proportion of whom were afflicted with some form of combat fatigue. The malady accounted for one in seven of all hospital admissions, a rate that might even have exceeded gunshot wounds. One commander estimated that in a single microcosmic attack that gained eight hundred yards of Okinawan soil, combat fatigue accounted for an eye-opening 25 percent of the unit's losses. Of course the notion that these men were not battle casualties was absurd—the same was largely true for those evacuated with dysentery, malaria, typhus, and other diseases. To wit, a Tenth Army correlation analysis found that a higher incidence of traditional battle casualties inevitably led to more supposed nonbattle casualties.

The preponderance of Japanese artillery and mortar fire wore on the psyches of many soldiers, especially veterans who were surprised at the volume of enemy shells compared with their previous combat experiences; "therefore their preconceived notions got a violent shock when they ran into so much here all of a sudden," Colonel Lawrence Potter, a XXIV Corps surgeon, told a historian. Private Russell Davis, who had seen heavy action on Peleliu with the 1st Marine Division, later testified that "we were out of practice and our nerves were not in shape for the slam of the guns." A theater medical report asserted that "the admission rate was in direct proportion to the amount of artillery fire the unit received. Cases were typical [sic] manifest by confusion, disorientation, amnesia, incoherent speech, tremor, startle pattern and other indications of emotional stress." Another treating physician described the casualties as victims of "severe anxiety and fear neuroses. These 'battle fatigues' were brought to the aid stations trembling violently, glassy-eyed, crouched and flinching, and many were crying hysterically. Old, hardened soldiers broke up the same as new troops." Some lost touch with reality, others just the will to carry on, wearing "expressions of idiots or simpletons knocked too witless to be afraid any more," Corporal Eugene Sledge, the Marine mortarman, later wrote with somber eloquence. "They ranged in their reactions from a state of dull detachment seemingly unaware of their surroundings, to quiet sobbing, or all the way to wild screaming and shouting." He and other frontline fighters quietly sympathized, with the unspoken understanding that they, too, might fall prey to combat fatigue just as easily as to enemy ordnance.

Every bit as much as the steady shellfire, the daily hopelessness of intense combat, the lack of sleep each night for fear of Japanese infiltrators, and the constant exposure to frontline privations of filth, lousy weather, and food all accumulated like a debt that must ultimately be paid. Even the bravest hit their breaking point, either randomly or as a result of some traumatic event. When a buddy of Private Glenn Searles fell asleep on watch one night, allowing a Japanese soldier to come close to killing several men with a grenade, he "spent the rest of the night in the bottom of our hole crying. He was evacuated the next day with combat fatigue." The last time Searles saw him, he was lying on a stretcher, encased in a straitjacket, waiting to go home. "When I spoke to him, he could not meet my eyes. He was a brave soldier. What a pity!" During the savage fighting for the Maeda Escarpment, a tank platoon leader who was assigned to support an important attack by 96th Division infantrymen became so terrified that he lost control of himself. Brigadier General Claudius Easley, the hard-charging, incredibly courageous assistant division commander of the 96th Division, climbed onto the tank turret and sternly told him to carry on in support of the infantry soldiers. "I want you to listen carefully, because I am giving you a direct order. I am *ordering* you to take this tank and get in front of these other four tanks and lead your platoon through that cut in the hill. I want you to go down and give them proper support and I mean I want you to do it *right now!*" Ashen-faced, quivering, and crying, the lieutenant closed his eyes, shook his head, and replied, "I cannot do that. I just can't," and sank down into his turret, sobbing. General Easley ordered him relieved and physically removed from the tank. The crew had to manhandle the lieutenant's limp, quaking body out of the Sherman. "It was pitiful," Lieutenant Bob Green, who replaced him, later wrote sadly. "He was weeping loudly and had soiled his clothes. Someone led him away, and I never saw or heard of him again."

Commanders readily understood that this kind of overweening fear and panic could spread like a contagion, so they quickly evacuated anyone with symptoms of mental or emotional breakdown. By now the Army had developed a dedicated infrastructure to deal with the problem. On Okinawa, rest camps were established a few miles behind the lines where neuropsychiatrists and other specialists treated their patients, always with the hope of returning them to duty, in part for obvious military reasons but also because they had found that combat fatigue symptoms tended to harden into permanent mental disabilities for those who never returned to their units. Moreover, the majority wanted to return. "It is a general principle that the nearer the front they are treated, the better is the chance of getting these men back to duty," wrote Captain DeWitt Smith, a doctor in the 27th Division, in a thoughtful study of battle fatigue within the division. "They are treated initially with rest, which removes one of the factors that is most responsible for the combat failures. They are given plenty of sedatives to enable them to sleep, then they are fed a couple of meals, and soon after that they are put to work. Fatigue and hunger and lack of sleep have led to his breakdown, and if they are corrected, in many cases he recovers." Most combat fatigue cases were initially evacuated to the 82nd Field Hospital, a unit that specialized in their treatment, after which they then spent seven days in a rest camp. "The goal . . . was to keep every man as busy as possible in one way or another," Lieutenant Paul Leach, the embedded 77th Division historian, wrote of the treatment approach. "They were given clean clothes and made to clean themselves up. Many men were put on details, while others attended supervised athletics, specially selected movies, information and education classes, or organized games conducted by the Red Cross." Division records documented the return of 76 percent of the patients to the line with the claim that only 10 percent "failed to hold up in combat." Other units were not as fortunate. Tenth Army as a whole evacuated about half of its Army and Marine combat fatigue victims off Okinawa in the course of the battle.[25]

The constant stream of casualties, whatever their cause, created a voracious demand for replacements, especially in frontline infantry units. Buckner's forces operated chronically under strength, though their mere access to any replacements at all provided them with a huge edge over the Japanese, who could not replace any of the men they lost. As the fighting killed or sidelined more American troops, Buckner appealed for help from his administrative superior Lieutenant General Robert Richardson, whose Pacific Ocean Areas headquarters functioned as the highest Army command under Nimitz's auspices. Inexplicably, Richardson's personnel section had estimated that Tenth Army would need only 9,000 replacements over a two-month period, a totally inadequate number. Richardson scoured the central and south Pacific for bodies. The manpower demands of a global war nearing its climax guaranteed fallow ground for Richardson. In the course of the fighting on Okinawa, he was able to ship 671 officers and 13,686 enlisted men to Tenth Army, though only 12,777 soldiers actually made it to the island, and many were only minimally trained. They arrived in five separate waves from April 14 to May 10; most processed through the 74th Replacement Battalion, and 95 percent went to one of the four Army infantry divisions. Another 11,147 Navy hospital corpsmen and Marines, split about evenly between the 1st and 6th Marine Divisions, reinforced Major General Roy Geiger's III Amphibious Corps. Proud veteran leathernecks were shocked and dismayed to realize that some of their newcomers were draftees. The infusion of nearly 24,000 soldiers, sailors, and Marines certainly helped Tenth Army, but Buckner actually needed two or even three times that many to keep his combat units anywhere near full strength. "The replacements that did arrive in Okinawa were not sufficient to fill up organizations during combat," General Bruce wrote in an analysis of personnel policies during the battle. "This division was . . . forced to continue fighting under strength. This resulted in a drastic lowering of morale when the officer and soldier felt he had to continue on the job without additional help until he was killed or wounded." At the height of the fighting, Bruce confided to Richardson's chief of staff that "due to the high losses from combat, climate . . . this is not the same division as it was when we left Oahu."

The hard-pressed survivors welcomed help from anyone, even new men whom they did not yet know or trust. "They were glad to see you," said PFC Martin Allday, who on May 1 joined a rifle squad in the 96th Division that had been whittled down to only two men by the desperate Maeda Escarpment fighting. "They'd had the heck kicked out of them." Many of the new men were brave and eager to fight—perhaps more so than jaded veterans who had little remaining stomach for chancing the unforgiving law of averages—but too often they lacked familiarity with weapons and proper combat tactics. Staff Sergeant Alfred Junkin of the 307th Infantry Regiment, whose platoon was completely destroyed on two occasions during the costly fighting, observed a number of rookie mistakes that stemmed from inadequate training. Several froze up rather than fire at enemy soldiers. Another attempted to open fire but found that he had forgotten to reload his rifle. "Our 30 replacements showed great courage but were too new to the job," he wrote to his battalion commander. "I deplore the necessity for taking green recruits who hardly know how to load a rifle into combat. I believe that you will agree that these teenage youngsters fight with great courage, but are just too green and inexperienced to do the job." Green or not, the infusion of fresh manpower allowed Buckner to sustain continual operations.

By contrast, every man whom Ushijima lost hastened the demise of his army because he could not replace any of them. Imperial General Headquarters had officially informed him that he could expect no resupply or reinforcements. So, even if Buckner could recoup only one-third of his manpower losses, he still enjoyed a distinct advantage that became steadily more pronounced over the many weeks of heavy fighting. As 32nd Army slowly bled to death among the hills and caves of the Shuri Line and Japanese defenses began to buckle under the weight of continued American attacks, Ushijima had to decide where his beloved army would make its last stand. The commanders convened in Ushijima's headquarters cave on the evening of May 21 and enjoyed a convivial meal of canned clams and canned pineapples. They debated among three options: stay in place and defend Shuri unto annihilation, retreat to the Chinen Peninsula, or withdraw to prepared positions on the Kiyan Peninsula at Okinawa's southern coast. They quickly dismissed the idea of a movement to the Chinen Peninsula as an impossibility because of impassable hills and mud-engorged roads. The division commanders felt that the honor of the Imperial Army demanded that they defend Shuri to the last. True to form, the relentlessly rational Colonel Yahara argued for a withdrawal to Kiyan because it offered the opportunity to prolong the battle and damage the Americans more than would a Shuri stand. This time he got his way. Ushijima elected to retreat to Kiyan while a few courageous stay-behinds fought a delaying action. Medics gave concoctions of condensed milk, water, and cyanide to badly wounded men and advised them cheerlessly, "Achieve your glorious end like a Japanese soldier." Starting on May 25 and continuing for several nights thereafter, the remnants of 32nd Army sloshed south in a nightmarish retreat, harassed by waves of artillery fire, under cover of clouds and rain, away from the largely unsuspecting Americans, to settle into new lines. In the tortured recollection of one participant, the route was "truly horrible and muddy and full of artillery craters with corpses, swollen two and three times normal size, floating in them."

The horrendous conditions made it difficult for the Americans to chase them down, but an equal or even greater factor in Ushijima's escape was their ignorance of his intentions. Intelligence officers at XXIV Corps and Tenth Army uniformly believed that 32nd Army would hunker down for a last stand at Shuri. "Japs will hole up in Shuri," Colonel Louis Ely, Tenth Army's intelligence officer, incorrectly assured his boss. Even as the Japanese were streaming south, Buckner ventured that "they don't appear to be falling back." In any event, enough of 32nd Army escaped to present Tenth Army with persistent resistance once Buckner's forces divined the abandonment of the Shuri Line and began to trail behind the retreating enemy. About 20 percent of Ushijima's combat troops still remained in service, though most were armed only with their own personal weapons. Just one-fifth of the army's machine guns and 10 percent of its heavy weapons survived the retreat.[26]

Though successful militarily, Ushijima's withdrawal proved disastrous for the population of southern Okinawa. Many had remained in their homes or had taken shelter in caves with the expectation that the Japanese would fight to extinction at the Shuri Line, sparing everything to the south from becoming a battle zone. Instead, as Japanese troops streamed southward, Okinawans became ensnarled in the fighting, especially as they attempted to flee to the south. Anticipating this terrible situation, Ei Shimada, the island's governor, had urged Ushijima to keep his men at Shuri, but to no avail. The Americans dropped leaflets instructing Okinawans to stay off the roads and away from military weaponry, vehicles, and Japanese troops. The leaflets further urged them to wear white to distinguish themselves from combatants and to surrender immediately to any Americans whom they encountered. But far too many were confused into inaction by such an overwhelming situation, or ignorant of the instructions or terribly frightened of the Americans because the Japanese had assured them that the bewildering foreigners would torture, rape, and murder them with impunity. Their unenviable circumstances reflected their nebulous status amid such a monumental death struggle. "What was it that Okinawans were supposed to gain or lose in the throes of war?" Masahide Ota, a teenage Boeitai militia member who later became governor of Okinawa, asked pointedly decades after the war.

The question cut to the quick of the hopeless situation in which the locals found themselves once this unwanted war came to their homeland. They were culturally similar to the Japanese, but they enjoyed no status as equals. The Japanese expected their loyalty almost as an entitlement, but with little sense of inclusion, respect, or equivalence as repayment. The Americans did distinguish between the Okinawans and the Japanese—though, to be sure, the average young soldier or Marine sometimes had difficulty grasping these distinctions—but they had no way of knowing the extent of local loyalty to Japan, and thus what sort of threat the average person might have posed. Even so, Buckner and his staff had planned extensively to care for the people on this heavily populated island. The general issued strict instructions, as did his key commanders, to behave with correct compassion toward the locals. "It is expressly forbidden to kill, injure, or mistreat any persons acting in good faith while endeavoring to surrender or after being taken into custody," General Geiger wrote in a III Amphibious Corps general order. "Civilians and prisoners of war will be treated with humanity, and their persons and honor will be respected. Rape and other mistreatments will be severely and quickly punished. All religious customs and taboos not interfering with military operations will be respected. Dead bodies will not be mutilated. Looting and pillaging are strictly forbidden." One impressed staff officer in the 96th Division testified that "we were even cautioned not to use or desecrate the Okinawa tombs."

Tenth Army's Military Government Section under Brigadier General William Crist attempted to provide for all the necessities of life. Every division in Tenth Army brought along 70,000 individual rations of canned fish, soybeans, and rice to help feed Okinawans, plus medical supplies to care for them. "They have been living in caves and dugouts for some time and need a lot of cleaning up," Buckner wrote to Adele. "They say that we give them more and better food than they have gotten since the war started." The smooth invasion and the relatively low-intensity conquest of the north afforded the opportunity for civilians to harvest their own crops. Crist's section interned civilians in barbed wire compounds and then crowded villages where they received medical care and food and worked on farms or at carrying supplies for the Americans. By the end of April, some 126,876 Okinawans had come under the control of Crist's military government, and, because of the stalemated front, the number had grown to only 144,331 by the end of May.

An overworked cadre of 170 counterintelligence corps interpreters, many of whom were Japanese Americans or Okinawan Americans, screened every person for their background, education, home, family information, and perceived loyalty to the Japanese. "The screening serves as a means of getting acquainted with the natives and letting them become acquainted with the Americans so that each may learn something about the other and know their proper relationship, both present and future," a counterintelligence corps document explained. Aided by educated Okinawans who agreed to function as assistants, the interpreters screened people in groups of thirty or forty at a time. "The persons being screened are much less reticent and more likely to talk when their own people are asking the questions than they would be if a Nisei or a language officer were to question one of them. The whole atmosphere in the screening rooms is one of friendliness, courtesy, and respect."

To the Okinawans, the invaders appeared physically large, endowed with oddly shaped round eyes, and equipped with terrifying means of destruction. The understandable Okinawan fear of the Americans gave way to friendliness and accommodation as they came to realize that the Yanks meant them no harm. "Our main concern was to keep alive," Yasuharu Gibo, a local man, later commented. Most were more than happy to stay under American control. The 96th Division recorded only two instances of locals trying to escape from camps or villages. The Americans quickly realized that they had little to fear from Okinawans, most of whom were less than committed to the Japanese cause and wanted little more than to be left alone to live in peace. A Tenth Army analysis determined that only 1 out of every 9,200 individuals posed any semblance of a threat.

Civilians were issued military-style dog tags for identification and sent to live and work in military-supervised villages away from the fighting. American soldiers generally viewed the locals sympathetically, albeit with a tinge of patronizing racial condescension. "The civilians on this island are a ragged group living in flea bitten, dirty straw and brick homes," PFC Horace Floyd of the 96th Division wrote to his family. "They are dressed in nothing short of rags, and the older people especially the women are very frail and shrivelled [sic] up." Captain Charles Lidster, a quartermaster working behind the lines among Okinawans in a secure environment, minutely described them in a letter to his sister as having "a mixture of features of their ancestors which are both Chinese and Japanese and Mongoloid. Their faces are round and flat with slanted eyes and they are more brown than yellow. They are all short and stocky. In spite of their apparent intelligence, they kept their goats, chickens and sometimes their pigs right in their huts with them. The young girls, about 10 to 14, carry tiny babies on their backs to work in the fields. It doesn't seem to hurt the baby as they never cry. Everyone . . . lives in centralized areas where most of the farms [are]. They go out in the fields in the morning and work all day. The men carry big baskets on a pole across their shoulders and the women carry a big basket on their head. Most everyone goes barefooted. These rice-burners think nothing of defecating and urinating right out in the open. When they are working in our Battalion Laundry, we have to watch them to make them conform to our ideas of sanitation. They are crazy about American cigarettes. They will do most anything for one single cigarette. I threw a handful of camels towards a bunch of 9 to 12 year olds, and the darndest scramble started."

The children especially tugged at American hearts. "Nearly all of us gave them all the candy and rations we could spare," one Marine later wrote. "They were quicker to lose their fear of us than the older people, and we had some good laughs with them." Private First Class Jeff Crabtree of the 96th Division voluntarily risked his life several times to recover babies and children from besieged caves. "I have seen and helped so many babies since I have been here," he wrote poignantly to his own six-year-old son back home. "Some of them are starved, some are wounded, and all of them are so badly scared. I have taken a lot of chances . . . but I think it is worth it, don't you?" Specially fitted American medical installations cared for thousands of civilians who became sick or were wounded. One hospital alone treated 1,180 local patients during the May fighting. Reflecting the views of many Americans, an admiring XXIV Corps officer asserted that the civilians "exhibited a great deal of fortitude in the midst of their misfortune."

The chaotic, desperate situation in the wake of 32nd Army's retreat afforded little opportunity for nobility and niceties, nor much chance for the Americans to identify, screen, and get to know local people as they had in secure areas up north. Battle-zone firepower, confusion, despair, and occasional atrocities ruled the day. Desperate, wild-eyed Japanese soldiers pressed sharpened bamboo poles or grenades into the hands of reluctant civilians and commanded them to attack the Americans. Most of the would-be assailants ditched their weapons at the first opportunity and fled. "I'll never forget how frightened I was and all others I met were also," Kosuke Matayoshi, a young refugee, later said. As exhausted, thirsty, hungry, terrified Okinawans meandered south in an effort to escape the fighting, they instead became engulfed in it, creating an epic tragedy of human suffering and death on such a scale as to mark local history forever. One Japanese doctor described them as "wandering and sleeping here and there in mountain caves and riversides, crying and weeping . . . near death, overwhelmed by hideous fatigue." Towns were snuffed out in minutes by the fighting. Artillery and mortar shells blasted people to pieces. The hips of one Home Guard militiaman were shattered by an explosion. He lay in a pool of blood and bled to death, gazing in dismay at the dismembered remains of his wife and three children nearby, all of whom had fallen prey to the same shell. Matayoshi saw thirty older men, women, and children die when an aerial bomb scored a direct hit on the community shelter where they had taken refuge. Some civilians were murdered, robbed, or raped by Japanese servicemen or, in a few cases, GIs.

Roads, trails, valleys, and their environs were littered with bloated, maggot-infested bodies of people killed by the dizzying array of deadly firepower. Tokuyo Higashionna, a young school principal, recalled years later the sight of "utter horror . . . dead everywhere . . . everywhere. There were corpses of all sorts—mothers with a dead child on their backs—live children on the backs of dead mothers. It was literally Hell. When I think of those days I pray God will not let that happen again. Even today to think of it gives me the chills." Injured children were abandoned by the sides of roads, plaintively begging for help from any passerby. "It was so pitiable," shuddered Miyagi Kikuko, a member of the Himeyuri Student Corps, the group of local teenage girls mobilized for duty as nurses. "I still hear those cries today." Wounded civilians moldered in their own filth, their cuts and breaks inundated with maggots. "Pus would squirt in our faces," Kikuko recalled of attempting to treat them. "Gas gangrene, tetanus, and brain fever were common. Those with brain fever were no longer human beings. They'd tear their clothes off because of their pain, tear off their dressings." Elderly people who had never left their villages became lost and died of exposure or starvation. Other civilians were shredded in the cross fire by the bullets and grenades of innumerable firefights. Captain Donald Mulford, a historian embedded with the 96th Division, wrote of one wasted battleground village as "a living, stinking testimonial to the horror that war brings to a civilian population. The natives here had been caught, partly by the force of circumstance, and partly by a fear of the advancing Americans bred of constant propaganda from the Japanese Army. Consequently they huddled in their holes, refusing to give up until burned or blasted out—some killing themselves and their children rather than face the horrors they had been led to expect. The sickly sweet smell of death [hung] like an unseen mist over the rubble. One had to walk carefully for the dead were everywhere. Against the base of a stone wall was the naked body of an infant about a year old. No one seemed interested except the hundreds of flies that swarmed over it."

As Mulford indicated, a few Okinawans chose suicide rather than risk defilement by the Americans. Private John Sloup of the 7th Division watched horrified as a father killed his family and then himself. "He shot each child in the temple, shot his wife in the temple and then shot himself in the temple. I don't know why. I never did know." In some cases, Japanese soldiers donned civilian clothes in an attempt to ambush the Americans by posing as a local. Even worse, they occasionally herded Okinawans in front of themselves as bait or a shield during attacks on American positions. "They were pushing Okinawans ahead of them[selves] and we were behind a stone wall . . . and we had machine guns," Private Peter Bourgeois, a combat medic in the 382nd Infantry Regiment, 96th Division, sadly recalled. "Those machine guns were firing all night as they were coming in. You couldn't tell the difference between the Japanese and the Okinawans. A lot of Okinawans got killed." Untold numbers of locals unwisely took refuge inside caves or burial tombs either on their own or alongside Japanese defenders. In either instance, they often found themselves shelled, flamed, blasted, shot, or sealed off by American troops who had correctly come to view these places as resistance nests. In some fortunate, but too infrequent, instances, they managed to make face-to-face contact with the Americans before they opened fire. Inside one cave, Staff Sergeant Jean Rowland, a dismounted tanker, "found a very old lady . . . rolled up in a quilt and left to die." He arranged to have her evacuated and cared for by medics. She gratefully gave him an ornate teapot that he ended up sending home.

The luckiest among the local population made it through the American lines to become haggard, poverty-stricken refugees. "The depressed and tired to the bone little people, dressed mostly in black or dark blue, were of all ages," Captain Appleman, the XXIV Corps historian, noted in his journal after witnessing streams of Okinawans trudging northward. "Many were old, sparsely bearded men and bent, heavily wrinkled women, old long before their years according to American standards. Many little girls of six years were carrying on their backs baby sisters or brothers. Their burden seemed as large as they were, and in some cases the dangling feet of their loads came half way down between their knees and ankles." Somewhere between 100,000 and 150,000 Okinawans lost their lives, primarily from late May to late June, one-quarter to one-third of what the population had been on Love Day, a monumental bloodbath that marked one of the war's truly terrible tragedies.[27]

The end also neared for Ushijima and his remnants. For nearly three weeks in June, the Tenth Army battered away at a five-mile-long last-ditch line anchored along the Yaeju Dake and Yuza Dake hill masses, consuming the last of 32nd Army's combat power like starvation vaporizing muscle. The battlefield steadily constricted, to the point where Tenth Army could only employ elements of the 1st and 6th Marine Divisions and the 7th and 96th Infantry Divisions to do the fighting. "The picture is one of several thousand troops resisting in the rugged coral and limestone hills with individuals and small groups each determined to fight to the death in hopes of inflicting as many casualties as possible on our forces," a XXIV Corps report summarized of the methodical, climactic fighting.

Buckner continued to circulate among the combat units, visiting the front almost every day. His steady courage may have been exceeded only by his zest for documenting seemingly every moment for his own personal memories, a surprising avocation for a man who generally shunned and disliked the media. He maintained a diary and found time almost every day to jot down an entry. On the evening of June 17, he recorded, "Inspected naval base development on East coast. No progress by our XXIV Corps and stiffer resistance as result of Japs' 32nd Div [sic] remnants reinforcing line there. About 700 yds progress in units of III Phipcorps zone." He continued to indulge his love of photography, carrying his camera and taking snapshots almost everywhere he went. At 1315 on June 18, with his trusty camera in hand, he visited the front to watch a Marine attack. As was his custom, he wore a helmet with all three of his shiny stars proudly displayed. In spite of warnings from the regimental commander that the area was less than secure, he and a small entourage made their way to a forward observation post nestled into some coral boulders. At the outpost, several Marines asked the general to remove his helmet for fear of drawing enemy fire. A battalion command post on a nearby hill mass even radioed a warning that they could easily see the stars. Buckner had heard similar warnings many times before during his frontline visits and he well understood the danger, but he firmly believed that a senior leader must inspire his troops by his visibility, an opinion shared by nearly all World War II American generals. Even so, he eventually agreed to put on a different helmet as he watched the action.

By now, though, a Japanese artillery crew had spotted him. They unleashed a quick batch of half a dozen shells that exploded in the vicinity of the post. A hunk of coral ripped a hole in Buckner's chest, knocking him to the ground. Incredibly, everyone else was untouched. A frantic radio operator called for help: "General Buckner is hit!" The general's aide-de-camp, Major Frank Hubbard, and several Marines hurriedly placed him on a poncho and dragged him to the battalion aid station. Buckner asked them if anyone else was hit. He smiled almost dreamily when he found out that everyone was okay. At the aid station, a doctor and a corpsman frantically worked on Buckner. A Marine grasped his hand and assured him, "You are going home. General, you are homeward bound." Nearby, someone recited the Twenty-third Psalm. In a matter of a few minutes, Buckner died. At that sad moment, he became the highest-ranking American military officer killed by enemy fire in World War II. That evening, Brigadier General Post, his chief of staff, shared the bad news with Tenth Army's saddened staff. Buckner's remains were placed in a simple coffin and buried the next morning with a quiet ceremony in the 7th Infantry Division's new cemetery on the island. "Essentially he was a kindly man, and his forte was sturdy common sense rather than brilliance," Major John Stevens, Tenth Army's historian, wrote in tribute. Among Buckner's personal effects was the bottle of liquor that Nimitz had given him back in April. It remained unopened.

Before the invasion, Buckner had designated old friend Geiger as his successor in the event of his death. Geiger thus became the first Marine ever to command a field army, though his tenure lasted only four days until none other than General Joseph Stilwell replaced him. Because Tenth Army would eventually come under MacArthur's command, and knowing that Army leaders would never accede to a permanent Marine commander, Nimitz yielded the choice to MacArthur. The SWPA commander could have had his pick of successful European theater commanders, but he wanted no outsiders on his turf. His first choice for command of Tenth Army would have been Lieutenant General Griswold, the tough-minded XIV Corps commander, but General George Marshall, Army chief of staff, did not want someone without previous experience commanding an army. So MacArthur chose Stilwell, whom he had known and held in high esteem for four decades, since their days at West Point. Stilwell was conveniently close by, circulating on official visits around the Pacific theater, almost as if looking for a job. He held a characteristically caustic and low opinion of Buckner, whose management of the battle had not impressed him. "[He] is tiresome," Stilwell sniped in his private diary prior to Buckner's death. "I tried to tell him what I had seen [in Burma] but he knew it all. Keeps repeating wisecracks. There is NO tactical thinking or push. No plan was ever discussed . . . to hasten the fight or help the divs."[28]

The news of Buckner's death reached Ushijima in the austere, cramped, besieged cave at Mabuni that now served as 32nd Army headquarters. Ushijima had probably never expected to outlive Buckner. The staff was gleeful over his death, but the Japanese general was oddly saddened by the demise of his adversary. "He looked grim, as if mourning Buckner's death," Colonel Yahara later wrote. "Ushijima never spoke ill of others. I had always felt he was a great man, and now I admired him more than ever." On the evening of June 17, a special Tenth Army surrender entreaty, sent personally by Buckner a few days earlier, reached 32nd Army headquarters. "Like myself you are an infantry general, long schooled and experienced in infantry warfare. You must surely realize the pitiful plight of your defense forces. You know that no reinforcements can reach you. The destruction of all Japanese resistance on the island is merely a matter of days." No matter how rational the appeal seemed to the Americans—and most any other reasonable individual, at least in the abstract—the Japanese gave it no consideration. Staff officers and Ushijima reacted to the message with amused contempt; many must have wondered if the Americans had really learned anything about their adversaries after fighting them across so many thousands of miles and so many blood-soaked battlefields. When Ushijima read the message, he smiled and remarked, with droll brevity, "The enemy has made me an expert on infantry warfare." Yahara later commented that the message was "an affront to Japanese tradition."

Maybe so, but Buckner was absolutely correct about the imminent demise of Ushijima's army. By the evening of June 21, he had run out of combat troops to defend his headquarters. Nothing substantial stood between the Americans a few hundred yards away and Ushijima's cramped cave. He sent farewell dispatches to Tokyo and one last communication to his remaining troops. "My Beloved Soldiers: You have all fought courageously for nearly three months. You have discharged your duty. Your bravery and loyalty brighten the future. The battlefield is now in such chaos that all communications have ceased. It is impossible for me to command you. Every man in these fortifications will follow his superior officer's order and fight to the end for the sake of the motherland. This is my final order. Do not suffer the shame of being taken prisoner. You will live for eternity. Farewell."

He and Cho resolved to commit suicide rather than risk any chance of getting captured. They ordered the younger staff officers, including Yahara, to attempt to make it to Japan or continue the fight on Okinawa as guerrillas. When Yahara requested permission to commit suicide with the generals, Ushijima forbade it. "If you die there will be no one left who knows the truth about the battle of Okinawa. Bear the temporary shame but endure it. This is an order of your Army commander." Since the retreat from Shuri and the onset of imminent defeat, Cho's mood had swung between apocalyptic paranoia and fatalistic good humor. "I think you are spies," he roared one day at Japanese war correspondents. "I'll cut you down with my sword." To one such reporter, it seemed that the chief of staff was "almost crazed at the prospect" of defeat. To the soldiers and especially Yahara, he presented a much more noble face. During a tearful, sake-soaked goodbye with the colonel, he reminisced, "We drank in Saigon before the war started. Do you remember the beautiful movie we saw at the theater across from the Majestic Hotel? We shared much pain together, and now we face our final day." They were polar opposites and yet they had an unlikely bond. "We could hardly be good friends, yet our human relationship was warm," Yahara later ruminated.

Ushijima characteristically behaved with more stoicism as the end neared. Late on the night of June 21, he put on his full dress uniform and convened with Cho for a final meal of rice, miso soup, canned meats, cabbage, potatoes, fish cakes, salmon, pineapples, tea, whiskey, and sake. When they finished their meal shortly before dawn on June 22, they drank farewell toasts to each other and exchanged final poems. With Cho in the lead, they made their way out onto a narrow ledge, just outside the cave, overlooking the sea. Ushijima probably felt warm in his dress uniform. He fanned himself with a locally made fan. Cho wore over his uniform a white silk kimono with an inscription on the back: "The offering of one's life is to fulfill the duties towards the Emperor and the Country. Cho Isamu." He looked over his shoulder at Yahara. "For future generations, you will bear witness to how I died."

Once outside, the two generals knelt down on a white cloth and waited a few moments for the sun to rise so they could see what they were doing. First Ushijima and then Cho plunged the hara-kiri dagger into his abdomen. An instant later, a sword-wielding captain quickly lopped off their heads. The soldier witnesses placed the remains under nearby rocks and then scattered in every direction "like a collapsed dam," in Yahara's recollection. Hours later, American soldiers from the 32nd Infantry Regiment, 7th Division, found the bodies of the two generals and, with the help of prisoners, positively identified them. The Americans buried their remains with military honors. On Cho's body, they found one last message from the verbose chief of staff: "22nd Day, Sixth Month, 20th Year of the Showa Era, I depart without regret, fear, shame or obligations. Age at departure, 51 years." That same day, Tenth Army headquarters declared an end to the battle. A color guard representing Tenth Army, both corps, and every division stood at attention beneath a flagpole as a band played "The Star-Spangled Banner" and the American flag was raised. Against the backdrop of a blue sky, the flag swayed gracefully and flapped in the gentle breeze, almost as if gazing solemnly over the blood-doused places where so many had recently died.[29]

The usual ragged patrol and cave-clearing operations went on for several more weeks. Soldiers and Marines exterminated anyone who continued to resist, usually from caves, tombs, or bunkers in bypassed areas. They also rousted thousands of civilians from shelters and caves and attempted to persuade surviving enemy soldiers to give up. Like hundreds of other interpreters, Tech 3 Takejiro Higa, who had grown up on Okinawa and emigrated to Hawaii, coaxed as many people as possible, whether they were Japanese military or local, to surrender to American custody. "I did not fire a single shot out of my rifle. With the portable megaphone, English-Japanese dictionary, notes, pencil and my mouth, I was able to fulfill my obligation as a citizen [of the U.S.] and . . . I was able to help people I grew up with. To give some comfort to those hiding in [a] cave, I used to introduce myself." Unfortunately, in spite of the best efforts of Higa and his comrades, some soldiers and civilians still chose to resist or kill themselves. "If the people believed in us a little more, perhaps, we could have saved many more. This saddens me. I did my best but my best, perhaps, wasn't good enough. How sad."

By one estimate, nearly 9,000 Japanese military personnel were killed or committed suicide in self-sacrificial last-ditch battles during the last week of June. But for the first time in the entire war, meaningful numbers of Japanese troops began to give up. As of late April 1945, the United States had taken only 3,260 Japanese prisoners of war. A few were housed at Camp Iroquois on Ewa Beach, Oahu; the rest were scattered among POW camps at Angel Island, California; Clarinda, Iowa; and Fort McCoy, Wisconsin, where they were generally treated well, under the dictates of the Geneva Convention. Tenth Army had taken only 403 military prisoners in April and scarcely many more in May; the vast majority of these men were wounded or incapacitated and could not resist capture.

The reluctance of combat soldiers and Marines to take prisoners played a part in these tiny POW numbers, but the real reason for them was the prevailing Japanese notion that surrender was unthinkable and dishonorable. In late June, as the battle ended, this cultural peer pressure finally began to fray as sizable numbers of enemy troops surrendered or allowed themselves to be captured. Exhausted, starving, in some cases disillusioned, Japanese soldiers discovered that if they could survive the first few minutes of an encounter with the Americans, they could expect decent treatment, a remarkable circumstance considering the ferocity of the battle, the American propensity to equate dead

Japanese with progress, and the war's constant underpinning of cultural and racial hatred. "We treated them with respect," Lieutenant Robert Muehrcke, a rifle platoon leader in the 96th Division, asserted. "We did not push them around, beat or abuse them." For fear of hidden weapons, the Americans forced them to shed their clothes, gave them water and chocolate, interrogated them, and moved them to a barbed-wire-enclosed POW compound guarded by military policemen. "I was given C rations and realized I would not be slain," one prisoner fondly recalled many years later. "I was starved when captured and very uncertain for the future. But the treatment at the camp was with warm feeling, food rationed and adequate. As my feelings calmed, I thought [that] the Americans have . . . treated us in accord with proper methods."

In the last eleven days of June, XXIV Corps took 2,910 POWs and another 2,519 unarmed Japanese laborers. At one point, the corps was taking 400 prisoners each day. On a single day in June, Tenth Army captured 977, an enormous number by the standards of this war. In total, the Americans on Okinawa captured 7,401 military prisoners, 3,339 laborers, and 15 Japanese civilians, by far the largest POW haul of the war to date. Among the captives was Colonel Yahara, who had disguised himself as a civilian and attempted to escape before coming under American control with a group of refugees. In late July, a fellow internee identified Yahara to the surprised Americans, who treated him with cordial professionalism and engaged him in many in-depth conversations that yielded excellent intelligence on the Japanese conduct of the battle. One American interrogator described him as "an extremely shrewd individual blessed with a glib tongue and a very rational way of thinking. His memory and powers of observation are excellent and the reliability of his information is far above that of the average officer POW." Yahara survived the war and even wrote a revealing memoir about his experiences and the intricacies of 32nd Army headquarters, never relenting from his belief in the correctness of the defensive strategy of attrition and the folly of the two counteroffensives. "It was clear that the foolish ideas of a decisive air offensive and suicide assaults had resulted in irreversible failures," he wrote scathingly. "They were bad strategy and bad tactics. We could have accomplished much more than we did if only [we] had stayed with the attrition strategy instead of yielding to offensive tactics. We could have saved at least one-quarter and perhaps even a third of our forces until the end of hostilities."

As it was, their accomplishments were hardly minimal. At Okinawa and the Ryukyus, the Allies captured key air and sea bases on Japan's doorstep a mere 350 miles away from Kyushu, isolating the home islands and bringing the country's war leadership to the brink of collapse. The two great American theaters—overseen by MacArthur and Nimitz—at last came together, in preparation for the final assault on Japan itself. But the price was steep, a troubling harbinger for what might well beckon in the home islands. In the immediate aftermath of the Okinawa fighting, General Hodge, the highly experienced XXIV Corps commander, described the battle as "by far the worst we have had to date in the Pacific." The Americans suffered 49,151 battle casualties, including 12,520 fatalities. The toll included 4,582 soldiers killed in action, 95 missing in action, 18,099 wounded, 2,398 Marine dead and missing, and 13,708 wounded. Okinawa was the deadliest battle in the history of the US Navy. A total of 4,907 sailors were killed and 4,824 wounded. Thirty-six ships were sunk and another 368 damaged, mostly by kamikazes. The Navy also lost 763 planes. The Royal Navy's Task Force 57 added another 85 killed and 4 damaged fleet carriers.

The Japanese lost a mind-boggling 7,800 planes and, according to Tenth Army records, 107,539 killed, some of whom were probably Okinawan militia fighters or civilians. The battle marked the end of the Imperial Navy as any sort of modern fighting force. The American wolf's presence at the door of the sacred home soil completed the isolation of the Japanese home islands to the east and the west and facilitated the powerful strategic bombing campaign that had now begun to consume Japan's cities in flames. The battle featured some of the most ferocious naval and ground combat in human history. Ironically and tragically, it brought widespread death and destruction to a land that had mostly known peace, marking a seminal moment in the history of the Okinawan people.

Although Japan was militarily defeated well before Okinawa, the battle brought the country's doom into sharp and immediate focus. With Japan facing imminent destruction by air, sea, and land, the question now was whether Japanese leaders would choose to fight to total extinction on their own soil, as they had in so many other places around the Pacific and Asia, or if they would stop short of this apocalypse and find some way to end the war. Interestingly, Okinawa was the only battle of the war in which neither commanding general survived, a fitting, powerful symbol of the war's accelerating cost to both sides as the ground war climaxed. "Every single person who survived the battle for Okinawa knew they were lucky to still be alive," Major Art Shaw, an artillery officer in the 96th Division, later wrote with bald honesty. He and the other survivors began to prepare for a climactic invasion of Japan, though most could hardly bear the thought of what promised to be an even bigger bloodletting than Okinawa. "The men understood they were still faced with only two alternatives: life or death," Shaw affirmed. "The odds were decidedly in favor of death." With a radio station now operating on the island, Stilwell took to the airwaves on the Fourth of July and gave a typically earthy, no-frills speech to the hardened veterans of Tenth Army. "The harder we pour it on, the sooner we'll all go home. This has been a tough fight; nobody but the men who've fought it can possibly realize how tough. If we are going to get the war over as soon as possible we've got to keep going. Extra sweat we put into it now will pay off as we close in on the Jap in his home islands." Indeed, like a powerful storm nearly spent, the war neared a final resolution. The outcome of this struggle was certain; who would live to see the end of it was not.[30]

5

Final Act

I n captivity, the tormented survivors of nearly three years of nightmarish incarceration at the hands of the Japanese held on, bleak day
by bleak day, earnestly hoping for ultimate deliverance. As Japan
sank into a state of desperation, the privation, neglect, and mistreatment
of prisoners had only worsened. The Japanese were struggling to feed
themselves, much less enemy prisoners whom they considered nothing
more than dishonored, nonhuman chattel. Ugly, apocalyptic rumors
circulated that the Japanese planned to slaughter all their prisoners
rather than see them liberated by the Allies. Fortunately, the rumors
had no basis in fact, but the prisoners could not have known this.

At Yodogawa near the Japanese city of Osaka, twenty-six-year-old
Private Michael Campbell, a former foster child and infantryman, continued to toil away as a slave in a steel mill. He and the other prisoners
subsisted on starvation-level rations of steamed rice, augmented with a
little barley, corn, millet, and the occasional low-grade meat, fish, or potatoes. Hunger pangs had long ago given way to torpor. The men expended nearly every ounce of their energy just to make it through their
eight to ten hours in shifts in the mills. On average, each prisoner had
lost between sixty and eighty pounds. They battled depression and bick-
ered constantly. "Many men were so run down physically and so harassed mentally they could hardly be trusted alone," commented Captain
John Olson, a West Pointer who, for the general health and welfare of
the prisoners, struggled mightily to maintain some semblance of discipline amid such a disorderly, degraded environment. "Brow beaten by the
Japanese and dubious of their chances of survival, most prisoners were
resentful of any form of control by men who were in the same predica-
ment as they." As a last resort, he even utilized corporal punishment as

a means of keeping the prisoners from descending into starved anarchy. "I deplore the use of it, but the circumstances left it as the only resort," he told a war crimes investigator after the war. "I employed it for stealing from Americans, eating garbage, and once for insubordination that threatened the whole camp. No one fully trusted anyone else." An official US Army study later described the Yodogawa prisoners as "automatons of men who lived with suspicion of human-kind. They were becoming quarrelsome among themselves and to an extent vicious."

The nearness of Allied victory offered the only ray of hope for Campbell, Olson, and the others. The private and the captain had forged an unlikely friendship around their mutual professional military admiration for discipline as well as illicit sharing of war news. They were electrified to find out about the invasion of Okinawa. But privately, both men struggled to ward off total despair, particularly the captain, who often found himself consumed with guilt over what he perceived as his failure to lead with the principles he had been taught at West Point. He poured out his anguish in unsent letters to his mother. "If ever there was a place more full of intrigue, distrust, and dishonesty than a prison camp, I pray I will never see it," he scrawled in pencil on June 30. "I seem to have a most exaggerated idea and standard of conduct to which no one else adheres. It has been a long, dreary struggle. Mentally and physically we have suffered. To me the mental tortures have far exceeded the [physical]."

When B-29s bombed nearby Osaka in March, the prisoners saw firsthand evidence of Japan's impending demise. Private Campbell was so transfixed at the sight of the planes that, even as Japanese guards fled for cover, he stood in place as bombs rained down uncomfortably close. "They were the biggest planes that I had ever seen," he later wrote with wonderment. "I was too awestruck and fascinated to run and hide. I just stood there and watched the bombs drop through the factory roof. Fires sprang up and flames were roaring through the buildings." In response to the bombings, the Japanese moved Campbell and the others by train and truck to Oeyama, a camp on Honshu's western coast where they put the prisoners to work either in a nickel mine or as stevedores in Miyazu Harbor.

The men lived in decrepit barracks with no indoor latrines or plumbing. Adjacent to the mess hall, kitchen grease and waste had accumulated into a squalid cesspool. Food consisted of half-cooked rice laced, in Campbell's recollection, "with all kinds of dirt, glass, worms, rat dung, and grit in it." He spent his days at the docks unloading cargo from barges and then laboriously loading it onto boxcars at a nearby rail line. He nearly died one day when a guard caught him trying to steal beans from a load of cargo. The guard beat him and dragged him before the camp commander, who told him through an interpreter, "You swine, how dare you steal food from us. You have violated one of our strictest rules. Stealing is a very serious offense and you are going to be punished." The guard and the interpreter threw him into the seething cesspool. "They forced me to sit and the water came up to my chin. The guard then drew out his sword and started swinging at my head. I had no choice but to duck my head under the filthy water. He did this repeatedly and laughed with glee." When the guard tired of his cruel sport, the interpreter shouted obscenities and hurled rocks at Campbell, forcing him to plunge again into the noxious water. "Finally he too had enough and departed. I slowly managed to extricate myself from the gooey sewage and climbed out of the cesspool. I went to a nearby spigot and washed off." For Campbell and his fellow prisoners, life had now boiled down to a waiting game, nothing more than a daily, almost hourly attempt to fend off death long enough to outlast the Japanese Empire.

Four hundred miles to the south, on the island of Kyushu, at Fukuoka #17, the same struggle preoccupied Private Lester Tenney, a former tanker from Chicago who had survived the Bataan Death March and, by now, nearly three years of slavery, toiling in a coal mine owned by the Mitsui Coal Mining Company. Conditions at Fukuoka #17 were predictably awful and getting worse during the early months of 1945, with rations generally consisting of little more than steamed rice and a few vegetables. "All of the prisoners were skeletons, having lost in weight an average of around 60 pounds per man," a US Army report on camp conditions documented. The Japanese pilfered from a recent shipment of Red Cross boxes and refused to issue them individually to the prisoners. Only grudgingly did they allow the prisoners' mess officer to disseminate some of the meat, butter, and milk among the daily rations. "I made numerous protests to the Japanese Camp Commander against

this method of distribution . . . which promptly brought me a face slap-
ping and the remark that the Red Cross items would be issued as the
Japanese Camp Commander decided," Major John Mamerow, the ranking prisoner, later testified in an official report.

Prisoners worked twelve-hour days in the mine to produce a fixed
quota of coal, with only three days off per month. Anyone who fell short
of his quota risked a beating or some other form of torture. "We had lost
all the weight, strength, and energy we could afford," Tenney later wrote.
"There was nothing left to lose, except our lives." He and the others
seldom had the sort of adequate footgear or clothing they needed to
work in the watery, chilly underground tunnels, where they hacked and
shoveled coal for hours. Streetwise and glib, Tenney had established an
illicit trading organization that provided him with some extra necessities in addition to helping him establish friendships with fellow prisoners and Japanese civilian overseers. Similar to Campbell, the military
authorities had caught him breaking their draconian rules, and he had
counted himself fortunate to survive the experience with nothing more
than beatings and solitary confinement. "Our monotonous routine—get
up, eat some rice, walk to and from the mine, shovel and load coal, suffer beatings by the Japanese for the slightest infractions, take a shower,
go to bed—was a sorry and unpleasant one but one we had to follow,"
Tenney later wrote with glum precision.

The thought of making it back home to his wife, Laura, whom he had
married before deploying to the Philippines, helped him make it through
each terrible day, and solidified in him a determination to survive. At
the same time, the news of Japanese battlefield defeats and the onset of
the bombing campaign against the home islands greatly angered the
guards and civilian overseers. The skinny, diseased prisoners represented convenient scapegoats for their collective wrath; beatings became
more common and arbitrary. Tenney had already had teeth knocked
out, his nose and other bones broken, and his shoulder injured badly
enough that Captain Thomas Hewlett, the prisoners' courageous doctor
and relentless advocate, had considered amputating the arm before deciding instead to immobilize it with a makeshift sling. Tenney walked
with a limp that originated when an overseer had smashed him in the
left hip with a pickax. Through it all, he had almost become inured to

the pain. "After having so many beatings . . . nothing's gonna make any difference any more," he later reflected. In the wake of one raid during which half a dozen American fighters strafed the Japanese side of the camp, the guards cut prisoner rations in half and beat up Tenney and several other men. Defiant and tough as gristle, Tenney refused to show them any inkling of the pain he felt. "We got the message: the Allies were winning the war, and time would soon tell the story of how the rising sun fell," he later wrote. "When I was beaten that night for a minor infraction of the regulations, I stood tall and took it with pride. Their time was coming, I thought, maybe not today, but soon, real soon."

Japan's demise could not come soon enough for Lieutenant Colonel Harold "Johnny" Johnson, a West Point–trained officer and Bataan Death March survivor with an almost religious passion for ethical leadership. "I think of him as being anchored in spiritual values," a colleague once commented of Johnson. "He has an inner intensity." Johnson had managed to survive a hellish three-month sea journey from the Philippines to Japan, an almost surreal odyssey that claimed the lives of over 70 percent of the prisoners. During the journey, as prisoners died of starvation, disease, and dehydration, Johnson had traded his West Point ring to one of the guards in exchange for a small amount of food and water that he divided evenly among the men under his charge. By the time Johnson made it to Japan in late January 1945, his weight had dropped to less than 100 pounds. He hardly had the strength to raise his arms or walk. For the next three months he could do little else besides attempt to recuperate. On February 22, his birthday, he managed to weigh himself. "I was just coming down with pneumonia and I weighed ninety-two pounds," he later commented.

The Japanese had moved Johnson and the others away from the Philippines to make sure they were not liberated by advancing American armies. In late April 1945, with the possibility that Japan itself might become an invasion target, they once again moved Johnson and 139 other Americans, this time to a camp in Inchon, Korea, where they joined a few dozen British and Australian prisoners who had been there for over two years. The Yanks quickly forged close friendships with their allies. On the Fourth of July, the British prisoners magnanimously prepared cakes from their carefully husbanded, scarce supplies of sugar, chocolate, flour, and milk and presented them to the Americans. Living standards and treatment at this camp were actually decent, at least by the abysmal, appalling standards of Japanese captivity. Prisoners lived in sturdy barracks, slept on mat-covered platforms, and had access to regular hot-water showers. Under the supervision of a Japanese sergeant, British and American cooks prepared three meals a day, comprising a diet of about 2,000 calories, enough to stave off starvation and disease if not necessarily hunger. "The basic food rationing consisted of a bowl of soup and a small bowl of rice in the morning and evening, a bun and a bowl of soup at noon," an Army report on camp conditions testified. "The bun was made of half wheat flour and half soya bean meal." In the recollection of Lieutenant Colonel Armand Hopkins, the buns "badly needed salt, but [they were] a great treat nonetheless, especially for us Americans who, since the surrender had scarcely tasted anything made of wheat flour." The meals were augmented once a week with strips of fish or vegetables cultivated in a garden tended by the prisoners. "Every piece of fish that I received had its share of bones, but even bones have some food value, and I, being a stubborn soul, found that they could be masticated if they were mixed with rice and chewed long enough," Lieutenant Colonel Irvin Alexander, who arrived alongside Johnson, later wrote. Unlike in Fukuoka #17, the Japanese authorities twice per month allowed prisoners access to the Red Cross packages in their entirety.

With better food and more stability, Lieutenant Colonel Johnson slowly warded off pneumonia and put on some weight. The Japanese put the prisoners to work hauling firewood and sewing uniforms, a comparatively easy occupation to the many other POWs elsewhere who toiled in mines or factories or as stevedores. Universally respected and trusted for his honesty, Johnson served as the work detail officer. In this capacity, he constantly fenced with the Japanese to spare his fellow prisoners as much harm as possible. "It was just a continuous struggle, argument, argument, argument all the time," he recalled decades later. "We were always trying to figure out ways to outwit them without them losing face among themselves or overtly with us." Occasional conversations with Korean guards and glances at newspapers supplied them with highlights of the war's progress. Johnson otherwise filled the many empty hours thinking of his wife, Dorothy, and, true to his character, caring for the welfare of his fellow prisoners. He sensed that, like a finish line in the distance, the end of the war was near, and he was fiercely determined to see it.

No one felt more responsibility for the survival of as many prisoners as possible than Lieutenant General Jonathan Wainwright, the ranking American in Japanese custody. His stark circumstances belied his seniority. Scion of a military family, with a West Point pedigree and an Army-wide reputation as a hard-drinking, courageous straight shooter, he had, in May 1942, reluctantly surrendered a starving, checkmated Allied military force in the Philippines. During three years of subsequent captivity he had endured beatings, humiliation, slave labor, and the same privations as any other prisoner, interrupted only by occasional spates of decent treatment, usually when the Japanese wanted to use him as a propaganda piece. He had spent the bitterly cold, forlorn winter of 1945 at an isolated small camp near Sian in Manchuria. Temperatures sometimes plunged as low as 45 degrees below zero Fahrenheit. Wainwright slept fully clothed and still could not keep from shivering heavily. A soldier to the core, and imbued with an almost incredible selflessness, he did his best to maintain a military bearing and attend to the welfare of his fellow prisoners. But his degraded, impoverished circumstances and his poor physical condition made this extraordinarily difficult. For years, as a nod to his lankiness, he had affectionately been known in Army circles by the nickname "Skinny." By now, the moniker "Scrawny" probably would have fit him even better; his weight had plunged to just under 130 pounds. His cheeks were hollow, his arms spindly, his eyes sad. To keep his balance and avoid limping, he leaned on a walking stick whenever he traversed any substantial distance. The half dozen cheap Japanese cigarettes he smoked each day undoubtedly contributed to his feebleness. He was sixty-one years old but, in his wasted, melancholy condition, he looked at least a decade older.

Meals at Sian consisted of "corn-meal mush for breakfast, a thick gruel for lunch, vegetables and a kind of soya curd for dinner," Wainwright later wrote. Occasionally, he and the other prisoners received a bit of bread and some of the contents of Red Cross packages. Wainwright now had no work requirements and no real official duties. Though he had indications that the American people and his superiors in Washington held him in high regard, he still sometimes worried that he would be court-martialed and reviled in American society for surrendering his command in the Philippines to the Japanese back in 1942. Bored and restless, he spent his days sharpening the limited supply of razor blades available to the prisoner population. On a good day, when he had a little energy, he could sharpen twenty blades. He carefully maintained two of his own that he alternated periodically. "We did what we could to occupy our minds," he later reflected. To that end, he read anything he could, but books were scarce. He read and reread the limited offerings. He had nearly memorized *Oliver Wiswell* and *Northwest Passage* by Kenneth Roberts, as well as *The Long Rifle* by Stewart Edward White.

He spent most of his time playing solitaire and carefully recording the results. By springtime, he had documented the completion of more than 7,500 games, with the goal of reaching 10,000. Ironically, due to the isolation of Sian in Manchuria's wilderness, he knew less about the war situation than did many thousands of lower-ranking Allied prisoners sprinkled amid other camps throughout the dying Japanese Empire. He knew the Allies were winning. He had no idea of the Okinawa invasion, nor the bombing of Japan. At times, Wainwright heard stories that the Japanese were near capitulation, but he refused to believe this. "In captivity it is easy to grasp at any comforting rumor," he wrote with a skepticism born of many hard-knock disappointments. He figured that the Allies would have to invade Japan to finish the war. To do that, they would need a major staging base near Japan, and he doubted they could seize one until 1946. By his ultimate estimate as a military professional, he believed the titanic campaign to conquer the Japanese home islands could not possibly end until at least 1947, meaning he must face at least two more years of captivity, a depressing thought that sometimes made it hard to fend off total despondency.[1]

If he had known the true state of the war, and the advanced nature of Allied invasion plans, he would have felt considerably better. "Although the will to fight remains strong," Brigadier General Charles Willoughby, MacArthur's intelligence chief, wrote in a late March assessment of the Japanese, "current patterns are purely those of delaying action whereby they hope to gain sufficient time to regroup on a new

Pacific battle position whose MLR [main line of resistance] is frankly . . . to be the shores of the Empire itself." On March 29, the Joint Chiefs had officially set in motion the plans for Operation Downfall, the two-phase invasion of Japan. Downfall envisioned an invasion of Kyushu, dubbed Operation Olympic, on November 1, 1945, followed four months later by Operation Coronet, the invasion of Honshu during which the Americans planned to take Tokyo and the heavily populated Kanto Plain, the critical core of the Japanese homeland. The purpose of Olympic centered around establishing major bases on southern Kyushu in support of Coronet, the climactic knockout blow.

The Joint Chiefs appointed MacArthur commander in chief of Army Forces in the Pacific, with control of all ground forces, including Marines, plus most Army Air Force units except the Marianas-based B-29s. Admiral Nimitz was to have control over all naval forces. In essence, the Chiefs intended to phase out the respective theater commands of the general and the admiral in favor of a division of responsibilities—MacArthur would run ground operations and Nimitz naval operations, an arrangement that made sense in terms of mission suitability and also maintained peace between the Army and the Navy as equal partners instead of adversaries struggling for ultimate mastery of Downfall.

During the spring and summer of 1945, even as Yamashita stubbornly held out in northern Luzon and Ushijima fought to the finish on Okinawa, MacArthur's staff planned intensively for Olympic and Coronet. The Americans planned to amass the greatest fleet in history, with 3,000 warships, highlighted by 22 battleships, 63 aircraft carriers of varying tonnage, and 50 cruisers. General Krueger's Sixth Army would swell to include fourteen divisions apportioned among four corps, an amphibious assault force of 650,000 troops. The order of battle included the 3rd, 4th, and 5th Marine Divisions organized into the V Marine Amphibious Corps. Coronet was even more ambitious. It involved two field armies, the Eighth and the First, and even envisioned the eventual usage of British, French, Canadian, and Australian combat units. The two field armies were to converge in a pincers maneuver on Tokyo with Lieutenant General Eichelberger's Eighth Army playing a leading role. For the task, he was to have nine divisions, including two armored divisions, under his command.

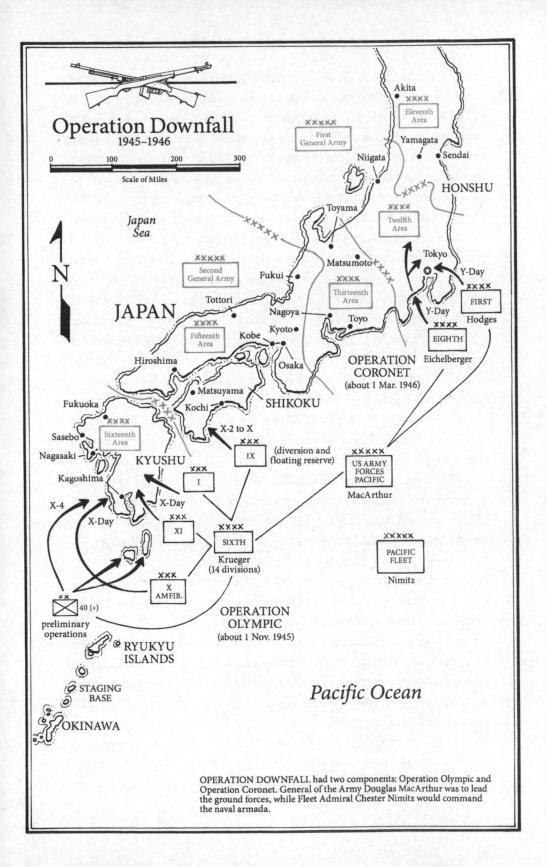

Operation Downfall
1945–1946

Scale of Miles

0 100 200 300

N

Japan Sea

HONSHU

Akita
×××× Eleventh Area

Yamagata
Sendai

First General Army ×××××

Niigata

Toyama

Twelfth Area ××××

JAPAN

Tokyo
Y-Day

Second General Army ×××××

Fukui

Matsumoto +++

×××× FIRST
Hodges

Tottori

Nagoya

Thirteenth Area ××××

Y-Day

Fifteenth Area ××××

Kyoto
Kobe

Toyo

EIGHTH ××××
Eichelberger

Hiroshima

Osaka

OPERATION CORONET
(about 1 Mar. 1946)

Matsuyama

SHIKOKU

Fukuoka

Kochi

X-2 to X

US ARMY FORCES PACIFIC ×××××

MacArthur

Sixteenth Area ×××

IX ×××

(diversion and floating reserve)

Sasebo

Nagasaki

KYUSHU

I ×××

Kagoshima

X-Day

X-4

XI ×××

SIXTH ××××
Krueger
(14 divisions)

PACIFIC FLEET ×××××

Nimitz

X-Day

X AMFIB. ×××

×× 40 (+)

preliminary operations

OPERATION OLYMPIC
(about 1 Nov. 1945)

RYUKYU ISLANDS

STAGING BASE

Pacific Ocean

OKINAWA

OPERATION DOWNFALL had two components: Operation Olympic and Operation Coronet. General of the Army Douglas MacArthur was to lead the ground forces, while Fleet Admiral Chester Nimitz would command the naval armada.

By contrast to the Luzon campaign, MacArthur had this time better fitted his key Army commanders to their missions. Krueger was well suited to do the job of carrying out a massive set-piece invasion with incremental, limited geographic objectives to establish bases; Eichelberger was perfectly cast for the rapid-exploitation-maneuver campaign that undoubtedly would have characterized Coronet. For the gargantuan task of supporting these operations, the Chiefs afforded MacArthur control of two major logistical organizations, the newly created Western Pacific Base Command under Lieutenant General Wilhelm Styer and Lieutenant General Robert Richardson's existing Army Forces, Middle Pacific Command. As the summer unfolded, their soldiers toiled feverishly to amass Downfall's vital supplies and sinews. For Olympic, Army Forces, Middle Pacific Command alone compiled incredible quantities of matériel: 5 million pounds of spare parts for engineering equipment, a temporary reserve of 1,450,000 C ration meals, 850,000 K rations, 2,500,000 10-in-1 rations, 21 tons of bulk coffee, 24 tons of canned milk, 135 tons of fruit juice, 33 tons of jam, 24,990 field jackets, 331,500 pounds of dynamite, 377,646 bags of cement, 3,818,970 gallons of asphalt, 30,379,320 board feet of lumber, and 50,530 metric tons of ammunition for ground forces, among a myriad of other items.[2]

The Japanese correctly anticipated Allied intentions. Fully expecting an invasion of southern Kyushu, they heavily reinforced the island from March through early August. By the second week of August, the Sixteenth Area Army, the force charged with defending Kyushu, had grown to a strength of 600,000 troops, with more scheduled to arrive in succeeding weeks. The Imperial Navy's surface ships were, of course, no longer a significant factor, but Okinawa had proven that this hardly mattered. Hundreds of suicide boats and a disturbing 5,000 kamikaze aircraft were available. Japanese commanders wisely intended this time to target troop transports and supply ships, the crucial vessels upon which the success of the invasion hinged. Many of the kamikaze planes were obsolete and the pilots barely trained. But even if only 10 to 20 percent made it to their targets, they could wreak havoc on the American fleet. Ominously, the Japanese concentrated their ground troops and fortifications at the exact beaches where the Americans intended to invade. Buttressed by the prospect of mass kamikaze support, combat on their home soil, equality in numbers with the invaders, and the availability of much defensible terrain, the Imperial Army reoriented its anti-invasion tactics back to defending at the waterline.

Ultra intercepts provided the Americans with a largely accurate picture of the troubling Japanese buildup, exacerbating high-level concerns about the distinct possibility that Krueger's army would incur prohibitive casualties. By August, Nimitz, King, and Marshall all began to have doubts about the wisdom of following through with the plan to invade Kyushu on November 1. Their understandable concerns, and those expressed later by Harry Truman, who had succeeded Roosevelt as president after his death on April 12, contributed to a long-enduring but pointless postwar debate over preinvasion casualty estimates for Olympic that ranged from a low of about 50,000 casualties to an otherworldly high of one million fatalities. Regardless of any contemporary casualty estimates or exaggerated postwar claims, Olympic promised to be costly, exacting a blood debt that was likely to mirror those paid in such campaigns as Luzon and Okinawa. It only made good sense to consider other ways of ending the war. Each segment of the American military and policy-making establishment tended to see the solution through its own lens. Naval thinkers advocated bombardment and blockade. The Army Air Forces naturally looked to the intensification of strategic bombing to force Japan to surrender. Led by Joseph Grew, who had served ten years before the war as ambassador to Japan, some in the State Department argued for diplomacy as the key to ending the war, specifically by amending the policy of unconditional surrender to allow for the perpetuation of the emperor in postwar Japan.

MacArthur, as a ground commander and a highly experienced, successful practitioner of amphibious warfare, saw invasion as the best way to bring Japan to its knees. Even in the face of the obvious Japanese buildup on Kyushu, he remained an unrelenting proponent of Olympic. When General Marshall expressed reservations about proceeding with the invasion, MacArthur argued strongly against postponement or cancellation. He downplayed the disturbing reports of the burgeoning Japanese military presence on Kyushu, and assured the chief of staff that American planes would heavily degrade the island's defenders. "Throughout the Southwest Pacific Area campaigns, as we have neared an operation, intelligence has invariably pointed to greatly increased enemy forces," he intoned. "Without exception, this buildup has been found to be erroneous. In this particular case, the destruction that is going on in Japan would seem to indicate that it is very probable that the enemy is resorting to deception." MacArthur's contentions had little basis in fact. In spite of constant sorties, the planes had not prevented the Japanese from reinforcing Kyushu. If Leyte, Luzon, Iwo Jima, and Okinawa served as any guidepost, air attacks were unlikely to have a decisive impact on well-fortified, dug-in Japanese troops. Nor were the reports of Japanese strength exaggerated or the product of an orchestrated deception plan. MacArthur's stubborn adherence to Olympic probably did not stem, as some analysts have intimated, from a vainglorious desire to preside over history's greatest invasion. Instead, as a ground commander, he quite naturally looked to land warfare as a means to ultimate victory. When events outside his control overtook Downfall's relevance, he happily discarded his advocacy of invasion in favor of peaceful occupation.

In truth, no matter what course of action the Americans chose to pursue, the ultimate decision on the war's final act rested with the Japanese. The Allied powers issued the Potsdam Declaration on July 26 stipulating unconditional surrender, postwar occupation, transformation of the Japanese government, and the punishment of war criminals, and hinting at but not guaranteeing the perpetuation of the emperor. In response, Japan neither overtly accepted these terms nor pursued constructive negotiations. Even though the Japanese were clearly beaten militarily by August, they were still potent enough to exercise the curious and frightening sort of power that revolved around their own choices, of the sort exerted by a grenade-wielding man who is cornered in a room by his enemies. Only the cornered man could decide on mutual destruction, self-sacrifice, or defusion. With their cities incinerated by incendiary raids, their armies in retreat, a hostile navy of enormous power at their shores, and their homeland under threat of imminent invasion, the Japanese ultimately had to choose between the nihilistic course of fighting to a bloody extinction or finding some other way out of the vise grip in which they now found themselves.

Postwar recriminations over the atomic bombings notwithstanding, the bare fact was that the Japanese did not decisively resolve these choices among themselves until they sustained the dual body blows of two nuclear bombings and Soviet entry into the war. Even then, when the emperor himself decreed to the government's inner circle of decision makers that the war must end, and when he took the unprecedented step of recording a special Imperial Rescript message to this effect for broadcast to the entire nation, he faced a coup by midlevel officers from the 1st Imperial Guards Division, the unit dedicated to the mission of protecting his palace and his family. Determined to fight on even if that led to the total destruction of Japan and the annihilation of its people, the plotters rallied soldiers to their side; killed Lieutenant General Tokeshi Mori, their unsupportive division commander; and isolated the emperor in his palace for several hours while they searched in vain for the vinyl records on which technicians had recorded his broadcast. By their actions, they showed that they were willing to defy the authority of the emperor, the very sovereign whom they viewed as god on earth and had sworn to defend unto the death. Frustrated in their attempt to destroy the records, they seized control of a Tokyo radio studio where the ringleader, Major Kenji Hatanaka, put a pistol to the head of a broadcaster and ordered him to yield his microphone. The announcer courageously refused and bought enough time for an engineer to disconnect the station's radio tower. In the meantime, another group of hotheads attempted unsuccessfully to assassinate Kantaro Suzuki, the retired admiral who had served as prime minister since April 7 and presided over a military-dominated cabinet.

Though all these plotters ultimately failed, the mere fact of their efforts demonstrated that some Japanese who were uncomfortably close to levers of power were determined to choose the route of mutual destruction, a stark truth usually ignored by latter-year moralizers against the use of the atomic bomb. Had the coup warriors succeeded, the war and its bloodshed would likely have continued, at least until Hirohito managed to find some other way to stop it, conceivably even after Olympic had begun. From Truman on down, no American at this point understood the extent and significance of the abortive coup efforts. As it was, the Japanese government on August 15 accepted Allied surrender terms, with the mutual agreement that the institution of the emperor would continue, subject to the authority of the Allied occupation forces. Hirohito's melancholy message was broadcast to a nation that had never before heard the sound of his voice. He avoided any explicit mention of surrender or defeat, but communicated these realities in roundabout phrases, referring to a war that "has developed not necessarily to Japan's advantage, while the general trends of the world have turned against her interest." As an unstated allusion to Japan's defeat and the coming occupation, he concluded his address with the loaded, meaningful declaration that "we have resolved to pave the way for a grand peace for all the generations to come by enduring the unendurable and suffering what is unsufferable."[3]

Among the GIs, rumors of Japan's impending capitulation had already circulated for several days. The official, momentous news spread with lightning rapidity all over the Pacific and Asia, prompting many raucous celebrations, a nearly universal outpouring of victory-induced jubilation and relief unique to World War II, at least for Americans. Ships in Manila Harbor shot colored flares, blew whistles, and, at night, bounced searchlight rays off low-hanging clouds. Filipinos hugged Americans and shouted "Victory Joe!" or "Give me one cigarette, Joe!" The excitement prompted some men to celebrate irresponsibly by foolishly shooting off ordnance, leading to unnecessary casualties in numbers that remain undocumented and obscured. One Eighth Army staff officer remembered that "thousands and thousands of tracer bullets fired from automatic weapons arched their light trails into the . . . dark sky."

Most soldiers received the news with a mixture of shock and the joyful release of competing emotions. "The boys here took it in varying degrees of excitement," Lieutenant Florance Chapman, a nurse in Manila who had spent many weeks treating battle casualties, wrote to her mother, "from the 'throw-her-over-your-head' variety in a moment of wildest happiness, to the very quiet face, knowing he wasn't thinking of the future, but looking back on the shock and horror, the loss of his buddy, uselessly. I can never explain how I felt. I wanted to cry and be by myself. I wanted to laugh and shriek and jump around with the boys." In northern Luzon, Lieutenant Noel Seeburg and his comrades in the 129th Infantry Regiment, 37th Division, were watching a Laurel and Hardy movie when the regimental adjutant unplugged the projector and announced the news. "Absolute silence immediately fell for one long moment, as the full implication of the announcement burst inside each individual's brain," he soon thereafter wrote to his family. "No more wet foxholes, no more screaming shells, no more snapping bullets, no more sights of mutilated bodies. Pandemonium broke loose and the night air was vibrant with the paean of victory from the Regiment's throat. The feeling that struck me was indescribable. It was as though a burden that I had unconsciously been carrying were suddenly removed and a new and wonderful feeling of freedom and lightness took possession of me. The majority of us went quietly to our tents and sat down on our cots and talked far into the night about the repercussions and ramifications" of the war's end. Like untold thousands of other GIs, Private Russell McLogan and his buddies in a 6th Division rifle company had no access to liquor, but he felt they hardly needed it to have a good time. "We were already high on peace and deliverance."

Many of those who had engaged in the bloodiest fighting barely celebrated at all. "My heart grows sad when I think of all my fallen comrades who are not here to hear the wonderful news," Lieutenant Warren Anderson, a platoon leader in the 32nd Division, wrote somberly to his family. "But for them our happiness would be complete." Lieutenant Bob Green, the tank commander who had seen heavy action on Okinawa, testified to his mother of a somber mood around his 763rd Tank Battalion. "There was hardly any celebrating at all. It sure was a pity it couldn't have happened in time to save all those boys on Okinawa. I guess that's what we are all thinking." Private David Williams of the 38th Division similarly attested to a prevailing mood of pensive reverence over exultant jubilation. "Here among us not one loud voice was heard, but our thoughts would have, most likely, put the best prayers to shame."

In Chungking, Lieutenant General Wedemeyer was reviewing his plans for an offensive to reclaim Hong Kong and Canton when he received a message transmitting the news. An elated Chiang Kai-shek had already heard. "I thanked God that the mercy he gave me was so great," he told his diary of his reaction. In a radio address to the Chinese people, he pontificated, "Our faith in justice through black and hopeless days and eight long years of struggle has today been rewarded." He invited Wedemeyer to make the short two-mile journey to his residence for a small celebration. When Wedemeyer attempted to get there by jeep, he found himself engulfed in an enormous crowd of jubilant revelers so numerous as to make any movement of his jeep impossible. "Increasingly their cries and laughter were punctuated by the explosion of firecrackers," he later fondly recalled. When they spotted Wedemeyer, their mood became even more jovial. "While I held firmly onto the steering wheel of my jeep, the vehicle was raised completely from the ground by many willing hands which carried their load for several hundred yards in a spontaneous triumphal procession." When they finally set the jeep down, a bemused and amazed Wedemeyer drove back to his headquarters, where he waited several hours for the excitement to calm down before he finally made it to Chiang's house. In Manila, Generals Eichelberger and MacArthur shared a few nice moments of self-congratulation. "They haven't gotten my scalp yet, Bob!" a jubilant MacArthur exclaimed in reference to an inside joke they had often shared earlier in the war to the effect that both of their scalps were always on the line. In a communiqué, MacArthur eloquently wrote, "I thank a merciful God that this mighty struggle is about to end. I shall at once take steps to stop hostilities and further bloodshed." Brigadier General Clovis Byers, Eichelberger's chief of staff, later described to his wife, Marie, a climate of relieved wonderment: "The reaction of everyone was still strange. I imagine it could best be described as a feeling of incredulity. To most it had looked as though the finish was so far away and some of the most difficult action of the entire war was in front of us. And then suddenly the whole bottom dropped out of everything. It was a wonderful feeling of relaxation."[4]

The word filtered raggedly to Allied POWs, usually in the form of a gradual improvement in conditions—the surrender agreement mandated immediate proper treatment of POWs and threatened punishment for those who defied this order—and grudging announcements of the momentous news by their Japanese captors. In Inchon, Lieutenant Colonel Johnson and the other Allied prisoners were gathered together and "told that the Emperor and Roosevelt had agreed to get along." Apparently, the camp commander, and many of the prisoners, did not even know that Roosevelt had died four months earlier. "My chief emotion was a lump in my throat, and it took some effort to keep tears from my eyes," Lieutenant Colonel Armand Hopkins confided to his diary in the wake of the announcement. The newly freed men broke into a nearby food storehouse and ate anything they wanted. At Fukuoka #17, Private Lester Tenney and his fellow prisoners were marched to the mine for yet another day of hard labor, but then mysteriously told to go back to camp, where they were fed a generous meal and given full Red Cross packages. A surge of excitement coursed through the ranks as they speculated that the war was over. Tenney figured the best way to tell for sure was to defy the usual stricture of bowing to a Japanese guard. "I spoke to him in Japanese but I wouldn't stand at attention. I just said . . . sort of a greeting and he just looked at me . . . and finally he stood at attention and bowed to me. That's when I knew the war was over." Later, the Japanese gathered them together on the camp's main parade ground. As they stood at attention, the commander abruptly told them, "America and Japan now friends. War is over." With that, he and the other guards hopped onto trucks and left. "For a moment no one spoke a word," Tenney later wrote of the surreal moment. "The silence was overwhelming. Then we realized we were free. We cheered. We had won!" Tenney breathed a deep sigh of relief that he would live to see his family and Laura again. Captain Hewlett, the courageous doctor, estimated that 126 POWs had died at Fukuoka #17 over a two-year period. "Forty-eight deaths attributed to pneumonia, thirty-five to deficiency disease, fourteen to colitis, eight to injuries, six to tuberculosis, five to executions, and ten to miscellaneous diseases," he later reported.

Private Michael Campbell had noticed for several days a distinct relaxation in the harshness of his captivity at Oeyama. Meals were more substantial, supervision from the guards significantly more lax and easygoing, until work calls ended altogether. The prisoners excitedly speculated that their liberation was near. A dignified-looking Imperial Army officer soon visited them and confirmed what they had already sensed. "Our glorious emperor has decreed that the status of war that currently exists between you and us is terminated. The war is over for you gentlemen and you are no longer prisoners of war. I am sorry for any of the hardships that you have endured and hope that you will forgive us." As a token of this new friendship, he gave them a huge sow for slaughter. "I sank to the ground and sobbed," Campbell later wrote reverently of this wonderful moment. "Some of the POWs started whooping and bellowing. Others were too overcome. The big sow was slaughtered and turned over to the mess hall crew. They prepared a big feast of roasted pork. We all ate heartily and spent many hours talking. The air was filled [with the sound of] laughing and happy men."

At Sian, one of General Wainwright's aides excitedly burst into his room, congratulated him, and claimed that the war had ended. The hard-edged old cavalryman refused to believe him. But the next morning, the Japanese confirmed the fantastic news. "By order of the emperor, the war has now been amicably terminated," an interpreter contended. Wainwright and the others were so excited and vindicated by the obvious Allied victory that they burst out laughing. "There was no stopping the laughter," the general later wrote. "It came up in me, and in the others, with an irresistible force: something born of a combination of our relief, the look on the Jap's face, the blind preposterousness of his beginning, the release from years of tension, the utter, utter joy over having survived to see this blessed day."

Liberation did not yet mean repatriation, though. Scattered throughout as many as three hundred camps around the freshly dead Japanese Empire, most of the prisoners endured two to three oddly anticlimactic weeks of limbo, waiting in place or roaming around in an attempt to return to Allied control. Buttressed by reasonably good intelligence and accurate Japanese information as to the location of the camps, the various Allied commands arranged for supply drops by bombers. The capacity and range of Marianas-based B-29s made them an ideal fit for this mission of mercy. Engineers installed special platforms inside bomb bays and devised ingenious means of packing them full of food, clothing, medical supplies, and other items inside fifty-gallon drums outfitted with red, white, or blue parachutes. The food consisted mainly of C rations, soup, vitamins, and fruit juices. For easy identification, prisoners in some instances painted "PW" atop a barracks building; at other camps, the bomber crewmen simply flew low and pored over maps and photos until they found the right spot or saw prisoners waving to them. Once in place above their "targets," the

bombers slowed their airspeed to 160 miles per hour or less and jetti-
soned their loads from less than one thousand feet. "I got more pleasure
out of this mission than all the others put together," Captain Miller
Anderson, a highly experienced combat bombardier in the 16th Bomb
Group, wrote to his sister after one run. "To be taking food, candy,
smokes, clothing and medical supplies to men who have probably been
without for two or three years just makes me glow with pride."

On the ground, the former prisoners reveled in the receipt of this
modern-day manna from heaven. "We were overjoyed at the abundance
of food," Private Michael Campbell commented of the drops at Oeyama.
"It was all passed out to each POW." Private First Class Lee Davis later
recalled of a drop at Inchon camp, "We saw the crew members waving
out of the bomb bays. We thought they were waving at us. They really
wanted to get us out of the way, but we were too happy to even think
right." The concerns of the crewmen were valid. The rapidly descending
drums could be dangerous. In more than one instance, former prisoners
were struck and killed or sustained broken bones. Nor were the aviators
immune to losses. A troubling eight planes failed to return from relief
missions, with the loss of 77 crewmen. Over a three-week period, the
Army Air Forces utilized 1,066 planes on 900 effective sorties. The aircraft dropped 4,470 tons of supplies. Their Santa-like bounty included
movies, projectors, ice cream, beer, blood plasma, gum, jam, magazines,
and books, the combination of which now became available in staggering quantities for the recuperating men. Indeed, as the operation unfolded, Richardson's Army Forces, Middle Pacific Command processed
and dispensed some 120 pounds of C rations, 129 pounds of K rations,
66 pounds of vitamin tablets, 90 pounds of canned soup, 92 pounds of
fruit, 56 pounds of candy, 50 pounds of gum, 52 pounds of boxed
matches, 42 pounds of cigarettes, 62 pounds of soap, 50 pounds of bulk
sugar, 57 pounds of evaporated milk, and 200 pounds of beer.

Former prisoners gathered parachutes, fashioned them into oversize
American flags, and proudly draped them inside barracks or atop roofs
or flew them from flagpoles that had previously displayed only the Rising Sun. In Asia, the supply drops were abetted by Office of Strategic
Services teams that parachuted in and made contact with the newly
liberated men. "This personnel, equipped with a minimum of medical

supplies, some emergency rations, and radio sets which could reach the
U.S. radio net in China, gave us early information of conditions in the
camps . . . where food or supplies could be parachuted, and the necessary information to what was most urgently needed," Major General
Henry Aurand, Wedemeyer's supply officer who oversaw the massive
relief effort, later wrote of their contributions. Among the freed men,
proscriptions from camp physicians to limit food consumption went for
naught. The men ate almost anything they could, even when they experienced terrible cramps and diarrhea, and looked forward impatiently
to permanent repatriation.[5]

As the experiences of the POWs indicated, the Japanese surrender was
similar to a simple handshake business deal with myriad difficult details
to formalize. An anticipatory limbo consumed the entire second half of
August as Allied and Japanese leaders labored to implement the terms
of the surrender agreement. In China, Chiang Kai-shek, with a worried
eye on his impending showdown with the communists, took whatever
steps he could to make sure that Japanese troops surrendered to Nationalist formations and no one else. He wrote to President Truman to af-
firm that the agreement with the Japanese mandated this in order to
prevent "the surrender of any Japanese Forces in China including puppets and armed bands cooperating with the Japanese to any armed
Chinese political parties or Chinese partisans. The surrender of all
Japanese arms and equipment shall be made only to officials of the National Government of China to be designated to you by me. All Japanese
commanders in the China theater (other than those opposing the Russians) should be held strictly accountable for full compliance with the
above directive." Neither Chiang nor Truman truly had enough power
to bring this concept to full fruition, and, of course, after demolishing
Japan's Kwantung Army in Manchuria, the Soviets, as Chiang hinted,
phased out hostilities according to their own agenda. They captured
nearly 600,000 Kwantung Army soldiers—a stunningly huge number
considering the general Japanese abhorrence of becoming a prisoner—
and worked many as slave laborers well into the next decade. Mao's
soldiers trailed the Soviet advance and ended up with enough Japanese

arms and equipment to strengthen CCP military forces and communist influence in Manchuria for the eventual Chinese Civil War.

With the concurrence of the Soviet, Chinese, and British governments, Truman appointed MacArthur the Supreme Commander for the Allied Powers in Japan (SCAP). In this capacity, MacArthur and his staff took the lead in working with the Japanese on the surrender arrangements. On MacArthur's orders, a sixteen-man delegation of Japanese officers led by Lieutenant General Toroshiro Kawabe of the Imperial Army General Staff arrived in Manila on the evening of August 19 aboard an American plane. In an unusual moment of vindictiveness, the otherwise gentlemanly MacArthur forced them to fly under the call sign "Bataan." At Nichols Field, they were escorted off their plane by tall, husky military policemen. "The humiliated, myopic little men . . . in their ill-fitting, ribbon-bedecked uniforms came humbly down the steps of the large American aircraft, their sabres rattling on the airplane's steps, to confront the dignified, giant Americans," Lieutenant Colonel Weldon "Dusty" Rhoades, MacArthur's pilot and a personal eyewitness to their arrival, noted in his diary. "Their proffered handshakes were politely but unostentatiously ignored. Their swords and hara-kiri knives seemed so completely out of order." Hundreds of American soldiers, from privates to generals, gawked, with more curiosity than malice, at the visitors whose faces were, in the recollection of Brigadier General Bonner Fellers of MacArthur's staff, "very set and serious." To Lieutenant Rogers, the stenographer, they looked "small and frightened." According to the young lieutenant, Brigadier General Charles Willoughby, MacArthur's officious intelligence chief, afforded them an especially chilly reception. "[He] towered over them, and his arrogance was properly displayed. He stared down at them with haughty contempt."

Cars drove the visitors to temporary quarters and then to Manila's City Hall building, where they removed their sidearms and swords and stacked them on Rhoades's desk. Mindful of preserving an almost imperial mystique, MacArthur did not personally meet with them. Instead, a group of staff officers, headed by Sutherland, sat down with the Japanese in a spacious, map-covered City Hall conference room and worked through the night. Both sides were careful to observe correct protocols of hierarchy and decorum. Sutherland sat opposite Kawabe, and the others in places according to their respective ranks and jobs. Led by Sutherland's strict demeanor, the Americans issued instructions for surrender procedures and the coming occupation of Japan. Translations and correct wording took up much of their time. A dignified mood, one of "coldly correct formality," in the description of one SWPA staffer, prevailed.

Besides agreeing to the language of the surrender documents, the most significant, and troubling, issue pertained to the possibility that diehards in Japan might still seek to perpetuate hostilities. The Americans wanted to send occupation troops into Japan within four days, but the Japanese persuaded them to delay for at least a week until they could be sure they had quelled all rebellious elements—the request in itself a revealing tribute to the intransigence of some fanatical Japanese in spite of the country's horrendous state. The Japanese officers were especially concerned about disquieting rumors that kamikaze pilots based at Atsugi airfield, where the Americans were scheduled to land, might stage a mass attack. In that sense, one might view the two-and-a-half-week interlude between the emperor's broadcast and the formal surrender ceremony in Tokyo Bay as a necessary cooling-off period for Japanese authorities to identify and suppress any remaining violent dissenters.

In the meantime, individual Japanese soldiers and units began giving themselves up. "If we depend on America, our country will survive and there will be spring again," one of them professed to his diary. "Will the enemy forgive us? I want to go back alive and analyze why Japan acted so foolishly. Never before in history was anything so foolish done." When Private Takeji Nagata and his starving comrades in a remote corner of Luzon surrendered, they sat for a time together in a stupor. "We were in shock. No one talked. Later we realized that our dream was coming true. We were alive and were going home soon. We didn't much care any more about the loss of the war." Many of the GIs had seldom seen a live Japanese, much less any who were willing to surrender. They often found themselves intrigued and bemused by their new captives. Lieutenant Philip Hostetter, a physician in the 24th Division, watched small groups of bedraggled Japanese trickle into the American lines and noted that "they saluted everyone. Our men would stop their vehicles and give them a ride to Headquarters. G.I.s driving in with several former enemies in the back seat became a common sight, and certainly a strange one." On Cebu, where Lieutenant Buckner Creel and the 77th Division had gone for a rest after the terrible Okinawa fighting, he was amazed to witness an entire organized enemy battalion lay down its arms "complete with all equipment including mountain guns. We disarmed, fed, and provided them with medical attention. Most were malnourished and suffering from the various tropical diseases that abounded there. The Japanese were no problem. Our biggest job was protecting them from the Philippinos [sic] who became quite aggressive after we had disarmed the Japanese." Staff Sergeant Milton Weitz supervised a group of two dozen prisoners and made sure they were fed, clothed, housed, and given medical attention, an experience that, in his eyes, fleshed out their humanity. In a letter to his sister, he judged them as "obedient and willing to work. They seem meek, very unsoldier like, and appear to be kind of dull witted. Regarding their physical appearance—average height is 5'5" brown skinned flabby appearance, and hardly what you would call fine looking. Somehow I don't harbor any hatred for them. I merely feel indifferent toward them, perhaps a bit sorry for them." But many of those who had fought them so ferociously and lost buddies in combat found it nearly impossible to let go of the hatred. "I am always amazed, when I look at the dirty innocuous little rats," an unrepentant Major General Roscoe Woodruff, commander of the 24th Division, wrote to Eichelberger, "how they could have accomplished so much in these areas [the Philippines] in the early days of the war." Speaking for many thousands who could not yet set aside their hostility, Private Charles Card still looked upon the Japanese as "dangerous animals and unhuman. I continue to mistrust, dislike, and consider the Japanese as enemies."[6]

Regardless, the feelings of individuals mattered less now than the formalities of ending the war. Eight days after the Japanese delegation had visited Manila, Admiral Halsey's Third Fleet entered Yokohama Harbor and then Tokyo Bay within forty-eight hours. An advance team of Army engineers and communication specialists landed without incident at Atsugi on the morning of August 28. The Japanese treated them to a carefully prepared lunch, augmented by pitchers of orange juice and glasses of wine. Colonel Charles Tench, the team commander, radioed MacArthur, "Landing of advance party proceeding according to plan. Reception by Japanese entirely correct." Two days later, the main vanguard of the SCAP commander's occupation army began arriving. At dawn, C-54 Skymasters carrying the leading troops of the hard-fighting 11th Airborne Division descended on Atsugi. In a classic example of hurry up and wait, the division two weeks earlier had hastily redeployed by air from the Philippines to Okinawa in anticipation of an immediate occupation mission. Instead, they had languished in the Okinawan mud, subsisting on C rations and K rations, eagerly waiting for the word to move out. At last, they boarded their silver C-54s at 0100 on August 30 for the five-hour flight from Kadena airfield on Okinawa to Atsugi. The first plane landed at 0600. Major General Joseph Swing, the redoubtable division commander, stepped onto Japanese soil first, followed by his staff. A delegation of Japanese officers greeted them with polite deference. For hours, C-54s arrived at the rate of one every four minutes, bringing with them everything from riflemen to signalmen to honor guardsmen and bandsmen. In the hundreds and then the thousands, sagging under the weight of full field packs, they skittered out of the planes and moved into position around the airfield. For fear that some unreconciled, fanatical kamikaze pilots might attempt to attack the American aerial armada, the Japanese had removed the propellers from every plane in the vicinity.

At 0730, Swing's troopers raised the first American flag of the occupation army even as planes continued to fill the cloudless azure skies overhead, like a majestic aviation conga line. "The sky for eight hundred miles was full of noise and traffic," Lieutenant General Eichelberger marveled. His plane approached the field around midday. He had not been to Japan since twenty-five years before, when he had visited as a young lieutenant colonel. "One of the most thrilling parts . . . was when we first began to go low over Japanese territory," he later wrote to Emma. "I was surprised at the small amount of destruction all the way up to the airstrip." Once on the ground, he greeted the Japanese officers and mixed easily with newspapermen and cameramen, mostly Japanese, who were on hand to document the momentous occasion. "This is the beachhead where I was supposed to land," he said, in an allusion to Operation Coronet. "I never expected to reach it in a plane without a shot being fired at me."

Hovering beneath the surface, like a mild but nagging headache, were American concerns that the Japanese at the field might still spring an ambush of some kind or that other suicidal rebels might launch attacks. "Trouble may arise either from Jap special attack units and unreconciled militarists against the orders of the Emperor, or from the civilian population antagonistic to the Japanese military authorities," fretted a planning document for the 1st Cavalry Division, one of the first units scheduled to arrive for the occupation. "High standards of conduct on the part of all American Occupation Forces are mandatory and will duly impress the Japanese population." Out of security concerns, Eichelberger had asked MacArthur to give him two days to establish the Eighth Army's occupation divisions and gauge the local mood. MacArthur had no intention of missing out on the sublime opportunity to lead the way into Japan. He gave Eichelberger two hours. At 1400, the SCAP commander's C-54, nicknamed "Bataan" of course, landed at Atsugi. "I touched down exactly on schedule," Lieutenant Colonel Rhoades noted in his diary. "It was with the greatest sigh of relief I've ever breathed. The boss was here, safe and sound, and my most important mission of the war had ended."

MacArthur evinced little concern about the security situation. Two weeks of coordinating the occupation with the Japanese and his understanding of the emperor's central role in maintaining social control in Japanese society had allayed any fears he otherwise might have had. Before boarding his aircraft that morning, he had told his traveling party to leave their pistols behind. He correctly understood the counterintuitive reality that, to the Japanese, they would actually appear more powerful unarmed than armed. "Years of overseas duty had schooled me well in the lessons of the Orient and, what was probably more important, had taught the Far East that I was its friend," he later wrote, with characteristic pomposity, of his decision to carry no sidearms. With his cap in place on top of his head and his distinctive corncob pipe protruding from his mouth, MacArthur emerged from the plane door and descended the ladder steps onto the tarmac as the band struck up a marching tune. An honor guard stood at attention, as did the band. General Swing stood resolutely nearby, both supervising and observing. Sutherland and other staffers emerged from the plane while MacArthur casually looked around and puffed on his pipe. A crush of photographers and officers greeted them. Still worried about security, Eichelberger greeted MacArthur with a handshake and an anxious smile. "Bob, from Melbourne to Tokyo is a long way," MacArthur asserted genially; "this is the payoff." Of this valedictory moment, Eichelberger later wrote, with wry appreciation, "I thought it was too. But I wasn't quite sure what the payoff would be."

MacArthur thanked the band and exchanged brief pleasantries with some of the 11th Airborne soldiers. The party moved on to a fleet of about twenty ramshackle civilian vehicles that the Japanese had provided for their transportation. Japan's fuel and transportation capabilities were in such an advanced state of decrepitude that most of the vehicles burned charcoal instead of gasoline. MacArthur, Sutherland, and Eichelberger climbed into an American-made Lincoln automobile—the finest car the Japanese could find—and the convoy set off for the Hotel New Grand twenty miles away in war-ravaged Yokohama. Vehicle breakdowns and poor roads stretched the journey into two hours. For most of the route, on either side of the road, armed Japanese soldiers stood guard with their backs to the convoy. "They were on both sides of the road, twenty or thirty feet off it . . . rifles at the ready," Lieutenant Colonel Roger Egeberg, MacArthur's physician, later wrote. At first, many of the Americans, including the worried Eichelberger, wondered if this represented a sign of disrespect or some kind of imminent danger. He and the others need not have worried. "It finally dawned on me that this solid wall of men was there to assist in guarding the Supreme Commander and that the turning away of faces was an obeisance, which previously had been accorded only to the Emperor himself," Eichelberger later wrote.

Without incident, they made it to Yokohama, a coastal city where a May 29 incendiary raid had consumed nearly seven square miles of urban landscape. Egeberg found himself amazed at "the massive total devastation that lay about us. Here and there a standing building of concrete showed by its starkness and contrast the extent of the rubble that lay about it." Entire blocks were gone. Destitute civilians listlessly picked through the ruins. "What a kick to stare at the arrogant, ugly, moon-faced, buck-toothed, bowlegged bastards, and realize where this put them," General Stilwell vindictively razzed to his diary upon viewing the remains of Yokohama. Only a few seemingly random undamaged pockets remained, including the site of the Hotel New Grand, an eighteen-year-old structure where many Westerners had stayed before the war. A sign on a nearby factory roof enthused, "Three Cheers for the U.S. Navy and Army." The polite hotel staff checked MacArthur in to Suite 315, the finest room available. "The manager was in a managerial frenzy lest the food and service be anything less than perfect," a correspondent for *Time* magazine reported. "Houseboys brought cold bottles of beer and urged U.S. officers to drink their beer, shower, and not to be late for dinner."

Outside, Eichelberger posted five hundred paratroopers in a perimeter guard around the hotel. Only then did he cease worrying about his boss's personal safety. Perhaps inwardly relieved, MacArthur told members of his entourage, "Boys, this is the greatest adventure in military history. Here we sit protected by one or two battalions of the Eleventh Airborne looking right down the throats of twelve or fourteen [Japanese] combat divisions." Considering the war's incredible ferocity, it was indeed remarkable that he and the other Americans now had nothing to fear from their former adversaries, a rapid dissipation of overt hostilities that had few other historical precedents.

The Japanese were probably even more relieved to find that they had little to fear from their new occupiers. Many had worried about the possibility of widespread atrocities. But instances of violence and criminal behavior on the part of the GIs were nonexistent. One Japanese naval officer expressed amazement at their "civilized" and "friendly" behavior. A Japanese reporter described a group of newly arrived naval aviators as "very light-hearted and agreeable. They did not show any attitude, whether in speech or manner of boasting of their victory. The agreeable attitude shown by these pilots is something of which every Japanese must be ever mindful when coming into contact with U.S. occupational forces from now on." After absorbing years of wartime propaganda as only an adolescent boy can, Sasaki Naokata fully expected the

Americans to look precisely like "glaring demons with horns sprouting from their heads. We were disappointed, of course. No horns at all." He was amazed at their normal appearance and their propensity to hand out chocolate bars. Schoolmates who had interacted closely with them assured him, "Americans, they're good people." Captain Randy Seligman, an American physician who was astonished at the lack of overt hostility he witnessed from the locals, wrote to a friend, "The Japs have found us to be courteous, kind, clean, inoffensive, and souvenir-mad. We haven't raped any women, bayoneted any babies, tortured any of their men, or looted any of their property. Naturally we don't patronize them, slap them on the back, or become palsy-walsies. But we have treated them fairly and decently. They, in their turn, have been docile, obliging, and cooperative. Only some of the ex-soldiers glare at us with a burning hatred. We walk around un-armed and unmolested both day and night."[7]

Once ensconced at the Hotel New Grand, MacArthur and his headquarters staff focused on their final planning for the formal surrender, scheduled to take place on September 2 aboard the USS *Missouri* as a tribute to President Truman's home state. In fact, his daughter, Margaret, had commissioned the ship. On the evening of August 31, as MacArthur sat down to dinner, a staffer notified him of the arrival of a special visitor, Lieutenant General Jonathan Wainwright. Aided by an OSS team, Soviet soldiers, and his fellow prisoners, Wainwright had embarked upon a stressful, meandering freedom odyssey from his remote camp in Sian to Wedemeyer's headquarters in Chungking, where he had finally begun to grasp the pleasant fact that his countrymen viewed him as a hero rather than a pariah. "We all admire you here," Wedemeyer told him. "Everybody does." In Chungking he received the Distinguished Service Cross in a quiet, tearful ceremony as well as an inscribed photograph of his beloved wife, Adele, who had nearly collapsed with joy at her house in Skaneateles, New York, when she heard the news that her husband had returned to Allied control. "I am very happy today," she wrote on the photograph. "Waiting impatiently for your return." He had replied with a loving note of his own and assured her that he would be home soon.

Wainwright ate delicious meals, acquired a fresh uniform of Wedemeyer's that draped unevenly over his gaunt frame, caught up with old friends, and gradually became accustomed to the dizzying array of new American equipment, weaponry, and matériel that attested to the country's powerful largesse. With a special invitation to the surrender ceremony, he flew to Japan by way of Manila, where he gawked sadly at the ruins of a city he loved, and made it to Yokohama early in the evening on August 31. When MacArthur heard the news of his arrival, he got up from the long dinner table where he and about two dozen others were dining on steak, fish, rice, vegetables, and soup to greet Wainwright in the lobby. But before the supreme commander had advanced more than a few paces, the door swung open and Wainwright entered the large room, leaning heavily on a cane as he hobbled along. For a few moments, a distinct hush came over the room. MacArthur and his entourage, some of whom had served in the first Philippines campaign, were aghast at their old comrade's diminished appearance. "His eyes were sunken and there were pits in his cheeks," MacArthur later wrote poignantly. "His hair was snow white and his skin was like old shoe leather."

MacArthur took him in his arms with an uneven hug. The two generals were so overcome with emotion that they had difficulty speaking. They had known each other for nearly half a century. For MacArthur, this moment of reunion must have been charged with a bevy of contrasting feelings. Wainwright had suffered the misfortune that might well have been MacArthur's had President Roosevelt not ordered him out of the Philippines before the collapse of the Allied military position in 1942. MacArthur might well have felt more than a tinge of guilt over this, and he probably worried that Wainwright would deeply resent him. For at least a year after Wainwright had surrendered this army, MacArthur privately begrudged that he had capitulated at all, and he had even opposed a War Department Medal of Honor nomination for him. But MacArthur's heart had since softened. He had great personal affection for Wainwright, whom he called "Jim" in reference to an old West Point nickname, and he now understood something of Wainwright's steadfast leadership during years of captivity as well as how much his old colleague had suffered under the Japanese. MacArthur hugged him, shook him affectionately, and blurted, "I'm glad to see you." Wainwright could think of nothing more to say than "I'm glad to see *you*."

MacArthur ushered him to the dinner table. The others pumped Wainwright's hand and greeted him enthusiastically with multiple recitations of his most common nickname: "Skinny!" Some even clapped in appreciation at his presence. As they all dug into a meal that Wainwright could only have dreamed of just a few weeks earlier, MacArthur offered him any command he wanted. Wainwright admitted that in captivity he had long believed that his surrender in the Philippines would disqualify him from any such position of responsibility ever again. "Why, Jim, you can have any one you want," MacArthur assured him. He asked only for a corps in MacArthur's army, and he readily agreed. The exchange was more symbolic than tangible. A corps-level command would actually have represented a demotion for Wainwright, and he did not end up serving in MacArthur's occupation army. In truth, the promise meant that MacArthur would have been happy to serve with Wainwright again and vice versa, a kind of mutual affirmation that mirrored the country's adulation of Wainwright. "I've been waiting for this day for more than three years," he emoted to reporters after dinner that evening. "I couldn't be happier."[8]

For the Americans, the war had begun when the Japanese attacked the battleships of the Pacific Fleet at Pearl Harbor; perhaps, then, it was only fitting that the war would officially end nearly four years later aboard a battleship. Commissioned on June 11, 1944, the USS *Missouri* was the third ship in US Navy history to carry the proud name of that great Midwestern state. She had fought at Iwo Jima and Okinawa, and survived kamikaze attacks. Third Fleet commander Admiral William Halsey had made *Missouri* his flagship on May 18. For several days, as August turned into September, the crew had prepared intensively for a surrender ceremony conceived and orchestrated like a magnum opus by MacArthur. The crowning moment might have led to an awkward showdown between the Army and the Navy over whether he or Nimitz should preside, a kind of unpleasant aftertaste from the division of command that had prevailed throughout the war. But the White House brokered a wise compromise. As the senior officer, MacArthur was to preside over the ceremony and sign the surrender documents on behalf of all the Allied nations in his capacity as Supreme Commander for the Allied Powers. Nimitz would sign on behalf of the United States. The five-star flags of the general and the admiral would fly equally over the ship. Personalities undoubtedly played a role in this compromise as well. The humble Nimitz probably had little desire to take on the central role in the proceedings. He was only too happy to cede that job to MacArthur, an undisputed master of stagecraft and a first-rate wordsmith.

In planning the ceremony, MacArthur and his staff left nothing to chance. The general wrote and rewrote his remarks several times, aiming to strike just the right tone. "He was determined that [they] should be strong, not vindictive, but he was already looking beyond," Egeberg, his physician, later commented. "It was to become a step on the way to rebuilding Japan." The names of every participant, every witness, every officer, even every reporter and photographer were committed to a master list and sent to Halsey. The schedule was exacting, minute, and timed almost to the second. Participants were to be served toast and coffee as they waited to board destroyers to carry them to *Missouri*. Everyone was to arrive aboard the battleship by 0830. Once aboard, "Navy officer guides will receive personnel as they board the *Missouri* and will indicate their positions for the ceremony," Colonel H. Bennett Whipple, MacArthur's headquarters commandant, wrote in a carefully prepared set of instructions dictated by the supreme commander himself. The instructions even determined the order in which the representatives of other Allied nations would board the ship—China, United Kingdom, USSR, Australia, Canada, France, Netherlands, and New Zealand. Captain Stuart Murray, *Missouri*'s skipper, and his officers, in Halsey's recollection, "rehearsed every step of it, provided for every nuance of etiquette, and smoothed away even the possibility of a bobble." Murray used off-duty sailors to serve as stand-ins for the participants and marked the exact spots where they were supposed to observe the proceedings. At least twenty times his sailors simulated and rehearsed the arrival of the eleven-man Japanese delegation. Not all the preparations went smoothly. During a final rehearsal on the afternoon of September 1, when a band played "The Admiral's March" to simulate the arrival of

Nimitz, his stand-in, a beefy chief boatswain's mate nicknamed "Two Gut," froze up and murmured, "I'll be damned! Me an admiral!"

The next morning, MacArthur and his cortege arose at 0430 and ate a breakfast of eggs, toast, jam, and bacon, accompanied by coffee. The group included an appreciative Wainwright, who later wrote, "I am eternally grateful to MacArthur for seeing to it that I was a party to the drama." To Lieutenant Colonel Egeberg, Wainwright looked "happy in a subdued way." At the Yokohama Custom House pier, an honor guard and a band greeted them. Colonel Whipple, the headquarters commandant and de facto stage manager, herded them onto the destroyer USS *Buchanan,* where they got under way at 0730. On the journey, they ate yet another breakfast. Outside, clumps of drifting gray clouds intermittently obscured the rays of the sun. The late-summer day was of the sort where one feels cool in the shade and warm in the sunshine. Allied naval might dominated Tokyo Bay. Some 260 ships of all sizes were spread out at anchor, almost as far as the eye could see. In their midst, a convoy carrying occupation troops from the 1st Cavalry Division glided into the harbor. "Literally hundreds of U.S. warcraft came into view, giant battleships, cruisers, destroyers, aircraft carriers, tenders and a few wandering native craft clearing debris out of the bay," the division's after-action report soon thereafter chronicled dramatically. "By the big battleship Missouri, the convoy steamed. On its decks could be seen hundreds of white-clad sailors in formation awaiting the arrival of General MacArthur, high-ranking representatives of all the Allied powers and the tiny Japanese ex-dignitaries who were coming to fix an unwilling signature on the dotted line."

An army of 225 reporters and 75 photographers from all over the world arrived at *Missouri* first and spread out to their assigned vantage points. To provide the cameramen with a choice view, sailors had constructed a wooden platform atop the veranda deck near turret number two, adjacent to a cloth-covered rectangular table where a chair was in place on one side for MacArthur and another on the other side for the Japanese signers. A microphone stand was perched behind MacArthur's chair. Some 148 flag and general officers arrived in the course of the morning. The Americans were clad in khaki uniforms, no ties, with shirts open at the collars. Representatives from the other Allied powers wore their own unique dress uniforms, varying from Soviet forest blue to Chinese olive drab and British and French khaki. On a nearby bulkhead, the original American flag that Commodore Perry had once flown during his 1853 expedition to Tokyo was mounted consequentially inside a glass frame, a mute reminder of the century-long historical forces that had led to the events of this day. At Admiral Halsey's behest, Lieutenant John Breymer had shepherded the old flag from its permanent home at the US Naval Academy in Annapolis along a circuitous, breakneck journey across America and the Pacific, all the way to the USS *Missouri*.

Alongside turret number two, the senior officers milled about the deck, conversing in the jovial tones of historic victors, enjoying a sublime moment of vindication and self-congratulation afforded to all too few in modern warfare. Their ranks included Generals Stilwell, Krueger, and Eichelberger, each of whom viewed the moment with his own unique individuality. "To us it marked the triumphant culmination of the bitterly fought war in which thousands of our comrades had died," the formal Krueger later commented meaningfully. Stilwell was seemingly less awed, telling his diary that night, "I took a crap & then went on deck." The garrulous Eichelberger chatted with anyone he could, except Krueger, whom he studiously avoided. "There were foreigners of all nationalities and I had a chance to talk to them all," he later wrote Emma. "Russians, Chinese, French, Aussies etc., were all there. We were lined up according to diagram. My place was on the front row of the Army section."[9]

Nimitz arrived first and then MacArthur. Both were piped aboard and greeted enthusiastically by Halsey. The Third Fleet commander was thrilled and moved to see Wainwright, an old friend whom he had not seen since they attended the War College together in 1933, when Halsey was a commander and Wainwright a lieutenant colonel. "I could not trust my voice," Halsey wrote years later. "I just leaned over the rail and grabbed his hand." Wainwright's bony face lit up at the sight of his old friend. "It was a thrill to be back with a man who had done so much for his country," he later gushed. With many salutes and handshakes, Halsey, Nimitz, and MacArthur made their way to the veranda deck adjacent to turret number two, where the flag officers and generals were so engrossed in their chatter that Commander Horace Bird, the ship's gunnery officer, had to bellow at the top of his lungs, "Attention, all hands!" to snap them out of it and get them into formation. They quickly came to attention as the three briskly strode past them. MacArthur grinned at members of Halsey's staff, many of whom he had known since 1942, and said, "It's grand having so many of my side-kicks from the shoestring . . . days meeting me here at the end of the road!"

Halsey led MacArthur and Nimitz to his cabin and offered them coffee. Both declined. MacArthur's stomach was churning with a nervousness that sometimes beset him on momentous occasions. "He was getting taut and, I thought, wanted to be alone," Egeberg correctly mused. MacArthur retired into the admiral's private restroom. "I could hear him retching, and I asked him if he wanted me to get a doctor," Lieutenant Colonel Rhoades, who was standing immediately outside, subsequently told his diary. "He replied that he would be all right in a moment." Fortunately, MacArthur was right. The upset stomach passed and he returned to the veranda deck just as a boat carrying the Japanese delegation arrived at 0856. Their leader, Foreign Affairs Minister Mamoru Shigemitsu, was clad in a formal suit and a silk top hat, as were two other civilians in the group. The military men wore dark green dress uniforms and peaked caps.

In 1932, Shigemitsu had lost a leg to a bomb detonated in Shanghai by a Korean independence advocate. Hobbled by an artificial leg and aided only by a cane, he had a difficult time exiting the boat and ascending the ladder onto the *Missouri*. Knowing of Shigemitsu's infirmity, Captain Murray's sailors had previously strapped swab handles onto their legs to estimate how long it might take "Peg-Leg Pete," as they irreverently called Shigemitsu, to make it onto the deck. At last, after several uncomfortable moments with only the clacking of Shigemitsu's artificial limb piercing the silence, he and the others made their way to the veranda deck, where they stood mutely and formally in three distinct lines. Shigemitsu and General Yoshijiro Umezu of the Imperial General Staff, an unrepentant hawk who had opposed the capitulation, stood together in the front rank, waiting for MacArthur to speak. To Lieutenant General Robert Richardson, watching from only yards away, the uniforms worn by Umezu and the other military men appeared "unpressed, shabby, [with] very shoddy material." Hundreds of onlookers packed together in any open spot they could find and gawked at the Japanese. Photographers snapped still shots or took motion pictures. To the right of the Japanese envoys, easily within their peripheral vision, four lines of admirals and generals stared at them. Most watched impassively, almost curiously, but some could not conceal their contempt for the Japanese. "Stilwell bristled like a dog at the sight of an enemy," Theodore White of *Time* magazine reported to his readers. "Kenney curled his lips in a visible sneer." Indeed, Kenney later admitted, "I believe that I disliked them that day more than at any time during the war." Halsey scowled malevolently at them, typical for such an unambiguous man whose hatred of the Japanese bordered on a barbarous bloodthirstiness. "The way to win this war is to kill Japs, kill Japs, and kill more Japs," he had once famously told the press; he often concluded messages with the menacing tagline "Keep 'em dying."

The visitors resisted what must have been a nearly irresistible urge to return the gazes of so many hundreds of recent adversaries. "We were, I felt, being subjected to the torture of the pillory," diplomat Toshikazu Kase, a forty-two-year-old English-speaking alumnus of Harvard and Amherst, later wrote of his emotions as he stood behind Shigemitsu. "There were a million eyes beating on us in a million shafts of a rattling storm of arrows barbed with fire. I felt their keenness sink into my body with a sharp physical pain. Never have I realized that the glance of glaring eyes could hurt so much. We waited for a few minutes standing in the public gaze like penitent boys awaiting the dreaded schoolmaster. I tried to preserve with the utmost sangfroid the dignity of defeat, but it was difficult and every minute seemed to contain ages. Tears rose in my throat and quickly gathered to the eyes, flooding them." Like a guilty pleasure, Stilwell maliciously enjoyed their discomfort. "Terrible experience for those bastards," he remarked with smug satisfaction to his diary. "The downfall of Japan in complete disaster, & they had to stand & take it. They stood stiffly and suffered. How we loved it."

Everyone stood at attention while a recorded version of "The Star-Spangled Banner" played over the ship's loudspeakers. At last, when the music ended, MacArthur strode to the microphone, his manner purposeful and dignified. His hands trembled slightly as he read from his prepared statement. "We are gathered here, representatives of the major warring powers, to conclude agreement whereby peace may be restored. The issues, involving divergent ideals and ideologies, have been determined on the battlefields of the world and hence are not for our discussion or debate. Nor is it for us here to meet, representing as we do a majority of the people of the earth, in a spirit of distrust, malice or hatred. But rather it is for us, both victors and vanquished, to rise to that higher dignity which alone befits the sacred purposes we are about to serve, committing all our people unreservedly to faithful compliance with the understanding they are here formally to assume. It is my earnest hope, and indeed the hope of all mankind that from this solemn occasion a better world shall emerge out of the blood and carnage of the past—a world dedicated to the dignity of man and the fulfillment of his most cherished wish for freedom, tolerance and justice. The terms and conditions upon which surrender of the Japanese Imperial Forces is here to be given and accepted are contained in the instrument of surrender before you."

Impressed by the magnanimous tone of the statement, Kase later wrote approvingly, "Never has the truth of the line 'peace has her victories no less renowned than war' been more eloquently demonstrated." Egeberg commented insightfully that the short speech represented "a look forward rather than a recounting of the past. It set the tone at a high level for this historic occasion." Colonel Sidney Mashbir, the Japanese-speaking officer who had headed up MacArthur's Allied Translator and Interpreter Section, which had played such a key role in gathering valuable intelligence that helped win the war, later remarked admiringly that "his statements brooked no denial, but they were not swaggering. It was the kind of thing that made you proud to be there and proud to know that you were a part of it."

MacArthur invited the Japanese to come forward and sign the two-page surrender document bound in a canvas holder. The second of eight paragraphs in the document declared unambiguously, "We hereby proclaim the Unconditional Surrender to the Allied Powers of the Japanese Imperial Headquarters and all of Japanese Armed Forces and All Armed Forces under Japanese Control wherever situated." When Shigemitsu had difficulty determining the proper place to affix his signature, MacArthur summoned his own chief of staff and barked crisply, "Sutherland, show him where to sign." Sutherland, the man who had served MacArthur in such an able and duplicitous fashion for nearly a decade, hastened forward and pointed to the proper spot. The foreign minister signed on behalf of the emperor and the Japanese government and the general for Imperial General Headquarters. At 0908, when they were finished, MacArthur sat down to sign for the Allied powers a different, leather-bound copy of the document. He summoned Wainwright and Lieutenant General Arthur Percival, who had surrendered British forces at Singapore in February 1942. They stood at attention behind him as he carefully signed his name with multiple pens, and then handed one apiece to Wainwright and Percival. Moved by this thoughtful gesture on MacArthur's part to recognize their collective ordeal, Wainwright later described the historic pen as "a wholly unexpected and very great gift."

Led by Nimitz, the other signers in their turn sat and, in most instances with at least one of their countrymen observing over their shoulders, scrawled their signatures. When they finished, MacArthur returned to the microphone and stated gravely, "Let us pray that peace be now restored to the world and that God will preserve it always. These proceedings are now closed." At nearly the same moment, the gray clouds dissipated and, almost as if by magic, an overflight of many hundreds of B-29s and naval aircraft appeared overhead, buzzing by in proud formations. "For the next half hour the air was dark with one of the mightiest displays of air power—peacetime air power—ever seen in the Pacific," radio correspondent Bill Dunn of CBS told his listeners.

The Japanese left USS *Missouri* by the same boat that had delivered them. The ceremony had lasted less than thirty minutes. On the way back to Tokyo, Kase scribbled a quick report of the proceedings for Shigemitsu to present to the emperor, who was, according to the foreign minister, relieved that the event had gone so smoothly, a good harbinger for a reasonable occupation. An equally allayed Shigemitsu regarded the outcome as "a painful but profitable task," a strong indication that the victor's treatment of the Japanese people would be tinged with cultural understanding and lofty forbearance. Impressed by the ennobling, forward-thinking tone of the entire ceremony, and especially

MacArthur's speech, Kase could not help but admit to himself that the mood would have been far different had Japan triumphed. "I raised a question whether it would have been possible for us, had we been victorious, to embrace the vanquished with a similar magnanimity. Clearly it would have been different. Indeed, a distance inexpressible by numbers separates . . . America from Japan. After all, we were not beaten on the battlefield by dint of superior arms. We were defeated in the spiritual contest by virtue of a nobler idea. The real issue was moral—beyond all the powers of algebra to compute."

As if to prove Kase's insightful point, MacArthur later that same day broadcast worldwide another speech, one that summoned to the surface the very best in his nature, and perhaps also that of the country he served. "A new era is upon us," he intoned at one point poignantly. "Even the lesson of victory itself brings with it profound concern, both for our future security and the survival of civilization. . . . We have had our last chance. If we do not now devise some greater and more equitable system, Armageddon will be at our door. The problem basically is theological and involves a spiritual recrudescence and improvement of human character that will synchronize with our almost matchless advance in science, art, literature and all material and cultural development of the past two thousand years. It must be of the spirit if we are to save the flesh. . . . We are committed by the Potsdam Declaration of principles to see that the Japanese people are liberated." And, in the moment of this ennobling utterance, the hostility and hatred of war—at least between these belligerents that had tragically bludgeoned one another for four long years—now yielded to a more high-minded hope for a better future.[10]

Epilogue

For the survivors, life went on. The future unfolded rapidly for the many individuals who had shaped the conflict and had also, in their turn, been shaped by it. "I had traveled over 30,000 miles in my army career, taken part in four major campaigns, and participated in eight assault landings," Francis "Bernie" Catanzaro, a rifleman who served with the 41st Infantry Division, wrote five decades after the war. "I estimated that I spent about 170 nights sleeping in foxholes. I had suffered malaria, hepatitis, jaundice, dysentery, and jungle rot but had not missed a day of combat. The hardships I endured would favorably affect the way I would live the rest of my life. I did not feel that I had done anything heroic or extraordinary; nevertheless I was proud of what I had accomplished." As true as his feelings were for many hundreds of thousands of GIs who went home and lived long postwar lives, they also applied to many of their former adversaries as well. In the wake of the official surrender, hundreds of thousands of Japanese servicemen eagerly laid down their arms in locales far and wide over the vast theater of war, from New Guinea to Bougainville, Rabaul, Java, Borneo, Thailand, Burma, Vietnam, Formosa, Korea, the Philippines, Manchuria, Japan itself, and innumerable smaller places. MacArthur's headquarters and Japan's foreign office estimated the capitulation of 3,240,485 soldiers and sailors and 2,788,333 civilians by late 1946, many of whom still awaited repatriation at that time from Western Allied or Soviet captivity. A few Japanese famously either did not get the word that the war was over, refused to believe it, or simply determined to fight on. One group of two dozen soldiers on Peleliu did not surrender until April 1947. Shoichi Yokoi, a Japanese soldier on Guam and perhaps the best known of all the holdouts, did not surrender until 1972.

Most bowed to reality, though. General Tomoyuki Yamashita, the ranking Japanese commander in the Philippines, spent the second half of August 1945 in frequent communication with the Americans and immediately ceased all hostilities, but he put off the final capitulation of his 40,000 bedraggled, hungry stalwarts until the same morning on which his government surrendered. Some of his officers had urged him to kill himself rather than be taken prisoner. "I have killed many enemies and I am afraid some friends, too," he replied evenly. "I must pay for this. In my wildest dreams, I never believe I can return to Japan. But if I kill myself, someone else will have to take the blame instead of me. I must take this responsibility alone; that is why I have decided to live." Even as the USS *Missouri* ceremony unfolded in faraway Tokyo Bay, Yamashita at Kiangan, deep in the wilds of northern Luzon, turned himself in to the 32nd Infantry Division, an appropriate honor for a hard-fighting unit that had won the first American ground victory of World War II at Buna in December 1942. The mood was almost jovial as soldiers and reporters gathered around to catch a glimpse of the legendary "Tiger of Malaya," who had fought such a masterful delaying action on Luzon. Had the war continued and the Allied invasion of Japan taken place, the protracted resistance of Yamashita's Fourteenth Area Army might well have absorbed valuable resources and troops at the expense of the campaign in Japan. MacArthur's forces never completely subdued this adversary; only the end of the war accomplished that.

The Americans led Yamashita and his group to an unassuming house with a peaked roof where they briefly rested. Flashbulbs constantly popped as photographers and individual soldiers commemorated the occasion, to the point where Lieutenant General Akira Muto, Yamashita's English-speaking chief of staff, quipped, "The war is over. We've had enough of those mortars." Everyone laughed. Among the troops, the mood was equally casual. An American lieutenant remembered that the GIs and newly surrendered Japanese soldiers soon established a "brisk exchange of battle flags and other souvenirs for sugar, powdered coffee, chocolate, cigarettes and the like." Yamashita's party was transported by trucks and cars along a damaged road to Baguio, the beautiful resort town that had once functioned as the summer capital for American imperial overseers. Many of the Filipinos who glimpsed the surrendering Japanese were in anything but a forgiving mood. "Natives who were repairing the road used abusive language and threw dirt at us," Muto later wrote. "The insults coming from the Filipinos . . . were unbearable."

The formal surrender ceremony took place the next day inside the concrete mansion that had once been home to Francis Sayre, the High Commissioner to the Philippines. In attendance were Percival, who had once surrendered to Yamashita at Singapore, and Wainwright. The pair had traveled by plane alongside several other generals for much of the previous day and night. Wainwright knew Baguio well. He had once lived there when he commanded the Philippine Division. He noted sadly that the site of his old house "was now a hole in the ground." Sayre's house, though, remained largely unscathed, an ideal site for the historic event. "A long table had been placed down the center of the reception room," Wainwright wrote descriptively. "On the side of it were what remained of Commissioner Sayre's fine carved chairs. Stools and folding chairs were placed on the other side. On a table near the conference room were placed all the swords taken from the Jap officers. The place swarmed with ranking Army, Navy, and Marine officers . . . correspondents and cameramen." The actual signing took only a few moments. Once again, Percival and Wainwright received pens. "Thus ended the ceremonies that brought to an end in the Philippines active hostilities which had begun with the bombing by the Japanese of Clark Field shortly after the notorious Pearl Harbor raid forty-four months earlier," an official US Army report of the proceedings chronicled majestically.

Yamashita and the others were trundled off into captivity. On MacArthur's orders, the Americans subsequently charged him with war crimes for the atrocities perpetrated by Japanese troops in Manila and elsewhere. If the USS *Missouri* ceremony had brought out the best in MacArthur, the treatment of Yamashita brought out the worst, reflecting little more than a desire to dishonor and punish the Japanese general for Japan's crimes in the Philippines. In November 1945, during dramatic trial testimony inside a Manila courtroom located within sight of Intramuros, where hundreds of Filipinos had fallen prey to mass executions and other barbarities, Yamashita denied knowledge of any war crimes, or any complicity in ordering them. He emphasized that he was out of communication with many segments of his army, including the Manila garrison that committed terrible depredations. "I wish to say that I absolutely did not order this, nor did I receive the order to do this from any superior authority, nor did I ever permit such a thing, or if I had known of it would I have condoned such a thing, and I will swear to heaven and earth concerning these points. That is all I have to say." Regardless, the court held him responsible for the actions of his troops and sentenced him to death by hanging. The United States Supreme Court declined to overturn the sentence. In a dissenting opinion, Justice Frank Murphy predicted correctly that the decision would set a troubling precedent that commanders could be held legally responsible for crimes committed by soldiers beyond their ability to control and against their express wishes. "An uncurbed spirit of revenge and retribution masked in formal legal procedure for purposes of dealing with a fallen enemy commander, can do more lasting harm than all of the atrocities giving rise to that spirit." Murphy sensed that the verdict stemmed from a thirst for vengeance rather than justice. Someone had to pay for what the Japanese had done in the Philippines. Rear Admiral Sanji Iwabuchi, the man most responsible, was dead. In his stead, Yamashita served as a convenient scapegoat. He was hanged on February 23, 1946. For many of the same reasons, Lieutenant General Muto, his chief of staff, followed him to the gallows on December 23, 1948.[1]

When Wainwright had watched Yamashita taken unceremoniously into custody, he turned to Lieutenant General Wilhelm Styer, whose headquarters was responsible for his care, and asked sympathetically, "This might seem a little strange, coming from me, but I hope Yamashita is shown the courtesy due his rank, in the matter of personal accommodations, housing, and food." Styer assured him of the proper treatment, and held true to his promise. Wainwright's request revealed much about his personal character. After years of mistreatment, at a time when he might understandably have wished to see the same degradation meted out to a defeated enemy, he instead advocated for fair play and decency. Seldom in American history has a military professional so deserved and received the mantle of hero from his countrymen. In the whirlwind days that followed the war's end, Wainwright returned home to an almost hysterically enthusiastic welcome. The Army promoted him to four-star rank, awarded him the Medal of Honor, and, on September 10, staged a triumphant parade for him in Washington, DC, that drew 400,000 admirers to the Mall area to hear him speak.

Shortly before the speech, he was reunited with Adele, whom he had not seen in four years. Both found it difficult to suppress their tears of joy. "The men who fought on Bataan and Corregidor were never beaten in spirit," he told the enormous crowd. "Exhausted by thinning supply and the ordeal of terrific pounding by siege guns and bombers, it was useless to continue the struggle. We surrendered as honorable soldiers. The tables are now completely turned. No humane person could desire that the Japs be forced to endure what many of our men went through." With the exultant cheers of the crowd ringing in their ears, he and Adele climbed into an open-top Packard at the head of a motorcade bound for the Capitol. Lampposts were adorned with posters that displayed his image and the phrase "Welcome 'Skinny.'" Along the streets, another 300,000 well-wishers jockeyed for a close look at the general. One woman slipped through a police cordon and jumped onto the car's running board. The surprised Wainwrights graciously shook hands with her. "I'll never forget this day," she gushed. Wainwright addressed both houses of Congress and then met personally with President Truman, who enthusiastically draped the Medal of Honor around his scrawny neck.

Three days later, four million cheering New Yorkers turned out for a ticker tape parade in his honor. The general sat on the back of an open-top car, waving mightily at the sea of faces around him. Policemen on motorcycles coasted on either flank. The revelers expended a remarkable five hundred tons of confetti along the twenty-two-mile route. Upstate, Skaneateles held a "Peace Pageant" parade for its favorite son and daughter. Some twenty thousand people turned up, a huge number for such a small town. "The parade included forty big American flags carried by forty men in mass formation," Nellie Glass, a resident, recalled. "What a beautiful sight! A great thrill of pride swept through me, and for such an American as Jonathan Wainwright."

He had become one of the most famous men in America. He was inundated with letters, speaking requests, endorsement offers, keys to cities, honorary degrees, awards, memberships, and interview inquiries. "Do I *have* to accept all these invitations," he wrote at one point to Dwight Eisenhower, one of the few people in the country who could understand and relate to what he was experiencing. The pliant Wainwright had difficulty telling people no. As the postwar months and years unfolded, Wainwright's fame and the adulation for him became suffocating. He traveled constantly. Everyone seemed to want something from him. "They never left him alone, these hangers-on, these sycophants riding on the coattails of the great," Duane Schultz, Wainwright's finest biographer, vividly wrote. He could scarcely go out to dinner without being accosted by well-meaning but intrusive fans. Some pressed in just to touch him; others tried to tear the stars from his uniform. His mail arrived in the tons. He struck a lucrative deal to publish his memoirs. Considerate and honest by nature, he tried manfully to accommodate his many well-wishers, but this was impossible.

In captivity he had worried incessantly about living his postincarceration days as a reviled pariah. Instead, he became the opposite, beloved, lionized, revered, a goodness to the point of excess, "alone in his hero's cage," as a West Point classmate once succinctly described his silky burden. Wainwright stayed in the Army until 1947 when he turned sixty-four, the mandatory retirement age, and he bought a home in San Antonio. As a civilian for the first time since his teen years, he lent his name to multiple insurance companies and a supermarket chain. He frequently attended military reunions of the many comrades with whom he had served—POW organizations, men who had fought under him at Bataan and Corregidor, West Point classmates, and more. He and Adele had always been heavy drinkers but, after so many years of privation and stress, and the new persistent pressures of fame, their alcohol consumption became problematic. Soon Adele could not take it anymore. "The strain of the long wait, the worry over his treatment as a prisoner, the lack of positive information as to his whereabouts, and finally the terrific excitement amid the wild acclaim of our people, continuing for so long, brought on a serious collapse," a friend of hers sadly related. She experienced an emotional and physical breakdown. Numerous treatments failed to improve her condition. Eventually, she required permanent hospitalization at Emory John Brady Hospital in

Colorado Springs, leaving him alone as a veritable widower. He drank excessively and constantly in both public and private. Everywhere he went, people plied him with drinks.

He imbibed so profusely that some Army officials privately worried that his public intoxication might bring embarrassment to the service. At home he lived an ironically lonely life surrounded by party-time pseudo friends who cared mainly about having a good time or getting something from him. "The drinking parties at his residence were endless," one true friend commented. "These sorts of parties were common among a large percentage of military, but not so extensively as in Wainwright's case. Everybody barged in constantly, sort of a 'hanging on the coattails' syndrome." Eventually the years of physical privation in captivity, combined with the frenetic, alcohol-soaked life of fame, took their toll. Wainwright suffered a debilitating stroke on August 13, 1953, lapsed into a coma, and died on September 2, exactly eight years to the day after he had stood behind MacArthur during the surrender ceremony aboard USS *Missouri*. Even in death, he was afforded no privacy from obsequious crowds of acquaintances who gathered in the hospital room and outside in hallways to witness his demise. Adele's condition was such that she could not attend his funeral. In fact, her caregivers at Emory John Brady Hospital could not even bring themselves to inform her of Jonathan's death until well after he was buried.[2]

Lieutenant Colonel Harold "Johnny" Johnson and the other former prisoners of the Inchon camp returned to American control on September 7 and 8 when soldiers of the 7th Infantry Division landed to begin an occupation of southern Korea by Major General Hodge's XXIV Corps. The Soviets and the Americans had agreed to jointly occupy the country temporarily to disarm the Japanese and lay the foundation for some sort of ill-defined independent Korea. The XXIV Corps ultimately swelled to include the 6th and 40th Infantry Divisions in addition to the 7th. The joint occupation, of course, eventually hardened into a north-south split in Korea as the Cold War developed. On that golden day in September 1945, though, Johnson and the others happily gathered at Inchon's wharves and boarded a Manila-bound transport ship. They were amazed at the sight of prodigious American military power in the Philippines. "It was bewildering, but pleasantly so, after our long

Rip-van-Winkle-like separation from normal life," Lieutenant Colonel Armand Hopkins, who was part of Johnson's group, later wrote. "We were wide-eyed gawkers."

A couple of weeks later, Johnson reached Hawaii, where he placed a call to his wife, Dorothy, in South Dakota, but she was out to lunch with some visiting cousins. He left a message for her: "Colonel Johnson has just left for the mainland." The message was her first inkling that he was alive and homeward bound. She practically collapsed with relief. She traveled to San Francisco, where they enjoyed a grand reunion and a week together at the St. Francis Hotel. They shared a strong bond that endured the many years of separation and privation. In captivity, Johnson had kept himself going by keeping a diary in the form of a long letter to Dorothy. When they were back together again, their readjustment was reasonably smooth. He was delighted to find that his daughter, whom he had not seen since she was just a few months old, immediately accepted him, as if he had never been gone. Johnson decided to stay in the Army. To get himself back in good physical condition, he took to refereeing basketball games, something he had enjoyed doing before the war. "To test my stamina in February, 1946, I refereed alone thirteen ball games in three days at a little country tournament. I did it so I figured I was in pretty good shape."

He bought a new West Point ring to replace the one he had traded to guards for food aboard the hellish *Brazil Maru*. "We are starting anew," he told Dorothy, a statement that applied to more than just the ring. He returned to Korea in 1950 as a battalion commander and then a regimental commander in the 1st Cavalry Division and saw even heavier combat than he had experienced on Bataan in 1942. He became the operations officer for I Corps. One of his superiors described him as "the most outstanding officer I know." Johnson attended the National War College, headed up the Command and General Staff College at Fort Leavenworth, and served in numerous key staff positions. In 1964, he was promoted to four-star general and was appointed Army chief of staff, a position he held for the next four years as the Vietnam War escalated. Johnson's experiences as a POW exacerbated his already powerful sense of duty and the overarching importance of integrity. He had seen the most desperate and terrible of situations, and somehow this brought out the best in him. He was determined to expect the same of others. "Of all the things that we have in the Army," he once said, "our most treasured possession is the integrity of the Army as a whole, and each one of these instances that we let somebody skip by is an erosion of this integrity. When you don't have integrity in the Army, you don't have an Army."

As chief of staff, Johnson made nine trips to Vietnam. The war's complexities and contentiousness seriously challenged even a man of his remarkable abilities and character. He could not help but wonder if American strategic aims in Southeast Asia were worth the terrible price they elicited. "This thought tears mercilessly at the heart and soul of every thinking person," he once told a rapt audience during a speech to the Association of the United States Army. "I read the casualty lists as they come to me day by day. I write a personal letter to every family that loses a son, or a husband, or a brother. I can assure you from the bottom of my heart that I ask myself this question day and night, and if I did not have an answer I would not be able to take the first step each morning that leads from my quarters to my office." With the mission in Vietnam far from completed, and the war far from finished, he retired in July 1968 to live a quiet life alongside Dorothy. He died in September 1983.[3]

Private Michael Campbell and the other survivors of Oeyama linked up with newly arrived Honshu occupation troops from the XI Corps about a week after the USS *Missouri* surrender ceremony. Campbell was still well underweight and dressed in a filthy POW uniform. After the hell of captivity, he became deeply emotional when he saw his first American soldier. "I was so happy to see him that I threw my arms around him," he wrote solemnly. "I was sobbing how glad I was to be free. He was so embarrassed that all he could do was swallow and I could see his adam's apple jerking up and down." A brass band played the national anthem until the former prisoners became so overcome with emotion that the music died out as everyone, bandsmen and the liberated alike, simply stood together sobbing. The repatriated men were given new clothes and copious amounts of food and were subjected to extensive physical and mental examinations, as well as interrogations about their comportment as prisoners. In addition to finding out who might have collaborated too closely with the Japanese by betraying their fellow prisoners, the interrogators hoped to account for the fate of every prisoner and gather information to prosecute Japanese war criminals. An adjutant general's memo had ordered soldiers who were processing newly recovered prisoners to take careful note of their physical condition and emotional well-being: "The particular points to be noted and recorded are as follows: 1) Depression. 2) Resentment and bitterness. 3) Sense of guilt. 4) Apathy, lack of interest, restricted initiative. 5) Attitude toward authority. 6) Attitude toward further service. 7) Anxiety. 8) Self confidence and self respect. 9) Concern over health. 10) Existence of domestic troubles."

Campbell's group was shipped from Japan to a tent city outside Manila, where they waited to go home. The mess hall was accessible to them all day and night. They could eat anything they wanted. He was promoted to corporal, bumping his pay from $50 to $66 per month. After four long years away from the United States, Campbell finally arrived in San Francisco on October 15. Like many other former POWs, he required hospitalization to recuperate from his physical infirmities. Gradually, he improved and went home to Flint, Michigan. He decided to reenlist and negotiated a sweetheart deal with the Army that earned him half a year of leave time, an enlistment bonus, and his choice of duty station. "With plenty of money, a car, and recovering health, my spirits soared. I fell into a routine of working out at the YMCA during the day, roller-skating at night, and dating girls in between." During one skating session, he literally bumped into Priscilla "Peg" Marion, the woman who soon thereafter became his wife. The couple had three children. Campbell ended up serving in the Army for another quarter century. He deployed to West Berlin but was fortunate enough to avoid the wars in Korea and Vietnam. He retired in 1971 with the rank of sergeant major.

True to Private Lester Tenney's proactive, energetic nature, he refused to stay put at Fukuoka #17 after the Japanese surrender and wait for American soldiers to come to him. George Weller of *The Chicago Daily News* made it to the camp, interviewed Tenney and others from Chicago, and told them that the Americans had just landed at Kanoya on Kyushu's south coast, some two hundred miles away. Tenney's left arm was still bound in a sling and he knew that Captain Hewlett, his doctor, was still thinking very seriously about amputating it. This concern, and the extreme desire to get out of Fukuoka #17 and meet up with the newly arrived American military forces, prompted him to set off with a friend for Kanoya. "All I knew was that I was going to see my family and, of course, Laura," he later commented. After a long journey by train, boat, and truck, they made it to Kanoya, where they joyfully met up with a newly arrived unit from the Army Air Forces. They were fed well, slept on clean sheets, and treated like special guests. "We were like kids at a picnic, eating and eating until we could not hold any more."

They were flown to Okinawa, where Tenney had a joyful chance meeting with his brother Willard, a member of a naval construction battalion. Willard brought him up to speed on family news, but seemed deliberately to avoid mentioning Laura. Just when Lester began to wonder what was wrong, his brother grew serious and said, "You know, Les, Laura was informed that you were missing in action, presumed dead. She waited three years. [She] thought you were killed in action. Les, Laura got married a few months ago." The terrible news devastated Tenney. He had managed to survive the Bataan Death March and over three years of captivity in part by sustaining himself with the thought of reuniting with Laura. "In addition to all my other surviving, I had to survive that also," he later commented.

Tenney returned home to the South Side of Chicago and a jubilant reunion with his family. He even got together with Laura and found out that not only was she remarried; she was also pregnant. Racked with guilt and remorse, she apologized profusely. Instead of lashing out at her to assuage his own grief, he forgave her and wished her nothing but happiness. "Despite my heartbreak, I realized that the dream of being with her was one of the reasons I never gave up and never stopped believing that one day I would return. For that I was eternally grateful, but our relationship was over, and there was no sense in crying about it any longer." He spent a year in the hospital recuperating from his physical injuries and kept his arm. When he left the Army in 1946, he went to college on the GI Bill and earned a PhD in finance. He remarried in 1959, became a professor at Arizona State University and San Diego State University, founded his own successful financial planning company, and retired in 1993.

In retirement, he wrote a memoir, joined with other former POWs to sue Japanese mining companies for reparations, and lobbied the Japanese government to apologize for the mistreatment of prisoners. He served as the national commander of the Defenders of Bataan and Corregidor, told his story to American audiences far and wide, and even traveled to Japan to speak to schoolchildren about his experiences. Along the way, Tenney decided that nothing good would come from holding a permanent grudge against his captors. He cultivated Japanese friends and once arranged for a Japanese prime minister to speak to an ex-POW group. "I've learned to forgive," he once said, "but I'll never forget." He died in 2017 at the age of ninety-six, a highly esteemed figure among his countrymen and a quintessential, consummate survivor of the worst that the Japanese and war itself could throw at him.[4]

The senior officers who had so shaped and influenced the course and outcome of the war—and were themselves so profoundly defined by it—moved on to their own postbellum triumphs and tragedies. Lieutenant General Richard Sutherland, MacArthur's long-serving chief of staff, knew he had lost influence with his boss after the terrible row they had over Elaine Bessemer-Clark, Sutherland's Australian mistress, in 1944. Either out of sheer spite or in a ham-fisted attempt to usurp MacArthur's authority, Sutherland had knowingly disobeyed a direct order from MacArthur not to station Bessemer-Clark at SWPA headquarters in the Philippines. When MacArthur found out, a volcanic argument had ensued. The SWPA chief did not fire Sutherland, but their relationship never recovered, and the byzantine Sutherland well understood that his days as MacArthur's most influential confidant were over. Shortly after the occupation of Japan began, Sutherland decided to retire. Major General Paul Mueller, the commander of the 81st Infantry Division, succeeded him, though Major General Courtney Whitney actually came to fill Sutherland's old role as the most influential, and universally disliked, member of the staff. Such was the distance between Sutherland and MacArthur that when Sutherland left Tokyo in December 1945, the supreme commander barely thanked or even acknowledged his long years of service. An embittered Sutherland enlisted Lieutenant Colonel Rhoades, the pilot, to fly him home by way of Brisbane, where he was briefly reunited with Elaine, much to Rhoades's frustration. He disliked her and wanted to spend Christmas with his family back in the States; in the event they did make it to Washington by December 23. During the many hours in the air together, Sutherland poured out his resentment against MacArthur, whom he felt had used him until he no longer needed him. "Sutherland said MacArthur never gave him a complete explanation why he had fallen into disfavor," Rhoades wrote of their conversation. "As a result he ended up a bitter and disillusioned soldier."

Sutherland continued to admire his former boss's intellect, once claiming to his young adult daughter, Natalie, that MacArthur "could read an article in the newspaper and seven years later quote it to you verbatim and not leave a word out. He said he had never seen a memory like MacArthur had." Regardless of his respect for MacArthur's mind, his resentment of him only grew, to the point where he dismissed him as little more than "an egomaniac." The two men who had worked together so intimately for years saw each other only once more, at a birthday dinner, exchanging just a brief handshake. Initially, when Sutherland returned home to Natalie and his wife, Josephine, he was moody, irritable, and rude (traits that many of those who served with him in the Army would have readily recognized). Elaine continued to write him long, passionate love letters. Inevitably, Josephine found one of them, confronted her husband, and tearfully threatened to divorce him. At this, Sutherland broke down sobbing, confessed his transgressions, promised to cut Elaine loose, and begged his wife to forgive him. Josephine agreed, and they resumed what had generally been a happy marriage. Natalie intercepted and destroyed any other incoming letters from Elaine, and Sutherland never communicated with her again. The Sutherlands moved to Florida and lived there until Josephine's death from a stroke at age sixty in 1957. He married Virginia Shaw Root in 1962, but then suffered a paralyzing stroke of his own. Sutherland whiled away his final months in a wheelchair, watching golfers play at a course near his home. He died in 1966, a thoroughly respected but almost universally disliked man in Army circles.[5]

Albert Wedemeyer stayed on as American commander in China into 1946, during the formative stages of the Chinese Civil War. When he briefly went home to the United States for a medical leave, the Truman administration contemplated appointing him ambassador to China, but backed down in the face of CCP objections due to his staunch anticom-munist views. Instead, Truman sent him back to China in 1947 to report on the situation. Wedemeyer strongly, and vainly, recommended exten-sive military support for Chiang and the Nationalists. Disaffected by American policy in Asia and deeply saddened by the communist victory in 1949, Wedemeyer retired from the Army in 1951 as a lieutenant gen-eral, though Congress three years later retroactively promoted him to four star. He took a job as executive vice president of AVCO, a manufac-turing conglomerate, wrote a memoir, and became involved in conser-vative Republican politics. Every bit a strategist and an intellectual, he remained a relentless Cold Warrior for the rest of his life, and an ardent critic of American postwar policy in Asia. But he never lost his intrinsic optimism for the progress of humanity. "Gradually, as the spirit of soli-darity, which has its genesis in common interests, spreads, mankind may one day attain that goal of a world state dedicated for all, realistic-ally capable of promoting equity and opportunity for all, regardless of race, color, creed, or social status," he once wrote with admirable hu-manistic idealism. He died in 1989 at the age of ninety-two.

Wedemeyer's predecessor, General Joseph Stilwell, continued as Tenth Army commander until it was deactivated in October 1945, after which, for a short time, he headed up an equipment board that made recommendations for future strategy before assuming command of Sixth Army at the Presidio in the San Francisco area. In spite of his seemingly vigorous constitution, he did not take good care of himself. Years of accumulated stress and inveterate smoking undoubtedly took a toll on his health. He was diagnosed with stomach cancer in 1946 at the age of sixty-three. On October 12 of that year, he died following sur-gery for the cancer. His ashes were scattered over the same Pacific Ocean waters he had once enjoyed viewing from his home in Carmel. His widow, Win, allowed correspondent Theodore White access to her late husband's papers, diary entries, and journals and authorized their pub-lication in an edited format in 1948. The general's sharp literary tongue and vituperative criticism of Chiang made for provocative reading so soon after World War II, even as the Chinese Civil War raged. The caustic writings have shaped historical perception of him ever since. But, to some extent, they stemmed from his habit of working through problems by writing about them and privately venting his frustrations. "He rarely made notes on things that were going well, the 'good things', because there was no worry about them," one of his close aides wrote years after his death.

Unlike Wedemeyer, Stilwell did not have the opportunity to write a memoir, shape latter-year perceptions of himself, or to reflect on his actions with the benefit of hindsight. In the decades that followed his death, Stilwell became a kind of symbol for the tragic failure of the wartime Sino-American alliance, reviled by some as a bigoted, vindictive knave who had undercut Chiang and unwittingly paved the way for a communist triumph, lionized by others as a courageous whistleblower who exposed the fatal repression and dysfunction of the Nationalist regime. In truth, he and his actions conformed to neither stereotype. "He was a highly sophisticated man in his understanding of painting and literature (both Western and oriental), his fluent knowledge of French, Spanish and Chinese, as well as English, and his wide travels which had given him an understanding of customs, thinking, and habits in many countries of Europe, Latin America and of course the Far East," Brigadier General Frank Dorn, one of his closest staff members, wrote perceptively of him years after the war. In the end, though, Stilwell's strengths as a cultural observer, an inspirational leader, and a military tactician could never offset his near total inability to see beyond his own presuppositions to find some way to achieve American strategic aims in China.[6]

By the war's end, General Walter Krueger was beginning to feel his age. He had logged forty-seven years in the Army, including almost three years overseas during World War II, commanding operation after operation from New Guinea to Tokyo. He had overseen the largest concentrations of American ground troops in the Pacific theater and, on Luzon, fought the largest battle of the war. He had dedicated himself completely to his command, to the point where he had not even allowed himself to take a drink during his entire time overseas. He had not seen his wife, Grace, for nearly three years, an eternity for a man so faithfully and sincerely committed to the woman he loved. He oversaw Sixth Army's occupation of Japan during the fall of 1945, but then decided to retire and go home when his sixty-fifth birthday arrived in January 1946.

Before he left, MacArthur gratefully decorated him with the Distinguished Service Cross. An honor guard and band from one of Krueger's favorite units, the 1st Cavalry Division, saw him off at Yokosuka. The band played "Deep in the Heart of Texas" as a tribute to his retirement destination in San Antonio. The battleship USS *New Jersey* carried him across the Pacific, back to the country that, from childhood onward, the German-born Krueger had so fervently made his own. He and Grace bought a home in San Antonio—the first they had ever owned—and settled down to a quiet life as empty-nest retirees. Krueger participated in numerous civic organizations and gave frequent talks at Army staff colleges. Prompted by his love of military history and a desire to tell Sixth Army's story, he spent nearly six years working on a wartime memoir, a project for which he eventually developed little passion, nor much motivation. "Every day I plug away at my book," he wrote to a friend in 1949, "but progress is slow. I often wish that I had never undertaken the task. I am staring at it daily and when it is finished, I shall really rest." He stuck with the project, and the end result was *From Down Under to Nippon,* published in 1953, an extraordinarily dry book that mainly just regurgitated wartime Sixth Army operations reports instead of sharing much about Krueger's personal perspective. The general's failure to tell his story in any kind of compelling fashion reflected an otherwise thoughtful man who struggled for most of his life to communicate effectively. In that sense, he proved himself much more an intellectual consumer than producer.

His postwar life was marked by tragedy and personal problems. He did not plan his finances well. He had allowed a large tax bill to accrue during the war, to the point where he and Grace were forced to rely on the charity of friends to help them afford their house. He described the tax bill as similar to "a veritable Sword of Damocles over my head." As a result, the Kruegers had to watch every penny, a humiliating circumstance for a retired full general. Even worse, Grace's health deteriorated. She suffered from high blood pressure and coronary artery disease, acutely enough to cause frequent hospitalizations and almost constant nausea and pain. "Grace is not at all well," he wrote to his lifelong friend Colonel Fay Brabson, "and does not seem to get better." She died on May

13, 1956, leaving him crushed, melancholy, and "terribly lonely." He openly spoke of joining her as soon as he could.

Problems with his children only added to Walter's nightmarish retirement years. The Kruegers had three children, Jimmie, Walter Junior, and Dorothy. Both sons graduated from West Point, Jimmie in 1926 and Walter in 1931. Walter enjoyed a successful military career and retired as a colonel. But Jimmie and Dorothy had serious problems. Jimmie was banished from the Army in 1947 for actions unbecoming an officer, a charge that stemmed from a drinking problem. Fortunately, he found a good job at an engineering firm and put his life back on track. The same could not be said for Dorothy. Sheltered but rebellious, she struggled with mental illness, alcoholism, and narcotics abuse. In 1934, at age twenty-two, she married Aubrey Smith, a 1930 West Point graduate and highly regarded, innovative officer who commanded the 306th Infantry Regiment, 77th Infantry Division, during World War II and earned a Silver Star for his courageous leadership at Okinawa.

The couple had a son and a daughter. Dorothy's personal issues led to constant tension in the marriage and the unique embarrassment that came with their life in the military fishbowl. She became known for neurotic outbursts and once knocked down the wife of another officer. As the daughter of a famous general and the wife of an ambitious colonel with a promising future in the Army, she could hardly hope for any privacy. Nowhere was this more true than when Colonel Smith was assigned to Tokyo as chief of the Army's Far East Command plans and supply section, a prominent staff position on General Mark Clark's United Nations Command. Dorothy viewed herself as an impediment to her husband's career. She told a friend that she wanted to commit suicide and even, on one occasion, slashed her wrists. But she was actually more a danger to Aubrey than to herself. On the evening of October 3, 1952, she stabbed her sleeping husband in the side with a ten-inch hunting knife. As he lay bleeding to death, Dorothy sat beside him, clad only in bra and panties, and told their Japanese maid, "I'm sorry I didn't get him in the heart."

Colonel Smith died at a Tokyo hospital within a few hours. Dorothy was tried in a military court, found guilty of murder, and sentenced to life in prison at hard labor. Her devastated father filed an appeal on her behalf, arguing that her trial was unconstitutional because a military court had no jurisdiction over a civilian. The case, known as *Kinsella v. Krueger,* went all the way to the Supreme Court in 1956. In a 6–2 decision, the court ruled in Krueger's favor, declaring that civilians could not be subject to military trial. Dorothy was released from prison and moved in with her father. "Dorothy . . . is getting along well and busy with her secretarial course at a local business college," Krueger told Brabson in an upbeat 1958 letter. "Her son's wife gave birth to a baby girl on April 20th—my eighth great grandchild!" But Dorothy's problems persisted. She suffered a nervous breakdown that required hospitalization. She eventually got out of the hospital, settled in as a medical secretary, and lived into her eighties, dying in 1996.

The general was plagued with his own health troubles. He suffered from back pain so acute that he could hardly sit for more than a few minutes. Arteriosclerosis sapped his energy. Glaucoma diminished his vision, almost to the point of blindness. He had hernia and kidney surgeries. More than physical maladies, he battled loneliness and the depression inherent in so many family difficulties. When Brabson became obsessed with regret over his failure to make general during his Army career, Krueger remonstrated with him with a heart-wrenching exploration of his own unhappiness. "I wish you would compare your situation with mine for a moment. You are fortunate in having a loving wife by your side and three wonderful children. I, on the other hand, have lost my precious wife, my son Jimmie's [Army] career ended in disgrace and my only daughter's tragic actions broke my heart. All the promotions and honors that have come to me cannot possibly outweigh these heartaches and disappointments. If true happiness is the aim of life— and I believe it is—then you are more fortunate than I and I would gladly trade with you." Saddened by years of heartache, Krueger died in 1967 of pneumonia exacerbated by his arteriosclerosis, a relatively humble and anonymous end for such a remarkable, self-made man who had commanded more ground soldiers than all but a few other generals in American history.[7]

Krueger's nemesis, Lieutenant General Robert Eichelberger, enjoyed a much better postwar life, though, ironically, he could have benefited from Krueger's wise advice about true happiness. Joined in Japan by Emma, Eichelberger stayed on as Eighth Army commander and quickly established a friendly, approachable reputation among the Japanese. He was known to give rides to hitchhikers and trade trinkets with street vendors. When he retired in 1948, Hirohito and his wife invited the Eichelbergers to lunch, a rare sign of imperial respect. Gifts from everyday Japanese poured into his office. A crowd of 50,000 people gathered to see them off when they boarded the USNS *Buckner*. Some shed tears. One admirer told him, "General, it is a tragedy you are leaving us." Eichelberger was especially moved by the gratitude of an elderly rickshaw driver who "as my ship pulled out . . . waved and waved while tears made furrows down his leathery face." Much to Eichelberger's resentment, MacArthur demonstrated far less appreciation. Their final meeting was awkward and stilted. Neither expressed any appreciation to the other. "This is a very interesting phase of his character that he would let an officer who has run his occupation for so many years and who has been in my opinion largely responsible for its success leave here without recognition of his services," he groused to his diary that evening, referring angrily to MacArthur as "one person who forgot to thank me and wish me well after six years of service in the Pacific!" The two generals never saw each other again.

Eichelberger initially lived in Washington, DC, where he served his last few months in the Army and officially retired at the end of 1948. Congress retroactively promoted him to four-star general in 1954. For a time he worked as a Far East expert consultant to Assistant Secretary of the Army Tracy Voorhees until he soured on working for a man whom he described as "a pretty good single-handed talker himself and doesn't need a consultant very much." He was offered or considered a vast array of jobs, including the presidency of the University of Vermont, a UN peacekeeping position in Kashmir, the head of the CIA in the Pacific, and management of several chemical companies.

In the end, none of these opportunities represented the right fit for him. He could afford to be choosy. He and Emma were financially secure. She had inherited a sizable sum of money from a bachelor brother. He received a generous Army pension and made extra income by writing magazine articles and making speaking appearances. In June

1951, the Eichelbergers moved to Asheville, North Carolina, Emma's hometown, and bought a beautiful two-story home, where they lived for five years until moving to another fine house on a golf course. Eichelberger loved the Asheville area. "To me, Western North Carolina is one of the beauty spots of the world," he once wrote a friend.

A natural communicator, Eichelberger yearned to tell the story of his military life and bring attention to the exploits of the Eighth Army. Surprisingly, in view of his glibness and his strong literary skills, he enlisted the assistance of a ghostwriter, Milton MacKaye, though he soon found himself exasperated with MacKaye's laziness and hard-drinking lifestyle. With MacKaye's dubious help, Eichelberger wrote seven serialized articles about his World War II experiences and published them in the August and September 1949 editions of *The Saturday Evening Post*. The response was largely positive. Eichelberger received personal kudos from such luminaries as George Marshall and Eleanor Roosevelt. A less enamored Krueger thought that Eichelberger had claimed too much recognition for himself and his army, at the expense of Sixth Army. "It is difficult for me to understand . . . why anyone should attempt to claim more credit than is due him," Krueger wrote privately to Brabson. "I have been urged to refute many of his statements, but have declined, for it would be beneath my dignity to do so." The articles formed the critical mass of Eichelberger's memoir—again with MacKaye aboard as a ghostwriter—published in 1950 under the title *Our Jungle Road to Tokyo*, a well-written, engaging book that has generally held up under historical scrutiny.

The success of the book only added to Eichelberger's comfortable financial circumstances. He traveled the world, donated his time to many civic organizations, attended football games, fished, and became a passionate golfer. He felt immense relief "knowing that when I awake I do not have to go to some office and plow through a basket of papers. I have more time for thought and reading than I have ever had in my life." But the fact that he had so much time on his hands also turned out to be unfortunate. Sensitive and reflective by nature, in retirement he came to spend far too much energy stewing about the past. The resentment he had so long harbored against Sutherland, Krueger, and MacArthur hardened into outright hostility, if not hatred. He felt that

Sutherland had connived behind his back to sabotage his operations and supplant him as I Corps and later Eighth Army commander. He could not abide what he perceived as Krueger's chronic rudeness and disrespect, as well as his perception that Krueger had attempted to keep him from getting the Eighth Army command. "These two men were full of deceit and it is hard to forgive those who make one's way difficult with an enemy to fight," Eichelberger wrote in 1959 to Clovis Byers, who by then was a lieutenant general serving in the Pentagon. Two years later, he told Byers of Krueger, "I have no intention of speaking to him in heaven or hell."

Eichelberger felt more hurt than hatred for MacArthur. From Buna to Japan, MacArthur had leaned heavily on Eichelberger when he needed him, but had never, in the latter's view, properly rewarded him for his many achievements. During the war and the occupation, Eichelberger knew it was in his best interests to get along well with MacArthur. In retirement, he had no such concerns. With the proverbial gloves off, Eichelberger let himself grow more upset by the year over MacArthur's high-handed behavior to deny him a Medal of Honor for Buna, a major command in Europe, and, in general, the kind of public recognition that Eichelberger craved. At the risk of delving into psychohistory, one cannot help but come to the conclusion that Eichelberger's feelings about MacArthur were reminiscent of the resentment he had developed for his father, whose dismissive attitude toward his son and failure to recognize his achievements created in Eichelberger a lifelong ambition to distinguish himself. Eichelberger was shocked and revolted by the public adulation for MacArthur that so prevailed in American culture during the 1950s. Privately, he viewed his former boss as highly overrated, far short of a great battle captain. "General MacA seemed to feel that whatever impression he gave the American people was what counted and what really happened did not seem very important," Eichelberger once commented in a private memo. In a letter to Brigadier General Clifford Bluemel, an old friend who had been captured in 1942 as part of the doomed Philippines garrison and whose personal feelings for MacArthur smacked of intense hatred, Eichelberger sniped, "He knew less about enlisted men and what makes them tick than any high ranking officer I have ever known." For a time, Eichelberger contemplated writing a tell-all book to expose MacArthur's many warts, but he wisely shelved the idea. A relieved Byers affirmed that Eichelberger had little to gain from penning such a catty tome. "If you were to mention some of the facts that you and I know would be justified in using, the two people [Krueger and MacArthur] most concerned could be influenced in no way," Byers told him. "Their national reputation will be well evaluated by historians as they consider the events that took place."

Equally conscious of historical posterity, Eichelberger dictated, over the course of many years, hundreds of pages of recollections, comments, and anecdotes to Virginia Westall, his personal secretary and close friend, who referred to him affectionately as "Sir Robert." The topics ranged from recapitulations of the many battles he had fought to his childhood memories and leadership philosophies to many cutting critiques of MacArthur, Krueger, and Sutherland, alongside warm words of admiration for Dwight Eisenhower, Joseph Swing, Jonathan Wainwright, and a host of others, especially the soldiers he had once led. Eichelberger's preoccupation with the past began to indulge his petty side. Once, when Sutherland tried to get together with Eichelberger in Washington, the former Eighth Army commander refused to see him. Eichelberger declined to attend SWPA reunion dinners scheduled in New York each year on the occasion of MacArthur's birthday. When Byers did attend, MacArthur invariably and warmly asked for Eichelberger. "Tell me, Clovis, how is that grand old chief of yours?" the former SWPA commander would ask. Perhaps if Eichelberger had gone to these dinners, his natural friendliness and affability might have led to conversations of mutual understanding with his old antagonists and softened his feelings. But he would not, or could not, bring himself to take that leap. As it was, he developed a close friendship with the noted historian Jay Luvaas, who at the time worked at Duke University. Like so many others, Luvaas came to revere the charismatic general. Eventually, Eichelberger entrusted his voluminous dictations and other personal papers, including the copious letters he had written to Emma during the war, to the university under Luvaas's worthy stewardship. Emma felt that the letters she had written to her husband during the war were too private to include in the Duke material, an understandable sentiment, but then she went to the unfortunate extreme of destroying them. Even so, Eichelberger's papers proved a precious resource for generations of historians, a uniquely detailed and revealing exploration into the experiences of an important, and highly overlooked, general.

Though Eichelberger's postwar health was generally good, he did experience some problems. His gallbladder had to be removed in 1950. He once dealt with a blood clot in his lung. As he entered his seventies, he battled high blood pressure and elevated blood sugar levels. He began to have prostate problems. On September 25, 1961, he underwent exploratory prostate surgery at Memorial Mission Hospital in Asheville. A few days before, he told Byers, "This will be a minor operation." He was wrong. He survived the operation but his condition soon worsened due to pulmonary problems. Pneumonia set in, and he died the next day at age seventy-five. In an edited book of Eichelberger's letters to Emma, published in 1972, Luvaas warmly eulogized the general as "one of the most colorful and attractive individuals it has been my good fortune to meet," one who genuinely liked all people, no matter their background. "Because of his lively curiosity, vitality, and basic optimism, he never became an old man. Above all he was honest. He possessed a magnetic sense of humor, sturdy integrity, and a lofty concept of duty and patriotism." By any fair measure, he was the finest American ground commander of the Pacific War, an inspiring, albeit flawed, man who made a major contribution to Allied victory and the strategic aims of the postwar occupation. Emma died in 1972. She and Robert are buried together at Arlington National Cemetery.[8]

Unlike the other key senior generals of the Pacific War, MacArthur commanded troops in combat again. He oversaw the highly successful occupation of Japan, transforming that country from an aggressive, militaristic, repressive predator into a vibrant, economically prosperous world leader under a tolerant, representative government. This remarkable accomplishment was probably MacArthur's finest hour. Then, when communist North Korea invaded noncommunist South Korea in June 1950, MacArthur, at age seventy, assumed command of a United Nations force with the strategic objective of repelling the invaders to preserve the prewar status quo division of the peninsula. Running the war from Tokyo, MacArthur presided over the buildup of American and South Korean ground forces in the embattled Pusan perimeter during the late summer. He then engineered an outflanking amphibious invasion of Inchon on September 15 by the 1st Marine Division that sent the North Koreans into headlong retreat back across the 38th parallel. Had UN forces simply halted at the parallel with Seoul liberated and the South Korean government restored, MacArthur might well have claimed a victory for the ages, though he doubtless would have subjected himself to much criticism from ardent Cold Warriors for not snuffing out communism in all of Korea.

Indeed, with North Korean military forces in disarray, the temptation, for both MacArthur and Washington policy makers, to advance north and dismantle the communist regime proved almost irresistible. But a troubling specter hovered behind the veneer of this post-Inchon military triumph. Mao and the CCP had triumphed in the Chinese Civil War the year before and had established control over the country's armed forces. A strong possibility existed that Mao might use those forces to intervene in Korea and save the north's communist regime. At an October 15 meeting on Wake Island, President Truman asked MacArthur about just this possibility. MacArthur assured him that the Chinese were highly unlikely to get into the war. The general described the war as won and asserted that his armies had little to fear from the Chinese even if they did get involved. "Had they interfered in the first or second months it would have been decisive. We are no longer fearful of their intervention. Formal resistance will end . . . by Thanksgiving." It was one of the most colossal and tragic miscalculations in modern military history, one for which MacArthur and the newly established Central Intelligence Agency deserved equal shares of the blame. It also marked the beginning of the end of his career. With United Nations forces approaching the Korean-Chinese border in November, Mao launched a major offensive that hurled MacArthur's armies back into South Korea and completely changed the nature of the war from a regional conflict into a serious Asian landmass showdown between leading Cold War powers.

Rather than risk having this burgeoning struggle escalate into World War III, a chastened Truman now sought little more than to attain the original objective of fighting a limited war to maintain the sovereignty of noncommunist South Korea, a strategy with which MacArthur ardently and rebelliously disagreed. The old warrior viewed Chinese entry as an opportunity to destroy communism in Asia and advocated a strategy of widening the war with a counteroffensive into Manchuria and perhaps even the use of atomic weapons or radioactive waste to limit communist troop movements. The man who had so movingly wished for world peace aboard the USS *Missouri* five years earlier now seemed to have embraced the notion of world war. He did not appear to grasp that if the American-led UN side was fighting a frustrating limited war, so, too, were the communists. When he publicly criticized and opposed Truman administration war policy, the president on April 11, 1951, took the politically unpopular action of firing him and ending his half-century military career.

The widespread anger over his relief was exceeded only by the almost hysterically enthusiastic reception he received upon coming home to the United States for the first time in a decade and a half. A Gallup poll revealed that two-thirds of the American people disapproved of MacArthur's removal. A young senator from California named Richard Nixon reported that he received almost 5,000 telegrams and 10,000 letters, almost 100 to 1 in favor of MacArthur. "The happiest group in the country . . . will be the communists and their stooges," he sniffed. One of his Republican colleagues called for Truman's impeachment and ranted conspiratorially, "This country today is in the hands of a secret inner coterie which is directed by agents of the Soviet Union." When the plane carrying MacArthur, Jean, and Arthur landed at the San Francisco airport, thousands of excited well-wishers were on hand to welcome them. In Washington, he addressed a joint meeting of Congress, famously declaring that "old soldiers never die, they just fade away. And like the old soldiers of that ballad, I now close my military career and just fade away—an old soldier who tried to do his duty as God gave him the light to see that duty." In New York, hundreds of thousands turned out to cheer him along a nineteen-mile parade route. The revelers dumped 2,852 tons of confetti and other paper onto the procession, exceeding Wainwright's by a factor of almost 6 to 1. Chicago staged yet another ticker tape parade for him, and he spoke to a packed house at Soldier Field. Observing the pandemonium from afar in Asheville, Eichelberger found himself almost nauseated by the public fawning over the deposed general. Privately, Eichelberger called MacArthur's retreat from North Korea the "worst defeat the American Army has ever suffered."

MacArthur and his family settled into a new penthouse apartment home in Suite 37A at the Waldorf Towers in New York. The retired general hoped that the public adulation of him might lead the Republican Party to draft him as its presidential nominee in 1952 (he had no intention of actively campaigning). The Senate investigated his relief and MacArthur gave expansive testimony, outlining his aggressive views on Cold War strategy and the Korean War. Once the sheen wore off the initial adoration of MacArthur, the American public, and many of his greatest congressional admirers, shied away from the general's ideas as they began to realize how overstretched the country was just to fight the limited war in Korea and how costly, in lives and treasure, would be the escalation that MacArthur apparently envisioned. His political star waned and his 1952 nomination went nowhere. Instead, the party chose Dwight Eisenhower, the longtime aide for whom MacArthur had developed such a sub-rosa antipathy, and he, of course, became president.

MacArthur settled in to post-military life as a highly respected, if not quite universally revered, military statesman. He received six honorary doctorates and almost every possible civic honor. Schools, parks, airports, streets, and buildings were named after him. He became chairman of Remington Rand, a manufacturer of typewriters and other business machines. He sometimes advised the Eisenhower and Kennedy administrations on military and policy matters. Every year on the occasion of his birthday, he convened in a ballroom at the Waldorf-Astoria Hotel with his SWPA cronies for a convivial stag dinner and, usually, a speech by the old commander. At the 1953 dinner, with Krueger absent just a few months after his daughter had killed her husband, MacArthur lionized him: "The past year has treated him with one of the cruel strokes of fate. We miss him tonight, the vacant chair looms very large upon the horizon of this table. I don't think that history has given him credit for his greatness. I think he stands unexcelled in the history of our traditions." He even compared Krueger to General Thomas "Stonewall" Jackson, the eccentric, audacious Confederate commander, a generous but awkwardly inappropriate equivalence between generals of such radically different dispositions.

MacArthur himself yearned for comparison to both Jackson and Robert E. Lee, even though his own father had fought for the Union and earned the Medal of Honor for his valor. Near the end of World War II, Douglas Southall Freeman, author of the famous book *Lee's Lieutenants*, a revealing but somewhat Lost Cause–influenced, hagiographic exploration of Confederate commanders, had approached MacArthur about the possibility of writing a similar study of SWPA. In one letter, Freeman hailed MacArthur as the "inheritor of the boldness and the strategy" of Lee and Jackson. In an unctuous reply, MacArthur had lobbied stridently for Freeman to make this comparison at a prominent place in his book. "I have taken the liberty of inserting it in pencil for your consideration. It would link me with my teachers." For whatever reason, the author never followed through on the project.

MacArthur made one final trip to the Philippines in 1961, at the age of eighty-one with his health declining, and the next year, he received the prestigious Sylvanus Thayer Award, given to the American citizen who best embodies the West Point motto of "Duty, Honor, Country." To accept the award, he visited his alma mater one last time and addressed the Corps of Cadets. Age had not diminished his outstanding, arresting oratorical skills. "The shadows are lengthening for me," he intoned movingly. "The twilight is here. My days of old have vanished—tone and tint.... In my dreams I hear again the crash of guns, the rattle of musketry, the strange, mournful mutter of the battlefield. But in the evening of my memory I come back to West Point. Always there echoes and re-echoes: Duty, honor, country. Today marks my final roll call with you. But I want you to know that when I cross the river, my last conscious thoughts will be of the corps, and the corps, and the corps. I bid you farewell." By the time he finished, according to one witness, "There were tears in the eyes of big strapping cadets who wouldn't have shed one before a firing squad." In 1964, near the end of his life, MacArthur published a memoir entitled *Reminiscences*. Heavily influenced by the byzantine Courtney Whitney, the book careened between self-aggrandizing reproductions of congratulatory messages the general had received from numerous prominent figures over the course of his career and fascinating, beautifully written descriptions and insights. MacArthur died on April 5, 1964, at Walter Reed Hospital of biliary cirrhosis, a liver problem that led to the deterioration of his abdominal cavity. He left behind a long shadow as a compelling and troubling figure, a commander of enormous intellect and impact, but one of enduring controversy that may well never cease, his vexing legacy making him something of an American Montgomery.[9]

Of course, from a broader viewpoint, the war itself generated its own legacies. The Army had transformed from a chronically understrength, underequipped provincial force into a highly modern, lavishly supplied, sophisticated, professionally led military organization, perhaps soldier for soldier the most effective ground army on earth in 1945. In plain terms, the Army found itself with enough professionals at all levels to pull off this remarkable transition but not so many as to cripple the institution with careerism. For Americans as a whole, the formal end of hostilities marked the conclusion of a conveniently precise victory narrative. But in actuality, for millions of Asians, and even the victors themselves, the end of World War II initiated over a half century dominated by postcolonial strife, bloodshed, and death. In the summer of 1945, Wedemeyer had presciently described the continent, in a cable to the Joint Chiefs, as "an enormous pot, seething and boiling, the fumes of which may readily snuff out the advancements gained by Allied sacrifices the past several years." Without any question, China was at the center of it all, the geopolitical driver and tone setter, dominating events of the Asia-Pacific Rim in much the same way that the United States loomed large over everything in the Western Hemisphere. The dominant American cultural narrative of World War II, heavily influenced by the triumphal residue of the Europe First strategy that struck down the horrendous evils of Nazism, tended to see China as a tertiary, backwater theater, an interpretation that, in retrospect, seems very wrongheaded, perhaps even precisely backward. Chiang invited Mao to Chungking for six weeks during the fall of 1945 in hopes of brokering some sort of compromise to forestall civil war. The visit settled nothing, nor did numerous futile American attempts at arbitration. Years of bitter war ensued.

The communist victory in 1949 was, at a minimum, the most important event in the history of the Cold War and, at a maximum, the most important event of modern post–World War II history. The triumph of the Soviet Union in Europe spread communism to much of that continent and set the tone for decades of associated European conflict, much of it frightening but most of it bloodless. By contrast, Mao's victory had a similar but much worse effect in Asia. It solidified within the world's most populous, and previously fractious, backward country an extraordinarily murderous but highly effective regime, one that modernized this sleeping giant and cast off its historical shackles of Western imperialism, even as it consistently devised effective new means of inhuman repression. It also exported communism to much of Asia and its environs and sparked enormous bloodshed. If Mao had lost to Chiang, it is difficult to imagine that the Soviet Union could have had anything like the same sort of influence in Asia, especially with the obstacle of a Nationalist China in its way.

Like a major earthquake with heavy aftershocks, the Chinese communist victory led, directly or indirectly, to a slew of terrible postcolonial wars or instances of genocide, from Indonesia to Manchuria, that cost some ten million lives. This appalling death toll does not even include the many millions of Chinese who lost their lives as a result of Maoist persecution, starvation, disease, and exposure. Nor does it take into account the radicalizing, polarizing effect that the condescendingly termed "loss of China" had on American politics for decades, highlighted, of course, by the disturbing rise of Senator Joseph McCarthy, one of the most infamous demagogues in American history. In this light, perhaps it is no coincidence that since World War II, nearly every American conflict has taken place somewhere on the Asian landmass. The country's two largest post–World War II wars, Korea and Vietnam, would never have occurred in the absence of a communist China. Indeed, one could argue that they were fought primarily to curtail Chinese influence on the southern periphery of Asia and limit its expansion to the Pacific regions where Americans had shed so much blood during World War II.

Nowhere was this more true than in the Philippines, the very nexus of the American war against Japan, where the US had fought two major campaigns. Guerrillas had, of course, played a significant role in the liberation of the archipelago from the Japanese. Eichelberger once told Colonel Wendell Fertig, who on Mindanao had led one of the largest insurgent organizations, "I would say that the Philippine guerrillas rendered valuable assistance and almost in direct ratio to the value of their leadership. The Japanese were forced to maintain heavy guards on convoys and at strategic points, thanks to the guerrillas. They had to maintain larger forces of troops in the Philippines than otherwise would have been necessary." In response to the local resistance, the Japanese had made the classic mistake of terrorizing the population. Whitney, whom MacArthur had charged with the complicated task of coordinating SWPA operations with guerrillas and overseeing civil affairs, told Fertig, "We were fortunate in the Philippines in being opposed by a ruthless enemy whose very brutality gave the measure of his stupidity and insured a strong spiritual resistance to him." As in Europe, the resistance groups reflected the diverse political components of the larger whole—ideological, cultural, geographical, ethnic, religious, and the like, many yearning for revenge against real or perceived collaborators, another stark similarity to Europe. With the common Japanese enemy now gone, these guerrilla groups morphed into power centers that contested ferociously for influence in postwar political battles that were made even more intense by the Philippines' status as a newly independent country.

Here, as in so many other places around Asia and the Pacific, the Americans had to find some way to reconcile imperialism's putrid aftertaste with the rise of a menacing Soviet- and Chinese-sponsored second- and third-world communist nationalism. Upon war's end, Tech Sergeant William Owens, a counterintelligence corps specialist who had become enmeshed in the ruthless world of local politics, felt little more than cynicism and foreboding for the future of the country. "In a Manila Bay sunset of red, purple, gold, I thought of the Philippines more than I thought of home," he wrote of leaving the islands. "Bitterly I recalled what cynical Americans had named as the four freedoms of the Philippines: freedom to starve, freedom to stagnate, freedom to revolt from democracy, freedom to go from one political form to another until chaos or authoritarianism rules. I had arrived in the Philippines in darkness; I was leaving the Philippines in darkness." Communist Huk-balahaps (or Huk) guerrillas who had fought the Japanese during the war established an aggressive, grassroots agrarian insurgency that seized upon the general climate of want and misery, and the corruption of the new government in Manila, to come frighteningly close to seizing power. "Morally the Philippine government is bankrupt," Fertig wrote sadly after the war. "When chided about graft and dishonesty in government, they reply, 'We learned from the Americans.'"

Eichelberger's bromide about leadership came to fruition in this instance as well. The preternaturally honest Ramon Magsaysay, himself a former guerrilla and onetime auto mechanic, became defense minister and later the elected president. With close assistance from Edward Lansdale, an innovative, unconventional CIA adviser, Magsaysay masterminded a powerful counterinsurgency that defeated the Huks. If this turnaround had not happened, then the former colony where the American people had invested so much wartime blood and treasure, where some of the greatest naval and land battles in modern history had played out, where more than 21,000 Americans had become prisoners of war, where MacArthur had invested American prestige to an almost spiritual degree, would have become a hostile country, a sort of Pacific Cuba, affiliated with the communist bloc. Instead, the Philippines became a bulwark within an American-sponsored alliance network of anticommunist states stretching from the Horn of Africa to Japan, encompassing Thailand, Malaysia, Indonesia, Chiang's Taiwan, South Korea, and, with all-too-tragic brevity, South Vietnam.

The very inclusion of an economically and politically transformed Japan revealed a stunning postwar geopolitical shift almost reminiscent of musical chairs. From MacArthur on down to the most fuzzy-cheeked eighteen-year-old private, few American soldiers during the war could have anticipated that, within only a few short years, the Japanese would become trusted, reliable allies and the Chinese implacable enemies. If the war itself seems almost unnecessary and wasteful in that retrospective light, it is well to remember that only the horrendous cost and bloodshed of the conflict changed Japanese attitudes and afforded the

United States the opportunity to occupy the country and transform it in its own image.

Perhaps inevitably, the transformation had a darker side, too, bought in part with the stomach-churning price tag of more than a few unpunished or paroled war criminals granted by the American government in the wake of a treaty that formally ended the occupation in 1952. The newly elected Eisenhower administration subsequently freed scores of those who had mistreated Allied prisoners and committed other war crimes. The freedom roll even included some murderers like Petty Officer Second Class Yukitauna Tanaka, who had executed an American prisoner in October 1944. "Under U.S. control his prison rating has varied from 'satisfactory' to 'superior,' receiving the latter rating 5 of the 27 months rated and receiving the next highest rating of 'excellent' 12 of the 27 months," Conrad Snow, chairman of the Board of Clemency and Parole, wrote in flowery legal language. "Under Japanese Government control he has been rated as 'very excellent.' He is 31 years of age, single, and apparently in good health. If paroled, he will engage in farming and attempt to improve the living conditions of the family which consists of his father and mother, and 3 brothers and a sister." The new president's initials at the bottom of the document spelled freedom for Tanaka.

Less surprising was the establishment of enduring blood brother-style alliances with New Zealand and Australia, both of which by necessity during the war embraced an enduring, seminal geostrategic security shift away from their original British mother country and into league with the United States. Some one million Americans passed through Australia or were stationed there during the war years, the beginning of a long-term cross-pollinating cultural melding that has never since abated. No accident, then, that the Australians have fought shoulder to shoulder with their US partners in every major American conflict since World War II.

The cost, human and otherwise, of maintaining the Cold War and post–Cold War American order in the Pacific and Asia forever resists any firm calculation. The unsettling wastage at war's end provided the first glimpse into this long-term investment. As American armies had migrated north late in the war, their once vital South Pacific bases had already become backwaters. The end of hostilities turned them, and most of the newer bases, into wasteful ghost towns. The untabulated wastage surely ran into the tens of millions of dollars. Lieutenant Colonel Rhoades, MacArthur's pilot, once heard his chief grouse, to no avail, against this profligate squander. "Some of this material was new, some slightly used or slightly damaged," Rhoades documented in his diary. "MacArthur's innate conservative nature rebelled against such waste." Warehouses and equipment were abandoned outright or sold to local merchants at bargain-basement prices. Planes, tanks, trucks, jeeps, bulldozers, and other vehicles and an untold variety of equipment were left to rot in jungle wilds or even dumped into the ocean. On Guadalcanal, the sale of 13,277 tons of fuel and supplies netted only $26,354, about one-quarter of its original cost. Some 58,831 measurement tons of matériel that had cost the taxpayers nearly 20 million dollars was abandoned or destroyed on this island alone, a microcosm for uncounted other places. By and large, the Philippines and Chiang's China benefited the most from this largesse, inheriting, pilfering, or purchasing almost anything the Americans no longer wanted.

From the soldier's perspective, the savagery of Pacific theater fighting cast the longest shadow of all. The dehumanizing brutality of the war marked the participants like some sort of martial scarlet letter. The Japanese refusal to observe any semblance of what the Americans viewed as legitimate rules of warfare established the pattern for every American enemy since then. From Korea to Iraq, American soldiers, in their turn, struggled mightily, and sometimes unsuccessfully, to define their own moral parameters, especially within the ethically ambiguous environment of counterinsurgent warfare and often in a media-charged climate of bitter self-recrimination. Perhaps in that limited sense, No Gun Ri, My Lai, and Abu Ghraib owed some small measure of ancestry to the barbarism the Army had experienced in so many Pacific locales. Without any question, the Vietnam-era obsession with body counts hearkened greatly to the customs of the Pacific War, when more than a few Army commanders emphasized kill ratios and inflated body counts in official reports. Tactically, the Army, in yet another Pacific War hangover, far too often ceded the night to its enemies and retreated its combat units into terrified perimeters underneath an umbrella of protective firepower, until the advent of the night-vision era of the late-twentieth century. The war foretold a great future for American sea power, air-power, and special operations, all of which served as the powerful fist behind the alliance of like-minded states in containing communism during the Cold War and endlessly battling Chinese influence and Muslim extremism in its aftermath. Latter-year Army Rangers and Special Forces soldiers could recognize many of their own experiences in those of Merrill's Marauders, Wendell Fertig, and a host of other American guerrilla warriors against the Japanese. The war against Japan anticipated the central importance of ground power for American security interests, in tandem, of course, with submarines, carrier groups, fleets of bombers, and other potent implements of sea power and air-power; indeed, the war had clearly demonstrated the crucial long-term importance of interservice cooperation and coordination. Even so, the ground troops manned the many American bases around the Pacific Rim and, from Korea to Afghanistan, did the vast majority of the fighting and dying, suffering 90 percent of the casualties in time of war, all during an era when some thought that nuclear weapons or precision munitions or hyper communications had made them obsolete or redundant. Naval forces and aircraft had played an undeniable, cutting-edge, seminal role in the Pacific War, but, from Bataan in 1942 to Okinawa in 1945, the fighting was ultimately consummated—and the will of one side eventually prevailed over the other—on the ground. In that sense, for the Army at least, the conclusion of the Pacific War actually represented far more a beginning than an ending.[10]

The success of that will came at a fearful, timeless price. Some 12,935 American POWs of the Japanese did not survive, a 37 percent death rate that bespeaks their horrendous mistreatment. Most of the survivors endured some sort of physical or emotional malady stemming from captivity. "I would say that more than half of former prisoners of war, in the Asiatic theater, are suffering from various degrees of constitutional ailments," one physician noted years after the war. "It is my opinion that a very high percentage have damage to their gastrointestinal and neurological systems from which there will probably be no complete recovery. I believe there is also a relatively high percentage who have suffered cardiac damage which will manifest itself only as time goes on. Also, a smaller percentage who are no longer useful citizens due to mental conditions brought about by the horrors of prison life." Another examining doctor flatly stated that "these men will never be the same."

The war never truly ended for these former prisoners, but they had, at least, survived. The United States suffered approximately 359,000 overseas fatalities in World War II. A total of 111,606 Americans were killed or went missing somewhere in the Pacific or Asia. Thousands were lost or buried at sea, consumed by fire in plane crashes or vehicle explosions, or simply disappeared into remote jungles or mountain wilds. The Navy lost 31,157 killed in the effort to subdue Japan, a number that far exceeded the total fatalities suffered by the sea service in all previous American wars. The Army Air Forces lost 15,694 killed or missing. Some 19,733 Marines lost their lives, a disquieting 3.6 percent fatality rate that revealed much about the incredible gallantry and hard fighting of the Marine Corps on so many bloody Pacific battlefields. The greatest plurality of American deaths, 41,592, occurred among Army ground soldiers, a 2.3 percent death rate for the 1.8 million who served in the war against Japan.[11]

In the immediate aftermath of the war, these fallen GIs, and the bodies of their comrades from the other military services, lay in graves scattered over more than a third of the globe's surface, spread among 133 Pacific-area cemeteries, 9 in China, and 59 in what had been the Burma-India theater. Overworked and undermanned graves registration units, and occasionally local laborers, had interred them as carefully and reverently as battle conditions permitted, a thankless, traumatic, and often horrifying job. "Some stared wide-eyed, others had died in the middle of a scream, and their mouths hung open," Private Thomas Dowling, a graves registration soldier, later commented grimly. "Others had no face at all. The work was nightmarish and it ate at our hearts . . . cracked some of us, darkened the spirits of others, and numbed the rest."

By and large, the dead were concentrated in places where the fighting had raged most fiercely, especially from Guadalcanal to Luzon and Tarawa to Okinawa. Their nation did not intend for them to stay there permanently. With the passage of Public Law 383 on May 16, 1946, Congress earmarked the hefty sum of $190,869,000 to return them to their homeland. Nearly unprecedented in human history, the American government's "Return of the World War II Dead Program" epitomized the country's wealth and its republican commitment to the value of its citizens' lives. It also reflected predominant American attitudes about the vitally important nature of carefully preserved and stored corporeal remains as both tangible and symbolic reminders of the mourned.

Just as the Army had done so much of the fighting around every corner of the earth, it also assumed the primary responsibility for carrying out the program by means of the Quartermaster Corps Graves Registration Service. All over America, the anguished next of kin filled out Quartermaster General Form 345, an official document that allowed them to choose whether to have their soldier returned at government expense for burial at a cemetery of their choice or forever remain overseas at rest in one of fifteen military cemeteries maintained by the American Battle Monuments Commission. In some cases, the decision led to terrible, grief-stricken arguments within families whose trauma and melancholy over their loss would never abate. Heedless of these painful internal disputes, the polling continued over many months, culminating in 1947. Sixty-one percent of the families chose to bring their fallen soldier home. The retrieval teams and their civilian partners numbered only 13,311 members at the program's peak. Everywhere that Americans had traversed in World War II, figuratively to the end of the earth and beyond, from European towns to remote Pacific islands, forlorn jungles, and Asian mountain chains, the teams traveled to recover the venerated dead, braving heat, cold, monsoons, privation, loneliness, and even occasional unstable political circumstances. "Sweating American soldiers were dragging soggy corpses out of the ooze of Waikumete Cemetery, Auckland, last week," John Scarfe, a reporter for *The New Zealand Observer,* wrote of a recovery operation in his country. "It was a gruesome scene. In a tree-lined plot were opened graves. Coffins lay around to receive the decomposed dead. Shovels were rammed into mounds of mud piled beside the holes, and desolate white crosses stuck askew in the ground. In dungarees and gum-boots, the grave-gang worked. They were an average looking crew. There were city men and smalltown boys. In green-cloth denims, rubber gloves and heavy boots, they pried from the sticky earth reluctant bodies which had lain there for two or three years."

Worldwide, the teams recovered and identified 280,835 remains, 170,752 of which were earmarked for return to the States. Only 10,356, a mere 3.7 percent, still remained unidentified, a crowning tribute to the exacting, efficient work of the wartime graves registration units that had, in the vast majority of cases, collected the dead men—and, in a few cases, women—from the disparate geographic areas where they had died and then buried them in carefully organized temporary cemeteries. Many of the corpses had been laid to rest in sheets, blankets, or makeshift clothes. The recovery teams found that this preserved them better than did some improperly ventilated wooden coffins and even some metal caskets. "When the body, clad in uniform and wrapped only in a blanket or shelter-half, is buried in well-drained soil above the permanent water line, the remains are invariably found after 2 years in a 'dry' condition, all body liquids and results of decomposition having been absorbed by the earth," the Graves Registration historian explained. Even in ideal conditions, though, mold, mildew, and insects had too often degraded the remains and rotted clothing and footgear. In problematic conditions, with remote or shoddy burials, the bodies were horribly decomposed by the elements.

One by one, at sites all over the Pacific and Asia, the recovery soldiers laboriously disinterred all the bodies they could find and transferred them into specially designed burial containers. "Upon exhumation, remains are thoroughly sprayed with deodorant and/or disinfectant solutions, wrapped in clean mattress covers, if available, and placed in envelopes," Colonel C. R. Hutchins, an officer involved in running the operation, reported to higher headquarters in 1947. "The open side is then folded into a double fold and sealed with waterproof cement. Cement, liquid, tent patching, available within theater, has been found most satisfactory." The envelopes, or body bags, measured six feet four inches in length and three feet in width and, according to Hutchins, were closed tightly "with electric heat sealing."

Similar to the way the Americans fought the war, here, too, they liberally expended equipment and matériel. To dry up bodily fluids and minimize their stench, crews sprayed a powdery hardening compound into any remaining body cavities such as the abdomen and the skull. Command directives recommended the usage of between two and five pounds of compound per body, one gallon of deodorant spray for every twenty remains, and one pair of gloves for every three to five remains. Once collected, the newly encased bodies were placed in steel-reinforced caskets and shipped with appropriate ceremony and military honors, usually aboard LSTs, from the various Pacific theater locales to specially designated concentration areas. By the late summer of 1947, the hard-working teams had amassed 73,252 bodies for shipment home, including 30,387 at Manila Mausoleum, 2,027 in Yokohama, 3,500 in Calcutta, 23,132 on Saipan, and 14,206 in Honolulu. At every step of the way, from the original burial spots to the collection points, clerks maintained meticulous interment, reinterment, and identification records, minimizing any chance that next of kin might receive the wrong body. "This notable accomplishment had required weeks and months of unpleasant, arduous toil on barren Pacific atolls, in hot, swampy jungles, and in rugged and remote spots throughout the vast Pacific and on the Asiatic mainland," the Army's historians of the program asserted proudly of the recoveries.[12]

At last, on September 30, 1947, at Pearl Harbor, where the American war had begun, the first set of 3,027 returning Pacific War dead were ready for their final journey home aboard the US Army Transport (USAT) *Honda Knot,* a 4,000-ton Liberty ship. For this trip, and the ten successive voyages that other funeral ships coming from Pacific locales would make in the months ahead, the caskets were placed in specially designed steel crates, generally with two caskets per crate. The *Honda Knot*'s crew made sure the ship was in the best possible condition to receive these most honored of guests. The decks and superstructure gleamed with a fresh coat of paint, as did the loading equipment on the dock. All over the harbor, ships flew their flags at half-staff. Carefully organized convoys of tractor trailers ferried the crates from the mausoleum to the harbor. Honor guards from every branch of the armed forces stood at attention and then at parade rest as the casket-laden crates were carefully loaded aboard *Honda Knot.*

The ship's voyage to San Francisco, the port of reception for the

Pacific theater, took ten days (European theater dead came home via New York). At noon on October 10, seemingly with somber resolution, *Honda Knot* sailed under the Golden Gate Bridge and into the bay from which many of her deceased passengers had undoubtedly set forth on their terminal journeys to the Pacific War. An unseen cannon boomed somewhere in the hills as the solitary ship dropped anchor opposite Marina Green, where hundreds gathered for a sober memorial service. The group included Mayor Roger Lapham, Secretary of the Navy John Sullivan, General Mark Clark, senior Protestant, Catholic, and Jewish clergy, and scores of veterans and civic and business leaders. One chronicler later described the short ceremony as "impressively dignified." It represented the culmination of months of preparation and rehearsals by the Army to receive the remains properly and begin their ultimate return to their next of kin, all under the hot glare of friendly but intense anticipatory media coverage.

In the ceremony's aftermath, respectful port crews unloaded the crates, each of which was now firmly draped with an American flag and escorted by a serviceman, and placed them aboard trailers bound for rail depots. At the same time, telegrams were sent to the families informing them of their dead soldier's arrival. In another revealing indicator of the elaborate planning and preparation behind this most hallowed of enterprises, the Army had established fifteen major distribution centers around the country, chosen for their geographic location and proximity to railheads. Their names read like a tour of American geography: New York City, Schenectady, Philadelphia, Charlotte, Atlanta, Memphis, Columbus (Ohio), Chicago, Kansas City, Fort Worth, San Antonio, Auburn (Washington), Mira Loma (California), the Utah Distribution Center, and, of course, San Francisco.

At the cost of $1,000,003, the Army Transportation Corps had commissioned the American Car and Foundry Company to convert some of their existing rolling stock into 118 specially modified mortuary railcars. Another contract, with the Pennsylvania and Southern Pacific Railroad companies, arranged for the conversion of some baggage cars for mortuary purposes. The inside of each car was fitted with a locking device to hold the crates in place. The typical train consisted of 12 to 15 cars, each of which held between fifty and sixty-six remains stacked in three rows, held firmly in place by the locks. Each train was designated with a Military Authorization Identification Number whose records referred to each of the caskets not as cargo but as "Passenger, Deceased."

At the distribution centers, when the remains were ready for movement, military authorities sent another telegram to the family with an estimated time of arrival. Carefully chosen and trained military escorts now assumed responsibility for the journey by rail to the final destination. Every one of them was required to view a training film entitled *Your Proudest Duty*. The escort was a member of the same service as the deceased and had equal or higher rank. Many were combat veterans who had volunteered for this most heart-wrenching of duties. They were held by their superiors to the highest standards for dress, comportment, and interpersonal skills. They rode either in a coach or a sleeper car, depending on the length of the trip. During the mission, they were forbidden from consuming any alcohol. "Upon arrival at their destination, escorts were expected to help and comfort the bereaved in every possible manner, including attendance at the funeral if this was requested," the Army's historians of the program wrote of the escorts. "In each case, the escort was directed to remove the American flag from the casket and present it to the next of kin. In many cases, the escort represented the only personal contact made with relatives. For this reason, he often was 'leaned upon' by bereaved families, funeral directors, veterans' groups, and others. To some families, he almost became another 'son.'" One grieving father, typical of many thousands, wrote gratefully to the commander of his area's distribution center, "The Government couldn't have selected a better man, a perfect gentleman in every respect, so considerate of the family and so helpful in every way, relieving us of many of the details. The escort's very presence made us a lot braver and our burden a lot lighter."

News of the imminent arrival of escort and "passenger" routinely spread through local media or just by word of mouth, prompting frequent warm welcomes from a dizzying host of well-wisher organizations— the American Legion, the Veterans of Foreign Wars, the Catholic War Veterans, the Jewish War Veterans, Military Order of the Purple Heart, the Gold Star Mothers, the American Veterans of World War II, and, most significant, a veterans association representing the unit of the deceased. Before groups large and small, in major cities, midsize towns, small towns, and remote, isolated country outposts alike, the flag-draped caskets were ceremonially buried, with full military honors, wherever the next of kin chose, at a price of $564.50 per funeral. Seventy-eight percent buried them in a private cemetery or a family plot, almost all the rest in a national military cemetery. A tiny handful, 751 in total, were shipped to Canada, Mexico, or another country for interment.

In practically every region, Americans felt compelled to gather publicly to pay homage to the dead. Some towns organized solemn processions to escort coffins to cemeteries. In Chicago, a nighttime crowd of 80,000 gathered at Soldier Field to pay tribute to the sacrifice of ten local men whose caskets were placed in a prominent spot alongside the stands. Together the Chicagoans held lighted candles aloft in total silence as a tribute. Among the throng was the mayor and the governor of Illinois. In Kansas City, Missouri, 2,500 people gathered at the site of the Liberty Memorial, dedicated two decades earlier in tribute to local veterans of World War I, for a tasteful service in tribute to fallen soldiers who hailed from the eight states served by the local distribution center. A similar-size crowd assembled on Veterans Day in Albany to honor that city's war dead.

Here and in so many more anonymous, tear-soaked gatherings around the United States, the living paid reverent tribute to the dead brought to them, at such time, expense, and effort, by the *Honda Knot* and its US Army Transport successors, *Cardinal O'Connell, Dalton Victory, Walter Schwenk, George Boyce,* and others. Among those whose mortal remnants now rested forever in their home soil were soldiers from every corner of the Pacific War. Their grim roll call included PFC Edward Kuntz, a coast artilleryman who died in captivity in the Philippines; Private James Henson, once a member of the 192nd Tank Battalion who died of beriberi while in captivity; Sergeant Frank Simmons, who succumbed to pneumonia after suffering a wound somewhere in the South Pacific; PFC Norman Petschauer, killed in the Battle of Saipan while serving with the 27th Infantry Division; PFC Louis Profeda, once captain of his high school football team, killed at Buna in 1942; PFC Herman Staub, killed with the 41st Division at nearby Gona; Sergeant John Zangerle of the 37th Division, killed as he and his soldiers assaulted a fortified building in the Battle of Manila; Captain Richard Charles Ufford, a company commander in the 96th Division who was killed on Leyte in October 1944; Lieutenant Alfred Rossman, who died of what the Army vaguely dubbed "nonbattle causes"; PFC Monroe Hicks, whose hometown paper in Sikeston, Missouri, identified him as both a returning hero and a "colored" soldier; Lieutenant Buford Cooper, an engineer who was killed in a vehicle accident on the Stilwell Road; Private Jacob Kampman, a nineteen-year-old infantryman killed on Negros in the Philippines on April 27, 1945, while fighting with the 40th Division; and many more whose identities remain more obscure.

Reflecting on the often tortuous, always costly path to victory, General Eichelberger, the man who had commanded the operation that cost young Kampman's life, once ruminated in a moving Memorial Day speech, "I go back now over the long road that now lies behind us. I see the dead lying on the beach at Buna and along the bloody, jungle-covered Sanananda Trail. I see the magnificent 32nd Division and their Australian comrades, green and untried in the bitter jungle warfare that was their lot. I see the gallant regimental combat teams of the Americal Division—of the 40th and 41st Divisions—slugging it out cave by cave with the Japanese on Cebu and Negros, at Zamboanga and in the Sulu Archipelago. All of these have paid the price. The names of their dead adorn the honor rolls of a thousand American communities. We must build, with a firm hand, a permanent structure of world peace. Such can be the only memorial worthy of our dead, the only memorial acceptable to our conscience." In 1951, after six years and the shipment home of 171,539 fallen Americans from both Europe and the Pacific, and the expenditure of $163,869,000, the "Return of the World War II Dead" repatriation program officially ended. The mourning never really did.[13]

Acknowledgments

I can never hope to assign proper credit and thanks to all the people who made this third volume of the Victory in the Pacific series possible, most of whom I have already thanked for their contributions to the first two volumes, but I must express my gratitude again here. So many people assisted me, in fact, that for every one I mention here, two or three others could probably lay claim to some role, especially because my research and writing occupied the better part of a decade. For those whom I have not mentioned, usually out of consideration for brevity, I offer my deep apologies and assurances that I have greatly appreciated your assistance. The input of so many knowledgeable, helpful people does not, of course, change the fact that I am solely responsible for any errors of commission or omission.

The dedicated military archivists at the National Archives and Records Administration embody professionalism and expertise, none more so than the dean of them all, Tim Nenninger, Branch Chief for Modern Military Records, who was kind enough to lead me to an incredibly rich vein of primary source material during my months in residence. The same was true for the remarkable staff at the United States Military History Institute (now known as the Army Heritage and Education Center), the leading repository of Army history and one of my favorite places on earth. Shannon Schwaller expertly processed my massive list of requests and, in the process, saved me a tremendous amount of time and consternation. Steve Bye always took the lead to access whatever I needed in a timely and efficient manner. During my visit to the Hoover Institution Library and Archives at Stanford University, Carol Leadenham helped me find a fascinating array of firsthand material from among dozens of individual papers collections. This book is much the better for her assistance. Elizabeth Dunn and the staff at the David M. Rubenstein Rare Book and Manuscript Library on the campus of Duke University made General Robert Eichelberger's vast collection of correspondence, dictations, reports, musings, and photographs available to me in full. There is no way to overstate the importance of the Eichelberger papers, not only in bringing the general himself to life but also the story of the war as a whole.

In spite of many bureaucratic challenges, Susan Lintelmann and Suzanne Christoff of the United States Military Academy Library helped me access the library's vast array of individual papers collections, much of it from graduates who became prisoners of the Japanese. Genoa Stanford at the Donovan Research Library, Fort Benning, Georgia, made an extensive assemblage of Infantry School papers from Pacific War veterans available to me. Laura Farley at the Wisconsin Veterans Museum in Madison provided me with a fascinating group of letters and other firsthand accounts. Chris Kolakowski, who became the director of the museum as I was working on the previous volume, also was kind enough to share primary source material and useful personal wisdom with me. Mary Hope, senior archivist at the Army's Office of Medical History, Fort Sam Houston, Texas, and Carlos Alvarado, her assistant, made sure I had access to a rich trove of oral histories and interviews from Army nurses who served in the Pacific. Reagan Grau at the National Museum of the Pacific War in Fredericksburg, Texas, took the time and trouble to give me digital versions of hundreds of original oral histories from Army and Marine veterans. The stewards of the extensive oral history archive at the University of North Texas in Denton, J. Todd Moye and Amy Hedrick, kindly made a vast collection of individual accounts available to me in digital format.

The almost limitless collection of letters, diaries, interviews, and other primary source material at the National WWII Museum in New Orleans is a relatively underutilized archive. Lindsay Barnes and Nathan Huegen helped me tap into this remarkable resource both on site during my visit and at distance as well. Frank Shirer at the US Army Center of Military History (CMH) in Washington, DC, went the extra mile to compile for me in digital format much of the American and

Japanese institutional history of the war, from command reports to special studies to Japanese monographs and postwar interviews, as well as fascinating, overlooked theater and battle histories, allowing me to bring a vividness and immediacy to the chapters that otherwise might not have been possible. I do not know that mere words can convey my appreciation to Frank. During my visit to CMH, Siobhan Blevins Shaw kindly helped me access even more of this insider's Pacific War.

The Eisenhower Presidential Library and Museum in Abilene, Kansas, might seem like an odd place to look for revealing source material from the American war with Japan. But a great many Army veterans of the war, from generals on down, donated their fascinating papers to this library, as did many units that fought in theater. In addition, Eisenhower's letters and writings from his purgatorial days as an aide to MacArthur offer a rich portrait of the SWPA commander and his proclivities. I am grateful to Kevin Bailey and Tim Rives for making my visit to Abilene so productive. At Fort Riley, just down the road from Abilene, Bob Smith, director of the US Cavalry Museum in Fort Riley, was kind enough to make a remarkable, and surprisingly underutilized, collection of 112th Cavalry Regiment material available to me during my all-too-brief visit. The Mecca for all things MacArthur is, not surprisingly, the MacArthur Memorial Archives and Museum in Norfolk, Virginia. Chris Kolakowski, who was director at the time of my visit, and Jim Zobel, the archivist, set new records for cordiality and helpfulness during my extensive visit. I was absolutely blown away by the richness of the MacArthur Memorial's Pacific War collections, and especially by the impressive expertise of Chris and Jim on the Army in the war. I would like to thank Jennifer Bryan and her staff at the United States Naval Academy Special Collections and Archives of the Nimitz Library for helping me access a diverse blend of source material that allowed me to delve deeply into naval operations and the leadership of Admirals Nimitz, Spruance, and Halsey. During my year in residence at the Naval Academy as the Leo A. Shifrin Distinguished Chair of Military History, Rick Ruth and his colleagues in the History Department warmly welcomed me as one of their own. This book is much the richer for many, many wonderful conversations with my fellow department faculty members and the persistent enthusiasm of my midshipmen.

At the Association of the United States Army, the redoubtable Roger Cirillo, the muse of all modern Army historians, was kind enough to share, over the course of some long conversations, much knowledge and many productive suggestions. My good friend Kevin Hymel, another sage on the World War II Army and a leading expert on General George Patton, conducted the photo research and provided much good advice over the many years since I first shared my vision for the series with him over dinner at a restaurant in Portland, Maine. During the course of many conversations, Robert von Maier, the sagacious editor of *Global War Studies* and director of the burgeoning think tank Brecourt Academic, helped shape my focus and enhanced my understanding of the vast and diverse assortment of topics covered by this series. The National Endowment for the Humanities (NEH) awarded this project a prestigious, and much-needed, Public Scholar Grant, and I am deeply appreciative. The vital support and partnership of the NEH, especially with Mark Silver and his team, made possible a level of depth and complexity to the research that I otherwise could not have attempted.

Closer to home, the staff at the State Historical Society of Missouri worked hard to provide me with individual access to a fascinating archive of several thousand letters written by servicemen and -women during the war. At Missouri University of Science and Technology in Rolla, where I am a faculty member, the library and interlibrary loan staffs tirelessly fulfilled my dizzying range of requests for rare and not-so-rare books, articles, and dissertations. My colleagues in the Department of History and Political Science remain a daily source of inspiration and excellence: Diana Ahmad, Andrew Behrendt, Petra DeWitt, Larry "Legend" Gragg, Tseggai Isaac, Chris Ketcherside, Alanna Krolikowski, Michael Meagher, Justin Pope, Jeff Schramm, Kate Sheppard, all of our distinguished emeriti, and especially our outstanding department chairs, Michael Bruening and Shannon Fogg. Another thank-you—of so many over the years—goes to Robin Collier, our world-class department administrative assistant and guiding light.

I would like to thank my dear friend Rick Britton, a cartographer of singular talent, for once again producing an absorbing set of original maps that have done much to illuminate my prose. Many thanks go to Brent Howard, executive editor at Dutton, whose keen insight into good storytelling and good scholarship sets him apart from his peers. I greatly appreciate his belief in my work and the innumerable ways he continues to improve it with his relentlessly good judgment and unfailing professional eye. I am incredibly lucky that he is my editor. Michael Congdon, my brilliant agent and friend, helped guide and shape this work, so much so that, if not for his efforts, I do not believe it would have come to fruition. I greatly appreciate his wise counsel and especially his willingness to listen to my pessimistic diatribes about the remote chances for any of my favorite sports teams to win a championship each season.

I am especially grateful to friends and family, all of whom seem inexplicably resolved to put up with me, and all of whom have helped sustain me during the long gestation process for this book: Pat O'Donnell, Mitch Yockelson, Joe Balkoski, Paul Clifford, Paul Woodadge, Sean Roarty, Michael Roarty, Mike Chopp, Steve Loher, Steve Kutheis, Steve Vincent, John Villier, Jon Krone, Professor Dave Cohen, James Gavin McManus, the late Tom Fleming, the late Russ Buhite, the late Dick Hyde, Charlie Schneider, Don Patton, Curtis Fears, Don Rebman, Bob Kaemmerlen, Ron Kurtz, Joe Carcagno, all of my 7th Infantry Regiment Cottonbaler buddies, my numerous friends at the National WWII Museum, and many more friends than I have space to mention.

I'm extremely blessed to be part of a loving and supportive family. On the Woody side, I am very grateful to Nancy, Doug, Tonya, David, Angee, and my nephews and nieces for many acts of kindness and a lot of laughs over the years. My dear father-in-law and fellow St. Louis Cardinals fan, Nelson Woody, did not live to see this book come to fruition, but his spirit is all over it. He and Ruth, my mother-in law, are like bonus parents. I cannot ever repay them for all their love and support. A special thank-you to my elder siblings, Mike and Nancy, for a lifetime of support and friendship. The same goes for my brother-in-law, John Anderson. My nieces, Kelly and Erin, are grown women now, and far smarter and more focused than I was at their age (or, let's be honest, even at my present age!). My teenage nephew, Michael, is already taller than I am—which admittedly might not be saying much—and he is making us all proud with his intelligence and athleticism. Thank you all for many moments of affection and warmth. I have been blessed with incredible and supportive parents. Michael and Mary Jane McManus have given me such a great life that I could never possibly repay them, though I do try, probably ineffectively. Perhaps a simple and sincere thank-you will suffice. As always, my wife and soul mate, Nancy, has borne the greatest cross, enduring long absences and my deep absorption with this project. Naturally, to her go my deepest and most heartfelt thanks, not just for her enduring and true love but for indulging my lifelong passion for words on paper. . . .

John C. McManus
St. Louis, Missouri

Notes

1. Crusade

1. General Douglas MacArthur, letter to Jean MacArthur, January 8, 1945, Record Group 10, Box 7, Folder 21, General Douglas MacArthur Private Correspondence; Dr. Paul Rogers, letter to Brigadier General LeGrand "Pick" Diller, October 30, 1984, Record Group 46, Box 1, Folder 4, Paul Rogers Papers, both at Douglas MacArthur Memorial Archives (DMMA), Norfolk, VA; Brigadier General Clyde Eddleman, "The Lingayen Operation," speech given to the Army and Navy Staff College, February 4, 1946, Clyde Eddleman Papers, Box 1; Major General Oscar Griswold diary, December 12, 15, 1944, Oscar Griswold Papers, Box 1, both at US Army Heritage and Education Center (USAHEC), Carlisle, PA; Sixth Army on Luzon, Lingayen to Manila, 9 January–3 March, 1945, pp. 1–7, Record Group 407, Entry 427, Box 1957, Folder 106-0.3, National Archives and Records Administration II (NA), College Park, MD; USS *Boise* entry at www.historyofwar.org and www.navsource.org; Douglas MacArthur, *Reports of General MacArthur*, vol. 1, *The Campaigns of MacArthur in the Pacific* (Washington, DC: Center of Military History, 1966), 254–58; Robert Coakley and Richard Leighton, *United States Army in World War II, The War Department: Global Logistics and Strategy, 1943–1945* (Washington, DC: Center of Military History, United States Army, 1968), 835–37; Robert Ross Smith, *United States Army in World War II, The War in the Pacific: Triumph in the Philippines* (Washington, DC: Center of Military History, United States Army, 1963), 26–30; Samuel Eliot Morison, *History of United States Naval Operations in World War II*, vol. 13, *The Liberation of the Philippines: Luzon, Mindanao, the Visayas, 1944–1945* (Annapolis, MD: Naval Institute Press, 2012 reprint), 94–95, 115–18; Weldon E. "Dusty" Rhoades, *Flying MacArthur to Victory* (College Station: Texas A&M University Press, 1987), 524; Walter Krueger, *From Down Under to Nippon: The Story of the Sixth Army in World War II* (Washington, DC: Combat Forces Press, 1953), 220–22; D. Clayton James, *The Years of MacArthur*, vol. 2, *1941–1945* (Boston: Houghton Mifflin, 1975), 616–22; Walter R. Borneman, *MacArthur at War: World War II in the Pacific* (New York: Little, Brown, 2012), 458–59. Eddleman estimated the total number of SWPA soldiers at 204,000. The only other World War II Army ground general who had received a Medal of Honor by 1945 was Theodore Roosevelt Jr., son of the president of the same name, for his actions at Utah Beach on D-Day. The Roosevelts and MacArthurs are the only father-son recipients. General Jonathan Wainwright would eventually receive the medal, but in January 1945, he was still in captivity.
2. 3rd Amphibious Force, Report of Luzon Operation, Enclosure H, 2, February 5, 1945, MS416, World War II Battle Operations and Reports, Box 36, Folder 1, Special Collections and Archives, United States Naval Academy (USNA), Annapolis,

MD; Lieutenant Stanley Caplan, Oral History, 5, April 13, 1945, Record Group 38, Entry P11, Box 5, Records of the Chief of Naval Operations, World War II Oral Histories and Interviews, 1942–1945, NA; Brigadier General Bonner Fellers, letter to Dorothy Fellers, January 8, 1945, Record Group 44A, Box 2, Folder 1, Bonner F. Fellers Papers, DMMA; Griswold diary, January 8, 1945, USAHEC; Aviation Ordnanceman José "Andy" Chacón, personal account, at www.usmilitariaforum.com; John Deane Potter, *The Life and Death of a Japanese General* (New York: Signet Books, 1962), 128, 133–34; Morison, *History of United States Naval Operations in World War II*, vol. 13, 98–115, 325–26; James, *The Years of MacArthur*, vol. 2, 619–20; Roger O. Egeberg, *The General: MacArthur and the Man He Called "Doc"* (Washington, DC: Oak Mountain Press, 1993), 100; Smith, *Triumph in the Philippines*, 60–67; Douglas MacArthur, *Reminiscences* (New York: Da Capo Press, 1964), 240–41.

3.   Southwest Pacific Area, G2 Monthly Summary of Enemy Dispositions, December 31, 1944, Record Group 3, Box 19, Folder 2, Records of Headquarters, Southwest Pacific Area, 1942–1945; Southwest Pacific Area, G2 Estimate of Enemy Capabilities in the Luzon Area, January 15, 1945, Record Group 4, Box 22, Folder 6, Records of Headquarters, US Army Forces in the Pacific, 1942–1947; General Clyde Eddleman, Interview with Dr. D. Clayton James, June 29, 1971, Record Group 49, Miscellaneous File, Part II, all at DMMA; General Clyde Eddleman, Oral History, 1975, pp. 22–23, Clyde Eddleman Papers, Box 2, United States Army Military History Institute (USAMHI), Carlisle, PA; General Walter Krueger, "Responsibilities in a Joint Operation," lecture, Armed Forces Staff College, April 18, 1947, Walter Krueger Papers, Box 12, United States Military Academy Library Archives (USMA), West Point, NY; Sixth Army on Luzon: An Intelligence Summary, pp. 151–52, Combined Arms Research Library (CARL), Fort Leavenworth, KS; Michael Bigelow, "Intelligence in the Philippines," *Military Intelligence Professional Bulletin*, April–June 1995; Krueger, *From Down Under to Nippon*, 218–19; Edward J. Drea, *MacArthur's ULTRA: Codebreaking and the War Against Japan, 1942–1945* (Lawrence: University Press of Kansas, 1992), 180–87; Borneman, *MacArthur at War*, 457.

4.   Japanese Monograph #4, Philippines Operations Record, Phase III, July–November 1944, Fourteenth Area Army Plans, 8-5.1 AC4; Japanese Monograph #8, Philippine Operations Record, Phase III, December 1944–August 1945, Shimbu Group, 8-5.1 AC8; Japanese Monograph #9, Philippines Operations Record, Phase III, December 1944–August 1945, Kembu Group, 8-5.1, AC9; Lieutenant General Akira Muto, unpublished memoir, pp. 14–15, in Translations of Japanese Documents, Volume I, 8-5.1 AD1 V1, all at US Army Center of Military History (CMH), Washington, DC; Lieutenant General Akira Muto, trial testimony, November 22, 1945, pp. 3010–13, *United States of America versus Tomoyuki Yamashita*; General Tomoyuki Yamashita, trial testimony, November 28, 1945, 3527, *United States of America versus Tomoyuki Yamashita*, both in Volumes 21–34 of official trial records at www.loc.gov; Smith, *Triumph in the Philippines*, 88–100; J. Potter, *Life and Death of a Japanese General*, 125–31.

5.   Transport Division Six, Operation Report of Luzon Island, Enclosure A, January 17, 1945, MS416, World War II Battle and Operations Reports, Box 34, Folder 2, USNA; 37th Infantry Division, Life Aboard the Transports, Record Group 407, Entry 427, Box 8605, Folder 337-0.3.0; 129th Infantry Regiment, Historical Data, Luzon Campaign, Record Group 407, Entry 427, Box 8733, Folder 337-INF-129-0.3.0; 40th Infantry Division, History, Luzon, Panay, Negros, Record Group 407, Entry 427, Box 8870, Folder 340-0; 43rd Infantry Division, Narrative History, Luzon Campaign, 1 December 1944–1 November 1945, Record Group 407, Entry 427, Box

9151, Folder 343-0.3; Sixth Army on Luzon, Lingayen to Manila, p. 10, all at NA; Muto unpublished memoir, p. 27, CMH; Griswold diary, January 8, 1945, US-AMHI; Lieutenant Howard McKenzie, letter to wife, January 20, 1945, Folder 2128, Accession #286, at State Historical Society of Missouri Research Center (SHSM), Columbia, MO; Brigadier General Bonner Fellers, letter to Dorothy Fellers, January 9, 1945; Major General Richard Marshall, Deputy Chief of Staff, Memorandum, Official Party to Accompany the C-in-C Ashore on 9 January, 1945, in Record Group 44A, Box 2, Folders 1 and 7, respectively, Bonner F. Fellers Papers; William Dunn, broadcast transcript, January 15, 1945, Record Group 52, Box 3, Folder 46, William J. Dunn Papers, all at DMMA; Muto trial testimony, November 22, 1945, p. 3028, www.loc.gov; Joseph Connor, "Shore Party," *World War II*, January–February 2017, 43; Major General Hugh J. Casey, *Engineers of the Southwest Pacific, 1941-1945*, vol. 6, *Airfield and Base Development* (Reports of Operations, United States Army Forces in the Far East, 1951), 323; Smith, *Triumph in the Philippines*, 69–83; Morison, *History of United States Naval Operations in World War* II, vol. 13, 123–36; James, *The Years of MacArthur*, vol. 2, 621–22; J. Potter, *Life and Death of a Japanese General*, 132–33; MacArthur, *Reminiscences*, 242–43.

6. Transport Division Five, Action Report, Lingayen Gulf, p. 5, January 22, 1945, MS416, World War II Battle Operations and Reports, Box 34, Folder 5, USNA; Colonel Herbert Vogel, "Logistical Support in the Lingayen Operation," lecture, Army and Navy Staff College, pp. 2–4, February 4, 1946, Walter Krueger Papers, Box 25; General Walter Krueger, "The Luzon Campaign of 1945," United States Army Command and General Staff College, lecture, p. 12, April 6, 1954, Walter Krueger Papers, Box 12; Krueger, "The Commander's Appreciation of Logistics," p. 33; General Clyde Eddleman, letter to Dr. William Leary, August 13, 1985, Walter Krueger Papers, Box 40, all at USMA; Eddleman, Oral History, pp. 32–33, Clyde Eddleman Papers, Box 2; Griswold diary, January 12–13, 1945, both at USAMHI; Masterson, "United States Army Transportation in the Southwest Pacific Area," p. 455, CMH; Sixth Army, Report of the Luzon Campaign, 9 January–30 June 1945, Volume IV, The Engineer, p. 29; Lieutenant Colonel Charles Ritchie, "Quartermastering, Australia to Tokyo, 14 December 1943 to 11 August 1946: Personal Experiences of a Base and Intermediate Section Quartermaster," School of Combined Arms Regular Course, 1946–1947, United States Army Command and General Staff College, Leavenworth, KS, pp. 8–9, both at CARL; Wesley Frank Craven and James Lea Cate, eds., *The Army Air Forces in World War II*, vol. 5, *The Pacific, Matterhorn to Nagasaki, June 1944 to August 1945* (Washington, DC: Office of Air Force History, 1983), 418; Karl C. Dod, *United States Army in World War II: The Technical Services, The Corps of Engineers: The War Against Japan* (Washington, DC: Office of the Chief of Military History, United States Army, 1966), 600–606; Casey, *Engineers of the Southwest Pacific*, 6:342–43; James, *The Years of MacArthur*, vol. 2, 627–30; William M. Leary, ed., *We Shall Return! MacArthur's Commanders and the Defeat of Japan* (Lexington: University Press of Kentucky, 1988), 79; Krueger, *From Down Under to Nippon*, 227–28, 234; Smith, *Triumph in the Philippines*, 120–21, 131–33, 141–42. Eddleman, in his letter to Dr. Leary, also made the claim that MacArthur wanted to liberate Manila in time for his birthday.

7. XIV Corps M1 Operation, After Action Report, pp. 220–21; Sixth Army, Report of the Luzon Campaign, The Engineer, p. 8, both at CARL; Major General Loren Windom, Oral History, 1984–1985, p. 42, Loren G. Windom Papers, Vertical Files, Box 44, Folder 11; Griswold diary, January 19–20, 1945, both at USAMHI; Krueger, "The Commander's Appreciation of Logistics," p. 32, USMA; Dod, *Corps of*

Engineers: The War Against Japan, 595–606; Egeberg, *The General,* 114–15; Smith, *Triumph in the Philippines,* 129–30.

8. Lieutenant Colonel Walter Krueger Jr., letter to Dr. William Leary, May 20, 1985; Lieutenant Colonel David Gray, Impressions of General Krueger, July 28, 1985; Lieutenant General Jack Tolson, letter to Dr. William Leary, May 10, 1984, all in Walter Krueger Papers, Box 40; Krueger, "Responsibilities of a Joint Operation," all at USMA; General Walter Krueger, Biographical Sketch; General George Decker, letter to Mr. Ben Decherd, January 21, 1961, both in Walter Krueger Papers, Box 1; General Walter Krueger, letter to Colonel Fay Brabson, September 5, 1947, Fay Brabson Papers, Box 6; Lieutenant General Richard Sutherland, Interview with Dr. Louis Morton, November 12, 1946, Louis Morton Papers, Box 2; Lieutenant Colonel Ellis Blake, World War II Veterans Survey #6347; Lieutenant General Arthur Collins, Oral History, 1982, p. 136, Arthur S. Collins Papers, Box 1; Griswold diary, January 31, February 9, 1945, all at USAMHI; Major General Roscoe Woodruff, Interview with Dr. D. Clayton James, September 8, 1971, p. 19, Record Group 49, Box 4, D. Clayton James Collection; Fellers, Interview with James, p. 20, both at DMMA; Lieutenant General Robert Eichelberger, letters to Emma Eichelberger, February 14, 22, 1945, Box 9, Robert Eichelberger Papers; Lieutenant General Robert Eichelberger, Dictations, 1948, Zamboanga and the Philippines, p. 12, Box 69, Robert Eichelberger Papers; Eichelberger diary, February 21, 1945, all at David M. Rubenstein Rare Book and Manuscript Library, Duke University (DU), Durham, NC; Lieutenant General Robert Richardson diary, August 22, September 7, 1945, copy in author's possession courtesy of Mr. Rob Richardson (grandson of the general); Arthur S. Collins Jr., "Walter Krueger: An Infantry Great," *Infantry* 73, no. 1 (January–February 1983): 15–19; Russell E. McLogan, *Boy Soldier: Coming of Age in World War II* (Reading, MI: Terrus Press, 1998), 136; James M. Scott, *Rampage: MacArthur, Yamashita, and the Battle of Manila* (New York: W. W. Norton, 2018), 128; Egeberg, *The General,* 115; Leary, *We Shall Return!,* 83; Paul P. Rogers, *The Bitter Years: MacArthur and Sutherland* (New York: Praeger, 1990), 257; Kevin C. Holzimmer, *General Walter Krueger: Unsung Hero of the Pacific War* (Lawrence: University Press of Kansas, 2007), 215–26; Jay Luvaas, ed., *Dear Miss Em: General Eichelberger's War in the Pacific, 1942–1945* (Westport, CT: Greenwood Press, 1972), 216. A few of Krueger's commanders, most notably Horace Fuller, did come to hate him.

9. Sixth Army on Luzon, Cave Warfare in the Mountains, p. 2, Record Group 407, Entry 427, Box 1957, Folder 106-0.3; Sixth Army on Luzon, Lingayen to Manila, p. 20; 40th Infantry Division, History, pp. 17–18; 129th Infantry Regiment, Historical Data, all at NA; 37th Infantry Division, After Action Report, Luzon, 1 November 1944–30 June 1945, pp. 28–36, CARL; Japanese Monograph #9, Kembu Group, CMH; Lieutenant Colonel Morris Naudts, "The Operations of the 129th Infantry Regiment (37th Infantry Division) in the Battle for Clark Field and Fort Stotsenburg, Luzon, Philippine Islands, 27 January–3 February 1945: Personal Experiences of a Battalion Executive Officer," Advanced Infantry Officers Course, 1947–1948, Fort Benning, GA, pp. 16, 21, 31–32, Donovan Research Library (DRL), Fort Benning, GA; Tech Sergeant Philip Hauser, letter to Mrs. Helen Hauser, September 1945, Folder 1261, Accession #2779, SHSM; Lieutenant General Robert Eichelberger, letter to Emma Eichelberger, January 23, 1945, Box 9, Robert Eichelberger Papers, DU; Griswold diary, January 26, 1945, USAMHI; Craven and Cate, *Army Air Forces in World War II,* 5:419–29; George C. Kenney, *General Kenney Reports: A Personal History of the Pacific War* (Washington, DC: Office of Air Force History, 1987), 513–15; Dod, *Corps of Engineers: The War Against Japan,* 598;

Luvaas, *Dear Miss Em,* 198; Smith, *Triumph in the Philippines,* 167–86. For more information on the experiences of the 26th Cavalry Regiment on Bataan in 1942, see the first volume of this series, *Fire and Fortitude,* 119.

10. Griswold diary, February 4, 1945, USAMHI; Frazier Hunt, *The Untold Story of Douglas MacArthur* (New York: Devin-Adair Company, 1954), 361–63; Floyd W. Radike, *Across the Dark Islands: The War in the Pacific* (New York: Ballantine Books, 2003), 211–12; William Manchester, *American Caesar: Douglas MacArthur, 1880–1964* (New York: Dell, 1978), 479–82; MacArthur, *Reminiscences,* 244; Smith, *Triumph in the Philippines,* 155–60; Borneman, *MacArthur at War,* 462–64; James, *The Years of MacArthur,* vol. 2, 628–31; Egeberg, *The General,* 113–31.

11. 6th Ranger Infantry Battalion, Report on Mission at the Pangatian Prison Camp, 383.6; Muto unpublished memoir, pp. 19–20, both at CMH; Lieutenant Colonel Stephen Sitter, Oral History, September 12, 1945, pp. 6–7, Record Group 112, Entry 302, Surgeon General, Inspections Branch, Box 223, Interview Number 188; Major Emil Reed, Medical Corps, 26th Cavalry Regiment, Report of Activities of Prison Camp Number 1, Cabanatuan, March 23, 1945, p. 5; Sixth Army on Luzon, Lingayen to Manila, pp. 21–23, all at NA; Bob Prince, letter to Mr. William Breuer, June 11, 1985, William Breuer Papers, Box 4, USAMHI; Captain George Monsarrat, "Operations of Company C (Reinforced) 6th Ranger Infantry Battalion in the Liberation of Allied Prisoners of War, at Pangatian Prison, in the Vicinity of Cabanatuan, 28–31 January 1945 (Luzon Campaign): Personal Observation by Headquarters Company Commander," Advanced Infantry Officers Course, 1949–1950, Fort Benning, GA, pp. 8–22, DRL; Mr. E. G. Baumgardner, Interview with Mr. William Dunn, February 1, 1945, Record Group 52, Box 3, Folder 48, William J. Dunn Papers, DMMA; Robert Prince, Interview with Mr. Eddie Graham, September 17, 2004, pp. 6–10, Nimitz Education and Research Center, National Museum of the Pacific War (NMPW), Fredericksburg, TX; Bess Fields, letter in *Philippine Postscripts,* March 1945; Brian Bushong, "The Contributions of NCOs in the Cabanatuan Raid," unpublished paper, March 3, 2006, copy in author's possession; Henry Mucci, "We Swore We'd Die or Do It," *Saturday Evening Post,* April 7, 1945; Lieutenant Colonel Henry Mucci, "Rescue at Cabanatuan," *Infantry Journal,* April 1945; Captain Ray Stroupe, "Rescue by the Rangers," *Military Review,* December 1945; Hampton Sides, *Ghost Soldiers: The Epic Account of World War II's Greatest Rescue Mission* (New York: Anchor Books, 2002), 247–50; William B. Breuer, *Retaking the Philippines: America's Return to Corregidor and Bataan, October 1944–March 1945* (New York: St. Martin's Press, 1986), 129–36; William B. Breuer, *The Great Raid on Cabanatuan: Rescuing the Doomed Ghosts of Bataan and Corregidor* (New York: John Wiley & Sons, 1994), 178–232; Robert W. Black, *Rangers in World War II* (New York: Ballantine Books, 1992), 273–86; Lance Q. Zedric, *Silent Warriors of World War II: The Alamo Scouts Behind Japanese Lines* (Ventura: Pathfinder Publishing of California, 1995), 187–99. For more information on the Palawan massacre, see Stephen L. Moore, *As Good as Dead: The Daring Escape of American POWs from a Japanese Death Camp* (New York: NAL Caliber, 2016). About two dozen of the liberated men at Cabanatuan came from other Allied nations. The overfeeding of emaciated liberated prisoners was common in both Europe and the Pacific. Mucci and Prince received the Distinguished Cross; all other officers received the Silver Star, and the enlisted men were all decorated with the Bronze Star. The Cabanatuan liberation was made famous by the 2005 movie *The Great Raid* starring Benjamin Bratt and James Franco.

12. 5th Cavalry Regiment, Historical Report, Luzon Campaign, p. 6, 5th Cavalry Regiment Records, Box 497, Dwight D. Eisenhower Library (EL), Abilene, KS;

Lieutenant Colonel Glines Perez, Interview with Dr. D. Clayton James, May 25, 1977, p. 29, Record Group 49, Box 6, D. Clayton James Collection; William Swan, unpublished memoir, p. 3, Record Group 15, Box 59, Folder 3, Contributions from the Public Collection; William Dunn broadcast, February 2, 1945, Record Group 52, Box 3, Folder 48, William J. Dunn Papers, all at DMMA; Fred Faiz, Interview with Mr. Ed Metzler, July 2, 2007, p. 21, NMPW; Madeline Ullom, Interview with Colonel James Hunn, April 9, 1983, no pagination; Rose Rieper Meier, Interview with Major Margaret Lauer, March 12, 1984, p. 19, both at Army Nurse Corps Collection, Army Medical Department Center of History and Heritage Museum (AMEDD), Fort Sam Houston, TX; The anecdote about Chase's fiery aggressiveness is related in Sergeant Warren E. Matha, Recollections, copy in the author's possession courtesy of his son Warren Matha; World War II entries at www.first -team.us; Elizabeth Collins, "The 'Angels of Bataan,'" *Soldier's Magazine*, no date; Carl Mydans, "My God, It's Carl Mydans," *Life*, February 19, 1945; Elizabeth M. Norman, *We Band of Angels: The Untold Story of the American Women Trapped on Bataan* (New York: Random House Paperback, 2013), 199–200; Abraham V. H. Hartendorp, *The Santo Tomas Story* (New York: McGraw-Hill, 1964), 397–402; James, *The Years of MacArthur*, vol. 2, 631–33; William C. Chase, *Front Line General: The Commands of William C. Chase: An Autobiography* (Houston, TX: Pacesetter Press, 1975), 81–87; Smith, *Triumph in the Philippines*, 217–21. Among the Army nurses, one was a trained dietician and another a physical therapist.

13. Brigadier General Bonner Fellers and Colonel Andrew Soriano, Memorandum for Commander-in-Chief, February 5, 1945, p. 1, Bonner Fellers Papers, Box 3, Folder 2, Hoover Institution Library and Archives, Stanford University (HIA), Palo Alto, CA; William Dunn broadcasts, February 3–4, 1945, Record Group 52, Box 3, Folder 48, William J. Dunn Papers; Swan, unpublished memoir, pp. 3–4; Perez interview, p. 3, all at DMMA; Major James Telfer, Oral History, August 21, 1945, Record Group 112, Entry 302, Surgeon General, Inspections Branch, Box 223, Interview Number 185; Lieutenant Ruby Motley, Oral History, April 26, 1945, Record Group 112, Entry 302, Surgeon General, Inspections Branch, Box 221, Interview Number 149, both at NA; Bertha Dworsky Henderson, Interview with Colonel Mary Horan, no date; Phyllis Arnold Adams, Interview with Colonel Mary Quinn, March 10, 1987; Meier interview, pp. 20–23, all at AMEDD; Ethel Sally Blaine Millett, Interview with Major Patricia Rikli, April 9, 1983, Army Nurse Corps Collection, Series III, Oral History, Box 50, Folder 10, USAMHI; Ethel Sally Blaine Millett, Interview with Mr. Floyd Cox, April 24, 2000, pp. 22–23; John Hencke, Interview with Mr. Eddie Graham, January 31, 2002, p. 8, both at NMPW; XIV Corps, AAR, p. 84, CARL; Matha, Recollections; "68 Heroines of Bataan Arrive in Tears of Joy," *Chicago Sunday Tribune*, February 25, 1945; Rupert Wilkinson, "Standoff at Santo Tomas," *World War II*, March–April 2014, 58–64; Mydans, "My God, It's Carl Mydans"; Collins, "The 'Angels of Bataan'"; Chase, *Front Line General*, 86–89; Hartendorp, *Santo Tomas Story*, 405–20; Norman, *We Band of Angels*, 204–8; Scott, *Rampage*, 142.

14. 37th Infantry Division, AAR, Luzon, pp. 36–42, CARL; Fellers and Soriano, Memo for C-in-C, pp. 1–2, HIA; Major Warren Wilson POW diary, February 4, 1945, Record Group 407, Philippine Archives Collection, Box 143B, Folder 7; Colonel Carlton Vanderboget, Oral History, May 21, 1945, p. 8, Record Group 112, Entry 302, Surgeon General, Inspections Branch, Box 222, Interview Number 153; Sergeant Charles Sadler, Oral History, July 21, 1945, p. 10, Record Group 112, Entry 302, Surgeon General, Inspections Branch, Box 223, Interview Number 177, all at NA; Sergeant Ike Thomas POW diary, February 3–5, 1945, at www.mansell.com; Stanley

Frankel, "B Stands for Beer," *37th Infantry Division Veterans News,* no date, p. vii; David L. Hardee, *Bataan Survivor: A POW's Account of Japanese Captivity in World War II,* edited by Frank A. Blazich Jr. (Columbia: University of Missouri Press, 2016), 191–93; Gerald Astor, *Crisis in the Pacific: The Battles for the Philippine Islands by the Men Who Fought Them—An Oral History* (New York: Dell, 2002), 530–31; Scott, *Rampage,* 174–79. With the Battle of Manila raging uncomfortably close to Bilibid, the 37th Division soldiers initially evacuated the liberated prisoners away from the prison, with orders to leave all possessions behind. When they returned a few days later, they found that most of those possessions had been stolen or looted.

15. Sixth Army on Luzon, Lingayen to Manila, p. 17; Wilson POW diary, February 7, 1945, both at NA; Brigadier General Bonner Fellers, letter to Dorothy Fellers, February 3, 1945, Record Group 44A, Box 2, Folder 1, Bonner F. Fellers Papers; Major James Chabot, Interview with Dr. D. Clayton James, July 2, 1971, pp. 43–44, Record Group 49, Miscellaneous File, Part I; Gaetano Faillace Interview with D. Clayton James, p. 34, all at DMMA; General Headquarters, Southwest Pacific Area, Communiqué, February 6, 1945; Griswold diary, February 7, 1945, both at USAMHI; "Urban Operations, An Historical Casebook: The Battle of Manila," by Dr. Thomas Huber, Combined Arms Center, Combat Studies Institute, CARL; Smith, *Triumph in the Philippines,* 240–60, 308; Hartendorp, *Santo Tomas Story,* 418; Egeberg, *The General,* 135–39; MacArthur, *Reminiscences,* 247–48; Norman, *We Band of Angels,* 208; Sidney Huff, with Joe Alex Morris, *My Fifteen Years with General MacArthur: A First-Hand Account of America's Greatest Soldier* (New York: Paperback Library, 1964), 97–99; Chase, *Front Line General,* 96–99; J. Potter, *Life and Death of a Japanese General,* 133–36; James, *The Years of MacArthur,* vol. 2, 633–40.

16. XIV Corps, Combat in Manila, pp. 2, 14–15, 32–33, July 1, 1945, Record Group 407, Entry 427, Box 1957, Folder 106-0.3; Colonel William Walsh, XIV Corps, Report of Investigation of Atrocities Committed by Japanese Imperial Forces in Intramuros (Walled City) Manila, PI during February 1945, p. 3, Record Group 407, Philippine Archives Collection, Box 245; ATIS Significant Items, #151-175, Record Group 496, Entry 134, Box 651, Records of the General Headquarters, SWPA/USAFP, ATIS Administrative Records, 1942–1945; Sixth Army on Luzon, Lingayen to Manila, p. 37, all at NA; *Sack of Manila,* United States Government Pamphlet, pp. 6–9, 14, 370.2, CMH; Lieutenant Colonel Herald Smith, "The Operations of the 148th Infantry Regiment (37th Infantry Division) at Manila, Luzon, Philippine Islands, 9 January–3 March 1945: Personal Experiences of a Regimental Intelligence Officer," p. 24, Advanced Infantry Officers Course, 1947–1948, Fort Benning, GA, DRL; Brigadier General Bonner Fellers, letter to family, February 14, 1945, Record Group 44A, Box 2, Folder 1, Bonner F. Fellers Papers, DMMA; XIV Corps, AAR, p. 87; Huber, "Battle of Manila," both at CARL; Lieutenant Obaru Fukuzo diary, February 13, 1945, Obaru Fukuzo Papers, Box 1, USAMHI; Anthony Arthur, *Deliverance at Los Baños: The Dramatic True Story of Survival and Triumph in a Japanese Internment Camp* (New York: St. Martin's Press, 1985), 184; J. Potter, *Life and Death of a Japanese General,* 137–38; Scott, *Rampage,* 512. Scott's book is the finest secondary account of the infamous atrocities, and also of the battle as a whole.

17. Eighth Army, Report of Commanding General on the Mike Six and Seven Operations, 29 January–1 February 1945, Foreword, Record Group 407, Entry 427, Box 2238, Folder 108-0.5; Eighth Army, Night Operations in the Pacific Ocean Areas, March 18, 1945, Record Group 337, Entry 15A, Box 60, Folder 274; Eighth Army, Report of Tactical Interrogation of Former Colonel Masatoshi Fujishige, p. 5, Record Group 407, Entry 427, Box 2287, Folder 108-2.13; 11th Airborne Division, After

Action Report, Luzon Campaign, p. 3, Record Group 407, Entry 427, Box 6546, Folder 311-0.3, all at NA; Colonel Joseph Swing, Officer Efficiency Report, prepared by Major General Innis Swift; Major General Joseph Swing, letter to General Peyton March, January 25, 1945, both in Joseph Swing Papers, Box 1, USMA; Lieutenant General Joseph Swing, Interview with Mr. Ed Edwin, Oral History Research Office, Columbia University, June 21, 1967, Joseph Swing Papers, Vertical Files, Box 42, Folder 10, USAMHI; Lieutenant General Robert Eichelberger, letters to Emma Eichelberger, January 30, 31, February 2, 9, 1945, Box 9, Robert Eichelberger Papers; Lieutenant General Robert Eichelberger, Dictations, January 2, 1953, Box 20, Robert Eichelberger Papers; Lieutenant General Robert Eichelberger, Dictations, 1948, Zamboanga and Philippines, pp. 3–4; Lieutenant General Robert Eichelberger, "The Dash for Manila," unpublished article, p. 13, Box 69, Robert Eichelberger Papers; General Robert Eichelberger, Dictations, 1958, p. 5, Box 73, Robert Eichelberger Papers, all at DU; Major Isaac Hoppenstein, "The Operations of the 187th Glider Infantry Regiment (11th Airborne Division) in the Landing at Nasugbu, Luzon, Philippine Islands, 31 January–3 February 1945: Personal Experiences of a Regimental Supply Officer," Advanced Infantry Officers Course, 1947–1948, Fort Benning, GA, pp. 10–11, 19, 28, DRL; Captain Harrison John Merritt, "The Operations of Company 'G' 187th Glider Infantry Regiment (11th Airborne Division) in the Attack on Nichols Field, Luzon, Philippine Islands, 13–15 February 1945: Personal Experience of a Company Commander," Advanced Infantry Officers Course, 1947–1948, Fort Benning, GA, p. 6, DRL; Edward Sebree, "Leadership at Higher Levels of Command," p. 32, copy in author's possession; Martin Blumenson, ed., *The Patton Papers, 1940–1945* (Boston: Houghton Mifflin, 1974), 398; Edward M. Flanagan Jr., *The Angels: A History of the 11th Airborne Division, 1943–1946* (Washington, DC: Infantry Journal Press, 1948), 67–77; Robert L. Eichelberger, *Our Jungle Road to Tokyo* (New York: Viking Press, 1950), 188–92; Paul Chwialkowski, *In Caesar's Shadow: The Life of General Robert Eichelberger* (Westport, CT: Greenwood Press, 1993), 115–18; Luvaas, *Dear Miss Em,* 205–8, 214; Smith, *Triumph in the Philippines,* 221–31. During the invasion of Bataan, Eighth Army headquarters controlled the XI Corps, but within a day, control of the corps passed to Sixth Army headquarters. One of the officers who went into the Nasugbu area ahead of the invasion forces was Captain John Richmond of the 503rd Parachute Infantry Regiment. He returned with an erroneous report that the area was defended by 14,000 Japanese. Eichelberger correctly put no stock in these numbers and decided to go ahead with the invasion.

18. 188th Glider Infantry Regiment, History, Luzon Campaign, 31 January–31 March 1945, Record Group 407, Entry 427, Box 6557, Folder 311-INF-188-0; 11th Airborne Division, AAR, Luzon, both at NA; Pacific Warfare Board, Report #11, Parachute Field Artillery, June 19, 1945, p. 1; Captain John Coulter, "The Operations of the Headquarters Company, Third Battalion, 511th Parachute Infantry (11th ABN Div) in the Attack on Manila, 3–13 February, 1945: Personal Experience of a Company Commander," Advanced Infantry Officers Course, 1946–1947, Fort Benning, GA, p. 6; Captain Edwin Jeffress, "Operations of the 2nd Battalion, 511th Parachute Infantry (11th Airborne Division) in the Battle of Southern Manila, 3–10 February: Personal Experience of a Battalion Intelligence Officer," Advanced Infantry Officers Course, 1948–1949, Fort Benning, GA, p. 19, all at DRL; PFC Walter Cass, letter to mother, February 14, 1945, Folder 463, Accession #933, SHSM; Major Matthew Sweeney, "American Airborne Operations in the Pacific Theater: Extending Operational Reach and Creating Operational Shock," Monograph, p. 24, School of Advanced Military Studies, United States Army Command and General Staff College, 2014,

Fort Leavenworth, KS, CARL; Flanagan, *The Angels,* 75–80; Smith, *Triumph in the Philippines,* 224–31; Craven and Cate, *Army Air Forces in World War II,* 5:425–27; Eichelberger, *Our Jungle Road to Tokyo,* 194.

19. 11th Airborne Division, AAR, Luzon, p. 5; 188th Glider Infantry Regiment, History, Luzon Campaign, p. 7, both at NA; Major General Joseph Swing, letter to General Peyton March, March 4, 1945, Joseph Swing Papers, Box 1; D. Gray, Impressions of General Krueger, both at USMA; Muto, unpublished memoir, p. 29, CMH; Muto trial testimony, November 22, 1945, pp. 3062–65, www.loc.gov; James Augustin, unpublished memoir, no pagination, World War II Veterans Survey #8281; Lieutenant General Robert Eichelberger, Dictations, December 11, 1952, p. 138, Robert Eichelberger Papers, Box 1, Folder 3, both at USAMHI; Lieutenant General Robert Eichelberger, letters to Emma Eichelberger, February 7–8, 11, 1945; Brigadier General Charles Willoughby, letter to Lieutenant General Robert Eichelberger, March 4, 1945; Brigadier General William Dunckel, letter to Lieutenant General Robert Eichelberger, March 3, 1945, all in Box 9, Robert Eichelberger Papers; Eichelberger diary, February 3, 1945, all at DU; Brigadier General Clovis Byers, letter to Marie Byers, March 5, 1945, Clovis Byers Papers, Box 9, Folder 9–10, HIA; Cass, letter, SHSM; Jeffress, "Operations of the 2nd Battalion, 511th Parachute Infantry," p. 33, DRL; Deane Marks, "'The Day the Tank Blew Up,'" *Winds Aloft,* January 1990, 12–14; Flanagan, *The Angels,* 83–85; Luvaas, *Dear Miss Em,* 209, 213–15; Eichelberger, *Our Jungle Road to Tokyo,* 195–97; Smith, *Triumph in the Philippines,* 268–73; John F. Shortal, *Forged by Fire: Robert L. Eichelberger and the Pacific War* (Columbia: University of South Carolina Press, 1987), 105–13; Chwialkowski, *In Caesar's Shadow,* 118–24. Lieutenant General Yokoyama did launch a small counterattack in an attempt to open up a route into Manila through which Iwabuchi's troops might escape, but the 112th Cavalry Regiment repulsed the attack.

20. Sixth Army, Combat Notes, Number 7, May 1945, p. 10, Record Group 337, Entry 15A, Box 71, Folder 491; Pacific Warfare Board, Battle Experiences Against the Japanese, Number 39, p. 1, August 4, 1945, Record Group 337, Entry 15A, Box 59, Folder 222; Colonel Ingomar Oseth, "Observer Report on Operations of Sixth Army, SWPA, 26 November 1944–27 February, 1945," pp. 22–23, April 10, 1945, Record Group 337, Entry 15A, Box 60, Folder 273; Major General Oscar Griswold, phone conversation with Brigadier General George Decker, February 15, 1945, Record Group 338, Entry P50487, Box 1, Folder 3; XIV Corps, Combat in Manila, pp. 39–40, all at NA; Warren Fitch, World War II Veterans Survey #8294; Edwin Hanson, unpublished memoir, p. 36, World War II Veterans Survey, no number; Griswold diary, February 10–17, 1945, all at USAMHI; H. Smith, "Operations of the 148th Infantry Regiment," p. 30, DRL; Matha, Recollections; Major John Gordon, "Battle in the Streets—Manila 1945," *Field Artillery Journal,* August 1990, 28; Astor, *Crisis in the Pacific,* 536–37; Smith, *Triumph in the Philippines,* 237, 294–97. In the 1960s, Dewey Boulevard was renamed for Manuel Roxas, who served as president of the Philippines from 1946 to 1948.

21. Sixth Army on Luzon, Lingayen to Manila, p. 33; XIV Corps, Combat in Manila, p. 47; Walsh, Report of Investigation of Atrocities, pp. 1–8; 129th Infantry Regiment, Historical Data, Luzon Campaign, all at NA; *Sack of Manila* pamphlet, pp. 18–19, CMH; 7th Cavalry Regiment, Historical Report, Luzon Island Campaign, 7th Cavalry Regiment Records, Box 499; 12th Cavalry Regiment, History of Luzon Campaign, 12th Cavalry Regiment Records, Box 505; 5th Cavalry Regiment, Luzon Historical Report, all at EL; XIV Corps, AAR, p. 123; Huber, "Battle of Manila"; 37th Infantry Division, AAR, Luzon, pp. 49–88, all at CARL; Brigadier General Clovis Byers, letter to Mr. John Pollard, February 9, 1945, Clovis Byers

Papers, Box 3, Folder 3-7, HIA; Captain Glenn Steckel, "The Role of Field Artillery in the Siege on Intramuros, Manila, Philippine Islands," The Armored School, May 7, 1948; Hanson, unpublished memoir, p. 36; Griswold diary, February 23, 1945, all at USAMHI; PFC Joseph Jones, letter to parents, circa 1945, Folder 1514, Accession #1259, SHSM; World War II entries at www.first-team.us; Major Nelson H. Randall, "The Battle of Manila," *Field Artillery Journal,* August 1945, 450–56; Gordon, "Battle in the Streets," 28; Frank Gibney, ed., *Senso: The Japanese Remember the Pacific War* (Armonk, NY: M. E. Sharpe, 1995), 149–50; Smith, *Triumph in the Philippines,* 297–308; MacArthur, *Reminiscences,* 247; James, *The Years of MacArthur,* vol. 2, 644–47; Rogers, *The Bitter Years,* 263–66; Scott, *Rampage,* 403–5, 417–19, 422–37.

22. Sixth Army on Luzon, Clearing Batangas and Bicol, 3 March–30 June 1945, pp. 1–4, Record Group 407, Entry 427, Box 1957, Folder 106-0.3; Sixth Army, Combat Notes, Number 7, pp. 31–39, both at NA; Major Robert Kennington, "The Operations of the Los Banos Force (1st Battalion, 511th Parachute Infantry and 1st Battalion, 188th Glider Infantry) 11th Airborne Division, in the Liberation of Internees from the Los Banos Internment Camp, Luzon, Philippine Islands, 23 February 1945: Personal Experience of a Battalion Operations Officer," Advanced Infantry Officers Course, 1947–1948, Fort Benning, GA, p. 14, DRL; Terry Santos, Interview with Mr. Eddie Graham, no date, NMPW; Dorothy Still Terrill, Interview with Lieutenant Colonel James Vail, April 9, 1983, pp. 18–19, AMEDD; Lyman "Tex" Black, Interview with Juan Lopez, no date, AFC/2001/001/48982; Ronald S. Morgan, Interview with Jane Cohen, May 21, 2003, AFC/2001/001/10010, both at Library of Congress, Veterans History Project (LOC), Washington, DC; Major General Joseph Swing, letter to General Peyton March, March 24, 1945, Joseph Swing Papers, Box 1, USMA; Henry Burgess, "Reminiscences of the 11th Airborne Division Raid on Los Banos," 1985, pp. 10–23; Henry Burgess, letter to Mr. William Breuer, May 22, 1985, both in William Breuer Papers, Box 4, USAMHI; Mr. Paul Leary, letter to Mrs. Edith Doiron, April 14, 1945; Lieutenant William Mayberry, letter to Mrs. Edith Doiron, February 25, 1945, Bernice Rehorst Collection, #2001.344, National WWII Museum (WWIIM), New Orleans, LA; XIV Corps, AAR, p. 159, CARL; Martin Squires, letter to Lieutenant General Edward Flanagan, February 11, 1984, Record Group 43, Box 9, Folder 29, Weldon B. Hester Papers, DMMA; American Foreign Service, Report of Death of an American Citizen, Walter Scott Price, March 18, 1945, at www.findagrave.com; Donald Roberts, "Angels to the Rescue," *Military Heritage,* August 2001, 78–86; Major Peter Foss, "Angels of Los Baños," *Infantry Journal,* May–June 1945, 52–55; Lieutenant Colonel Louis A. Walsh, "The Raid on Los Baños," *Infantry Journal,* October 1945, 26–29; Edward Lahti, "Memoirs of an Angel," self-published, 1944, pp. 77–83; Bart Hagerman, *USA Airborne: 50th Anniversary, 1940–1990* (Nashville: Turner Publishing, 1990), 180; Edward M. Flanagan Jr., *The Los Baños Raid: The 11th Airborne Jumps at Dawn* (Novato, CA: Presidio Press, 1986); Bruce Henderson, *Rescue at Los Baños: The Most Daring Prison Camp Raid of World War II* (New York: William Morrow, 2015); Arthur, *Deliverance at Los Baños,* 180–85; Flanagan, *The Angels,* 93–98; Breuer, *Retaking the Philippines,* 168–78. I did not cite any specific page numbers for the Flanagan, Henderson, and Arthur Los Baños books because I drew from the entirety of each.

2. Grind and Dash

1. Japanese Monograph #8, CMH; XI Corps, Historical Report, Luzon, 1945, pp. 5–9, Record Group 407, Entry 427, Box 3569, Folder 211-0.3; Pacific Warfare Board Report, Battle Experiences Against the Japanese, Number 74, p. 1, Record Group 337,

Entry 15A, Box 59, Folder 245; Sixth Army on Luzon, Batangas and Bicol, pp. 36–42, all at NA; 503rd Parachute Infantry Regiment, Historical Report on Corregidor Island Operation, March 6, 1945, p. 2, 503rd Parachute Infantry Regiment Records, Box 1533, EL; Brigadier General George Jones, Recollections and Comments on Corregidor Operation; Lieutenant General Jack Tolson, letter to Mr. William Breuer, July 10, 1985, both in William Breuer Papers, Box 4, USAMHI; Brigadier General George Jones, letter to Lieutenant General Edward Flanagan, October 10, 1986; Dick Williams, unpublished memoir, p. 4, in Record Group 43, Box 9, Folders 20 and 31 respectively, Weldon B. Hester Papers, DMMA; Don Abbot, personal account, at www.503prct.org; Sadashichi Yamagishi, personal account; William Calhoun, personal account; 503rd Parachute Infantry Regiment, Unit Journal, June–August 1944, S3 Journal, February 15, 1945, all in 503rd Parachute Infantry Regiment section of www.corregidor.org; Captain Arthur Brinson, "The Battle of Zigzag Pass," Advanced Officer Class #1, The Armored School, May 5, 1948, Fort Knox, KY; Major Lester Levine, "The Operations of the 503rd Parachute Infantry Regiment in the Attack on Corregidor Island, 16 February–2 March 1945: Personal Experience of a Regimental Adjutant," Advanced Infantry Officers Course, 1947–1948, Fort Benning, GA, p. 13, both at DRL; Lieutenant Colonel Edward Jenkins, "The Corregidor Operation," *Military Review*, April 1946, 57–62; Major Thomas Hardman, "Drop on Corregidor," *Coast Artillery Journal*, July–August 1945, 20–21; J. James Fahey, *Pacific War Diary, 1942–1945: The Secret Diary of an American Sailor* (Boston: Houghton Mifflin, 1963), 282; Gerard M. Devlin, *Back to Corregidor: America Retakes the Rock* (New York: St. Martin's Press, 1992), 27–43; James H. Belote and William M. Belote, *Corregidor: The Saga of a Fortress* (New York: Harper & Row, 1967), 204–15; Chase, *Front Line General*, 99–109; Krueger, *From Down Under to Nippon*, 260–67; Craven and Cate, *Army Air Forces in World War II*, 5:430–34; Drea, *MacArthur's ULTRA*, 199; Breuer, *Retaking the Philippines*, 179–92; Smith, *Triumph in the Philippines*, 315–41. Belote and Belote on page 215 vaguely assert that Itagaki was warned "by Tokyo" about the possibility of an American airborne drop. According to Levine, a captured diary confirmed this warning.

2. 503rd Parachute Infantry Regiment, History Report on Corregidor Island Operation, EL; Pacific Warfare Board Report, Battle Experiences Against the Japanese, Number 72, August 23, 1945, p. 1, Record Group 337, Entry 15A, Box 59, Folder 243; Pacific Warfare Board Report, Battle Experiences Against the Japanese, Number 75, August 30, 1945, p. 1, Record Group 337, Entry 15A, Box 59, Folder 246, all at NA; Captain Magnus Smith, "Operations of the 'Rock Force' (503rd RCT Reinforced) in the Recapture of Corregidor Island, 16 February–8 March 1945: Personal Experience of an Assistant Regimental Operations Officer," Advanced Infantry Officers Course, 1949–1950, Fort Benning, GA, p. 20; Captain Donald Crawford, "Operations of 503d Parachute Regimental Combat Team in Capture of Corregidor Island 16 February–2 March 1945: Personal Experience of a Regimental Assistant S-1," Advanced Infantry Officers Course, 1948–1949, Fort Benning, GA, p. 25; Lieutenant Edward Flash, "The Operations of the 2d Battalion, 503d Parachute Infantry Regimental Combat Team in the Recapture of Corregidor Island, 16 February–23 February 1945: Personal Observation of a Parachute Rifle Platoon Leader," Advanced Infantry Officers Course, 1949–1950, Fort Benning, GA, p. 10; Major Lawson Caskey, "The Operations of the 503d Parachute Infantry Regimental Combat Team in the Recapture of Corregidor Island, 16 February–8 March 1945: Personal Observations of a Parachute Battalion Commander," Advanced Infantry Officers Course, 1948–1949, Fort Benning, GA, pp. 12–15; Major John H. Blair, "Operations

of the 3d Battalion, 503d Parachute Infantry Regiment in the Landing on Corregidor, P.I., 16 February–2 March 1945: Personal Experience of a Battalion Staff Officer," Advanced Infantry Officers Course, 1949–1950, Fort Benning, GA, p. 14; Pacific Warfare Board, Battle Experiences Against the Japanese, Number 11, June 19, 1945, pp. 2–4, all at DRL; August "Gus" Schanze, unpublished memoir, p. 37, A. E. Schanze Papers, Box 1; Donald Lundy, letter to Mr. William Breuer, May 4, 1985; Lieutenant Colonel John Lackey, "The Rock Operation or the Return to Corregidor"; Walter Gonko, letter to Mr. William Breuer, July 9, 1985; Jones, Recollections and Comments; Jones, letter to Breuer; Tolson, letter to Breuer, all in William Breuer Papers, Box 4, USAMHI; Harris Mitchell, letter to Lieutenant General Edward Flanagan, September 1, 1986, Record Group 43, Box 9, Folder 24, Weldon B. Hester Papers; Williams, unpublished memoir, pp. 4–9, both at DMMA; Tony Sierra, Interview with Mr. Dick Brzezinski, February 26, 2004, NMPW; Sergeant Frank O'Neill, letter to Mrs. J. P. O'Neill, 1945, Folder 2229, Accession #2795, SHSM; Calhoun account, on 503rd Parachute Infantry, February 15, 1945, page of www.corregidor.org; Edward M. Flanagan Jr., "Corregidor: The Rock Force Assault," *Army* 45 (February 1995): 52–56; Jenkins, "The Corregidor Operation," 61–62; Hardman, "Drop on Corregidor," 21–22; Morison, *History of United States Naval Operations in World War II*, vol. 13, 198–205; Devlin, *Back to Corregidor*, 44–61; Breuer, *Retaking the Philippines*, 198–214; Belote and Belote, *Corregidor*, 214–22; Fahey, *Pacific War Diary*, 287–89; Craven and Cate, *Army Air Forces in World War II*, 5:431–33; Smith, *Triumph in the Philippines*, 342–45. Schanze was Eighth Army's personnel officer.

3. Task Group 78.3 Action Report, Mariveles-Corregidor Landings, 15–16 February 1945, Enclosure B, p. 3, Enclosure C, p. 2, June 29, 1945, MS416, World War II Battle Operations and Reports, Box 49, Folder 6, USNA; Pacific Warfare Board Report, Battle Experiences Against the Japanese, Number 76, p. 1, August 31, 1945, Record Group 337, Entry 15A, Box 59, Folder 247; Battle Experiences Against the Japanese, Number 74, p. 1; XI Corps, Historical Report, Luzon, p. 12, all at NA; Captain Hudson Hill, "The Operations of Company 'E,' 503d Parachute Regiment at Wheeler Point, Island of Corregidor, Philippine Islands, 23 February, 1945: Personal Experience of a Company Commander," Advanced Infantry Officers Course, 1947–1948, Fort Benning, GA, p. 36; Crawford, "Operations of 503d Regimental Combat Team," pp. 31–33; Battle Experiences Against the Japanese, Number 11, p. 3, all at DRL; 503rd Parachute Infantry Regiment, AAR, Supply Officer Report, p. 4, EL; Harry Akune, Interview with Mr. Jerry Mannering, September 21, 2008, p. 19; Ben Guthrie, Interview with Mr. Ed Smith, February 26, 2004, p. 39, both at NMPW; Brigadier General George Jones, letter to US Army Intelligence Center, April 17, 1995, Record Group 15, Box 70, Folder 1, Contributions from the Public Collection; Joe Gray, unpublished memoir, p. 2, Record Group 43, Box 9, Folder 15, Weldon B. Hester Papers; Williams, unpublished memoir, p. 21, all at DMMA; Lieutenant Colonel Edward Postlethwait, Interview with Dr. William Belote, January 1964, William and James Belote Papers, Box 1; Lieutenant Colonel Edward Postlethwait, "The Recapture of Corregidor," speech, p. 11, William Breuer Papers, Box 4, both at USAMHI; Private Ralph Frey, letter to Mrs. Merrit Frey, June 15, 1945, Folder 949, Accession #1047, SHSM; Smith, *Triumph in the Philippines*, 344–46; Belote and Belote, *Corregidor*, 215–16, 222–27; Devlin, *Back to Corregidor*, 48–49, 58–59; Jan Valtin, *Children of Yesterday: The 24th Infantry Division in the Philippines* (New York: Readers' Press, 1946 original, 2014 reprint), 268–77. Private

Frey was a member of the 151st Infantry Regiment, 38th Infantry Division, a unit that fought in the last stages of the Corregidor battle.

4. Colonel J. A. McCallan, Use of DDT Powder in Sixth Army, Philippines, p. 2, Record Group 112, Entry 31, Surgeon General, Administrative Records, Box 228, NA; 503rd Parachute Infantry Regiment, AAR, p. 9, EL; Private Arthur Smith, letter to family, March 27, 1945, Record Group 15, Box 11, Folder 14, Contributions from the Public Collection (also available in World War II Veterans Survey #1889 at USAMHI); Harold Templeman, "The Return to Corregidor," no pagination, Record Group 43, Box 9, Folder 4, Weldon B. Hester Papers; Anonymous sergeant major, letter to Lieutenant General Edward Flanagan, no date, Record Group 43, Box 9, Folder 30, Weldon B. Hester Papers; Don Abbot, unpublished memoir, no pagination, Record Group 43, Box 9, Folder 8, Weldon B. Hester Papers; Henry Gibson, letter to Lieutenant General Edward Flanagan, August 8, 1986, Record Group 43, Box 9, Folder 14, Weldon B. Hester Papers; Weldon B. Hester, Recollections, Record Group 43, Box 9, Folder 7, Weldon B. Hester Papers; Walter Gonko, letter; J. Gray, unpublished memoir, p. 2; Williams, unpublished memoir, pp. 20–24, all at DMMA; Victor Erdahl, Interview with Mr. Metzler, February 27, 2004, p. 11; Sierra interview, both at NMPW; "Louis," letter to Mrs. Anna Mae Miller, March 11, 1945, Folder 1964, Accession #1431; O'Neill, letter, both at SHSM; 503rd Parachute Infantry Regiment Casualty List at www.503prct.org; Caskey, "The Operations of the 503d Parachute Infantry Regimental Combat Team," p. 21, DRL; Flanagan, "Corregidor," 58; Valtin, *Children of Yesterday,* 280–84; Breuer, *Retaking the Philippines,* 239–57; Devlin, *Back to Corregidor,* 140–41, 176–218; Belote and Belote, *Corregidor,* 242–51; Smith, *Triumph in the Philippines,* 348–50; Rogers, *The Bitter Years,* 264–65; Borneman, *MacArthur at War,* 469–71; James, *The Years of MacArthur,* vol. 2, 651–53. Two Red Cross units operated on Corregidor during the battle. Weldon Hester's was attached to the 3rd Battalion, 34th Infantry Regiment; the other, led by Harold Templeman, actually jumped in with the 503rd. In the aftermath of the Corregidor battle, the Americans also secured or neutralized smaller islands around the harbor.

5. 1st Infantry Regiment, History of the Northern Luzon Campaign, Record Group 407, Entry 427, Box 6097, Folder 306-INF-1-0.3; Major General Charles Hall, Phone Conversation with Brigadier General George Decker, March 8, 1945, Record Group 338, Entry P50487, Box 1, Folder 3; 103rd Infantry Regiment, History, Philippines, 1 January–31 May 1945, p. 9, Record Group 407, Entry 427, Box 9183, Folder 343-INF-103-0; Memoirs of Company M, 130th Infantry Regiment, p. 11, Record Group 407, Entry 427, Box 8125, Folder 333-INF-130.7.0; Lieutenant Colonel Robert Vance statement in 128th Infantry Regiment, Lessons Learned, Action on Hill 505 and Luzon Combat Actions, June 1945, Record Group 407, Entry 427, Box 8038, Folder 332-INF-128-0.3; 130th Infantry Regiment, History of the Luzon Campaign, 10 February–30 June 1945, Record Group 407, Entry 427, Box 8121, Folder 333-INF-130-0.3, all at NA; SWPA Planning Conference Notes, August 10, 16, 1944, DMMA; 7th Cavalry Regiment, Historical Report, Luzon Island Campaign, EL; Lieutenant Edward Guhl, letter to mother, Edward Guhl Papers, Box 3, Folder 3-1; Milton Pearce, unpublished memoir, p. 164, World War II Veterans Survey #5161; Augustin, unpublished memoir, all at USAMHI; PFC Robert Myerson, letter to Mr. Joseph Myerson, February 1945, Folder 2068, Accession #2515; PFC Henry Burger Jr., letter to Mr. Henry Burger Sr., August 21, 1945, Folder 376, Accession #365; Frey, letter, all at SHSM; Brinson, "Battle of Zigzag Pass," p. 12; McLogan, *Boy Soldier,* 121, 140.

6. Pacific Warfare Board, Battle Experiences Against the Japanese, Number 31, July 30, 1945, p. 2, Record Group 337, Entry 15A, Box 58, Folder 219; Pacific Warfare Board, Battle Experiences Against the Japanese, Number 54, August 12, 1945, p. 1, Record Group 337, Entry 15A, Box 59, Folder 231; 43rd Infantry Division, G2, Language Section, Captured Japanese Diary, Lieutenant Hasegawa, March 2, 1945, Record Group 165, Entry 79, Box 407, Captured Documents; X Corps Headquarters, 167th Language Detachment, Captured Japanese Diary, Anonymous, June 16, 1945, Record Group 496, Entry 441, Box 2700, Records of the General Headquarters, SWPA, Psychological Warfare Branch General File, 1942–1945; Sixth Army, Combat Notes, Number 9, July 1945, p. 39, Record Group 407, Entry 427, Box 1998, Folder 106-3.01; Anonymous Imperial Army soldier diary, March 1945, Record Group 165, Entry 79, Box 412, Captured Documents; Oseth, "Observer Report on Operations of Sixth Army, Statements of High Ranking Officers," p. 1; Sixth Army on Luzon, Cave Warfare in the Mountains, pp. 51–52, and Hill and Mountain Fighting West of Fort Stotsenburg, Want in the Midst of Plenty, p. 7; 130th Infantry Regiment, History of the Luzon Campaign; Captain Roger King, "Capture of Infanta," Armor School Monograph, 1947, p. 10; Howard Cooksey, Oral History, p. 23, Howard Cooksey Papers, Box 1, both at USAMHI; Lieutenant Noel Seeburg, letter to "Folks," May 9, 1945, Noel Seeburg Collection, #2007.299, WWIIM; Keith Barress, Interview with Mr. Dan Lucas, October 18, 2001, AFC/2001/001/01684, LOC; Private Raymond Lansford, letter to parents, June 30, 1945, Folder 1709, Accession #1364; Staff Sergeant Jay Gruenfeld, letter to Ms. Crofts, February 18, 1945, Folder 1140, Accession #2752, both at SHSM; Radike, *Across the Dark Islands,* 213; McLogan, *Boy Soldier,* 143; Anthony Arthur, *Bushmasters: America's Jungle Warriors of World War II* (New York: St. Martin's Press, 1987), 159.

7. Mr. James Clark, letter to General Walter Krueger, July 16, 1945; General Walter Krueger, letter to Mr. James Clark, July 30, 1945; General Walter Krueger, letter to Mrs. Nellie Patrick, March 17, 1945, all in Walter Krueger Papers, Box 9; Krueger, "Commander's Appreciation of Logistics," p. 33, all at USMA; 127th Infantry Regiment, History of the Luzon Campaign, 27 January–30 June 1945, Major Louis Sass Surgeon Report, p. 2, Record Group 407, Entry 427, Box 8015, Folder 332-INF-0.3; Major John Olwin, Experiences and Impressions of a Surgical Team Attached to Medical Units Closely Supporting Combat Troops, pp. 7–8, Record Group 112, Entry 31, Surgeon General, Administrative Records, Box 78; Report of Neuropsychiatric Consultants, Lingayen and San Fabian, July 1945, Record Group 112, Entry 31, Surgeon General, Administrative Records, Box 77; US Army Forces, Western Pacific, Psychiatric Diseases and Organic Neurological Diseases, SWPA, January–July 1945, charts, Record Group 495, Entry 250, US Army Forces, Western Pacific, Box 1623, Folder 1; 36th Evacuation Hospital, Quarterly Medical History, Second Quarter 1945, July 8, 1945, p. 5, Record Group 112, Entry UD1012, Surgeon General, HUMEDS, Box 82; 3rd Field Hospital, Quarterly Historical Report, March 1945, p. 9, Record Group 112, Entry UD1012, Surgeon General, HUMEDS, Box 62; 130th Infantry Regiment, History of Luzon Campaign, all at NA; Colonel Floyd Wergeland, "Survey of Effectivness of Army Service Force Trained Medical Department Units and Personnel in SWPA and POA," US Army Medical Department, 1945, pp. 11–16, Vertical Files, Box 65, Folder 10; Charles Hanks, unpublished memoir, p. 36, Charles E. Hanks Papers, Vertical Files, Box 7, Folder 88; Robert LaChaussee, World War II Veterans Survey #3120; Colonel Bruce Palmer, Oral History, p. 349, all at USAMHI; Floyd Gilbert, unpublished memoir, p. 86, WWIIM; PFC Leon Clement, letter to Mrs. W. W. Clement, September 12, 1945, Folder 510, Accession #377, SHSM; V. G. Rowley, Interview with Mr. Mark Van Ells, September 25, 1995,

p. 20, Wisconsin Veterans Museum (WVM), Madison, WI; John C. McManus, *The Americans at Normandy: The Summer of 1944—The American War from the Beaches to Falaise* (New York: TOR Forge, 2004), 437; Mary Ellen Condon-Rall and Albert E. Cowdrey, *United States Army in World War II, The Medical Department: Medical Service in the War Against Japan* (Washington, DC: Center of Military History, United States Army, 1998), 333–51; Krueger, *From Down Under to Nippon,* 318; Smith, *Triumph in the Philippines,* 383, 652–55; John C. McManus, *Fire and Fortitude: The U.S. Army in the Pacific War, 1941–1943* (New York: Dutton Caliber, 2019), 436–40. Lieutenant William Clark is buried at Gate of Heaven Cemetery in the Cincinnati, Ohio, area.

8. Kazunobu Miyakaki et al., "History of the Himeji 39th Infantry Regiment 10th Division Imperial Japanese Army: The Untold Story Behind the Battle of Bataan in 1945," self-published, 1993, pp. 53, 63, Record Group 43, Box 9, Folder 6, Weldon B. Hester Papers, DMMA; ATIS Advanced Echelon, XIV Corps, Captured Imperial Japanese Army soldier diaries, Anonymous, February 13, 17, 1945; Sergeant Teruo Furunishi diary, April–June 1945, both in Record Group 496, Entry 441, Box 2700, Records of the General Headquarters, SWPA Psychological Warfare Branch General File, 1942–1945; Lieutenant Kumura diary, March 10, 1945, in Defects Arising from the Doctrine of "Spiritual Superiority" as Factors in Japanese Military Psychology, a Research Report, October 10, 1945, Record Group 165, Entry 79, Box 339, Report #76; ATIS Information Bulletin, Japanese Violation of the Laws of War, April 29, 1944, Record Group 165, Entry 79, Box 314, Bulletin #20; Hasegawa diary, March 5, 1945, all at NA; Fukuzo diary, January 27, 1945, USAMHI; Muto, unpublished memoir, pp. 34–42, CMH; Burger, letter, SHSM; Gibney, *Senso,* 141–47, 156–58; J. Potter, *Life and Death of a Japanese General,* 141–46; Flanagan, *The Angels,* 119–20. Miyazaki's brother was a captain in the 39th Infantry Regiment who died fighting on Bataan.

9. Sixth Army, Report of the Luzon Campaign, The Engineer, pp. 164–65; Army Service Forces, Major Supply Problems in Overseas Theaters During the Fiscal Year 1945, Record Group 319, Entry 48, Box 7, Global Logistics and Strategy, 1940–1943, both at NA; Vogel, "Logistical Support in the Lingayen Operation," p. 5, USMA; Ritchie, "Quartermastering Australia to Tokyo," p. 11; Sixth Army, Report of the Luzon Campaign, The Engineer, p. 11, both at CARL; 339th Engineer Combat Battalion, "This is an Engineer's War," p. 17, DMMA; Masterson, "United States Army Transportation in the Southwest Pacific Area," pp. 456, 679, 701–8, CMH; "Luzon," *Quartermaster Review,* July–August 1945, 24–25; Collins, "Walter Krueger: An Infantry Great," 18; Casey, *Engineers of the Southwest Pacific,* 6:354–67; Alvin P. Stauffer, *The Quartermaster Corps: Operations in the War Against Japan* (Washington, DC: Center of Military History, United States Army, 2004), 280–82; Krueger, *From Down Under to Nippon,* 322–23; Smith, *Triumph in the Philippines,* 362–63.

10. Dr. Karl Compton, letter to Lieutenant General Richard Sutherland, November 23, 1945; Report on Philippine Civil Affairs, Volume I, August 25, 1945, p. 7, Record Group 200, Entry 19810 (A1), Richard Sutherland Papers, Boxes 57 and 58 respectively; Army Service Forces, Supply Problems in Overseas Theaters, both at NA; History of US Army Services of Supply Southwest Pacific and Army Forces Western Pacific, 1941–30 June 1946, Luzon Base Section, US Army Services of Supply from 13 February to 1 April 1945, no pagination, 8-5.8 AA V18; Masterson, "United States Army Transportation in the Southwest Pacific Area," pp. 461–67, Appendix 44, p. 1, Appendix 45, p. 11, both at CMH; William Dunn, broadcast transcript, June 10, 1945, Record Group 52, Box 3, Folder 50, William J. Dunn

Papers, DMMA; Jean Smith, unpublished memoir, p. 87, Jean Smith Papers, Box 1, USAMHI; Ritchie, "Quartermastering Australia to Tokyo," p. 10, CARL; Rear Admiral William A. Sullivan entry, www.arlingtoncemetery.net; David Smollar, "A World War II Story of the Philippines: Letters of the Medical Officer of Philippine Civil Affairs Unit #17," *Journal of History of the Philippines* 61, no. 1 (January–December 2015): 19–20; James, *The Years of MacArthur,* vol. 2, 653; Rogers, *The Bitter Years,* 264; Condon-Rall and Cowdrey, *Medical Service in the War Against Japan,* 418–20; Krueger, *From Down Under to Nippon,* 324–25; Scott, *Rampage,* 459. In the Philippines that year, the Army measured a ton at 2,240 pounds instead of the conventional 2,000 pounds. I thank David Smollar for providing me with a copy of his fine article.

11. History of US Army Services of Supply Southwest Pacific . . . Luzon Base Section, CMH; N. B. Sauve, unpublished memoir, p. 90, N. B. Sauve Papers, Box 1; Johnny, letter to Fred, November 1, 1945, in Frederic Cramer material, both at USAMHI; Sergeant Minnie Foster, letter to family, June 1945, Folder 935, Accession #2409; Corporal Robert Landers, letter to friends, July 21, 1945, Folder 1709, Accession #1364, both at SHSM; Rogers, *The Bitter Years,* 265; Scott, *Rampage,* 433.

12. Dr. Earl Moore and Lieutenant Colonel Thomas Sternberg, Venereal Disease in the US Army in the Philippine Islands, and Recommendations for their Control, June 5, 1945, Record Group 29C, Box 2, Folder 1, Richard J. Marshall Papers, DMMA; History of US Army Services of Supply Southwest Pacific . . . Luzon Base Section, CMH; Melvin Benham, World War II Veterans Survey #9147; Wergeland, "Survey of Effectiveness of ASF Trained Medical Department Units," p. 11; Sergeant Joseph Steinbacher journal/memoir, pp. 72–73, all at USAMHI; 36th Evacuation Hospital, Quarterly Medical History, p. 11; 3rd Field Hospital, Quarterly Historical Report, pp. 13–14, both at NA; Condon-Rall and Cowdrey, *Medical Service in the War Against Japan,* 421; Egeberg, *The General,* 165–67; Scott, *Rampage,* 431–32.

13. Private Al Carleton, letter to Ms. Jessie White, February 14, 1944, Record Group 496, Entry 74, Box 456, Records of the General Headquarters, SWPA/USAFP, Personal Letters Held by Theater Censor, NA; Multiple Organizations, Joint Statement on Full Utilization of Negro Nurses in Armed Forces, March 19, 1945; National Nursing Council for War Service and National Association of Colored Graduate Nurses, Joint Statement, March 14, 1945, in Army Nurse Corps Collection, Series II, Official Papers, Box 6, Folder 6; WACs in SWPA, partial history manuscript, pp. 1–2, Jean Smith Papers, Box 1; Lieutenant Martha Wayman, letter to Ruth, June 13, 1945, Martha Wayman Papers, Box 2, all at USAMHI; Mildred Ferguson, unpublished memoir, p. 16, World War II Participants and Contemporaries Collection, Pat Schmidt Folder; Hostetter, unpublished memoir, p. 36, both at EL; D. Gray, Impressions of General Krueger, USMA; Lieutenant Margaret Carlson, letter to Mr. Henry Josten, July 17, 1945, Folder 432, Accession #839, SHSM; "The Army Nurse Corps," www.history.army.mil; Mattie E. Treadwell, *United States Army in World War II, Special Studies: The Women's Army Corps* (Washington, DC: Center of Military History, United States Army, 1991), 418–51; McManus, *Fire and Fortitude,* 441.

14. Headquarters, Eighth Army, Questions About Performance of 93rd Infantry Division, July 9, 1945, Record Group 407, Entry 427, Box 11329, Folder 393-0.1; Generals George Marshall and Douglas MacArthur, Radiograms, March 3–4, 1945, Record Group 200, Entry 19810 (A1), Richard Sutherland Papers, Box 41, both at NA; Anonymous letter to *Pittsburgh Courier,* October–November 1945; Mr. Walter White, rough draft of February 12, 1945, article for *New York Post,* both in Leonard Russell Boyd Papers, Box 1; Captain Joseph Pruden, Chaplain Corps,

"American Soldier Filipino Relationships," October 20, 1945, Leonard Russell Boyd Papers, Box 2, all at HIA; George Ridout, Interview with Mr. Walter Valentine, May 21, 2005, AFC/2001/001/32824, LOC; Lieutenant General Ira Eaker, Comments, War Department Special Board on Negro Manpower, November 24, 1945, Alvan C. Gillem Papers, Box 1, EL; General Robert Eichelberger, letter to Mr. William Gordon, September 14, 1956, Box 20, Robert Eichelberger Papers, DU; Chris Dixon, *African Americans and the Pacific War, 1941–1945: Race, Nationality, and the Fight for Freedom* (Cambridge, UK: Cambridge University Press, 2018), 246–48; Ulysses Lee, *United States Army in World War II: The Employment of Negro Troops* (Washington, DC: Office of the Chief of Military History, United States Army, 1966), 529–35; Robert F. Jefferson, *Fighting for Hope: African American Troops of the 93rd in World War II and Postwar America* (Baltimore: Johns Hopkins University Press, 2008), 215–17. Eichelberger, in his letter to Gordon, expressed ambivalence about African American troops. He respected their garrison discipline, but he also seemed to buy into the contemporary condescending notion that they posed some sort of special threat to white women.

15. Brigadier General Clovis Byers, letter to Marie Byers, March 31, 1945, Clovis Byers Papers, Box 9, Folder 9–10; Brigadier General Bonner Fellers, letter to Admiral Husband Kimmel, March 6, 1967, Bonner Fellers Papers, Box 22, Folder 7, both at HIA; Lieutenant General Robert Eichelberger, letter to Emma Eichelberger, February 22, 1945, Box 9, Robert Eichelberger Papers; Eichelberger diary, February 21, 1945, both at DU; "Emil Bachrach–Bachrach Motors," at www.lougopal.com/manila; MacArthur, *Reminiscences*, 251; Luvaas, *Dear Miss Em*, 225–26; Egeberg, *The General*, 163, 184; Huff, *My Fifteen Years with General MacArthur*, 99–102; Manchester, *American Caesar*, 493–94; James, *The Years of MacArthur*, vol. 2, 660–64, 802–3; Scott, *Rampage*, 437.

16. Eighth Army, Operational Monograph on the Panay Negros Operation, 9-2.8 AB V3; Eighth Army, Staff Study of the Japanese Operations on Mindanao Island, 8-5.4 AA8; Eighth Army, Operational Monograph on the Mindanao Operation, 9-2.8 AB V5; Eighth Army, Staff Study of the Japanese Operation on Negros Island, 8-5.4 AA9; Eighth Army, Staff Study of the Japanese Operation on Panay Island, 8-5.4 AA11; Eighth Army, Staff Study of Japanese Operations in Zamboanga, 1944–1945, 8-5.4 AA1; Eighth Army, Operational Monograph on the Zamboanga Zulu Archipelago, 9-2.8 AB2 V4; Japanese Monograph #6; Tomochika, True Facts of the Leyte Operation, all at CMH; History of X Corps on Mindanao, 17 April–30 June 1945, Record Group 407, Entry 427, Box 3532, Folder 210-0; Outstanding Differences and Similarities in the Manner of Performance of the Americal Infantry Division on Cebu . . . and the 24th Infantry Division on Mindanao, Record Group 407, Entry 427, Box 6611, Folder 324-0.1; Major General Roscoe Woodruff, A Narrative Account of the 24th Infantry Division on Mindanao, Record Group 407, Entry 427, Box 6612, Folder 324-0.3; 31st Infantry Division, History of the Mindanao Campaign, Record Group 407, Entry 427, Box 7733, Folder 331-0.2; Major Cleary, Eighth Army Observer Report on Palawan, March 20, 1945, Record Group 407, Entry 427, Box 2291, Folder 108-3.01, 40th Division, History, Luzon, Panay, Negros, all at NA; Americal Division, Report of V2 Operation, 26 March–20 June 1945, William Howard Arnold Papers, Box 1; 503rd Parachute Infantry Regiment, Historical Report on Negros Island Operation, June 28, 1945, 503rd Parachute Infantry Regiment Records, Box 1533, both at EL; Major General William "Duke" Arnold, Oral History, 1975, pp. 146–47, William Howard Arnold Papers, Box 3, USAMHI; Lieutenant General Robert Eichelberger, letters to Emma Eichelberger, March 29, May 16, 1945, Boxes 9 and 10, Robert Eichelberger Papers; Eighth Army

Staff Study of Japanese Operations on Jolo Island, April 19, 1945–September 16, 1945, Box 38, Robert Eichelberger Papers; Lieutenant General Clovis Byers, letter to General Robert Eichelberger, February 21, 1958, Box 21, Robert Eichelberger Papers; Eichelberger, Dictations, 1948, Zamboanga and Philippines, p. 9; Eichelberger diary, multiple entries, March–May 1945, all at DU; Brigadier General Clovis Byers, letter to Marie Byers, April 19, 1945, Clovis Byers Papers, box 9–10; Brigadier General Clovis Byers, letter to Miriam, Wallie, and Bruce, May 15, 1945, Clovis Byers Papers, Box 3, Folder 3-9, all at HIA; Lieutenant General Robert Eichelberger, "The Amphibious Eighth," *Army Navy Journal*, December 1945; MacArthur, *Reports of General MacArthur*, vol. 1, *Campaigns*, 327–55; Francis D. Cronin, *Under the Southern Cross: The Saga of the Americal Division* (Washington, DC: Combat Forces Press, 1951), 273–54; Chwialkowski, *In Caesar's Shadow*, 131–37; Shortal, *Forged by Fire*, 114–24; Smith, *Triumph in the Philippines*, 583–626; Eichelberger, *Our Jungle Road to Tokyo*, 200–202, 216, 220–23, 232; Luvaas, *Dear Miss Em*, 227–40, 265–66.

17. Colonel Wendell Fertig, letter to Mr. John Keats, January 31, 1958, Record Group 53, Box 6, Folder 9, Wendell W. Fertig Papers; Lieutenant General Robert Eichelberger, letter to Sue, April 29, 1945, Record Group 41, Box 2, Folder 10, Robert Eichelberger Papers, both at DMMA; Lieutenant General Robert Eichelberger, letters to Emma Eichelberger, March 2, April 1, 10, 18, 28, 1945, Box 9, Robert Eichelberger Papers; Major Robert White, letter to Mrs. Emma Eichelberger, June 21, 1945, Box 10, Robert Eichelberger Papers; Brigadier General Clovis Byers, Memo of Saturday, March 30; Interview with General MacArthur, April 9, 1945, interspersed with Eichelberger, diary; Eichelberger diary entries, March 23, April 10, 28, 1945; Eichelberger Dictations, 1948, Zamboanga and Philippines, p. 9, all at DU; Brigadier General Clovis Byers, letters to Marie Byers, March 31, April 7, 1945, Clovis Byers Papers, Box 9, Folder 9–10, HIA; Memo of President Eisenhower's Conference with Prime Minister Menzies, June 8, 1960, Dwight D. Eisenhower Diary Series, Box 50, EL; Eichelberger, "Eighth Army Operations in the Philippines, 1945," *Army Navy Journal*; Fahey, *Pacific War Diary*, 307; MacArthur, *Reports of General MacArthur*, vol. 1, *Campaigns*, 353–55; Luvaas, *Dear Miss Em*, 24, 228–29, 243–60; Smith, *Triumph in the Philippines*, 640–58, 692; Eichelberger, *Our Jungle Road to Tokyo*, 243–44; Chwialkowski, *In Caesar's Shadow*, 137–42; Shortal, *Forged in Fire*, 124–26.

3. Hope and Grief

1. General Albert Wedemeyer, interview, no date, Albert Wedemeyer Papers, Box 6, Folder 3, HIA; Captain Alexander von Plinsky, "General Albert C. Wedemeyer's Missions in China 1944–1947: An Attempt to Achieve the Impossible," Master's Thesis, 1991, Fort Leavenworth, KS, pp. 4–12; Major Neil Stark, "Engaged in Debate: Major Albert C. Wedemeyer and the 1941 Victory Plan in Historical Memory," School of Advanced Military Studies, United States Army Command and General Staff College, 2017, pp. 1–14, both at CARL; Richardson diary, March 31, 1945; General Albert Coady Wedemeyer entry at www.arlingtoncemetery.net; Charles F. Romanus and Riley Sunderland, *United States Army in World War II: China-Burma-India Theater: Time Runs Out in CBI* (Washington, DC: Office of the Chief of Military History, United States Army, 1959), 15–16; Albert Wedemeyer, *Wedemeyer Reports! An Objective, Dispassionate Examination of World War II, Postwar Policies, and Grand Strategy* (New York: Henry Holt & Company, 1958), 267–74; Jim Lacey, *Keep from All Thoughtful Men: How U.S. Economists Won World War II* (Annapolis, MD: Naval Institute Press, 2011); John J. McLaughlin, *General Albert*

C. Wedemeyer: America's Unsung Strategist in World War II (Philadelphia and Oxford: Casemate, 2012), 13–48, 70–76. McLaughlin's biography is very favorable, and he credits Wedemeyer as the true mastermind of the Victory Plan. Lacey, on the other hand, argued that all evidence of Wedemeyer's supposed integral contributions came from Wedemeyer himself. Stark strikes a middle ground, acknowledging Wedemeyer as one important voice among several.

2. General Albert Wedemeyer, untitled writings on World War II, no date, p. 4, Albert Wedemeyer Papers, Box 6, Folder 32; Major General Albert Wedemeyer, letter to Major General J. Edwin Hull, November 25, 1944, Albert Wedemeyer Papers, Box 81, Folder 35; General Albert Wedemeyer, letter to Mr. John Hart, May 25, 1960; Brigadier General Frank Dorn, letter to Mr. John Hart, July 20, 1960, both in John Hart Papers, Box 1, all at HIA; General Albert Wedemeyer, Interview with Dr. D. Clayton James, July 6, 1971, p. 19, Record Group 49, Box 4, D. Clayton James Collection, DMMA; Richardson diary, September 7, 1945; Romanus and Sunderland, *Time Runs Out in CBI,* 258; McLaughlin, *General Albert C. Wedemeyer,* 120–25; Wedemeyer, *Wedemeyer Reports!,* 304. In postwar communications with historians, Wedemeyer repeatedly stated that he felt especially betrayed by Stilwell because Wedemeyer had expressly written to General Marshall to recommend Stilwell for promotion to four-star rank while Wedemeyer served as Mountbatten's deputy. The idea of a two-star general with fifteen fewer years of Army service somehow recommending a promotion for a more senior three-star general who served in a different command is patently absurd, and an alarming indication of Wedemeyer's tendency toward self-aggrandizing pomposity. Brigadier General Frank Dorn, a key Stilwell aide and loyalist, grew to hate Wedemeyer because the latter fired him after taking command. Dorn wrote voluminous letters to historian John Hart with fascinating in-depth analyses of many key CBI personalities, including Wedemeyer, of whom he once wrote: "He not only was a scatterbrain politically, but seldom knew what the hell he was talking about in anything. He liked the sound of his own voice." In another scathing letter, he denounced Wedemeyer as a "primary horse's ass and liar." Dorn also claimed that Stilwell held a similarly low opinion of General Embick, Wedemeyer's father-in-law. The Dorn letters and other fascinating material can be found in Box 1 of the John Hart Papers at HIA.

3. US Army China Theater, "History of the China Theater," Chapters I and II, 8-6.3 AA V1 C2; Historical Section, Headquarters, United States Army Forces, India-Burma Theater, "History of the India-Burma Theater 25 October 1944–23 June 1945," Chapter II, no pagination, 8-6.2 AB V1 and 2, CY3, both at CMH; Von Plinsky, "General Albert C. Wedemeyer's Missions in China," p. 21, CARL; Richard B. Frank, *Tower of Skulls: A History of the Asia-Pacific War, July 1937–May 1942* (New York: W. W. Norton, 2020), 3, 86–95; Jonathan Fenby, *Chiang Kai-shek: China's Generalissimo and the Nation He Lost* (New York: Carroll & Graf Publishers, 2003), 431–33; Jay Taylor, *The Generalissimo: Chiang Kai-shek and the Struggle for Modern China* (Cambridge, MA: Belknap Press of Harvard University Press, 2009), 296–99; Romanus and Sunderland, *Time Runs Out in CBI,* 15–45; Wedemeyer, *Wedemeyer Reports!,* 271; Max Hastings, *Retribution: The Battle for Japan, 1944–45* (New York: Vintage Books, 2007), 219–22, 404–6; Rana Mitter, *Forgotten Ally: China's World War II, 1937–1945* (Boston: Mariner Books, 2013), 347–50.

4. Patrick Hurley, letter to Major General Orlando Ward, January 11, 1952, Record Group 319, Entry 76, Box 11, Records of the Office of the Chief of Military History, Stilwell's Command Problems; Lieutenant General Albert Wedemeyer, Instructions for American Liaison Groups with the Chinese Army, February 18, 1945, Record Group 337, Entry 15A, Box 64, Folder 360, both at NA; Major General

Albert Wedemeyer, letter to General George Marshall, December 10, 1944, Albert Wedemeyer Papers, Box 82, Folder 23; General Albert Wedemeyer, Untitled Writings on Chiang, no date, Albert Wedemeyer Papers, Box 6, Folder 27; Wedemeyer, undated postwar interview, all at HIA; Von Plinsky, "General Albert C. Wedemeyer's Missions in China," pp. 16–17, 40–43, CARL; Romanus and Sunderland, *Time Runs Out in CBI*, 52–55, 165–67; Taylor, *The Generalissimo*, 296–97; Wedemeyer, *Wedemeyer Reports!*, 295–97; McLaughlin, *General Albert C. Wedemeyer*, 127–29. Hurley tended to be emotional and voluble. At one point, he grew angry with Wedemeyer and stopped speaking to him for a few days. He soon apologized profusely and, in his correspondence with the general, even professed love for him. Bemused by this behavior, the even-tempered Wedemeyer maintained a very correct, if not exactly effusive or warm, posture toward the ambassador. For more on this, see their correspondence in the Albert Wedemeyer Papers, Box 81, Folder 36, HIA.

5. Lieutenant Colonel Vann Kennedy, notes from anonymous interviewer, May 7, 1945, Frank Dorn Papers, Box 4, Folder 8; Major General Albert Wedemeyer, letter to Major General Lawrence Kuter, November 20, 1944, Albert Wedemeyer Papers, Box 82, Folder 3; Wedemeyer, letter to Hull, all at HIA; Japanese Monograph Number 133, CMH; Leo J. Daugherty, *The Allied Resupply Effort in the China-Burma-India Theater During World War II* (Jefferson, NC, and London: McFarland & Company, 2008), 175–76; Craven and Cate, *Army Air Forces in World War II*, 5:252–53; Romanus and Sunderland, *Time Runs Out in CBI*, 52, 142–50, 178–79; Wedemeyer, *Wedemeyer Reports!*, 290–93; Taylor, *The Generalissimo*, 296–97.

6. Historical Section, Headquarters, United States Army Forces, India-Burma Theater, "History of Northern Combat Area Command, China-Burma-India Theater and Burma Theater, 1943–1945, Appendix 1, 5332 D. Brigade (Prov.), India-Burma Theater, 16 July 1944–8 March 1945," 8-6.2 AE V4; "History of Northern Combat Area Command, China-Burma-India Theater and India-Burma Theater, 1943–1945," 8-6.2 AE V2 and V3, CY1; "History of the India-Burma Theater," all at CMH; 475th Infantry Regiment, History of the Regimental Intelligence and Reconnaissance Platoon, November 1944–February 1945, Record Group 407, Entry 427, Box 17055, Folder INRG-475-0.3; 475th Infantry Regiment, Unit Histories, A through C Companies, November 1944–February 1945, and Unit Histories and Patrol Reports, Medical Detachment, E through G Companies, January–February 1945, Record Group 407, Entry 427, Box 17056, Folder INRG-475-0.7; 475th Infantry Regiment, Medical History, November 15, 1944–February 15, 1945, Record Group 407, Entry 427, Box 17058, Folder INRG-475-26.0, all at NA; Tech 5 Walter Pippin, letter to family, February 16, 1945, Folder 2345, Accession #1571; Lieutenant Robert Jones, letter to Mrs. C. Rosa Jones, February 7–8, 1945, Folder 1517, Accession #2461, both at SHSM; Major George Jordan, "The Operations of 2d Squadron, 124th Cavalry Regiment Special in the Battle of Knight's Hill, 29 January–2 February 1945, Personal Experiences of a Squadron Commander," Advanced Infantry Officers Class, 1948–1949, Fort Benning, GA, p. 27, DRL; *Central Burma*, pamphlet, pp. 15–19, CMH; Eric Morris, "The Uncommon Commoner," *Military History Quarterly (MHQ)*, Spring 1995, 20–30; Romanus and Sunderland, *Time Runs Out in CBI*, 213–23.

7. Brigadier General Lewis Pick, letter to Brigadier General Frederick "Fritz" Strong, February 23, 1945, Frederick Strong Papers, Box 2, USMA; "History of India-Burma Theater," Chapter VI, 8-6.2 AB V1 and 2, CY3, CMH; Sergeant Dave Richardson, "Truck Convoy to China" and "With the First Convoy to China over the

Ledo-Burma Road," *Yank,* March 23, 1945; Deton Brooks, "Negro Engineers Write History in Heroic Job on Key Ledo Road," *Chicago Defender,* November 4, 1944; Deton Brooks, "China Denies Bar on Negro Troops," *Chicago Defender,* February 17, 1945; "The Ledo Road" photo collection at www.cbi-theater.com; William Collins King, *Building for Victory: World War II in China, Burma, and India and the 1875th Engineer Aviation Battalion* (Lanham, MD: Taylor Trade Publishing, 2004), 137–38; Dod, *Corps of Engineers: The War Against Japan,* 473–74; Daugherty, *Allied Resupply Effort in the China-Burma-India Theater,* 133–36.

8. "A History of Soldier Morale in the CBI and IB Theaters, 1944–1945," p. 28, Record Group 319, Entry 77, Box 6, Records of the Office of the Chief of Military History, Time Runs Out in CBI, NA; Historical Section, India-Burma Theater, "History of the India-Burma Theater, 1 March 1944–31 June [*sic*] 1946," Volume I, pp. 147–61, 8-6.2 AC VI CY1; "History of the India-Burma Theater," Chapter VI, both at CMH; Kenneth Clyde Anderson, "U.S. Army Pipelines in India (The Not So Glamorous Corps of Engineers)," Vertical Files, Box 74, Folder 5; Lieutenant Charles "Chuck" Whalen, 628th Quartermaster Refrigeration Company, biography and recollections, p. 4, Charles Whalen Papers, Box 1, both at USAMHI; Pick, letter to Strong, USMA; Sergeant Clifford Miller, letter to Mrs. Jack O'Hara, July 4, 1945, Folder 1965, Accession #2139; Private Robert Chisman, letter to family, April 4, 1945, Folder 495, Accession #882; "Bill," letter to Ms. Eleanor Butts, April 20, 1945, Folder 397, Accession #714, all at SHSM; Nancy Brockbank, "The Context of Heroism: The African American Experience on the Ledo Road," Master's Thesis, Eastern Michigan University, 1998, pp. 99–101; Nelson Grant Tayman, "Stilwell Road: Land Route to China," *National Geographic,* June 1945; Deton Brooks, "Ledo Road Battle Just Beginning, Writer Says," *Chicago Defender,* April 28, 1945; Walter Orey, personal memoir; Photos of Ledo Road Signs, both at www.cbi-theater.com; Benjamin King, Richard C. Biggs, and Eric R. Criner, *Spearhead of Logistics: A History of the United States Army Transportation Corps* (Fort Eustis, VA, and Washington, DC: US Army Transportation Center and Center of Military History, 2001), 174–75; Winston Churchill, *The Second World War,* vol. 5, *Closing the Ring* (New York: Bantam Books, 1963), 480; Leslie Anders, *The Ledo Road: General Joseph W. Stilwell's Highway to China* (Norman: University of Oklahoma Press, 1965), 218–44; Dod, *Corps of Engineers: The War Against Japan,* 662–66; Romanus and Sunderland, *Time Runs Out in CBI,* 317–18; W. King, *Building for Victory,* 138–39.

9. "History of the China Theater," Volume I, Chapter IV, pp. 11–12, Chapter V, pp. 77–81, CMH; Major George Kuite, Oral History, August 9, 1945, p. 4, Record Group 112, Entry 302, Surgeon General, Inspections Branch, Box 223, Interview Number 182; Captain Malcolm Bouton, Oral History, April 4, 1945, pp. 5–6, Record Group 112, Entry 302, Surgeon General, Inspections Branch, Box 221, Interview Number 143; Lieutenant Colonel John Regan, Oral History, September 8, 1945, p. 3, Record Group 112, Entry 302, Surgeon General, Inspections Branch, Box 223, Interview Number 187; 48th Evacuation Hospital, History, 1944–February 20, 1945, p. 5, Record Group 112, Entry UD1012, Surgeon General, HUMEDS, Box 82; Captain Leonard Ramey, Contagious Diseases in District B, Base Section Number 1, Record Group 112, Entry 31, Surgeon General, Administrative Records, Box 13, all at NA; *What You Should Know About China,* pamphlet, p. 6, Hiram Boone Collection, #2002.210, WWIIM; Special Service Division, Army Service Forces, United States Army, *Pocket Guide to China,* at www.cbi-theater.com/booklet/guide-to-china.html; Samuel Stouffer et al., *The American Soldier: Combat and Its Aftermath* (Studies in Social

Psychology series, vol. 2 of 4) (Princeton, NJ: Princeton University Press, 1949), 627–29; Peter Schrijvers, *Bloody Pacific: American Soldiers at War with Japan* (New York: Palgrave Macmillan, 2010), 145–46.

10. Captain Hymen Stein and Corporal Ralph Strand, 14th Evacuation Hospital, A Reconditioning Program, p. 4, Record Group 112, Entry UD1012, Surgeon General, HUMEDS, Box 78; Major Anthony Niccoli, Memorandum to the Commanding General, Headquarters, Advance Section, India-Burma Theater, May 29, 1945, Record Group 159, Entry 26F, Office of the Inspector General, Box 57, Folder 333.9, both at NA; Mr. Frank Bolden, letter to Mr. P. L. Prattis, no date; Lieutenant Colonel George Hibbert, War Correspondent Isaacs and First Convoy, May 4, 1945; Colonel Albert Johnson, War Correspondent Harold Isaacs' Activities in Relation to Negro Troops in China, May 11, 1945; Major General Robert McClure, Memo for Chiang Kai-shek, December 20, 1944; Major General Gilbert Cheves, Memo to the Inspector General, China Theater, Newspaper Correspondents, Negro Question, May 7, 1945; Mr. Harold Isaacs, Notes from Press Conference with Generals Cheves and Pick, February 5, 1945; Mr. Harold Isaacs, Notes from Press Conference with Generals Cheves and Merrill, Mr. Brooks and Mr. Bolden, February 6, 1945; Mr. Deton Brooks and Mr. Frank Bolden, Notes from Press Conference with Generals Cheves, McClure, and Lieutenant Colonel Hibbert, February 8, 1945; Lieutenant General Albert Wedemeyer, Secret Memo for General Douglas MacArthur, August 21, 1945, all in Albert Wedemeyer Papers, Box 87, Folder 1, HIA; "History of the China Theater," Volume I, Chapter III, pp. 38–39; "History of the India-Burma Theater," Chapter VIII, both at CMH; Brockbank, "Context of Heroism," pp. 114–42; Deton Brooks, "Calcutta Social Whirl Happy Escape from Burma Jungle for Colored GIs," *Chicago Defender,* January 27, 1945; Deton Brooks, "Pat O'Brien Pays Tribute to Negro Army Engineers," *Chicago Defender,* January 6, 1945; Deton Brooks, "First Negro MPs in India Burma Theater," *Chicago Defender,* April 28, 1945; Brooks, "Ledo Road Battle Just Beginning," *Chicago Defender*; Lee, *Employment of Negro Troops,* 616–19; Daugherty, *Allied Resupply Effort in the China-Burma-India Theater,* 190–93; Romanus and Sunderland, *Time Runs Out in CBI,* 297–98, 347–48.

11. General Albert Wedemeyer, letter to Sutherland *[sic]* and Romanus, April 21, 1950, Record Group 319, Entry 75, Box 7, Records of the Office of the Chief of Military History, Stilwell's Mission to China; General Albert Wedemeyer, letter to General John Stokes, February 17, 1956; General Albert Wedemeyer, letters to Major General A. Cooper Smith, February 9, 19, July 12, 1954, Record Group 319, Entry 77, Box 9, Records of the Office of the Chief of Military History, Time Runs Out in CBI; Patrick Hurley, letter to Major General R. W. Stephens, December 15, 1956, Record Group 319, Entry 77, Box 9, Records of the Office of the Chief of Military History, Time Runs Out in CBI; Hurley, letter to Ward, all at NA; "History of the China Theater," Volume II, Chapter VII, p. 11, CMH; Mr. John Davies, "The Generalissimo's Dilemma," p. 1, Frank Dorn Papers, Box 2, Folder 1; Lieutenant General Albert Wedemeyer, Report on Conscription in China, Albert Wedemeyer Papers, Box 85, Folder 4; Lieutenant General Albert Wedemeyer, letter to Major General J. Edwin Hull, June 7, 1945, Albert Wedemeyer Papers, Box 81, Folder 35, all at HIA; Hastings, *Retribution,* 410–13; Mitter, *Forgotten Ally,* 350–55; Taylor, *The Generalissimo,* 304–10; Wedemeyer, *Wedemeyer Reports!,* 285–87, 302–36; Charles F. Romanus and Riley Sunderland, *United States Army in World War II: China-Burma-India Theater: Stilwell's Mission to China* (Washington, DC: Office of the Chief of Military History, United States Army, 1987), 371–74; Romanus and Sunderland, *Time Runs Out in CBI,* 368–85.

4. Doorstep

1. Major Roy Appleman, "The XXIV Corps in the Conquest of Okinawa," Volume 1, December 1945, pp. 3–10, 8-5.3 ABv1, CMH; Bruce Gudmundsson, "Okinawa," *MHQ*, Spring 1995, 64–65; George Feifer, "The Ghosts of Okinawa," *MHQ*, Summer 1997, 64–65; Roy E. Appleman, James M. Burns, Russell A. Gugeler, and John Stevens, *United States Army in World War II: The War in the Pacific, Okinawa: The Last Battle* (Washington, DC: Center of Military History, United States Army, 1948), 7–14; Samuel Eliot Morison, *History of United States Naval Operations in World War II*, vol. 14, *Victory in the Pacific, 1945* (Boston: Little, Brown, 1960), 33–86; Benis M. Frank and Henry I. Shaw, *History of U.S. Marine Corps Operations in World War II*, vol. 5, *Victory and Occupation* (Washington, DC: Historical Branch, G-3 Division, Headquarters, US Marine Corps, 1968), 31–39; George Feifer, *Tennozan: The Battle of Okinawa and the Atomic Bomb* (New York: Ticknor & Fields, 1992), 58–77. Weapons were not unknown on the island of Okinawa, but traditionally they remained in the hands of an elite few. There is a vast literature on the Battle of Iwo Jima. For this overview I have relied mainly on George Garand and Truman Strobridge, *History of U.S. Marine Corps Operations in World War II*, vol. 4, *Western Pacific Operations* (Washington, DC: Historical Division, Headquarters, US Marine Corps, 1971), 443–728. The Army's 147th Infantry Regiment landed on Iwo on March 20, 1945, participated in the elimination of the last vestiges of Japanese resistance, and then garrisoned the island. But three Marine divisions, the 3rd, 4th, and 5th, did the vast majority of the ground fighting on Iwo.

2. Imperial Japanese Army, Staff Comments on Questions—Okinawa, December 1945, Record Group 319, Entry 64, Box 3, Records of the Office of the Chief of Military History, Okinawa the Last Battle; Personalities of the 32nd Army, Interrogation Summaries, July–August 1945, Record Group 319, Entry 64, Box 5, Records of the Office of the Chief of Military History, Okinawa the Last Battle; Colonel Hiromichi Yahara, POW Interrogation Report, August 23, 1945, pp. 1–4, Record Group 127, Box 254, World War II Area Geographic Files, Folder A28-1.5, all at NA; Japanese Monograph Number 135, Okinawa Operations Record, March–June 1945, 8-5.1 AC135; Appleman, "XXIV Corps in the Conquest of Okinawa," Volume 1, pp. 71–74, both at CMH; Colonel Hiromichi Yahara, letter to Dr. Belote, no date; Colonel Ysuneo Shimura, Interview with Drs. James and William Belote, July 19, 1967; Mr. Kunishige Tanaka, Interview with Drs. James and William Belote, August 13, 1967, all in William and James Belote Papers, Box 3, USAMHI; Thomas Huber, "Japan's Battle of Okinawa, April–June 1945," Leavenworth Papers, Number 18, pp. 2–6, 21–24, CARL; Sharon Lacey, "Into the Inferno," *World War II*, July–August 2015, 41–42; Hiromichi Yahara, *The Battle for Okinawa: A Japanese Officer's Eyewitness Account of the Last Great Campaign of World War II* (New York: John Wiley & Sons, 1995), 3–19, 207–10; James H. Belote and William M. Belote, *Typhoon of Steel: The Battle for Okinawa* (New York: Harper & Row, 1970), 14–21; Robert Leckie, *Okinawa: The Last Battle of World War II* (New York: Penguin Books, 1995), 28–31; Frank and Shaw, *Victory and Occupation*, 39–46; Feifer, *Tennozan*, 76–77; John Toland, *The Rising Sun: The Decline and Fall of the Japanese Empire, 1936–1945*, vol. 2 (New York: Random House, 1970), 877–78.

3. Japanese Monograph Number 135, pp. 29–44; Appleman, "XXIV Corps in the Conquest of Okinawa," Volume 1, pp. 38–41, 46–74, both at CMH; Shimura interview, USAMHI; Huber, "Japan's Battle of Okinawa," pp. 8–21, CARL; S. Lacey, "Into the Inferno," 36–37; Haruko Taya Cook and Theodore F. Cook, *Japan at War:*

An Oral History (New York: New Press, 1992), 254–55; Appleman et al., *Okinawa: The Last Battle,* 10–17, 87–96; Frank and Shaw, *Victory and Occupation,* 46–56; Belote and Belote, *Typhoon of Steel,* 34–36; Yahara, *The Battle for Okinawa,* 19–6. The Japanese called the Okinawan teenage boys the Blood and Iron Student Corps. Ushijima and his staff were galled by the fact that the 9th Division never even made it to the Philippines. Thanks to the ubiquity of American submarines and planes, the ships carrying the division made it only as far as Formosa.

4. Fifth Fleet, Action Report, Ryukyus Operation through 27 May 1945, Part II, pp. 1–3, MS416, World War II Battle Operations and Reports, Box 49, Folder 2, USNA; 96th Infantry Division, Action Report, Ryukyu Campaign, Chapter IV, p. 1, CARL; US Pacific Fleet and Pacific Ocean Areas, Joint Staff Study: Iceberg Operation, pp. 5–7, copy in author's possession courtesy of Mr. Christopher Kolakowski, Director, WVM; Ian W. Toll, *Twilight of the Gods: War in the Western Pacific, 1944–1945* (New York: W. W. Norton, 2020), 104–5; Morison, *History of United States Naval Operations in World War II,* vol. 14, 156–62, 372–88; Appleman et al., *Okinawa: The Last Battle,* 41–43; Worrall Reed Carter, *Beans, Bullets, and Black Oil: The Story of Fleet Logistics Afloat in the Pacific During World War II* (Washington, DC: Department of the Navy, 1953), 342–47; Frank and Shaw, *Victory and Occupation,* 59–62, 70–73. The Battle of Okinawa entry at www.historyofwar.org contains an excellent, well-researched order of battle overview. Throughout the last year of the war, Nimitz rotated his two primary commanders, Spruance and Halsey, in command of the operational fleet. This made for confusing unit designations. When Spruance was in charge, the command was known as the Fifth Fleet. Under Halsey, it was the Third Fleet. Spruance commanded until May 27, 1945, when Halsey took over and oversaw naval operations for the rest of the Okinawa campaign.

5. Lieutenant General Simon Bolivar Buckner Jr., Biographical Notes, Record Group 407, Entry 427, Box 2443, Folder 110-1.19, NA; Lieutenant General Simon Buckner, letter to Adele Buckner, March 26, 1945, in A. P. Jenkins, editor, "Lieutenant General Simon Bolivar Buckner: Private Letters Relating to the Battle of Okinawa," Simon Bolivar Buckner Papers, Box 1; Lieutenant General Simon Bolivar Buckner Jr. diary contains many references to athletic activities, Simon Bolivar Buckner Papers, Box 1, EL; William Buckner, Interview with Mr. Brainard Parrish, September 17, 2005, p. 5, NMPW; Captain Russell Gugeler, "Operations of the 7th Infantry Division on Okinawa, 1 April–22 June 1945," Volume 1, pp. 8–9, 8-5.3 AAv1, CMH; PFC Ellis Moore, letter to Peggy, April 16, 1945, USAMHI; David Wittels, "These Are the Generals," *Saturday Evening Post,* May 8, 1943, 102; "Buck's Battle," *Time,* April 16, 1945, 32; Sharon Lacey, "The Peacemaker," *World War II,* July–August 2013, 43–47; Nicholas Evan Sarantakes, ed., *Seven Stars: The Okinawa Battle Diaries of Simon Bolivar Buckner, Jr., and Joseph Stilwell* (College Station: Texas A&M University Press, 2004), 3–9; Appleman et al., *Okinawa: The Last Battle,* 25–27, 492; Battle of Okinawa entry at www.historyofwar.org. For an in-depth discussion of what is generally known as the Smith versus Smith controversy, see pages 362–71 and 391–97 of *Island Infernos: The U.S. Army's Pacific War Odyssey, 1944,* the second book in this trilogy. Admirals Spruance and Turner both preferred Marine Lieutenant General Holland Smith to command Tenth Army, but after the Saipan fiasco, there was no chance that Lieutenant General Robert Richardson or any other Army leader would ever again allow soldiers to come under Holland Smith's control. In that sense, Buckner was a compromise choice as Tenth Army commander, owing to his ability to lead a unified interservice team.

6. Captain Paul Leach, The Operations of the 77th Infantry Division in the Kerama Retto, Record Group 319, Entry 64, Box 3, Records of the Office of the Chief of Military History, Okinawa the Last Battle, NA; Appleman, "XXIV Corps in the Conquest of Okinawa," Volume 1, pp. 31–33, CMH; Glenn Searles, unpublished memoir, p. 14, copy in author's possession; Men Who Were There, *Ours to Hold It High: The History of the 77th Infantry Division in World War II*, ed. Max Myers (Washington, DC: Infantry Journal Press, 1947), 228–39; Appleman et al., *Okinawa: The Last Battle*, 52–60; Morison, *History of United States Naval Operations in World War II*, vol. 14, 117–29; Belote and Belote, *Typhoon of Steel*, 43–46.

7. Tenth Army Report of Operations in the Ryukyu Campaign, September 3, 1945, Chapter 11, Section V, pp. 1, 6, Record Group 337, Entry 15A, Box 76, Folder 607, NA; Tenth Army, Amphibious Operations, Capture of Okinawa (Ryukyus Operation), 27 March to 21 June 1945, Volume 1, Chapter 2, p. 36, CARL; Appleman, "XXIV Corps in the Conquest of Okinawa," Volume 1, pp. 34–40, CMH; Morison, *History of United States Naval Operations in World War II*, vol. 14, 130–40; Appleman et al., *Okinawa: The Last Battle*, 14–17, 45–47, 64–70; Feifer, *Tennozan*, 88–93.

8. Captain Lauren Soth, 96th Infantry Division Deadeyes on Okinawa, no pagination, Record Group 319, Entry 64, Box 3, Records of the Office of the Chief of Military History, Okinawa the Last Battle; 7th Infantry Division, Operations Report on Ryukyus-Okinawa Campaign, p. 39, Record Group 127, Box 255, World War II Area Geographic Files, Folder A32-5-1; 6th Marine Division, Special Action Report, Phase I, Record Group 127, World War II Area Geographic Files, Folder A32-1, all at NA; 96th Infantry Division, Action Report, Chapter VII, p. 3, CARL; Captain Leo Smith, "The Landing on Okinawa and the Securing of the Beachhead by the 2d Battalion, 383d Infantry (96th Division) 1 April to 8 April, Personal Experience of a Battalion S-3," Advanced Infantry Officers Course, 1947–1948, Fort Benning, GA, p. 7, DRL; Corporal Aram Philibosian, letter to Philip, September 5, 1945, Folder 2328, Accession #1580, SHSM; Lloyd Pierson, unpublished memoir, p. 29, World War II Veterans Survey #8977, USAMHI; Lieutenant General Simon Buckner, letter to Adele Buckner, April 1, 1945, in Jenkins, editor, "Private Letters Relating to the Battle of Okinawa," EL; Appleman, "XXIV Corps in the Conquest of Okinawa," Volume 1, pp. 88–91; Gugeler, "Operations of the 7th Infantry Division on Okinawa," Volume 1, 124–33, both at CMH; S. Lacey, "Into the Inferno," 36; E. B. Sledge, *With the Old Breed: At Peleliu and Okinawa* (New York: Oxford University Press, 1990), 188; Donald O. Dencker, *Love Company: Infantry Combat Against the Japanese, World War II: Leyte and Okinawa* (Manhattan, KS: Sunflower University Press, 2002), 163–64; Appleman et al., *Okinawa: The Last Battle*, 72–75; Yahara, *The Battle for Okinawa*, xxii–xiv; Belote and Belote, *Typhoon of Steel*, 53–63; Sarantakes, *Seven Stars*, 30; Edmund G. Love, *The Hourglass: History of the 7th Infantry Division in World War II* (Washington, DC: Infantry Journal Press, 1950), 299.

9. Army Service Forces, 205th Hospital Ship Complement, USS *Comfort*, Report of Activities on the Night of April 28, 1945, World War II Battle Operations and Reports, Box 43, Folder 5; Fifth Fleet Action Report, Section G, Medical Report, p. 7, both at USNA; Appleman, "XXIV Corps in the Conquest of Okinawa," Volume 1, pp. 97–103, CMH; Richard Spencer, unpublished memoir, pp. 18–19, World War II Veterans Survey, no number; Major General Andrew Bruce, letter to Colonel Vincent Tanzola, January 18, 1945; Major General Andrew Bruce, letter to Mrs. Vincent Tanzola, April 4, 1945; Major General Andrew Bruce, Memo for Major General John Hodge, April 22, 1945, in Andrew Bruce Papers, Boxes 6 and 8 respectively, all at USAMHI; Lieutenant Larry McDonnell, letter to family, circa

1945, Folder 2104, Accession #2040; Seaman Harry Hymon, letter to Elsie Hymon, September 9, 1945, Folder 1420, Accession #2856; Donald Gutglueck, letter to parents, May 28, 1945, Folder 1147, Accession #1086; Yeoman Second Class W. L. "Bud" Wissel, letter to parents, circa 1945, Folder 3274, Accession #2646; Seaman Second Class William Oyler, letter to Mr. William Oyler, circa 1945, Folder 2249, Accession #2794, all at SHSM; Kanji Suzuki as told to Tadaeo Morimoto, translated by Kan Sugahara, "A Kamikaze's Story," *MHQ*, Spring 1995, 44–47; Chris Klein, "When a US Hospital Ship was Attacked by a Kamikaze Pilot in World War II," May 1, 2020, at www.history.com; "Poland Nurse Killed in War to Be Honored at Waterville," *Lewiston Evening Journal*, circa 1945, on www.ww2veteranshistory project.org, accessed 2019; Morison, *History of United States Naval Operations in World War II*, vol. 14, 180–98, 233–47, 390–92; Appleman et al., *Okinawa: The Last Battle*, 96–102, 360–64; *Ours to Hold It High*, 253–54; Feifer, *Tennozan*, 204–5; Charles O. West, *Second to None: The Story of the 305th Infantry in World War II* (Washington, DC: Infantry Journal Press, 1949), 159; Gerald Astor, *Operation Iceberg: The Invasion and Conquest of Okinawa in World War II—An Oral History* (New York: Dell, 1995), 187; Cook and Cook, *Japan at War*, 324–25; Toll, *Twilight of the Gods*, 372–75. Astor claims that Bruce had considered relieving Tanzola before his death. Bruce's April 22 report to Hodge seems to corroborate Bruce's presence aboard *Chilton* during the kamikaze attack.

10. Captain Paul Leach, Ie Shima, pp. 1, 12–13, Record Group 319, Entry 64, Box 5, Records of the Office of the Chief of Military History, Okinawa the Last Battle, NA; 77th Infantry Division, Battle of Ie Shima; Major General Andrew Bruce, letter to Lieutenant General Simon Buckner, April 20, 1945, both in Andrew Bruce Papers, Box 8; Captain Randy Seligman, letter to Lieutenant Mary Jane Anderson, April 28, 1945, all at USAMHI; Major Mills Brown, "The Operations of the 306th Infantry (77th Infantry Division) on Ie Shima 16 April–21 April 1945, Personal Experiences of a Regimental Operations Officer," Advanced Infantry Officers Course, 1947–1948, Fort Benning, GA, pp. 18–19, DRL; Searles, unpublished memoir, p. 18; George R. Nelson, *I Company: The First and Last to Fight on Okinawa*, self-published (Bloomington, IN, 2003), 217–18, 229; Appleman et al., *Okinawa: The Last Battle*, 149–62; West, *Second to None*, 167; Morison, *History of United States Naval Operations in World War II*, vol. 14, 239–41; *Ours to Hold It High*, 258–64; Belote and Belote, *Typhoon of Steel*, 180–81.

11. Sergeant Richard Hutchison, letter to parents, April 20, 1945, Folder 1415, Accession #1160, SHSM; Major General Andrew Bruce, letter to Major General John Hodge, April 19, 1945, Andrew Bruce Papers, Box 8; Statement of General Bruce on the Death of Ernie Pyle; Major General Andrew Bruce, letter to Mrs. Jerry Pyle, April 30, 1945; Mrs. Jerry Pyle, letter to Major General Andrew Bruce, July 30, 1945; Major General Andrew Bruce, letters to Mr. Lee Miller, September 27, December 7, 1945, all in Andrew Bruce Papers, Box 10; R. D. and Minnie Warman, letter to Major General Andrew Bruce, circa 1945; Major General Andrew Bruce, letters to Mr. and Mrs. Warman, July 19, August 31, 1945; Captain Vincent Calandrillo, Memo for Commanding General, 77th Infantry Division, August 28, 1945, all in Andrew Bruce Papers, Box 11; PFC Ellis Moore, letter to Aunt Janie, May 6, 1945, all at USAMHI; Searles, unpublished memoir, p. 18; Nelson, *I Company: First and Last to Fight*, p. 219–21; Roy Morris Jr., "'Ernie Was One of Us,'" *MHQ*, Autumn 2020, 36–45; Belote and Belote, *Typhoon of Steel*, 177–78; Appleman et al., *Okinawa: The Last Battle*, 162–83; *Ours to Hold It High*, 264–81; Astor, *Operation Iceberg*, 270–71. Hutchison was an antiaircraft soldier who saw Pyle's body. His account corroborates every detail related in the other sources. Geraldine Pyle

struggled with alcoholism and suicidal depression. The couple had actually divorced in the spring of 1942 and remarried a year later. She survived several suicide attempts, but on November 21, 1945, she died of acute uremia.

12. Lieutenant Russell Gugeler, Notes from Interview with Lieutenant Colonel James Green, April 28, 1945, Record Group 319, Entry 64, Box 4, Records of the Office of the Chief of Military History, Okinawa the Last Battle; 7th Infantry Division, Operations Report, both at NA; Gugeler, "Operations of the 7th Infantry Division on Okinawa," Volume 1, pp. 36–37; Appleman, "XXIV Corps in the Conquest of Okinawa," Volume 1, pp. 110–19, both at CMH; Captain John Blair, "The Operations of 'E' Company, 381st Infantry (96th Infantry Division) in the Attack and Consolidation of Positions on Kakazu West, Okinawa, 10–15 April 1945, Personal Experience of a Company Commander," Advanced Infantry Officers Course, 1949–1950, Fort Benning, GA, p. 7, DRL; 96th Infantry Division, Action Report, Chapter VII, p. 11, CARL; Bob Green, *Okinawa Odyssey* (Albany, TX: Bright Sky Press, 2004), 114; Art Shaw, with Robert L. Wise, *82 Days on Okinawa: One American's Unforgettable Firsthand Account of the Pacific War's Greatest Battle* (New York: William Morrow, 2020), 64; Orlando R. Davidson, J. Carl Willems, and Joseph A. Kahl, *The Deadeyes: The Story of the 96th Infantry Division* (Washington, DC: Infantry Journal Press, 1947), 102–13; Appleman et al., *Okinawa: The Last Battle,* 107–25; Love, *The Hourglass,* 304; Astor, *Operation Iceberg,* 229.

13. 32nd Army Direction Number 12, March 12, 1945, in Tenth Army G2 translations of captured Japanese documents, Record Group 407, Entry 427, Box 2453, Folder 110-2.9; Lieutenant Jesse Rogers, Combat Interviews, April 12–13, 1945, Record Group 319, Entry 64, Box 5, Records of the Office of the Chief of Military History, Okinawa the Last Battle; 7th Infantry Division, Operations Report, all at NA; Captain Donald Mulford and Lieutenant Jesse Rogers, "96th Division Action on Okinawa, 1 April–30 June 1945," Volume 1, pp. 58–64, 8-5.3 ACvl; Gugeler, "Operations of the 7th Infantry Division on Okinawa," Volume 1, p. 87; Japanese Monograph Number 135, pp. 62–67, all at CMH; Huber, "Japan's Battle of Okinawa," pp. 30–35, 41–47, CARL; Blair, "Operations of 'E' Company, 381st Infantry," pp. 31–32, DRL; Beauford Anderson Medal of Honor citation and other information at www .arlingtoncemetery.net; Davidson et al., *The Deadeyes,* 112–13; Belote and Belote, *Typhoon of Steel,* 136–40; Appleman et al., *Okinawa: The Last Battle,* 130–37. The Imperial Army sometimes named units after their commanders.

14. 27th Infantry Division, Nansei Shoto, Phase I, Record Group 407, Entry 427, Box 7210, Folder 327-0.3; 382nd Infantry Regiment, After Action Report, Ryukyus Operation, 1 April–30 June 1945, Chapter VIII, Infantry Combat, p. 2, Record Group 407, Entry 427, Box 11554, Folder 396-INF-382-0.3; Captain Roy Appleman, Historian's journal, June 1945, p. 2, Record Group 319, Entry 64, Box 4, Records of the Office of the Chief of Military History, Okinawa the Last Battle; Battle Lessons and Enemy Tank Tactics, Based on the Combat Experience of the Kaya Detachment, pp. 2–3, in Tenth Army G2 Translation Number 85; Tenth Army Report of Operations, Chapter 11, Section IX, p. 2, all at NA; Captain Edmund Love, "Narrative of the Operations of the 27th Infantry Division on Okinawa," Chapter IV, 8-5.3 AD; Captain Donald Mulford and Lieutenant Jesse Rogers, "96th Division Action on Okinawa, 1 April–30 June 1945," Volume 2, pp. 17–33, 8-5.3 ACv2; Appleman, "XXIV Corps in the Conquest of Okinawa," Volume 1, pp. 150–65, all at CMH; Melvin Coobs World War II Veterans Survey #2403, USAMHI; Lieutenant General Simon Buckner, letter to Adele Buckner, April 14, 1945, in Jenkins, editor, "Private Letters Relating to the Battle of Okinawa"; Lieutenant General Simon Buckner diary, April 15–25, 1945, both at EL; Sarantakes, *Seven Stars,* 39; Dencker,

Love Company, 193; Edmund G. Love, *The 27th Infantry Division in World War II* (Nashville: Battery Press, 1949), 531–49; Appleman et al., *Okinawa: The Last Battle*, 184–207.

15. Major General Andrew Bruce, letter to Lieutenant General Simon Buckner, April 20, 1945; Major General Andrew Bruce, letter to Major General John Hodge, April 19, 1945; Major General Andrew Bruce, letter to Brigadier General Walter Dumas, April 15, 1945, all in Andrew Bruce Papers, Box 8; Major General Andrew Bruce, Statement about article "General Buckner's Decision Against a Second Landing on Okinawa," Andrew Bruce Papers, Box 10; Yahara, letter to Belote, all at USAMHI; Major General Andrew Bruce, letter to Major General Harry Maloney, December 11, 1948; Brigadier General Oliver Smith, letter to Brigadier General Harry Maloney, July 30, 1946; Brigadier General Lawrence Schick, letter to Lieutenant Colonel John Stevens, June 13, 1946; Brigadier General David Blakelock, letter to Lieutenant Colonel John Stevens, February 8, 1946, all in Record Group 319, Entry 64, Box 4, Records of the Office of the Chief of Military History, Okinawa the Last Battle; Yahara, Interrogation Report, p. 7, all at NA; Lieutenant General Simon Buckner, letter to Adele Buckner, April 27, 1945, in Jenkins, editor, "Private Letters Relating to the Battle of Okinawa," EL; Admiral Chester Nimitz, Graybooks, Volume VI, Summary, April 22–24, 1945; Historical Division, Department of the Army, "General Buckner's Decision Against a Second Landing on Okinawa," *Military Review*, November 1948, 8–10; Sarantakes, *Seven Stars*, 48; E. B. Potter, *Nimitz* (Annapolis, MD: Naval Institute Press, 1976), 373–76; Frank and Shaw, *Victory and Occupation*, 195–97; Appleman et al., *Okinawa: The Last Battle*, 258–64, 491; Yahara, *The Battle for Okinawa*, 213; Morison, *History of United States Naval Operations in World War II*, vol. 14, 390–91; Belote and Belote, *Typhoon of Steel*, 212–14. Major General Pedro Del Valle, commander of the 1st Marine Division, and Major General Lemuel Shepherd, commander of the 6th Marine Division, both favored a second amphibious landing.

16. Major General John Hodge, letter to Major Roy Appleman, February 1, 1946; Brigadier General Elwyn Post, letter to Lieutenant Colonel John Stevens, June 10, 1946; Bruce, letter to Maloney, all in Record Group 319, Entry 64, Records of the Office of the Chief of Military History, Okinawa the Last Battle; Appleman, Historian's journal, July 1, 1945, all at NA; Brigadier General Elwyn "E.D." Post, memo for Major General Andrew Bruce, April 21, 1945, Andrew Bruce Papers, Box 10; Brigadier General Edwin Randle, letter to Major General Andrew Bruce, May 12, 1949, Andrew Bruce Papers, Box 6, both at USAMHI; General Joseph Stilwell diary, June 5, 1945, www.hoover.org; Historical Division, "General Buckner's Decision Against a Second Landing on Okinawa," 9–13; Belote and Belote, *Typhoon of Steel*, 213–14; Frank and Shaw, *Victory and Occupation*, 195–97; E. Potter, *Nimitz*, 375; Appleman et al., *Okinawa: The Last Battle*, 258–64. In Hodge's letter to Appleman, the XXIV Corps commander defended Buckner's decision, even though he was clearly on the record in the spring of 1945 as favoring a second invasion. Most likely, Hodge withheld his criticism of Buckner's decision out of respect for the memory of a general who lost his life in combat less than a year before Hodge wrote the letter.

17. Master Sergeant James MacGregor Burns, Historian's journal, May 21, 1945; Major John Stevens, Historian's journal, May 1945, both in Record Group 319, Entry 64, Box 4, Records of the Office of the Chief of Military History, Okinawa the Last Battle; Lieutenant Colonel Robert Williams, Observer Report on the Okinawa Operation, May 1, 1945, Record Group 127, Box 272, World War II Area Geographic Files, Folder A96-2; Tenth Army, Report of Operations, Chapter 8, p. 2, all at NA;

Major Joseph Vering, "The Operations of the 382d Infantry (96th Infantry Division) in the Penetration of the Japanese Naha-Shuri-Yonabaru Line, on Okinawa, 10 May–31 May 1945, Personal Experience of a Company Commander," Advanced Infantry Officers Course, Fort Benning, GA, pp. 10, 24, DRL; Appleman, "XXIV Corps in the Conquest of Okinawa," Volume 2, 8-5.3 AVv2, pp. 255–57, CMH; Herman Buffington, unpublished memoir, no pagination, AFC/2001/001/70500, LOC; Combat Lessons Number 9, Rank and File in Combat, p. 21, CARL; Astor, *Operation Iceberg*, 469–70.

18. Captain Bernard Borning, "Ryukyus Campaign, Artillery on Okinawa," pp. 12–19, 8-5.3 FA, CMH; Tenth Army, Amphibious Operations, Capture of Okinawa, Volume 1, Chapter 2, pp. 36–41, CARL; Tenth Army, Report of Operations, Chapter 11, Section V, p. 19, Section VII, p. 6; 7th Infantry Division, Report of Operations, pp. 68–69, both at NA; Captain Lawrence Fawcett, "Operations of the 81-MM Mortar Platoon, Company 'D,' 305th Infantry (77th Division) in Support of the 1st Battalion During the Advance on Shuri, Okinawa, 7–15 May 1945, Personal Experience of an 81-mm Mortar Platoon Leader," Advanced Infantry Officers Course, 1948–1949, Fort Benning, GA, p. 28, DRL; Martin Allday, Interview with Dr. Ronald Marcello, October 8, 1994, Number 1047, p. 20, University of North Texas Oral History Collection (UNT), Denton, TX; Appleman et al., *Okinawa: The Last Battle*, 498–501.

19. Infantry sergeant comments are in: Notes from conference in S Room, June 21, 1945, p. 20, Record Group 337, Entry 15A, Box 72, Folder 512; 382nd, AAR, Chapter VIII, Infantry Combat, p. 2; 7th Infantry Division, Report of Operations, pp. 68–69, all at NA; 96th Infantry Division, Action Report, Chapter IX, pp. 4, 13–14; Combat Lessons Number 9, Rank and File in Combat, p. 22, both at CARL; Major General Andrew Bruce, letter to Admiral Chester Nimitz, May 3, 1945; Major General Andrew Bruce, letter to Mrs. J. D. Kreiss, May 1, 1945, both in Andrew Bruce Papers, Box 10; Mrs. Martha Bruce, letter to Major General Andrew Bruce, May 1945, Andrew Bruce Papers, Box 7; John Moore, World War II Veterans Survey #4648, all at USAMHI; Allday interview, p. 26, UNT; Captain Pat LaValle, letter to Ms. Clara Ridolofo, June 6, 1945, Folder 1727, Accession #1350, SHSM; Buffington, unpublished memoir, LOC; Searles, unpublished memoir, p. 24; Appleman et al., *Okinawa: The Last Battle*, 256.

20. Pacific Warfare Board Report, Battle Experiences Against the Japanese, Number 50, August 11, 1945, p. 2, Record Group 337, Entry 15A, Box 59, Folder 230; Lieutenant Paul Leach, Historian's journal, May 16, 1945, Record Group 319, Entry 64, Box 4, Records of the Office of the Chief of Military History, Okinawa the Last Battle; Sergeant Bert Balmer, "Japanese Counter-Tactics against U.S. Infantry-Tank Teams," pp. 13–22, Record Group 319, Entry 64, Box 3, Records of the Office of the Chief of Military History, Okinawa the Last Battle; 382nd Infantry Regiment, AAR, Chapter VIII, Infantry Combat, p. 2; Williams, Observer Report on the Okinawa Operation, p. 34; Tenth Army, Report of Operations, Chapter 11, Section IX, p. 7, all at NA; Major J. L. Balthis et al., "Armor on Okinawa," Committee 1, Officers Advanced Course, The Armored School, 1948–1949, Fort Knox, KY, pp. 2, 57–60, 71–72, 142–43, DRL; Captain Dennis Neill, "A Tank Company on Okinawa," Advanced Officers Class #1, 1948, The Armored School, Fort Knox, KY, p. 13; 713th Tank Battalion, After Action Report, 10 November 1944 through 30 June 1945, pp. 1–2, Chapter VII, pp. 1–2; 711th Tank Battalion, After Action Report, no pagination; Huber, "Japan's Battle of Okinawa," pp. 67–69, all at CARL; Appleman, "XXIV Corps in the Conquest of Okinawa," Volume 2, pp. 201–2, CMH; John Ryan, Interview with Mr. Clarence Brick, September 13, 2003, p. 10, NMPW; Frank

and Shaw, *Victory and Occupation,* 386; Green, *Okinawa Odyssey,* 68–70, 132, 144, 155–57; Astor, *Operation Iceberg,* 304–5; Appleman et al., *Okinawa: The Last Battle,* 386–87. The Americans also used flame tanks in the Battle of Iwo Jima.

21. Appleman, "XXIV Corps in the Conquest of Okinawa," Volume 2, pp. 304–28; Japanese Monograph Number 135, pp. 77–84, both at CMH; Marvin Schroeder, unpublished memoir, p. 6, World War II Veterans Survey, no number; Koichi Ito, Interview with Drs. James and William Belote, July 20, 1967, William and James Belote Papers, Box 3, both at USAMHI; Yahara Interrogation Report, pp. 8–9, NA; Huber, "Japan's Battle of Okinawa," pp. 82–91, CARL; Belote and Belote, *Typhoon of Steel,* 218–19; Appleman et al., *Okinawa: The Last Battle,* 283–302; Yahara, *The Battle for Okinawa,* 41–44, 53–55.

22. Master Sergeant James MacGregor Burns, Correspondent's Briefing, May 27, 1945, Historian's journal, May 21, 1945; Appleman, Historian's journal, June 2, 4, 1945; Leach, Historian's journal, May 9, 1945; Soth, 96th Infantry Division Deadeyes on Okinawa, no pagination, all at NA; Captain Donald Mulford and Lieutenant Jesse Rogers, "96th Division Action on Okinawa, 1 April–30 June 1945," Volume 3, pp. 140–41, 8-5.3 ACv3; Major Roy Appleman, "XXIV Corps in the Conquest of Okinawa, 1 April–22 June 1945," Volume 3, pp. 430–31, 458–60, 8-5.3 ABv3, both at CMH; Spencer, unpublished memoir, p. 22, USAMHI; PFC Horace Floyd, letter to family, June 5, 1945, Folder 924, Accession #1036; PFC Frank Kittek, letter to family, September 9, 1945, Folder 1650, Accession #1304, both at SHSM; Edmund Austin, Oral History, p. 6, NMPW; Allday interview, pp. 34–35, UNT; Jean Rowland, handwritten notes, copy in author's possession courtesy of Dr. Paul Rowland; Nicholas Evan Sarantakes, "Interservice Relations: The Army and the Marines at the Battle of Okinawa," *Infantry* 89, no. 1 (January–April 1999): 12–15; Sarantakes, *Seven Stars,* 78–80; Appleman et al., *Okinawa: The Last Battle,* 422–23; Sledge, *With the Old Breed,* 223, 258, 283–84. Columnist David Lawrence of the *Washington Evening Star,* from the distant vantage point of the capital, excoriated Buckner for deciding against a second landing. Lawrence argued that Buckner's decision was evidence of the Army's hidebound, conservative outlook in contrast to the more innovative Marines, who knew more about amphibious invasions. Needless to say, the argument had no basis in any fact, and only revealed Lawrence's complete ignorance of the Army's extensive amphibious-warfare experience as well as the particulars of how many Army officers favored the second landing at Okinawa.

23. Lieutenant Paul Leach, Historical Report, Okinawa Campaign, pp. 16–21, Record Group 319, Entry 64, Box 3, Records of the Office of the Chief of Military History, Okinawa the Last Battle; Leach, Historian's journal, May 6, 1945; Tenth Army, Report of Operations, Chapter 11, Section XV, pp. 1, 24–26, all at NA; Mulford and Rogers, "96th Division Action on Okinawa," Volume 2, p. 50, CMH; PFC Paul Kaup, letter to parents, May 31, 1945, Folder 1579, Accession #2709; Tech 4 Nathan Model, letter to parents, July 3, 1945, Folder 1864, Accession #2268, both at SHSM; Spencer, unpublished memoir, p. 21, USAMHI; Desmond Doss, video interview, no date, AFC/2001/001/89672; Desmond Doss, Oral History, no date, AFC/2001/001/33796; Desmond Doss, Personal Narrative, video interview with Michael Willie, April 14, 2003, AFC/2001/001/32978; Buffington, unpublished memoir, no pagination, LOC; Searles, unpublished memoir, pp. 25–26; Katie Lange, "PFC Desmond Doss: The Unlikely Hero Behind 'Hacksaw Ridge,'" at www.army.mil; also see more information at www.desmondoss.com; Captain Lauren K. Soth, "Hacksaw Ridge on Okinawa," *Infantry Journal,* August 1945, 11; *Ours to Hold It High,* 303–7; Condon-Rall and Cowdrey, *Medical Service in the War Against Japan,*

395; Appleman et al., *Okinawa: The Last Battle,* 282–83; Sledge, *With the Old Breed,* 257. The contemporary sources claim that Doss saved fifty men. Postwar sources put the number at seventy-five or more, but Doss himself disagreed with that larger tally. "I didn't see how it could possibly be over fifty and I still don't," he commented decades later in an interview. He was immortalized in the 2016 movie *Hacksaw Ridge.* My wife Nancy's grandfather was a veteran of the 77th Division in World War I. When Nancy was a child, her family lived in the Chattanooga, Tennessee, area, as did Desmond Doss. During one of her grandfather's visits, my father-in-law took him to Doss's house for an impromptu visit. The two 77th Division veterans of different wars seemed to share an immediate bond and spent a pleasant afternoon together. Doss subsequently paid a visit to their church's Cub Scout pack, which included my brother-in-law, and taught them how to tie knots as he had at Hacksaw Ridge.

24. 106th Infantry Regiment, Unit Report, Okinawa, p. 20, Record Group 407, Entry 427, Box 7315, Folder 327-INF-106-0.3; 148th General Hospital, Annual Report, 1945, p. 6, Record Group 112, Entry UD1012, Surgeon General, HUMEDS, Box 37; Lieutenant Paul Leach, Notes on the Okinawa Campaign, Record Group 319, Entry 64, Box 3, Records of the Office of the Chief of Military History, Okinawa the Last Battle; Leach, Historian's journal, May 5, 1945, all at NA; Army Ground Forces, Battle Casualties, Study, p. 12, CMH; Administrative History of Medical Activities in the Middle Pacific, Office of the Surgeon, 1946, pp. 26–27, US Army Forces Middle Pacific, Office of the Surgeon Collection, Box 1, Block 8; Lieutenant Catharine Breisacher, History of Nursing Activities on Okinawa, pp. 1–2, Medical Corps, 233rd General Hospital, Box 1; Legion of Merit Recommendation and Supporting Affidavits for Lieutenant James Wong, Surgeon, 3rd Battalion, 305th Infantry Regiment, December 20, 1945, Andrew Bruce Papers, Box 7; Gage Rodman, unpublished memoir, pp. 1–8, letter to parents, May 14, 1945, Gage Rodman Papers, Box 5; John Tobey, World War II Veterans Survey, no number, all at USAMHI; Lieutenant General Simon Buckner, letter to Adele Buckner, May 3, 1945, in Jenkins, editor, "Private Letters Relating to the Battle of Okinawa," EL; Lieutenant Richard R. Beck, "With the Army on Okinawa," *Military Surgeon* 97, no. 3 (September 1945): 232–34; Sarantakes, *Seven Stars,* 50; Condon-Rall and Cowdrey, *Medical Service in the War Against Japan,* 401, 406–8; Appleman et al., *Okinawa: The Last Battle,* 412–15.

25. Captain Donald Mulford, Historian's journal, May 26, 1945, Record Group 319, Entry 64, Box 4, Records of the Office of the Chief of Military History, Okinawa the Last Battle; Leach, Notes on the Okinawa Campaign; Tenth Army, Report of Operations, Chapter 9, Section IV, p. 1, Chapter 11, Section I, Figure 12, all at NA; Statistics of the Pacific Campaigns, OPRST 050, CMH; Administrative History of Medical Activities in the Middle Pacific, Office of the Surgeon, Neuropsychiatry, 1946, p. 11, US Army Forces Middle Pacific, Office of the Surgeon Collection, Box 1, Block 16; Captain DeWitt Smith, Personal Adjustment in the Division, November 3, 1944, p. 4, US Army Forces, Middle Pacific, Office of the Surgeon General Collection, Box 1, Block 16, all at USAMHI; Fawcett, "Operations of the 81-MM Mortar Platoon," p. 22, DRL; Searles, unpublished memoir, pp. 26–27; Russell Davis, *Marine at War* (Boston: Little, Brown, 1961), 209; Green, *Okinawa Odyssey,* 140–41; Condon-Rall and Cowdrey, *Medical Service in the War Against Japan,* 403–4; Appleman et al., *Okinawa: The Last Battle,* 384–87, 473, 490–91; Sledge, *With the Old Breed,* 270–71.

26. Master Sergeant James MacGregor Burns, Major John Stevens, Historian's journals, May 18, 19, 21, 1945; Tenth Army Report of Operations, Chapter 11, Section I,

pp. 16–22; Yahara, Interrogation Report, pp. 8–9, all at NA; United States Army Forces in the Pacific Ocean Areas, Participation in the Okinawa Operation, pp. 9–10, 370.2; Japanese Monograph Number 135, pp. 89–99, both at CMH; 77th Infantry Division, G1 Study, June 10, 1945, p. 3, Andrew Bruce Papers, Box 7; Major General Andrew Bruce, letter to Major General Clark Ruffner, May 23, 1945, Andrew Bruce Papers, Box 10; Staff Sergeant Alfred Junkin, letter to Lieutenant Colonel Gerald Cooney, May 21, 1945, Andrew Bruce Papers, Box 8, all at US-AMHI; Allday interview, p. 14, UNT; Huber, "Japan's Battle of Okinawa," pp. 92–102, CARL; Cook and Cook, *Japan at War,* 357; Yahara, *The Battle for Okinawa,* 71–103; Appleman et al., *Okinawa: The Last Battle,* 387–402, 488.

27. Tenth Army Civil Affairs Plan for Okinawa and III Amphibious Corps General Order #33, Instruction to Troops Concerning Military Government, Record Group 127, Box 278, World War II Area Geographic Files, Folder B16-3; Counterintelligence Corps on Okinawa, July 8, 1945, pp. 1–4, Record Group 337, Entry 15A, Box 63, Folder 354; Tenth Army Report of Operations, Chapter 9, Section II, p. 1; Appleman, Historian's journal, June 22, 1945; Stevens, Historian's journal, June 19, 1945, claims that Tenth Army had recorded only five rape cases and two felonious assaults by that time, all these sources at NA; Kosuke Matayoshi, Interview with Drs. James and William Belote, July 12, 1967; Tokuyu Higashionna, Interview with Drs. James and William Belote, July 12, 1967, both in William and James Belote Papers, Box 3, USAMHI; Lieutenant General Simon Buckner, letter to Adele Buckner, April 17, 1945, in Jenkins, editor, "Private Letters Relating to the Battle of Okinawa," EL; Mulford and Rogers, "96th Division Action on Okinawa," Volume 3, pp. 264–65; Appleman, "XXIV Corps in the Conquest of Okinawa," Volume 1, pp. 137–42; Captain Charles Lidster, letter to Mrs. R. M. Dennison, August 2, 1945, Folder 1764, Accession #2758; PFC Jeff Crabtree, letter to My Boy Danny, Folder 592, Accession #899; Floyd letter, all at SHSM; John Sloup, Interview with Mr. Floyd Cox, July 19, 2002, p. 14; Peter Bourgeois, Interview with Mr. Richard Misenhimer, January 18, 2002, p. 12, both at NMPW; Feifer, "The Ghosts of Okinawa," 63–69; Feifer, *Tennozan,* 446–63, 533; Cook and Cook, *Japan at War,* 357–58; Sarantakes, *Seven Stars,* 41; Appleman et al., *Okinawa: The Last Battle,* 415–19; Astor, *Operation Iceberg,* 245; Condon-Rall and Cowdrey, *Medical Service in the War Against Japan,* 408–9; Belote and Belote, *Typhoon of Steel,* 184–89; Sledge, *With the Old Breed,* 199.

28. Major John Stevens, Historian's journal, June 18, 1945; Captain Roy Appleman, Historian's journal, June 19, 1945, both at NA; Major Roy Appleman, "The XXIV Corps in the Conquest of Okinawa, 1 April–22 June 1945," Volume 4, pp. 584–87, 8-5.3 ABv4, CMH; Buckner, diary, June 17, 1945, EL; Stilwell diary, June 5–6, 1945; "General's Burial," *Time,* July 2, 1945, 30; "Buckner's Creed," *Newsweek,* July 2, 1945, 33–34; S. Lacey, "The Peacemaker," 47; Sarantakes, *Seven Stars,* 83–84, 87–89; Frank and Shaw, *Victory and Occupation,* 353–54; Astor, *Operation Iceberg,* 492–93; Belote and Belote, *Typhoon of Steel,* 307–8; Appleman et al., *Okinawa: The Last Battle,* 461. Buckner was observing an attack by the newly arrived 8th Marine Regiment when he was killed. The 8th was organically part of the 2nd Marine Division, but on Okinawa it was temporarily under the control of the 1st Marine Division. Lesley McNair was a three-star general like Buckner, but McNair was killed in Normandy by friendly fire, not due to enemy action.

29. Captain Russell Gugeler, "Operations of the 7th Infantry Division on Okinawa, 1 April–22 June 1945," Volume 3, pp. 495–99, 8-5.3 AAv3; Appleman, "XXIV Corps in the Conquest of Okinawa," Volume 4, pp. 606–12, both at CMH; Tokuzo

Makiminato, Interview with Drs. James and William Belote, July 13, 1967, William and James Belote Papers, Box 3, USAMHI; 7th Infantry Division telegram relating to discovery of the bodies of Lieutenant Generals Ushijima and Cho, Loren Erickson Collection, #2009.196, WWIIM; Yahara Interrogation, p. 8, NA; Huber, "Japan's Battle of Okinawa," pp. 111–16, CARL; S. Lacey, "Into the Inferno," 42–43; Toland, *Decline and Fall of the Japanese Empire,* 895; Belote and Belote, *Typhoon of Steel,* 317–18; Frank and Shaw, *Victory and Occupation,* 365–68; Appleman et al., *Okinawa: The Last Battle,* 470–71; Yahara, *The Battle for Okinawa,* 134–56. After the war, unproven stories circulated that Cho and Ushijima shot themselves rather than commit ritual hara-kiri, a somewhat scurrilous accusation because this would have been a less honorable means of suicide. The contemporary American sources seem to confirm that both generals committed hara-kiri.

30. Provost Marshal Statement to House of Representatives, April 26, 1945, and Provost Marshal Semi-Monthly Report on Prisoners of War as of August 1, 1945, both part of Provost Marshal Prisoner of War Operations, Tabs 11-116, 4-4.3 AAv3Cl; Appleman, "XXIV Corps in the Conquest of Okinawa," Volume 4, pp. 625–32, both at CMH; Major General John Hodge, Interview with Captain Roy Appleman, notes recorded in Historian's journal, June 19, 1945; Tenth Army, Report of Operations, Chapter 9, Section II, p. 3, Section IV, p. 1, both at NA; Major James Emerson, "Military Police Operations in the Okinawa Campaign," pp. 39–41, Master's Thesis, United States Army Command and General Staff College, 1995, Fort Leavenworth, KS; Huber, "Japan's Battle of Okinawa," pp. 118–20, both at CARL; Takejiro Higa Questionnaire, Record Group 15, Box 70, Folder 4, Contributions from the Public Collection, DMMA; Higashionna interview, USAMHI; David Hobbs, "The Royal Navy's Pacific Strike Force," January 2013, www.usni.org; Okinawa entry at www .historyofwar.org; Shaw, *82 Days on Okinawa,* 307; Frank and Shaw, *Victory and Occupation,* 368–70; Sarantakes, *Seven Stars,* 92–93; Astor, *Operation Iceberg,* 334–35; Appleman et al., *Okinawa: The Last Battle,* 384, 465, 473–74, 489–91; Morison, *History of United States Naval Operations in World War II,* vol. 14, 282, 389–92; Yahara, *The Battle for Okinawa,* 159–97, 220.

5. Final Act

1. Prisoner of War Camps in Japan and Japanese Controlled Areas as Taken from Reports of Interned American Prisoners, pp. 76–83, 4-4.5A AA Cl; "Prisoners of War Camps in Areas Other Than the Four Principal Islands of Japan," pp. 35–36, 4-4.5A AB C5, both at CMH; Mamerow Report on Fukuoka 17, NA; Captain John Olson, POW Statement, letters to mother, June 30, July 24, 1945, John Olson Papers, Box 1; Captain John Olson, letter to Mr. Simon Nash, April 23, 1947, John Olson, Box 6; Michael Campbell, unpublished memoir, pp. 133–36; Johnson, Oral Histories, January 27, February 7, 1972, all at USAMHI; Tenney interview, LOC; Hopkins, unpublished memoir, pp. 119–21, USMA; Osaka Oeyama page and OSA-03 Roster at www.mansell.com; Martin Blumenson, "Harold K. Johnson: Most Remarkable Man," *Army,* August 1968, 20; Dominic Caraccilo, editor, *Surviving Bataan and Beyond: Colonel Irvin Alexander's Odyssey as a Japanese Prisoner of War* (Mechanicsburg, PA: Stackpole Books, 1999), 224; Lester I. Tenney, *My Hitch in Hell: The Bataan Death March* (Washington, DC: Potomac Books, 1995), 168–72; Lewis Sorley, *Honorable Warrior: General Harold K. Johnson and the Ethics of Command* (Lawrence: University Press of Kansas, 1998), 77–78; Jonathan M. Wainwright, *General Wainwright's Story,* edited by Robert Considine (Westport, CT: Greenwood Press, 1945), 252–57; Duane Schultz, *Hero of Bataan: The Story of*

General Jonathan M. Wainwright (New York: St. Martin's Press, 1981), 384–86. The Japanese referred to Inchon as Jinsen.

2. General Headquarters, US Army Forces Pacific, "'Downfall': Strategic Plan for Operation in the Japanese Archipelago," May 1945; "'Downfall': Strategic Plan, G2, Estimate of Enemy Situation," March 1945, both in Collection of 20th Century Military Records, 1918–1959, Series II, Library Reference Publications, Box 21, EL; Conference Memorandum for the Record, Future of the Pacific War, March 12, 1945, Record Group 319, Entry 64, Box 5, Records of the Office of the Chief of Military History, Okinawa the Last Battle, NA; United States Army Forces in the Pacific Ocean Area, Final Participation Report, Final Phase of the Pacific War, June–September 1945, pp. 36–49, 95–131, 370.2, CMH; MacArthur, *Reports of General MacArthur*, vol. 1, *Campaigns*, 387–430; Edward Drea, "Previews of Hell," *MHQ*, Spring 1995, 74–81; Richard B. Frank, *Downfall: The End of the Imperial Japanese Empire* (New York: Random House, 1999); John Ray Skates, *The Invasion of Japan: Alternative to the Bomb* (Columbia: University of South Carolina Press, 1994), 171; James, *The Years of MacArthur*, vol. 2, 723–26; Drea, *MacArthur's ULTRA*, 202–25; Krueger, *From Down Under to Nippon*, 334. The Frank and Skates books are so well researched and comprehensive that their entire contents have informed my discussion of Downfall.

3. Thomas B. Allen and Norman Polmar, "The Voice of the Crane," *MHQ*, Spring 1995, 98–102; Drea, "Previews of Hell," 74–80; Harry S. Truman, *Memoirs*, vol. 1, *1945: Year of Decisions* (New York: Da Capo Press, 1955), 265, 417; Hastings, *Retribution*, 444–81, 504–12; Drea, *MacArthur's ULTRA*, 222–23; Skates, *The Invasion of Japan*, 77, 109, 234–57; Frank, *Downfall*, 308–60; Toland, *Decline and Fall of the Japanese Empire*, 1002–72; Toll, *Twilight of the Gods*, 652–89, 720–42. After the war, MacArthur derided the decision to drop the atomic bomb and claimed that Soviet entry into the war was unnecessary for victory. But he lodged no contemporary opposition to the bomb's use and was on record during the war as approving of Soviet entry on the Allied side.

4. Dr. Karl Compton, letter to Lieutenant General Richard Sutherland, November 23, 1945, Record Group 200, Entry 19810, (A1), Richard Sutherland Papers, Box 57, NA; Colonel August "Gus" Schanze, unpublished memoir, unpaginated, A. E. Schanze Papers, USAMHI; Lieutenant Noel Seeburg, letter to family, August 11, 1945, Noel Seeburg Collection, #2007.299, WWIIM; Lieutenant Florance Chapman, letter to mother, circa 1945, Folder 479, Accession #879; Lieutenant Warren Anderson, letter to family, August 15, 1945, Folder 64, Accession #683; Private David Williams, letter to Miss Foote, September 16, 1945, Folder 3240, Accession #175, all at SHSM; Lieutenant General Albert Wedemeyer, Memo for Chiang, August 14, 1945, Albert Wedemeyer Papers, Box 85, Folder 4; General Albert Wedemeyer, untitled writings on World War II, no pagination, Albert Wedemeyer Papers, Box 6, Folder 32; Brigadier General Clovis Byers, letter to Marie Myers, August 15, 1945, Clovis Byers, Box 9, Folder 9–11, all HIA; Lieutenant General Robert Eichelberger, letter to Emma Eichelberger, August 16, 1945, Box 10, Robert Eichelberger Papers, DU; MacArthur, *Reports of General MacArthur*, vol. 1, *Campaigns*, 442–46; McLogan, *Boy Soldier*, 263; Green, *Okinawa Odyssey*, 184; Mitter, *Forgotten Ally*, 362; Luvaas, *Dear Miss Em*, 301.

5. United States Army in the Pacific Ocean Area, Final Participation Report, pp. 51–52, CMH; Major General Henry Aurand, unpublished memoir, no pagination, Henry Aurand Papers, Box 2; Headquarters, Service of Supply, China Theater, staff conference, August 22, 1945, Henry Aurand Papers, Box 27, both at EL; Hopkins, unpublished memoir, p. 122, USMA; Campbell, unpublished memoir, pp. 138–43;

Harold Johnson, Oral History, January 27, 1972, both at USAMHI; Captain Miller Anderson, letter to Mrs. Leota Hening, circa 1945, Folder 59, Accession #2112, SHSM; Tenney interview, LOC; Wainwright, *General Wainwright's Story*, 258–59; Schultz, *Hero of Bataan*, 386–89; Craven and Cate, *Army Air Forces in World War II*, 5:733–34; Donald Knox, ed., *Death March: The Survivors of Bataan* (New York: Harcourt, Brace, Jovanovich, 1981), 440, 445–47; E. Bartlett Kerr, *Surrender and Survival: The Experience of American POWs in the Pacific, 1941–1945* (New York: William Morrow, 1985), 283–85; Tenney, *My Hitch in Hell*, 172–73.

6. General George Marshall, classified message to General Douglas MacArthur, August 11, 1945; President Harry Truman, Directive to the Supreme Commander for the Allied Powers, August 14, 1945, Record Group 15, Box 13, Folder 6, Contributions from the Public Collection; Brigadier General Bonner Fellers, letter to Nancy Jane Fellers, August 20, 1945, Record Group 44a, Box 2, Folder 1, Bonner F. Fellers Papers; Colonel Sidney Mashbir, Interview with Dr. D. Clayton James, September 1, 1971, Record Group 49, Box 3, D. Clayton James Collection, all at DMMA; Generalissimo Chiang Kai-shek, letter to President Harry Truman, August 13, 1945, Albert Wedemeyer Papers, Box 81, Folder 36, HIA; Commander Tadakazu Yoshioka diary, circa 1945, Record Group 165, Entry 79, Box 287, ADVATIS, Current Translations, #173–74, NA; Staff Sergeant Milton Weitz, letter to Mrs. Jack Hirsch, September 10, 1945, Folder 3180, Accession #2616, SHSM; Charles Card, World War II Veterans Survey #2274; Takeji Nagata, unpublished memoir, no pagination; Buckner Creel, World War II Veterans Survey #2899, all at USAMHI; Major General Roscoe Woodruff, letter to Lieutenant General Robert Eichelberger, September 14, 1945, Box 16, Robert Eichelberger Papers, DU; Hostetter, unpublished memoir, p. 252, EL; Stanley Weintraub, "The Three-Week War," *MHQ*, Spring 1995, 95; MacArthur, *Reports of General MacArthur*, vol. 1, *Campaigns*, 446–49; Rogers, *The Bitter Years*, 302; James, *The Years of MacArthur*, vol. 2, 776–78; Rhoades, *Flying MacArthur to Victory*, 437. Shortly before the surrender, Sutherland had just gone back to the United States for a brief leave. MacArthur summoned him back immediately, necessitating a hectic, exhausting return trip for Sutherland to get back in time to receive the Japanese delegation.

7. Major General William Chase, Change No. 1 to Enclosure 1 to Field Order 34, August 23, 1945, 5th Cavalry Regiment Records, Box 497, EL; Mashbir interview, DMMA; Captain Randy Seligman, letter to "Dearest All," October 10, 1945, USAMHI; Stilwell diary, September 1, 1945; "Uncle Bob" and "The Last Beachhead," *Time*, September 10, 1945; Cook and Cook, *Japan at War*, 468–69; James, *The Years of MacArthur*, vol. 2, 784–87; Rhoades, *Flying MacArthur to Victory*, 446; Eichelberger, *Our Jungle Road to Tokyo*, 261–65; MacArthur, *Reminiscences*, 269–70; Luvaas, *Dear Miss Em*, 306; Flanagan, *The Angels*, 147–55; Egeberg, *The General*, 196–202.

8. Mashbir interview, DMMA; Egeberg, *The General*, 205–6; Wainwright, *General Wainwright's Story*, 272–78; Schultz, *Hero of Bataan*, 388–89, 400–402; James, *The Years of MacArthur*, vol. 2, 150–51; MacArthur, *Reminiscences*, 271–72; Manchester, *American Caesar*, 524–25.

9. Colonel H. Bennett Whipple, Instructions for Personnel Attending Surrender Ceremony, September 2, 1945, Record Group 29c, Box 2, Folder 1, Richard J. Marshall Papers; Major General Richard Marshall diary, September 2, 1945, Record Group 29c, Box 4, Folder 4, Richard J. Marshall Papers; LeGrande "Pick" Diller, Oral History, September 26, 1982, p. 19, Record Group 32, Oral History #23, all at DMMA; Lieutenant General Robert Eichelberger, letter to Emma Eichelberger, September 2, 1945, Box 10, Robert Eichelberger Papers, DU; 1st Cavalry Division,

Historical Narrative, July 1–September 30 1945, 5th Cavalry Regiment Records, Box 497, EL; Lieutenant John Breymer, Oral History, September 19, 1945, Record Group 38, Entry P11, Box 3, Records of the Office of the Chief of Naval History, World War II Oral Histories and Interviews, 1942–1945, NA; Stilwell diary, September 2, 1945; E. B. Potter, *Bull Halsey* (Annapolis, MD: Naval Institute Press, 1985), 353–55; Wainwright, *General Wainwright's Story,* 279–80; Egeberg, *The General,* 206–10; Toll, *Twilight of the Gods,* 757; Rhoades, *Flying MacArthur to Victory,* 452; Luvaas, *Dear Miss Em,* 307; James, *The Years of MacArthur,* vol. 2, 788–89; Krueger, *From Down Under to Nippon,* 339; Manchester, *American Caesar,* 525–26.

10. Proclamation by Emperor of Japan and Instrument of Surrender, Stephen Chamberlin Papers, Box 7, Terms of Surrender Correspondence File, USAMHI; Stilwell diary, September 2, 1945; William Dunn, broadcast transcript, September 2, 1945, Record Group 52, Box 3, Folder 53; Marshall diary, September 2, 1945; Mashbir interview, all at DMMA; Lieutenant General Robert Eichelberger, letter to Emma Eichelberger, September 2, 1945, DU; Breymer, Oral History, NA; Richardson diary, September 2, 7, 1945; Admiral Stuart Murray, Oral History, February 1971, at www.usni.org; MacArthur, *Reports of General MacArthur,* vol. 1, *Campaigns,* 453–54; Theodore White, "Peace Be Now Restored," *Time,* September 10, 1945; William F. Halsey and J. Bryan Halsey III, *Admiral Halsey's Story* (New York: Whittlesey House, 1947), 281; E. Potter, *Bull Halsey,* 356–61; James, *The Years of MacArthur,* vol. 2, 789–92; Wainwright, *General Wainwright's Story,* 279–81; MacArthur, *Reminiscences,* 272–80; Manchester, *American Caesar,* 527–31; Barbara W. Tuchman, *Stilwell and the American Experience in China, 1911–45* (New York: Macmillan, 1970), 522; Egeberg, *The General,* 210–19; Rhoades, *Flying MacArthur to Victory,* 252; George C. Kenney, *The MacArthur I Know* (New York: Duell, Sloane and Pearce, 1951), 186–91; Toll, *Twilight of the Gods,* 113; Luvaas, *Dear Miss Em,* 308; Toland, *Decline and Fall of the Japanese Empire,* 1074–78; Schultz, *Hero of Bataan,* 402–3. Surrender ceremony footage at www.youtube.com. The flyover was timed so well because, soon after MacArthur signed the document, he ordered Halsey to contact the planes and give them the go-ahead to overfly the bay. Mashbir served as host and escort for the Japanese during the ceremony. The only wrinkle in the ceremony occurred when Colonel Lawrence Cosgrave, the Canadian representative, signed on the wrong line. When the Japanese expressed reservations, Sutherland simply stepped in and made the necessary corrections to the document by hand. Toshikazu Kase's niece is none other than Yoko Ono.

Epilogue

1. Jerry Angel, unpublished memoir, 12, World War II Veterans Survey #134, USAMHI; Muto, unpublished memoir, 75–80, CMH; Yamashita trial testimony, November 30, 1945, pp. 3656–57, www.loc.gov; "Surrender at Baguio: A Record of Events and Proceedings Relating to the Surrender of Japanese Forces in the Philippines," September 3, 1945, copy in author's possession; MacArthur, *Reports of General MacArthur,* vol. 1, *Campaigns,* 460; "After World War II Ends, Some Japanese Soldiers Carry on the Fight," at www.usnhistory.navylive.dodlive.mil; Mike Lanchin, "Shoichi Yokoi, the Japanese Soldier Who Held Out on Guam," at www.bbc.com; also information on holdouts at www.pacificwrecks.com; Weintraub, "The Three-Week War," 95; D. Clayton James, *The Years of MacArthur,* vol. 3, *Triumph and Disaster, 1945–1964* (Boston: Houghton Mifflin, 1985), 94–97; Francis Catanzaro, *With the 41st Division in the Southwest Pacific: A Foot Soldier's Story* (Bloomington and Indianapolis: Indiana University Press, 2002), 184–86; James H. Hallas, *The Devil's Anvil: The Assault on Peleliu* (Westport, CT: Praeger, 1994),

283–84; Scott, *Rampage,* 493–506; Schultz, *Hero of Bataan,* 404–5; Wainwright, *General Wainwright's Story,* 283–86; J. Potter, *Life and Death of a Japanese General,* 148–51, 162–76. Muto was executed not just for the Manila atrocities but also for playing an alleged role in the Rape of Nanking in his capacity as vice chief of staff of the China Expeditionary Force.

2. General Jonathan Wainwright, letter to Lieutenant General Robert Eichelberger, October 15, 1945, Box 10, Robert Eichelberger Papers, DU; The Skaneateles Historical Society Newsletter, September–October 2020, at www.skaneateleshistoricalsociety.org; Duane Colt Denfield, "Wainwright, General Jonathan Mayhew, IV (1883–1953)," at www.historylink.org; General Jonathan Mayhew Wainwright IV, at www.arlingtoncemetery.net; Wainwright, *General Wainwright's Story,* 286–96; Schultz, *Hero of Bataan,* 412–40. Parade footage at www.youtube.com. Wainwright remained adamantly loyal to MacArthur for the rest of his life. He even gave a presidential-nominating speech for him at the 1948 Republican Convention. Adele died in 1970.

3. Harold Johnson, Interview with Dr. D. Clayton James, July 8, 1971, Harold K. Johnson Papers, Series VI, Oral Histories, Box 201, Folder 1, DMMA; Johnson, Oral Histories, January 27, February 7, 1972, USAMHI; Hopkins, unpublished memoir, p. 132, USMA; Major R. R. Kroells, "On the Back of a Grasshopper: The XXIV Corps and the Korean Occupation," School of Advanced Military Studies, 2016, United States Army Command and General Staff College, Fort Leavenworth, KS, CARL; General Harold Keith Johnson at www.armyhistory.org; General Harold Keith Johnson, at www.arlingtoncemetery.net; General Harold Keith Johnson at www.findagrave.com; "Renaissance in the Ranks," *Time,* December 10, 1965; Blumenson, "Harold K. Johnson" 21–26; Sorley, *Honorable Warrior,* 80–84, 107, 246, and entire contents of chapter 9 through epilogue. Inchon was, of course, the site of the 1st Marine Division invasion on September 15, 1950, during the Korean War.

4. War Department, Adjutant General's Office, Procedures for Processing, Return and Reassignment of Recovered Personnel, August 17, 1945, Harold K. Johnson Papers, Series II, Official Papers, 122; Campbell, unpublished memoir, pp. 140–44, 147–50, both at USAMHI; Tenney interview, LOC; Lester Tenney interviews, Raymond Mason lecture at the National WWII Museum, on www.youtube.com; Peter Maas, "'They Should Have Their Day in Court,'" *Parade,* June 17, 2001; John Wilkens and Peter Rowe, "Carlsbad's Lester Tenney, a Bataan Death March Survivor, Dies at 96," *San Diego Union-Tribune,* February 24, 2017; Tenney, *My Hitch in Hell,* 175–210.

5. Mrs. Natalie Carney, letters to Dr. Paul Rogers, September 5, December 14, 1983, September 27, November 30, December 5, 1984; Dr. Paul Rogers, letters to Mrs. Natalie Carney, September 22, December 3, 1984, Record Group 46, Box 1, Folder 3, Paul Rogers Papers; Natalie Carney, Interview with Jim Zobel, November 18, 2010, all at DMMA; Lieutenant General Richard Sutherland, Interview with Dr. Louis Morton, November 12, 1946, p. 24, Louis Morton Papers, Box 2, USAMHI; Lieutenant General Richard Kerens Sutherland at www.arlingtoncemetery.net; Rhoades, *Flying MacArthur to Victory,* 496–505, 522–24; Rogers, *The Bitter Years,* 306–7.

6. Brigadier General Frank Dorn, letters to Mr. John Hart, July 4, September 29, 1960, John Hart Papers, Box 1, HIA; General Albert Coady Wedemeyer, General Joseph Warren Stilwell, both at www.arlingtoncemetery.net; General Albert Coady Wedemeyer, General Joseph Warren Stilwell, both at www.findagrave.com; Wedemeyer, *Wedemeyer Reports!,* 433–40; McLaughlin, *General Albert C. Wedemeyer,* 199–213; Joseph W. Stilwell, *Stilwell Papers,* edited by Theodore H. White (New

York: William Sloane Associates, 1948); Tuchman, *Stilwell and the American Experience in China*, 523–31.

7. Colonel Walter Krueger Jr., letters to Dr. Walther Nardini, September 24, October 12, 1976, Walter Krueger Papers, Box 1; General Walter Krueger, letters to Colonel Fay Brabson, April 4, 1948, January 22, 1949, March 16, 1955, September 25, 1957, April 26, 1958, August 23, 1959, September 26, 1960, Fay Brabson Papers, Box 6, all at USAMHI; "Neurotic Explosion," *Time,* January 19, 1953; General Walter Krueger, Colonel Aubrey D. Smith, both at www.arlingtoncemetery.net; General Walter Krueger, Mrs. Grace Krueger, Colonel Aubrey D. Smith, Mrs. Dorothy K. Smith, all at www.findagrave.com; Kinsella versus Krueger records, at www .supremejustia.com and www.caselaw.com; Krueger, *From Down Under to Nippon,* 345–71; Holzimmer, *General Walter Krueger,* 1–3, 241–54.

8. General Robert Eichelberger, letters to Dr. Samuel Milner, March 8, November 10, 1954, 370.2, CMH; General Robert Eichelberger, letter to Colonel Wendell Fertig, April 16, 1953, Record Group 53, Box 4, Folder 10, Wendell W. Fertig Papers, DMMA; General Walter Krueger, letter to Colonel Fay Brabson, October 7, 1950, Fay Brabson Papers, Box 6, USAMHI; Lieutenant General Clovis Byers, letter to General Robert Eichelberger, February 12, 1959; General Robert Eichelberger, letter to Lieutenant General Clovis Byers, February 27, 1959, both in Box 22, Robert Eichelberger Papers; General Robert Eichelberger, letter to Lieutenant General Clovis Byers, February 17, 1961, Box 23, Robert Eichelberger Papers; General Robert Eichelberger, letter to Brigadier General Clifford Bluemel, September 12, 1958, Box 21, Robert Eichelberger Papers; General Robert Eichelberger, Dictations, "General MacArthur as a Soldier," circa 1954, p. S-3, Box 73, Robert Eichelberger Papers, all at DU; "Uncle Bob," *Time,* August 16, 1948; Eichelberger articles, *Saturday Evening Post,* August 13, 20, 27, September 3, 10, 17, 24, 1949; General Robert Eichelberger entry at www.remarkableohio.org; General Robert Lawrence Eichelberger, at www.arlingtoncemetery.net; General Robert Lawrence Eichelberger, Emmaline Adelaide "Emma" Gudger Eichelberger, both at www.findagrave.com; James, *The Years of MacArthur,* vol. 3, 83; Eichelberger, *Our Jungle Road to Tokyo,* 268–79; Shortal, *Forged by Fire,* 127–30; Chwialkowski, *In Caesar's Shadow,* 149–62, 173–90, 205–8; Luvaas, *Dear Miss Em,* ix–xvi.

9. General Douglas MacArthur, speech, January 26, 1953, William Gill Papers, Box 1, USAMHI; Dr. Douglas Southall Freeman, letter to General Douglas MacArthur, December 29, 1944; General Douglas MacArthur, letter to Dr. Douglas Southall Freeman, May 30, 1945, Record Group 10, Box 4, Folder 38, General Douglas MacArthur Private Correspondence, DMMA; "The Little Man Who Dared," "Homeward Bound," "MacArthur's Career," "Action on M-Day," "MacArthur v. Truman," "Jubilation & Foreboding," all in *Time,* April 23, 1951; "Red China Is Too High a Price for a Truce in Korea," *Saturday Evening Post,* April 21, 1951; General Douglas MacArthur, at www.findagrave.com; H. W. Brands, *The General vs. the President: MacArthur and Truman at the Brink of Nuclear War* (New York: Doubleday, 2016); Harry S. Truman, *Memoirs*, vol. 2, *1946–1952: Years of Trial and Hope* (New York: Da Capo Press, 1956), 364–70, 414–16, 440–52; MacArthur, *Reminiscences,* 327–426; Manchester, *American Caesar,* 773–94; Huff, *My Fifteen Years with General MacArthur,* 136–42; Chwialkowski, *In Caesar's Shadow,* 182; James, *The Years of MacArthur,* vol. 3, 507–8 and chapters 13 through 20. MacArthur and Jean are buried in prominent graves at the MacArthur Memorial in Norfolk, Virginia.

10. Colonel Wendell Fertig, memo for Major General Robert McClure, Psychological Climate of Southeast Asia, December 11, 1952, p. 9, Record Group 53, Box 15, Folder 10, Wendell W. Fertig Papers; Major General Courtney Whitney, letter to Colonel

Wendell Fertig, April 23, 1953, Record Group 53, Box 6, Folder 38, Wendell W. Fertig Papers; Eichelberger, letter to Fertig, all at DMMA; Recommendation for Parole of Yukitauna Tanaka, March 16, 1953, located within file of multiple parole recommendations, Dwight David Eisenhower Records as President, White House Central Files, 1953–1961, Confidential Files Series, Box 100, EL; "American War and Military Operations Casualties: Lists and Statistics," at www.fas.org; Weintraub, "The Three-Week War," 93; William Owens, *Eye-Deep in Hell: A Memoir of the Liberation of the Philippines, 1944–1945* (Dallas, TX: Southern Methodist University Press, 1989), 235; Paul Thomas Chamberlin, *The Cold War's Killing Fields: Rethinking the Long Peace* (New York: Harper, 2018), 8; Taylor, *The Generalissimo,* 319–24; Rhoades, *Flying MacArthur to Victory,* 497; Stauffer, *Quartermaster Corps,* 322–25; McManus, *Fire and Fortitude,* 193–230. For more information on the persistent need for ground combat soldiers in the nuclear age, and the tendency for modern wars to be decided on the ground, see my book *Grunts: Inside the American Infantry Combat Experience, World War II Through Iraq* (New York: NAL Caliber, 2010).

11. *The Japanese Story, American Ex-POW Inc., National Medical Research Committee, Packet #10,* p. 58, USAMHI; Army Battle Casualties and Nonbattle Deaths in World War II: Final Report, 7 December 1941–31 December 1946," 8–9, at www .ibiblio.org; "Casualties," in Pacific War Encyclopedia at www.pwencyl.com; Casualties, US Navy and Marine Corps Personnel Killed and Wounded in Wars, Conflict, Terrorist Acts, and Other Hostile Incidents, at www.usnavy.mil; Cole Kingseed, "The Pacific War: The U.S. Army's Forgotten Theater of World War II," *Army,* August 2013, 52; Veterans Administration, Office of Planning and Program Evaluation, *POW: Study of Former Prisoners of War* (Washington, DC: US Government Printing Office, 1980), 10; Erna Risch and Chester Kieffer, *United States Army in World War II: The Technical Services, The Quartermaster Corps: Organization, Supply, and Services,* subseries vol. 2 of 4 (Washington, DC: Center of Military History, Department of the Army, 1995), 402.

12. Colonel C. R. Hutchins, letter to Commander-in-Chief, Far East Command, February 7, 1947, Record Group 92, Entry 1894, Records of the Quartermaster General, Graves Registration, Box 421, Folder 468; Lieutenant Colonel T. H. Metz, Memorial Division, Plans and Inspections Branch, Report of Official Travel, September 16, 1947, p. 11, Record Group 92, Entry 1894, Records of the Quartermaster General, Graves Registration, Box 448, Folder 333.1; for background information, I also relied on Report of Graves Registration and Disposition of Remains Activities, October 31, 1947; December 31, 1947, Record Group 92, Entry 1894, Records of the Quartermaster General, Graves Registration, Box 424, Folder 319.1; Headquarters, Graves Registration Service, India-Burma Zone, Plan to Accomplish Graves Registration Service Mission, India-Burma Zone, November 8, 1946, Record Group 92, Entry 1894, Records of the Quartermaster General, Graves Registration, Box 425, Folder 319.1; Colonel Ira Evans, Tentative Operational Schedules for the Return of World War II Dead Program, November 27, 1946, Record Group 92, Entry 1894, Records of the Quartermaster General, Graves Registration, Box 441, Folder 293; Brigadier General William Campbell, Chief Quartermaster, US Army Forces, Pacific, letter to Mr. W. M. Hines, Sr., Office of the Quartermaster General, April 4, 1946, Record Group 92, Entry 1894, Records of the Quartermaster General, Graves Registration, Box 439, Folder 293; Colonel N. E. Waldron, Headquarters, American Graves Registration Service, Pacific Zone, letter to Brigadier General Kester Hastings, Chief, Memorial Division, Quartermaster, January 20, 1949, Record Group 92, Entry 1894, Records of the Quartermaster General,

Graves Registration, Box 551, Folder 293, all at NA; David Colley, "The Last Detail," *World War II,* February 2007, 60–64; Joseph Connor, "A Grave Task"; James
Murrie and Naomi Jeffery Petersen, "The Last Train Home," both at www.history
net.com; Edward Steere, *The Graves Registration Service in World War II* (Washington, DC: Historical Section, Office of the Quartermaster General, 1951), 185;
Edward Steere and Thayer Boardman, *Final Disposition of World War II Dead,
1945–1951* (Washington, DC: Historical Branch, Office of the Quartermaster General, 1957), 395–97, 402–4, 528–29, 690–91; Risch and Kieffer, *Quartermaster
Corps: Organization, Supply, and Services,* vol. 2, 402–4. Dowling served in the
European theater but his experiences were identical to Graves Registration soldiers who operated in the Pacific and Asia. A nationwide steel workers strike in
1946 created a shortage of caskets that forced the Army to delay the return of
World War II dead until the fall of 1947.

13. Lieutenant General Robert Eichelberger, Memorial Day speech, May 30, 1945, Box
69, Robert Eichelberger Papers, DU; Murrie and Petersen, "The Last Train Home";
detailed information on USAT ships and servicemen available at www.iagenweb
.org; USAT *Honda Knot* specifications and history, at www.navsource.org; Private
James Henson, www.bataanproject.com; Lieutenant Buford Cooper, www
.rootsweb.com; "Casualties Brought Back to the United States by the USS *[sic]
Honda Knot,*" Sergeant Frank Simmons, PFC Louis Profeda, PFC Herman Staub,
Sergeant John Zangerle, Lieutenant Alfred Rossman, Private Jacob Kampman, all
at www.findagrave.com; Captain Richard Charles Uffner, www.ancestry.com;
"War Dead Arrive Today on Transport *Honda Knot,* Sikeston Colored Soldiers
Aboard" and "Captain Richard Charles Uffner Rites to Be Tuesday at 4 P.M.,"
Mason City Globe Gazette, September 17, 1948, both at www.newspapers.com; PFC
Norman Petschauer entry, "In Remembrance and Honor of the Brave U.S. Servicemen Who Made the Ultimate Sacrifice in the Marianas Campaign During World
War II," at www.nps.gov; Davidson et al., *The Deadeyes,* 255; Nathan Prefer, *Leyte
1944: The Soldiers' Battle* (Philadelphia and Oxford: Casemate, 2012), 66; Steere
and Boardman, *Final Disposition of World War II Dead,* 533–34, 654–63, 672–78,
685–93; Risch and Kieffer, *Quartermaster Corps: Organization, Supply, and Services,* vol. 2, 404. Also see Eichelberger postwar memorial service speech on www
.youtube.com.

Selected Bibliography

Archives and Manuscript Collections

Abilene, KS. Dwight D. Eisenhower Library (EL).

Annapolis, MD. Special Collections and Archives, United States Naval Academy (USNA).

Carlisle, PA. United States Army Military History Institute (USAMHI).

College Park, MD. National Archives and Records Administration II (NA).

Columbia, MO. State Historical Society of Missouri Research Center (SHSM).

Denton, TX. University of North Texas Oral History Collection (UNT).

Durham, NC. David M. Rubenstein Rare Book and Manuscript Library, Duke University (DU).

Fort Benning, GA. Donovan Research Library (DRL).

Fort Leavenworth, KS. Combined Arms Research Library (CARL).

Fort Riley, KS. United States Cavalry Museum (USCM).

Fort Sam Houston, TX. Army Nurse Corps Collection, Army Medical Department Center of History and Heritage (AMEDD).

Fredericksburg, TX. Nimitz Education and Research Center, National Museum of the Pacific War (NMPW).

Knoxville, TN. University of Tennessee Special Collections Library, Repository of the Center for the Study of War and Society (SCUTK).

Madison, WI. Wisconsin Veterans Museum (WVM).

New Orleans, LA. National WWII Museum (WWIIM).

Norfolk, VA. Douglas MacArthur Memorial Archives (DMMA).

Palo Alto, CA. Hoover Institution Library and Archives, Stanford University (HIA).

Quantico, VA. United States Marine Corps History and Museums Division (USMCHD).

San Diego, CA. Special Collections Library, San Diego State University (SDSU).

Washington, DC. Library of Congress, Veterans History Project (LOC).

Washington, DC. US Army Center of Military History (CMH).

West Point, NY. United States Military Academy Library Archives (USMA).

Books

Anders, Leslie. *The Ledo Road: General Joseph W. Stilwell's Highway to China*. Norman: University of Oklahoma Press, 1965.

Appleman, Roy E., James M. Burns, Russell A. Gugeler, and John Stevens. *United States Army in World War II: The War in the Pacific, Okinawa: The Last Battle*. Washington, DC: Center of Military History, United States Army, 1948.

Arthur, Anthony. *Bushmasters: America's Jungle Warriors of World War II*. New York: St. Martin's Press, 1987.

——. *Deliverance at Los Baños: The Dramatic True Story of Survival and Triumph in a Japanese Internment Camp.* New York: St. Martin's Press, 1985.

Astor, Gerald. *Operation Iceberg: The Invasion and Conquest of Okinawa in World War II—An Oral History.* New York: Dell, 1995.

Barbey, Daniel E. *MacArthur's Amphibious Navy: Seventh Amphibious Force Operations, 1943–1945.* Annapolis, MD: United States Naval Institute, 1969.

Belote, James H., and William M. Belote. *Corregidor: The Saga of a Fortress.* New York: Harper & Row, 1967.

——. *Typhoon of Steel: The Battle for Okinawa.* New York: Harper & Row, 1970.

Black, Robert W. *Rangers in World War II.* New York: Ballantine Books, 1992.

Blumenson, Martin, ed. *The Patton Papers, 1940–1945.* Boston: Houghton Mifflin, 1974.

Borneman, Walter R. *The Admirals: Nimitz, Halsey, Leahy, and King—The Five-Star Admirals Who Won the War at Sea.* New York: Little, Brown, 2012.

——. *MacArthur at War: World War II in the Pacific.* New York: Little, Brown, 2016.

Brands, H. W. *The General vs. the President: MacArthur and Truman at the Brink of Nuclear War.* New York: Doubleday, 2016.

Breuer, William B. *The Great Raid on Cabanatuan: Rescuing the Doomed Ghosts of Bataan and Corregidor.* New York: John Wiley & Sons, 1994.

——. *Retaking the Philippines: America's Return to Corregidor and Bataan, October 1944–March 1945.* New York: St. Martin's Press, 1986.

Carter, Worrall Reed. *Beans, Bullets, and Black Oil: The Story of Fleet Logistics Afloat in the Pacific During World War II.* Washington, DC: Department of the Navy, 1953.

Casey, Hugh J. *Engineers of the Southwest Pacific, 1941–1945.* Vol. 1, *Engineers in Theater Operations.* Reports of Operations, United States Army Forces in the Far East, 1947.

——. *Engineers of the Southwest Pacific, 1941–1945.* Vol. 6, *Airfield and Base Development.* Reports of Operations, United States Army Forces in the Far East, 1951.

Catanzaro, Francis. *With the 41st Division in the Southwest Pacific: A Foot Soldier's Story.* Bloomington and Indianapolis: Indiana University Press, 2002.

Chamberlin, Paul Thomas. *The Cold War's Killing Fields: Rethinking the Long Peace.* New York: Harper, 2018.

Chase, William C. *Front Line General: The Commands of William C. Chase: An Autobiography.* Houston, TX: Pacesetter Press, 1975.

Churchill, Winston S. *The Second World War.* Vol. 5, *Closing the Ring.* New York: Bantam Books, 1963.

Chwialkowski, Paul. *In Caesar's Shadow: The Life of General Robert Eichelberger.* Westport, CT: Greenwood Press, 1993.

Condon-Rall, Mary Ellen, and Albert E. Cowdrey. *United States Army in World War II, The Medical Department: Medical Service in the War Against Japan.* Washington, DC: Center of Military History, United States Army, 1998.

Cook, Haruko Taya, and Theodore F. Cook. *Japan at War: An Oral History.* New York: New Press, 1992.

Craven, Wesley Frank, and James Lea Cate, eds. *The Army Air Forces in World War II.* Vol. 5, *The Pacific, Matterhorn to Nagasaki, June 1944 to August 1945.* Washington, DC: Office of Air Force History, 1983.

Cronin, Francis D. *Under the Southern Cross: The Saga of the Americal Division.* Washington, DC: Combat Forces Press, 1951.

Daugherty, Leo J. *The Allied Resupply Effort in the China-Burma-India Theater During World War II.* Jefferson, NC, and London: McFarland & Company, 2008.

Davidson, Orlando R., J. Carl Willems, and Joseph A. Kahl. *The Deadeyes: The Story of the 96th Infantry Division*. Washington, DC: Infantry Journal Press, 1947.

Davis, Russell. *Marine at War*. Boston: Little, Brown, 1961.

Dean, Peter J. *MacArthur's Coalition: US and Australian Military Operations in the Southwest Pacific Area, 1942–1945*. Lawrence: University Press of Kansas, 2018.

Dencker, Donald O. *Love Company: Infantry Combat Against the Japanese, World War II: Leyte and Okinawa*. Manhattan, KS: Sunflower University Press, 2002.

Devlin, Gerard M. *Back to Corregidor: America Retakes the Rock*. New York: St. Martin's Press, 1992.

Dixon, Chris. *African Americans and the Pacific War, 1941–1945: Race, Nationality, and the Fight for Freedom*. Cambridge: Cambridge University Press, 2018.

Dod, Karl C. *United States Army in World War II: The Technical Services, The Corps of Engineers: The War Against Japan*. Washington, DC: Office of the Chief of Military History, United States Army, 1966.

Drea, Edward J. *MacArthur's ULTRA: Codebreaking and the War Against Japan, 1942–1945*. Lawrence: University Press of Kansas, 1992.

Egeberg, Roger O. *The General: MacArthur and the Man He Called "Doc."* Washington, DC: Oak Mountain Press, 1993.

Eichelberger, Robert L. *Our Jungle Road to Tokyo*. New York: Viking Press, 1950.

Fahey, James J. *Pacific War Diary, 1942–1945: The Secret Diary of an American Sailor*. Boston: Houghton Mifflin, 1963.

Feifer, George. *Tennozan: The Battle of Okinawa and the Atomic Bomb*. New York: Ticknor & Fields, 1992.

Fenby, Jonathan. *Chiang Kai-shek: China's Generalissimo and the Nation He Lost*. New York: Carroll & Graf Publishers, 2003.

Flanagan, Edward M., Jr. *The Angels: A History of the 11th Airborne Division, 1943–1946*. Washington, DC: Infantry Journal Press, 1948.

———. *The Los Baños Raid: The 11th Airborne Jumps at Dawn*. Novato, CA: Presidio Press, 1986.

Frank, Benis M., and Henry I. Shaw Jr. *History of U.S. Marine Corps Operations in World War II*. Vol. 5, *Victory and Occupation*. Washington, DC: Historical Branch, G-3 Division, Headquarters, United States Marine Corps, 1968.

Frank, Richard B. *Downfall: The End of the Imperial Japanese Empire*. New York: Random House, 1999.

———. *Tower of Skulls: A History of the Asia-Pacific War, July 1937–May 1942*. New York: W. W. Norton, 2020.

Garand, George W., and Truman R. Strobridge. *History of United States Marine Corps Operations in World War II*. Vol. 4, *Western Pacific Operations*. Washington, DC: Historical Division, Headquarters, United States Marine Corps, 1971.

Gibney, Frank, ed. *Senso: The Japanese Remember the Pacific War*. Translated by Beth Cary. Armonk, NY: M. E. Sharpe, 1995.

Green, Bob. *Okinawa Odyssey*. Albany, TX: Bright Sky Press, 2004.

Griffith, Thomas E., Jr. *MacArthur's Airman: General George C. Kenney and the War in the Southwest Pacific*. Lawrence: University Press of Kansas, 1998.

Hagerman, Bart, ed. *USA Airborne: 50th Anniversary, 1940–1990*. Nashville: Turner Publishing, 1990.

Halsey, William F., and J. Bryan Halsey III. *Admiral Halsey's Story*. New York: Whittlesey House, 1947.

Hardee, David L. *Bataan Survivor: A POW's Account of Japanese Captivity in World War II*. Edited by Frank A. Blazich Jr. Columbia: University of Missouri Press, 2016.

Hartendorp, Abraham V. H. *The Santo Tomas Story*. New York: McGraw-Hill, 1964.

Hastings, Max. *Retribution: The Battle for Japan, 1944–45*. New York: Vintage Books, 2007.

Henderson, Bruce. *Rescue at Los Baños: The Most Daring Prison Camp Raid of World War II*. New York: William Morrow, 2015.

Herman, Arthur. *Douglas MacArthur: American Warrior*. New York: Random House, 2016.

Holzimmer, Kevin C. *General Walter Krueger: Unsung Hero of the Pacific War*. Lawrence: University Press of Kansas, 2007.

Huff, Sidney, with Joe Alex Morris. *My Fifteen Years with General MacArthur: A First-Hand Account of America's Greatest Soldier*. New York: Paperback Library, 1964.

Hunt, Frazier. *The Untold Story of Douglas MacArthur*. New York: Devin-Adair Company, 1954.

James, D. Clayton. *The Years of MacArthur*. Vol. 2, *1941–1945*. Boston: Houghton Mifflin, 1975.

———. *The Years of MacArthur*. Vol. 3, *Triumph and Disaster, 1945–1964*. Boston: Houghton Mifflin, 1985.

Jefferson, Robert F. *Fighting for Hope: African American Troops of the 93rd Infantry Division in World War II and Postwar America*. Baltimore: Johns Hopkins University Press, 2008.

Kenney, George C. *General Kenney Reports: A Personal History of the Pacific War*. Washington, DC: Office of Air Force History, 1987.

———. *The MacArthur I Know*. New York: Duell, Sloane and Pearce, 1951.

Kerr, E. Bartlett. *Surrender and Survival: The Experience of American POWs in the Pacific, 1941–1945*. New York: William Morrow, 1985.

King, Benjamin, Richard C. Biggs, and Eric R. Criner. *Spearhead of Logistics: A History of the United States Army Transportation Corps*. Fort Eustis, VA, and Washington, DC: US Army Transportation Center and Center of Military History, 2001.

King, William Collins. *Building for Victory: World War II in China, Burma, and India and the 1875th Engineer Aviation Battalion*. Lanham, MD: Taylor Trade Publishing, 2004.

Knox, Donald, ed. *Death March: The Survivors of Bataan*. New York: Harcourt, Brace, Jovanovich, 1981.

Krueger, Walter. *From Down Under to Nippon: The Story of the Sixth Army in World War II*. Washington, DC: Combat Forces Press, 1953.

Lacey, Jim. *Keep from All Thoughtful Men: How U.S. Economists Won World War II*. Annapolis, MD: Naval Institute Press, 2011.

Leahy, William D. *I Was There: The Personal Story of the Chief of Staff to Presidents Roosevelt and Truman Based on His Notes and Diaries Made at the Time*. New York: McGraw-Hill, 1950.

Leary, William M., ed. *We Shall Return! MacArthur's Commanders and the Defeat of Japan*. Lexington: University Press of Kentucky, 1988.

Leckie, Robert. *Okinawa: The Last Battle of World War II*. New York: Penguin Books, 1995.

Lee, Ulysses. *United States Army in World War II: The Employment of Negro Troops*. Washington, DC: Office of the Chief of Military History, United States Army, 1966.

Love, Edmund G. *The Hourglass: History of the 7th Infantry Division in World War II*. Washington, DC: Infantry Journal Press, 1950.

———. *The 27th Infantry Division in World War II*. Nashville: Battery Press, 1949.

Luvaas, Jay, ed. *Dear Miss Em: General Eichelberger's War in the Pacific, 1942–1945*. Westport, CT: Greenwood Press, 1972.

MacArthur, Douglas. *Reminiscences*. New York: Da Capo Press, 1964.

———. *Reports of General MacArthur*. Vol. 1, *The Campaigns of MacArthur in the Pacific*. Washington, DC: Center of Military History, 1966, 1994.

———. *Reports of General MacArthur*. Vol. 2, *Japanese Operations in the Southwest Pacific*. Washington, DC: Center of Military History, 1966, 1994.

Manchester, William. *American Caesar: Douglas MacArthur, 1880–1964*. New York: Dell, 1978.

McCallus, Joseph P. *The MacArthur Highway and Other Relics of American Empire in the Philippines*. Washington, DC: Potomac Books, 2010.

McCartney, William F. *The Jungleers: A History of the 41st Infantry Division*. Washington, DC: Infantry Journal Press, 1948.

McLaughlin, John J. *General Albert C. Wedemeyer: America's Unsung Strategist in World War II*. Philadelphia and Oxford: Casemate, 2012.

McLogan, Russell E. *Boy Soldier: Coming of Age in World War II*. Reading, MI: Terrus Press, 1998.

McManus, John C. *The Americans at Normandy: The Summer of 1944—The American War from the Beaches to Falaise*. New York: TOR Forge, 2004.

———. *Fire and Fortitude: The U.S. Army in the Pacific War, 1941–1943*. New York: Dutton, 2019.

———. *Grunts: Inside the American Infantry Combat Experience, World War II Through Iraq*. New York: NAL Caliber, 2010.

———. *Island Infernos: The U.S. Army's Pacific War Odyssey, 1944*. New York: Dutton, 2021.

McMillan, George. *The Old Breed: A History of the First Marine Division in World War II*. Washington, DC: Infantry Journal Press, 1949.

Men Who Were There. *Ours to Hold It High: The History of the 77th Infantry Division in World War II*. Edited by Max Myers. Washington, DC: Infantry Journal Press, 1947.

Mitter, Rana. *Forgotten Ally: China's World War II, 1937–1945*. Boston: Mariner Books, 2013.

Moore, Stephen L. *As Good as Dead: The Daring Escape of American POWs from a Japanese Death Camp*. New York: NAL Caliber, 2016.

Morison, Samuel Eliot. *History of United States Naval Operations in World War II*. Vol. 13, *The Liberation of the Philippines: Luzon, Mindanao, the Visayas, 1944–1945*. Annapolis, MD: Naval Institute Press, 2012 reprint.

———. *History of United States Naval Operations in World War II*. Vol. 14, *Victory in the Pacific, 1945*. Boston: Little, Brown, 1960.

Motley, Mary Penick, ed. *The Invisible Soldier: The Experience of the Black Soldier, World War II*. Detroit: Wayne State University Press, 1975.

Murphy, Edward F. *Heroes of WWII*. New York: Ballantine Books, 1990.

Norman, Elizabeth M. *We Band of Angels: The Untold Story of the American Women Trapped on Bataan*. New York: Random House Paperback, 2013.

O'Donnell, Patrick K. *Into the Rising Sun: In Their Own Words, World War II's Pacific Veterans Reveal the Heart of Combat*. New York: Free Press, 2002.

Owens, William A. *Eye-Deep in Hell: A Memoir of the Liberation of the Philippines, 1944–45*. Dallas: Southern Methodist University Press, 1989.

Potter, E. B. *Bull Halsey*. Annapolis, MD: Naval Institute Press, 1985.

——. *Nimitz*. Annapolis, MD: Naval Institute Press, 1976.

Potter, John Deane. *The Life and Death of a Japanese General*. New York: Signet Books, 1962.

Radike, Floyd W. *Across the Dark Islands: The War in the Pacific*. New York: Ballantine Books, 2003.

Rhoades, Weldon E. "Dusty." *Flying MacArthur to Victory*. College Station: Texas A&M University Press, 1987.

Risch, Erna, and Chester Kieffer. *United States Army in World War II: The Technical Services, The Quartermaster Corps: Organization, Supply, and Services*, subseries vol. 2 of 4. Washington, DC: Center of Military History, Department of the Army, 1995.

Rogers, Paul P. *The Bitter Years: MacArthur and Sutherland*. New York: Praeger, 1990.

Romanus, Charles F., and Riley Sunderland. *United States Army in World War II: China-Burma-India Theater: Stilwell's Mission to China*. Washington, DC: Office of the Chief of Military History, Department of the Army, 1956.

——. *United States Army in World War II: China-Burma-India Theater: Time Runs Out in CBI*. Washington, DC: Office of the Chief of Military History, Department of the Army, 1959.

Sarantakes, Nicholas Evan, ed. *Seven Stars: The Okinawa Battle Diaries of Simon Bolivar Buckner, Jr., and Joseph Stilwell*. College Station: Texas A&M University Press, 2004.

Schaller, Michael. *Douglas MacArthur: The Far Eastern General*. New York: Oxford University Press, 1989.

Schrijvers, Peter. *Bloody Pacific: American Soldiers at War with Japan*. New York: Palgrave Macmillan, 2010.

Schultz, Duane. *Hero of Bataan: The Story of General Jonathan M. Wainwright*. New York: St. Martin's Press, 1981.

Scott, James M. *Rampage: MacArthur, Yamashita, and the Battle of Manila*. New York: W. W. Norton, 2018.

Shaw, Art, with Robert L. Wise. *82 Days on Okinawa: One American's Unforgettable Firsthand Account of the Pacific War's Greatest Battle*. New York: William Morrow, 2020.

Shortal, John F. *Forged by Fire: Robert L. Eichelberger and the Pacific War*. Columbia: University of South Carolina Press, 1987.

Sides, Hampton. *Ghost Soldiers: The Epic Account of World War II's Greatest Rescue Mission*. New York: Anchor Books, 2002.

Skates, John Ray. *The Invasion of Japan: Alternative to the Bomb*. Columbia: University of South Carolina Press, 1994.

Sledge, E. B. *With the Old Breed: At Peleliu and Okinawa*. New York: Oxford University Press, 1990.

Smith, Robert Ross. *United States Army in World War II, The War in the Pacific: Triumph in the Philippines*. Washington, DC: Center of Military History, United States Army, 1963.

Sorley, Lewis. *Honorable Warrior: General Harold K. Johnson and the Ethics of Command*. Lawrence: University Press of Kansas, 1998.

Spector, Ronald H. *Eagle Against the Sun: The American War with Japan*. New York: Vintage Books, 1985.

Stauffer, Alvin P. *The Quartermaster Corps: Operations in the War Against Japan*. Washington, DC: Center of Military History, United States Army, 2004.

Steere, Edward. *The Graves Registration Service in World War II*. Washington, DC: Historical Section, Office of the Quartermaster General, 1951.

Steere, Edward, and Thayer M. Boardman. *Final Disposition of World War II Dead, 1945–51.* Washington, DC: Historical Branch, Office of the Quartermaster General, 1957.

Stilwell, Joseph W. *The Stilwell Papers.* Edited by Theodore H. White. New York: William Sloane Associates, 1948.

Stouffer, Samuel A., et al. *The American Soldier: Combat and Its Aftermath.* (Studies in Social Psychology series, vol. 2 of 4). Princeton, NJ: Princeton University Press, 1949.

Tapert, Annette, ed. *Lines of Battle: Letters from American Servicemen, 1941–1945.* New York: Times Books, 1987.

Taylor, Jay. *The Generalissimo: Chiang Kai-shek and the Struggle for Modern China.* Cambridge, MA: Belknap Press of Harvard University Press, 2009.

Tenney, Lester I. *My Hitch in Hell: The Bataan Death March.* Washington, DC: Potomac Books, 1995.

Toland, John. *The Rising Sun: The Decline and Fall of the Japanese Empire, 1936–1945,* vol. 2 of 2. New York: Random House, 1970.

Toll, Ian W. *Twilight of the Gods: War in the Western Pacific, 1944–1945.* New York: W. W. Norton, 2020.

Treadwell, Mattie E. *United States Army in World War II, Special Studies: The Women's Army Corps.* Washington, DC: Center of Military History, United States Army, 1991.

Truman, Harry S. *Memoirs.* Vol. 1, *1945: Year of Decisions.* New York: Da Capo Press, 1955.

———. *Memoirs.* Vol. 2, *1946–1952: Years of Trial and Hope.* New York: Da Capo Press, 1956.

Tuchman, Barbara W. *Stilwell and the American Experience in China, 1911–45.* New York: Macmillan, 1970.

United States Strategic Bombing Survey (Pacific), Naval Analysis Division. *The Campaigns of the Pacific War.* Washington, DC: US Government Printing Office, 1946.

———. *Interrogations of Japanese Officials* (2 vols). Washington, DC: US Government Printing Office, 1946.

Valtin, Jan. *Children of Yesterday: The 24th Infantry Division in the Philippines.* New York: Readers' Press, 1946 original, 2014 reprint.

Veterans Administration, Office of Planning and Program Evaluation. *POW: Study of Former Prisoners of War.* Washington, DC: US Government Printing Office, 1980.

Wainwright, Jonathan M. *General Wainwright's Story.* Edited by Robert Considine. Westport, CT: Greenwood Press, 1945.

Waterford, Van. *Prisoners of the Japanese in World War II.* Jefferson, NC: McFarland & Company, 1994.

Wedemeyer, Albert. *Wedemeyer Reports! An Objective, Dispassionate Examination of World War II, Postwar Policies, and Grand Strategy.* New York: Henry Holt & Company, 1958.

West, Charles O. *Second to None: The Story of the 305th Infantry in World War II.* Washington, DC: Infantry Journal Press, 1949.

Willoughby, Charles A., and John Chamberlain. *MacArthur, 1941–1951.* New York: McGraw-Hill, 1954.

Yahara, Hiromichi. *The Battle for Okinawa: A Japanese Officer's Eyewitness Account of the Last Great Campaign of World War II.* New York: John Wiley & Sons, 1995.

Zedric, Lance Q. *Silent Warriors of World War II: The Alamo Scouts Behind Japanese Lines.* Ventura: Pathfinder Publishing of California, 1995.

Index

About the Author

John C. McManus is Curators' Distinguished Professor of US military history at the Missouri University of Science and Technology (Missouri S&T). As one of the nation's leading military historians, a recipient of the prestigious Gilder Lehrman Prize for Military History, and the author of fourteen previous well-received books on the topic, he is in frequent demand as a speaker and expert commentator. In addition to dozens of local and national radio programs, he has appeared on CNN, Fox News, C-SPAN, the Military Channel, the Discovery Channel, the National Geographic Channel, Netflix, the Smithsonian Network, the History Channel, and PBS, among others. He also served as historical adviser for the bestselling book and documentary *Salinger*, the latter of which appeared nationwide in theaters and on PBS's *American Masters* series. During the 2018–19 academic year, he was in residence at the US Naval Academy as the Leo A. Shifrin Distinguished Chair of Military History, a visiting professorship. He hosts two World War II–oriented podcasts, *Someone Talked!* and *We Have Ways of Making You Talk in the USA*.